THE VENETIAN PATRICIATE

THE VENETIAN PATRICIATE

Reality versus Myth

DONALD E. QUELLER

UNIVERSITY OF ILLINOIS PRESS

Urbana and Chicago

Publication of this work was supported in part by a grant
from the Gladys Krieble Delmas Foundation.

LIBRARY OF CONGRESS CATALOGING IN PUBLICATION DATA

Queller, Donald E.
  The Venetian patriciate; reality versus myth.

  Bibliography: p.
  Includes index.
    1. Italy—Nobility—History.   2. Venice (Italy)—Social conditions.
  2. Venice (Italy)—History—697–1508.
  I. Title.
  HT653.I8Q45 1986   305.5'223'094531   84-28041
  ISBN 0-252-01144-9

To the community of Venetianists. May we continue to have our differences, for scholarship would be a dull affair without them, but may we continue to have them with respect, affection, and the true spirit of scholarship. I have profited by your labors and your unselfish help.

Contents

Preface

THIS IS an avowedly one-sided book. It is an attack upon that portion of the myth of Venice which holds that the Venetian patriciate was extraordinarily patriotic, self-sacrificing, decorous, and wise. The other, the mythic side, has been presented many times, and scarcely needs to be reviewed. If there are readers of this book who are not familiar with it, they will find in Chapter 1 a plethora of examples. There is even some truth in it, but only a very partial truth. A great deal of rubbish needs to be cleared away before we can have a clear view of the Venetian nobility.

Let it be clear at the outset that I do not consider the Venetian nobles to have been peculiarly unpatriotic, selfish, rude, and stupid. They were pretty much like any other elite, generally self-serving but occasionally capable of great sacrifices in the interest of the Republic. Some outstanding individuals, indeed, carved out patriotic careers more or less in conformity with the myth. Our biographies of Venetian nobles, with the exception of Frederic Lane's Andrea Barbarigo, have been drawn from this small group, and historians have incorrectly extrapolated from this evidence a mythic view of the patriciate as a whole.[1]

What was really unusual about the Venetian nobility was its rigid character after the early fourteenth century. The rich commoner did not usually rise into the elite, and, more important for my concerns, the poor noble did not drop out of the patriciate. A key to much of what follows is that many, probably most, nobles were poor.

The chronological limits of the book run approximately from the formation of the closed patriciate (with a few glances backward) to the Battle of Agnadello in 1509. The reason for the *terminus a quo* is obvious: the distinctive Venetian patriciate came into existence at that time, or rather, as Stanley Chojnacki has taught us, it evolved over the next generation. The reason for the *terminus ad quem* is that it is generally conceded that the Venetian patriciate became decadent in the sixteenth century and remained so for the remainder of the history of the Republic. Scholars used to believe that this was a result of economic depression following upon the discoveries of the Cape route and the New World and the trauma of the War of the League of Cambrai. We have since learned, however, that the sixteenth century in Venice was not a time of depression but of sustained prosperity. If the sixteenth-century nobility was truly decadent, and if that demoralization cannot be traced to a cause peculiar to that time, then it seems worth raising the question whether those sixteenth-century patricians were, in fact, very different from their forebears. It is my argument that they were not, that there is abundant evidence that the nobles of the fifteenth century were generally as driven by self-interest as those of the sixteenth and as most men, and that there is some evidence for the fourteenth and even thirteenth centuries. Prior to that there is precious little evidence, of course, as any medievalist familiar with the paucity of documentation before the late thirteenth century would expect.

I AM NOT so naive an iconoclast as to believe that myths are fit only for destruction. Myths, of course, are social and historical realities, which have consequences in the realms of ideals and behavior. This subject is treated to some extent in Chapter 1, but the main thrust of the book is to expose the myth as a myth, rather than as an accurate reflection of the character of the ruling class.

Critics will no doubt charge me with being a Venetophobe (or a patriciophobe), as I have been charged with being a Venetophile by reviewers of my book on the Fourth Crusade. I think I am neither, nor, I hope, schizoid. It is the traditional view of the Venetian patriciate that is split: the same scholars hold that the rulers of Venice were models of altruism in favor of the state, but monsters of greed when it came to individual or communal profit. The literature on the patriciate is characterized by the positive myth, that on the Crusades by the negative one. The latter portrays the Venetians as greedy, deceitful, crafty, devoid of religion, worshipping only profit. It is very widespread, especially among Byzantinists, most of all in their treatment of Doge Enrico Dandolo. It, too, is worthy of extended treatment. Both the positive and the negative myths should be pricked, and the Venetian ruling class should be viewed as reasonably normal human beings. The contrast between reality and the positive myth is the subject of this work, and so, like the King of Brobdingnag questioning Gulliver about English government—but, alas, without Swift's art—this book will challenge the mythic view.[2]

To this end I have combed the legislation of the Great Council, the Senate, and the Ten, and I have sampled other archival collections. I have also made considerable use of the diarists of the late fifteenth and early sixteenth centuries and of other narrative sources. From the fourteenth century, Venetian laws were provided with preambles explaining why the legislation was needed. These have been a mine of information for me. I concede that they may sometimes be self-denigrating and hyperbolic. When the drafters declare that the act against which they are legislating occurred "every day," we need not believe that this was literally true. We may fairly conclude, however, that it happened quite often. When they use a more general phrase, such as "many times," I think we may safely assume that the disapproved deed was committed frequently. I have made allowance for hyperbole. These laws, on the other hand, are the most solemn sorts of public acts, formulated by officials in a position to know the facts and passed by the patricians themselves. Those of the Great Council may be taken even more seriously, perhaps, than those of the Senate or the Ten. The more restrictive bodies were dominated by the rich and the powerful and the leaders who proposed the legislation were often among those who had the wealth, leisure, and incentive to devote themselves to the state as prescribed by the myth. They would be more prone to excoriate in excessive terms their poorer brethren, who missed the mark widely. The Great Council, on the other hand, included the numerous poor nobles whose deeds were so often denounced. They would be less likely to approve highly exaggerated condemnations of their own acts. Among the narrative sources, too much reliance upon the *Diarii* of Girolamo Priuli could legitimately be criticized, for Priuli was, indeed, a Jeremiah, and may have distorted the deeds of his fellow nobles. He interpreted the defeat at Agnadello, for example, as God's punishment for the sins of *broglio,* corrupt justice, arrogant rule, and perjury, as well as improper clothing, sexual license, and sodomy.[3] Marino Sanuto, on the other hand, may have occasionally allowed his disappointment in his own political career and some touch of jealousy of more successful patricians to find expression. Even allowing for such factors, however, their testimonies will still bear a great deal of weight. Generally, I allow the documents to speak for themselves in Chapters 2 through 7. My paraphrases are very close to the originals, and in some crucial cases a direct translation is given in the text or the original in the footnotes. In the conclusion of each chapter and in the concluding chapter I attempt to synthesize the evidence, making allowances for its selectivity, the possibility of exaggeration, the circumstances, and the various other issues that a historian must consider in dealing with his documents. Much of the evidence, as might be expected, is scrappy, bits and pieces not worth much individually but collectively forming a very convincing case. I ask the reader's understanding, then, as I build my argument, sometimes with boulders but often with pebbles. Knowing how reluctant we historians are to relinquish received opinion (unless we are the authors of the revisions), I am not very hopeful for its immediate acceptance, but my aim is to lay to rest, once and for all, the confusion of the myth of the Venetian patriciate with the actual patricians.

IN THE COURSE of studying how the nobles abused their privileged status I have discovered a great deal about how Venetian government worked from the late thirteenth century to the early sixteenth, and it is hoped that the reader will find some of this information useful for understanding Venice.

ANOTHER interesting by-product of the research has been that the patriciate, which has traditionally been pictured not only as noble in character but as "pompously grave, puritanically rigid, and crushingly dull,"[4] is seen in more human terms. Nobles had trouble paying the rent, they cheated on expense accounts, they politicked for petty jobs, they gossiped about affairs of state in church and at parties. That there were poor nobles is no new discovery, but it seems to me that the poverty of many of the patricians has never been adequately emphasized. If I have succeeded in depriving the nobles of their overblown reputation, perhaps I have also contributed in restoring what is really theirs, their ordinary humanity.

I WISH to thank the Guggenheim Foundation for the opportunity to spend a year working in the Archivio di Stato and the Marciana and also the staffs of those institutions, especially the always helpful and learned Dr. Maria Francesca Tiepolo. I also wish to thank the Institute for Advanced Study, and especially Professor Kenneth Setton, for the opportunity to spend a blissfully sheltered year writing a large part of the book. The Gladys Krieble Delmas Foundation enabled me to make a short trip to Venice to pick up loose ends, and it has also generously granted a subvention to the University of Illinois Press toward publication. Patricia Hollahan contributed an extraordinarily thorough copyediting of the manuscript, for which I am grateful. I also feel a debt of gratitude to the community of Venetianists, and particularly to those scholars, such as Robert Finlay, Guido Ruggiero, Edward Muir, and

Margaret King, who have made their manuscripts or proofs available to me before publication. They and others, and Finlay above all, have been generous in sharing information and advice.

The Venetian Patriciate

I

The Myth of the Patriciate

ITS HISTORY

There may be no place on earth as charming as Venice, and it beguiles us into believing myths. Every society probably embodies its ideals in myths about its own nature and its heroes.[1] We Anglo-Americans have our myths, of course: a Magna Carta very different from the charter of 1215, the English yeoman, Washington and the cherry tree, the brooding Lincoln, our conviction of our own moral superiority, to name but a few. If there is anything extraordinary about the myth of Venice it lies in its endurance.[2] Charles Rose has broken down the myth of Venice into three essential elements: the idea of liberty or freedom, the superiority of the constitution, and the virtues of the nobility.[3] Much has been written about the first two, and especially about the constitution, which we need not repeat here, for we are directly concerned only with the myth of the patriciate.[4]

The myth of Venice, according to Franco Gaeta, reached its developed form only in the late Quattrocento or in the Cinquecento, although Gina Fasoli has certainly shown that elements of the myth of Venice reach as far back as the liberation of the body of St. Mark in the ninth century and she believes that it was fully formed by the middle of the fourteenth century.[5] The first example that I have found of the mythologizing of the patriciate is in Martino da Canal's propaganda piece, *Les estoires de Venise,* which antedates the Serrata del Maggior Consiglio of 1297–98 by some quarter-century. His use of French, the lingua franca of the thirteenth century, helped to achieve a broad circulation of his encomium. The author was not an official historian, such as Venice was later to employ, although he does seem to have been an employee of the ducal *curia*. He depicts other cities split by civil discord, while Venice was a block of granite. He lauds the nobility of Venice and makes the outrageous claim, which echoes in the historical literature of the present, that among the Venetians the community alone was valued, not the interests of individuals.[6] Jacopo Bertaldo, who probably wrote his uncompleted work on Venetian courts between 1311 and his death in 1315, describes the Venetians of the preceding century as "bound together by pure love," governing themselves most purely and discreetly through a complex of customs.[7] The execution of Doge Marin Falier in 1355 raised the reputation of the oligarchic government for decisiveness, efficiency, and severity. Malcontents feared more than ever to plot against it, while the nobles, now a closed caste which monopolized political power and enjoyed most of its benefits, rejoiced in its wisdom and strength. No hint was allowed to appear of a rift in the ruling class dedicated to political concord and the exaltation of the state.[8]

Early in the fifteenth century Lorenzo de Monacis wrote in praise of the Venetian nobility:

> flesh and blood are not the true subject of nobility, but excellent and virtuous customs. . . . that devoted and most powerful order of its Great Council, from which depends the entire government of the Republic, is so regulated that no one can rise to it and to the government of the Fatherland unless elevated legitimately by reputation. Many [elsewhere] on account of power acquired through robberies by sea or by land, or treacherous acts, or invasions, or factions, or extortions, or usuries, or riches acquired badly in some other way are called nobles by false opinion. . . . But the city of Venice should cause envy, for, the facts agree with what is said, by the contrary acts and customs it ascends the mount of true nobility. For the first care of its youth was a certain judgment of great spirit and of native nobility, and a clear presage of future glory.[9]

The funeral oration of a prominent noble, of course, provided a natural setting for the praise, not only of the individual, but of his family and of the state. As a genre, it can reveal a great deal about the ideals of a society. Leonardo Giustinian's eulogy for Giorgio Loredan is a good example of the use of this form to set forth and reinforce the ideal of the noble patrician. He lauds the Loredan family for its centuries of distinguished service to the Republic before proceeding to the praise of Venice itself. The dead man had fled leisure to give his body and mind to the military and civil requirements of the *patria,* for he knew that he had been born and educated to this end. He had endured heat, cold, and vigils in campaigns on land and sea. In the domestic offices to which he was called he conducted himself with modesty, integrity, prudence, and constancy. He accepted all burdens of state, not only at home, but in distant lands.[10] Pierleone-Leonardo Giustinian also described the life of a patrician: he did not fail in his public or private duty; every day he went to the court and to Rialto; every day he helped his friends and aided the Republic with his talent, experience, and authority.[11] Pietro Barozzi, delivering a eulogy of Cristoforo Moro, recounted how swiftly one duty was piled upon another. Moro barely had a chance to catch a little breath after one mission, when the Senate ordered him upon another. He obeyed that body with the greatest zeal, as one who bore freely all the labors of the Republic, who did not withdraw from any inconveniences, who was deterred by no perils. Barozzi also noted the supposed tradition by which no Venetian noble was exalted above any other.[12]

In Venice, unlike Florence, the humanistic movement was led by distinguished nobles, such as Leonardo Giustinian, men who were procurators of St. Mark, ambassadors, *podestà,* commanders of the fleets, and the like. Francesco Barbaro, a leader of these humanistic nobles, expressed the belief that happiness, among a free people, consisted of devotion to the common welfare, dealing with important matters, and enjoying a reputation for wisdom. Bernardo Giustinian followed the humanistic approach to history as a series of examples for contemporaries. He romanticized the founders of Venice as paragons of civil responsibility.[13] In that Golden Age great concord and love reigned among them. The public welfare was everything, private wealth was not considered. This led to peace and justice, for who would injure another, if the injury were considered done to all? Fraud, deceit, lying, rapine were far from their minds.[14] The noble class existed from the very beginning and, of course, was worthy of praise.[15]

Official historians serve as another source of myths. Many scholars have believed that Venice acquired in Marcantonio Sabellico its first official historian, but Gilbert has argued convincingly that the government did not pay Sabellico to devote all his time to writing a history of Venice, but rather rewarded him for the history presented to the doge and the Senate with a lectureship in the school of St. Mark.[16] Sabellico was a learned humanist with no particular competence as a historian or in political affairs, but he possessed an exalted style and knew how to pull together the strands of the Venetian tradition in a way that satisfied the propagandist aims of the leading nobles.[17] His account of the release of Vettor Pisani from prison to take command against the Genoese provides a model for noble attitudes and behavior, and, indeed, the history was intended as a store of such *exempla*.[18] Marino Sanuto's youthful *Cronachetta*, dedicated in 1493 to Doge Agostino Barbarigo, also reflects a desire to exalt Venice and its patriciate. The foundation of the city in 421 was not at the hands of shepherds, like Rome's, but of nobles and powerful men. Some believe these were Cisalpine Gauls, but others think the founders were Trojans, the followers of Antenor.[19] These early inhabitants were not proud, nor did they esteem riches, although they were rich, but they respected *pietà* and innocence. They did not dress ornately or seek honor, but, content and happy, they undertook the tasks of government for the good of the Commune. One did not differ from another. As Cassiodorus wrote, poor and rich were equal.[20] Venice has been ruled with marvelous order, says Sanuto, without seditions among the people or discord among the patricians.[21] In his more mature *Diarii,* however, Sanuto hardly shows himself an apologist. As we shall see abundantly, his criticisms and his complaints against the government and the patricians are almost as mordant as those of his contemporary Priuli.[22]

The *Poema de omni Venetorum excellentia* of Francesco Arrigoni contains some glowing passages on the Venetian patriciate. He stresses patrician gravity and sobriety. The young nobles are carefully trained for their responsibilities. They engage in humanistic studies, traverse the seas, and go to war. They enter the Great Council at an early age so that they can accustom themselves to affairs of state. Thus, no one can govern subjects better than the Venetian nobles, for they themselves are governed by a strict code enforced by the state. They do justice to all equally. They are held together by love and concord, and no faction troubles them.[23] If anyone fails in his duty, punishment is swift, so that each will be wary of how he conducts himself in office.[24] In an absolutely terrible poem, *La summa gloria de Venetia,* published in 1501, Francesco Allegri also writes that the nobles do not care who has more gold, for they are all equal and honor is accorded to age. No one has ever seen anything so fine as the Great Council; not even the Romans had anything to compare with it.[25]

Thus, in quasi-official histories, patriotic little chronicles for the schools, and family histories, in eulogies, poems, and public art the elements of the myth of the patriciate were propagated in Venice.[26] We can also trace the prehistory of the myth of the Venetian patriciate abroad from scattered references to its virtues to a relatively systematic fifteenth-century myth.

In the first half of the thirteenth century an English Franciscan named Bartholomew of Glanville lauded the Venetian ruling class in a widely circulated text: "[Venice] rules most justly, protects her subjects and defends them from enemies most powerfully; she subjects the Republic and the civil power to just laws. She does not ignore or permit to remain within her boundaries any sect contrary to the divine regulations. I think that to refer to the singular probity of this people is superfluous since the power, circumspection, foresight, unity and concord of citizens, and love of justice tempered with clemency of the Venetians is known to all nations."[27] A few years later, probably in 1262, Rolandino of Padua, rejoicing in the deliverance from Ezzelino da Romano, exulted in the happiness of the Venetian commune, whose citizens had so much regard for their community.[28] A pseudo-Dante letter of 1314 displays at one and the same time the great reputation which Venice enjoyed abroad and the disillusionment of the author of the letter. He had expected to find in Venice noble Catos and rigorous censors of depraved customs. Instead he beheld a "truly miserable and badly behaved people." They were insolently oppressed, vilely governed, and cruelly vexed by new men, destroyers of the ancient law and authors of unjust corruptions. He found the venerable fathers afflicted with obtuse and bestial ignorance.[29] This is most amusing, for he is referring precisely to the post-Serrata patriciate in the process of becoming the famed nobility of Venice. In fairness to the fathers, the author seems to have been piqued because they did not want to listen to his Latin oration.[30] In contrast, Robey and Law have called attention for the first time to the praise of Venice in Benzo of Alessandria's *Chronicon* of about 1320. In rolling rhetoric Benzo finds the Venetians illustrious for prudence, venerated for age, regarded for their customs, and strong in eloquence. Their principles are laudable, especially their regard for the common welfare. They have enjoyed peace for a long time. They cultivate justice. Curiously, nobility does not prevail, according to Benzo, but the suffrage of all.[31] By this last Benzo probably means that there was not a dominating elite within the patriciate, but that all of them were equal, which is, of course, not the case in fact, but it was constitutionally true and in conformity with the myth.

By the time the classical notions of the Renaissance humanists were brought to bear upon the image of Venice only that city and Florence remained strong republics. Florence and Venice were in contrast, however, a polarity that I think crucial for the spread of the myth of Venice. Florence was always volatile, subject to revolutions. Venice seemed unchanging, and, indeed, as against Florence, its constitution was stable.[32] Petrarch's hospitable reception in Venice and the house on the Bacino that he received are well-known. It is hardly surprising that he responded with praise for the city "rich in gold, but richer in repute; strong in power, but stronger in virtue; built on solid marble, but more stably and solidly established on the more secure foundations of its citizens' concord, fortified and made safe by the intelligence and wisdom of its sons, rather than by the sea which surrounds the city."[33] With the coming of the Quattrocento, the myth begins to emerge as something more than scattered comments in favor of the Venetian patriciate. The humanist Pier Paolo Vergerio composed a *De republica veneta* containing many of the standard assertions concerning the civic virtues of the Venetian rulers: temperance, constancy in affairs of state, lack of interest in personal gain, love of honor and glory.[34]

Like the author of the pseudo-Dante letter, Gian Francesco Poggio-Bracciolini underwent an amazing change of attitude with regard to Venice, but in the opposite direction. In his *De nobilitate* about 1440 he lashed out at the Venetian nobles, who, however absurd, foolish, silly, and destitute, esteemed themselves learned and wise above other citizens.[35] In 1459, however, in his old age, he wrote the oration *In laudem rei publicae Venetorum,* not because he was actually so fond of the Venetians, but because he was miffed at the Florentine government over taxes. First he wrote *In fidei violatores* blasting Florence, then turned in the oration to praise the rival republic. Venice is for Poggio little more than an instrument with which to beat Florence.[36] Still, it is one of the best panegyrics of Venice of the fifteenth century. According to Poggio, the Serenissima is the only state to match Cicero's ideal of aristocratic government under which the best men devote themselves to governing.[37] The Venetian nobles are completely intent upon public service and lay aside all care for private affairs.[38] Venice is free from all those vices and outrages which bring about the fall of other cities. There is no dissension, discord, faction, or open hatred, because all devote themselves to the safety of the Republic. Commoners have no place in government, but only the nobles, and the best among them, bear the rule.[39] He praises the modesty of the young, the authority of the old, the gravity of men, and the dignity of the Great Council.[40] It is especially worthy of praise that the laws are stable and of long life, and they are not varied from day to day for anyone, but keep their sanction perpetually.[41] It is remarkable that the petty grievances of a malcontented humanist should contribute to the myth of the Venetian patriciate. Florentine taxes have helped make Venetians great!

Pope Pius II (Eneo Silvio Piccolomini) was no friend of the Venetians of his day. He denounced them to the Venetian ambassador, Bernardo Giustinian, in scathing terms, which still, however, show some elements of the favorable side of the myth. For the Venetians, he declared, outside of their Republic, which they hold for a god, nothing is sacred, nothing is respected. Everything is just to them that is good for the state. It is legitimate if it will increase their dominion. Our fathers, he continued, held the justice of Venice in great veneration. They esteemed Venetians as sober, modest, and devoted to religion. Now, however, there is no faith, or moderation, or justice. In place of the old-time virtue there is avarice, cupidity, ambition, envy, cruelty, lust, and all the base instincts.[42] Here we have both the positive and the negative myths of Venice, the unfavorable assigned to the present, the favorable relegated to the past. This chronological organization of mythic elements will be detected again and again. The ancients will be idealized as models for their frail descendants. It is the topos of the Golden Age.

Whatever Poggio's petty motives for his praise of Venice, it was influential in Florence. In 1482 the Venetian noble Pietro Dolfin wrote from there that the whole of Florence shared Poggio's high estimation of Venice. Gilbert believes, probably correctly, that this really only means that the aristocratic circle around Lorenzo de' Medici in which Dolfin himself moved admired Venetian government, but that in itself is quite significant. Before the end of the Quattrocento the Florentines, their confidence shattered after the flight of Piero de' Medici, had turned their gaze from troubled Florence to the tranquility of Venice. Enthusiasts like Bernardo Rucellai, one of the *ottimati* who hoped to secure their own status by adopting a constitution on the Venetian model, urged not only the harmony of Venice, but the patriotism of her citizens (read "nobles"), who were accustomed to place the public welfare before their own interests.[43] Under the leadership of Savonarola and Soderini the Florentines adopted a new constitution modeled upon the mythological Serenissima, although their actual knowledge of Venetian government was spotty and superficial. In the process they helped to formulate the myth of Venice.[44]

The War of the League of Cambrai was a turning point in the development of the myth of Venice. That Venetian institutions could undergo the trials of defeat, ultimately gain the victory, and survive basically unchanged confirmed their reputation for stability. In the hands of publicists like Donato Giannotti, who presented the Venetian model with a knowledge and detail previously unknown in Florence, the Serenissima achieved at worst parity with Rome as an exemplar of the ideal mixed constitution of classical antiquity.[45]

The sceptical Machiavelli, however, resisted the allure of the Venetian myth, though even he found some virtues in Venice.[46] He despised their dependence upon the arms of *condottieri*, and possibly he could not bring himself to find in any contemporary polity a rival to his beloved Rome.[47] Venice was not so free from faction as it was reputed, according to Machiavelli, for no city was more torn by dissension.[48] He was more surprised that the Venetians were able to hold the empire than that they had acquired it. He did not esteem them very highly.[49]

As the War of the League of Cambrai proved a watershed for the Venetian myth as seen from Florence, so, naturally, it was also in Venice itself.[50] While the myth as received in Florence and Venice was essentially one and the same, there are subtle differences in motives, settings, and uses. At a distance and beset by their own problems, the Florentines, for the most part, perceived only the success of Venice in maintaining its independence and its republican government. Venetians, however, while unquestionably proud of their accomplishment, knew all too well how close the Republic had come to disaster. They set to work on the myth in a conscious effort to restore Venetian prestige, which they perceived to have been damaged. That is why the Venetians placed the mythical Venice in the past. It was their ancestors who had established the ideally balanced, mixed constitution, and it was those patricians of long ago who set the examples of virtue, wisdom, and patriotism.[51] This, in turn, is related to the radical, republican use of the myth in Florence and its conservative, aristocratic value in Venice.

Chambers reports the "eloquent and disingenuous harangue" that Antonio Loredan delivered to a group of commoners summoned into the hall of the Great Council in October 1509, a few months after the defeat of Agnadello. He informed them how well-off they were as civil servants and merchants in contrast to the duty-bound patricians, who had only temporary government jobs, bore heavy expenses, and risked their lives in war. "We make do with the odour of the state, and you eat the roast meat; we bear the name, and you the prizes; we the leaves, and you the fruit."[52]

In 1516, after a half-century during which Valla, George of Trebizond, the younger Filelfo, and Biondo had been put forward as candidates, the Senate finally named Andrea Navagero, a patrician, the first official historian of the Republic.[53] Navagero's responsibility was to brush up the image of Venice, which the Senate thought had been tarnished by the war. Unfortunately, Navagero never wrote the history that was expected of him.[54] His funeral oration in 1521 for Doge Leonardo Loredan, however, is a token of his good faith. Loredan, according to the eulogy, was the ideal Venetian patrician, whose entire life was dedicated to the state without any regard for his own interests. The patriciate which governed Venice produced such men as this and raised them to the highest offices.[55]

As Donato Giannotti codified the myth of Venice in Florence, so did the patrician and prelate Gasparo Contarini in Venice. His *De magistrati-*

bus et republica Venetorum was written in the early 1520s, a few years
before Gianotti's work, and published in Paris in 1543, three years after
the Florentine's book had appeared.[56] He wrote in a period in which the
Republic had been badly shaken, though it had survived, not without
gaining its measure of glory. The patriciate, of which Contarini was a
very prominent member, strove to affirm its rule and the social structure upon which it was based. The character, dignity, and functions of
the nobility needed reinforcement. Contarini writes that the ancestors
of the Venetians were not moved by personal ambition or the desire for
fickle fame, but by the common welfare. This was the spirit in which
they founded the Republic.[57] Contarini is compelled to marvel at the
wisdom, spirit, and incredible love of country of their ancestors.
Athens, Sparta, and Rome, of course, could boast some noble citizens,
but they were not numerous enough to prevail over the multitude, and
so did not do their countries much good. The Venetians, though,
united themselves in their zeal for Venice, setting aside private benefit
and honor. A proof of this selflessness is the absence of monuments to
individuals.[58]

Pietro Bembo became the successor to Navagero as official historian,
and he did produce a history, which picked up where Sabellico had left
off. It was, as desired, an *apologia* for Venice. He took as his prototype
for Venetian government an old, gray-haired, eloquent, wise, God-
fearing, prudent, and modest senator, full of patriotic and moral idealism. Bembo marred his work, however, by grinding his own axes
against the Grimani and others, so the Ten had the book expurgated
and named no successor for thirty-two years after Bembo's death.[59] In
1579 the post was reinstated in favor of Paolo Paruta.[60] He depicted the
nobles as pursuing riches, civil honors, and greatness. In the crises of
the sixteenth century the ruling class had displayed its virtues, which
were now represented as those of diplomatic wisdom and adroitness,
rather than morality.[61] About this time Francesco Sansovino celebrated
the character of the Venetian patriciate. He described their "grave aspect, regal presence, firm faith, constant spirit, secure counsel, great
clemency, with a knowledge of affairs and a great love of country."
Government was in the hands of the very best chosen from among
themselves by the best citizens. They were not ambitious to have political office, but sacrificed their own interests for the benefit of the state
when duty called.[62] Still in the early seventeenth century Giovanni Botero and Traiano Boccalini lauded the solidarity of the patriciate and its
dedication to public service, which enabled Venice to survive unchanged in constitution or social structure.[63]

The subject of the influence of the myth of Venice abroad in the sixteenth and seventeenth centuries and even later is one that has attracted considerable attention from scholars such as Fink, Chabod, Bouwsma, and Haitsma Mulier.[64] Gaeta pictures Venice after its emergence from the trials of the War of the League of Cambrai entering "with spread sails into the sphere of the political mythology of sixteenth century Europe."[65] Many saw the secret of her success in the devotion of the patricians to the public welfare.[66] In 1565 Salvago wrote in praise of the Venetian patricians that they gave their all in the public service, "aspiring to legations and magistracies without intermission, not sparing to accept them, but performing them, however difficult or expensive; besides this they give honor to their elders, a general applause to the best among them, a salutary emulation of the greater men who through honest competition generate utility and pleasure rather than scandal and harm through civil tumult."[67]

Outside of Italy the myth of the Venetian patriciate seems to have been especially influential in France. A minor but interesting manifestation of the prestige of Venice in France was provided by the reply of Francis I's messenger, of whom Benvenuto Cellini demanded the significance of the "naturalization papers" that the king had conferred upon him. "This is more of an honor," the envoy replied, "than being made a Venetian nobleman."[68] Jean Bodin did his bit toward furthering the prestige of Venice, for he believed that the patricians of the Republic excelled in laws and political wisdom, although he proclaimed republican Venice's inferiority to monarchical France.[69] Bodin had the knowledge and the insight to understand, however, that the myth of mixed government did not correspond to the facts, that even nominally the government was in the hands of some two thousand members of the nobility, and in fact was controlled by a much smaller number of the real elite.[70] Etienne de la Boétie, that passsionate foe of tyrants, regarded Venetians as the highest example of devotion to liberty.[71]

Gonzalo Fernandez de Oviedo, the Spanish historian of the Indies in the mid-sixteenth century, praised the Senate and Signoria of Venice for wisdom and prudence. They knew how to govern better than anyone. He noted that the Venetians did not have a king, but were ruled by their good sense and their municipal ordinances.[72]

We now owe to Haitsma Mulier's *Myth of Venice* a detailed and learned account of the influence of the myth upon seventeenth-century political thought, especially in the Dutch Republic. From the early sixteenth century, Dutchmen marvelled at Venice, "full of wisdom and full of prudence, full of wealth and full of power."[73] They were drawn to the Venetian example through their studies at Padua and their knowledge of Italian, through the affinity of the two states as republics and through common enmity toward the papacy.[74]

The myth of Venice was also of some importance, along with admiration for the Dutch Republic, in the political controversies in England in the mid–seventeenth century.[75] Lewkenor's translation of Contarini's *De magistratibus* appeared in 1599, offering English readers the classical version of the Venetian myth.[76] James Howell enthused over the Venetian patriciate: "Now, there are few or none who are greater *Patriotts* than the Venetian Gentlemen, their prime study is the public good and glory of their Contrey, and civil *prudence* is their principal *trade* whereunto they arrive in a high measure; yet as it may be easily observed, though these Gentlemen are extraordinary wise when they are *conjunct,* take them single they are but as other Men." The title of Howell's book is of more than passing interest: *SPQV, a survey of the signorie of Venice.*[77] James Harrington had a strong bias in favor of an enlightened patriciate, such as that of Venice was supposed to be. Englishmen continued to show a strong interest in Venetian government even after the Restoration, for Hale has counted at least ten books dealing with the subject in some way between 1668 and 1672.[78]

ITS NATURE

The myth of the Venetian patriciate makes the claim that no other aristocracy has so deserved the power that it held.[79] If it was not theoretically an aristocracy of merit, contended Giuseppe Maranini, certainly it was so in fact.[80] The nobles who formed the Great Council were born to rank and to government and accustomed to attend to the affairs of state with thoughtful wisdom.[81] Vittorio Siri wrote that in Venice "the nobles busy themselves with no other exercise than that of civic prudence, which is practiced by persons of the finest judgment well instructed in the affairs of princes."[82] The poet Arrigoni tells us that some of them pursued scholarship and others the works of war. The young men were introduced into the Great Council so that they would learn how to conduct domestic and foreign affairs better and more prudently. That is why no people were governed with so much reason.[83] The young venerated the old, and rarely did a noble of less than ripe years and experience attain the highest offices.[84] In age and wisdom, but also in regal presence, authority, decorum, and gravity, the mythological model of the Venetian noble calls to mind the procurators of San Marco painted by Tintoretto.[85] Arrigoni exults in the majesty of gatherings of the venerable fathers when they assembled in the Great Council.[86] Cardinal Agostino Valier described the Senate as "a place of gravity, a school of judgment, a shelter of prudence, the honor of Italy, an archive of the affairs of the world, the daily history of the most important actions, the father of eloquence, the master of modesty, the defender of true liberty."[87]

The patriciate, according to the myth, was duty-ridden.[88] Its characteristic sense of responsibility for the people is enshrined in the words of the ever-popular Jacob Burckhardt.[89] The patricians' impartial rule over the lower classes made them universally admired.[90] They were also too astute to burden unduly the conquered peoples. They left their subjects their local customs, treated them justly, and made them loyal and devoted.[91] Hence both the people of Venice and of the subject states loved and venerated the Venetian nobles and rejoiced to obey them.[92]

Again and again recurs the theme of the Venetian patrician sacrificing his individual interests on the altar of the Republic. Rucellai reported it in Florence at the end of the fifteenth century.[93] In modern times Charles Diehl has given it exuberant expression. The nobles, whose birth gave them the right to govern the state, in turn offered to it the most admirable devotion. From infancy the young noble was raised to believe that he owed his entire being to the Republic. All his life he willingly subordinated his own interests to the state. He could not refuse public office. He moved from one duty to another—administration, arms, diplomacy—always working for the good of the city. Even if it was necessary to be ruthless, brutal, and faithless, he would do it for the *patria*. Diehl sees an incontestable beauty in this selfless dedication.[94] Charles Yriarte's old (1874) biography of Marcantonio Barbaro stands as another monument to the mythical patrician. From the age of twenty-five the patrician belonged to the Republic. He owed it his mind, his illustrious name, his special skills as a lawyer, diplomat, or soldier. Whatever his aspirations, he could not withdraw from public life. "Apart from the state, he has no personality." "[H]is innermost existence disappears in his political existence, and we have difficulty in recovering any trace of it." The family was not important. Some nobles, richer in birth or talent than in money, accepted the penalty for refusing costly office, but only because they realized that their financial means did not permit them to represent the Republic adequately. Yriarte's hero, Barbaro, died as he had lived, in the service of the Republic. The dominant idea of his whole life was love of the *patria,* its glory and its interest. It seems that this sentiment dominated all of patrician life. Yriarte concludes with a panegyric to patriotism, which "ought to be the law of our life."[95] Another writer who romanticized patrician devotion to the state was Giuseppe Volpi and, although sometimes in a less unctuous form, it was a commonplace.[96] A seventeenth-century biographer of a Venetian saint, Girolamo Miani, who was a nobleman of no great significance, tells how hard it was for him to give up the service of his country. "[I]t is indeed a peculiar character of the Venetians, instilled into them by nature, to love affairs of state with such loyal and harmonious sentiments that they have the reputation of far surpassing all other nations in their love and sense of duty towards their country."[97] The light of dawn, according to Enrico Besta, often found the devoted senators still in their chamber toiling in the interest of the Republic.[98]

As seen by the myth, the patrician was bound by the laws as by a chain of iron, anxious to defend the weak against the strong, unwilling to accept gifts, and scornful of his friends who wanted favors. As Ludovico Foscarini exhorted Bernardo Giustinian: "[Y]ou most prudent consul of the Fatherland, defend liberty, exercise justice, cultivate the good, direct the hesitating, care for those who bear injuries on account of their weakness, and strongly resist worthless men, especially the ambitious and the more powerful."[99] The same Foscarini professed that when he entered upon a governorship he put off the person of Ludovico and put on the public person.[100]

ITS USES

An obvious function of the myth of Venice was to give sanction to the exercise of power by the patriciate. Ruling classes generally spawn myths, ideologies, fake sciences, and lies to justify their grasp on power. Social Darwinism was the bastard extrapolation from biology, for example, by which capitalists, *nouveaux riches,* and a variety of swindlers rationalized their dominion. The Aryan race theory of the Nazis lies at the nasty end of the spectrum of ideas by which ruling groups have sought to justify their role.[101] At its most successful such a myth or ideology salves the consciences of the elite and contributes to the submission of their inferiors. Alain Dufour is rightly critical, however, of the Marxist view which sees in historical myths merely an instrument of domination. He points out that historical myths are not simply invented by the dominant group and imposed upon inferiors, but that they are born collectively in the minds of those, the exploited and the exploiters, who accept them. The claim set forth must have a certain credibility to be effective: there is usually some relation of myth to reality.[102] Tht is why Gaeta says that the myth is set in the past or in the present and not, like utopias, in the future or outside the time frame.[103] A myth set in the past, almost certainly an unreal past, like that of the Venetian patriciate, commonly serves to point up and try to correct the real or imagined decadence of the present.[104] The conscientious paternalism of a few Venetian nobles provided sufficient relationship to reality to sustain the myth for centuries.

Another, more generous, altogether more sophisticated way of looking at myth is that it serves as an ideal, which is effective in attracting behavior toward itself, although it is unattainable. The goal must not be set so high, however, by a myth totally lacking correspondence with reality, that it is incapable of attracting aspiration. Such an unrealistic myth could even have an adverse effect on behavior.[105] As will appear in later chapters, especially the one on *broglio,* I believe that precisely this contrary reaction occurred in Venice. It would be hard to deny, though, that some patricians, and among them many of those who had taken the teachings of the humanists to heart, like Zaccaria Trevisan, Francesco Barbaro, and Ludovico Foscarini, were inspired by the myth to try to conduct their lives according to its highest standards.[106]

George C. Homans makes several observations in a modern context which are pertinent to the Venetian patriciate. One is that the more the members of a group interact, the more alike they become in their norms, their sentiments, and their activities. They are, however, more alike in their norms than in their overt behaviors.[107] The members of the noble class in Venice interacted a great deal (although we would like to know more about this); at any rate, it is quite clear that the norms embodied in the myth were widely shared among them, as witness the support for those norms in the votes of the Great Council, even though large numbers of the very same people acted in gross contravention of them. Another extremely relevant observation by Homans is that the higher the rank of a person within a group, the more likely he is to conform to the norms of the group. He admits that it works both ways: the person who conforms to the norms of the group gains rank; but it is also true that, if we take rank as the independent variable, the higher the rank the more closely the individual will come to the norm.[108] Already the recurrence of names like Francesco Barbaro, Ludovico Foscarini, Bernardo Giustinian, and Gasparo Contarini illustrate Homans's point. As our study progresses it will deal very largely with nobles who fall considerably lower on the scale. Our traditional mythologized view of the Venetian patriciate has been distorted by concentration upon a few of these figures of very high rank.

THE MYTH UNDER ATTACK

The present work, of course, makes no claim to being the first to challenge the myth of the unified, patriotic, and self-denying patriciate. Cessi, Cracco, and Gilbert stand out among those who over the last half-century have examined the documents relevant to their various subjects and raised objections to the traditional view of the Venetian nobility.

Priority belongs to Roberto Cessi, who, while studying the fiscal measures and arrangements of the Republic, discovered that this area was a battleground of interest groups. As early as 1925 Cessi's introduction to *La regolazione delle entrate e delle spese (sec. XIII–XIV)* showed that a powerful, monopolizing aristocracy, whose wealth was based on the Levantine trade, was struggling successfully to gain control of fiscal policy and turn it to their own interests. It was a bitter struggle, since these policies were not in the interests of less prosperous nobles. Cessi cracked the facade of the unified and self-sacrificing nobility.[109]

No one, however, appears to have paid much attention to the damage for a generation, in spite of the great reputation achieved by Cessi. The critical study of the myth itself, which began with Fasoli's article in 1958, and was continued by Gaeta and Pecchioli, raised new doubts about the real character of the nobility.[110] Fasoli's lectures on Venetian history at the University of Bologna have also contributed to spreading the view that Venice was hardly free from intrigues and corruption, which were covered up by the official historians. She argues that individuals could be shown by official historians to have failed, but they must be properly punished; the virtues of the ruling class, however, could not be called in question. This was propaganda for internal and external consumption, she contends, not a serious effort to understand Venetian society as it really worked.[111]

Angelo Ventura's study of *Nobiltà e popolo* in the Veneto does not confront our subject head-on, but it does offer some insights, especially with regard to the relationship of the patrician government and the *terraferma*. He remarks on the patrimonial attitude of the nobles toward the state. The documents often speak of *stato nostro,* and this should be understood quite literally with full force given to the possessive pronoun. The state was the collective possession of the patriciate. Ventura believes in the strength of Venetian " 'patriotism'—the consciousness, that is, of the general interest, which transcends the single individual." This was based, however, upon the common awareness of being members of a class to whom the Republic belonged, and it referred primarily to the noble class, not the state itself. The state was placed above the individual, according to Ventura, but not above the class with which it was identical.[112] He is very critical of that part of the myth of Venice, and especially of its embodiment in Samuele Romanin, which views Venice in contrast to Lombard tyranny as a sort of benevolent federal government, leaving to the towns of the mainland their municipal liberties. The Venetian government, according to this view, was the protector of common people and especially of the peasants.[113] We hear much about the loyal cry of "Marco! Marco!" raised by the common people on the mainland after Agnadello, but Ventura presents evidence of their attempts to resist their Venetian landlords, who came to try to collect their rents in the Padovano with armed escorts of twenty-five or thirty soldiers.[114]

Giorgio Cracco has extended and reformulated in dialectical terms Cessi's interpretation, tracing the overthrow of the open government of the twelfth century by an increasingly narrow group of rich Levantine merchants.[115] He begins with the limitations on the doge in the twelfth century and the rise of the merchant class, full of enterprise and patriotism.[116] Venice underwent a great crisis, beginning in the late thirteenth century, and out of this crisis over the course of two centuries arose the Venice of the myth. It carried in itself and even nourished the germs of its own decadence.[117] The state had passed into the hands of a very narrow body of families who turned its policies to serve their own interests in trade with the East, regardless of the harm that was done to the people and even to the lesser nobles. The result was an increasing disparity of wealth and power between the elite within the patriciate and all others.[118]

My limited studies on Venetian ambassadors can claim a small role in the attack on the myth. Diplomacy is an activity in which the Venetian patriciate was supposed to be at its very best. It is also one dominated by the rich and influential, for only those with money could afford the financial sacrifice of most embassies and a succession of important diplomatic missions was an essential element in rising to the highest offices and honors. So, we should expect conduct approaching the norm established by the myth, and sometimes we observe it. In very many cases, however, nobles went to ridiculous lengths to escape election or to avoid serving, and when they did accept they cheated egregiously on their expense accounts. The dedication of the nobles to Venetian diplomacy has been grossly overrated.[119]

Frederic C. Lane, who seems to have read everything on Venetian history, has also picked up the critical attitude toward the myth, although his work is basically traditional. He points out that in Venice, as in Florence, the republican ideal of office as a reward for public service was corrupted by awarding power to men for serving private interests.[120] Contrary to the ideal that the office should seek the man, Lane finds the solicitation of desirable offices so repeatedly forbidden that it must have been practiced.[121] The corrupting pressures upon the Great Council by would-be officeholders increased after the nominating powers of the Signoria and the Senate were restricted and later by the fiscal strains of the War of the League of Cambrai.[122] He tells of the hardening of class lines in the second half of the fourteenth century and the fracturing of the nobility by family rivalries and financial interests.[123] Lane also gives a worldly-wise description of the rise of the myth of solidarity among the noble class in the sixteenth century, when internal strife in other Italian cities was so strong that Venetians could be induced to overlook the bloody factionalism that had dominated the earlier centuries of their history.[124]

Felix Gilbert has been highly critical of the myth, although the criticism is scattered among his articles. In "Venetian Diplomacy before Pavia: From Reality to Myth," for example, he criticizes the sixteenth-century official historiographers who propagated the myth of Venetian wisdom, responsibility, and foresight. Venetian statesmen were not only loyal, according to this view, but they did not make serious diplomatic mistakes. The myth smothered the critical sense, not only of sixteenth-century historians, but of such modern scholars as Kretschmayr, Cessi, and Cozzi. The myth of the excellence of Venice actually arose out of Venetian weakness. It was an ideological refuge for the city-republic after the arbitrament of affairs had passed into the hands of great powers. Gilbert's own finding is that in the conduct of the diplomacy preceding the battle of Pavia the Venetians did not display any particular foresight or wisdom.[125]

Without tackling the myth directly, Stanley Chojnacki has raised questions about it. He recounts the challenge by Cessi, Cracco, Bouwsma, and Gilbert and wonders, indeed, if they have not thrown the myth out altogether. For Chojnacki, it is the vulneratiblity of the idea of class solidarity that leads in turn to the fall of the idea of patrician civic loyalty.[126] He also criticizes that aspect of the myth which sees in the constitutional reform of the late thirteenth century a fixing not only of constitutional forms but also of the substantive reality of Venetian politics and society.[127]

Robert Finlay's fine *Politics in Renaissance Venice,* in which he displays a highly developed sense of the way in which politics actually works, has recently exposed the real and very corrupt workings of Venetian government in the late fifteenth and sixteenth centuries. He takes refuge, however, from the conclusion that his copious evidence would seem to compel in the Panglossian conclusion that "pervasive corruption made for civic concord."[128]

Guido Ruggiero has also recently shown that the Venetian nobles were not peaceful but, contrary to the myth, violent. It is true that collectively they desired law and order, but individually they were prone to acts of violence. This was true because they perceived themselves as nobles in the feudal tradition. They read or listened to feudal literature and they held jousts in the Piazza San Marco. When crossed by a petty official or refused by a baker's wife, they reacted arrogantly and often violently.[129]

Valuable as the above-mentioned works have been, none of the critics, perhaps with the exception of Cracco, has undertaken a frontal attack upon the myth of the patriciate. Some of them, moreover, most notably Cessi, have on the whole or in part reverted to the myth.

THE LIVING MYTH

The myth, in fact, is very much alive. As Haitsma Mulier puts it, "[A] myth can be very stubborn in its existence and hard to refute by rational argument."[130] The iconoclastic English constitutional historian, George O. Sayles, bitterly comments: "Hard experience has taught me that it is impossible to destroy a national myth, in England or in any other country. When I read recent textbooks on history and law, I cannot even share the optimism of Max Planck in his final testimony: 'A new scientific truth does not triumph by convincing its opponents and making them see the light but rather because its opponents eventually die and a new generation grows up that is familiar with it.' "[131] Such is the force of myth that even the finest scholars cling tenaciously, as Gilbert charges, to theses that are untenable.[132]

The present section marks the culmination of this introductory chapter and is of the utmost importance for the significance of the whole book. Here I shall try to prove that I am not tilting against windmills, but against a real dragon of a myth—with a very long tail, wounded slightly but far from defeated. In order to appreciate its strength, we shall seek out the beast first in several old, but still very influential works, then in popularizations, and finally in the writings of respected modern scholars, some of them of the highest (and most highly deserved) eminence.

Pompeo Molmenti and Horatio Brown are of the old school, of

course, and no claim is made that they represent current scholarship, but they are still listened to and the Venice of the myth lives in their works. According to Molmenti, a Venetian patriot, his countrymen in their quest for sound judgment scorned the lofty theorizing of the Florentines, which led to dissension. They were ambitious, but always ready to lay aside the posts of honor to return to private life.[133] Their striking energy was able to move in an orderly fashion because of the virtues of the Venetian constitution, the pieces of which fit together like the wheels of a watch.[134] While this constitution delivered all power into the hands of the nobility, the people, after a few attempts to overthrow it, came to recognize the benefits of patrician rule, for "the aristocracy discharged its political duties with that equity which unites divergencies and corrects inequities." The commoner absorbed himself in his prosperous trade or craft, and he looked upon the patriciate as his protector. He even gained some sense of participation through the guilds, which the prudent aristocracy favored.[135] Legal procedure was applied with spotless honesty.[136] Even in the bitter times of the early sixteenth century, Venice was notable for the prudence of her foreign policy, forethought for domestic affairs, clarity of vision, consideration only for the profit or loss of Venice, the common sense of the patricians, and their admiration and worship for noble conduct.[137] In the sixteenth century, it is true, vice spread, but many nobles, like Andrea Morosini, who called for the death of his reprobate son, displayed the old Venetian virtues.[138]

Horatio Brown, the English Venetophile, is so full of praise for the Venice of the Golden Age that his words appear almost fit to be set to music. Brown is one of those who saw the sixteenth century as a period of moral, economic, and political decline. The aristocracy then turned to luxury, country estates, lavish expenditures, and turned away from the austere pursuit of gain which had made Venice great.[139] Even so, not long before the fall of the Republic the doge could still boast of the Venetian reputation for prudence.[140] Brown presents the familiar selflessness of the Venetian patriciate in its most overripe condition:

Perhaps in no state of importance equal to that of Venice are we left in such obscurity as to personal details regarding its great men; material for biographies of leading Venetian statesmen and soldiers is singularly scanty. Venice demanded and secured the effacement of the individual, and impressed upon its citizens, one and all, that the state was everything, the individual nothing. The consequence is that the life of a distinguished Venetian, in so far as we can recover it, is little more than a bare record of the offices he filled;

his policy, his ability, his achievements are rarely associated with his own name, and are to be looked for not in the history of the man but in the development of the state.[141]

Watch for echoes of this enthusiasm in later scholars.

René Guerdan's *Sérénissime* is a quite recent work of *vulgarisation,* not bad, typical of its genre. That signifies, however, a large admixture of romantic rubbish. For more than ten centuries, according to Guerdan, Venice was the great revolutionary state of the West. Birth did not confer privileges, but duties. Power rested upon law. Justice conferred upon the regime the character of a democracy.[142] Venice was the only modern state in the West for eleven centuries.[143] Guerdan is given to the sweeping statement embracing vast periods, rather than to the meticulous study of process.

William McNeill's *Venice: The Hinge of Europe* (1974) also generally presents the traditional, mythological view of the patriciate, although with a bit more caution than usual. The rigor of the mold of the Venetian aristocrats—their sense of duty, selflessness, and the like—made their monopoly of power more or less tolerable to the other classes. "Flagrant abuses of power were likely to be punished; political office was not often used for naked self-aggrandizement. . . ."[144] Such statements are adequately hedged, although even a very sophisticated and suggestive mind like McNeill's is still no substitute for reading the sources and the literature.

The recent *Venice: The Rise to Empire* (1977) by Lord Norwich is another good book of its type, but it too reiterates elements of the Venetian myth. The author recounts that few Venetian nobles considered high office anything but a responsibility, which they would prefer to avoid. Civic duties, however, at home or abroad, had to be accepted under heavy legal penalties.[145] The constricted area in which the Venetians lived forced upon them a sense of cooperation manifested most clearly in their daily affairs. Among the nobles, everyone knew everybody else, and this fostered a sense of mutual trust not commonly found elsewhere.[146]

That the myth of Venice lives in well-known but antiquated works and works of *vulgarisation* does not prove that it should be taken seriously by scholars. It is time to see, therefore, whether it can be found in good contemporary scholarly literature. Let it be stressed that no disrespect is intended toward the authors of these works. On the contrary, they have been selected because they are fine scholars, some the very best. The point is that even in their writings either traces of the myth survive or, at least, the myth is unchallenged. This is not surprising: we do not easily abandon ideas to which we have become accustomed.[147]

Let us begin with two distinguished Venetian historians, Gino Luzzatto and Roberto Cessi. As an economic historian, Luzzatto had less occasion to deal with our subject, but the myth does appear fairly prominently in his article "Les activités économiques du patriciat vénitien," an admirable and interesting study. It is the nature of aristocratic regimes, he says, to repress individualism. That is why the history of Venice is so poor in biographical material. It is possible, however, to trace in general terms the career of a typical Venetian patrician.[148] The young noble was likely to go to sea to learn navigation and commerce, as well as to gain wealth. When he reached maturity, however, at about forty, he gave up his journeying and settled in Venice. It was time to take up public duties and to climb the scale of offices and honors. From now on public service occupied most of his time. He sat in the councils, participated in ordinary and extraordinary commissions, filled the collegial magistracies. These were obligations, which it was not easy to escape.[149] Luzzatto records how the Commune in time of need in 1187 turned for money to its citizens, "true lovers of our land, who can and are accustomed to succor our *patria* in the time of its necessity." While some of those who were called upon to contribute preallocated shares were commoners, the great majority were nobles, members of those families that furnished judges, magistrates, and councillors.[150] Luzzatto does give us, on the other hand, a very hardheaded picture of the way in which the patricians took advantage of their political monopoly to further their economic interests.[151] There were patricians, of course, who conform to Luzzatto's model, but they were that minority of wealthy, powerful, and generally patriotic (though not selfless, as Luzzatto notes) nobles which has for so long distorted our view of the Venetian patriciate as a whole.

It is strange to find Roberto Cessi named again here after we have credited him with leading the attack on the myth of the Venetian patriciate, but his two-volume *Repubblica di Venezia* contains a lot of old-fashioned romanticizing. On the very first page he waxes eloquent about the eternal memory of a glorious past.[152] By the beginning of the thirteenth century, he writes, Venice was known for sagacious diplomacy and military virtue in international affairs and for temperance and mature reflection at home.[153] He rightly criticizes those who see in the alleged Serrata of the Great Council a struggle between a popular party, which lost its ancestral rights, and an aristocratic one, which imposed a tyranny of the few upon the many. No such clash developed during the slow evolution of the noble class, which gained through long experience its social position, its political power, and its character. Venice remained free from the turmoil of Guelfs and Ghibellines, symbols of internal rancor. Her enviable harmony, simple customs, hard work, and industry won her the esteem and trust of both Italians and foreigners.[154] One cannot find, according to Cessi, in the Tiepolo episodes, from Lorenzo in the mid-thirteenth century to Baiamonte in the early fourteenth, the echo of a class struggle in which the people were deprived of liberty. This people in its *arengo* continued to perform acts of sovereignty. It remained noted for wisdom and prudence above all others in Italy. The ruling class did not arise out of conflict, but through natural development.[155] The result of constitutional reform of the late thirteenth century was a harmony based upon the firm homogeneity of the ruling class, capable of eliminating every possibility of the exercise of public functions for personal advantage.[156] In the embellishment of the city in the fifteenth century, private citizens played their part, assuming the burden as a public duty, just as they assumed public offices.[157] At the end of the fifteenth and the beginning of the sixteenth century "the holy Republic" with sagacity and wisdom offered its sons the most propitious means for enjoying mainland benefices without pride, without moral and material luxury, without offending human or divine laws.[158]

Consider too the fine work of Yves Renouard, who nevertheless presents a thoroughly mythological view of the Venetian patriciate. In looking at the patricians before the so-called Serrata he sees nothing of the unrestrained individualism which characterized Genoa. A collective sense which had grown over six centuries showed itself everywhere. There were no familial conspiracies, no factional undertakings, no banishments of whole blocs of the population. Venice was ruled by an experienced aristocracy, passionate for the welfare of the city and capable of personal sacrifice to that end. The sense of community and the discipline of the nobles enabled them to define themselves through the regulations and institutions of the state.[159] Their unity was nurtured through centuries of struggle against a hostile environment, for Venice could live only through a great act of will and energy. It was as fragile, enthuses Renouard, as the glass that was made there. Its isolation fathered that sense of community shared by the people, although possessed in the highest degree by the nobles. The Venetian men of affairs made fine administrators because of their innate sense of being at the service of the state.[160] The nobles had a long tradition of seeing their well-being only in terms of the collectivity. This intense patriotism allowed the state to impose upon them constraints that were at the same time firm and moderate, and always useful to the society.[161] It is surprising that the aristocracy did not split into two hostile groups, but it preserved its unity and its national feeling. It was this spirit that led patricians to seek burdensome offices. The Venetian patriciate offered the rare example of a class that held full power, yet knew how to restrain itself. Thus it was able to govern for several centuries without arousing too much opposition, because it kept its attention upon the general interest of the country.[162] Venice, Renouard insists, is by double title a masterwork of man: for its physical being, its monuments erected in the midst of the water and upon the sands; for its collective spirit that assures its survival and glory.[163]

Like Cessi, it is surprising to find Gina Fasoli a propagator of the myth of Venice, but her mimeographed lectures for a course in the history of Venice at Bologna in 1957–58 constitute largely a panegyric of the island republic. The Venetian constitution, studied and praised by Venetians and foreigners, appears a model of perfection. The true perfection of the Venetian political system was not in a mixed constitution, however, but in the spirit of the citizens who manned the government. The history of Venice through the centuries is a great example of will, activity, courage, perseverance, sense of responsibility, and social solidarity. Even its decadence has exemplary value.[164] Fasoli presents here a quite old-fashioned view of the constitutional reform of 1297.[165] She shares the enthusiasm for the mythical virtues of the patriciate: shrewdness, realism, capacity to sacrifice themselves for the common welfare and the greatness of their city, which they love passionately.[166] The Venetian nobles fell under a double influence: that of the eulogistic histories, to which they were exposed from youth, and from which not even we are completely freed; that of the broad-minded diplomatic *relazioni,* which were widely known and studied.[167] She quotes Maranini on the willing submission of the lower classes "with a trust that is the best proof of the goodness of Venetian government."[168] Every act of government appeared as the fruit of an anonymous and sovereign will above and beyond individual wills. That is why the word Signoria came to signify, not only the doge and his councillors, but the state itself, and why *serenissima,* the adjective applied to the Signoria, came to stand by itself for the Republic, la Serenissima.[169] No other state, not even Rome, arose from such unpromising beginnings to become a vast colonial empire, which defended Christianity so valorously for centuries against the barbarian enemy.[170] Fasoli's romanticism is especially difficult to understand, since the lectures were delivered at just about the time when she must have been finishing her very learned article on the origins of the myth. Admittedly, mimeographed lectures for students do not constitute the most scholarly format, but they are the work of a justly distinguished savant in a field in which she has great expertise. Perhaps what we see in Cessi's case, and especially in Fasoli's, is that in the monographic work based very carefully upon documents, step by step, we follow where the evidence leads us, regardless of preconceptions; in works of synthesis, however, we tend to fall back upon the received wisdom, building a wall in our minds about our hard-won scholarly knowledge, and refusing to accept the implications that necessarily follow from it.[171]

Even Cracco is capable of momentary reversion to the myth. He writes that to struggle, to sacrifice themselves for the state, to conserve and increase its internal cohesion, to increase its weight and prestige vis-à-vis foreigners, to make it splendid, religious, celebrated, and opulent became the nobles' chief ideal. They abandoned into the hands of relatives their risky mercantile careers to turn themselves into sedentary political figures permanently burdened with the exercise of power.[172]

William Bouwsma, who is one of the most distinguished students of Venice and by no means a mythographer, nonetheless does inadvertently disseminate the myth of the patriciate. His problem is typical of intellectual historians, whose interests and researches often cause them to fail to distinguish clearly between political ideas and ideals, on the one hand, and political practice, on the other. Bouwsma presents quite correctly the *formal* political structure of Venice, as well as favorable Venetian and foreign views on Venetian politics, but he has not paid much attention to political reality. He describes the constitutional equality of all nobles, who recognized no superior, had no hierarchy of status among them, and sat in their assembly, the Great Council, in any seat that was not already occupied.[173] At the formal level this also is true, but behind the constitutional facade in fact were not only disparities in ability and wealth, as he says, but family connections, patronage, and a quite recognizable hierarchy. He states that the Venetian aristocracy "existed to serve the state, in governorships, embassies, major administrative positions, or naval commands."[174] In context he is merely defining the Venetian nobility as those who were constitutionally eligible to elect to office and to hold office, but the reader is not warned that the Venetian aristocracy was normally self-serving or that only a small elite among them was able to aspire to these exalted posts. Bouwsma praises the virtues of Leonardo Donà, who was one of those nobles who did approach the ideal set by the myth. Donà, according to Bouwsma, stands as the result of the evolution of a political type that required centuries. He had a religious devotion to public service, in which he professed to submerge his identity: "I should like to be known in the Roman curia as ambassador of Venice . . . , and not as

Leonardo Donà; and equally in Venice as senator of that fatherland . . . and not by my private name." Bouwsma believes that Donà may have remained celibate for civic, as much as religious, reasons. He was reserved, imperturbable, almost inhuman in his control. Young nobles considered him a Pythagoras and an oracle.[175] Such men enabled Venice to keep alive "the political attitudes and values of the Renaissance, through her own political writings and above all through her survival as living proof of their validity. . . . In this way Venice helped to transmit the political tradition of the Renaissance to the Enlightenment, and thus she prepared the way for the fruitful recognition of the political achievement of England."[176] If we keep in mind that Bouwsma is dealing with the history of a complex of ideas, we remain on solid ground. It was, indeed, the *myth* of Venice which kept the tradition of Renaissance republicanism alive.[177]

Patricia Labalme waxes eloquent on the virtues of Bernardo Giustinian and his ancestors, who, indeed, like Donà, were among the Venetian nobles who came closest to the ideal. As a member of one of the great noble families he was molded, as Labalme sees it, for public responsibility, and he spent his life in the fulfillment of political obligations. He had before him in the persons of his uncles, Lorenzo and Marco, and his father, Leonardo, models of Venetian nobility.[178] As Bernardo portrayed it, Lorenzo Giustinian accepted the patriarchate for the sake of Venice, "on behalf of whose honor he could refuse no labor, so much did it deserve from him."[179] Bernardo's father, Leonardo, described in verse the lighthearted loves of his youth, but when he entered the Great Council he rejected these frivolities with all the sternness of Prince Hal become king. Labalme says: "[U]pon reaching his majority and donning the sober cloak of the Venetian patrician, he put away with the colored vestments of boyhood the vagaries of his past. His life became, then, not a song, but a service, not a choice, but an acquiescence, and from the day on which he presented himself to the Great Council, giving proof of his nobility, he dedicated himself to the Republic."[180] Leonardo himself wrote that it had never been possible to separate him from his civic duty, "although I have often resisted."[181] The last is an interesting comment. Bernardo was born a patrician, trained to be a statesman, active as a diplomat, and also educated as a humanist. He saw his life as service to the state. Even his humanistic endeavors were for the glory of Venice. All his activities were simply aspects of a single patriotic devotion.[182] Labalme's explanation of the inferiority of Venetian humanistic culture, certainly inferior vis-à-vis Florence, is that the monuments of Venice might not crowd the shelves of libraries, but, in their day, they crowded the Rialto and San Marco.

For these monuments were the men themselves, "formed by their education, sensitive to their society, dedicated to their political tasks."[183] Like Bernardo himself and many other propagators of the myth in the Renaissance, Labalme places the Golden Age in the past. By Bernardo's death in 1488 the tradition of an exclusive and dedicated aristocracy was becoming a thing of the past.[184] There is no reason to doubt that Leonardo, his brothers, and his son Bernardo were praiseworthy members of the Venetian nobility, although we should perhaps be a bit wary of accepting their own evaluations and Labalme's rhetoric is extreme. As we shall see, however, even if it is true, such idealism was far from typical.

The evidence cited above makes it clear that the myth of the Venetian patriciate lives, not only in popularizations of romantic bent, but in the work of serious scholars, upon whom the romantic also exercises its charms. Some of the statements are wildly fanciful; some are partly true; some are true enough, although not placed in the context of the complicated makeup and motivations of a nobility that was not as single-mindedly patriotic as had been believed. My purpose has not been to condemn scholarly works which are, in fact, praiseworthy, some in the highest degree, but to demonstrate the tenacity of the myth.

II

Welfare Jobs for the Nobles

Now LET US turn from the heady realm of political mythology to the humdrum of real life as reflected in Venetian legislation, records of trials, the diarists, and other sources. There we shall discover how the nobles exploited the Commune to provide for their own welfare, how they struggled for offices but evaded responsibilities, how they succumbed to various forms of corruption, and otherwise violated the norms set before them by the myth.

The Venetian patriciate, in fact, used the government largely for its own benefit. In this it was like other elites, except in Venice, since the early fourteenth century, the patriciate was a closed caste with a monopoly upon political authority. When we speak of the Venetian nobility or patriciate we tend to think of the owners of the great *palazzi* on the Grand Canal, of Tintoretto's portraits, of doges, procurators of St. Mark, *savi grandi,* and members of the Ten, and so we have misled ourselves. Some patricians were exceedingly rich, and some of these held the highest offices, many of which required a very great outlay of personal funds. Some were moderately prosperous. Others were poor, and their numbers increased greatly in the course of the profound economic changes of the fifteenth century. Yet, although fallen from the economic elite, they remained members of the nobility and of the Great Council. Poor nobles, like the rich, were full members of the class which possessed the state, and the ideology of the medieval city-state entitled them to an equal share in its benefits. What they received was frequently jobs. The often petty positions for which we shall see them struggling were in many cases created, not because of the necessities of government, but simply or in large measure to enable the participation of impoverished nobles in the state and to provide incomes for them.

The patrician government was, in a very important sense, a welfare scheme for the poorer members of the ruling class.[1]

On several occasions Luzzatto has analyzed the very interesting *estimo* of 1379. He reminds us that the document possesses at least great relative value, like our real property tax lists, for example, although its absolute value in terms of actual wealth may be doubted. Here are the results in tabular form as given by Luzzatto:

TABLE I		nobili	popolani
Sopra la 50.000	lire a grossi	1	
da 50.000 a 35.000	" " "	4	1
da 35.000 a 20.000	" " "	20	5
da 20.000 a 10.000	" " "	66	20
da 10.000 a 5.000	" " "	158	48
da 5.000 a 3.000	" " "	145	88
da 3.000 a 1.000	" " "	386	214
da 1.000 a 300	" " "	431	541
		1211	917

Quite alone at the top stood the fabulously rich noble Federico Cornaro with a patrimony self-assessed at 60,000 *lire a grossi*. Many other indices—still according to Luzzatto—confirm that we can accept as "rich" those with a patrimony of 20,000 *lire a grossi* or more, or 25 nobles and 6 commoners. The 224 nobles with a patrimony below 20,000 but more than 5,000 were scarcely prosperous. The 962[2] between 5,000 and 300 had patrimonies which were less than middling. We must not forget, however, that (to quote Luzzatto) "a good number of nobles are purely and simply omitted, because their patrimonies did not reach the minimum of 300 *lire*. They belong to the category of poor nobles, sad heritage of the period of decline, but which the years of the greatest prosperity did not succeed in liquidating completely. How did they live? Their only resources were the income from modest jobs that the state reserved for them, joined to the assistance of richer nobles."[3]

Luzzatto further informs us that a century later the maldistribution of wealth among the nobility had not improved, but had, in fact, become more pronounced. Sanuto reports that the majority of the 3,000 nobles of his day lived under serious financial difficulties, and Priuli goes as far as to assert that almost three-quarters of the patricians were poor and dependent upon public offices for their livelihood.[4] Contarini exhorted bishops to give a high priority to relieving the poor of noble birth.[5] Impoverished nobles sometimes contrived to eke out a living in ways less reputable than seeking public office. The Milanese ambassador Taddeo Vimercate reported in 1492 that, although it would not have been believable to him if he had not received the information from a reliable and well-informed source, 111 nobles (almost 5 percent of the patriciate) had just been exiled for being pimps.[6] Others begged. These "shamefaced poor" of noble blood had the privilege of soliciting alms with their faces covered.[7] Once the patricians for want of capital gave up their old mercantile practices many of them had no honest and nonpublic means of making ends meet.[8] Increasing pressure provoked proposals for relief.[9] Two of the heads of the Quaranta, a body noted as a haven for poor nobles,[10] advanced a scheme in 1492 for extending aid to all impoverished nobles at the expense of officeholders, who would be required to serve one-third of their terms without salary. The College and the Ten, dominated by the rich and the powerful, beat back the project and sent the proposers into exile.[11] The economic hardship of many patricians is also illustrated by Niccolò Morosini's construction of small, rent-free housing units for poor noblemen, each unit consisting of two rooms, a kitchen, and an area at canal level for storage.[12]

It is understandable, then, that public salaries meant a great deal to poor nobles, more and more so as time passed, the division between rich and poor became sharper, and increasing numbers of poor nobles accumulated at the bottom of the patriciate. In 1486 the six *capi di sestiere* were expelled from office and deprived of the Great Council and eligibility for other offices for six months for attempting to interfere with the retinues of the *governadori*. They begged for mercy: "considering their miserable calamity on account of the weight of the penalty which they suffered and damage because some of them gained their living from that, and the misery of their families." They asked to be allowed to enter the Great Council and to be eligible for other offices in order that "these poor gentlemen can live under your shade and enjoy and participate in that in which they have participated in the past."[13] A few months later Michele Salomon appealed for an end to his exile. He describes himself as in the greatest calamity, misery, and tears, along with his numerous family, which included grown daughters, as well as sons. He has no way of supporting them, so he begs for repatriation and the benefits of nobility which he enjoyed before his condemnation.[14] Another document of 1490 requests that the appellants "should participate in the benefit . . . of our magistracies and governorships with which our nobles *for the most part* live and sustain their families."[15] In 1501 Pietro Hieronymo and Alvise Bragadin appealed their condemnation by the Ten to deprivation of councils and offices for ten years as a result of a certain verbal altercation with Niccolò Zorzi at his house. They claimed to be in the greatest anxiety and grief on account of this infinite adversity, and they requested the enjoyment of the grace of the Signoria, like the other nobles.[16] In 1420 the Great Council deprived large numbers of patricians of their seats and the right to be elected to office on account of nonpayment of forced loans. The Senate noted in 1433 that such nobles were appearing daily before the Signoria pleading their poverty and the impossibility of paying the impositions. They requested that they should no longer be deprived because of their poverty of the privileges that their ancestors had bequeathed and that nature had conceded to them. The Senate, indeed, held that it was pious and just to help these "powerless ones."[17]

Salaries were sometimes reduced in cases of financial emergency for the state with more or less hardship upon the nobles. The exigencies of the Turkish war, in fact, caused the Senate to decree in December 1500 that everyone should have to serve the Republic without salary for the next year. Pietro Dolfin declared that never in his seventy-four years had he seen Venice reduced to such an extremity.[18] We can imagine the hardship to officeholders who had counted desperately upon those salaries. In fact, when the measure was renewed a year later a noble named Giovanni Antonio Minio, who was a successful advocate but who had enjoyed little political prominence, made a speech in the Great Council assailing the measure as unfair to the poor nobles, who lacked the means to live. They had been born the heirs of the benefices of the Republic, but by this measure they were deprived. The nobility, he asserted, was divided into the poor, the middling, and the rich, but the poor and middling bore all the burdens of the state, while the rich were not forced to pay what they owed. The proposed renewal was snatching the bread from the mouths of the poor nobles, who would be driven to the poorhouse by their lack of skills to earn a living in any other manner. There was also the danger that unpaid service would become the custom. Worse still, those who were elected would be prey to the temptation to commit injustice, to sell judgment, to rob the public. The doge angrily challenged Minio, arguing the necessity of the case and charging that the advocate was trying to sow dissension among the nobility and build a party for himself. The measure was passed with a large majority, and Minio was promptly fined three thousand ducats and exiled for life to Arbe.[19]

The situation certainly did not improve over the later centuries of the Venetian Republic.[20] Lane points out that the sum of more than 200,000 ducats a year paid in salaries annually to between 700 and 1,000 nobles was a very substantial contribution to the income of the patriciate.[21] Venice spent almost all of its liberal income on these salaries, not building up a treasury so that when large sums were needed the government had to impose levies which burdened the whole population.[22]

Maranini recalled an unnamed scholar, an expert on Venetian magistracies, whom he respected, arguing that Venetian administration consisted of a disorganized muddle of divided and subdivided offices as a result of the effort to give employment to the greatest possible number of nobles. Maranini did not agree with this contention, although others have and he himself conceded that the government took measures to provide for poor nobles, perhaps less out of charity than from a concern for the prestige of the aristocracy.[23] Such a cautious scholar as Lane has come very close to accepting Priuli's hint[24] that Venetian conquests on the mainland were at least partly motivated by the patrician desire for jobs. Although the subject cities retained their own laws and magistracies, and Venice sent out only a few officials to each, as the conquests increased a very considerable number of jobs paying from 100 to 500 ducats a year were provided. A significant number of Venetian nobles depended upon these for their livelihood and dignity.[25]

The evidence that very large numbers of nobles depended upon public office to eke out a meager living is absolutely overwhelming.[26] James Williamson has put it in appropriately crass and modern terms: "Venice provided 'jobs for the boys' when needed." He points to the large number of positions created in 1442 and 1450, two years in which attendance at the Great Council was high. Since the council was most occupied with election and members attended for the most part in pursuit of jobs and salaries, if not for themselves, for relatives, friends, clients, or patrons, the heavy attendance is an indicator of the need for jobs. Williamson believes that the posts were almost certainly unnecessary, designed primarily to provide relief for poor nobles. The retreat of these impoverished patricians from the pursuit of commerce to government offices may well be a more important trend in the fifteenth century than the increasing tendency of the rich to invest their capital in land.[27] The quest for public salaries, of course, was not unique to Venice. Philip Jones tells us that in late medieval Italy the desire "to gain access, as the Florentines put it, to the public 'manger,' the *mangiatoia*," was widespread and a common subject of complaint.[28]

The demand for offices by the Venetian nobility was so intense that the Signoria found itself granting to them by *grazia*[29] posts that belonged by customs to *cittadini* and other subjects. Sometimes this was done even in violation of provisions and concessions made to the provincials. There was much complaining, but still the nobles feverishly petitioned for positions. The Ten in 1455 called for the election of a *zonta* of twenty nobles in order that the problem should be considered. Meanwhile, no such *grazia* should be granted.[30] Two days later the Ten returned to the same problem. They noted that both the Senate and the Great Council had tried to give order to the election of nobles to offices, but neither the law nor orderly process was being followed. Very many offices by which *cittadini* and other subjects were accustomed to live were being granted by the Signoria to nobles. Complaints issued not only from the deprived non-nobles, but also from those nobles who did not receive the spoils, for they said that such favors were granted on account of friendship and not on the basis of equality. Since neither the Senate nor the Great Council was obeyed and neither penalties nor oaths did any good, the Ten declared that all *grazie* considered by the Signoria but not yet acted upon by the appropriate council should be revoked, although those already passed by the Great Council or the Forty should stand. Once the term of the grantee was ended, however, no one should be sent in his place until the Ten had declared which offices belong to nobles. Then all offices should be filled by election, according to a law of 1450.[31] A couple of weeks later the Ten and its Zonta began to determine which posts belonged to nobles.[32] At least one bit of documentary evidence states clearly that some government positions were sinecures. In 1424 the *podestà* of the Lido, whose term had ended but whose successor had not yet been named, was allowed by the Senate to repatriate himself on the grounds that his predecessors had been accustomed to spend their time at Venice or elsewhere than the Lido, because they had little to do, since there were only five or six families to govern there.[33]

Clearly the government was anxious to expand the number of jobs available to destitute patricians. In 1454 the Senate appointed a representative to consult with one Master Ferlino, who was proposing a scheme which would provide jobs for more than two hundred nobles at incomes of two hundred ducats a year or more at modest cost to the state. The Senate jumped at the chance, "because the multiplication of our nobles rightly induces the Signoria to be watchful that they should be able to live with honor."[34] We do not know the nature of the plan or the outcome, but the Senate was still dealing with Ferlino five months later.[35]

BALESTRIERI DELLA POPA

The most striking of the jobs created for the nobles were those of the *balestrieri della popa* or bowmen of the quarterdeck. They originaly performed the martial function of ordinary bowmen, but, as nobles, the *balestrieri della popa* mingled with the officers and the merchants and dined at the captain's table. Sometimes they were known as *nobeli di galia*.[36] They had been obliged to qualify at shooting matches where the selection was made. They received a salary, free passage, food, and the right to carry a certain amount of merchandise for trading.[37] In time the positions became handouts for poor nobles. The eligible age was lowered from twenty to eighteen, and even younger boys were sometimes allowed.[38] Even a blind noble and a woman received *balestrierie*.[39] The large number, in itself, shows that the position had lost its original military function and become a sinecure.[40]

The *balestrieria* was a means of preparing young nobles for a career by means of on-the-job training, observing more experienced men perform their tasks. They were not formally apprenticed, as commoners often were, but they went to sea at an early age, often in the company of a father, uncle, or older brother. The Senate created the institution of the *balestrieri della popa* to encourage this training and to assist the poorer nobles to get a start.[41] As the Maggior Consiglio, perhaps already rather anachronistically, put it in 1493, the major reason for the *balestrieri* was "to make our gentlemen experienced and expert at seafaring, which, as everyone understands, is the principal foundation of our state. . . ."[42] Or, as the same council declared in 1357, "it would be honorable and useful for our land to cause our nobles, by whom it is necessary that this land be governed, to go about the world and to investigate it, so that they might be able to be wisely instructed and tested in the affairs of the Commune and to expose their persons in honors and labors when it will be necessary."[43] Lane's Andrea Barbarigo got his start in just this manner. His noble father had been financially ruined by a heavy fine for violation of the rules of navigation on the galleys of Alexandria, which he commanded in 1417. In the following year young Andrea began his career with a very modest capital of two hundred ducats as a *balestriere della popa*.[44] The commercial depression of the fifteenth century, by reducing the number of galleys and other ships, diminished the opportunities for poor nobles to get a start as *balestrieri*,[45] but Benedetto Sanuto's advice to his younger brother, who was going abroad as a *balestriere* for the first time, shows that the educational function of the institution was still somewhat viable as late as the mid-sixteenth century.[46]

Marino Sanuto acknowledges that another purpose was to provide an income for nobles who had no offices or income, and were not able to exercise any trade. At that time the salary was sixty ducats or more a year, which could be raised to a total of one hundred to two hundred ducats with profits from trading.[47] In this way many poor families were sustained.[48] An act of 1397 refers to an earlier law allowing each merchant galley to carry up to four noble *balestrieri* among the normal complement of bowmen. The act of 1397 instead requires that three such *balestrieri* had to be employed with a fourth optional.[49] In 1400 the fourth *balestriere* was also required.[50] In 1421 the Senate required that the four roundships which were about to set out against the pirates each should have two *balestrieri della popa*.[51] The six roundships appointed for the voyage to Syria in 1433 were also required to carry two *nobiles ballistarios* each, "because there are in Venice many poor nobles."[52] Since the number of poor young nobles had multiplied so exceedingly, the Senate in 1437 raised the number of noble *balestrieri* per merhcant galley to six.[53] A motion to raise the number to eight was defeated in 1455,[54] but in 1483 such a proposal was passed.[55] In Sanuto's time every merchant galley was required to carry eight *nobeli di galia,* light galleys two, roundships above six hundred *botte* also two, and roundships between four hundred and six hundred *botte* one.[56] For the total number of nobles who profited from this welfare scheme in a year we find in the sources differing estimates. The Ten states in 1448 that it was more than 150.[57] In 1500 the Senate estimated that 120 to 130 out of about 250 who presented themselves were chosen as *balestrieri*.[58] Approximately twenty years later Contarini declared that 200 or more nobles gained the benefits.[59] The variation, of course, is related both to the decline in the number of ships and the increase in the number required for each.

According to the act of 1397 the noble *balestrieri* were to be elected from among the nobles at least twenty years old, but not yet forty, by a special committee or *collegio*. They were to provide their own crossbows and other arms.[60] Later the choice came into the hands of the Quaranta criminale, one of its more valued prerogatives.[61] The shooting exercises at which candidates qualified for the remunerative assignment were sometimes riotous. The Senate lamented in 1421 that "little order has been followed and many dishonest acts committed." The intention of the law was that the better bowmen and the more poverty-stricken should be chosen, but under pressure from some nobles and others who were always standing by the less sufficient were actually elected. The Senate decreed that henceforth the *patroni* of the Arsenal, where the shooting took place, should prevent the entry of unauthorized persons.[62] By 1444, however, the exercise was filled with a thousand disorders and as many infractions, primarily because of the absence of those officials who were supposed to help the committee. Lists were set up for each of the *sestieri* of Venice, but competitors entered whatever lists they wished without tickets and they shot as many times as they wished. The specified officials were obliged to be at their stations, so that competitors should shoot only in the lists of their own *sestieri* and should not have two or three tries. Everyone who shot had to have a ticket, and no one should have entered the lists without a crossbow, because six or eight had been entering together, and one of them had been shooting for the others.[63] The stakes were high, at least for poor nobles, and the chaos seems even worse than the disorder surrounding elections in the Great Council.

Balestrierie, moreover, were often granted by *grazia.* The Senate overwhelmingly voted in 1445 to make Giovanni Capello a *balestriere della popa,* "just as has been done in similar cases for many." The circumstances were that his brother Giorgio had gone down with the goods of both of them on the ship of Carlo Loredan.[64] In very early 1498 the Great Council sought to assist those nobles who had suffered because of the shipwreck of two triremes in the Gulf of Quarnero and of a roundship on the Flanders run. To the fathers, sons, or brothers of those who drowned they granted one *balestrieria* a year for four years; to those who were saved but lost their goods, one per year for two years. Giovanni Orio, who was returning from a tour as councillor in Candia with goods occupying seveteen *bocche,* and who escaped only with his life, was given six *balestrieri* over four years. He had also lost a son and his goods on the Flemish voyage. Others, too, received the favors of the state.[65] A couple of months later one *balestrieria* a year for two years was allotted to each of four nobles who had been on the Morosini galley. Sanuto, however, disapproved of the measure.[66] Four *balestrierie,* one a year for four years, were also allocated by the Great Council to the four brothers of Paolo Foscari, who had been drowned in Flanders—undoubtedly in the same shipwreck as Orio's son.[67] Early in 1499 an unusually generous grant of eight *balestrierie* was made to the wife of Geronimo Zorzi, who was in prison for homicide and assassination. Domenico Malipiero remonstrates that "thus the treasure which serves for the feeding of poor, needy gentlemen has been dispensed to someone to whom it ought not."[68] In 1500 the Great Council granted a *balestrieria* for life to Leonardo Lombardo, who had become blind, so that he would have a means of supporting his family.[69]

The government was especially likely, of course, to provide for those who had sacrificed themselves for the Republic, using its power of patronage to grant what amounted to pensions.[70] The four sons of Bernardo Cicogna, captain of the Barbary galleys, who had lost his life in action against French pirates, received in 1498 a grant of two *balestrierie* each for the two succeeding years. Sanuto notes that although the measure passed there were many negative votes.[71] A sixteen-year-old *nobele di galia,* Giovanni Contarini, was awarded one *balestrieria* a year for life in recognition of his loss of an arm in the same fight.[72] In 1500 the Great Council voted two positions (or one) as *balestriere* for life to the five sons of Giovanni Alvise (or Giovanni Andrea) Cocco. Their father had died in the battle at Modon, and he had left no money, having squandered it on gambling and women. Pietro Dolfin complains of this act, because other poor nobles would be deprived of this source of support, while the beneficiaries should enjoy it even if they rose to positions of wealth and prestige.[73] In 1501 the Senate and the Great Council took action to prevent the erosion of the rights of the Forty to elect *balestrieri della popa*. Whereas 120 or 130 should have been elected there, the number had been reduced to 30 or 32 by the *grazie* passed in the Great Council. In the future no *balestrieri* should be named by *grazia* unless with the consent of all six councillors, all three heads of the Forty and five-sixths of the Great Council with at least 900 members voting. An amendment abrogated all concessions for a time or for life of *balestrieri*. *Nobeli di galia* should be named by the Quaranta criminale, according to custom.[74]

The salaries of the *nobeli di galia* were a burden on commerce, the patron of the galley being responsible, except that the public treasury paid in the case of naval expeditions. Private *patroni* were also responsible for the costs of passage and food.[75]

As the welfare function of the *balestrieri della popa* grew at the expense of the military and educational functions, nobles who were elected to these remunerative positions increasingly sent substitutes in their places. In 1423 we hear of noble *balestrieri* selling their places to others for a kickback of part of the pay. The Senate required that the elected noble go unless he were ill.[76] Nevertheless, only nine years later we learn that the majority of those elected were substituting someone else in their places. An investigation was undertaken, and the officials of armament were ordered not to accept any uncertified *balestriere*.[77] Sickness in the family and unsuitable age came to be accepted excuses, and those elected were permitted to send instead sons, brothers, or other relatives who were of the required age.[78] The privilege of substituting was even extended to those who felt that they could not go on account of the press of their affairs. It was pointed out, moreover, that some did not have sons or brothers, so, in the interest of equity, those elected were allowed to substitute any noble they wished who met the age requirement and was acceptable to the Signoria.[79] And so it came about that the positions were sold, which, protested the Great Council, was against the intentions of their ancestors, who had established the *balestrieri della popa*. The council therefore decided that those who were elected must either go themselves or send a brother or son of the appropriate age.[80] In discussing a law of 1501 which again prohibited the selling of the privilege, Priuli lets us know just what had been happening and why it was so contrary to the intention of the law. Patrons of galleys and roundships had been buying the positions themselves in order not to suffer the costs of the *balestrieri nobeli*. In consequence, says the diarist, where there were supposed to be eight young nobles receiving training and experience in maritime affairs and commerce, there were only one or two. This was very detrimental, of course, to the effort to strengthen the seafaring tradition. The new law provided that any salary and expenses not spent as intended by the government had to be paid instead to the Arsenal, so that the patron could not avoid the expense. Those elected could still send, however, a father or a brother.[81] Apparently, like so many well-intentioned Venetian laws, the legislation did not have any lasting effect. Sanuto's *Cronachetta* and Contarini's *De magistratibus,* at any rate, inform us that those who did not wish to go on the voyages sold the privilege to other nobles.[82]

Despite the opportunities open to the *balestrieri della popa,* there was throughout the fifteenth and early sixteenth centuries some reluctance to take the job.[83] Contarini and Priuli find this an increasing problem, as noble engagement in commerce declined and patricians ever more avidly sought salaried public offices close to home.[84]

Analogous to the young *balestrieri della popa* were the older nobles for whom provision was made by a decree of the Senate in 1433. Many nobles who were expert officers and had been patrons of ships and admirals of the galleys suffered from penury when they grew a little older. It was necessary, the Senate believed, for the Republic to provide for maritime commerce, upon which the growth of the city was based, and it would be useful for the ships to have an experienced person who could in case of necessity command or give counsel. So it was decided that every roundship of over 400 *botte* should employ at not less than five ducats a month a noble of at least forty years of age who had been patron or pilot of a roundship or admiral, councillor, captain, or patron of the galleys. He should eat at the captain's table, like the young *balestrieri nobeli,* and should be able to carry a bit of merchandise for trading, like all seamen.[85] A year and a half later we learn that the law was not being observed, so new steps were taken to enforce it.[86]

QUARANTA

The Council of Forty, which multiplied in the course of the fifteenth century to two and then three councils, was another means of providing an income to poor nobles. For a long time it was not so, for, like the Great Council and the Senate, the Forty offered no remuneration, but in 1454 pay was begun. Many members of the Quaranta, the act declared, had been in great necessity.[87] Priuli stated that the nobles of the Quaranta criminale were poor, unable to pay their taxes, had little to lose, and heeded only their own advantage.[88] In fact, the Forty had become a refuge for poorer nobles. The rich did not seek the office, according to Contarini, and would have been easily defeated if they had. Through this highest judicial body of the Republic the poor nobles were not only subsidized financially, but, in conformity with the ideal of the medieval city-state, they were allowed a role in government beyond their participation in the Great Council and in minor offices.[89] We have just seen that the Quaranta criminale gained the privilege of dispensing the valuable *balestrierie,* and in the chapter on *broglio* we will learn that the Quaranta was a center of that much-favored and much criticized activity. Pullan likens the elected heads of the Quaranta to the Roman tribunes, defending the rights, not of the people, but of the poor nobility.[90]

ADVOCATES

Still another device employed by the oligarchy to subsidize poorer members of the patriciate was the election by the Great Council of official attorneys whom plaintiffs and defendants in civil cases were required to employ for a fee. During our period, at any rate, they had to be nobles, though they did not have to be educated in the law or even to know very much, although it was thought that they at least ought to have knowledge of the statutes. In fact, the position was often a sinecure, for litigants who cared for their causes hired skilled lawyers and left the official attorneys to their ease, although they still had to pay them. In the early sixteenth century there were twenty-four advocates, twenty for the courts at the ducal palace and four for the Rialto. A position as public advocate was another early step in the career of Andrea Barbarigo.[91]

CASTELLANIES AND OTHER COMMANDS

The Venetian Empire offered many opportunities for jobs for poor nobles. Among other positions, castellanies and commands were used in peacetime to provide employment. If peacetime changed suddenly to wartime, *tant pis.* A *grazia* of 1311 granted the castellany of Castro

Nuovo of Crete to Giovanni Zancarolo, who had been captured in the war over Ferrara and had spent eleven months in prison.[92] In 1317 Andrea Cornaro of Crete was granted a castellany, because in the defense of the island he and his house had raised a force of cavalry, on account of which he fell into poverty.[93] Marino Trevisan was rewarded *per grazia* for his service in the army of Ferrara in the same year. First he received the right to export grain from Apulia, but, when he did not exercise it, he was granted instead a castellany in Crete.[94] On the same day the Great Council gave the castellany of Belforte to Bompledo Grisoni for two years following the completion of the term of the incumbent, because of the grave injuries suffered to his two very valuable horses.[95] Graziano Zorzi gained a grace in 1400 because his family had expended almost all their wealth over the years in the Republic's wars.[96] In 1442 the Great Council showed concern for the many poor nobles who lacked assistance. The honor of the Signoria demanded that it provide for these unfortunates, so various castellanies, a position as *podestà,* and a constableship were devoted to this cause.[97] But here there is no indication that these were to be a reward for service or a compensation for unexpected losses, as in the earlier examples. The act seems to provide means for the relief of poor nobles generally. The Senate objected in 1450 to the daily grants by the Signoria of fortified places at the petition of many nobles. Because these fortifications were so important to the state, the Senate claimed the right to approve or disapprove all *grazie* granting castles or allowing their exchange, except that the Collegio should have the power to dispose of them in time of war or other necessity.[98] A few months later the sovereign Great Council asserted that all castellanies and offices, many of which had been granted by grace, should now be filled by election in that assembly.[99] In 1501 provision was made for the survivors of nobles who had died fighting the Turks at Modon. The four sons of Alvise Michiel received the castellany of Mestre for fifteen years. It was worth two hundred ducats a year.[100] Geronimo and Alessandro Malipiero, brothers of Giovanni, who also had given his life at Modon and merited a greater reward, received the castellany of the Castella Sarasinesca at Padua. It was worth 120 ducats a year.[101]

The voracious demand for offices on Crete, as well as the liberality with which they were granted, is the subject of an act of the Great Council of 1304. Such offices, with some significant exceptions, could only be granted henceforth with the consent of five of the Council of Six, thirty of the Forty, and two-thirds of the Great Council.[102] In an attempt to preserve positions for the nobility the Senate decreed in 1356 that all the officials appointed by the rector of Canea, except for scribes and appraisers of grain, should be either nobles of the Venetian Great Council or of that of Canea itself.[103] The Senate in 1385 took note of the demands for castellanies and other offices and possessions on Crete granted by *grazie* for life or at the good pleasure of the Signoria. Notable damage to the Commune resulted, because the Signoria was often deceived. In the future no such *grazia* could be granted until after the two most recent ex-dukes of Crete were consulted and letters had been sent to the rectors who would have jurisdiction over the desired offices asking their advice.[104] The principle of the welfate state for nobles was clearly stated by the Great Council in 1388: the Signoria was accustomed to come to the aid of its noble citizens in their necessity, especially to those who had become poor through no fault of their own. The Republic could not allow its "begging nobles" to be totally abandoned. Raniero Premarin, who had often conducted himself faithfully and in a praiseworthy manner in the service of the state, had been reduced to straitened circumstances by having to feed four little children. So he was granted a castellany in Crete or some other position there for two years.[105] Later in the same year the Great Council came to the aid of Pietro Loredan, who was burdened with a very large family and could hardly live in Venice. He received the headships of the *avogadori* in Candia.[106] A few months later the council similarily had pity on Lorenzo Bon, who bore poverty with his numerous family, by making him a judge in Candia. The government could not accept that its noble citizens should be forced miserably to beg.[107] The Senate complained in 1394 that the act of 1385 concerning petitions for castellanies and other offices and possessions was not being observed, because the heads of the Forty moved exceptions to it every day in favor of insufficient and undeserving nobles. So they raised the penalty, which probably had little effect.[108]

In 1399 the Senate by *grazia* granted the castle of Bicorne in Crete to Antonio Premarin on account of his poverty. He was the son of the late Raniero Premarin, who had received a castellany by *grazia* because of his poverty and large family eleven years previously.[109] What happened to Antonio is unknown, but seventeen months later the same castellany was given *per grazia* to his brother Andrea.[110] In 1420 the Senate also complained that the law of 1356 reserving offices under the rector of Canea for nobles was not being obeyed, for the offices were given to rustics and other low persons. The rector was commanded to appoint nobles under penalty of two hundred ducats.[111] In 1459 the Great Council found that not only was the government of Crete appointing commoners to positions reserved for nobles, but that the Great Council itself was doing so, and it took measures to see that such posts as commanders of the Cretan galleys, advocates, and *balestrieri* should be filled by nobles.[112]

We will not attempt to list the many offices which might serve for the financial relief of hard-pressed patricians, partly because it would be extensive, and partly because inclusion would depend upon the degree of impoverishment of the office seeker. Occasionally we do find a list of some of the offices exploited for this purpose. An act of the Great Council in 1392 speaks of minor offices held regularly by poor nobles, who could not by any means have supported themselves and their families from the incomes, which had been reduced during the War of Chioggia and were now raised. The act specifies: judges with large salaries; *avvocati proprii;* collectors of customs on wine; the Five of peace, who were among the chief officers of police; the officials holding office at Rialto; the salt officials; the *vicedomino* of the Lombards; officials over gold leaf; officials of the Fondaco dei Tedeschi; rope officials; *officiales publicorum;* officials over cloth of gold; officials of the Levant; consuls of merchants; and paymasters of the troops.[113] A list of 1442 might not be worth recording, except for its prologue (or *arenga*), which declares that the number of nobles has greatly increased and continues to grow, so that care must be taken to find governorships and offices for them. The act provides for the election of the following: governor of Argos; treasurer of Nauplia; councillors of Canea; captain of the fortress of Corfu; captain of the fortress of Modon; captain of the fortress of Negroponte; the treasurer of Sebenico; the treasurer of Capodistria, etc.[114] These were not at all minor jobs, and they carried quite handsome salaries and perquisites. It is true, however, that at least some of them required the maintenance of households and horses. There is a similar act of 1444.[115] Sanuto also informs us that the positions of collectors for the governors and *appuntatori a San Marco* were sinecures for needy nobles.[116]

We have already dealt with the substitution of relatives as *balestrieri della popa* and even of the sale of such posts. Other offices, too, came to be considered a form of property in which one had a vested right. In 1459 the Senate complained that when a governor or a captain died, his son

43

or another relative had the place and, of course, the income, which brought great peril to the land. Provision was therefore made for the prompt election of a successor in case of the death of a *podestà,* captain, *provveditore,* or governor.[117] Still, substitutions continued to be made. Niccolò Zio had been chosen one of the Cinque a pace by the Ten "for himself and his son." Niccolò, however, was too old to serve, and his son was absent with the doge, so Niccolò sought permission to name a suitable substitute. It was granted until the return of his son.[118] This entire attitude that public office is a source of income, not a responsibility, may be charitable, but it is a poor way to staff a government. Not only is the position often treated as a sinecure, but even a hardworking recipient of such a position is not likely to be well chosen for the task.

DISTRIBUTION OF OFFICES

Although individual nobles avidly sought to be in office as often as possible, it was the often-professed collective will of the patriciate that there should be a certain equality in government, as much as possible, so that all nobles should participate in the honors and burdens (not to mention the incomes) of the land according to their conditions.[119] A couple of decades before the Serrata del Maggior Consiglio, the Great Council had already established that a salaried official could not have a second office, whether salaried or unsalaried.[120] A variation on the holding of multiple offices was the reservation of a second position. In 1386 the Great Council pointed to the bad custom that captains of the galleys, finding themselves in the city, were elected to governorships, which they managed to have reserved, meanwhile remaining captains. It was not proper that one noble should have two such notable positions, but rather that all should participate. Such persons, therefore, could have their choice, but must give up one or the other.[121] Another gambit was to be elected from one closely related office to another, as from official of silver money to official of gold money and vice versa at the mint. This was prohibited in 1432.[122]

Nobody was expected to be allowed to enjoy the fruits of public office continuously, but it was intended that offices should circulate, inspiring a small hope in everybody rather than satisfying a few. It was for this reason that the terms of office were short, averaging perhaps twelve to sixteen months and, with the exception of the dogeship and the regular procuratorships of St. Mark, not exceeding three years.[123] This is stated explicitly in an act of 1454. The practice had been that castellans held office for three, four, or even five years, so it was fixed that their terms should be no longer than two years; governorships and offices on the mainland which had been held for two years ought to be for only one, except for some specified governorships.[124] Less than a year later, though, the Great Council was complaining that governors were succeeding in prolonging their terms to the detriment of others who were waiting for the jobs.[125] An act of the Great Council in 1490 directed against the prolongation of terms of offices declares that it is appropriate that all should share equally in those public positions "with which the majority of our nobles live and sustain their families."[126]

We are not concerned, however, nor were the Venetian nobles, just with individuals, but with families, which stood between the individuals and the state, and which in Venice were as important as either. An equitable distribution of incomes, honors, and responsibilities was therefore desired, not just among individuals, but among families, so the number of members of a family who could hold certain positions was limited. Even before the Serrata salt officials, officials at Rialto, and judges and officials of the palace could not have as colleagues anyone of the same lineage (*schiata*).[127] The same council decided in 1481 that nobles related to *podestà,* captains, dukes, castellans, treasurers, and other officials could not serve in the same places. The degree of relationship should be the same as that for which they would have to leave the Great Council.[128] This was revoked in 1485, however, in favor of the old rule which only prohibited relatives serving in offices in which they would have occasion to judge the same causes.[129] All of the above may reflect some concern for conflict of interest, as well as a desire to pass the offices around, but the case of the *balestrieri della popa* (1493) is absolutely clear: no more than one or at most two from one family could be elected in one year. The act defined the family as those living together in one house and not emancipated, and its intention clearly was to distribute the welfare.[130]

CONTUMACIA

Contumacia as used here does not mean "contumacy" in the English sense of defiance, a meaning which is shared by Italian, but rather it is more like the alternative Italian meaning of quarantine. It signifies the practice of excluding officeholders after the expiration of their terms of office for a specified time from the same post, from various positions or (with some exceptions) from all offices. This was one of the most effective means by which the Venetian constitution provided for a broad distribution among the patricians of the spoils of office.[131] There were, it is true, reasons for the practice that had more relevance to the public good: by this means it was assured that many of the ruling class had a chance to learn something of government, very often in several offices; the Venetians also had a healthy respect for the darker side of human nature, believing that men could not be trusted with long exercise of power.[132] The more exalted reasons, however, are rarely mentioned in the laws, while the intention to share the benefits of office-holding on a broad basis (among the patricians, of course) is freely and frequently stated.[133]

The first act on the subject that I have found was passed by the Great Council in 1280, and it was experimental. It provided that after the duke of Crete, the *baiuli* of Acre, Tyre, and Negroponte, the castellans of Coron, the counts of Zara and Ragusa, the *podestà* of Capodistria, Parenzo, and Chioggia end their terms of office they could not be elected to any of the specified offices for two years. The act was to be in force for six years.[134]

In 1281 the Great Council took the first step toward what was to become a more or less general rule, declaring that neither councillors nor their sons should hold councillorships for a period as long as that they had served.[135] The same council in 1290 reaffirmed an act, although they could not find the original in the official records, which provided that no officials except the Small Council and the Council of Forty could be reelected into the same office until they had vacated it for a year.[136] In 1300 the Senate provided that castellans and officials, except advocates, had to remain out of office for as long as they had been in it.[137] A senatorial act of 1386 refers to the practice of excluding captains of the Gulf and other similar rectors from reelection for one year, and it provides that captains of merchant galleys should also not be eligible for reelection for the same voyage for a succeeding year.[138] The Great Council noticed in 1393 that the judgeships and advocateships in the courts of the ducal palace were all in the hands of a very few, who moved from one to the other, whereas it was the intention of the ancestors of the patricians that many should participate, so it was decreed that a judge or an advocate of the palace might not succeed in any such positions until one year after leaving office.[139] Another statesmanlike reason for *contumacia* turns up in an act of the Great Council of 1395. The right of appeal against the decisions of their rectors had been allowed to the citizens of the subject territories in the interest of justice, but this proved ineffective as long as potential appellants feared that the same rector against whom they were appealing would be reelected to office. It was therefore provided that rectors should stand aside from office as long as they had stood in it.[140] An act of the Great Council in

1408 refers to the fact that almost all officials and judges are denied reelection either for a year or as long as their term of office. It adds that advocates of the commune should have a six-month period of contumacy.[141] Nonetheless, in 1419 the Great Council declared that in the elections of many officials it is provided that they can be reelected, so that such officials enjoy their offices for many years. In the interest of broader participation in government, however, it was established that they could not be reelected unless they had been out of office for as long as they had been in it.[142] The Senate voted fifty to zero in 1419 for a proposal that the *savi del consiglio* should have a period of *contumacia* for six months, but the measure may have failed for want of a quorum.[143] As usual the Venetian legislation on this subject does not fall into a consistent pattern, indicating either that there are lost acts or that laws were unenforced and forgotten, for in 1428 the Great Council, ignoring the act of 1395, noted that rectors at more than forty ducats were required to stand aside as long as they had been in office. It extended the rule to rectors at less than forty ducats and also to most other officials serving abroad.[144] The rule was sufficiently generalized by 1432 that the Great Council alluded to laws requiring that anyone "who will have been in any office should not be in it unless he will have vacated it for as long as he stood in it."[145] Finally in 1443 the Great Council ruled that all Venetian officials, with a few exceptions, should stay out of office for as long as they had served.[146]

In some cases the restriction was more severe. In 1410 the Great Council objected that only a few nobles held governorships, because after a short time they were reelected. Henceforth no *podestà*, captain, count, or rector on *terraferma* or in the maritime empire as far as the further limit of the Gulf of Quarnero could be reelected into his office for four years in order that all should participate in the benefits of office.[147] A few days later the council decided that captains of the merchant galleys to Flanders, Romania, Beirut, and Alexandria should be ineligible to be captains for the same voyages for five years, in order that more nobles should exercise themselves in seamanship. Concerning this the council was completely serious, and not merely rationalizing the division of the spoils. A captain of a merchant galley, however, could be elected captain of the Gulf, but a captain of the Gulf could not be reelected for three years.[148] Within a month the act was amended to prohibit the election of captains of merchant galleys to a similar post for the other voyages for two years.[149] In 1418 the act on *podestà*, captains, counts, and rectors was extended to embrace other rectors, consuls, *baiuli*, and castellans.[150]

By 1450, according to the Great Council, the old provisions concerning *contumacia* were no longer effective in distributing offices equitably, because the number of nobles had increased so much. It therefore adopted the sweeping general rule that without exception no officer receiving a salary or provision from the Signoria or from any community or person subject to the Signoria should after leaving his post receive any office until a period of time equal to his previous tenure had elapsed. He also should not be reelected to the same office within four years.[151]

Priuli tells us that in 1500 the Senate decreed that the *savi* of the Pien Collegio should be subject to *contumacia* equal to the term of their office, but the act was quickly revoked.[152] Sanuto, on the other hand, at almost the same time reports that the *contumacia* of the *savi del consiglio* and *di terraferma* was raised from three months to six.[153] Seven months later Antonio Tron, who had been one of the sponsors of the above act, proposed in the Collegio an act to impose a *contumacia* upon the *savi agli ordini* for as long as they held office. Paolo Pisani and Sanuto himself, who held that office, spoke against the measure, and the doge ordered Tron not to push it.[154] The reason for the opposition, I suspect, is that *savio agli ordini* was an honorable position on the fringes of power either for young nobles climbing the ladder or a consolation prize for older ones, like Sanuto, who never broke into the inner circle. The Senate, again on the initiative of Antonio Tron, in 1500 referred to the general act of 1450 with praise, but noted that in the succeeding fifty years many official positions both within the city and outside it had been created which had been exempted from the rule. They were therefore brought under the provision of exclusion from all salaried office for the same time as the term of office and *contumacia* of four years for the same office.[155]

On the other hand, exceptions were included in some of the laws on *contumacia*. The early act of 1290 prohibiting the holding of the same office without the lapse of a year excluded the Small Council and the Forty.[156] The Great Council noticed in 1420 that the prohibition against reelection could be harmful to the Republic; in this case the reelection of one official of gold money was allowed, because that office was a craft (*misterium*) concerning which men do not know much unless they have experience of it.[157] The most obvious exceptions had to do with the necessities of war. The 1395 law on rectors was to be binding only in peacetime.[158] Similarly the acts of 1410 on sea captains provided that in time of war they should be elected as it seemed better and more secure for the state.[159] From the *contumacia* law of 1443 members of the Council of Six, procurators of Saint Mark, advocates of the Commune, the Forty, officials of the night, and the heads of the *sestieri,* and the old and new auditors of sentences were excepted.[160] The general act of 1450, in spite of its *nemine exceptato,* did exempt the Council of Six, the procurators of Saint Mark, the advocates of the Commune, the Forty, and the *balestrieri nobeli,* as well as sea captains in wartime.[161] An act of the Senate in 1506 reaffirmed *contumacia,* but exempted councillors, those in place of procurators, advocates of the Commune, all called *savi,* captains-general of the sea, provisors of the fleet, captains of the Gulf, captains of the galleys of the *mude,* captains of the coast of the March, *sopracomiti,* and judges of the court and of the council.[162]

As in other areas, the laws on this subject were badly enforced. The Senate objected in 1461 that some rectors and officials did not report the date of their entry into their functions, and therefore the laws on *contumacia* could not be enforced. The Senate decreed the keeping of a double set of records in the chancellor's office and in the Office of Old Accounts.[163] It obviously did not work, because only a little over a year later the Ten legislated against some presumptuous nobles who allowed themselves to be elected to positions even though they were under the ban of *contumacia,* thus depriving another noble, "who would have lived from the income of that benefice for that period."[164]

LARGE NUMBERS of Venetian patricians were poor. The patriciate was hereditary and did not change in composition very readily or very much with the rise and fall of fortunes. There was very little upward mobility into the ruling class and almost none downward out of it. As times got harder in the fifteenth century, we clearly are not speaking of *relative* poverty among the nobility nor of genteel poverty (pimping is not genteel) but, for some nobles at any rate, real indigence.

One means of coping with poverty among the ruling class was to exploit the resources of the state to provide jobs, some of which had genuine responsibilities and many of which did not. Usually when we speak of the Venetian Republic or another state being the property of the ruling class, we have in mind the power of a wealthy elite, and this is one face of the Venetian coin. On the other side, though, we see the Republic as a vast endowment for the support of less fortunate members of the patriciate.[165]

The Italian city-states typically regarded the state as the common possession of the citizens (in the case of Venice, read "nobles"), whose benefits and burdens should be shared more or less equally among them. It did not, therefore, require any radical change of direction for the Venetian government to seek to provide positions for nobles, not only by legislating short terms and ineligibility for reelection, which were common practices, but also by multiplying offices and fragmenting functions. The lack of a rational bureaucratic order may indeed, as Stella, following Muazzo, pointed out, have protected individuals and the public against oppression through sheer inefficiency.[166] The trade-off, of course, was that the government was not well run. There was also a high price for the inefficiency of a spoils system in a very immediate and obvious sense. Vergerio tells us that, in spite of the large income to the treasury from the imposts on goods being imported and exported, almost everything was eaten up in interest payments and the salaries of magistrates.[167] Another problem was the failure to enforce laws and the tendency to grant exceptions from them. With regard to the act of 1501 requiring that *balestrieri* must be elected in the Quaranta, Priuli remarked: "Even this act, however, has not been observed, nor was there a need to propose such acts on this subject, because it had been provided for by our ancestors. It was only necessary to put into execution without favoritism what had already been ordained. Where the benefits and the misdeeds of the Venetian nobles were treated, however, and especially those of the multitude on account of *broglio*, they plug up their eyes."[168] Surely this tendency to adopt measures outside the law and even contrary to it contributed to the contempt for law that the Venetians themselves mocked with the maxim: *Una leze veneziana / dura una settimana.*[169]

There is nothing basically unworthy, of course, in providing for the poor. When the spoils of office are the instrument, however, government sacrifices other important objectives to compassion for the needy. Those who held offices were less likely to be competent and less inclined to serve the purposes of the state. While blind men and widows did not actually serve as bowmen, those who bought the positions from these beneficiaries of the spoils often did not possess any qualifications for helping to defend the vessel. The spoils system, moreover, is prone to abuse. Without rules that were consistently obeyed, appointments were subject to favoritism and caprice.[170] The use of offices for the purpose of relief, moreover, led to a disruptive competition for offices, which the Venetian government dreaded.

III

Broglio Onesto

THE VENETIAN ELECTORAL SYSTEM was based upon the idealistic but impractical notion that the office should seek the man, and not vice versa. Ermolao Barbaro, for example, in his funeral oration for Niccolò Marcello, praised the deceased because he had never sought office or solicited votes, but, when called upon by the Republic, had served with great zeal.[1] The nominators and electors were supposed to use their own uninfluenced judgments, free of pressure and even of arguments, to select the best candidates to serve the profit and honor of Venice.[2] From 1279 to 1509 those voting were obliged by oath to give their ballots to the best man, and not to aid their friends or injure their enemies fraudulently; in the latter year the custom was abrogated, because too many souls were jeopardized by false swearing.[3] Venice was a city-republic governed by a small, interrelated, and familiar political class, where the obligarchs confronted one another face-to-face from day to day. The Venetian political ideal, therefore, was less unreasonable than if it were applied to one of our huge and impersonal states—or even to a modern city comparable in size to medieval Venice but possessing a much broader political base. Even so, it was unrealistic and did not work.

With the dwindling of maritime and mercantile income nobles became increasingly eager for salaried offices.[4] The shift is illustrated in Lane's *Andrea Barbarigo,* for the grandsons of Andrea, the entrepreneur, turned to government careers, especially Giovanni Alvise, who was in office almost continuously from age twenty-five until his death at fifty-seven.[5] As long as there was a rough equivalence between the numbers of office seekers and the offices sought, campaigning, though it existed, was not the major problem that it became in the Quattrocento. Then, although the number of offices increased, it did not keep pace with the number of nobles clamoring for public employment.[6] By the end of the fifteenth century competition was fierce. James C. Davis estimates that there were about eight hundred government positions, but that perhaps no more than four hundred to five hundred nobles held office at a given time, due to pluralism. Thus somewhat fewer than one-fifth of the eligible nobles would be in public employment.[7] The story of Andrea Contarini, a poor noble from a distinguished clan, is well known. On 3 March 1499 he pushed past the doorkeeper of the Collegio, protesting excitedly to the doge and his colleagues that he was a noble of the house of Contarini, but he had only sixteen ducats of income a year and nine children on his shoulders. For sixteen years he had not held public office. He did not know how to gain his living with any trade. And because he owed sixty ducats to the government, the office of the *cazude* (*cadute*) sold the house that he lived in. He begged them to have pity on him and not to deprive him of the roof over his head.[8]

The desirable posts fell into two categories, the first composed of major offices which could prove extremely lucrative or especially powerful.[9] Holders of such offices found it expedient to utilize their authority in ways which might promote their further political ambitions. As procurator of San Marco, Francesco Foscari had distributed considerable sums of what were said to be unclaimed funds to poor nobles, thereby creating a personal political clientele in preparation for his campaign for the dogeship.[10] Priuli, who expressed disdain for the disreputable ways in which politicans strove for office, explicitly complained that patrician magistrates tolerated other nobles' misdeeds to avoid making political enemies.[11] While the upper echelons of the Venetian patriciate were thus engaged in efforts to retain their popularity and to accede to positions of considerable profit and influence, the less fortunate nobles scrambled for minor posts as a means of livelihood.[12] Poor nobles, left with the hope of public employment as a means of support after the decline of their commercial income, assiduously cultivated the more influential members of their class who frequently held higher offices and who could provide them with blocs of votes for election to less important, but at least moderately profitable, positions.[13] There was a chasm between the rich and powerful, of whom we normally think in connection with nobility, and the poor nobles, perhaps more so in Venice than elsewhere because of the relatively rigid nature of the noble class from early fourteenth century. The Spanish ambassador Bedmar at the beginning of the seventeenth century wrote of the unspeakable poverty of some nobles, whose daughters rotted at home on filthy mats, because they lacked clothes to go out. Politically, however, these miserable nobles retained their rights as members of the Great Council and clung to their status as their only remaining asset.[14] Priuli records the scorn that the real elite felt for the poor nobles who dominated the Great Council.[15] The problem of poverty among large portions of the patriciate undermined the ideal of Venetian politics and, combined with the attempts of more prosperous nobles to further their careers, made elections in Venice heated and vigorous.

These violations of the Venetian ideal that the office should seek the man were called *broglio*. The practice began, according to the *Cronaca Bemba,* as soon as the power to name officials passed from the doge to the Great Council. The name *broglio* was derived from that part of the Piazza San Marco from the Church of San Gimignano to the Church of Santa Maria del Broglio (of the orchard). Across the Piazzetta from the ducal palace citizens (after the Serrata, nobles) gathered before elections, especially those who wanted some office or magistracy, commending themselves and begging for support.[16] The word was very broad in its meaning, covering any attempts to influence the nominations and vote of others. The derived term *brogeto,* signifying the tallies of votes in the Senate, proves how widespread illegal campaigning was, not only in the Great Council, but among the more distinguished members of the Senate.[17]

For our purposes, we shall split *broglio* into two subheadings to be considered in this chapter and the next. The broad term covered offenses ranging from soliciting votes, calling attention to oneself, praising other patricians, casting one's vote so that it would be known and appreciated, and congratulating winners of elections to cheating and bribery. The one sort we moderns would consider normal campaigning, whereas the other would be electoral corruption, but the Venetians classified them under the common heading of *broglio,* against which the laws constantly strove. There is some historical justification for our distinction, however, although the evidence is late, for Robert Finlay has discovered in a seventeenth-century *Discorsetto* the designation *broglio onesto.*[18] This included such common political practices as calling all other nobles by name[19] or referring to someone as *magnificus.*[20] The present chapter, then, will deal with *broglio onesto,* the next one with electoral corruption.

In addition to distinguishing between *broglio onesto* and electoral corruption, we ought also to emphasize the distinction between the offices for which rich and poor nobles illegally campaigned. Giovanni Botero speculated in the seventeenth century that the Venetians consciously applied an equalizing scheme to public offices, assigning to the rich such posts as ambassadorships, which required large expenditures out of the holder's private purse, and to the poor offices bearing some remuneration.[21] More modestly Priuli, without suggesting any overall plan to redistribute wealth, distinguished between the governorships of the cities of *terraferma,* which required ostentation and the expenditure of one's own funds quite beyond one's salary, and the maritime governorships, where one spent little because of low prices.[22] Botero exaggerates, I believe. There was no overriding intent to smooth away the inequalities of wealth among the patriciate. Costly offices fell to the rich, because only they could bear them and because these offices were stepping-stones to the highest honors in the Republic. Offices bearing modest salaries were awarded to the poor nobles in a spirit of charity, it is true, but also to keep them from desperation and because only the poor would want them.

Thomas Jefferson believed that "Whenever a man has cast a longing eye on offices, a rottenness begins in his conduct." This is a dictum in which the Venetians would have readily concurred.[23] Venetian patricians desiring offices, or their family and friends, lined the steps of the ducal palace, chanted the names of their favorites, whispered pleas and inducements, and bet on the outcomes of elections. Within the chamber itself they stood on benches to be conspicuous, wandered about politicking, and followed the voting urns around the chamber to encourage and check on their potential supporters.[24] Early in the sixteenth century we find Priuli expressing a typical businessman's disdain of politicians, declaring that he had never held office, because he would not engage in these humiliating practices.[25] This illegal soliciting of votes was so commonplace that it could be done by giving a conventional sign. The *stola,* a strip of black cloth normally worn over the left shoulder, half in front and half behind, was folded and carried hanging from the arm as a sign that one wanted help or a favor. And so *calare stola* became synonymous with engaging in *broglio.*[26]

The great sixteenth-century propagators of the myth of Venice, Contarini and Giannotti, largely ignored the widespread and sordid quest for offices. As Charles Rose has recently pointed out, they "were satisfied to detail the machinery of government, without attempting to analyze the forces which drove it. Thus they preserved the panegyrical image of the Republic which such analysis would have destroyed in part."[27] Our task will be to examine *broglio* at some length and to correct this view.

Before proceeding, however, it will be necessary for understanding to describe the Venetian electoral process in detail. The combination of election and the use of lots which was employed in Venice has attracted

considerable attention and praise.[28] By far the largest number of offices
in the Venetian administration were conferred by elections held in the
Great Council,[29] and it is not surprising that the largest number of
extant laws on elections pertain to the practices in that assembly. Prior
to any election, as before votes on any measures, the members in attendance were to be counted,[30] and anyone not arriving in time to be
counted was to be excluded from participation in the election.[31] After
this process was completed, the council proceeded to the selection of
the members of the nominating committees. The manner for doing so
in the late thirteenth century, according to a statute of 1273, required
that a number of balls equal to the number of members who had been
counted in the council was to be placed in a single urn, and forty of
them were to be golden. Each member of the council walked to the urn
and drew a single ball; those who were fortunate enough to extract a
golden one remained in the chamber while all others departed. The
forty remaining then proceeded to the urn once more and drew another
ball. The urn had been refilled with forty balls, of which only nine were
golden; those who chose them comprised the single nominating committee, and any name approved by six of them was returned to the
Great Council as a nominee for whatever magistracy was being filled.[32]
It is not until 1279 that we hear of *electiones duplices,* in which two slates
of candidates were named and for which two nominating committees
were required. For such elections eighteen of the forty members chosen
in the first round of drawing would be retained, and the number of
golden balls placed in the urn in the second round was simply doubled
to select them.[33] In time four nominating committees came to be employed for the more important offices.[34]

A description of the fully developed process is offered by Gasparo
Contarini in his *De magistratibus.* Although his portrayal lacks historical
depth, it will be useful to give a rather detailed paraphrase of it.[35]

The process began with the *electio,* which we would call the nomination. The initial step was the choosing by lots of members of the Great
Council for positions on four nominating committees (or "hands") of
nine members each. For this purpose three urns were arranged at the
front of the chamber, one on each side, and one in the middle. The side
urns contained thirty golden balls and an indeterminate number of
silver balls, which could be replenished as needed; the middle urn contained sixty balls, of which thirty-six were golden. The golden balls
were all marked with a coded inscription, changed from election to
election, so that officials in charge of the election could make sure that
no member could secretly bring a golden ball to the palace with him
and thus obtain a seat on the nominating committees.[36]

After the urns had been prepared all the nobles were summoned to the side urns to draw a ball from one of them. The members of the Great Council were seated on benches on both sides of the hall, and the order in which the various benches proceeded to the urns for the drawing was determined by lot.[37] Each noble drew one ball, and the urns were placed at such a height that no one could know whether he had a golden or a silver ball until he had withdrawn it. A noble drawing a silver ball simply returned to his seat; one drawing a golden ball handed it at once to the councillor presiding over the urn, so that the latter could check the coded inscription to see that it was not counterfeit. The fortunate noble then proceeded to the middle urn. If he there drew a silver ball, he returned to his original seat; if a golden one, he took his place on the ducal platform as a member of one of the nominating committees. The name of each elector was proclaimed in order to implement a law that prohibited more than two members of the same family from being on the nominating committees for the same election. As each group of nine was formed it proceeded to a smaller chamber for its deliberations.[38]

Here, in descending order of age, the nominators drew lots numbered from one to nine from another urn. These numbers corresponded to a previously prepared list of vacant offices, and the drawer of a given number gained the right to nominate to the corresponding position. Each announced his choice for the position he had drawn, and, if the candidate received six of the nine votes, he was considered the nominee of that committee; if he did not receive six votes, then the same nominator would propose another name until a nominee was found.[39] This process went on independently in each of the four nominating committees, so that at its conclusion there would be four nominees for each office to be presented to the Great Council, unless, of course, the same candidate had been named more than once for the same office. There were also some minor offices which required only two nominating committees, in which case only the first two nominating committees made nominations. After the nominating process had been completed the nominators were dismissed, having no right to vote in the ensuing election or even to return to the floor.

The nomination (*electio*) was followed by election (*proba*) in the Great Council. The chief secretary announced to the council the candidates for each office, the nominating committee in which they had been named, and the originator of the nomination. When each nominee was named, he, his immediate family, and certain other specified relatives were required to leave the chamber until the vote on his candidacy had been completed. When all the nominees for a given office had departed, votes were taken on them individually. Two youths traversed each row of benches in the chamber carrying specially designed urns, the *bussuli,* which enclosed two compartments, one green and one white, which could be reached through a single opening. By inserting one's hand into the device one could drop a ball into either compartment secretly.[40] Secrecy was further insured by using balls made of linen as ballots, so that the sound of the falling ballot should not reveal the vote. Before balloting, each noble showed his ball to his neighbors, then he inserted his hand into the *bussulus,* dropping the ball into the white compartment for a positive vote, into the green for a negative. After all had voted, the *bussuli* were carried to the ducal platform, where they were emptied into two bowls, a white one for the positive votes, a green for those from the green compartments. The ducal councillors then counted the ballots, while the *bussuli* were returned to the carriers for use in the *proba* on the next candidate. Whichever of the four candidiates received the highest number of affirmative votes was elected (or approved), as long as that number constituted a majority of the whole council. If none of the four candidates received a majority, the process was voided and the election deferred until the next meeting of the Great Council.[41]

NOMINATIONS

A great deal of the illegal electioneering—and *all* electioneering was illegal—centered upon the nominations, for, if one desiring office could find one of those fortunates who drew the golden balls to nominate him, he would stand a good chance of election, since the nominating committees put up at most four candidates. It is true that the Senate or the Signoria sometimes added a nominee, who had a great advantage, but this was usually in the case of important offices, not for those petty offices for which the poor nobility strove. It has not been sufficiently recognized that most of the disapproved activity focused on the latter—not that the great were above illegal campaigning for the highest offices.

One was not allowed to harass the members of the nominating committees with pleas for office. An act of 1409 notes previous legislation which prohibited members of the Great Council from speaking to the nominating committees after they entered their chambers under penalty of 40 *s.,* but it continues that this penalty causes no dread, "for daily in the Great Council many nobles in the presence of the Signoria before the nominating committees enter their chambers, not having any respect for the Signoria, indulge in many dishonest practices." Henceforth, no member of the Great Council might speak to the nominators either before or after they entered their chambers under penalty of five pounds *parvorum*. Notice carefully what is prohibited here. Not only did office seekers speak to the nominators seated on the dais, but they actually intruded into the chambers of the nominating committees.[42] Within a month and a half this act was canceled by a new one, which again noted the daily dishonest acts in speaking to the members of the nominating committees and took additional measures to halt them.[43] Again in 1423 the Great Council was having difficulty with members of the Forty or other officials delegated to carry the balloting urns who seated themselves on the dais and from there urged their desire for office upon those attempting to draw the golden balls or upon those fortunates already seated upon the dais awaiting the completion of their nominating committee. This was prohibited to them and to all nobles, under penalty of exclusion from the Great Council—and so from elections—for six months.[44] Another and broader attack on the problem in 1424 mentions an old law that anyone speaking to nominators for the sake of getting himself or someone else nominated should be fined 20 *s.* Because of the antiquity of the law and the smallness of the fine, it was disobeyed by many. The penalty was changed to expulsion from the council for six months and a fine of fifty pounds.[45] The Senate also found in 1425 that its *scrutinii* were being corrupted by those asking for office or having others do it for them. Senators often responded favorably in order not to displease those asking the favor. Asking for votes for oneself or another was prohibited, as was recommending one's honor to a voter, under penalty of five hundred pounds and exclusion from the Great Council for four months. Those who failed to report such efforts were also made subject to the same penalties.[46]

The Great Council found in 1431 that the provisions for the integrity of nominations were not adequate in its new chambers. It was provided that during the whole period of nominations, from the beginning of the summons to the urns to draw for the golden balls until all the nominations were returned to the council no noble could go out the small door to the doge's right leading to the old hall, nor could he remain in the old hall or in the *liago* (or sunroom) at the corner of the building toward the Bacino and the prisons. These were favorite places for soliciting nominations. The penalty was twenty-five pounds and exclusion from the Great Council for six months.[47] In 1444 the Ten called attention to those who sought favors from judges and officials and those who pleaded with other nobles of the council for offices. Not only did they ask, in fact, but they tried to constrain them in dishonest ways. A new penalty of six months' banishment and a fine of two hundred *lire* was imposed.[48]

The Senate called attention to irregularities in its elections in 1454, stating that senators came together, spoke, and gained what they desired without any respect for the laws and the state. Henceforth when they were electing *savi ai ordini,* the Forty for criminal cases, or anything else, the nominators should go apart into the chancellery. Any noble who was not a member of the committee who went there should be expelled from the Senate for a year.[49] At this time, at any rate, the Senate seems to be using for some elections a procedure rather like that of the Great Council instead of the characteristic *scrutinio* with nominations from the floor. In 1460 the Ten found disorder in the election by the Forty of its three heads. Knowing that there were many things done in these elections which did not contribute to the peace and quiet of the state, the Ten had provided that councillors should administer an oath to the Forty that they would elect the heads who deserved the position. It turned out, however, that after the oaths were administered the members of the Forty came together and politicked, asking for help and coming to agreements much more scandalous and odious than before, on which account complaints and arguments had arisen. The Ten revised the system of election, so that the members of the Forty should draw golden balls for five seats on a nominating committee, which would meet apart, like those in the Great Council, to nominate five candidates. No one was to speak to them and they would swear not to nominate anyone who asked for it or had someone else ask for support for him.[50] It is worth noting, considering all the complaints against the nominating procedure in the Great Council, that it was considered worthy of imitation in other councils. In 1462, while Doge Pasquale Malipiero lay dying, the Ten took steps against *broglio* for that highest prize that the Republic had to offer.[51] The quite different and fantastically complicated process of electing a doge, of course, was designed precisely to prevent illegal electioneering. It only succeeded in making the lobbying more complicated.

It would appear from an act of the Ten in 1464 that all sorts of disorders were occurring within the nominating committees of the Great Council. The members did not sit, as they were supposed to do, but stood before the voting urn, so that they could watch their colleagues put their ballots in the white receptacle. Some even voted more than one ballot, a topic to which we shall return in the next chapter. They failed to leave the group if their fathers, sons, or brothers were nominated. They pleaded for votes from their colleagues, and even worse they went about to the other nominating committees to plead for candidates. Henceforth, they should not only be put under oath, but they should each receive a ballot in one of four colors, one color for each of the committees. Within their individual chambers, they should also sit down and receive their lots for nominating for the several offices. The one drawing the first office should make his nomination, cast his vote publicly (since the nominator's vote was hardly secret), and return to his seat, but each of the others, one by one, should cast his vote as secretly as he can, showing his ballot in the palm of his hand first. (This was probably to necessitate putting the entire hand into the neck of the urn, thus adding to the secrecy.) Only when all nine had voted should they rise again and stand by the urn to see the outcome of the vote. They were to leave when fathers, sons, or brothers were nominated. The penalty for failure to observe these rules was deprivation of the Great Council for a year. (Except that the penalty was two years for failure to vote secretly.) Speaking with electors from another committee was formerly subject to a fifty-*lire* fine and exclusion from the Council for six months, but was raised to a one-hundred-*lire* fine and two years' exclusion.[52] It did not work, for a year and a half later the Ten again complained of scandals caused by illegal associations and sects within the nominating committees. The provision of the law of 1464 requiring that they remain in their seats was to be enforced. It was made illegal for more than two of them to talk secretly, or, if two, it became illegal if one of them then talked secretly with another. Signals were also illegal. When the committee reported, three of them should be interrogated about whether there had been illegal politicking in the committee. If it were discovered, the guilty should be deprived of the Great Council and all offices for three years, and the accuser should receive a thousand *lire* from the guilty noble's goods.[53]

The Ten complained in 1466 that when the oath was administered to assure that nominations (and also votes in elections) had not been solicited, many, especially in the Senate, left the chamber to avoid taking the oath. Members were made responsible for declaring to the Signoria that they had missed the oath and for receiving it before the end of the session. If they failed to do this, they should be fined ten pounds and should lose their place in that council for six months.[54] As usual, the law failed to achieve its purpose. In 1480 the Ten complained of a plague of the same abuses, for few took care to follow the law exactly. When in the future there should be any nomination, scrutiny, or election, all the doors leading out of the chamber should be closed. An oath should be administered to all concerning whether their votes had been solicited. Anyone refusing to name those who asked him for votes was also guilty, unless he swore that he did not know them.[55] Nominations were also sometimes made by the Signoria (*per bancham*). The Great Council was up in arms in 1480 over the pleas and other usages which took place when the Signoria proceeded by scrutiny. They required nomination through electoral committees. The haughty and tiny Signoria, because of its many electoral misdeeds, was to follow the example of the huge and disorderly Great Council.[56]

A bad custom had developed, that the various electoral committees failed to meet in separate rooms, as was the intention, but mingled together. In 1484 the Ten decreed that each of the four must be conducted to a designated chamber by a notary, who should lock the door until they had finished their nominating, and that the notary should be forbidden to carry any messages or notes to the nominators or to say anything to anyone about what they were doing.[57] Within six months the Ten again had to take action against the same problem. They complained that the four nominating committees could speak together whenever they wished, because the rooms allocated to them were not suitable for prohibiting communication, so a reallocation of rooms for the four committees was made.[58]

In 1487 five nobles were prosecuted in the Ten for violation of the act of 1480 concerning the oath to be taken after nominations, scrutinies, and elections that one's voice had not been solicited. We learn that the act of 1480 had not been enforced and had not even been published from month to month in the Senate as required. Nonetheless, the disobedient nobles were held guilty and sentenced to deprivation of the Great Council for six months. All five were officials, four members of the Quaranta criminale and one official of the *cattavere*.[59] The failure to enforce the act of 1480 was typical. It is clear that Venice legislated too much, followed up too little.

In 1489 the Ten returned to the problem of soliciting nominations, for as the nobles ascended the stairs to the Great Council and at the doors they were harassed by crowds of those seeking office for themselves or relatives, and, even when the nominators were secluded in their various rooms, from down below those seeking offices yelled at them or thrust handbills (*apodisas*) toward them. The Ten decreed that this misbehavior should result in exclusion from offices for two years and a fine of one hundred ducats. Also those solicited who failed to report it should be subject to the same penalties.[60] Another curious custom had developed which required attention in 1489. The Venetians often awarded honorary Venetian nobility to various distinguished people, usually noblemen from northeastern Italy or the eastern Adriatic coast. When these honorary patricians visited the Great Council, the urns were presented to them in such a manner that they could see in and draw a golden ball, and then in the nominating committees they were awarded the first nomination, which was, of course, approved in the committee. Thus, nominations were made by those who, however well intentioned, were not familiar with the situation, but made their selections upon the basis of the importunate prayers of office seekers. In the future, the Ten said, they must draw balls at random, like others, and also draw in the customary descending order of age for the right to nominate within the committees. In short, they should be treated like any other members of the Great Council.[61] The Great Council took action in 1491 against those nobles who literally forced their way out of the hall of the Great Council, overwhelming the advocate of the Commune who was supposed to prevent them, to go to the head of the lower stairway in the view of the Signoria and the Senate for the sake of *broglio*. They should be deprived of the Great Council and of all office-holding for a year and should be imprisoned for two months.[62]

That much of the struggle for offices concerned poor nobles seeking humble, but paid, positions is true and important. Rich and powerful men also competed, however, for offices of great dignity, especially, according to a decree of the Ten in 1503, for the procuratorships of St. Mark. Next to the dogeship itself, these were the most exalted positions in Venice, and election was for life. This act noted the begging for nominations and votes and the much worse and more abominable custom of putting pressure on members of the Great Council to block some rival candidate. Of course this was in violation of the ideal of Venetian election by free vote according to personal knowledge and conscience. According to the act, an oath should be taken that no noble should wish to make procurator anyone who has said "Select me," or who has had someone say on his behalf "Select so-and-so" ("*tuome over tuo Itale*"). Other oaths were also required to try to assure that the election was run according to the ideal.[63]

Written exhortations to nominate and vote for someone were also known in Venice, although they were quite illegal, of course. A law of 1342 prohibited the passing of handbills (*cartoline*) in the ducal election, and, if such written propaganda were received, it was to be torn up and thrown away.[64] This prohibition was repeated in 1356 and 1382.[65] In the act of 1425 dealing with electioneering in scrutinies, mention is also made of communicating in writing one's desire for office for oneself, a family member, or anyone else.[66] A decree of the Ten in 1478 calls attention to the most evil and indecorous custom of many nobles, who, neglecting their honor and the propriety of the nobility, congregated in the Piazza San Marco and on the stairs of the palace shoving written pleas to be nominated for office at passing members of the Great Council or senators. Offenders were to lose the right to hold office for two years, pay a fine of 200 *l. parvorum,* and spend a month in prison.[67] The

Ten returned to the subject in 1484, recalling the law of 1478 but complaining that nobles standing near the doors of the Great Coucil and the Senate with their hands full of handbills, pressed their candidacies upon those entering. The Ten interpreted the act of 1478 as restricted to the doors and the interiors of the chambers, which it was not, in fact.[68] We also have already heard of the prohibition of 1489 against waving handbills at the windows of the chambers in which the nominating committees were meeting.[69] All in all, calling to potential nominators and thrusting handbills at them was scarcely conducive to the dignity of the patriciate, but there were other methods of making one's wishes known which were equally indecorous.

In the quest for offices, Venetian nobles sought to call attention to themselves by whatever means they could. In 1314 the Great Council felt compelled to prohibit anyone, while awaiting his turn to draw for the golden balls, from sitting or standing upon the raised benches in the area from the ducal throne to the door that the nominators enter under penalty of 20 *s. parvorum.*[70] Nobles seeking offices also liked to stand within the chancellery to call attention to themselves when the nominators were going there. (At this time the nominating committees met in the chancellery.) Standing there was prohibited in 1389.[71] In 1402 the Great Council again tried to deal with nobles who stood in various conspicuous places to gain attention, such as in the sunroom (*liago*) or at the bar where one goes into the sunroom. They even got in the way of those approaching the urns.[72] The Great Council ruled in 1423 that all nobles should sit in their proper places on the benches. These they were always allowed to select themselves, but, according to the act, once seated they had to remain so, except when going to the urns, or going as nominators, or carrying the voting urns.[73] We have already noted the prohibition in 1423 against taking a seat on the dais.[74]

If one failed on a given day, more elections were always coming up, so office seekers took care to make a big fuss over those who were elected, shaking hands and praising them. These practices were also forbidden in 1425.[75] Another act of 1442 made standing in the front of the Great Council illegal.[76] A decree of the Ten in 1480 prohibited standing at the door of the stairs when there was a nomination or election in the Senate and calling attention to oneself by signs or nods. Transgressors were to be fined one hundred ducats and incarcerated for six months, in addition to which they could not be elected to the desired office.[77]

It was impossible, however, to keep nobles from posting themselves in conspicuous places. This certainly was not the worst offense in the world, but imagine the lack of decorum as the *patres,* renowned for sober dignity, milled about jockeying for attention. In 1484 the Ten complained of the disorder as the nobles stood in front of or near the urns or at the heads of the benches in the sight of the Signoria or doing other things so that they would be noticed. They also went about crossing the paths of the departing nominating committees or following them, and speaking or nodding. The Ten recalled the act of 1423 requiring nobles to remain in their seats, insisting again that they must remain in place from the time of the first summons to the urns until the nominating committees have left the council. Violators should be fined 100 *l. parvorum* and be excluded from the council for a year if they did not speak, double the penalties if they did.[78] It was this desire to prevent the nominators from being influenced by visual signals from office seekers that led to the rule that those who selected a golden ball from the middle urn, gaining them a place on a nominating committee, must sit on the dais with their backs to the council until their "hand" of nine was completed.[79]

It is scarcely surprising that those hungry for office also sought to send messages to the secluded nominators. In 1413 the Great Council objected that very often nobles sent notaries of the court with messages to the nominators, and the fine—against the notaries—was raised.[80] In 1424 the council returned to the subject, prohibiting nobles from sending any boy or notary with an oral or written message to the nominating committees.[81] Legislation of 1438 refers to the many attempts to see to it that nominators should function without any outside pressure, which had not been entirely succesesful, so that once again notaries were ordered not to be in the rooms of the nominating committees except by the command of the Signoria.[82] The Ten also took action in 1484 against the carrying of messages to the nominators by the notaries who were responsible for locking nominating committees in their chambers.[83]

A new evil was introduced when unscrupulous nobles began to bring boys with them to the Great Council to do their dirty work. The act of 1438 mentioned above also complained of the many pleas and dealings carried out in this improper fashion. Nominators who listened to these boys were to lose their votes and pay ten *lire*. Anyone who sent a boy to speak with any nominator was to be deprived of the Great Council for six months, as well as of all offices and benefices for that time, and pay twenty-five *lire*.[84] As usual, it did not work, for we find the Great Council in 1443 strenuously objecting again to the practice of bringing boys to its meetings in such a multitude that there was "a puerile clamor and clatter." Certain of them, of course, dared to speak with nominators on behalf of candidates. Henceforth no boys (except those in the service of the chancellery) were to come to the Great Council under penalty to the fathers of one hundred *soldi*.[85] In 1492 the Ten took notice of the fact that this law was not being observed, and the Great Council had to put up, not only with the clamor of the boys, but their intercessions with nominators on behalf of fathers, brothers, and so on. The penalties were therefore raised.[86]

Another type of *broglio* was the exchange of nominations within the nominating committees. As early as 1253 the Great Council sought to deal with this in part by prohibiting any nominating committee for the Signoria from naming more than one of its own members.[87] A law of 1271 prohibits reciprocal nomination by the members of a nominating committee, which, of course, implies the nomination of more than one.[88] It appears to have been unsuccessful again, because two years later the Senate prohibited any nominator who had requested another to leave so that he could nominate him from in turn being nominated by the other.[89] In 1276 the law of 1253 was relaxed, allowing no more than two from one committee to be nominated, except for nonsalaried offices.[90] At this point the problem seems to have been dealt with satisfactorily, for we hear no more of it until 1480, when the Ten prohibited the exchange of lots, i.e., the numbers drawn entitling each nominator to nominate a candidate for a specific office.[91]

The Venetians sought to keep secret what occurred in the nominating committees, for its revelation would feed the fires of *broglio*. In 1307 there was a revision of the item in the capitulary of the nominators which required them to keep their proceedings secret under oath, which had proved ineffective, to provide for a fine of one hundred *soldi*, half of which should go to the accuser, whose identity would be kept secret.[92] There was more concern with the failure to vote secretly within the nominating comittee. Obviously, the nominator's vote could be public, since presumably he was voting for his candidate, but the others should not reveal how they were voting, because this would lead to pressures and vote-swapping, rather than to each voting according to his conscience. According to an act of the Great Council in 1376 anyone (except the one who made the nomination) who did not vote secretly should lose his vote in the committee.[93] The prohibition was repeated in 1421 under penalty of exclusion from the Great Council for six months and a fine of twenty-five *lire*.[94] When in 1464 the Ten tried to do away with disorders such as clustering around the voting urns to watch one's fellow nominators vote, it gave a description of the system as it should work. The nominators should sit down upon entering the chamber and receive their lots while sitting. The one who drew the right to nominate should then rise, make his nomination, and cast his ballot openly. Then he should promptly resume his seat, and only after he was seated should the second nominator cast his vote, then the third, and so on. Each should show his ballot to his colleagues held in the palm of his hand, not in the fingers, close his hand, insert it into both urns, and drop it as quietly as possible. Only after the last nominator had voted should they come to the urns to see the result, except that anyone who was nominated himself, or whose father or son or brother was nominated, should stay away from the urns.[95] In 1492 the Ten took action against those nominators who threw their ballots into the urns so that eveyone could see—thus currying favor with those for whom they voted. They were subjected to ten years' exclusion from offices and councils, as well as a fine of one hundred ducats.[96] In 1498, according to Sanuto, the Ten reformed scrutinies in the interest of each nominating his free choice of the best candidate. Instead of notaries circulating around the chamber to write down nominations on a list, each member, when he came to take the oath that he had not been solicited, should deposit his nomination in an urn.[97]

Throughout a period of about two and a half centuries, therefore, the Venetian government was constantly taking measures to try to ensure that the nomination of candidates for office was carried out without pressure and in the interest of the public welfare, while nobles who sought office and those who were eager to please the more powerful discovered various means of subverting such attempts.

ELECTIONS

The second and final stage in the electoral process in the Great Council was the *proba* (or election).[98] Some elections were conducted in other councils: the Quaranta criminale, for example, elected its own heads. The Senate gradually acquired the right to elect a considerable variety of important officials. Even in the more sober and presumably more responsible Senate, lobbying for office eventually tended to take a disproportionate place, so that in 1497 the Senate felt compelled to turn over to the Great Council elections to many offices, since all the lobbying that occurred prevented the senators from turning their attention to pressing public issues.[99] We are told in 1505 that this law had not been strictly observed, so it was repeated with an additional allocation to the Great Council of the offices and magistracies in recently acquired territory.[100]

The time frame of the electoral process was determined, in considerable measure, at least, by the concern over *broglio*. Originally, the final vote was held at a sitting subsequent to the nominations, or, at any rate, conclusion of the entire process could be postponed to a subsequent sitting because of the lateness of the hour or other reason. In 1462, however, the Ten decreed that if the whole process could not be finished the nominations should be considered void and it should begin anew with the drawing of the gold balls. Otherwise, campaigning of a very vigorous sort occurred overnight.[101] Finlay points out that after the reform the senatorial candidate had the advantage, not only of the prestige of the Senate, but also of the fact that he was nominated at least one day before the *electio* and the *proba* in the Great Council, so that he, his family, and friends had valuable time in which to round up support.[102]

The most obvious and most prominent (and to us moderns quite innocent) ploy was simply to ask others for their support, or have others ask on one's behalf: this was often done with great insistency. The first legislation on the subject known to me stems from the Great Council in 1417, when action was taken against friends and relatives of candidates who scattered themselves among the benches. When the *bussuli* approached, these supporters scurried among their neighbors pleading for their votes, saying "Dayla" or similar words.[103] In 1425 the Senate complained of candidates who, not caring for the good of the Commune but only their own welfare, begged for votes. The voters often complied, not wishing to displease them and anticipating reciprocity. The Senate declared that one must not ask for votes for oneself or others under penalty of fifty pounds and exclusion from the Great Council for four months. Recommending one's honor to another amounted to the same thing. Under the same penalty those solicited were bound to report it to the Signoria.[104] The penalty was increased in 1430, a certain indication that the act of 1425 was ineffective, and the Senate returned to the problem again in 1433.[105] The Great Council itself complained in 1434 of the many nobles who wrongfully went out of the council hall and returned to vote for those whose supporters had sought their ballots, neglecting to vote on other candidates, so that the number of votes cast on the opposing candidates fluctuated wildly. They were not departing, of course, just to seek a breath of fresh air, but to participate in *broglio*. It would not be very different from our modern representatives going out into the cloakrooms to make a deal, but it was against the ideals and principles of the Venetian constitution. Offenders, the council said, should be excluded from the Great Council for six months and fined twenty-five pounds.[106]

A wide-ranging reform of 1442 prohibited the supposedly proud Venetian nobles from wandering up and down the benches pleading for votes, saying, "Dayla, dayla."[107] A couple of years later the Ten provided that those who ask for votes for others should fall under the same penalties as those who tried to influence judges, namely exclusion from the council for six months and a fine of two hundred pounds.[108] In fact, the pressures on the ideal were severe. In 1449 the Ten declared that the system of elections and *scrutinii* in the Senate had been devised by their virtuous ancestors so that the most capable men would be obligated to assume the burdens of office, but since then elections have become vitiated and corrupted, so that "whoever does not beg for votes cannot be elected." Once more trying to enforce the rule against asking for votes for oneself or another, the Ten imposed a two-year ineligibility for offices and councils upon offenders.[109] Five days later, to encourage enforcement the Ten added that whoever should bring accusations resulting in convictions for this offense should have one hundred ducats from the goods of each guilty party and, of course, his identity should be kept secret.[110] On the same day, the Ten observed that what was prohibited to the members of the councils was done for them by notaries, who went about the chamber saying, "Elect so-and-so to such-and-such an office," or "Do not elect so-and-so, because he doesn't want to be elected," or "So-and-so has chosen such-and-such." If they did this henceforth, they were to be excluded from the chancery and any other official position for five years.[111] Notice the discrepancy in the period of exclusion for nobles and non-nobles, two years and five years respectively. The notaries, of course, were employees of the state, and should be expected to tend to their tasks without such shenanigans: but the patricians, on the other hand, were the possessors of the state, the monopolists of political power, who claimed a unique virtue. The discrepancy reveals, here as elsewhere, a sense that nobles had a right to offices, and if they overstepped propriety in seeking them—as they consistently did—it was an understandable and relatively forgivable offense. The Ten returned to the act of 1449 on elections and *scrutinii* in the Senate in 1457, declaring it a good act, but insufficient because the accusations against offenders were not forthcoming, so that lobbying became daily more customary. It was enacted that before a vote in the Senate fifteen senators would be selected by lot and questioned individually by the heads of the Ten and the advocates of the Commune under oath as to whether anyone had asked for their vote or nomination, or asked them simply to come to the Senate, or made any sign indicating what was wanted. If five of the fifteen had been solicited, the Signoria should banish the guilty nobles from all councils, offices, and benefices for two years. If the guilty party were a commoner, he should be banished from Venice for two years. (Notice again the discrepancy between deprivation of office and exile.) Furthermore, whoever was elected should take an oath that he had not solicited votes. There is also an interesting provision noting that some malevolent person might lobby for an enemy in order to get him fined. Therefore, if a candidate should be accused, not of lobbying but of causing votes to be solicited for him, he could clear himself by oath, and the actual culprit should be punished.[112] The Senate itself several months later revived the issue of asking for votes during balloting.[113]

In 1459 the Ten complained of elections of the heads in the Quaranta criminale and the Quaranta civile. So many pleas, understandings, and shady practices occurred that those who lawfully ought to have been elected failed. The Ten asserted that the votes of nobles should not be pressured in "these damnable and perilous ways," so they provided that the councillors should call the Forty before them one by one, asking each under oath whether his vote had been solicited. If five replied that this had occurred, then the offender should be expelled from the council and deprived of the Council of Forty, the Great Council, and all benefices and governorships for a year. He also had to pay the penalty for refusal of the headship.[114] That same year also saw the closing of a loophole that ambitious office-seekers had found in the 1457 law on *broglio* in the Senate in that, where both that body and the Great Council were involved in an election, they asked those who had a right to come to the Senate for their support in the Great Council.[115]

In the act of 1462 requiring that nominations and elections in the Great Council must be completed within the same day or begin anew, there is also a provision attempting to preserve secrecy surrounding the names of the nominees until they should be announced by the chancellor, because, as long as the Great Council remained ignorant of the nominees, pleadings and dealings could not take place.[116] The Ten remarked in 1466 that, in spite of many laws, some members moved about from place to place asking for votes. The new attempt to control *broglio* involved summoning those who carried the voting urns to appear before the Signoria and report under oath all illegal acts that they had observed.[117] In spite of all the laws on the subject, some of which have been omitted here, the Ten complained in 1472 that many went from bench to bench and followed the urns asking for votes and making promises, and, what was much worse, threatened those who wished to follow their conscience. In addition to other penalties under previous laws, anyone who solicited votes or caused them to be solicited between nomination and election was to be expelled from office.[118]

Broglio in the Collegio seems to have been unregulated until 1479, so that the pleading for office was so intense that it seemed that perforce the Collegio had to respond to prayers rather than to their consciences and the welfare of the Commune. The Senate simply applied the oath administered in the Senate also to the Collegio.[119]

Elections in the Great Council and scrutinies and elections in the Senate, of course, continued to be subject to illegal electioneering. When the oath was given to determine who had been solicited for votes by whom, according to the Ten in 1480, those who had been asked often left the chamber to avoid the oath. Sometimes they also dodged the issue by claiming to have been asked by everybody. So the Ten decreed that the doors should be closed and everyone should stay in his place. Those who moved about or avoided the oath should be imprisoned for four months and pay one hundred ducats. Those who asked more than four members for votes or signaled that they wanted votes or urged members to attend the session should suffer the previous penalties plus six months' imprisonment and a fine of two hundred ducats. The same applied to those who campaigned for another. It was added that no one should stand at the doors of the stairs for the purpose of displaying himself. If anyone who did this was elected, he should go to prison for six months, pay a fine of one hundred ducats, and be denied the office. The person who informed on him might have the office, if he could obtain over half the votes.[120] In 1482 the Ten took severe action against those who conspired together to plead for votes for friends and relatives. According to the same act, many young nobles, not yet eligible for the Great Council, came to meetings to make pleas for their relatives and friends. They were to be ineligible for the Great Council for ten years from the time when they would normally have been able to attend. Penalties under this act were most severe, so much so that they were probably rarely applied.[121]

One of the most desired posts was membership in the Zonta which the Ten often added to itself for important matters, and there was much illegal competition for it. In 1484 the Ten prohibited any efforts by aspirants to the Zonta to gain election under penalty of three years' exclusion from all secret councils.[122] There also was much competition for the three headships of the Quaranta civile, so that the Ten also in 1484 changed the method of election, providing that lots be drawn from the names of the sixteen candidates who received the highest number of votes in the nominating committees for the Forty.[123]

The Ten came to the obvious conclusion in 1491 that the multitude of oaths that were administered in the Great Council, the Senate, and the College against *broglio* only served to arouse disrespect for oaths. So they abolished them, requiring, however, that anyone whose vote was solicited must vote against the candidate for whom the favor was sought.[124]

The elections to the Zonta of the Senate became the object of legislation in 1496, as reported by Malipiero. The Ten prohibited revealing the names of those nominated before it was their turn to be voted on, for this increased the wheeling and dealing.[125] In 1497 the Ten required that, on the day after an election in the Senate, the advocates of the Commune and the heads of the Ten should summon by lot twenty-five of the Senate and the Zonta, ten of the Forty, and ten more of those entitled to attend the Senate by virtue of their offices and question them under oath whether their votes had been solicited by express words, signs, or nods. If three were found who had been so solicited, the offender should be deprived of all offices, governorships, and councils for five years and pay a fine of two hundred ducats.[126] But so many senators lied under oath that again in 1502 the Ten concluded that the oaths that were required after a scrutiny in the Senate to determine who had asked for votes only served to injure the majesty of Jesus Christ. Once again these oaths were abolished, although the oath requiring a negative vote against those for whom votes were asked was retained, as were all penalties against *broglio*.[127] This seems very nearly a repetition of the ineffectual act of 1491. The Venetian tendency to legislate freely, but to fail to carry out the legislation, was probably a much greater weakness than the really rather innocent crime of *broglio onesto*.

It is apparent from the above legislation that various nonverbal signs could be substituted for spoken requests for votes and that these too became prohibited. The act of 1457 providing for the questioning of fifteen senators specifies that they must count it *broglio* if anyone has kissed them or touched their cheeks or made any other sign.[128] An act of the Ten in 1491 reveals concern over those who applaud or rise from their seats when the names of favored nominees are announced. A penalty of six months' imprisonment and exclusion from the Great Council and from all offices for two years was imposed. The act was to apply to elections in the Senate, as well as the Great Council.[129] It certainly had no enduring effect, however, for within a year (January 1492) the Ten complained of the tumultuous disorder in the elections in the Great Council on the preceding Sunday, where Venetian nobles showed their approval or disapproval when a nominee's name was read by applauding, rising to their feet, or making some murmur of approval of disapproval. The Ten proceeded to pile on the penalties: ten years' exclusion from the Great Council and from all offices, as well as the loss of any office held, and a fine of two thousand pounds.[130] According to Priuli, electors illegally signaled to candidates that they intended to vote for them. Those who refrained from such practices, he says, were themselves kept out of office.[131]

Another device for appealing for votes was simply to take up a prominent position in the chamber. At a very early date (1276) the Great Council had to prohibit members from sitting on the tribune or on the other raised benches.[132] In 1430 also the Great Council complained of nominees and their relatives, who were supposed to leave the hall of the Great Council or the Senate during their *proba,* standing instead prominently displayed in the doorways where the sight of them would influence votes. Henceforth they should be fined fifty pounds and excluded from the council for six months.[133]

Supporters of some nominees sought to give them an advantage by according to them, beyond their own names, patronymics, offspring, and neighborhood, additional titles, saying that so-and-so was in such-and-such an office, and so on. It was declared in 1454 to be all right to include the offices held at the time of nomination and to declare it if his father had been doge or a procurator of St. Mark's, but no more.[134] A few months later it was discovered that the new law deprived the voters of identifications needed for intelligent voting, so it was amended to allow the introduction of one additional title.[135] In the wake of the recent Turkish war in 1501 the Ten found that nominees were getting announced along with the titles of fathers, brothers, or sons who had been killed, taken, burned, impaled, undone, ruined, and enslaved. Recollection of these sacrifices caused a commotion in the Great Council, with members rising to their feet. Many unsuitable candidates were being elected through sympathetic votes, so the practice was outlawed.[136] At about the same time, in fact, the Ten criticized and prohibited the practice ot attributing to candidates in the Great Council, the Senate, or the College titles which could not be substantiated by the records of the Commune.[137]

A means of currying favor, especially with the powerful, was to congratulate them on offices they received. Gratitude for such effusion could be expected to inspire support for one's own ambitions. In 1425 the Senate complained that this abuse in the Great Council had grown much worse than usual. Nobles committed such acts as shaking hands with a successful office seeker. All signs of rejoicing over another's triumph were outlawed under penalty of twenty-five pounds and two months' exclusion from the Council.[138] Apparently the law was not enforced in the long run, for in 1472 the Great Council essentially repeated it, giving the reasons as avoiding errors in voting and general lack of decorum.[139]

When the nominees were announced, and they and their relatives were supposed to leave the chamber, some, pretending to leave, took the opportunity to wander slowly among the benches, not only seeking but extorting votes, according to a law of 1491. Offenders were subjected to six months in prison and two years' exclusion from the Great Council and from all offices.[140]

The Ten discovered in 1498 that friends and relatives of young nobles who were being voted on in the Quaranta criminale for membership in the Great Council followed the urns about the chamber pleading for votes. This was prohibited under penalty of five years' exclusion from all councils, offices, and benefices.[141]

Of course, if those who bore the urns could urge the election of those they favored it would be a great and unfair advantage. That this was done comes first to our attention in an act of the Great Council in 1412. Members of the Forty and other officials chosen by lot were at that time entrusted with this task, and sometimes those to whom the lot did not fall sought the favor nonetheless, so that they could go about with the voting urn saying, "Dayla, dayla." Anyone who did this was to lose his place on the Forty or other position and pay a fine as if he had refused it.[142] Since the nobles of the Forty and other minor officials who bore the *bussuli* continued to abuse their position by asking for votes for their favorites, in 1469 the Senate took the job away from them and assigned it to sixteen young *cittadini originari* chosen by lot for the Great Council and to young notaries of the chancellery for the Senate.[143]

The ends of *broglio* were also favored if the powerful knew how their clients voted or, for that matter, if the votes of those of one clan or faction could be known to their allies. To minimize *broglio,* therefore, a secret ballot was important. In 1282 the Venetians gave up the use of wax ballots, which clattered as they fell into the *bussuli,* in favor of those made of cloth.[144] We hear no more of the problem of maintaining the secret vote for more than a century, when the Senate returned to it in 1424. In elections for *balestrieri* the vote must be secret, and those who failed to preserve secrecy should be fined fifty pounds, should lose whatever office they might have, and be ineligible to regain it for five years.[145] In 1433 the Great Council set forth in a preamble the Venetian electoral ideal: "[B]y our ancestors it was provided that in elections ballots should be cast secretly in order that each one should be obedient to his own conscience, which was holy and just. . . ." At present, however, the ancient custom was not obeyed, with much resulting scandal. Anyone who gave his ballot openly should be deprived for a year of all councils and offices and pay one hundred pounds.[146] The Ten noted in 1448 the need for secret ballots in all councils, although in the Ten itself the contrary was practiced. The Ten, it was then decided, should also vote secretly, and this should be achieved by each member placing his closed hand in each of the urns successively.[147] The Ten legislated on elections in the Great Council and the Senate in 1449, imposing two years' exclusion from office on those who failed to vote secretly.[148] About a month later the Ten required that the chancellor should announce the requirement that the ballot must be secret in every election in the Great Council or the Senate.[149]

We hear in 1455 of the conviction of Pietro da Mosto for giving his ballot openly. It is interesting for us to find someone convicted occasionally, for it is easy to get the impressions that the Venetians only passed laws, but did not enforce them.[150] His accuser was supposed to receive one hundred ducats from his goods, but nothing could be found because he was a pauper. This is significant, of course, for the whole subject of *broglio*. Paupers were tempted on the one hand to seek offices vigorously for the sake of the income and on the other to give their votes to please those who might help them. (Or, by the way, to those who might simply buy votes.) Provision was made for paying the accuser of da Mosto from communal funds.[151]

On 7 May 1484, the Ten amended the act of the previous 7 January (prohibiting asking for votes in elections to the Zonta of the Ten) to prohibit anyone from saying who nominated whom or who voted for whom in order to avoid the hatreds and enmities which were engendered by public knowledge of this information.[152] In a rather flowery preamble, the Ten in 1488 expatiated on the virtues and importance of the secret ballot, so that voters could in good conscience cast their ballots according to the merits of the nominees and not on account of importunities or other pressures. In spite of the laws, however, voting publicly was done frequently and boldly. In addition to all the previous requirements, an oath was to be administered from bench to bench in the Great Council and the Senate that each one had voted secretly. Anyone who placed his ballot openly should be subjected to the previously mentioned fine of one hundred ducats and also should be deprived of all offices and councils for two years.[153] A few months later the act was amended to include elections held in the Collegio.[154]

The most famous legislation in the history of the vain attempts to preserve secrecy in voting, and probably the best known in the whole struggle against *broglio*, is the act of 6 June 1492, adopting the ingenious Venetian voting urn designed by Antonio Tron. The device consisted essentially of two urns joined together, a white one and a green one, surmounted by a common sleeve. The voter inserted his hand into the sleeve and dropped the cloth ballot into the positive or negative urn, according to his conscience, and not—at least it was hoped—under pressure.[155] A week later the Ten voted to use the new urns with a third chamber added, also for votes such as *grazie,* where a *non sinceri* (not ready to decide) vote was possible.[156] In the same month, however, the Ten had to return to the quest of the secret ballot, for those wishing to curry favor threw their ballots into the urn in such a way that secrecy was lost. They were subjected to exclusion from councils and offices for ten years and a fine of one hundred ducats.[157]

The Ten in 1501 became fed up with the way in which the number of ballots cast for and against in the Great Council was circulated about the city and even abroad. Nobles guilty of leaking this information should be deprived of all offices and councils for four years. If secretaries or notaries were the culprits, they should be deprived of the chancellery for life and imprisoned for six months. Nobles or commoners who approached the place where the ballots were being counted for the sake of acquiring such information should be subject to the same penalties. Notice once again the apparent discrepancy in the severity of the penalty for the nobles and the secretaries or notaries.[158] In 1503 the Ten again tried to control the violations of secrecy concerning the numbers of votes received by various candidates. The councillors and heads of the Forty who counted the ballots were to be sworn not to tell or signal the count to anyone under penalty of one hundred ducats. The notaries who helped with the counting should likewise be sworn under penalty of permanent deprivation of office. Also the youths who bore the urns should not be allowed to say to anyone such things as: "So-and-so is doing well."[159] Additional minor measures to keep the numbers of votes secret were taken in 1507.[160]

It has been noted above that enforcement of the laws against *broglio* was a great problem, as it always is in the case of laws which run counter to common practice and common morality. In an attempt to make enforcement of the laws against *broglio* easier, the Ten decreed in 1478 that the doge, the councillors, the advocates of the Commune, and the heads of the Ten should be considered *creti,* i.e., offenders in the Great Council should be convicted on their word alone without argument.[161]

FACTIONS

What is behind all the legislation against *broglio,* of course, is fear of factions. This also helps to explain Venetian laxity in enforcing the laws against individual and petty offenders who sought, for example, to gain some office with an income by attracting the eye of a member of a nominating committee.[162] It was illegal and mildly disapproved, but it was not really dangerous, as factions were conceived to be. Even the faintest hint of political parties was not to be tolerated.

This threat was by no means peculiar to Venice. Jacques Heers gives an illuminating discussion of the efforts of French towns, especially, to limit the power and prestige of the clans through sumptuary legislation. Much of the attack upon luxury was directed toward a sort of "profusion of assembly." Great familial occasions, such as marriages, baptisms, and even funerals, provided an excuse for gathering relatives, friends, and clients around the head of clan and reaffirming the bonds that held them together, not only by association, but by feasting and the giving of gifts. The bigger the gathering, the greater the prestige of the clan, which strengthened their own unity and served notice of their power to others.[163] That is why marriages were celebrated in the open air—to accommodate the crowd and to publicize their numbers. Heers calls attention to an act of 1436 at Limoges, in which the magistrates condemned the habit of giving a banquet the day after a marriage, "where they serve pastries and roasts and everything that seems good to them." Little by little these banquets had become so important that there were as many people present as at the wedding itself. The same ordinance prohibited the guests at a baptism from eating at the home of the father of the child. The authorities of Limoges were also concerned about the size of escorts on various occasions. The number of people accompanying the godfathers and godmothers to the baptism was limited. When a young man went to visit his fiancée at her parents' home he could be attended by only so many. The same held for a visit by relatives of a pregnant woman. The government constantly tried to restrict these groups to a small number of close relatives. Thus they hoped to weaken the bonds of the powerful clans by reducing the occasions upon which they reaffirmed them. Or, at least, the authorities tried to diminish the visible signs of the clans' power and solidarity.[164]

Antonio Pilot's old (1904) study of Venetian *broglio* reflects the distaste of the Venetian government for these groupings in which the more powerful sought to gain supporters among the petty and the weaker enjoyed the patronage of the great.[165] In Venice in 1289, during the vacancy in the dogeship after the death of Giovanni Dandolo, it was prohibited to hold any gathering of people at one's house or elsewhere under penalty of one thousand pounds.[166] Apparently this became the rule, since the law found its way into a capitulary. There was legislation in 1298 against societies or *scuole* which were contrary to the oath of obedience to the Commune or to its profit and honor.[167]

Dinners were the subject of repeated legislation from the mid-fifteenth century. In 1454 the Ten passed an act which appears not to have gone into effect, which illustrates well the concern of the government for banquets at which conspiracies to gain office were hatched. The Ten comments on an old prohibition against having dinners for anyone other than kinsmen, except for marriages, etc. At that time, however, the act notes, many nobles not bound by blood nor even of comparable age gather together for dinners "in which, as experience teaches, other things than food are treated," and they make conspiracies very harmful to the honor of men who are not present. Therefore, except for feasts for kinsmen and for marriages, nobles were prohibited from having dinner parties. Up to three or four who were not relatives might be present, but, if there were more, all those present at the party had to leave the Great Council or the Forty when the vote concerned those who were present at the dinner, just as they had to for relatives.[168] In 1494 the Ten complained of societies of nobles holding many dinners which were harmful to God and the world and alien to the good and pacific customs of the city. These societies were the well-known *calze,* clubs of young nobles with their colorful and distinctive hose. It was prohibited to all nobles to give dinners for their clubs, even on the occasion of weddings. (The rules of the *calze* required the groom to entertain the society on such occasions.) Not only the person giving the party but the head of the house where it was held would be excluded for life from offices and benefices. Also those giving such a dinner should have their tithe doubled. Moreover, those attending should also fall under the penalty of ineligibility for office. The Ten went on to complain that such societies were growing. Henceforth, they were not to be allowed to exceed twenty-five members.[169] In November 1496 Giorgio Cornaro threw a huge feast for over one hundred nobles, ostensibly to celebrate the marriage of his daughter, but also probably to celebrate with his supporters his recent election as *podestà* of Brescia. Domenico Malipiero is critical of such means of exercising ambition by building up a coterie of followers.[170] The Ten again complained in 1497 of dinners at which deals were made either expressly or tacitly to gain by these detestable means honors which ought to be the reward of virtue. It was decreed that no noble, either before or after his election, might give a banquet for other nobles under penalty of perpetual privation of all offices. He should also have his tithe doubled. Anyone who attended such a feast should also be perpetually deprived of office. One could give up to three dinners in celebration of being elected, however, for closely related kinsmen up to the number of ten guests at each. Even for weddings one could only offer two dinners for relatives not to exceed forty each time.[171] The *calze* continued to enjoy their illegal feasts. The word "orgy," in fact, is suggested by an act of 1506, which reaffirms the law of 1497 and goes on to prohibit attendance at these feasts by women other than the wives of the male guests. The Ten apparently did not think that these dinners of the *calze* were innocent convivial gatherings, but, undoubtedly correctly, tabbed them as occasions for the rich to buy political support with all the sordid inducements employed by modern lobbyists.[172]

It is true, though, that the Venetian government was suspicious even of apparently innocent social relations among the patricians. During the interregnum following the death of Doge Giovanni Gradenigo in 1356, for example, nobles were not allowed to disrobe in another's house, i.e., to be overnight guests. It is obvious that political schemes were at issue, for the matter is linked with the passing of *cartoline*.[173]

It is small wonder, then, that baptisms came to be considered a source of factionalism. It is obvious that, like weddings, baptisms would be an occasion for gathering large numbers of kinsmen and allies, for munificence, and for outdoing rival clans, that gifts were given and that the bonds of kinship and friendship (including political friendship) were strengthened. It is also apparent that especially close bonds were created between the parents of the child and his godparents, but what is not so obvious is that the godparents could be numerous, as many as 150, and that a close bond was created among them, as well as with the family of the child, as *compari*.[174] Priuli and Sanuto tell us how nobles invited a multitude of other nobles to the christening of a child, making them *compari,* which created "the greatest bond of friendship," which was perilous to the Republic. Venetian nobles could not after 1505 have any other noble as godparent under a fine of two hundred ducats and exclusion from offices for five years. The godparents and the priest who performed the ceremony were also subject to the same penalty.[175]

Armorial display provided another means for asserting the solidarity and importance of the clan. An interesting act of 1266 prohibits anyone from wearing the armorial insignia of any great man, or having his arms at home, or bearing pictures of them, or displaying those arms in various ways.[176] This was not only directed toward maintaining public order against the all-too-historical feuds of Venetian Montagues and Capulets, but also against political factionalism. In the wake of the infamous conspiracy of 1310 the Council of Forty prohibited the bearing of the arms of the Querini and the Tiepolo:[177] the Ten repeated the prohibition in 1316.[178] By 1409 the lords of the night, who were responsible for exacting the fine of 100 *l.,* were reluctant to enforce the law against Giorgio Querini, who had displayed his family's red and white quartered arms. The Ten reminded them that it was their duty and imposed a penalty if they did not do it.[179] Some of the Querini of Crete tried to get around the law in 1421 by displaying red and yellow quartered arms, but the Ten took note, forbidding them such a display in any colors.[180] In 1489 the Ten prohibited Venetian governors in the subject cities from displaying their own arms, except for one painted (not sculpted) coat of arms inside the governor's palace. They had been accustomed to having their familial arms sculpted or painted, not only about the palace, but on gates, bridges, and other structures built during their terms.[181]

According to the Ten in 1417 many commanders of fleets and galleys had taken to displaying foreign arms. These roused the ire of some of those among whom the Venetians sailed and did business, which the government hoped to carry out in peace. So the display of foreign arms was prohibited on the galleys or in the piazza when crews were recruited. The sign of the cross and the effigy of the holy sepulcher, used on the yearly galleys bearing pilgrims, were excepted.[182] Within a year and a half, however, the Ten complained again of those who displayed the eagle or the lily on their galleys or at their recruiting benches. They were forbidden to display these symbols, whatever the color, under penalty of 500 *l.* and perpetual exclusion from the command of all galleys and roundships. They could show their own arms except, presumably, for the Querini and the Tiepolo.[183] Less than a year later, however, the Ten saw that the law was still not being enforced, because nobles who were found in violation pled that they had not been informed of the law. The Ten therefore provided that it should be read in the Great Council.[184]

Factions based on families might foment not only rebellion, as in the case of the Querini and Tiepolo clans, but also electoral conspiracies. By far the most infamous of Venetian electoral plots was the Cicogna conspiracy of 1432, which went beyond *broglio onesto* to real electoral cheating. The plot of 1432 also has implications, however, for the present matter. Marco Cicogna and four other nobles, Marco Magno, Benedetto Barbadeo, Zaccaria Contarini, and Andrea Pisani, organized a faction to aid one another secretly to gain offices.[185] The more remunerative and less onerous posts were those that they sought. It was no conspiracy to grab the levers of power in the state, for the positions were not the vital ones but sinecures or near sinecures. James Williamson has reported that the conspirators did not even belong to the important political groups. Some had important surnames, but many patricians of distinguished family were among the poor nobles. So, what we have is an illegal association among poorer nobles to gain for themselves more than their fair share of the largesse that the state offered to the nobility in the form of offices.[186] The charges against them point out that they dined together at Zaccaria's, Pisani's, and Paolo della Borole's houses.[187] They succeeded in upsetting the entire electoral process by flagrant cheating—which is the subject of the next chapter. Their association was considered contrary to the sound provisions of "our holy ancestors," a "horrible case," and when the plot was discovered the Great Council, whose members were far from disinterested in the allocation of sinecures, nearly rioted. Because of the danger of violence, the conspirators were allowed to escape for the time being.[188] Soon, however, they were taken. The leaders were tortured, and Contarini cracked under pressure and gave information on his associates.[189] Cicogna was convicted and sentenced to perpetual banishment.[190] The other leaders were sentenced to five years' banishment and deprivation of offices and councils for life.[191] The lesser members of the conspiracy received sentences ranging from one year's banishment and ten years' exclusion from offices and councils to deprivation of offices and councils for only one year.[192] In all the proceedings the emphasis is not upon the fact that they cheated egregiously in the elections, but that they formed a *compagnia* for coming to an understanding to aid one another to gain office. This reemphasized the point that the Venetians were relatively lax in enforcing the laws against *broglio* in the case of individual violations (even if gross cheating was involved), while they deeply feared political associations. As a result of the Cicogna conspiracy a new law was passed on 28 January 1433 against associations for aiding one another in the councils. The penalty was to be very heavy: perpetual banishment from all the possessions of Venice and a fine of one thousand pounds.[193] From 1436 to 1440, however, we find the Ten granting reductions in sentences to the Cicogna conspirators, including Cicogna himself.[194] Once more the Venetians did not consistently and firmly enforce the laws.

A new conspiracy to aid one another and relatives and friends of the conspirators to obtain offices was revealed in 1449. The Ten alluded to the existing laws against sects and conventicles, but declared that some nobles, nonetheless, dared to form open sects, so that when someone favored by the group was named in the Great Council, they distributed themselves at the heads of the benches or in the middle of the hall, and they pressured, entreated, begged, and forced others to give their ballots to the favored candidates. They also wanted to see the ballots cast openly. In the future, if anyone got up from his bench and went about the council urging people to vote for this one or that one, he was to be deprived of offices and councils for two years. Those who were solicited, moreover, should be excluded for one year if they did not immediately accuse the transgressor.[195]

Another plot to gain offices came to the surface in 1476. It was apparently thought to be quite widespread, but proved not to have anything like the scope of the Cicogna plot. Five nobles were convicted by the Ten and its Zonta. Domenico Arimondo and Bernardino Orio were charged and found guilty under the Cicogna conspiracy law, and were sentenced to perpetual exile from all Venetian possessions, as provided by that severe act. Luca Tron and Franco Malipiero, also charged with electoral conspiracy, suffered penalties of three and two years' deprivation, respectively, of offices and councils. Francesco Alberti was sentenced under the 1449 law for following the urns about the chamber asking for votes for others to two years' of ineligibility for offices and councils. It is interesting that in the midst of these documents we find a Jewish astrologer, Nicholas ben Jacob, taken into custody. We do not know on what charge, although presumably he was involved, nor do we learn what became of him. Three nobles charged in connection with the conspiracy were acquitted. Two of the advocates of the Commune tried three times to get the conviction of Giacomo Longo, but failed.[196] The Arimondo-Orio conspiracy gave rise to a new addition to the legislation on the subject. After the usual admonitions about rooting out "the most pernicious disease of sects," the Ten decreed that anyone who entered into an electoral conspiracy or even spoke to anyone concerning such a conspiracy must immediately report it under penalty of perpetual deprivation of all offices and coucils. All those who followed after the urns in the Great Council or the Senate asking that votes be given to some candidate, or indicating their desires in any way, or who remained in their places but indicated to those on the right or the left that they should vote in a certain way should be deprived of offices and councils for two years and fined one hundred pounds to be paid to the accuser.[197]

If I interpret correctly a series of documents of 1483, some faction in the Senate was trying to gain advantage in an election to the exalted post of captain-general of the sea by nominating enough of the most distinguished candidates for election in the Great Council so that much reballoting would be likely and the election would be delayed, because none would easily gain a majority. This practice is called a nursery of scandals, which could not be greater. A zonta was named for seeking out the guilty. A reward of 12,000 *l. parvorum* from the goods of the guilty, or, if necessary, from the Commune, was offered to informers. Even a participant could receive the reward and gain absolution for his own guilt by denouncing his allies. The law of 1476 on factions was reiterated.[198] A new law was passed by the Ten expediting elections in the Great Council, so that such delays would be less likely to occur.[199]

In 1487 there was a case involving nobles allegedly members of a society called the "Paladins" for helping one another to be elected. Although some of them were convicted of the lesser crime of asking for votes, they were found not guilty of forming a political sect.[200]

Benedetto Foscarini was the head of a conspiracy in 1491 to gain elections. He and his allies distributed themselves among the benches asking votes for fathers or friends of the group. The Ten sent Foscarini back to the college which had gained his confession to determine, with torture, if necessary, who were the candidates assisted and the allies who sought votes. Apparently Foscarini was guilty of an outburst against the Ten, and he was sentenced to five years' exile from Venice and an additional five years' exclusion from offices and councils. A few of the Ten were more vindictive, proposing that he be exiled to Cyprus for life.[201] Actually, Foscarini was the head of a band of the infamous *svizzeri,* who not only helped relatives and friends but sold their bloc of votes.[202]

It was bloc voting that the Venetians feared, not really the petty seeking after votes for minor offices by poor individuals. Among other acts, a great deal of what appears on the surface to be mere sumptuary legislation was directed against factions. All gatherings of nobles, especially dinner parties, were feared as occasions for forming factions. Baptisms were dreaded as occasions when the nobles might form very strong bonds among *compari*. In spite of these acts, there did emerge in the fifteeth century a number of significant attempts to form blocs to gain votes.

THE PATRICIATE established an unreasonable standard for Venetian politics, that men should not seek office but that the best should be chosen by their peers without pressure, influence, or argument. This was especially unrealistic since the same patricians used minor elective offices as a sort of welfare scheme for poor nobles. Maranini and others have been aware that there was a large amount of ineffectual legislation against office-seeking (the problem of *broglio* is a familiar one to Venetian scholars), but he praises the single-minded legislative effort to eradicate it.[203] To the propagators of the myth of Venice the dark cloud of evidence can always be turned inside out to reveal a silver lining. More respect should be paid to the evidence at its face value. What it tells us reveals, not, at least in this chapter, the depths of evil, but a long series of foolish attempts to legislate against the unconquerable petty weaknesses of humanity. Sometimes the legislation failed against the ambition of great men for the highest public offices, but much more often the obstacle was the desire of poor nobles to feed at the public trough, the *mangiatoia.*

We have not dealt here with what we moderns would consider to be dishonest ways of trying to fulfill these ambitions and desires, but only with *broglio onesto,* or simple campaigning for public office. Nobles tried to gain nominations by thrusting their candidacies upon nominators and potential nominators by words, handbills, signals, and messengers. Their underage sons overwhelmed serious proceedings with puerile clamor on behalf of fathers, uncles, and other relatives. The more decorous candidates simply stood or moved about in a conspicuous fashion. Congratulations and flattery were heaped upon possible future nominators. Once nominations were obtained similar devices were used to gain election. Nobles were asked openly for their votes—not a very serious crime, we would think, but in Venetian eyes an evil against which laws were constantly directed. It is revealing that those required to swear that their votes had not been solicited avoided naming the culprits by declaring that they had been demanded by everybody.

Not even the Venetian patriciate, for all its legislating, took *broglio onesto* too seriously. The laws were not consistently enforced. Patricians could peek through their fingers at the pitiful attempts of some poverty-stricken noble to obtain a small salary or even at the efforts of a grandee to gain the highest offices. These activities were legally disapproved, but generally tolerated. Moreover, since "everybody" was doing it—and that seems almost literally true—laxity of enforcement of the laws depended upon mutual back scratching. What was really feared and hated, so that discovery of a plot to control elections to petty offices caused a great uproar and a danger of violence, was faction, sect, or party. These were anathema.

There are not only defenders, like Maranini, of the Venetian attempts to outlaw *broglio,* but also defenders of the violations of these legislative attempts, in short, advocates of *broglio.* Finlay argues that it provided associations needed among the Venetian patricians, allowed an outlet for ambition, and prevented the political violence that occurred in other Italian city-states in the late Middle Ages. In this he is following some who are cited by Priuli (who does not agree):

Some say that lobbying and intrigue for offices are the salvation of the Republic of Venice, that is, the principal reason for [Venetian patricians] not offending or displeasing one another and for their maintaining tranquility, amity and peace. Without their intrigues, favors and enticements, there would begin among them the sort of seditions, parties and discords which exist in all the cities of the world. There would be such great conflict among patricians that the complete ruin of Venice would follow. But by reason of lobbying and offices, all [discords] remain subdued, and enmities, factions and sects are kept secret.[204]

There is some truth in the argument. Ambition and desire for gain were allowed some scope, although officially disapproved. Venice did maintain a stable government, although whether the virtue (or vice) of its nobility, its political structure, its topography of canals, bridges, and narrow *calli,* or some other factor is primarily responsible is open to debate. On the other hand the act of 1449 points out the great divisiveness induced by *broglio* and Priuli marveled that Venice had been able to endure it.[205] The failure of the legislation against *broglio,* like all efforts to impose laws that do not conform to powerful customs, created disrespect for law. It also led to much indecorous behavior, as the proud nobles of Venice circulated about the palace, jostling for favorable position, clamoring for nominations and votes, not only in the Great Council, but even in the ultradignified Senate. This is hardly our accustomed view of Venetian patricians.

If you look closely enough you can see that the winged lion's open book is really a palimpsest. Beneath the official inscription, "Pax tibi Marce, evangelista meus," can be discerned the real and enduring slogan of the Venetian Republic, "Dayla, dayla," or "Gimme, gimme!"

IV

Corrupt Elections

THERE STILL has been no thorough study of corruption in Venetian elections, especially for the period before the War of the League of Cambrai, although Robert Finlay's recent book offers considerable evidence for the late fifteenth and sixteenth centuries.[1] It is generally conceded, though, that the war had a very deleterious effect upon Venetian political morality and that electoral corruption was rife from then until the end of the Republic. Evidence abounds, however, that "the good old days" were less than good and that the *progenitores* were not more virtuous than their successors.[2]

Gasparo Contarini, who composed his *De magistratibus et republica Venetorum* after the War of the League of Cambrai to set before his countrymen in idealized form the *mores maiorum,* nonetheless inserted many parenthetical notes implying that the excellence of the governmental system was consistently undermined by patrician attempts to subvert it. The golden balls drawn to determine membership on the nominating committees, Contarini says, were coded "so that no fraud could occur," and more specifically "so that no one could bring a golden ball from home with him, hold it secretly in his hand and appear to have drawn it out of the urn, thus by fraud becoming an elector."[3] Before a nominating committee began its deliberations, its members were addressed by a secretary of the Commune, who "described to the electors the things prescribed by law to be observed in the choosing of magistrates. Also read to them are those senatorial decrees and other laws admonishing electors not to be corrupted by money or to make their choices through any fraud or deceit."[4] Before a *proba* was conducted in the Great Council, all prospective voters were warned by the chief secretary "that each of them was bound by divine and human laws to vote for the candidate who seemed the best of all and the most valuable to the Republic."[5] Most notable, however, is Contarini's explanation of why the sessions of the Great Council were not allowed to extend past sunset. "This was established for excellent cause," Contarini explained, "because if the matter of election was prolonged into night, it would have been difficult for the magistrates in charge of the assembly to control so great a multitude of citizens in any orderly fashion, or to prevent the citizens from doing anything contrary to the laws under cover of darkness."[6] The very complexity of the electoral process which Contarini and other humanist commentators found so laudable apparently resulted from the fact that, unless stringent controls were applied, the Venetian patriciate was expected to abuse it for personal advantage as a matter of course.

The ambivalent character of Contarini's description, emphasizing patrician loyalty and honor while intimating the existence of chicanery in elections, is mirrored in the elaborate *arenge* which Venetian legislators regulary used to introduce statutes. "There is nothing which can more surely and swiftly disturb, confuse and finally ruin the affairs of our state, so gloriously handed down to us through the grace and mercy of God and the virtue of our ancestors," a law of 1494 begins, "than that such a disease as the buying and selling of votes, which is said to occur in votes on governorships, offices, magistracies and other things conferred by our Great Council, should continue. . . . Such practices are known to occur on the part of those who, through such an ambitious and detestable mode, seek to achieve the dignities and other public benefits of our city."[7] Four years earlier the Council of Ten, after boasting that their predecessors had arranged all matters pertaining to the welfare of the state, including elections, with consummate wisdom, admitted nonetheless that "there exist some of our nobles who, with wicked intent and ambition to gain a seat on a nominating committee," were willing to engage in fraud to do so.[8] In 1419 the Great Council attributed the necessity for increasing penalties against electoral corruption to the fact that "everyone used to have greater reverence and fear than they do now."[9] Six decades later the Great Council bewailed the fact that it was the practice of granting large salaries to nobles for performing public business which had made them unwilling to serve except for their own benefit.[10] The Venetian legislators were extremely adept at portraying electoral duplicity among the patricians as an abominable perversion of an ancient norm, thereby fostering the idealized myth of the earlier patriciate and utilizing it as a model for their own times; Venetian legislative and judicial acts, however, offer no evidence, as we shall see, that the ideal was ever realized at any time from the thirteenth to the sixteenth century.

In this chapter, therefore, we turn from *broglio onesto* to such subjects as bribery, blatant cheating, and other measures considered corrupt by medieval Venetians and ourselves. Much of the evidence comes from Venetian legislation from the late thirteenth century until the beginning of the War of the League of Cambrai. In 1473 the Council of Ten remarked: "Many laws have been passed, both by the Great Council and the present council, to determine the mechanisms of elections, of coming to the urns and of casting ballots, all so that all fraud and clever deceit might be abolished and a proper and uncorrupted process might be preserved for the distribution of magistracies and offices in the Great Council."[11] By studying these laws and the problems they reveal we may gain a fuller appreciation of the attitudes and behavior of Venetian nobles in regard to election to office, and this in turn will cast light on the validity of the myth of the selfless patriciate.

THE GOLD BALLS

Noblemen fortunate enough to gain membership on a nominating committee could and did nominate friends and relatives; they could even sell their nominations for money or promised favors. In their quest for gold balls the patricians not only reduced the councils, and especially the Great Council, to disorder, but they cheated.

The first extant indication of malfeasance in the selecting of electors occurs in an act of the Great Council of 1319, the preface to which informs us that "the process does not seem sufficiently fit or honest, because of the many improper methods men use to be chosen." The law is unfortunately not specific about these improper methods, but that they must have been quite ingenious is suggested by the wholesale reorganization of the process for which the act provided. The Council of Forty was to prepare a list of all nobles eligible to participate in elections in the council, and the number of balls placed in the urn was to be determined by that listing. As names were read from the list, each noble would secure a ball from the urn; he would not, however, draw it himself. Instead a Venetian youth not more than twelve years old would be delegated to extract a ball from the urn as each noble was named. In succeeding years, the order of names on the Forty's list would be altered so that no fraud could be devised to take advantage of the new system.[12] The use of the boy to draw from the urn strongly suggests that nobles had not been drawing balls honestly and in a random fashion.

It cannot be determined whether this system was ever effectively employed, but if so it had certainly fallen into disuse by the early fifteenth century, when the Great Council was forced to take action against those who were improperly trying to increase their chances of drawing a golden ball from the urn. An act of 1419 notes that those who approached the urn with the occupants of a bench other than that on which they sat had regularly been punished by a fine of ten *soldi,* a sum which was no longer sufficient to restrain offenders; henceforth this offense would be punished by immediate expulsion from the Great Council, exclusion from all offices and councils for six months, and deprivation of the right to vote in elections. The key to the problem is found in the provision that the same penalties were to befall those who dared to go to the urn more than once.[13] Despite these measures, patricians in the Great Council continued their unseemly efforts to secure positions on the nominating committees. In 1430 the Great Council noted that many had been discovered drawing more than one ball from the urn in violation of the intention of the Venetian *antiqui;* surprisingly, however, no penalty was found to exist for this misdeed. The Council therefore voted that anyone drawing more than one ball from the urn should be at once expelled from the assembly and prohibited from participating in its deliberations for six months.[14]

In the preceding chapter we have already discussed the infamous Cicogna conspiracy of 1432, putting aside until now the aspects pertinent to real cheating, rather than mere campaigning for office.[15] Marco Cicogna, it will be recalled, headed a conspiracy of poor nobles to control petty elections in the Great Council. Each of the conspirators had a small tube up his sleeve, so that when he was called to draw a ball from the urn, he could drop a gold ball into his hand, get on a nominating committee, and nominate one of his associates.[16] The plan proved so effective that the council was unable to conduct a proper election. Sentences of banishment and deprivation of offices and councils were imposed upon thirty-eight conspirators.[17] The action of the Ten was swift and forceful, and it might be cited as rigorous enforcement of the laws against electoral corruption, but by 1440 the Ten had granted pardons to at least four of the principal conspirators.[18] The use of coded balls seems to have been an outcome of the Cicogna conspiracy.

At about the same time that the Cicogna plot occurred, the Senate was confronted by two cases involving improprieties in the selection of nominating committees in the Great Council. The first, in January of 1433, concerned Venceslao da Ripa, a former head of the Council of

Forty, who had been elected *camerario* of Brescia. It was charged that in his zeal to obtain that post, da Ripa had carefully arranged the gold balls in the first urn, and had informed nobles favorable to his candidacy how those balls were arranged and what benches would be called to the urns first. The Senate voted overwhelmingly to proceed on the indictment, and da Ripa was convicted and sentenced to three years' exclusion from office.[19] The following March, action was initiated against Marco Venier, who was charged with bribing two notaries of the chancellery to see to it that nobles who had promised to nominate his father to the governorship of Treviso were given the opportunity to do so. The first of the notaries, Apollonio Donati, had been responsible for calling nobles to the urns to draw their lots; the second had presided at the drawing of lots within the nominating committee, and his case will be discussed when we turn to that part of the procedure.[20] Donati, it was charged, had arranged for two of Venier's associates, Geronimo Molin and Giovanni Maria Contarini, to draw golden balls from the urn at which he stood guard. The Senate voted to exclude Venier from the Great Council for a year and to fine him two hundred pounds; Donati was condemned to perpetual exclusion from the ducal chancery.[21]

Nobles continued to wander about the chamber in an effort to approach the urn more than once. Although it was already required that nobles should remain in their seats and come to the urn only with those from the bench upon which they were originally seated, in 1442 the Great Council increased the penalty for violating this precautionary measure.[22]

Corruptly packing the nominating committees was a part, but only a small part, of the Pisani conspiracy of 1457. Bartolomeo Pisani, a head of the Forty, among other offenses, bribed two notaries in charge of the urns in the Great Council, Andrea della Costa and Paolonio Donati, to insure that electors favorable to Andrea Cornaro's candidacy for the Senate were selected and given the right to nominate.[23] To get information on how this had been accomplished, the Dieci offered to della Costa, who had fled Venice, a safe conduct to return temporarily to the city.[24] Both notaries were sentenced to perpetual exile.[25] Other aspects of the Pisani plot will be considered when we take up elections in the Great Council and in the Forty.[26] As a result of this conspiracy the Council of Ten legislated stringent regulations concerning the preparation of urns for the drawing of balls. The urns had often been prepared fraudulently to offer special opportunities for select nobles to obtain a golden ball. One reason this had occurred is that the *capi* of the Forty had taken it upon themselves to prepare the urns, instead of the ducal councillors designated to do so. (As we shall see, Pisani had engineered the election of two other heads of the Forty who were part of his conspiracy.) The Ten therefore decreed that the *capi* of the Forty should be prohibited from interfering with the councillors who were supposed to handle the matter. The same law attempted to regulate the order in which the various rows of benches would be called to the urns. This had regularly been done according to the whim *(beneplacitum)* of the officials in charge. This practice could lead to unfairness, since the officials might arrange the balls in the urn, inform their friends of the arrangement, and then call the benches on which those friends sat to the urns first, thereby giving them an excellent opportunity to secure a committee seat. Henceforth the names of the benches were to be inscribed on twelve small *schedulae,* which would be sealed and inserted into a special urn situated immediately before the doge. The councillor presiding over the election would then draw the schedules from the urn one by one and call the benches to draw their balls in the order in which their names had been drawn.[27]

In 1459 the Council of Ten took action against two nobles, Luca Polani and Antonio Coppo, charged with committing "dishonest acts" at one of the urns in the Great Council. They were expelled from the Great Council and from all offices and governorships for a year and jailed for two months.[28] A subsequent act reveals that they had approached the urns after the last benches had been called without waiting to be summoned. The Ten therefore decided to strengthen the two acts of 1419 penalizing those nobles who came to the urns out of order. It decreed that while the penalties stipulated in the legislation of 1419 should remain in force, anyone approaching the urns out of order should also be jailed for two months and excluded from the Great Council and from all other councils and benefices for a full year.[29]

It is clear that in the later fifteenth century incidents of malfeasance at the urns were growing more serious, for the punishments inflicted upon offenders became progressively heavier. In 1468 the Ten considered the case of one Pietro Marcello, who had visited an urn twice in an attempt to secure a gold ball. Determining that the penalties already legislated for this offense were inadequate, the Ten took the opportunity to decree a new set of penalties—a year's imprisonment and exclusion from the Great Council and all offices and benefices for a decade—and promptly imposed them on the unfortunate Marcello.[30] An ex post facto law was apparently not thought improper in Venice. In 1473 the Ten noted that although many laws existed to keep order in the first stage of *electio,* the approach to the urns was still "extremely confused and turbulent, . . . especially toward the close of elections, when no order is maintained and all, eagerly and in groups, want to put their hands into the urn." We can imagine the opportunities offered by such disorder for second and third attempts to draw a gold ball. To correct this situation, the Ten ordered that all regulations passed earlier concerning the order in which nobles should come to the urn should be absolutely observed. All patricians were to approach the urn with their own benches in the precise order in which they were seated upon them. Anyone not doing so, or daring to place his hand in the urn at the same time as those preceding or following him, should, on being seen by the doge, a councillor, or one of the *avogadori* or *capi* of the Ten, be immediately expelled from the Great Council for six months and fined fifty pounds. The same penalty was stipulated for anyone who was seen drawing more than one ball from the urn.[31]

The ineffectiveness of these statutes is suggested by the preface to a new act of the Ten in 1484, which notes that in spite of the many laws on the books many nobles persisted in going to the urn more than once in almost every council session. This and other prefaces to laws prove that we are not dealing with isolated abuses, but with ubiquitous corruption. The *arenge* may exaggerate, but if they claim offenses at nearly every session it is certain that offenses were frequent. The act stipulated that while all the provisions of earlier laws were to remain in force, such an offender was also to be punished by exclusion from all councils, offices, and benefices for the next ten years.[32] In 1489 the Ten observed that some nobles were making a practice of walking about the council chamber, saying that they had already been to the urn or that they had to leave the chamber because of kinship with an elector already chosen; their intention, however, was rather to find a place on the benches which had not yet been summoned to the urns. Such nobles were to be punished by exclusion from the Great Council for a year and fined two hundred ducats if they dared to come to the urn with the *ultimi banchi*. At the same time the Ten took action against those nobles who occasionally departed the chamber during elections by assigning a notary to guard the entrance of the hall. This notary could permit nobles to depart if they wished, but was to prevent them from returning until the election had been completed and the nominating committees were safely removed to their *camere*. The notary was bound to fulfill his duty under penalty of two months' imprisonment, and nobles who departed the council chamber and then returned to it by whatever means before the election had been finished were to be excluded from the Great Council for a year and fined two hundred ducats.[33] A few weeks later the Ten declared that there simply were not enough spaces for all the members of the Great Council to sit on the *banchi* whence they could be called in a relatively orderly fashion to the urns. They were compelled to stand, and thus many submitted to the temptation to mill about and take the opportunity to come to the urns more than once. The Ten assigned a place where the surplus nobles should stand and a bench with which they should come to the urns.[34]

In 1490, the Ten set a penalty for those nobles who, when they came to the urn, were lifting a number of balls above its lid in order to inspect them and choose a gold one. The punishment for such an offender was to be a month's imprisonment, exclusion from the Great Council for six months, and a fine of fifty pounds. The word of the doge, a ducal councillor, or one of the *avogadori* or the *capi* of the Ten who witnessed the deed was to suffice for the immediate execution of the penalty.[35] Still the cheating attempts to grab a gold ball continued. One Niccolò Barbo was expelled from the Great Council under the above act in 1493 for drawing two ballots from an urn.[36] On the same day another noble, Francesco Manolesso, was likewise expelled for leaving the bench where he was sitting to go to another bench which had been summoned to the urn.[37] The registers of the Great Council record the conviction of Tommaso Morosini in the following year for moving from his own bench to another.[38]

All of the statutes which the Great Council and the Council of Ten had passed through the fifteenth century appear to have had remarkably little effect. The prologue to a statute issued by the Ten in 1495 offers a graphic description of what was still occurring during the selection of the nominating committees. In the latest session of the Great Council, the act states, a virtual riot had arisen when the *ultimi banchi* had been summoned to the urns and the nobles suddenly realized that only one golden ball remained. "All proper order was abandoned around the urn," the act reports, "and the nobles, thrown into confusion, indulged in a loud and tumultuous brawl, each one striving eagerly and desiring through some violent means to thrust his hand into the urn and draw out the sole golden ball remaining in it." In response to this "most reckless and dangerous precedent," the Ten decreed that anyone engaging in such contentious behavior at the urn thereafter would be excluded from the Great Council and all state offices and benefices for two years, jailed for six months, and fined five hundred pounds. The offender was also to be declared ineligible for election to any official position until the fine had been paid. The Ten took this occasion to specify the precise routes by which nobles were to approach the urns and return to their benches, and stipulated the same stringent penalties noted above against anyone who failed to observe them.[39]

Perhaps it was with a sense of desperation that in 1497 the Council of

Ten added a supplementary penalty to the punishments specified by their act of 1468 for those going to the urn more than once: the loss of one's right to draw a ball from the urn in any of the councils of the Republic for the rest of the offender's life.[40] Whether this threat proved any more effective than those which had been devised over the previous two hundred years must be thought extremely questionable. Despite all its earlier warnings to the contrary, in fact, the Council of Ten granted grace in 1499 to Silvestro Geno, who had taken two balls from the urn, and Bernardino Minio, who had placed his hand in the urn twice. All penalties were remitted to both offenders.[41]

NOMINATING COMMITTEES

Since the Venetian patricians displayed such unseemly desire to gain a place on the nominating committees chosen from the Great Council, it is hardly surprising that the activity of those committees also had to be stringently regulated. It was certainly expected that those fortunate enough to have gained access to one of the committees would seek to use their position to advance their personal ambitions or those of their families. The electors were therefore prohibited from selecting more than one of their own number for nomination to the Signoria[42] or more than two of themselves for nomination to any offices whatsoever. Pointedly, however, the latter restriction was applicable only to nominations for offices which carried salaries; the state had little reason to fear that the electors would be prone to place their names in contention for offices which were not financially remunerative.[43] In 1273 the Great Council sought also to restrict the mere exchange of nominations among the electors. If one of them asked another to leave the chamber because he wished to nominate him, the elector so nominated could not in turn name for another office the man who had nominated him.[44]

The process to be observed in the nominating committees was also the subject of considerable concern. Upon entering their *camera*, it will be recalled, the members of the committee were to draw lots from an urn to determine the offices to which each would have the right to nominate. The *avogadori di comun* noted in 1408 that the drawing of lots had been improperly conducted and decreed that anyone who gave his lot to another or acted at all dishonestly in the drawing was to be fined twenty small *soldi*.[45] The third defendant in the previously mentioned Venier case of March 1433 was a notary, Pietro Azelino, who had given the right to nominate Marco Venier's father to Geronimo Molin. The notary was deprived of his post for three years as punishment.[46] In 1443 the Great

Council raised the fine levied against electors who exchanged their lots to one hundred pounds. The council also stipulated that the notaries conducting the nominating process were to place the lots into the urn immediately upon their entrance into the *camera,* and were to allow the electors to draw their lots only after the urn had received a thorough shaking. Any notary failing to follow correct procedure was also subject to the fine of one hundred pounds, as well as the loss of his office.[47]

The full scope of the corrupt practices which came to exist in the nominating committees is, however, revealed only in later statutes. The procedure was that after an elector had offered a name for nomination, the members of his committee proceeded to vote on the candidate by casting ballots in a single *bussulus.* A statute of the Council of Ten in 1456 reveals that electors were not only varying the order in which they voted and placing their ballots in the *bussulus* openly rather than secretly, but were even opening the *bussulus* without authorization and miscounting the results, thereby controlling the outcome of the *electio.* The Ten therefore decreed that henceforth a *bussulus* without a bottom was to be used; so long as it rested on a table, the ballots would remain hidden within it and voting could proceed normally. At the end of the balloting, however, the two final electors would lift the *bussulus* so that the ballots would immediately fall within the view of all without being touched by anyone. An elector who did not vote in proper order or who lifted the *bussulus* without authority to do so was to lose his right to vote in the election and to be excluded from the Great Council and all other councils and benefices for two years.[48]

The Ten returned to its regulation of the nominating process in 1464. The electors, the Ten observed, were still not performing their duties properly. They were supposed to remain seated during the votes on the various names suggested, except when they or a kinsman had been named, in which case they were to depart the *camera* entirely. In fact, however, electors were not leaving the chamber under those circumstances; rather they were actively soliciting affirmative votes for themselves and their relatives, standing at the *bussulus* to watch how their fellow electors voted, and in some situations placing more than one ballot in the *bussulus* themselves; occasionally they would even visit the *camere* of other committees to do some special pleading on their own behalf. This practice was intolerable, and the Ten therefore required that the electors take a solemn oath to fulfill their function faithfully and stipulated the precise manner in which that function was to be discharged. The electors were to take their seats immediately upon entering the chamber, listen to the oath they were required to swear, and then draw their lots in an orderly fashion. Balls of different colors,

marked to prevent multiple voting, would be provided for each nominating committee. In voting on proposed nominees, the electors were
to rise individually in the order in which their lots had been drawn,
place their ballots in the *bussulus,* and quickly return to their places.
After all had voted, the electors would return to the *bussulus* as a group
and count the ballots, recording the names of the nominee and of the
elector who had suggested him. Naturally, if an elector or one of his
relatives had been named, he was to absent himself from the *camera*
during the voting. If the nine members of a committee did not observe
this procedure in every detail, they were to lose their voting rights and
be excluded from the Great Council and all other councils, offices, and
benefices for a year. Each elector was bound by oath to report any
infractions to the doge, the *capi* of the Ten, or the *avogadori di comun.* At
the close of this elaborate act the Ten added several specific injunctions
as to how voting was to be conducted in the committees. The elector
who voted first on any prospective nominee, since he had openly
named the candidate, was also to vote on him openly; each of the other
electors was to vote secretly, showing his ballot to his fellows in his
hand (not, it was emphasized, in his fingers) and then, closing his hand,
inserting the ballot into the *bussulus.* Failure to follow this procedure
was to be punished by loss of voting rights and expulsion from the
Great Council and all offices and benefices for two years. Any elector
who placed more than one ballot in the *bussulus* was to suffer the
penalty for the same offense in *probe* of the Great Council: the loss of
the right hand. Any elector who dared to speak with an elector from
another committee was to be excluded from the Great Council for two
years and fined one hundred pounds, and if an elector had to leave the
camera for any valid reason he was to leave his ballots during his absence
with the councillor overseeing the session.[49]

ELECTIONS IN THE GREAT COUNCIL

Despite the difficulties which obviously attended the selection and voting of the nominating committees, slates of candidates for the vacant
magistracies were of course eventually reported to the Great Council
for *probatio.* Not surprisingly, the *probe* did not proceed without difficulties of their own. By 1275, for example, it had been found necessary
to decree that irregularities in the *probe* of ambassadors and *tractatores*
should not serve to invalidate the votes.[50] The greatest continuing problem was that nobles insisted on casting more than one ballot for or
against candidates in the *bussuli* carried through the council chamber.

The fact that the voting urns were carried from bench to bench, while the patricians were supposed to remain in their seats, represents an effort to avoid at this stage the disorder and dishonesty which occurred as the nobles filed to the stationary urns containing the golden balls which gave access to nominating committees.[51] The effort was not entirely successful. It came to be commonplace to see the vote totals on successive nominees vary, sometimes considerably, which probably indicates the casting of multiple votes. Sanuto accuses some nobles of inserting fistfuls of ballots into the urns.[52] The first suggestion of this practice occurs in an act of the Great Council of 1344, which rather naively ascribed the fact that too many ballots had been found in the *bussuli* to the fact that only two councillors had been counting them. Four councillors were therefore to be assigned that task, and the other two councillors, the *capi* of the Forty, the *avogadori di comun,* and other appropriate officials were to go about with the *bussuli* in their travels through the council chamber. If one of the councillors counting the ballots was forced to leave the chamber because of kinship with a nominee, another was to take his place.[53]

In 1375, however, an act of the Great Council specifically complained that *probe* in the council were being vitiated by some nobles' practice of casting more than one ballot. "It would be excellent," the preface to the act states bluntly, "if those whom the love of virtue does not restrain from this misdeed should at least be restrained by the terror of punishment." It was therefore decided that any noble placing more than one ballot in the *bussulus* was to be excluded perpetually from all governorships, offices, benefices, and councils of the Commune both within and without the city. Moreover, the *avogadori* were to have the option of proceeding with harsher penalties against the malefactor if the case seemed to warrant it. The *capi* of the Forty were required to read the statute to the assembled council every two months to assure that each voter was well acquainted with its provisions.[54]

This statute certainly did not solve the problem on a long-term basis. In 1396, for example, the *avogadori di comun* brought charges against Andrea Fontana, who, it was alleged, cast more than one ballot in a *proba* concerning the nomination of Giacobello Avanzago to a captaincy. The Senate, however, refused decisively to proceed against the accused in two ballots, both of which showed only six members favoring prosecution. Very likely the accused was innocent, possibly even the victim of harassment, but, in any event, multiple voting was still a vital concern.[55] In 1400, on the other hand, the Senate decided by a vote of 66 to 29 (with 35 *non sinceri*) that Alessandro Loredan should fall under the penalties imposed by the Great Council's statute of 1375 for casting more than one ballot. These penalties included perpetual exclusion from all governmental offices, councils, governorships, and benefices, as well as the possibility of further punishment by the *avogadori*.[56] In the following year, however, a motion that similar action be taken against Marco Polani was soundly defeated by the Senate, 82 to 9 (with 34 *non sinceri*).[57]

An act of the Great Council passed in 1409 noted that in many *probe* the number of ballots in the *bussuli* continued to exceed the number of eligible voters. When this occurred, the councillors counting the votes were habitually subtracting the excess from the affirmative ballots, although such a procedure did not insure a fair outcome. Henceforth, whenever an excess of votes was suspected, those ineligible to vote in the *proba* were to be expelled from the hall and a careful count made of the voters present. If that count agreed with the total number of votes in the original *proba,* the latter was to be considered valid; if not, the vote was to be repeated.[58] In 1433 the Great Council found it necessary to supplement its statute of 1375 concerning those who cast more than one ballot in elections by stipulating that, in order that offenders could be more easily apprehended, in every *proba* each voter would henceforth be required to demonstrate publicly that he had only one ballot in his hand before placing it in the *bussulus;* voters who failed to observe this regulation were to be subject to a fine of twenty *soldi*.[59]

The statute of 1409 which had provided for the repetition of *probe* in which an excess of ballots had been cast had to be revised in 1442. It seems that *probe* in which one candidate had gained favorable votes from more than half the Council and possessed more than one hundred votes above the total of his nearest rival were being repeated because a counting of the council had exhibited some slight variance from the total of the *probe*. Henceforth, in such cases the excess was to be subtracted from the victor's affirmative votes, and if he still had more votes than his competitors he was to be considered elected, provided that his total still exceeded a simple majority. If the subtraction brought the apparent victor to precisely the same vote total as his nearest rival, both were to be voted upon again in a runoff. In all other circumstances the law of 1409 was to remain in force.[60]

The continuing effort on the part of some nobles to place more than one ballot in the *bussulus* despite the penalties previously legislated led the Council of Ten to return to the problem in 1451. In April of that year the Dieci passed an act raising the fine for a voter who placed his hand in the *bussulus* without first publicly showing that he held only one ballot from twenty *soldi*—the amount specified by the Great Council in 1433—to ten pounds. The same act imposed an additional punishment for those convicted of casting more than one ballot in a *proba:* the amputation of the malefactor's right hand. Anyone who knew that such malfeasance had occurred and failed to report it to the proper authorities was to be subject to the same penalty.[61] We do have examples of the use of this Draconian penalty in the 1450s, but it was seldom employed thereafter, probably because it was considered too severe.[62]

Venice witnessed considerable political turmoil in 1457, for, in addition to the deposition of Doge Francesco Foscari, that year saw the occurrence of two conspiracies to subvert the electoral process. The first involved the efforts of Donato Cornaro to secure the election of his father, Giacomo, as *podestà* of Ravenna by enticing a group of fellow nobles to cast more than one ballot in his favor. Suspicion of complicity fell on the houses of Soranzo, Zane, Giustinian, and Civran, as well as Cornaro, and so the Council of Ten began its investigation by expelling Marco Cornaro and Niccolò Soranzo from its deliberations and electing a *zonta* of twelve members to conduct an inquiry.[63] On 11 February the Ten ordered the arrest of Paolo Giustinian, offering a reward of two hundred pounds to anyone who would turn him over to the authorities; penalties were also fixed for anyone who would harbor Giustinian or assist him to flee the Commune.[64] Five days later Giustinian was sentenced to perpetual exclusion from all councils, offices, and benefices and to exile at Candia in Crete, and was made liable to the amputation of his right hand and a fine of three thousand pounds if he were to violate his exile and be captured.[65] It was not until June that remaining members of the conspiracy were detained and sentenced. An order for the arrest of Donato Cornaro was issued on 14 June,[66] and six days later he was also exiled to Candia, with the proviso that if he ever broke confinement he was to be subject to immediate execution.[67] On the same day two other nobles whom Cornaro had induced to cast more than one ballot—Ettore Soranzo and Andrea Civran—were sentenced to perpetual exclusion from all councils, offices, and benefices and the amputation of their right hands.[68] It was also decided to proceed against Geronimo Zane, but the record of action against him breaks off without giving his sentence.[69] Another noble implicated in the venture, Adorno Contarini, however, was convicted in absentia and condemned to perpetual exile. If he dared ever to return to Venice, he was to be relieved of his right hand.[70]

It was unquestionably the Cornaro conspiracy which moved the Ten to complain of the excesses of ballots, which continued to be discovered in *probe* in the Great Council. The Council declared that the youths who had customarily been drafted to carry the *bussuli* were simply too young to understand their duties, a fact upon which unscrupulous nobles had seized in order to cast more than one ballot with impunity. The Ten therefore resolved to select notaries from the chancellery and noble youths of at least eighteen years of age to carry the *bussuli*. No one except those deputized by the Ten was to be allowed to fulfill this function, and those chosen were required to perform the duty under pain of a fine of twenty *soldi*. Nobles authorized to carry the *bussuli* were not to vote themselves until after their *banchi* had voted, and had to cast their ballots in full view of the doge to avoid being expelled from the Great Council for six months.[71]

While the Cornaro investigation was still in progress the Ten was confronted by the scandalous and complex effort of Bartolomeo Pisani to elect Andrea Cornaro to the Senate. Dolfin describes Pisani as between thirty and thirty-two years of age, stately and handsome, but audacious and eager to do damage to the Republic. He was in the habit of rigging elections in the hope of reward. Encouraged by Francesco da Canal, Pisani, who was then the only head of the Forty in office, engineered an elaborate electoral conspiracy. He rigged the election of heads of the Forty and bribed notaries to get Cornaro nominated. Then these *capi,* who also counted the ballots in *probe* of the Great Council at the time, falsified the votes for the senatorial position, so that Cornaro received a sizable majority.[72] The irregularity in the election of the *capi* of the Forty had been so blatant that the Dieci decided to investigate, and as a result the entire plot was discovered. Orders for the arrest of Pisani and the newly elected *capi* were issued and a *zonta* of fifteen elected to interrogate them, using torture if necessary; all rectors were also notified to detain them if they should be apprehended outside Venice.[73] In spite of these precautions, Pisani escaped, and the Ten had to condemn him in absentia, adding that if he were captured he was to be executed by hanging and his body left on the gallows for three days as an example to others.[74] The severity of the penalty reflects Pisani's repeated dishonest tampering with *electiones* and *probe*.[75] The unfortunate Paolo Giustinian, who had only recently been convicted of complicity in the conspiracy of Donato Cornaro,[76] was found to be implicated in Pisani's plot as well. The Ten therefore reaffirmed its sentence of perpetual exile for him, but added that if he ever violated his exile and was captured he was to lose his head as well as his hand.[77] Two bribed notaries were sentenced to perpetual exile.[78] Harsh penalties were also administered to others who had had a hand in Pisani's abortive venture. Andrea Cornaro had wisely fled the city, and so was sentenced to exile in absentia; his brother Marco, who had known of the plot and failed to report it, was banished for ten years, while Francesco Bon, Ludovico Lombardo, and Lorenzo Baffo, who were also guilty of concealing the crime, were banished for five years and deprived of all offices and benefices for a like period. Francesco da Canal received the same punishment.[79]

The Ten followed up the Pisani case with an act directed against the involvement of the *capi* of the Forty in counting the ballots in elections in the Great Council. A statute of 1344 had declared that four councillors should count the ballots, but the *capi* had usurped this function with the upshot which we have just seen. Blame was placed on the shoulders of the ducal councillors, and since, as the Ten believed, "it is necessary to provide that they be forced through a pecuniary penalty to do what they have not obeyed their oath to do," any councillors who henceforth allowed the *capi* of the Forty to count the ballots in their stead were to be fined one hundred ducats.[80]

The Council of Ten appointed a *collegio* in 1464 to investigate a recent election in the Great Council in which an excess of ballots had been found in the *bussuli*. The Ten also ordered the apprehension of two nobles, Pietro Querini and Pietro Erizzo, to be examined along with whoever else might be suspected.[81] Less than two weeks later the Ten sentenced Erizzo to six months' imprisonment and exclusion from the Great Council and all other councils, governships, offices, and benefices for two years.[82] It should be noted that this punishment, though hardly light, was not so harsh as that defined by statutes in force for casting more than one ballot; such an offense was to be punished by amputation of the criminal's right hand, as stipulated in 1451. There seems to be no evidence that action was ever taken against the second accused, Pietro Querini.

In 1472 the Great Council was forced to revise once more the regulations on the counting of ballots in its *probe*. If any candidate received a total of affirmative votes representing a simple majority of the council but the overall vote on his nomination exceeded the number of eligible voters, the excess was to be subtracted from the votes in support of his candidacy; if after this process he still had affirmative votes representing a simple majority and exceeding the total of any other candidate receiving a majority, he was to be considered approved. If, however, the subtraction reduced his total to less than a majority or left him tied with or losing to his closest competitor, balloting was to be repeated on the two candidates having the largest number of affirmative votes. If only one candidate possessed a majority in favorable votes and the subtraction of excess ballots from his total still left him with a majority, he was to be judged approved, but if not he was to be considered defeated.[83] Curiously, this statute seems to have returned the process to the same condition which had prevailed prior to the revisions of 1409, 1442, and 1462.

Another voting scandal came to light in August 1496 when two of the youths who carried the voting urns approached Giovanni Battista Foscarini, who had been elected to the Senate, and boasted (undoubtedly soliciting money, although this is not stated explicitly) that they had gained his election by tilting the urns, so that the negative votes were converted to positive. Foscarini, taking the advice of his brothers, reported them to the doge.[84] On 19 August the Council of Ten, after expelling one of its *capi,* Antonio Boldù, because of kinship, ordered the arrest of the two *ballotini,* Salvatore Nocente and Geronimo Frixo, and their interrogation by a *collegio,* which was authorized to use torture to extract the truth from them or from any other scribes, notaries, or youths suspected in the matter.[85] Giovanni Jacopo Bon, a nobleman who had recently been elected *sopracomito* of a galley, became implicated in what was revealed as a conspiracy to rig elections, and the Ten ordered his arrest and interrogation. A letter was sent to the Venetian provisors at Pisa, where he was believed to have fled, ordering his capture.[86] Confronted with the youths, and tortured, Bon stoutly maintained that they were lying, but he was convicted and sentenced to exile for life in Famagusta. If he dared to escape from Famagusta, anyone who captured him would receive a reward of two thousand pounds and Bon would be imprisoned for a year in Venice before being returned to his place of exile. Two of the *ballotini* were sentenced to perpetual exile in Retimo, while a third, Geronimo Stella, who was charged only with knowing about the crime and not reporting it, was banished for three years.[87] There was some difficulty in proceeding against Geronimo Frixo, who was Bon's principal coconspirator, apparently because of some question of clerical status,[88] but his conviction was announced on 29 September.[89] The ostensibly swift and determined justice meted out by the Dieci is thrown into some question, however, by an act dated 10 March complaining that Bon had not yet been transported to Famagusta. The Ten proceeded to make the financial arrangements to carry out its sentence.[90]

Every effort was to no avail, of course. In 1507 the Ten commented that "there are many who in a multitude of ways change the number of ballots at will."[91]

OTHER COUNCILS

Although the vast majority of legislative acts on Venetian elections are addressed to the nominating and voting procedures in the Great Council, there is evidence that elections held in various other councils of the

Republic were also susceptible to corrupting influences. In addition to nominations to magistracies made by committees of the Great Council, for example, nominations were provided by the Senate through its process of *scrutinio,* in which the senators had the opportunity to propose candidates upon whom all the senators then voted, with the candidate receiving the highest number of affirmative votes winning nomination.[92] In the case of some offices, the Senate not only nominated but elected by this process.[93] Freddy Thiriet reports that in 1430 the Signoria annulled the election of two *provedditori* of the Levant, because the scrutiny in the Senate was so disorderly that legitimate candidates were set aside.[94] It is not surprising, therefore, that the Venetian administration found it necessary to regulate the electoral process in the Senate as well as in the Great Council. The earliest extant indication of corruption in the senatorial electoral process is provided by an act passed by the Senate itself in 1440. This law was directed specifically against nobles who attempted to escape election to posts they did not want without incurring the penalties already fixed for refusal of office. Such nobles were utilizing alleged defects and disorders in the senatorial balloting as excuses for refusing with impunity to accept offices voted them by the Senate. The statute made no effort to suppress the improprieties acknowledged to exist in senatorial elections, but merely determined that they were not to be considered sufficient cause to permit refusal of office.[95]

In 1442 the Great Council claimed the right of approval of the members of the Zonta elected by the Senate on account of scandals in these elections.[96] Improprieties in senatorial ballotings are also revealed in an action of the Council of Ten in 1459. A motion passed unanimously in that year initiated an investigation of a vote in the Senate concerning the benefice of Santa Sophia in Padua, a vote in which an excess of ballots had been cast. The council required the *capi* of the Ten to pursue the matter and authorized monetary rewards and immunity from prosecution for anyone willing to give evidence regarding the misdeed,[97] but the results of the investigation have not been discovered.

More specific information on electoral corruption in the Senate is provided by a statute passed by the Senate in 1472, in which corruption was characterized as occurring daily in senatorial balloting. It appears that, just as in the Great Council, the senatorial votes were being plagued by some participants' insistence on casting more than the single ballot allotted them. The Senate therefore determined that prior to any *scrutinio,* the membership of the body was to be counted so that "errors" in balloting could be easily discerned, and that the participants should vote openly to prevent fraud. Moreover, if the *proba* on any candidate nominated by *scrutinio* revealed that more votes had been cast than the total number of senators participating, the vote was to be considered void and another balloting held.[98]

The Council of Forty was also responsible for the distribution of some offices through a procedure similar to that employed in the Senate, as well as for determining by vote the outcome of various legal cases. The elections of the *capi* of the Forty, for example, were held in the Council, and by 1457 the Council of Ten found it necessary to regulate them. A decree of that year forbade the *capi* of the Forty to conduct election of their successors, since deliberate miscounting of ballots had resulted from the practice. It was decided that councillors were henceforth to be delegated to oversee the elections of the *capi*.[99] This was a result of the very complex and thoroughly botched Pisani conspiracy.[100] In order to help him to falsify the results of the senatorial election in the Great Council, Pisani, who was the sole head of the Forty in office at the time, conducted a farcical election of *capi* in that body. When the results were announced, there was grumbling from the Forty, some saying, "I didn't vote for them!" and others replying, "Nor I!" The scandal spread all over town, and the heads of the Ten got wind of it and started the investigation that resulted in numerous convictions.[101]

In 1498 the Ten promulgated more thorough regulations concerning balloting in the Forty. No vote was to be permitted on a candidate until the nominee had departed the chamber and the doors had been securely closed. The election itself was to be conducted by two councillors and one of the *avogadori di comun,* who were obliged to insure that certain forms were strictly observed. Each voter was to show his ballot to those carrying the *bussuli* and, after voting, to show them his empty hand as well. No voter could follow the *bussuli* through the hall to make special pleas on behalf of a friend. If any voter claimed to have been responsible for some error in balloting, undoubtedly to invalidate a process whose outcome he found unsatisfactory, his claim was not to be sufficient cause for reballoting. No voter was to be allowed to touch the *bussuli* with the intention of emptying them or disturbing their contents. Anyone who transgressed any of these provisions would be subject to exclusion from the Council of Forty and all other councils, offices, benefices, and governorships for the next five years. Finally, the Ten extended the penalty for casting more than one ballot in *probe* of the Great Council—the loss of the offender's right hand—to elections in the Council of Forty and all other councils of the Republic. The same penalty was also to befall anyone who passed his ballot to another to be placed in the *bussulus.*[102] The possibility of corruption also existed in elections conducted by the Signoria or the Collegio.[103]

BRIBERY

Outright bribery played a major role in the corruption of Venetian elections. By the sixteenth century it was ubiquitous, as Sanuto claimed: "Votes are being bought for money. Everyone knows it; it is evident that no one can win an office of any importance who does not have a group of impoverished gentlemen to whom he has to give money before he is nominated and after being elected."[104] Some magistrates even sold lesser offices over which they had jurisdiction to unfortunates who could hope to recoup their investments and glean some profit from the posts.[105] Under these circumstances it is not surprising that the incidence of embezzlement in the Venetian administration rose markedly, because many jobs were filled by men forced by their wretchedness to extract profit greater than that offered by their salaries.[106]

As early as 1349 a decree of the Great Council, apparently no longer extant, imposed some penalties for trafficking in offices, benefices, and council seats, but the later enactment which refers to it states merely that its provisions had proven ineffective in ending the influence of money in the electoral process. This later statute, passed by the Great Council in 1364, imposed further punishments for buying, or attempting to buy, offices: deprivation from all offices, benefices, and councils for a year. If the offender was a *popularis,* he was to be exiled from St. Mark and the Rialto for the same period.[107] Such pronouncements had no enduring success, however, as the preface to an act of the Council of Ten passed in 1474 abundantly demonstrates. According to this document, many electors on nominating committees of the Great Council were accepting bribes for nominations and favorable votes from candidates. Those who offered such bribes and those who accepted them were to be equally liable to a penalty of exclusion from all governorships, offices, and benefices for five years and a fine of five hundred ducats; friends and relatives of candidates who offered bribes on their behalf were subject to the same punishments. After all elections had been concluded both the victors and those who had nominated them— now their sureties—were required to swear that money had played no part in the nominating process.

This same statute also addressed itself to a form of bribery in the nominating process which originated with the electors rather than the prospective nominees. Electors, the act states, were choosing nobles for lucrative positions with the intention of later extracting from them appointments to lesser positions which would prove remunerative; the result was that holders of *regimina* and their erstwhile nominators were collaborating in the abuse of the populace for personal gain. Electors were therefore forbidden to nominate anyone with this purpose in mind, and governors were prohibited from accepting money from anyone in return for lesser appointments; the punishment for either offense was to be a fine of five hundred ducats and exclusion from all offices, governorships, and benefices for five years. Newly elected governors were required to swear an oath that they had not made any prior arrangements to supply benefits for their nominators, and until such an oath had been taken and subscribed before the *capi* of the Ten their commissions were not to be issued. Any governor who did not observe his oath would be excluded perpetually from all governmental offices and benefices. The Ten added that the provisions of this statute were to be read in the Great Council twice every year to insure that they were well understood.[108]

In 1483, however, the Council of Ten complained that, despite the act of 1474, many nobles were still bribing the electors to obtain coveted nominations, with the result that whoever gave the most money to the members of the nominating committees was easily winning office. To the provisions of the statute of 1474, therefore, the Ten added the stipulation that anyone found guilty of direct or indirect bribery would also be deprived at once of any office, magistracy, dignity, or council seat to which he had been elected, excluded from all offices, benefices, and governorships for the next ten years, and fined five hundred ducats. Any elector who sought or accepted bribes from a prospective candidate was to suffer the same penalties.[109]

The first clear indication that has come to my attention of the infamous *svizzeri,* or mercenaries, although the name is not yet applied, is in a case of 1491. Benedetto Foscarini was convicted of threatening Paolo Barbo, lieutenant of Udine, who was to advance to many high offices, that if Barbo did not give him money he would by giving a sign see to it that a hundred votes would be cast against Barbo so that he would be defeated in every election. Foscarini was banished for five years and excluded from all offices for ten years.[110] The practice continued, of course. A decree of the Ten in 1494 established five years' exile and ten years' subsequent exclusion from all offices and councils as the penalty for offering or receiving bribes in elections. Moreover, if the bribery was not discovered until after the offender had begun or completed his tenure in the post he had fraudulently obtained, the criminal was also required to repay to the Commune all the salary and perquisites derived from the office.[111]

Pietro Dolfin declares that Antonio Tron's reform of 1500 denying to the Signoria the right to make nominations for office was inspired by the sale of such nominations to those offering the most.[112] If true, this is very interesting, because members of the Signoria were not usually poor nobles, and the offices were often among the highest in the Republic.

Sanuto reports a spate of cases of electoral corruption which came before the Council of Ten in 1508. The first centered upon the young Giovanni Vendramin, grandson of Doge Andrea Vendramin, who won the post of *podestà* and captain of Feltre through bribery. He had bribed two electors, Giovanni Battista Lion and Marin Querini, to nominate him for the position. Lion had received a house from the ambitious young man. Alvise Zancarolo and his brother Matteo had also received bribes for their support. On 13 August the Dieci sentenced Vendramin to deprivation of his office, banishment for two years, and exclusion from all offices and benefices for five years. Lion, Querini, and Matteo Zancarolo were excluded from office for eight years and Alvise Zancarolo for five.[113] Simultaneously the Council of Ten brought charges against three other nobles who had bribed their nominators. Lorenzo Capello was exiled and excluded from all offices and benefices for five years, and Geronimo Condulmer, his nominator and pledge, was also deprived of governmental offices for five years. Geronimo Giustinian was excluded from offices for six years, and his surety, Marin Cocco, for five. Almorò Donà was excluded from office for three years, and his pledge Matteo Minio for a like period.[114] Another nobleman, Francesco Foscari, was also convicted of bribery and sentenced to exclusion from all offices and benefices for five years, but no one was convicted with him.[115] The heads of the Ten refused to give Domenico Contarini, elected captain of Verona, his credentials because he had bribed his nominator for thirty ducats.[116] Notice that the penalties are all less than those prescribed by law in 1494. Nonetheless, Sanuto reports much unrest over the widespread selling of votes by unscrupulous nobles who raised to office whomever they wished.[117] The Ten responded to this evidence of widespread bribery with a new act of 25 August 1508, repeating virtually verbatim the complaints against bribery found in the act of 1494 and adding to the penalties earlier fixed against those giving or taking bribes the punishment of perpetual exile in any part of the Venetian territory which would seem proper to the Council of Ten, except the city of Venice itself.[118] Finlay quite properly makes the point, however, that those who had sufficient funds to buy votes also had enough money to buy pardons, as Vendramin did inside of ten months.[119] Corruption of elections in Venice had indeed become endemic before the War of the League of Cambrai.

All of this legislation against blatant electoral bribery in both *electiones* and *probe* notwithstanding, Sanuto attested that the practice was flourishing in 1515. In that year he reported that a group of poor nobles—the so-called *svizzeri*—were regularly calling at the homes of newly elected officials to demand money in recompense for the advancement their votes had accomplished. Although Sanuto attempted to downplay their importance, he nonetheless noted that the *svizzeri* were numerous and well-organized, even possessing a vocabulary of secret signs through which they could inform one inform one another which candidates should be approved and which rejected. All of this made Sanuto rather wistful about the "simpler" arrangement of earlier years, when an elector would merely invite contributions from interested parties with complete openness.[120] Moreover, despite calls that the Council of Ten should take action against the *svizzeri,* nothing was done, either because it was too difficult to single out those responsible or because too many persons were implicated.[121]

Emergency conditions in the early sixteenth century prompted measures which confused the issue of bribery in the electoral process. Beginning in 1515, the Republic's desperate need for funds to support its military expenses led to the introduction into the electoral process of loans to the government. Minor offices were sold, and the candidate's contributions to the coffers of the state became a factor in election to higher offices, although the largest contributor was not always successful.[122] It was a distasteful emergency measure and was not tantamount to legitimizing electoral bribery. Still, it violated the principle that only the qualifications of the candidate for the office should be considered, it did legitimize the role of money in elections, and it blurred the line between winning and buying offices, making it increasingly difficult to take effective measures against corruption.

ENFORCEMENT

Thus far our study has indicated that a continuous and increasing concern about electoral corruption existed in Venice from the thirteenth to the early sixteenth century, a concern explicable only by an assumption that such corruption was not a rare occurrence. The bewildering repetitiveness of much of the legislation which resulted, however, suggests further that the enforcement of the statutes on the books was irregular and haphazard. The laws are filled with complaints that prior statutes on the same subject had proven inadequate, and penalty was piled upon penalty in a vain effort to secure compliance. One aspect of Venetian political life which might have fostered this situation was the extremely fast turnover rate among administrative officials, brought about by the brief tenure for which almost all offices were entrusted to individual patricians.[123] A man who had participated in the framing of a statute was unlikely to be in a position to enforce it the following year, and his replacement might not even be aware of earlier legislation. Some statutes might well have been forgotten almost immediately after they were passed. In addition, the care with which administrators felt compelled to treat their fellow nobles to avoid antagonisms which might deprive them of other offices in the future undoubtedly encouraged laxity in enforcement of penal legislation.[124]

Another reason why the legislation against electoral corruption apparently failed so badly to achieve its intended effect might, however, be traced to the lack of efficient mechanisms to initiate and implement enforcement. It is interesting to note that virtually all the statutes against malfeasance in the electoral process place their greatest emphasis on charges brought against offenders by paid informants. One of the continuous threads in the laws on the subject consists of the promise of rewards for those serving as state's evidence in cases in which convictions were obtained. In 1375 the Great Council specified three hundred pounds as the reward for anyone successfully accusing a voter of having cast more than one ballot in a *proba;* this sum was raised to three thousand pounds in a statute of the Council of Ten in 1451, which added that if the accuser were an accomplice to the crime, he would in addition be granted immunity from prosecution.[125] In 1456 the Ten announced a reward of one hundred ducats to anyone successfully accusing an elector of having disturbed the *bussulus* in any way during the nominating process.[126] Accusers of those going to the urns more than once in an attempt to gain a seat on a nominating committee were promised five hundred ducats by the Ten in 1468, a sum lowered to one hundred ducats by the Ten in 1484 but returned to its former level in 1497.[127] Similar provisions were made for informants who reported instances of electoral bribery. In 1494 the Ten offered two hundred ducats to anyone accusing those who gave or received bribes in elections, and raised the sum to five hundred ducats in 1508.[128] In addition to these monetary rewards, informants were regularly assured that their names would be held in confidence and were often granted immunity from prosecution for any part they might have played in the offense they were reporting. It should be noted that the legislators attempted to insure that this governmental generosity would be assessed against the holdings of the convicted criminals rather than the state treasury; monetary rewards were to be drawn from the funds of those whose misdeeds had been reported whenever possible, although when an offender's personal wealth proved inadequate the state used its own resources to reward accusers.[129]

The Venetian legislators did not, however, consider it sufficient to solicit accusations of electoral corruption through promises of rewards; they also resorted to their favorite instrument, the heavy threat, in an attempt to secure useful information. These threats took the form of penalties against those who knew of wrongdoing but failed to report it to the appropriate authorities. In 1451, for example, the Council of Ten decreed that anyone who knew that a voter had cast more than one ballot in a *proba* of the Great Council and who did not inform the doge, the *capi* of the Ten, or the *avogadori* of the fact was to be subject to the penalties meted out to the offender himself, apparently including the amputation of his right hand. At the same time the Ten imposed a fine of twenty-five pounds upon carriers of the *bussuli* who failed to report a voter who had neglected to show that he had only one ballot in his hand before placing it in the *bussulus*.[130]

Clearly the Venetian legislators tried repeatedly to secure the cooperation, whether by promises or threats, of individual members of the patriciate in enforcing the legislation against electoral corruption. The apparent reluctance of nobles, even impoverished ones, to oblige might be explained in several ways. Promises of rewards for informants had to compete with bribes for nominations and votes which may not have been as large as the state's rewards individually but which were probably available more regularly. Threats of punishment for failure to report malfeasance would have been received with terror only if the malfeasance itself were continually and severely punished, but this does not seem to have been the case. Perhaps most important, one must wonder how seriously the assurances of confidentiality were taken by prospective informants. Rotation of offices among a relatively small number of families undoubtedly induced leaks of information, and a noble who knew of wrongdoing may well have thought it likelier that he could escape punishment by the government for withholding evidence than that he could avoid retaliation from a patrician family for having given testimony against its members. It was only natural, therefore, that a large share of the responsibility for enforcing the legislation against electoral corruption fell to the Commune's officials. In some cases, for example, attempts were made to counter apparent reluctance on the part of nonofficed nobles to accuse their fellows by making such accusations unnecessary. In 1473, the Council of Ten decreed that when a member of the Great Council violated the order for approaching the urns or proved overzealous in his attempts to draw a gold ballot, it was not necessary that a fellow voter report his conduct; his being seen by the doge or one of the councillors, *avogadori,* or *capi* of the Ten was sufficient for the execution of punishment, since no excuse could be heard and further proof was not required.[131]

The laws also offer bountiful evidence, however, that it was thought necessary to threaten the Republic's officials to insure that they would take appropriate action against those engaging in electoral corruption. One of the most regular features of the laws is an insistence that they should not be repealed and that recommendations of leniency in cases involving them should be prohibited entirely or at least made extremely difficult.[132] To discourage motions for repeal or leniency, the statutes frequently specified fines to be levied against officials recommending them. In 1457 the Council of Ten enjoined that a fine of one hundred ducats be assessed against anyone who attempted to alter its statute on the choosing of carriers of the *bussuli* in the Great Council or who suggested leniency in punishing infractions of it;[133] nonetheless, the Senate effectively repealed the Ten's statute in 1469 by decreeing an entirely new procedure,[134] but there is no record of any fines having been imposed as a result. In 1458, the Ten passed a comprehensive act on the order in which nobles were to approach the urns in the Great Council, and decreed that a fine of one thousand ducats should befall anyone who suggested revocation of the law or recommended leniency in a case concerning it.[135] In 1508 the Ten closed another statute against electoral bribery with the "express declaration" that in determining the penalty for an infraction no less stringent law could be utilized on pain of a fine of one thousand ducats.[136] Of course, even the Council of Ten realized that in some cases repeal of a statute would be beneficial or leniency might be appropriate in a particular judgment. Very often, therefore, the Ten added a proviso that revocation or leniency could be permitted, provided that certain conditions were met, among them a unanimous vote in the Council of Ten itself.[137] That such an "escape clause" seems to conflict with the original contention that the mere suggestion of repeal or leniency should be punishable by fine apparently did not overly concern the legislators; indeed, one must wonder how frequently the enormous fines stipulated in some statutes could possibly have been imposed.

In ordering officials to insure the observation of the various laws against electoral corruption, the framers of Venetian statutes often placed emphasis on the oaths those officials were required to swear to fulfill their functions faithfully. The Ten's statute of 1494 on electoral bribery, for example, placed its implementation in the hands of the *capi* of the Ten, who were to be bound by oath to see that its strictures were enforced.[138] Similarly, the councillors and *avogadori* designated by the

Ten's act of 1498 to oversee balloting in the Council of Forty were to swear that they would observe the statute in all its particulars.[139]

The Venetian legislators, however, had a healthy scepticism about the efficacy of such oaths. As the Council of Ten remarked in 1457, since officials were not fulfilling their oaths, "it is necessary to provide that they be forced through a monetary fine to do what they have not taken care to do because of their oath."[140] Strangely, the act in which this sentiment appears contains no imposition of fines against offending officials at all; the principle is employed, however, in various other statutes. In 1419, the Great Council had legislated that any councillor conducting an election who called the benches to the urns out of order was to be excluded from office for six months.[141] In 1431 the Senate decreed that officials who perverted the goal of secrecy in elections by revealing the vote totals of candidates in *probe* of any council should be punished by monetary fines.[142] In 1497 the Ten legislated that councillors conducting elections in the Great Council who failed to implement their statute against those approaching the urns more than once were to be fined one thousand ducats.[143]

THE RESULTS of investigation hardly support the mythical view of patrician excellence in the service of the Venetian state insofar as the electoral process was concerned. Extirpation of corrupt practices of various sorts was an increasing concern of Venetian legislators, and, as Lane has observed, every stage of the election procedure at Venice contained evidence that cheating was expected unless provisions were made to prevent it.[144] Indeed, the distinctive complexity of that procedure was perfected as a means, though not a very successful one, to curb corrupt practices. "In the Republic," Cozzi has rightly remarked, "which never had any illusions about human nature, the electoral system was set up in such a way that would offer the greatest possible protection; all the same, anyone who was inclined to cheat could find a way to do so."[145] Particularly in the fifteenth century, when the financial plight of many patricians became desperate, the frequency and variety of electoral corruption grew acute, as is evident from the amount of legislation on the subject from that period; such corruption was not, however, absent from Venetian life at any time during its recorded history, mythical notions to the contrary.

It seems quite clear that the Republic had little success in dealing with electoral corruption and was considerably confused in its numerous efforts. Some penalties, such as exclusion from the councils for six months for drawing more than one ball in an attempt to become an elector, were so minimal as to suggest that the offense was not really taken seriously. Others, such as the loss of the right hand, were so severe that they were almost never applied. Laws were reissued without apparent awareness that the legislation was already on the books, and sometimes the legislative bodies went full circle, returning to policies which had earlier been supplanted because they were inadequate.

While a significant amount of legislation against electoral corruption is available in extant records, moreover, it is clear that it was not enforced with sufficient rigor to control such practices. Indeed, by the second quarter of the sixteenth century the laws against corruption were so many and varied, and so openly violated, that they served only to confuse the distinction between legitimate and illegitimate practices.[146] A preliminary consideration of evidence on the prosecution of malefactors suggests that while firm action was occasionally taken, particularly in cases involving large-scale factionalism, the enforcement of the laws in less spectacular cases was vague and irregular at best. It is apparent that the necessity nobles felt for not antagonizing fellow patricians whose help they might later require or whose revenge they feared led them to refrain from supporting prosecution of offenders except in the most blatant cases. The spirit of the laws still extant might have been admirable, but their practical implementation was extremely weak.

Electoral corruption was clearly a fact of political life in Venice from the thirteenth to the sixteenth century. It coexisted with a myth of patrician self-sacrifice, which hardly conformed to what was currently occurring but which could be usefully employed to berate nobles for their failure to live up to the standards of their supposedly superior ancestors. It would obviously be unfair to place too great an emphasis on this fact; the present study has focused on evidence of electoral corruption in an attempt to redress a balance which has heretofore tended toward an uncritical acceptance of the idealized portraits drawn by popularizers and romantics, but the conclusions drawn should not veer too far in the opposite direction. Although corruption was omnipresent, there were numerous, if not effective, efforts to combat it. Insofar as its elections were concerned, Venetian life undoubtedly demonstrated a mixture of honesty and corruption no better, and perhaps no worse, than that found elsewhere.[147]

V
Evasion of Public Responsibilities

UP TO THIS POINT we have been concerned with the self-serving pursuit of public office by the Venetian patriciate. We now turn over the coin to observe the nobles' flight from civic responsibility.

The Italian city-republics demanded not only the taxes of their citizens, but their personal participation in public life. The tradition was born with the communes themselves; it was strengthened by the civic ideal which Roman and canon lawyers found in the *Code* and the *Digest;* and only recently we are becoming aware of the importance of the rhetorical tradition for the sense of public responsibility.[1] Peter Riesenberg argues convincingly that the awareness of the citizen's duty to share in his own person the burdens of government thus antedated the civic humanism of the fifteenth century based on classical literary culture.[2] In Venice, even before the Serrata del Maggior Consiglio and the subsequent creation of a closed political elite, the citizen was not free to indulge his personal interests to the neglect of public service.[3] Although we are about to call into question the extent to which the patricians practiced their professed beliefs, the civic ideal, like other ideals, had an effect, although an ambiguous one. The evidence that we shall examine in this chapter reveals the genuine collective belief of the Venetian patriciate in civic responsibility, as it also reveals the widespread irresponsibility of individual patricians. Molmenti has called our attention to the moral ambiguity of Giovanni Contarini's will, which left 50 *l.* to the Commune of Venice on account of the offices and councils where he should have been active, but had not.[4]

How do we reconcile the apparent contradiciton between the pursuit of public office and the rejection of it? Without knowing the detailed circumstances of each case we can achieve only an imperfect accommodation, but crucial in most instances was the distinction between desirable and undesirable offices. The problem is complicated, though, by the fact that a post which was highly attractive to one nobleman would often be quite unattractive to another. Election to a petty office with a modest income, so avidly sought by poor nobles, would be unthinkable—or a calculated insult—to a rich, distinguished, and mature patrician. Conversely, under most circumstances no one would consider electing a poor patrician to the highest offices of state, as doge, procurator of Saint Mark, *savio grande,* member of the Ten, or to the exacting and costly embassies and major governorships on *terraferma,* which were generally prerequisite to advancement to the highest positions.[5] It was not possible to rise to the highest offices without considerable wealth to meet the personal costs of the magnificence required of the embassies and governorships by means of which the powerful climbed the political ladder. Indeed, not only parsimony, but also (perhaps primarily) the intention to limit the access to real power to rich patricians lay behind the inadequate salaries requiring large outlays out-of-pocket.[6] It was ambition (and, to be sure, interest in the public welfare) which led some of those who could afford it to accept and even seek these costly posts.[7] Lane has pointed out how an expensive office, such as an embassy, especially if it seemed foredoomed to failure, was sometimes inflicted upon a political enemy. If he refused the position, he was subject to a fine and the loss of popularity for his lack of public spirit; if he accepted, he would lose money and probably fail in his task; and, in any event, he would be removed from the political scene at San Marco.[8] No wonder that it was difficult, occasionally impossible, to fill these dignified but backbreaking jobs.

Even the most exalted positions were occasionally refused. Stefano Giustinian in 1311 refused the dogeship itself, and in 1368 Andrea Contarini vainly sought to reject the honor, yielding only to the threat of banishment and confiscation.[9] Pantaleone Barbo declined a procuratorship of Saint Mark in 1366.[10] Usually, however, there was not much difficulty in finding nobles to be doge or procurator, but there were some problems in getting nobles to serve on the ducal council, the Avogaria del Comun, and in other exalted offices.[11]

Refusal and evasion of office was not, of course, a problem peculiar to the Venetian government and its patriciate. In Germany at Freiburg im Bresgau, for example, nominees for mayor offered money not to be elected.[12] Pullan has told us of the problems the Scuole had in the sixteenth and seventeenth centuries in getting members to accept office. The Council of Ten finally had to step in and impose a money penalty. Reluctant candidates, however, learned to use evasive tricks similar to those employed by Venetian nobles to escape public office: they used employment in government business as an excuse; they deliberately disqualified themselves by failing to pay their annual dues; or they achieved the same end by renting small houses from the Scuole, for the regulations provided that no tenant of the Scuole could hold office in it.[13]

REFUSAL OF OFFICE PROHIBITED

The Republic's claim on the services of the ruling class was sanctioned by a large number of acts prohibiting the refusal or resignation of office.[14] One was not free to pick and choose: if a nobleman wanted to enjoy the honors or the incomes of office, he ought not to have the right to refuse when the service of the state became a burden. As early as the late twelfth century the Great Council began to legislate against the refusal of public office.[15] The repeated legislation on the subject of refusal, the increasing weight of penalties, and the clear statements of concern over refusals prove that it simply is not true that there was "no major problem in recruiting."[16]

The earliest extant act on the subject was passed by the Great Council in 1185. It required that anyone elected to public office must accept within three days under penalty of ineligibility for all honors or offices and loss of all rights in court, unless, of course, he was excused for a legitimate reason.[17] Giacomo Zulian was sentenced under this act for refusing a magistracy in 1189.[18] It seems, however, that the act was evaded by avoiding notification of election, for a subsequent act in 1211 specified that acceptance must be given within three days after the electee was summoned either personally or by call outside his home. Refusal should be punished with a fine of 200 *l.*[19] Several months later the act was repeated with an additional clause prohibiting evasion on the grounds of a vow or an oath.[20] Mere willingness to accept the penalty rather than the office should not be tolerated, according to an act of 1229.[21] This was to remain a problem, however, through the centuries, especially since the penalties were often never actually paid. An act of 1257 appears to have weakened the government's position, for it distinguishes between refusal before and after acceptance, penalizing only the latter with a fine of 100 *l.*[22]

A key act of 1263, often subsequently cited and reaffirmed, returned to a more severe attitude, imposing a fine of ten large *soldi* and exclusion from salaried office for six months for refusing any office except for good reason validated by oath.[23] An interesting dispute concerning this key act of 1263 arose in 1328, when Tommaso Viaro wanted to refuse the grain office. He based his argument upon an act of 1319 which decreed that the *officiales frumenti,* after they had promised, could not refuse, except for going beyond the Gulf of Quarnero. From this, he argued, it followed that he could refuse before accepting without penalty, claiming that three or four other nobles had done it. Others argued that he was subject to the broader act of 1263, and that the later legislation had been intended to impose greater penalties on those re-signing the grain office after having accepted. The Great Council decided that he was subject to the penalty of the law of 1263.[24] The penalties were modified in 1339 because so many nobles were going abroad to escape office, which, especially in winter, was perilous and expensive. The fine was raised to twenty *soldi grossi,* but the penalty of exclusion from office was dropped. The act was passed on an experimental basis for two years, but was made permanent in 1341.[25]

The positions which were sometimes considered undesirable and most often refused were those of governors on the mainland, some in the maritime empire,[26] castellans, *provveditori* of fortresses, and above all ambassadors. A record of service in such posts was essential to attaining the most exalted offices, but their ceremonial demands in terms of retinue, horses, table, clothing, and so on were extremely expensive.[27] To a very large extent the costs had to be borne by the appointee, so it is hardly suprising that many nominees refused. In 1284 the Great Council decreed that ambassadors–elect might not negotiate over the size of the retinue and the expense to be assumed by the Republic, but must accept what was customary.[28]

In 1423 very many nobles had been declining to go to Zara as count or provisor, so the Great Council imposed a fine of two hundred ducats for refusing.[29] It returned to the general problem in 1454, lamenting that the Republic had special need for the services of citizens in times of wars and novelties, yet they continued to refuse ambassadorships and other undesirable offices. In the future they should not be able to refuse election as ambassador or provisor of the army or in cities, lands, castles, and other places without paying a penalty of 100 *l.* and being excluded from office for two years.[30] Again in 1479 the refusal of bur-densome offices abroad caused the Great Council to complain that the bad practice of paying for service to the state had made the nobles unwilling to serve except for their own benefit, rather than for the public welfare, "to which in this world above all things we are obligated." Anyone who refused a mission abroad should lose whatever office he held and pay three hundred ducats, in addition to whatever fine may have been specified in the particular case.[31] Nothing worked, as usual, although (also as usual) the penalties kept growing. Sanuto reports a case in 1501 when "everyone" was refusing an ambassadorship because the provision for expenses was not adequate. The Senate raised the penalty to five hundred ducats above and beyond other penalties.[32] In writing of the election of ambassadors, the author of the "Traité du gouvernement de Venise," probably composed in the very early sixteenth century, remarked on the heavy penalties imposed on those who refused.[33] All this is not to say, of course, that ambassadorships and commands of fortresses were always undesirable to all nobles. We have seen in earlier chapters how castellanies, for example, were sought by means of *broglio,* and even an ambassadorship could appear attractive on occasion.

The Republic had to be concerned, however, over the problem of refusal even of offices that were generally considered desirable, exalted, and honored, such as advocate of the Commune or ducal councillor. Refusal of the post of *avogadore di comun* was specifically prohibited under penalty of 200 *l.* by an act in 1259.[34] This was an office which was not really among those in the real and inner power structure, but it was a very respected position. Some nobles had quickly devised a means of escaping office by paying the penalty of ten *grossi* under the law of 1263, so in 1264 the Great Council decreed that anyone elected ducal councillor, elector of the year, advocate of the Commune, or *avvocato del proprio* must serve under the heavier penalties formerly established for those offices, and not get off with a mere ten *soldi.*[35] The councillors, at least, were within the inner circle. The advocates of the Commune were the subject of another law in 1272, requiring them to accept within three days under the prescribed penalties.[36] According to an act of 1287 covering a number of other offices as well, one could not refuse the Avogaria di Comun without being ineligible for other offices during the term of the office refused.[37]

The dogeship itself was the subject of a law of 1339 prohibiting refusal without the consent of the six councillors and a majority of the Great Council.[38] The Senate objected in 1373 that some members were refusing to draw lots from the urn, because they did not want to become nominators. They must do so under penalty of 10 *l.*[39] We have seen how nobles struggled for the right to nominate a relative or friend; reluctance to become a nominator probably was based on a desire to avoid political and social pressures. In 1407 the nobles originally elected as *savi del consiglio,* perhaps the most important officials in Venice short of the doge, refused. Of those elected to replace them, some were excused because they were not old enough and others refused, accepting the penalty. The penalty, however, was only 50 *l.,* which was not enough to keep them from refusing easily. For the time being, therefore, the Senate raised the fine to 100 *l*.[40] The Ten decreed in 1411 that none of its members might refuse the much more burdensome duties of head or inquisitor of that body.[41] These also were among the most important positions in the Republic. Again in 1417 the Great Council denied to those elected as ducal councillors the right to refuse. The council admitted that enough "good and sufficient" men were available, but the act would make it possible to have better ones.[42] In the midst of war in 1427 the Maggior Consiglio was disturbed that on account of the plague many worthy nobles had refused to become *savi del consiglio*. They escaped by going abroad, which was almost always accepted as an excuse.[43] For this time only, however, in order that better candidates might be found during the crisis, *savi grandi* might even be elected from among those who were prepared to go abroad.[44] In 1440 the Senate imposed a fine of 200 *l*. for refusing to serve as *savi di terraferma,* not as important as the *savi del consiglio* but still important members of the Pien Collegio.[45] A proposal was defeated in the Ten in 1497 to deny those elected as ducal councillors the right to refuse for any excuse other than old age.[46] It is very clear that there was considerable difficulty over the years in getting nobles to accept jobs as advocates of the Commune and ducal councillors, and some problem with such posts as *savi del consiglio* and *di terraferma,* heads and inquisitors of the Ten, and even a little indication of concern about the dogeship. Sometimes there were understandable reasons for the nobles' reluctance, such as desire not to be tied down in the city during time of plague, and I do not wish to suggest that Venetian patricians consistently refused the most important and prestigious posts in their government. The evidence is strong enough to demonstrate, however, that they were in no way uniquely selfless in their willingness to serve the state.

There is a third group of offices, neither those which were unusually distasteful, nor those which were among the most attractive to ambitious patricians, but ordinary offices, such as poorer nobles often desired. Despite the income which many of them offered, these also were sometimes rejected. The Great Council sought to prevent refusal of the office of judge of petitions in 1269.[47] A fine of 100 *l*. was established in 1277 for refusing to accept election to the Forty.[48] A law of 1287 specifies that anyone who turns down being judge of the palace, lord of the night, supraconsul or consul of the merchants, one of the old justices, one of the Five of peace or of the captains of the posts may not hold any office during the term of the office rejected.[49] Sometime in the thirteenth century a penalty of 100 *l*. was imposed for refusing the office of judge of the procurator.[50]

In 1319 the Council of Ten created a new magistracy for law enforcement, the six heads of the *sestieri,* alongside the lords of the night and the Five of peace, but after a year they voted to discontinue it. Ruggiero believes that the difficulty in obtaining nobles to undertake the tiresome and dangerous job may have been instrumental in this reversal. In any event, three months after the Ten had refused to renew the *capi di sestieri* the office was reinstituted by the Great Council, which made it more difficult to escape the responsibility by imposing a fine of 100 *l.*[51] The penalty for refusing to become a *giudice del proprio* was raised to 100 *l.* in 1331, because the old fine under the act of 1263 of 10 *soldi* made it too easy to refuse the office.[52] For the duration of the war the Senate decreed in 1411 that the penalties for refusing all judgeships and offices should be doubled.[53]

In 1444 begins an interesting series of acts concerning the reception of foreign ambassadors and other visiting dignitaries. It was the custom to assign Venetian nobles to meet and accompany the distinguished guests, probably as much for the purpose of keeping an eye on them as honoring them. It became difficult, however, to find nobles who were willing to sacrifice their time for this purpose, so a senatorial decree proposed by the doge established that those chosen for the task must fulfill it under penalty of loss of offices and exclusion from office for a year.[54] As usual, the legislation did not end the abuse, so the Senate provided in 1462 that every four months a panel of thirty nobles should be named by the College. During this period the members of the panel were required to attend foreign ambassadors and other guests when ordered to do so, but, once having been on the panel for four months, they would be ineligible to be on it again. Those who were refusing this duty could not really be excused on the grounds that there were too few nobles to perform all the required functions, at least in the judgment of the Senate, for the act declared that their number was great and notable.[55] This act cannot have been effective for long, because in 1483 the Senate returned to the subject without mentioning the panels of nobles. It decreed that patricians selected to fulfill this obligation must perform it under penalty of being entered in the books as debtors of the Commune in the amount of ten ducats. Until the amount was paid the offender should not be eligible for any office.[56] Again in 1502 the Senate returned to the same subject of nobles to accompany ambassadors and other distinguished guests. Saving and reserving all other acts on the subject, although quite typically the Senate does not seem to have been aware of what they were, a ten-ducat fine was decreed for refusal of this duty, but without any mention of ineligibility in case on nonpayment.[57] This task, which caused so much difficulty, was hardly one to be welcomed: it had no pay and it did not entail as a rule great honor. On the other hand, it was not at all burdensome in the same way as an ambassadorship. Expenses were minor, there was no danger, and the Venetian nobleman slept in his own bed. In short, it was a nuisance.

REASONS FOR REFUSAL

There is endless documentation of nobles refusing offices. In order to spare the reader citation after citation, this section will be limited to showing that the problem of refusal and resignation was a major one and to indicating the reasons why patricians declined to serve the Republic.

On 9 July 1382 the Senate attempted to elect an ambassador and *baiulo* to Constantinople.[58] Five nobles are listed as elected, each crossed out and accompanied by the word *reffutavit*. On 11 July, after agreeing to advance the ambassador three hundred ducats against his salary as *baiulo,* the Senate elected Luca Contarini, a ducal councillor, who had been one of the electees two days earlier; Contarini "refused with penalty." Finally Simone Dalmario appears to have accepted.[59] (This in itself, by the way, does not prove that he went promptly or at all, as we shall see in the next chapter.) At the beginning of 1390 the Senate sought an ambassador to congratulate Bayazid I on his succession. This was a distant embassy and such ceremonial missions required great expenses for ostentatious display. Such an ambassador, however, was free to accomplish his brief mission and return home. Three names are shown as elected, but are crossed out with the notation that "he refused with penalty." Francesco Querini seems to have accepted, but, lest he refuse after acceptance, on 17 January the Senate decreed that this would result in a fine of 100 *l.*[60] Only a short time later the Senate held an election for three provisors *pro recuperando terram nostram Argos.* Nine electees refused with penalty and two were excused as members of the Ten before three were found.[61] When in 1397 the Senate attempted to elect a commission to study the fortifications of the Lido and the channel of San Niccolò "almost everyone" (seven nobles) refused. A fine of 100 *l.* was decreed for declining this task, which would not seem to have been one requiring much expenditure, although it would surely require some time.[62] In 1405 the Senate reported that there was not anyone who wanted to go as *baiulo* to Cyprus, so measures had to be taken to see that the position of *vice-baiulo* remained filled. The decision to decline the top post in Cyprus was a significant political decision requiring consultation with family and friends, as we know from the letter of Ruggero Contarini, one of those who did refuse the job, to his brother.[63] The required age for the *capi di sestieri,* which seems to have been a very unpopular office, was lowered from twenty-five to twenty in 1408, because no one could be found to accept it under the old requirements.[64] When the Senate could not find anyone to accept an embassy in 1417 to protest Henry V's seizure of Venetian ships for his invasion of France, the mission had to be abandoned.[65] Since the Great Council had held many elections in 1441 to the post of *podestà* of Verona without finding anyone who would accept, the Senate proceeded to the election of a *vice-podestà.*[66]

Domenico Malipiero tells us how three nobles elected as a commission to review the accounts of ambassadors, provisors, and secretaries all refused, but accepted after they were reelected with a penalty for refusal of five hundred ducats.[67] The same author recounts how Cristoforo Moro in 1487 dodged a fine of five hundred ducats for refusing to become *provveditore* at Vicenza by going to Zara and staying a year.[68] In 1500 Niccolò Cornaro refused to become *provveditore* of the old castle at Corfu; then Angelo Querini accepted, but was subsequently excused on account of illness; Marco Zeno also refused; and finally Alvise da Canal, who wanted it very much, accepted.[69] There were great difficulties in filling offices, but sometimes jobs rejected by some were desired by others.

There were many reasons why members of the elite sometimes shunned public office. Some quite simply chose escape rather than involvement. This appears to have been the case with the young friends of Gasparo Contarini, all of whom were prime candidates for distinguished political careers. Vicenzo Querini became an ambassador not long after his return from Padua, but soon turned away from a public career with distaste to become a Camaldolensian monk. Tommaso Giustinian rejected from the outset the normative life of a wealthy patrician, ridiculed, in fact, the frenetic political and commercial activity, and promptly joined the Camaldolensians. Trifone Gabrieli served in the courts briefly before retreating to a life of contemplation and study with friends at his villa. Only Contarini himself pursued a patrician political career, but he of course, ended his career as a cardinal.[70] Ermolao Barbaro also provides an interesting and complex example. In *De coelibatu,* written at a tender age, he strongly repudiated responsibilities toward family and state in favor of learning and contemplation. He nonetheless entered upon a very active and distinguished career of public service until, as ambassador to Rome in 1491, he broke the law, defied the doge, saddened his aged father, and refused the entreaties of his friend by accepting and tenaciously refusing to give up papal appointment to the patriarchate of Aquileia. Under the circumstances, of course, he could not exercise his new office, so he remained in Rome (for he also was unable to return to Venice) and gave himself to classical scholarship.[71]

In spite of these well-known examples, however, Riesenberg is right in thinking that reluctance to serve "probably came as much from a desire to stay in the shop and make money as from conscious compliance with 'medieval' theories on the rejection of the worldly life."[72] Andrea Barbarigo, who was much less prominent than the Contarini circle or Barbaro, was considerably more typical of the patriciate. He, too, had a start on a career of officeholding, and abandoned it before he was thirty-two, not in favor of religious or scholarly withdrawal, but to throw himself into the pursuit of commercial gain.[73]

Although it is extremely difficult to separate convergent motives for refusing office, as it is for other matters, the documents make it clear that monetary rewards and personal costs were most important. In 1304 the government had considerable difficulty in finding ambassadors for a mission to Sardinia. A *grazia* in October informs us that Angelo Muazzo had refused it and had been fined twenty *soldi grossi*. Upon his plea that he could not go in an appropriate manner with the expenses allotted, he was forgiven the fine.[74] In November the Great Council declared that two ambassadors had refused the mission because they could not cover their expenses at two *soldi grossi* a day. It therefore decided to allow them thirty *soldi grossi* a day, a very considerable difference, which illustrates how costly an embassy must have been to the individual.[75] The Senate pointed out in 1349 that the labors demanded of the nobles were not remunerated adequately, so it made the provisorships to which it was electing, and which had been repeatedly refused, more attractive with a salary of 100 *l.*—and a similar penalty for refusal.[76] By the same year the judges of petitions had become overwhelmed by the number of cases, "on account of which our nobles would rather be in other positions in which a greater reward is drawn relative to the very great labor. . . ." The attempted solution was to increase the income by requiring the losing party to pay 3 *d.* per *l.* in the judgment for the benefit of the judges.[77] Another problem was that the shooting exercises for qualification as *balestrieri della popa,* as noted earlier, had become chaotic, because they were not adequately supervised. This, in turn, was due to the fact that the nobles were unwilling to assume the unpaid jobs as heads and inquisitors of the matches. A salary of forty *solidi grossorum* per half-year was added under a policy which was to be tried for six months.[78] In 1359 the salary of the consul of Alexandria was raised one hundred ducats to attract notable and sufficient candidates.[79] The office of the appraisers of gold was lacking officials in 1362 because of the modest salary, so the Great Council doubled it.[80] The Senate observed in 1392 that it was having difficulty in securing "the better and most favored citizens" to serve as dukes of Crete, because the office had become burdened with expenses that could not be covered by the exalted governor's salary and perquisites, so that the incumbent had to spend a lot of his own money. In order to stimulate the nobles to accept this position more freely the Senate proceeded to reduce the size of the retinue that the duke was required to maintain.[81] In the following year, because many nobles were refusing the *podestarie* of Torcello and Murano, the Senate raised the salaries from twenty to twenty-five *lire di grossi*.[82] (One would have thought that these governorships within the Venetian lagoon would have been attractive. The ceremonial expenses surely were not as high as those for the more important mainland governorships, but they must have been higher than could be covered by the income from the office.) Since they could not find anyone to assume the command of the fleet of Padua at the beginning of 1406, the Senate fixed a salary of one hundred ducats for the first month and a half and forty ducats per month thereafter.[83] The pay of the judge *magni salarii* was restored to its prewar level in 1408, because the Great Council could not find anyone to take the position.[84] The governorship of the town of Parenzo was burdensome to the incumbent, for he had to maintan a large retinue, and it was necessary to have someone good in the position, because of Parenzo's maritime importance, so the Senate in 1408 raised his salary.[85] Late in the same year the government restored (with some exceptions) the salaries of officials and judges as they were before the war with the Carraresi, because the majority of the positions were not being handled as they ought to be. Officials and judges had been compelled to pursue other sources of income in order to support their families. Therefore the income of the state had fallen and private persons had suffered unnecessary delays and expenses.[86] In 1430 the Senate repeatedly elected to the office of *podestà* and captain of Casalmaggiore without finding anyone who would accept. Finally they decided to offer, for this time, two hundred ducats beyond the amount specified in the commission (which by law had to be drawn up before election).[87]

The Forty was not yet salaried in 1451, and, in a law which tried to control absenteeism, the Great Council complained that "the Forty, not having any salary, either refuse the Council or do not come to the Council."[88] In 1459 we hear of patricians rejecting the office of *vice-domino* of Ferrara, not expressly because of low salary, but because the official responsible for paying was slow and difficult. Administrative changes were adopted to remedy the situation.[89] At any rate, the nobles refusing the post had professed that it was only the difficulty of obtaining the assigned salary that stood in their way, but four and a half months later Venice still found it impossible to send a *vice-domino* to Ferrara, solely on account of the skimpy salary, which did not cover costs. The Senate voted to assign an additional two hundred ducats.[90] Because of the poor income, many patricians were refusing the judgeship *del proprio*. What pay was allotted, moreover, was very hard to collect and the perquisites were not much, considering the hardships of the office. The Great Council considered this situation absurd, and so raised the salary and the perquisites.[91]

For the last four years, the Great Council observed in 1485, many nobles had refused the salt office of Chioggia, so the council raised the salary from four to eighteen ducats a month.[92] Pity the poor judges of petitions, according to the Great Council in the same year. Many had refused, because what they received in fees was small, they had to pay a special tax, they did not receive a salary, and their duties were heavy. They were awarded a salary of one hundred fifty ducats a year.[93] It was also hard to find nobles for *signori di notte* and *capi di sestieri* on account of small salary and perquisites.[94] At the same time no one could be found to accept the office of gold leaf, because of the poor salary. The raising of the salary in this case is interesting, because it was set at sixteen ducats a month, "so that they ought to have six ducats net a month."[95] In 1488 the Great Council lamented that *pagatori dell' armamento* might not be found on account of the hard work and small recompense, so they were awarded ten ducats a month plus perquisites. "For in this manner may be found nobles who, laying aside all their labors, will serve day and night, indefatigably and continuously, as the importance of the office demands and requires."[96] Over a period of a few months in 1492 the Maggior Consiglio elected many nobles to be castellan of Montefalcone, all of whom refused, and no one wanted to go on account of the most meager salary of five ducats a month. It should be augmented by another five ducats on condition that the increase should be taxed at the rate of 25 percent.[97]

A more general act of the Senate in 1493 makes a trenchant comment on all the above:

> There has been introduced for some time a certain pernicious and exceedingly detestable custom that when any of our nobles has been elected to any governorship, office or castellany or other thing, either before they accept or even after, they demand an increase of salary or other emolument, which is neither honest nor supportable. It is therefore salutary to avoid similar inconveniences,

which are the cause of many disorders. Therefore, let it be enacted that henceforth whenever anyone will have been elected to any governorship, office, castle, etc., no motion can be made concerning adding to it any salary, perquisite or emolument under penalty of 500 ducats to any councillor, head of the Forty, member of the College or anyone else moving or consenting to anything to the contrary. . . .

Moreover, all provisions, adaptations or increases which henceforth will be necessary to be made with regard to any governorship, magistracy or office should be understood and should be for those who will be elected after the said provisions, adaptations, etc., not, however, for those who will have been in the said governorships, offices, etc., nor for those who perchance will then have been elected. . . .[98]

The act seems to have been remarkably effective, for the type of act that I have illustrated above disappears from the registers, at least for the duration of the period covered by this study.

In defense of the Venetian patriciate (not of the myth, but of the real men), the salaries for public service were not only often inadequate, but in times of crisis they were reduced. On the occasion of the War of Chioggia there occurred a general reduction of salaries, of which we select a few representative examples: ducal councillors from ten ducats a month to five; the Forty from five ducats a month to two and a half; consuls of the merchants, twelve *l. grossorum* to eight; salt officials, twenty-six ducats per year to twenty; officials of the Fondaco dei Tedeschi, forty ducats a year to nothing (but they had perquisites).[99] The war with the Carrara led to a widespread reduction of salaries in 1404. Again, here are some examples: the councillors, who had been raised again to ten ducats, reduced once more to five; the Forty from eight ducats to four; the advocates of the Commune from one hundred *l. di grossi* per year to none, although the advocates did receive a portion of what they were responsible for collecting; the lords of the night from six ducats a month to none, although they also had some perquisites; the officials of grain for the new land from twelve *l. di grossi* to eight; the officials of the wine tax, who had no salary, had their perquisites reduced.[100] In late 1411 and early 1412 the Senate passed a mass of salary reductions on account of the Dalmation war. Again, here are a few examples: the ducal councillors, whose ten ducats per month had been restored, were reduced again to five; the Forty, who had been raised to ten, were also reduced to five; the officials of old, new, and newest accounts should also have half their salaries; judges of petitions should have only two-thirds of their fees; the *giudici del proprio* from ten *l. grossorum* to five. The Senate further decreed that anyone refusing or resigning office during the duration of the war should have a double penalty. They went on to reduce or suppress the salaries of various officials, many of them by name. Marino Magno, grain official in the new lands, was reduced from twelve *l. grossorum* to eight; Marco da Canal, another noble in the same office, from thirteen to nine; the procurators of Saint Mark from two hundred ducats a year to one hundred; the *vice-domini* of the Fondaco dei Tedeschi, who received twenty ducats a year, should have nothing for the duration of the war; the officials of gold leaf should be reduced in number from three to two and in salary from sixty ducats a year to forty; the officials of the wine tax, who have eight pence per amphora, should give two of those to the state; and so on at very great length. If these economies appear prima facie cruel, they are somewhat less so when it is recalled that jobs in Venice were a form of public welfare. As the Senate declared after enacting these reductions: it "is just and appropriate that those our faithful to whom the benefit is given by our Signoria of living honorably with their families, ought to feel some weight with regard to the said benefits during the present novelty."[101]

Through the fourteenth century the salaries of public officials were not taxed, although such officials might be pressured to invest significantly in the public debt. The heavy expenses of the wars on *terraferma* at the beginning of the fifteenth century first raised the issue of a tax on public salaries. On 1 April 1434 the government levied a tax of 10 percent on all salaries below four hundred ducats and 15 percent on those above that sum. On 7 November the Senate raised the levy to 30 percent and 40 percent respectively. This was all the more burdensome to those who were required to maintain a retinue out of their salaries or out of their private purses.[102] In 1488 the *magistrati straordinari* had lost by act of the Senate the income they had formerly received for issuing permits for ships to sail, reducing them to a condition in which they could hardly pay their taxes. In order to prevent them from refusing or resigning, the Great Council awarded them a salary of twelve ducats a month net.[103] In 1489 the Great Council noted that the salary of four hundred ducats a year of the governors of Arbe was so heavily taxed that they actually received only nine ducats and eight *grossi* per month. Lest they have cause to refuse, they should receive fifteen ducats a month.[104] Venetian nobles were very reluctant to accept positions in the maritime empire in 1501 on account of the danger of the Turks, and all the more so because a third of their salaries was being taxed away. The

Senate therefore decided to exempt from the taxes on public salaries all governors and magistrates beyond the Gulf of Quarnero.[105]

Unwillingness to sacrifice the time that could be used to pursue other interests was also an important reason for refusing or resigning office, although it is much more difficult to discern in the documents than the closely related financial motivation. Still, evidence of it does exist. In early 1440 Alvise Michiel expressed his willingness to serve as *sopracomito* of the lake (Garda), but he was not willing to neglect his own affairs for a long time. Since he was experienced in this matter the Senate badly wanted him to serve, so they agreed that he would be free to return to Venice without further license after four months.[106] The Senate was experiencing difficulty in 1483 in electing provisors for the Venetian camps on *Lago oscuro*. Under diverse pretexts many nobles had refused. Remedy had to be found, both because of the importance of the matter itself and in order to prevent so many of the most distinguished nobles from going into exile from Venice to escape service. The Senate therefore decreed that the two provisors who were to be elected should have to go for only two months. Anyone who would make a motion to make them remain longer against their will would be subject to a very large fine, and the provisors were also subjected to a very large fine if they should refuse.[107]

It has already been suggested that one reason, often mingled with others, for refusing offices was fear of danger. Giovanni Contarini refused a mission to Treviso in 1304 on account of the dangers due to the war with Padua and also because of an alleged technical flaw in his election. His request to be absolved from the penalty for refusal was denied.[108] When the government was finding it difficult to get an ambassador to go to Sardinia in 1304, Paolo da Mosto refused because of personal fear, and he was absolved from the penalty.[109] Later fear of the Turks became a more prominent reason for refusal. When the Senate tried to elect provisors to recover Argos in 1390 it had a terrible time. Nine nobles refused with penalty and two were excused as members of the Council of Ten. Danger is not mentioned as a reason, but it can probably be assumed. The Senate sought to overcome the reluctance of the nobles by raising the salary.[110] Positive or negative financial stimuli were about the only weapons that the government possessed against fear. Everyone who was elected as *podestà* and captain of Athens in 1395 refused to go, very likely because of fear of the Turks or partly for that reason. On 20 April the salary was raised from sixty *l. grossorum* to seventy, but a willing candidate was not found until 18 July.[111] This sort of delay in filling important positions was no minor matter, although it is a problem certainly not peculiar to the Venetians. The desire for money and the fear of danger were also probably intertwined in the Senate's search for a captain for the cogs scheduled to go to Tana in 1400. On 19 February the Senate turned down a motion to raise the salary from three hundred to four hundred ducats, but on 8 March they decided to add the extra one hundred ducats.[112] In early 1402 the Senate was most anxious to look to the defenses of the maritime empire, but many nobles refused to go as syndics to investigate conditions and report on them. Two of the needed four had accepted, however, and they were to proceed as quickly as possible to Modon and Coron and afterwards to Negroponte, Napoli di Romania, and then to Corfu and Durazzo. When the other two were obtained, they would go to Crete.[113] During this same period several nobles had declined to be *sopracomiti* of the galleys of Negroponte. In order to encourage the patricians to accept the commands the salary was raised from two hundred fifty to three hundred ducats.[114] The governorships of Modon and Coron, the eyes and ears of Venice in the East, were difficult to fill in 1438, so the salaries were increased.[115] The fear of the Turks was unquestionably a factor in this reluctance to serve. During a critical juncture in the Turkish War in the early 1470s many patricians refused to accept the governorship of Crete, so the salary was raised to one thousand ducats.[116]

At the end of the fifteenth century and the beginning of the sixteenth there was great difficulty in obtaining enough nobles for the important posts in the East. In 1499 Vettor Michiel, captain in Alexandria, refused to go as *provveditore* to Albania to see what needed to be done to defend against the Turks.[117] In 1501 Venice found it difficult to find a noble to serve as *luogotenente* to defend Cyprus against the Turks. No one wanted to go, according to Sanuto, into such a perilous place, in spite of the need. Pietro Marcello refused twice, "through fear of the Turks," according to Dolfin, which Sanuto also says, although he adds *ut dicitur*. Sanuto's indication that the suspicion of cowardice was being bruited about may be more telling than Dolfin's flat statement that Marcello was moved by fear. Niccolò Priuli finally accepted the mission.[118] Girolamo Priuli declares that on account of "these troubles and great fears of war with the Lord Turk there was not any noble in the city of Venice, and truly few, I say, of whatever condition and quality, who wish to go as governor or rector in the maritime empire with so much clear peril. . . ."[119] Just a few months later there was difficulty in replacing Giacomo Renier, who had died in office, as rector and *provveditore* of Napoli di Romania, because the nobles refused "through fear of the Turks." Finally, Marco Pizzamano accepted for a salary of three hundred ducats a year net, plus three hundred ducats as a gift.[120] In short, by the fifteenth century, and especially at the end of the century, Venetian nobles were refusing to do their civic duty out of fear of physical danger.[121]

Another danger was that of epidemic. When Ermolao Barbaro refused to serve the Republic during a raging plague and fled to Padua, he wrote rather apologetically to a friend that there were nobles whose assistance to the state was more valuable than his.[122] A telling proposal was made in the senate by Doge Francesco Foscari in 1425. Durazzo, the motion declared, was a pesthole, as was clear to everyone, since all the nobles sent there died. In the last two years the assignment had proved fatal to five nobles. Moreover, beyond the death of the nobles, the state suffered, "because, if they die before the completion of a year, they receive their salary for the whole year." Since it would be a good and pious act to prevent the deaths of nobles, the doge proposed that "our nobles ought not to be sent to the aforesaid governorship, but our commoners ought to be sent. . . ." The motion was defeated by the Senate, but not overwhelmingly: 42 in favor, 59 opposed, and 2 *non sinceri*.[123]

EXCUSES

There had to be, of course, legitimate and acceptable excuses for declining to serve the Republic. Perhaps Zaccaria Contarini laid it on a bit thick when he refused an embassy to Hungary in 1500: he had the responsibility for ten children; his wife was sick; he had previously served on ten embassies, three of them across the Alps; he had been exposed to the plague on one mission to Germany; his father and two other relatives had died from the hardships of serving as ambassadors.[124] It is perfectly credible, however, that all these things were true. The burdens upon a Venetian noble politically prominent enough to have had ten embassies, especially if he were not very rich, could be heavy indeed.

The first extant act prohibiting refusal of public offices in Venice in 1185 also provides in very general terms for excusing oneself from office for any cause that would be accepted as reasonable by the doge and the majority of his council.[125] No other acts make provision for excuses in quite such broad terms. It seems, however, that it continued to be true that an electee could excuse himself on any reasonable grounds, for almost three centuries later Bernardo Giustinian was excused from serving as one of the ceremonial ambassadors to congratulate Calixtus III on his election in order to look after his most important affairs. This was not among the specific acceptable excuses, which we shall consider shortly, but the mandatory five-hundred-ducat fine was waived. He was, however, reelected before the end of the year.[126] It might be pointed out that such a legation, while it was very expensive, did not last long.

A curious excuse that seems to have been employed successfully after the act of 1185 until it was prohibited in 1212 was the one of having taken an oath.[127] Presumably the electee averred that he had taken an oath to go on a pilgrimage, to look after the affairs of his widowed aunt, not to set foot outside Venetian territory, or whatever would serve.

Being either too young or too old was an acceptable excuse. Understandably electees could excuse themselves if they did not meet the required minimum age, as did some elected *savi agli ordini* in 1407 who had not reached the age of thirty.[128] Old age was a common excuse for refusing office, especially since the Venetians had a propensity toward gerontocracy. Nobles over seventy were allowed to refuse or resign the ducal council without penalty, according to an act of 1417.[129] Even without mandatory age limitations, old age could be accepted as an excuse, perhaps especially for missions abroad, very likely under the broad and general acts cited above.[130] Some electees apparently allowed their election to pass unchallenged, although age was a barrier, then, after deciding that they did not wish to serve, sought to be excused on account of age. An act of 1485 decreed that if the issue were not raised before the council adjourned, then it could not be used as an excuse.[131] Perhaps nobles even lied about their ages in order to escape unwanted offices, although evidence is understandably lacking.

Illness or infirmity was the most obvious excuse. The Great Council provided in 1259 that infirmity should be an excuse for not accepting the Avogaria di comun, provided that it seemed reasonable to the doge and his council and this was approved by a majority of the Great Council.[132] The well-known law of 1263 which imposed the fine of ten *soldi di grossi* and exclusion from office for six months for refusing did exempt from the penalties anyone who suffered some impediment of his person and who was willing to swear that this was his reason.[133] The act of 1272 levying a fine of twenty *soldi* upon those who refused embassies also provided for the acceptance of excuses touching one's person.[134] An act of 1283 imposing a fine of ten *soldi* for resigning any office after acceptance did allow such resignation on account of personal infirmity if it was confirmed by oath that such infirmity was the real reason.[135] In 1286 the Great Council declared that one could be excused from an embassy not only on account of his own sickness, but that of his father, mother, wife, child, or brother.[136] In 1304 a noble elected to go as ambassador to Zara was, in fact, excused after swearing that he could not go *occasione persone*.[137] When in 1322 Giacomo Dandolo was absolved by the Senate on account of infirmity from serving as ambassador in the Marches, the act included the familiar clause that *si consilium est contra sit revocatum,* explaining that this was because there was, indeed, a law stating that excuses should be approved in the Great Council.[138] With regard to the election of *provveditori* for Crete in 1342, the Great Council decreed that sickness should not be an excuse for anyone who had not let that sickness deter him from the fatigues of a voyage, although, upon approval of two-thirds of the Senate, genuine sickness should naturally be accepted.[139] In 1364 the Great Council observed that allegation of sickness was an easy way to avoid the penalty for refusing to serve. Unless the sickness was verified, the penalty had to be paid.[140] On 3 and 5 January 1397 four nobles excused themselves from serving as *savio del Lido,* three *propter defectum persone* and one on account of old age and weakness.[141] The act of 1404 against resignation from a mission abroad after acceptance provides that the excuse of sickness should only be valid with the approval of all six councillors, all three heads of the Forty, and four-fifths of the Senate.[142] This provision strongly suggests that the Great Council believed that the excuse was being abused. A different use of disease as an excuse for avoiding office is indicated in an act of the Great Council in 1405. In February the council had suspended for the duration of the war the right to refuse for the purpose of going abroad. In July the act was amended to allow the excuse to those who took their families abroad to escape the current epidemic.[143] The Great Council in 1480 accepted the excuse of ill health on the oath of the electee's physician, once again hinting at abuse by the patricians.[144] Not all who pled illness, of course, had their pleas accepted. Paolo Capello, elected *provveditore* in the field, an unpleasant task and one that involved some danger, protested that he was ill. Was running about the countryside indicated, he asked, for an unfortunate syphilitic? The Great Council, however, considered him alert and of sound mind, so he had to go.[145]

Provisions which were intended as penalties could be turned against the state as excuses of refusing office. A number of acts, for example, made indebtedness to the commune a bar to holding public office. It is clear that in the fifteenth century public debt was being employed to the advantage of the debtors to escape unwanted ambassadorships and other undesirable positions.[146] In 1448 debt was removed as an obstacle to a short list of such offices.[147]

A conflict of interest which would bar one from office could also be useful as an excuse. Tommaso Minotto was elected syndic to Negroponte in 1376, but declined on the grounds that he had a factor in Negroponte who did business on his behalf, while the commission of the syndics stated that they could not do business in Negroponte or have it done for them. He therefore claimed that he could refuse without penalty, just as wine tax officials, grain officials, the *ternarie* who collected various gabelles, and the salt officials could, and he was upheld.[148]

Much more common was the excuse that an office already held enabled an electee to refuse without penalty or that election to another office enabled him to resign a previous one. An act of the Great Council in 1259 which prohibited advocates of the Commune from refusing or resigning made several exceptions, among them the choice of accepting a command or a governorship.[149] Patricians commonly avoided serving as negotiators for the Commune by virtue of being officeholders, so in 1268 the Great Council declared that during the period of negotiations they would be relieved of their official duties. With this obstacle removed, the doge and his council were authorized to impose penalties on nobles who did not want to undertake the task.[150] A senatorial decree in 1349 declared that any noble should be eligible to become a judge of petitions except the ducal councillors, procurators (of San Marco), rectors, advocates of the Commune, auditors of sentences, patrons of the Arsenal, captains, ambassadors, provisors, and negotiators, the last three only if they were salaried for going abroad.[151] The judges, on the other hand, were free from election to the twelve commands, procuratorships, embassies to crowned heads, and the captaincies of the galleys.[152] According to the Great Council in 1381, an ancient law provided that members of the Ten and the Forty could not accept any other office without losing their seats on the Ten and the Forty. A more recent act provided that they should not lose those seats. In the interest of maintaining the prestige of these two councils, the Great Council decided that they could refuse other offices without penalty in order too remain in the Dieci and the Quaranta, but, if they accepted another post, they should be out of those two bodies.[153] In order to keep the best nobles in the ducal council, the Great Council ruled in 1408 that they should have the right of accepting or rejecting all other public positions, just as the Ten could do.[154]

Some nobles managed to be elected castellans of Durazzo, a well-paid post, for the sake of refusing other positions, so in 1422 the Senate made it a position for non-nobles and lowered the pay.[155] In 1427 the Great Council ruled that for the duration of the war the domestic governorships, offices, and councils which normally carried the privilege of refusing elections should not do so.[156] By 1440 the office of the advocates of the Commune and the advocates themselves were suffering because they were easily elected to many things. Henceforth, they could be elected only to a procuratorship, to one of the twelve major commands, or as ambassador to the pope or royalty.[157] In 1446, however, the Great Council eliminated the Zonta of the Ten as a refuge from unwanted legations and other tasks.[158] In 1448, when the Republic needed badly the services of its most highly qualified nobles, many were taking advantage of their offices to avoid unwanted assignments. None except the advocates of the Commune could refuse election for tasks concerned with the war.[159] In 1454 it was determined that only members of the Ten, ducal councillors, and advocates of the Commune should be able to refuse unpopular posts, such as embassies, without paying the fine.[160] In 1501 the Ten took a rather bizarre action. The Senate was having difficulty finding anyone who would go as orator to France, because the allowance for expenses was too restricted, so it passed an act imposing an additional penalty of five hundred ducats. Zorzi Emo, who had already refused, was elected again and tried to escape by claiming disorder in his election. The Ten then considered what it could do to save those who did not want to be ambassadors from penalties, so it decided to establish an office of three members *sopra le acque* who could not be elected *provveditori,* ambassadors, or members of the Collegio. Zorzi Emo was elected to this office, and then he was able to refuse the French embassy without penalty.[161]

Another useful ploy to dodge unwanted positions was the principle of contumacy, or ineligibility for reelection. This was a device for spreading the desirable jobs around, instead of letting them be monopolized by a few nobles repeatedly elected, but it could also be used to avoid office. The same act in 1427 which suspended the right of holders of domestic commands, offices, or councils to refuse elections also suspended contumacy, so that those who were needed for the duration of the war must either serve or pay the penalty, but these were wartime measures.[162] Contumacy was also among those objections that some nobles tried to raise after the council had adjourned, and this, along with age and debt to the Commune, could no longer be accepted, according to the act of 1485.[163]

The most common and the most sacrosanct, though possibly not the most obvious, excuse for not accepting office was that one was going abroad. The Venetian patriciate was always intensely conscious that the prosperity of the city depended upon foreign trade, and that activity was allowed precedence. In fact, their awareness of the importance of trade was so great that they probably believed it when it was no longer quite so true. In 1257 the Great Council prohibited councillors and electors from resigning "unless they go to Trani or Ragusa or beyond."[164] In 1259 the Great Council denied those elected advocates of the Commune the right to refuse office unless they were making a merchant journey beyond Ragusa, Monte San Angelo, or Milan.[165] In 1287 the Great Council established that no judge or official of the palace or Rialto could refuse or resign except if he made a journey beyond the Alps, the Gulf of Quarnero, and the Tronto. For a shorter journey or for illness he could also be absolved by the doge, a majority of the ducal council, and twenty of the Forty.[166]

The Great Council in 1329 complained that some nobles now and then refused office, saying that they were going abroad, then they delayed their departure endlessly. In the future, they were to leave within eight days after refusal or suffer double the penalty for refusing.[167] Fleeing abroad became a favorite device for escaping office. Since this entailed considerable costs and some risks for the nobles, however, the Great Council decided in 1339 that the refugees should free themselves from their voluntary exile by paying a fine of twenty *soldi* without any period of exclusion from office. In the interest of protecting bona fide merchants, though, the fine did not have to be paid by those who went abroad in a ship or a galley or those going abroad for at least two months. The act was originally to endure for a two-year trial, but it was made permanent at the end of that time.[168] In spite of this legislation, officials were escaping office by the abuse of "a most ancient law"[169] which imposed the penalty of loss of office if they left the city for fifteen days. Once again they had transformed a penalty into an advantage. In 1344 the Great Council decided that the more recent legislation had, in effect, repealed the earlier, so that this ploy would not work unless they remained abroad for at least two months.[170]

In spite of all the efforts of the government, patricians continued to use the excuse of going abroad as an easy means of escaping both public service and the fine for refusing it.[171] A motion was put forward in the Senate in 1389 that would have raised to four months the time that had to be spent abroad in order to escape the penalty for refusal, but it was defeated. Passed or not, however, the document contains the interesting and damning information that the majority of those elected as ambassadors, provisors, and other officers and benefices refuse on account of going abroad in order to escape the penalty for refusal. Worse, they then go to Murano or elsewhere and stay for two months solely to avoid paying the fine.[172] The defeat of the measure underscores the reluctance of the patricians to make it more difficult for them to dodge their responsibilities and lends credence to Lazzarini's belief that the many patrician residences on nearby Murano owed their existence to the two-month rule.[173] During the war with Padua the Great Council fixed the Gulf of Quarnero, the Tronto, and the Alps as the confines beyond which those wishing not to pay the fine for refusing had to go.[174] The practice of going abroad to escape both the office and the penalty had two bad effects, according to the Great Council in early 1405: the first was the risk that the work of the state simply would not be done; the second was the voluntary exile of so many experienced nobles, whose counsel had in the past been sound. The excuse of going abroad (along with the right to pay the fine rather than to accept the office) was therefore suspended for the duration of the war.[175] After a few months, however, the council backed off from the apparent meaning of this act, deciding that it had not been their intention to include those who went to distant parts for commerce or other affairs.[176]

Anyone who refused a position for the sake of going abroad, according to the Great Council in 1408, could not be elected to any other post during the time (in most cases, two months) which he was required to spend in foreign parts.[177] A special rule was passed by the Senate in 1416 for those who refused or resigned membership in the Council of Six, for they would have to remain abroad four months.[178] The act of 1427 which suspended for the duration of the war the right of certain officials to refuse other jobs did, however, retain the right to refuse for going abroad, although those employing it must leave within the prescribed term (one month, unless otherwise specified), which could in no way be extended.[179] The act making it more painful to refuse the Avogaria di Comun in 1439 provided that those choosing to go abroad must go beyond the Alps or the Gulf of Quarnero and remain four months.[180] In 1448 legislation that suspended for the duration of the war the right to refuse on account of conflicting offices or contumacy retained that right for those going abroad.[181]

We must not be misled into believing that Venetian legislation was consistently enforced. The Great Council in 1454 objected that in spite of the laws requiring those who refused or resigned for going abroad to go beyond certain limits (the current ones were the Alps and the Gulf of Quarnero), nobles in fact were escaping office by going to Padua, Treviso, or even Murano. This time the right to refuse for the purpose of going abroad was suspended.[182] With regard to a provisor elected in 1477, the Senate declared that if he refused in order to go abroad he would have to go beyond the Alps or the Gulf of Quarnero and remain for six months.[183] This longer term was embodied in general legislation in 1479. It raised the penalties for those refusing assignments abroad, but it continued to excuse nobles who passed beyond the Alps or the Gulf of Quarnero. They must now, however, leave within fifteen days and remain abroad for six months.[184] At least two points should be absolutely clear from the foregoing evidence: the Venetian government took foreign commerce very, very seriously; and Venetian nobles flagrantly abused the indulgence which was intended to further that interest.

From time to time, as we have seen, one or another of the councils tried to impose controls on the use of excuses to refuse or resign offices. It was an impossible task, though, to prevent the patricians from exploiting legitimate excuses for refusing or resigning for the purpose of dodging equally legitimate responsibilities.

RESIGNATIONS

The words *refutare, recusare, renunciare,* and so on signify both refusal to accept election and resignation after acceptance. Basically the Venetians thought of refusal and resignation as a single concept. Some documents, however, point clearly and specifically to acts of resignation, rather than refusal.

The principle was established as early as 1257: anyone who was elected to any office and consented to it, even tacitly, could not resign *(refutare)* under penalty of 100 *l.*[185] As noted previously, assignments abroad were generally considered undesirable, so the Great Council in 1269 added exclusion from all offices for a year to the normal penalty of 100 *l.* for refusing to go after accepting a mission or to remain at one's post as ordered by the doge.[186] Any rector in office who resigned before the expiration of his term would forfeit eligibility for other offices until the end of that term, according to a law of 1287.[187] In spite of all the legislation just mentioned, we find the Great Council objecting in 1315 that ambassadors who had accepted their elections and later resigned were getting away with paying only the penalty of twenty *soldi di grossi* established for refusals in general. As we have seen, this administration of the laws was typical of Venice. The council made it absolutely clear that the fine of twenty *soldi* was for those who refused to accept election; those who accepted and then resigned must pay 200 *l.*[188] Because the patrons of the Arsenal had originally been elected for life, they had been allowed to resign whenever they wished. When the term had been reduced to four years, however, they continued to resign at will, just as they had, without penalty. This did not seem reasonable to the Great Council in 1340, so they made the patrons subject to a fine of 100 *l.* for resigning.[189]

The difference in seriousness between refusing and resigning, although the same verb, *refutare,* is used for both, is made clear in a law of 1375. Loan officials had been subject to a fine of 100 *l.* for refusing, but their penalty for mere refusal was reduced to the normal twenty *solidi grossorum,* although the heavier penalty remained in effect for resigning.[190] The Great Council declared in 1404 that there was nothing more perilous to the state than those nobles who accepted embassies and other foreign missions and then resigned them. Those who resigned such missions henceforth should be out of any offices they held and should be excluded from all commands, offices, benefices, and councils for five years, in addition to the penalties already established.[191] The severity of these penalties should be emphasized; deprival of office for five years could be a disaster for the careers of the ambitious or for the finances of the poor.

The Ten faced a complicated problem in 1432. By their own act it was established that anyone who refused to be a head of the Ten or an inquisitor had to pay a fine of 100 *l.* But what if someone who was already head or inquisitor wished to resign, not only his special position, but from the Council of Ten? They decided that he could do that by paying the same penalty of ten *soldi di grossi* as any other member, but, if he wanted to resign as head or inquisitor, yet remain on the council, then he had to pay the heavier fine.[192] On the other hand, a special act providing for the election of advocates of the Commune in 1440 established a fine of five hundred ducats for refusing. Apparently such a heavy fine did not yet apply to those already in office, so the same penalty was extended to resignations.[193] There was a risk in 1455 that the Ten might be unable to function, since some resigned, some were elected to this or that, and one could receive permission to be abroad for a number of days. The Ten therefore decreed that anyone who refused or who accepted any position which would remove him from the council should not be considered off the council until his successor had been elected.[194]

The last half of the fifteenth century produced an interesting series of acts indicating that nobles were accepting offices so that they could have the title and then were quickly resigning, indeed resigning before they ever performed any functions. The series begins in 1468 with a complaint by the Ten about a custom by which members of the Forty, desirous of empty glory, titles of dignity, and offices that they did not exercise, accepted the headship of the council, and then promptly resigned. The Council of Forty ran through several such acceptances and resignations consecutively, which derogated from the dignity of the office. The title was to belong from now on only to those who served on the Signoria.[195] The Great Council took up the issue on a broader front in 1472 against the many who, desirous of vain glory, attributed to themselves titles of dignities and honors, offices and commands, that they had not executed because they had resigned them.[196] In 1486 the Maggior Consiglio was lamenting the condition of the *auditori vecchi delle sentenze,* the importance of which as a court of appeal for civil cases was well known. Considering the hard work and the difficulties of the position, however, the remuneration was very small, so no one for some time had wanted to serve until the end of his term or even for very long. Nobles accepted it for a short time, however, just to acquire the title, and then they resigned without having accomplished much, to the injury of the oppressed and the shame of the Signoria. The net pay was almost doubled to make the position more attractive.[197] Apparently the earlier legislation had not worked, for the Ten returned to the subject of the heads of the Forty in 1490. The custom of accepting the office merely for the sake of the title and then resigning had revived, so that sometimes in one day the Forty ran through eight successive elections of a head, "than which nothing could be more absurd." Anyone engaging in this practice in the future should not have the title and should be ineligible for the Council of Forty for two years.[198]

LACK OF ENFORCEMENT

The very repetition of laws dealing with the same problem may be the most common indicator that Venetian laws penalizing refusal and resignation of office were not consistently enforced. Occasionally an act specifies a penalty against those who fail to enforce the act.[199]

The granting of *grazie* via what we could call special legislation was one obstacle to serious enforcement of the laws. For example, in 1306 Jacopo Querini was absolved by the Great Council from paying the penalty of twenty *solidi grossorum* that he incurred for refusing to be ambassador to the king of Germany.[200] Sometimes the *grazia* was granted to relieve a noble of a genuine hardship, as when Niccolò Papacizza refused the money office because of another office that he held.[201] Although I have not found the act itself, there is later reference to a law of 1342 prohibiting release from the penalties for refusing offices, commands, and embassies.[202] The act of 1287 which had denied eligibility for other offices to rectors who resigned[203] had been evaded by the use of *grazie.* In 1348 the Great Council declared that this was to be permitted no longer under penalty of 100 *l.* to anyone moving such a *grazia.*[204] This seemed such a good idea that a month later the principle was extended.

Various officials had sought *grazie* for resigning without paying the fine, which not only resulted in a flood of resignations, but was also clearly inequitable, since some had to pay the penalty and others did not.[205] This act in turn was revised by the Great Council in 1352, so that it would apply to refusals before taking up office, as well as resignations afterwards.[206] Still, in spite of the clear intent of the legislation, in 1411 the Great Council discovered that many who paid the penalties were being reimbursed by *grazia*. Anyone moving such a *grazia* in the future should pay a fine equal to the amount that was to be reimbursed.[207]

The most common reason why penalties were not paid was plain negligence. The person who was fined did not bother to pay, and very often no one else bothered to make him do so. As early as 1291 there is evidence of difficulty in collecting these penalties.[208] An act of 1381 complained of the many cases of penalties for refusal of offices which went unpaid. The chamberlains of the Commune were ordered to collect these penalties within eight days of the time when they were due.[209] As usual it was of little avail, for similar legislation had to be passed in 1385, 1395, and 1401.[210] According to the Great Council in 1408 the fines were still not being collected, because either the chamberlains of the Commune were not notifying the debtors, or, if they did, the debtors were claiming that they had not been notified. Since the notifications were not written down, they escaped the memory of the officials or the debtors. Notification henceforth should not be required.[211] Still in 1441 the Senate averred that many nobles who had been fined for refusing offices had not bothered to pay. The Senate tried to encourage payment by allowing those who had incurred fines within the past ten years to pay within a month without additional penalty. If they did not, the chamberlains should collect with a penalty of two *soldi* per *lira*.[212] In 1447 many nobles who were debtors of the Commune for refusing offices or for other reasons still owed a sizable sum of money. They would have the remainder of the month of March to pay (it was 10 March), and, if they did not, their debts should be turned over to the officials of accounts of the ten offices, who could levy the fines against the debtors' capital and should have a quarter of what they collected.[213] Sanuto provides a list of the fines for refusing various offices, including the most exalted in state except for doge and procurator of St. Mark, adding, "which at the present time are not observed."[214] Obviously, it was extremely difficult or impossible to collect what was owed, making the fines a rather empty threat.

It seems that outright tampering with the records was another means by which one could refuse office and also avoid paying the penalty. In 1358 the Great Council recounted how many refused and were reported to the *camera* of the Commune as owing the penalty. The debtors were recorded, however, only in a single *folio,* which was accessible, so that some could cancel whatever they wished. The council provided for a more secure record of the debts.[215]

It is clear that the legislation against refusing or resigning office fell victim to Venetian ineptitude at enforcing their too-numerous laws.

OTHER EVASIONS OF OFFICE

Beyond openly refusing to serve or resigning office there were a number of other ways to try to avoid assuming unwanted responsibilities. A rather obvious method was what we might call negative *broglio,* or *broglio* in reverse, or simply campaigning *not* to be elected. The first mention of this comes from an act of the Great Council of 1274, or, rather, from its rubric. The act itself declares that "whoever henceforth will have been nominated for any office, after he will have been nominated in the council, cannot, taking the floor, say anything in the council, neither he nor anyone for him. . . ." If the rubric, however, correctly reveals the intention of the act, it was directed against negative *broglio,* for it declares "that anyone who will have been nominated cannot say in the council that he does not want to be [named]."[216]

There is no additional evidence of negative campaigning until 1427, when we learn that Venetian nobles nominated to serve as captain, ambassador, provisor, or *tractator* for the war or otherwise said to other nobles: "Don't elect me! Don't see me!" They also had the bearers of the urns and others do it for them. This negative campaigning was subjected to a fine of 100 *l.* and deprival of offices and councils for a year.[217] The Ten sought in 1439 to prevent its members from evading the duties of the headship. The habit of asking not to be elected had grown, and this was now prohibited under a penalty of 100 *l.,* loss of one's seat on the Dieci, and payment of the penalty for refusal or resignation.[218] In 1440 the Senate strengthened the legislation of 1427 which prohibited nominees from calling out, "Don't elect me! Don't see me!" Those who by head movements or other means indicated that they did not want to be elected were subjected to the same penalties.[219] The act of the Ten in 1449 which prohibited notaries from engaging in *broglio* to get nobles elected also prohibited them saying to voters, "do not elect so-and-so, because he does not want to be elected."[220] The Ten returned to the subject in 1467, unanimously imposing two years' exclusion from office upon those nobles who said in the council that they wished not to be elected.[221]

In the Collegio, a small body of twenty-six members, which often elected nobles to costly and unpopular embassies, the outcome could be affected by the relatives of a nominee voting for another candidate in order to protect their family. Relatives were therefore made ineligible to vote.[222] In 1483 the Ten reformed the law of 1480 on *broglio* to apply the same penalties upon those who campaigned on their own behalf or through sons, relative, or friends not to be nominated or elected.[223] By the end of the century the bad habit had arisen that nominees of the Senate for some undesirable position would gain the floor, offer their excuses, and not be elected. An act of 1499 prohibited them from making any statement at that time, either before the Senate or before the Signoria.[224]

Another device for trying to escape office was to evade notification of election. The act prohibiting refusal in 1185 seems to have been circumvented in this manner, for in 1211 it was provided that the electee must accept within three days of notification, either personally or by call outside his house.[225] The Great Council took action in 1268 against those who left town after their election. They were to be summoned at their homes, and if they did not appear they would have to pay twenty *soldi di grossi* and any other penalties and be ineligible for offices, the Great Council, the Forty, and the Senate for the term of the office which they had avoided.[226] Another attempt was made to tighten the law in 1269. If the electee had gone abroad before he was elected, nonetheless he would be summoned at his house to appear within three days, and, if he were in a place where he could come and did not, he should pay a penalty of forty *soldi di grossi*.[227] Anyone who had been selected as an elector for the year, and who had been summoned at his house, and did not come within three days to take the oath of office, would have to pay 50 *l.*[228] We hear no more of avoiding office by escaping notification, so this problem appears to have been handled successfully in the thirteenth century.

One could also try to avoid assuming an unwanted position on the grounds of technicalities. In 1295 the Great Council declared that although ambassadors and *tractatores* were supposed to be elected one by one, their elections should be binding even if this procedure had been violated.[229] In the fifteenth century unwilling and ingenious patricians who did not want to serve the state had rediscovered the technique of finding some flaw in their elections. This must have been somewhat commonplace, because in 1440 the Senate decreed that those elected must serve in spite of such defects or pay the penalty for refusing.[230] It seems that an election flawed by the participation of voters ineligible through some act of the Ten still worked for a time as a means to avoid an undesired election, for in 1461 the Great Council, fearing that the nobles could use this device to serve only in positions that they wanted, enacted that any objection to particular voters had to be raised before the balloting. Otherwise, the result could not be challenged.[231]

Many evaded unwanted offices and also the fine for refusing them by proclaiming their intention of going abroad on business. An act of 1410 required that they had to leave within a month,[232] but they wangled prolongations of their terms for departure, thus not serving, not paying the penalty, not going abroad, and not even being eligible for other unwanted offices. In 1441 the Senate prohibited such prolongations.[233]

A much-exploited device was to get oneself expelled from an un-wanted office by repeated absenteeism. At quite an early date, 1258, the Great Council legislated against going outside of Venice or beyond the boundaries for the purpose of escaping from office.[234] Keep in mind the Venetian disposition to favor going abroad, but it was not supposed to be done for the sake of evading responsibilities. An act of 1269 estab-lished that an officeholder who had been abroad fifteen days should lose his office. However, he should not leave Venice with the motive of getting out of his job.[235] Judges and officials of the palace and of Rialto were admonished in 1287 against going abroad in order not to be in office.[236] In 1294 the Five of peace were warned against going abroad for the purpose of losing their position. They had to satisfy the doge with an oath concerning their reason for going abroad.[237] An act of 1323 which provided for the election of six loan officials specified that they must not go abroad to escape the office without the license of the Signoria and a majority of the Forty.[238] In 1344 the Great Council complained of the many officials with liberal consciences who shed their offices by going abroad for fifteen days. Whereas a trip abroad, according to the Venetian list of priorities, should provide an excuse from office, it was the clear intention of the earlier legislation that this required a stay of at least two months. If the officeholders were absent from office for fifteen days they would lose their offices, but if they returned in less than two months, they were subject to the fine for resigning.[239] The loss of office after fifteen days of absence was intended to assure its functioning, not to provide an escape from it, so it was common in capitularies for officials to promise that they would not go abroad or remain away from office for this unpatriotic reason.[240] A more general act of 1364 lamented that many officials wishing to get out of office without paying a fine simply stayed away for fifteen days, if the office were a six-month one, or thirty days, if it were annual. Losing office for absence on account of sickness or for going abroad should continue to be acceptable excuses, but the reasons for absence should henceforth be examined by the officeholder's colleagues.[241]

A variation of this technique was to be absent from the city when an election occurred. The Great Council informs us in 1385 that nobles were avoiding the Avogaria di Comun in this way.[242] In 1389 we hear of elections of ambassadors, provisors, and others for missions abroad in which likely candidates departed for Murano or elsewhere on the day before the election. Henceforth, the act states, if they are to escape both election and penalty, they must have departed at least eight days before the election and must swear that their departure was not for the sake of evading responsibility.[243] In 1404 the Senate was attempting to elect a commission of *savi* to consider increasing or decreasing the public debt, but many were being excused for sickness by remaining at home and never taking up their responsibilities. The Senate was spending a lot of time electing successors to those absolved. In an attempt to tighten up procedures the Senate provided that no one could be absolved until he had entered office, although sickness that kept a *savio* at home should continue to be an excuse, provided that it was confirmed by oath that he stayed at home for no other reason. The Senate then proceeded to absolve three elected *savi*.[244] Bear in mind the Venetian proclivity for electing old men, who were naturally more liable to become ill. In 1406 the Great Council objected to the practice of members of the Forty who wished to be off the council. If they resigned they had to pay a fine of 200 *l.*, but if they were expelled for exceeding fifteen "points" for tardiness or absence they only had to pay 100 *l.* The majority of those who wanted to escape the council, therefore, deliberately failed to appear at the summons from the belfry for fifteen days. The Great Council tried to cope with the problem by reducing the fine for resigning to 100 *l.*[245]

By 1441, however, the act of 1389 on going to Murano or elsewhere was malfunctioning in that those whose simply wished to get out of office were abusing it—and presumably swearing falsely. Henceforth the noble elected should be summoned outside his house, and if he failed to appear within the allotted time, he would be fined unless absolved by two-thirds of the Senate.[246] Despite all efforts to halt the practice of leaving the city to escape being an ambassador, many nobles continued to abuse the law by spending a pleasant two months at Murano or some other nearby place. This inconvenience threatened to become a serious problem, so the Great Council yielded to the Senate, perhaps because it met more frequently, the right to impose penalties in order to prod those elected to accept their assignments and get on their ways.[247]

Membership on the Council of Ten was certainly considered a plum by wealthy, powerful, and politically involved members of the nobility, but the headship of the Ten was quite burdensome, for the *capo* on duty had the initiative in the Ten, saw to the execution of its judgments, supervised the prisons, possessed some judicial functions of his own, and held audiences three days a week. Members of the Ten escaped the headship by being absent for eight days, as a consequence of which they lost the headship without any other penalty. In 1488 the Ten decided that if an elected head did not appear to take up his responsibilities within three days without a "just impediment" accepted by the Ten he should be expelled, not only from the headship, but from the council. The inquisitors of the Ten were subjected to the same provision.[248] Nobles also sought to escape magistracies and offices secretly by points or resignations, so that they could be elected to other positions that they wanted. In 1493 the Ten assigned a secretary to keep a book recording carefully all such departures from office, so that those who were removed in these ways would not be chosen for more favored positions.[249]

A similarly devious device for escaping the burdens of office was to become a debtor of the Commune.[250] This, too, of course, had been intended as a punishment, not something for debtors to turn to their advantage. Under a law of 1254, ambassadors and others undertaking missions abroad were made ineligible for other offices if they failed to report or to return things that belonged to the Commune that had been entrusted to them for the mission. Nobles were exploiting this provision to make themselves ineligible, so in 1302 the Great Council decided that this would not work unless the delinquency had been declared before election. Otherwise, the delinquent still could not serve, but he had to pay the fine as if he had refused.[251] Again in 1317 the Great Council noted that nobles were exploiting the rule about exclusion from office on account of retaining possession of things belonging to the Republic. Some nobles who owed as little as about two *libre parvorum* refused to pay so that they would have a means of keeping out of jobs that did not please them. The Great Council therefore added to the penalties ineligibility for office for a year after payment of what was owed.[252] The act seems to have had little if any effect, because after only a little over a year the Great Council had returned to the problem. When nobles were elected to offices they did not want they were quick to find that they could not be elected because they had failed to make an accounting to the state. They did not make such a discovery, of course, if the office was a desired one. The Great Council again enacted that those who failed to submit their accounting or who owed the Commune might not hold office for a year after the accounts had been cleared.[253] Again there is no indication that the act was effective. Subsequent legislation, in fact, assumes that debtors of the Commune are ineligible for office only as long as they are in debt.

In 1401 the Great Council decided that debts should not be a bar to such unwanted offices as captain, *sopracomito*, provisor, *tractator*, or ambassador.[254] This was a pivotal act, reversed in 1412 but restored in 1413 with some slight changes in the list of offices affected.[255] The act of 1413 also does not seem to have cleared up the confusion, and, in fact, appears to have been ignored and unknown. At any rate, five years later the Great Council again laments the harm that comes to the Commune from the many *partes* and *ordines* prohibiting the election of debtors of the state. Again we learn that the intention was to penalize these debtors, in order that they might be more eager in paying their debts, but, on the contrary, it was the Commune that suffered. "There are many," the act declares, "who not only do not take care to pay, but with the highest zeal seek to be debtors of the Commune, in order that, if they should be elected to anything, they can protect themselves under the shelter of such a debt. . . ." The council provided once again that debtors could be elected.[256] In 1448 the Great Council tried once more to bring order to the confusion surrounding the question of the eligibility of debtors of the Commune for holding public office. This time the decision was that they would be eligible only for embassies, provisorships of the army, or the troops of Padua.[257] An act of 1458 states that "because debtors of the Commune cannot be elected except to embassies and provisorships of the army, oftentimes it happens that many held in high esteem by the councils, when they do not want to be elected to positions which are not pleasing to them, declare themselves debtors for some minimal debt." The act proceeds to add councillors and advocates of the Commune to the offices for which public debt should not be an obstacle.[258] In 1467 the Great Council again complained that the penalty imposed upon debtors of the Commune worked to the advantage of voluntary debtors, who used this device to escape the burdens of officeholding, since they could not be elected ducal councillors, advocates, *savi*, ambassadors, or provisors. (As if there had been no previous legislation on the subject.) The act proposed that these offices should be open to debtors, but it was defeated, possibly as somewhat redundant.[259] The confusion is again apparent when the Great Council says in 1468 that nobles who do not want to be councillors or advocates of the Commune or something else bribe (*habent modum intelligendi*) officials and scribes to record them as debtors of the Commune. The council placed a penalty on the officials and scribes who falsified the records.[260] Less than two years later the Senate took up the problem of nobles who had themselves declared debtors fraudulently for the sake of escaping office. They could not be recognized as debtors in the future without a highly specific record, and those who engaged in falsifying the record should be penalized.[261]

An effort to make debtors eligible to be councillors was proposed in 1497, in spite of the legislative history which suggests strongly that they already were, but it was defeated, possibly because unneeded.[262] In 1503 it was provided that of all of the offices filled by senatorial election only ambassadors and provisors of the army were excepted from the rule excluding debtors of the Republic from public office.[263] In 1504 the Great Council observed that many outstanding senators made themselves debtors in order to avoid election to the College. Therefore the College should be excepted from the rule excluding debtors.[264]

While the legislative history is very confused on the subject of exclusion for debt, it is perfectly clear that nobles became debtors of the Commune or even had themselves falsely declared debtors in order to evade the responsibilities which, according to the myth, they were so willing to undertake. This was just one of the ways in which they ducked and dodged in what appears a frantic effort to escape from unwanted offices.

ABSENTEEISM

In researching the life of Marcantonio Barbaro in the sixteenth century, Charles Yriarte leafed through thirty-four years of the sittings of the Senate and the Great Council, finding his patrician hero marked absent only twice, and that for illness, the second time only hours before his death.[265] No doubt Barbaro did show such devotion to duty, and surely so did a number of other such public-spirited Venetian patricians, but the evidence is quite clear that romantic generalizations concerning devotion to the state based upon the biographies of a few highly successful and famous political figures will not stand examination. Already in the 1930s Cassandro noticed the large mass of Venetian legislation on absenteeism: "[I]t returns upon its old steps, takes up old themes, it is a little like a sick person who can find no peace in his own bed."[266]

From 1269 we find frequent legislation attempting to restrain the absenteeism of officials and judges.[267] In 1394 the Council of Ten defeated a proposal which complained that in spite of many regulations requiring the heads of the *sestieri* (a major law-enforcement agency) to be present in their appointed places under heavy penalties, these penalties were not exacted. Therefore, "those heads of the *sestieri* do not take care to come nor to be present as they ought," with no small harm and delay to the affairs of state committed to them.[268] Ten years later the Ten returned to the same issue, and this time the measure passed.[269]

A new magistracy, the *appuntatori,* was established in 1406 to check up on judges and officials and their notaries and scribes. One *appuntatore* was to check both in the morning and after the ninth hour on the offices at the governmental center at San Marco, another on those at the commercial center near the Rialto bridge. Fines and loss of office after a number of absences *(puncti)* were fixed.[270] A rather damaging admission for the myth of the selfless patriciate is contained in an act of the Great Council in 1408, which states that because of the reduction of salaries and perquisites during the war with Padua the majority of offices and judgeships were not administered as well as they needed to be. It is conceded that these delinquent judges and officials were compelled by their low salaries to engage in private affairs in order to support their families, and the critical reader may well believe that their neglect of their public responsibilities was understandable and excusable. So it was, but the myth holds precisely that the Venetian nobles were deterred by no private sacrifice in their zeal for the public welfare. We can expose the mirage of the myth and still understand and sympathize with the plight of the patricians. With a number of exceptions the act of 1408 restores salaries and perquisites to their prewar level.[271] The Senate complained in 1444 that officials were not coming to their offices, sometimes remaining at home for five or six months. Their colleagues in office did not report them, as they should have, nor did the *appuntatori.* Henceforth, officials who were absent more than the permissible number of times would lose their offices. Their colleagues and the *appuntatori* had to report such lapses and the advocates of the Commune would be fined if they did not exact appropriate penalties.[272]

Absenteeism also caused problems at the *palio,* or shooting match, at which young nobles at one time qualified for much desired posts as *balestrieri,* or bowmen of the quarterdeck. On these occasions "a thousand disorders" occurred because the lords of the night, the heads of the *sestieri,* captains, and other officials responsible for keeping order were not found at their places nor were they to be seen at any time.[273] The admission that Venetian patrician officials did not attend to their duties because they were not paid strikes at the heart of the myth of the selfless patriciate. But such does seem to be the case. For example, the Quaranta criminale was finally put on salary in 1451, because without such a reward so many members were absent that sometimes the council could not function.[274] In 1499 officials and magistrates who were not members of the Collegio were forbidden to linger before that focus of power and information, because their absence from their offices was causing great harm to the city.[275]

It was necessary, of course, for the government to establish hours during which magistrates must be present for the performance of their duties, and there is a lot of surviving legislation on the subject. That it was ineffective is indicated by the complaint of the Great Council in 1311 that although the judges and officials of the palace and of Rialto came to their offices at the proper times in the morning, immediately or within half an hour they left to go about their own affairs.[276] By the late fourteenth century it seems that the standard hours of work were in the morning from a half-hour before the third hour (the *campana officialium*) until at least the third hour and in the afternoon from the ninth hour (the *campana longa*) at least until vespers. The rules, however, were badly observed, to the "great harm" of Venice, so a new system of checking was instituted in 1394 with a notary of the Signoria checking the offices and courts in the area of San Marco and another from the officials of accounts at Rialto.[277] Apparently the checking system instituted in 1394 did not work over the long run, for in 1421 the Senate provided once again for the appointment of two *appuntatori*, who should make their rounds immediately after the bells at the specified hours for beginning work and also around the third hour to see if anyone has merely put in an appearance and then left after the first inspection. Provisions were even made for fining the *appuntatori* if they should be absent.[278]

In 1440 the Senate objected to the fact that the *savi del consiglio* appeared for meetings of the Collegio only for about a half-hour in the morning, on account of which very little deliberation could occur. It therefore required that these powerful officeholders should come at the usual half-hour before the third hour and remain at least two and a half hours and similarly in the afternoons, except Wednesdays and Sundays when there would be meetings of the Great Council, from the ninth hour until the hour before sunset.[279] A year later a measure defeated in the Senate declares that, to the detriment of the Commune, the *savi del consiglio* were still not obeying this act.[280] Only a few months later, since the *savi del consiglio* and of *terraferma* still were not present often enough or long enough to carry out their responsibilities, the Senate removed the task of checking on them from the *appuntatori*, who were reluctant to penalize such powerful men, and transferred the charge to the higher-ranking heads of the Forty.[281] A senatorial act of 1449 declares that things could not be worse attended to, because the *appuntatori* fail to do their duty, conspiring with officeholders not to report them, so that everything tends to be neglected. Two new *appuntatori* should be elected for two-year terms, and they should be required to check every hour after the third hour, the ninth hour, and vespers. They should not be allowed in any way to enter into an agreement not to report absences.[282]

The government did not have the unrealistic aim, of course, of ending absenteeism, but tried only to keep it within reasonable limits. An act of 1360 in the capitulary of the officials of accounts seems to sum up the common rule that had evolved. Thirty days of abence, consecutively or not, but fifteen consecutive days abroad, should result in the loss of office.[283] This was for those with a tenure of one year; for those with a tenure of six months, fifteen days seems to have been the limit.

Many absences were caused by officials being out of the city. As early as 1268 there was legislation against those who had been elected and had accepted office leaving town. They were to be summoned, and if they did not return within the prescribed time they should pay twenty *solidi grossorum* and should be excluded from all political functions, including participation in the Great Council, during the term for which they had been elected.[284] In 1328 it was decided that those holding public office could not go beyond the Alps, the River Tronto, and the Gulf of Quarnero.[285]

The chief concern was to have enough officials on hand to conduct public business. In 1503, if the copy in the *Compilazioni leggi* is correct, advocates of the Commune had been neglecting to attend the meetings of the Ten. This was most important, for the advocate, while not given a vote, was supposed to exercise a constitutional restraint upon the Ten. Penalties had not been exacted. A large fine of a ducat was imposed.[286]

A small body of legislation deals with the failure of officials to respond to a lawful summons.[287] The Senate objected in 1502 that when the Signoria appointed gentlemen to honor visiting lords or ambassadors by going to meet them or accompanying them in the city often the task was not carried out. A very large fine of ten ducats was imposed.[288] Sanuto illustrates this point for us two years later. Because it was raining, only ten Venetian nobles went to greet a Turkish ambassador, and only one of them dressed in scarlet. The Signoria, says the diarist, when it heard this, took it very badly.[289]

Of course there were various acceptable excuses for absence from office. Thirteenth-century capitularies offer a typical list of legitimate excuses: being with the doge, one's own sickness or that of those relatives for whose sake one would have to leave the Great Council, going to a funeral or a wedding, or going abroad.[290] Because of the Venetian proclivity for electing nobles of advanced age, illness or other physical incapacity was often a reasonable excuse.[291] Marriage feasts (held out-doors in the *campi*) proved excessively tempting to officeholders, so it was provided that they could be excused only for weddings of those for whose sake they would have to leave the Great Council.[292] Two addi-tional excuses were allowed according to a decree of the Senate in 1421: for attending to charges against them or against relatives for whom they would have to leave the council or for going abroad according to their capitularies, but not otherwise.[293] All in all, this represents a rea-sonable list of excuses except that absence on account of weddings tended to be abused.

Priuli denounced the arrogance of Venetian noble judges who ne-glected their duties, delaying the administration of justice and thus denying the rights of individuals before the courts to reasonably prompt adjudication of their cases.[294] In spite of all excuses, we can confirm his judgment and add the other officials who were responsible for conducting the domestic affairs of Venice to the number of the guilty.

Those charged with embassies, governorships, and other functions abroad also did not often enough tend to their duties. The temptation for those assigned to nearby posts was especially great, for they liked to visit Venice to attend to their private affairs. In 1251 the Great Council prohibited the *podestà* of Chioggia from coming to Rialto on his own affairs for more than four days a month.[295] On the other hand, more distant governors did not invariably attend single-mindedly to the in-terests of the Republic. An act of 1256 requires that one at least among the *baiuli* and councillors of Tyre must remain at his post to conduct the governance of the colony and that absences should be limited to two months out of the year.[296] One of the main problems was that those assigned abroad often obtained license to visit Venice. The Great Coun-cil in 1283 prohibited rectors and other officials assigned beyond Rialto from coming to Venice, even if license had been granted, more than was permitted by their capitulary or commission.[297]

Many governors were excused on account of sickness from departing promptly for their posts. In 1304 the Great Council laid it down that they must either leave within a month or give up the position.[298] An act of 1308 refers to an earlier law requiring governors assigned beyond the Gulf of Quarnero to leave with the first ship. Interestingly, the act is repealed because the newly elected governor's predecessor would not yet have received license to return home, so that for a time the state would be paying two salaries for the same position, and would thus suffer great harm.[299] One reason that the Venetian and other governments had problems was that they were stingy. Again trying to deal with the transition from one governor to another, the Great Council in 1319 required that a governor or other official of Venice abroad must await the arrival of his successor before leaving for home.[300] Some governors promised to accept their offices, and then simply did not go. The Great Council in 1320 prohibited them from gaining any other governorship during the tenure of the first one.[301]

The Senate attempted in 1371 to cope with the problem of some officials in Candia who were conducting their private business abroad, appearing infrequently for the performance of their public duties. They had been elected in Venice, and had not been subject to firing by the duke of Crete and his councillors. In the future their attendance should be checked and the duke and his councillors could dismiss those who were absent more than was allowed by their capitularies.[302] The castellans in Crete, according to the Senate in 1403, were in the habit of running about the island on their own affairs, neglecting the custody of the castles and lands entrusted to their care. The Senate provided that they should not go to the city nor sleep outside their castles, with the exception that for the accomplishment of their missions the duke and councillors of Crete could give them permission to come to the city or to go about the island as many as four tiimes a year.[303] The Senate again complained that in the course of the war in 1413 provisors, heads, and captains of Venetian territories and other nobles sent to the army or other places withdrew from their posts and without special license they returned to Venice. This was a daily occurrence. In the future, those who left their posts were to pay the fine that they would have paid for refusing them, plus as much more, and they were to be excluded from all public offices for two years, which, as we know, was a very severe penalty to apply to a Venetian noble who had designs upon income from public employment.[304] The Senate again took action in 1471 against governors, chamberlains, and castellans, who received permission to be absent from their posts, and who, even when a deadline for return was given, made free to stay away as long as they wished. A two hundred-ducat fine was specified for those moving or voting to grant them leave to come to Venice or any place else.[305] As the weight of certain high offices abroad became heavier upon a limited number of qualified candidates in the fifteenth century, overburdened patricians, or those who thought they were, bombarded the government with requests for license to return home. In 1482 the Senate prohibited provisors, ambassadors, captains, *sopracomiti,* and others from coming home without the consent of the Senate under penalty of one thousand ducats to the official and another five hundred ducats to any councillor giving permission.[306] In 1506 the Senate passed yet another measure requiring officials abroad to obtain license from the Signoria to return home or else to stay at their posts. Priuli explains that they have been leaving inferiors to do their jobs, although they draw the salaries. The laws, he complains, are badly enforced because the patricians are so wrapped up in *broglio* that they were afraid to offend other patricians.[307]

Not only officials in Venice itself, therefore, but governors, ambassadors, military and naval officers, and other patricians sent abroad to serve the Republic were guilty of leaving their posts either unattended or in the hands of subordinates. Sometimes there were excuses, such as illness, which was all too common among the old men that Venice elected to important positions. Often, though, the negligent official was merely pursuing his own private interests, in Venice or abroad, or otherwise following his own desires.

Absenteeism from the councils was also a grave problem for the Republic. In 1345 the Great Council complained about patricians leaving the chamber, so they stationed an advocate of the Commune at the door to prevent it.[308] It is hardly surprising that in 1348, the year of the Black Death, there was at least a two-tiered problem of absenteeism: the Great Council was unable to function on account of poor attendance and the Forty was unable to carry out the task of electing additional members of the Great Council because of the same problem.[309] The plague was again at issue in September of 1478, when the Great Council anticipated difficulty in assembling a quorum of two hundred members to elect senators, so it required that on the appointed day all judges and officials, the members of the Forty, both civil and criminal, and also those who had been elected to the Senate must attend the Great Council under pain of loss of office.[310] In 1483 the Ten complained that when the *savi* or others received license to leave the Great Council, there was a great tumultuous rush about the unlocked doors by those trying to get out with them, and measures were taken to reduce the disorder.[311] In 1494 the Ten again returned to the problem of the great disorder created when the doors of the Great Council were opened to allow *savi* and others to depart. It was enacted that the Signoria should not have authority to allow them to leave once elections had begun.[312] Carlo Tron was convicted in 1499 of having a key made which would open the door of the Great Council, by the use of which he often left without license, setting a bad example. This was taken quite seriously, for he was sentenced to six months in prison, deprivation of the Great Council for a year, and loss of a minor office that he held.[313]

By 1500 it required 400 to have a quorum in the Great Council, and Sanuto tells of cases where business could not be conducted for want of attendance. On 28 November 1500 began the prosecution of Alvise Marcello, formerly captain of a fleet, for beheading a Venetian nobleman. There were not many present, says Sanuto, but 450, enough for a quorum.[314] On 2 December and 6 February, however, proceedings in the same case had to be suspended for want of a quorum.[315] The Great Council finally convicted Marcello on 11 February, but Priuli complains that only 682 nobles were present.[316] A year later Sanuto again reports poor attendance of 519 at the Great Council on account of heavy rain.[317] At this time the council had about 2500 members,[318] although many were always abroad on public or private business. Sanuto estimates a customary attendance of 1400 to 1500,[319] but the usual business of the council was the ever-popular *broglio*. Priuli, who did not share Sanuto's dedication to politics, boasted that he had not attended the Great Council for ten years.[320]

If one's individual vote counted for little in the Great Council, thus encouraging absenteeism, the Venetian government also had trouble concerning the attendance of the very powerful nobles of the Small Council. As early as 1229 the councillors' oath required that only in case of absolute necessity should they fail to respond to the bell summoning them to a meeting, and an early act also required that councillors should lose their office if absent for more than a month, later reduced to fifteen days.[321] They were not allowed to leave the island of Rialto, according to an act of 1275, without the permission of the doge and the other councillors, and at least four of them must remain to carry on business.[322] In 1309 the Great Council acted to enforce the presence of the councillors at various councils whose leadership they were supposed to provide.[323] It was noted in 1345 that their capitulary did not provide that they should be out of office for absence of fifteen days, whether consecutive or not, so that they could be absent for fourteen days, appear one day, be absent for another fourteen, and so on. The capitulary was changed to conform to those of other offices to avert this possibility.[324] A senatorial decree of 1375 points to the problem caused when councillors, in order to keep their number at the required four, failed to attend colleges to which they had been appointed. This worked to the special harm of prisoners, whose trials were delayed while they languished in their cells. It is therefore provided that in such cases heads of the Forty should replace councillors on the bench, while the latter attended their assigned colleges.[325] Councillors sometimes did have real enough difficulties with their busy schedules.

In 1488 occurred an instance in which two councillors were absent from the city and one of the remaining ones took ill, so that the Small Council was immobilized. Because of the importance of the case the head of the Ten for the week filled the vacant position.[326] As part of a major reform of the Quaranta criminale in 1491, the Ten decreed that if the absence of any councillor caused the Quaranta not to be in order, he should pay a fine of half a ducat.[327] Malipiero notes that a well-attended (1,670) Great Council was dismissed on 10 January 1496 because there were only three councillors.[328] Sanuto gives an example in 1499 of the hamstringing of the Senate, because only two councillors were present. Letters were read for about an hour, but no motions could be put. He mentions, by way of explanation, that the weather was bad.[329] A month later the College failed for want of the required four councillors.[330] In the following January the Great Council had to be dismissed two days in a row, to the great annoyance of many, because three councillors were ill. Sanuto points out that the fault lay in the election of so many old men.[331] On 28 June 1500 the Senate could only hear letters but not act, because there were only three councillors present. Again Sanuto blames the age of the councillors.[332] On 22 November the Great Council had to be dismissed for the same reason. Sanuto reports much complaining that in such weather the council should not be summoned, but, if it were, the councillors ought to come.[333] The Pien Collegio could not take up its important business on 4 November and 27 November 1503, lacking three councillors.[334] On 27 February it snowed, and only two councillors showed up for the Collegio.[335] One more appeared for a meeting of the Ten with the College and others in the afternoon, but, of course, nothing could be done.[336] So, there seems to have been a great deal of difficulty in assembling four councillors right around the year 1500. Granted that old age and illness are sometimes mentioned as the reason for the absence, still the Small Council was a crucial and highly placed body, essential to the functioning of the government. Bad weather is also mentioned several times. It is true that at this time severe storms may have made streets almost impassable and the use of gondolas difficult. Still, Venetian merchants probably made it to the Rialto under trying conditions, and we are here concerned with councillors, clearly among the crème de la crème of an elite allegedly possessing heroic virtues. If the councillors actually were so old and ill as to be quite unable to attend to their tasks, then we do have with Sanuto a valid criticism of the Venetian gerontocracy. One could, however, refuse office or resign for good cause. That they did not do so indicates either that they wished to serve the Republic in spite of their infirmities, or that they wished the honor of high office without assuming all its burdens, or a combination of both.

The Council of Forty was another of the most important constitutional organs, gradually specializing as the high court of Venice, controlling admission to the Great Council, and growing into three interrelated bodies, the Quaranta criminale, the Quaranta civile vecchia, and the Quaranta civile nuova. In 1307 the Great Council objected that the Forty (which was still a single entity) could not assemble a quorum of thirty for electing to the Great Council and other essential affairs, so it provided that when the Forty authorized its heads to summon it under penalty of ten *soldi,* that penalty should be paid by any member not present before the bell of the officials (half an hour before tierce) should stop ringing.[337] We have already mentioned the problem of deficient members in the Great Council during the Black Death of 1348, due, in part, to the inability of the Forty to muster its quorum of thirty for approving members of the Great Council, so the quorum was temporarily dropped to twenty-five.[338] In 1349 the Council of Forty itself, finding that attendance was poor when it was summoned for judicial business, tripled its daily salary and established a new fine for nonattendance.[339] The implication, of course, is that public service by the Venetian patriciate was largely mercenary. Ruggiero has discovered that the judicial sessions of the Forty had to be restructured in 1351 to prevent members from skipping the preliminary pleading.[340]

After a litany of acts declaring that "the Forty is assembled badly,"[341] the Great Council in 1390 ruled that members of the Forty who failed to attend for fifteen days, whether continuously or not, should be out of office.[342] An act of 1391 is introduced with a tribute to the importance of the Council of Forty, and goes on to restore the customary salary of its members, five ducats a month, which had been halved, presumably during the war. The act states that "on account of the smallness of the salary, the majority of the members of the council do not care to come at the sound of the bell."[343] To no avail. Again in 1393 the Great Council felt compelled to take action, because members of the Forty, "having no fear of the penalty, . . . do not care to come." So, new penalties were set, the fifteen-day rule was reiterated, and those who were expelled from office were to be fined 100 *l. parvorum,* in addition to other penalties.[344] Since the Forty often could not carry out its business because it lacked the required quorum, in 1403 its members were added to the list of those who were not allowed to attend during working hours the wedding celebrations held in the *campi,* unless these were their own marriages or those of a relative for whose sake they would have to leave the Great Council for conflict of interest.[345] In 1435 the Senate attempted to put an end to the bad practice of the heads of the Forty, who had been ordering nobles to excuse officials and members of the Forty for being absent.[346]

It seems that in the mid-fifteenth century the Quaranta criminale was unsalaried, for the Great Council noted in 1451 that for this reason nobles either refused or did not attend. It established a salary of four ducats a month and warned that for fifteen consecutive absences members should be expelled and fined as if they had refused.[347] An act of the Ten in 1455 takes note of the fact that salaries of the Forty were badly in arrears, and for that reason many members either did not come or did not remain at meetings. Or else they came only to vote, not hearing the case or the arguments of the parties. A certain case was decided with only nine ballots. To combat such dereliction, the Ten provided for the payment of the Forty, "so that they should be present to hear cases introduced before them and they should be able to render a good and well-considered judgment, as they are supposed to do." The act also provided that the Forty should be locked in their chamber.[348]

In 1491 the Ten issued a comprehensive act reforming the Quaranta criminale. It points out the importance to the state of equitable and expeditious justice and provides, among other things, that the Quaranta criminale should assemble at tierce and that the doors should be closed and locked during the entire meeting. It also declares that those absent for five days continuously or eight altogether should be dropped from the Forty and fined as if they had refused. Great delay, the act says, is caused when the Forty merely allow a case to be introduced, say that they do not want to hear any more, collect their pay for the day, and depart. Henceforth the advocates of the Commune must intervene in such a decision.[349]

The important Pien Collegio, which emerged in the late fourteenth and fifteenth centuries and gained control of the agenda of the Senate, also had trouble with attendance. It finally consisted of the Signoria plus three groups of *savi,* and there are many documents concerning absenteeism of the *savi* during the period when the Pien Collegio was slowly being formed.[350] Under the year 1499, when Sanuto himself was *savio agli ordini,* he mentions several times absenteeism from the Pien Collegio on account of bad weather. On 26 February there was a heavy snow, so more than half of the Collegio did not show up in the morning.[351] After dinner on the same day no one came.[352] On 8 March few appeared because of heavy rain.[353] On 13 December 1500, few of the Pien Collegio were present, perhaps because the Signoria was occupied with the reception of papal legate.[354] Again on 9 November 1502, few attended in the morning because of the rain, and none in the afternoon.[355] In 1503, on 17 November, the weather was awful after dinner, and only two of six councillors, two of six *savi del consiglio,* two of five *savi di terraferma,* and Sanuto alone among the five *savi agli ordini* appeared. There was important business at hand: among other things those present responded to a letter from the *provveditore* with the army by sending additional artillery.[356] Once more, in February of 1504, the Pien Collegio had only two councillors, two *savi del consiglio,* and three *di terraferma,* because of the great snow and the strange weather.[357]

Even the prominent politicians who held seats in the increasingly powerful and dreaded Council of Ten had a problem with absenteeism. We have a record of some absences from the Ten in 1331, although this is the only evidence found for the fourteenth century.[358] By 1412, though, the Ten was more frequently experiencing absenteeism. It required that those who were elected in place of the deficient must take their places within three days. Absence from meetings for three successive Wednesdays (the regular meeting day) should result in loss of office.[359] On 31 October 1426, there was a deficiency in the Council of Ten for carrying out some very important business.[360] Since the affairs of the Ten were so weighty, its capitulary provided that no member should receive permission to leave Venice without the consent of at least one of the heads of the Ten. The intention was that no more than one member should receive such license at a time, but sometimes two or three of the heads would grant permission, not knowing that their colleagues had done so. In 1427, therefore, the requirement was raised, so that license to be out of town had to be given by at least two of the heads.[361] A measure moved in the Ten in 1428 declared that members of the Ten who were absent were not recorded as they should be, but the effort to cause them to be recorded was defeated.[362] An attempt on 14 April 1434 to fine members of the Ten or advocates of the Commune who left the council during a sitting apparently failed due to the fact that only seven of the seventeen voting members were present, but a week later a similar act passed.[363] None of the Ten or the Zonta were allowed to leave town without license of the council under penalty of ten pounds, according to an act of 1447. Those summoned to meetings must come under the same penalty.[364] The rule that a member might not miss three consecutive Wednesdays was mentioned again in 1460, when Antonio Venier was given an extension in order to look to a lawsuit in which he was involved, but only because the next Wednesday would be Christmas Eve and the following one St. Silvester's Day, and the Council would not be meeting in any case.[365]

The Ten took action in 1462 against violators of the regulation that no member of the Ten should go abroad without the consent of at least two of the three heads. Not only members, but even the heads themselves, had been leaving the city at their pleasure. In the future no head was to leave, and members could do so only with the required license under penalty of exclusion from the Ten and the Senate for a year.[366]

The plague of 1485 made it difficult to assemble enough members of the Council of Ten. Measures were taken to fill the gaps of the dead and the ill and members were not allowed to go abroad without license of at least two-thirds of the whole council.[367] The council was embarrassed in 1489 by its inability because of unexcused absenteeism to deal with the case of Rizio Marino. It reaffirmed the fines for absence and, in addition, those on account of whose absence the council was unable to function should pay a ducat.[368]

The powerful Senate, when fully developed, consisted of about 300 members, some 230 with the right to vote. They included practically everyone of political importance. The number actually voting, according to Lane, averaged about 180, which, considering that many of these nobles had other governmental obligations, would not be bad.[369] Yet we possess a rather large amount of evidence concerning absenteeism.

Besta gives us the earliest information on the subject. The Great Council in 1290 imposed a fine of one *grosso* upon any senator who was not present at the last bell, reaffirming and modifying the act over the next few years.[370] In July of 1307 the galleys could not sail promptly because absenteeism prevented the Senate from functioning, so the Great Council raised the fine for nonattendance to two *grossi* when the Senate was summoned for expediting the galleys.[371] By 1316 there was already a rather confusing body of legislation on absence from the Senate, so the Great Council, in the interest of clarity and certainty, abrogated the previous laws, and once again affirmed the fine of one *grosso*. This act, too, was subsequently modified and refined.[372] Still, in June of 1341 the Senate was so badly attended that the business concerning Zara was postponed for a week. Any members who missed the coming session were to pay twenty *soldi*.[373]

In the decade from 1365 to 1374 there were frequent acts in the Senate reflecting the inability to muster a quorum of eighty, seventy, or even sixty for such important business as electing patrons of galleys or licensing them to depart, so exceptions were made to the regulations.[374] We know from a document of 1376 that members of the Zonta of the Senate (the number added to the basic sixty senators and the Quaranta) were removed from office if they failed to appear for a month, which seems remarkably liberal, considering the problem that we have seen.[375] In 1381 the Great Council again complained of the absences of senators and of the Zonta. Those who were not present when the bell stopped would be fined 10 s. and after eight such absences would be expelled from the council.[376] From 1382 to 1392 there is another flurry of acts making exceptions to the required quorum so that the galleys could sail.[377] The laws requiring a quorum to deal with the fleets and to elect patrons seem to have been almost as much honored in the breach as in the observance.

The Senate enjoined the officials of old and new accounts in 1402 to investigate certain exchanges made in Constantinople by the galleys under the captaincy of Niccolò Capello, reporting on the next day to the Senate, at least eighty members being present. It is no great surprise that eighty were not present, but they proceeded anyway.[378] In 1405 the Great Council declined to allow the Senate to proceed with a scrutiny for an advocate of the Commune in spite of the want of a quorum of seventy. Perhaps the Great Council was less lenient with the foibles of the senators than was the Senate itself.[379] When the Senate could not conduct its business for want of a quorum in 1409, those present postponed the agenda and declared a fine of one hundred *soldi* for those who would not attend "for the consideration of others who in the future do not want to come to this council."[380] In the same year the Senate failed to muster the required one hundred members for making the commission of ambassadors to Friuli, so it postponed the meeting, imposing a five-*lire* fine for nonattendance.[381]

There was another general complaint about poor attendance at the Senate in 1411, and it was provided that there should be a quorum of seventy for conducting any business at all.[382] Governors assigned beyond the Gulf of Quarnero could not have their terms for departure for their posts extended beyond two months without the consent of the Senate, at least eighty members being present. The Senate noted in 1412, however, that "rarely" were eighty members assembled on account of various public affairs. The law was therefore changed to specify seventy.[383] The plague drove many nobles out of town in 1416, so that the Senate could not assemble the required seventy members. The number required to do business was therefore lowered to sixty from 28 June to 29 September.[384] With only fifty-six present the Senate went ahead with the election of an advocate in 1427.[385] This document emphasizes one of the interesting aspects of Venetian government. The law of 1411 required that the Senate "non intelligatur tote congregatum, nec in ordine, nec in ipso possit aliquid tractatur" unless there was a quorum of seventy. Yet with only fifty-six present the law was suspended and the Senate proceeded to act as if a quorum were present. This is by no means a unique instance. Given the Venetian propensity for passing what amounted to merely hortatory legislation, the government probably could not have functioned at all without benign neglect of a good deal of it, but this neglect did entail a depreciation of the seriousness of law.

The Senate charged in 1440 that many of its members came at the summons and stood outside the doors of the chamber or just inside to listen to the reading of the letters (knowledge of which could be profitable at Rialto). When the reading of the letters was concluded they left without license. In an effort to halt this abuse the Senate decreed that nobody should stand outside the doors to hear letters or leave the chamber without license under penalty of three hundred *lire* and deprivation of the Senate for a year.[386] In 1478 the Great Council decisively defeated a measure to reduce the Senate's quorum temporarily to sixty on account of the plague. Instead it reaffirmed, since the size of the Senate was greater than ever, that seventy must be present. The law concerning the quorum was to be read every time the Senate met, and anyone who missed three meetings was to be out of the Senate.[387] In 1484 in a letter from Padua, Ermolao Barbaro confesses that he has attended the Senate only twice since his election, and the first time, the day on which he was admitted, he was late. He has been at Padua because of fear of the plague.[388] The Council of Ten in 1499 complained again of the senators who sneaked out of the chamber when the doors were opened for the doge to go in or out or for officials or magistrates who had license to come or go on account of their duties.[389] In connection with a prohibition against senators leaving the chamber, Maranini notes that the government not only wanted to maintain adequate numbers, but to prevent senators from dodging responsibility on delicate issues.[390] Although the event occurred in 1515, a few years after the end of our period, it is worth reporting Sanuto's remark that scarcely any senators appeared in their hall on the morning following an especially spectacular dramatic performance at ca' Pesaro.[391]

The excuse that senators were burdened with other and conflicting public responsibilities was a legitimate one, and the charge of civic irresponsibility should be tempered by this realization. The Senate, after all, was the basis for that very elite group which actually controlled the state, and, except for the Forty, did not consist of poor patricians seeking sinecures. The Forty, however, was an infamous refuge of salary-grubbing nobles. As was often the case in Venice, too much responsibility was reserved for too small an elite, while too many poor nobles sought salaries and shirked responsibilities.

An act of 1309 concerning the Council of Thirty-five is of considerable interest. It required a quorum of twenty-two, which was lacking, so the absentees were sent for in Rialto, in order that the council could proceed with a nomination. The delinquents replied that they did not want to come! The Great Council thereupon provided that the Council of Thirty-five could proceed with the number on hand.[392]

TARDINESS

Closely related to absenteeism, and also reflecting a lack of concern for duties, was tardiness. As early as 1261 the Great Council provided that when there was a meeting for elections and the bell ceased to ring the doors should be closed and no one should be admitted except officials of the palace.[393] An act of 1275 provided for the ringing of a bell, in the same measure as the *campana officialium* in the morning, immediately after the ninth hour. Before this bell finished ringing all the officials of Rialto were to be in their offices or lose their salary for the day and pay a fine of one *grosso*.[394]

By 1329, the members of the Ten had gotten into the habit of wandering about the palace after their appointed meeting time, so it was required under penalty that they be in their chamber before the bell for the ninth hour stopped ringing.[395] A law of 1374 points out that officials frequently were not present at the appointed time, and provides for notaries dispatched by the officials of the night and the Cinque alla pace to check them.[396] Two years later they returned to having an official's colleagues report his tardiness, because the law of 1374 "is not observed."[397] By 1381 the Senate was having trouble assembling on time. If members were not in the chamber when the bell stopped ringing, it should be noted, and eight such notices should result in removal from the Senate. The tardy should also pay a fine.[398] The Great Council complained in 1410 of the delays to public business caused by the tardiness of the councillors. They should be checked in the morning and in the afternoon, and, if they should be tardy or absent eight times, besides the usual fine, they should be out of office and fined 200 *l.*[399] The Ten was critical of itself in 1479, insisting that its members should be in place when the bell for their assembling stopped ringing, so that the doors could be closed.[400] The Senate decreed in 1483 that once the bell stopped ringing, its doors should be closed and locked, just as were the doors of the Great Council and the Ten.[401] On 23 July 1485, the Senate suspended this law through the end of October, because the majority of the Senate had left Venice for the summer on account of the inclemency of the air, and from Murano, Torcello, or the countryside they had trouble arriving on time. The doors, therefore, should not be closed and locked when the bell stopped, but rather at the discretion of the Signoria.[402]

There was also a very different kind of tardiness involving the failure of those elected for tasks abroad to depart for their posts expeditiously. This problem too plagued Venice from the time of the earliest registers of the Great Council in the thirteenth century throughout the medieval period and undoubtedly for the rest of the history of the Republic. In 1269 the Great Council imposed upon ambassadors and other officials who did not undertake their embassies or other missions when ordered to do so by the doge the same penalties they would have suffered if they had refused.[403] We do not hear more of this problem until 1374, but then it is serious. The majority of elected governors, according to the act, do not depart when they should, having discovered various ways and means of delaying. This causes great hardship, says the act, for the incumbent governors at the end of their terms sell their horses and other impedimenta, they dismiss their servants, and so the governorships are left ill provided. It also results in the incumbents being forced to remain at their posts, many times, for example, for eighteen months instead of the assigned year. Henceforth no more than eight days may be granted by way of extensions.[404] We have an example of delay from 1427, when Geronimo da Canal, elected ambassador to Mantua, kept saying daily that he was leaving, but did not go, while his unfortunate predecessor had to remain at his post. The Senate required him to leave by the next Sunday under penalty of two hundred ducats.[405] The Great Council complained in 1455 of those who had accepted and then did not actually go for one or two years, and it returned to the problem again and again.[406]

EVASION OF MILITARY RESPONSIBILITY[407]

For Molmenti, Lepanto was "brilliant proof that the Venetian patrician was ready at a moment's notice to abandon the pleasures of the city for the rude experiences of war."[408] In early centuries, it is true, the Venetians had been as warlike, for example, as the northern knights on the Fourth Crusade, whom they matched, at least, in valor and martial achievement.[409] Their military ardor, however, had faded with time. Philippe de Commynes marvels at the failure of the nobles to take an active part in the wars on the mainland at the end of the fifteenth century.[410] After the War of the League of Cambrai one of the *savi agli ordini* assigned to attend the Turkish ambassador informed the guest that the Venetians had come through a war against the combined kings of Europe without the loss of a single Venetian life. "Everything has been done with money and with the death of foreign soldiers."[411] Priuli lashed out against his fellow nobles:

> The Venetian prince and the fathers wish to stay at home, at ease and comfortable, and to sleep in their own beds, and to have vic-

tory, and this is difficult and almost impossible. And these Venetian lords excused themselves on account of not being accustomed to military activity and on account of this not being their practice and exercise. If they had gone to the army they would have caused more confusion rather than accomplishing anything, because, being of little heart and soul, they would have been the first to flee and put the whole army in confusion. . . . Truly, if the Venetian fathers wish to maintain and conserve their state in Italy, it will be necessary that the Venetian nobles—and I mean the *primi*—must take up the exercise and craft of arms and undertake military exercises, and do their deeds for themselves, as all the other lords of the world do, in order not to entrust themselves to aliens and foreigners. Otherwise they cannot conserve their state in Italy.[412]

Machiavelli noted with disapproval how the Venetians lost the *terraferma* in spite of a full treasury, because not gold, as common opinion has it, is the nerve of war, but rather good soldiers.[413]

One must beware, of course, of the records of trials of Venetian noblemen for losing battles. Venice tried and convicted some of her greatest heroes. Politics was nasty, and a military or naval defeat offered an opening to the political enemies of the vanquished commanders. Perhaps this is inevitable in a system in which there is no distinction between the politicians and the military leaders. With this word of caution, however, such records may still be useful to us.

The famous Vettor Pisani was one commander who suffered conviction and imprisonment for losing a battle. As a subordinate commander he had escaped punishment when his uncle, Niccolò Pisani, the captain-general, and some of Vettor's fellow *sopracomiti* were convicted for the defeat at Porto Longo in 1354.[414] In the War of Chioggia (1378–81), Vettor Pisani had risen to captain-general of the sea. Goaded by subordinates to take up a challenge that he preferred to decline and deceived as to the numbers of the Genoese fleet, he attacked vigorously near Pola, was overwhelmed when hidden Genoese galleys were thrown into the fray, and finally fled with a few galleys. He was charged with leading his fleet into battle in a disorderly fashion and with leaving the battle before it was ended, and he was found guilty on both counts, although a case for mitigating circumstances could certainly be made. The state's attorneys demanded capital punishment, which was fixed by law for leaving the battle. Although this was almost certainly a political trial, Pisani had, strictly speaking, violated the law. Under a compromise he was sentenced to five years' exclusion from governorships, offices, and councils and six months' imprisonment.[415] There were many trials at the end of the war. A captain named Marco Giustinian was sentenced to five years in prison and permanent loss of offices for abandoning his fortress without a fight. The severity of the punishment suggests that this may have been a true case of cowardice.[416] A commander of small craft before Chioggia, Giovanni Civran, was sentenced to six months' imprisonment, perpetual exclusion from all commands, and ten years' loss of all councils and offices. The offense is not specified, but, since capital punishment was proposed, it is likely that he left the scene of battle.[417] Andreolo Polani, who had been captain in the tower of Livenza, had abandoned it in a cowardly fashion, so that it fell into the hands of the enemy. He was sentenced to five years in prison and permanent ineligibility for all commands and positions in the empire.[418] The *sopracomiti,* Vittorio Duodo and Bertuccio Civran, who served in the fleet of the Gulf under Andrea Mocenigo, were convicted in 1430 of refusing the captain's order to engage the enemy at Gallipoli in an effort to take or burn his ships. Duodo escaped the death sentence, but received a year in prison, a fine of 500 *l.,* and permanent exclusion from the command of galleys. Civran got only six months in prison and a 500 *l.* fine.[419]

In 1432 the commanders of a Venetian fleet directed against the Genoese at Chios were arrested for their disorderly departure from the siege of the town. The merchant fleets of the previous fall had been impressed for duty. When the siege proved harder than anticipated, the commanders of the merchant galleys and the cogs began to grouse about the time lost from commerce, and when one high-ranking officer was killed and another wounded the Venetians lifted the siege and the merchant vessels went about their business.[420]

In 1483 Venice lost the town of Asola to the forces of the duke of Mantua. The patrician provisor, Niccolò Querini, was held responsible. He had governed badly, and by his will and consent, according to the Ten, the town passed into enemy hands. When he could have defended the very strong fortress, he abandoned it most wickedly and most vilely. The Ten exiled him to Crete for life.[421]

In the famous battles along the western coast of the Morea in August of 1499, while it is not absolutely transparent where blame should be placed, it is clear that the leadership became demoralized, that the commander did not adequately support his lieutenants, and that they did not obey him. The captain-general, Antonio Grimani (elected doge twenty-one years later), was not a traitor and perhaps was not a coward, but a leader must be judged by his ability to lead successfully, and in this Grimani certainly failed. The Turkish fleet was attempting to join the Turkish army in seizing Lepanto. Grimani first engaged it at

Porto Longo near Modone on 12 August. The two largest Venetian ships under Alban d'Armer and the newly arrived and very popular Andrea Loredan engaged the largest Turkish ship, which blew up, and all three burned. D'Armer was killed and Loredan, according to Priuli, faced with the choice of burning to death or falling into the hands of the enemy, raised the banner of St. Mark above his head, and, declaiming that he had been born and raised under it and now wished to die under it, marched into the flames. The Turks sent brigantines to pick up their survivors who had thrown themselves into the sea, but Grimani made no move to save d'Armer, Loredan (whom he had accused of disobedience to orders in 1494),[422] or the many Venetians who had jumped overboard. He had, however, ordered two lieutenants to attack, but both veered off to port and took to the sea—an unpleasant refrain, *prexenno la volta de mar,* haunting the whole series of engagements. Priuli excoriates them as cowards, not worthy to be called men. Grimani then lost heart, and gave up for the time being. He and his subordinates were blamed in Venice. He was even accused of having allowed Loredan to perish through jealousy. Perhaps Grimani did not attack because his plan of battle, which was not unreasonable, deprived him of the advantage—if it be such—of being in the forefront. Priuli, one of whose favorite themes is the unwillingness of the nobles to displease one another on account of *broglio,* says that this is the reason he failed to discipline his subordinates. Near Prote eight days later Andrea Basadonna, ordered by Grimani to attack with five galleys, lost courage once he got within range of the bombards, and he also took *la volta del mar.* He also went unpunished, although his *armiraio,* a commoner without vote in the Great Council, was replaced. Two days after that the captain-general and his *sopracomiti* failed to take advantage of another opportunity to destroy the Turkish fleet near Chiarenza, because they lacked courage, according to Priuli and Malipiero. Once more, on 25 August, off Akra Papas at the mouth of the Gulf of Patra, Grimani failed to stop the Turks. The galley commanders, save Marcantonio Contarini, refused to go to the aid of Lepanto, and so the besieged city fell. In the series of fights many nobles had conducted themselves with patriotism and honor, but the campaign was an absolute shambles. Grimani felt that he could do nothing because his lieutenants were cowardly; they had no heart for taking risks, perhaps because they remembered Grimani's failure to aid d'Armer and Loredan and their companions on the first day of the battle. Grimani was relieved of command and banished and Alvise Marcello, one of the worst offenders among the lieutenants, was sentenced to life imprisonment. Clearly the trial of Grimani before the Great Council had political and clannish aspects. Grimani's enemies were led by an ambitious advocate of the Commune, Niccolò Michiel, by his old rival Filippo Tron, and by Leonardo Loredan and his allies, embittered by the captain-general's abandonment of Andrea. Michiel had his eye on Grimani's procurator-ship of San Marco, and, as a reward for his very aggressive handling of the trial, he gained it. Ester Zille finds behind the personal ambitions and animosities the opposition of a party of *giovani*. Whatever Grimani's responsibility, the Venetian patriciate certainly had not covered itself with glory at the loss of Lepanto. It had displayed rivalry, jealousy, disobedience to commands, and lack of aggressiveness. Grimani's successor in the command peremptorily cut off the heads of delinquent subordinates.[423] The provisor of Lepanto, Giovanni Moro, also was convicted for handing the town over to the Turks.[424] The new captain-general also sentenced his *provveditore,* Geronimo Contarini, to two years' deprivation of that office and of captaincies and to remaining inside the Gulf during that time. The *provveditore* had failed to follow the flagship inside the Gulf of Prevesa, thinking it too dangerous, but instead withdrew to Corfu pretending illness.[425]

Once again it must be stressed that we cannot rely upon every one of the allegations of cowardice against unsuccessful commanders.[426] Especially where the penalties were relatively light we may suspect political harassment. Some cases, however, appear to be bona fide examples of dereliction of duty. And, whether the captain-general or his lieutenants were more responsible, the naval engagements leading to the loss of Lepanto in 1499 were a disgrace.

EVASION OF TAXES

Since the patricians monopolized power and exploited their control of the state to their own advantage, it was appropriate that they should pay for it, as Kretschmayr put it, "mit Gut und Blut."[427] So the myth of Venice would have it, at any rate. In a pinch it would even have been pragmatic, as Doge Leonardo Loredan declared in urging the patricians to pay their taxes in preparation for the war against the League of Cambrai: "[I]f we lose, we will lose a fine state; there will be no more Great Council . . ."[428]

In fact, like any elite, the patricians were not at all eager to levy taxes which would weigh heavily upon themselves.[429] Until the mid-fifteenth century the government subsisted basically upon indirect taxes, whose burden fell upon consumers and upon commerce.[430] These revenues would not suffice to confront the financial needs of major wars, when the Republic supplemented its income with loans, which very soon became forced loans. These bore interest and could be bought and sold on a more or less freely fluctuating market.[431] The wealthy patricians, who controlled the government, only consented to put their substance at the disposal of the state when the situation was desperate.[432] Moreover, for a long period the bonds of the Monte vecchio were not a bad investment, especially for those with sufficient money to move in and out of the market.[433] As the prices of bonds dropped, of course, real interest rose. Even considering the forced loan as a contribution, not as an investment, the burden was not heavy until the War of Chioggia. The rate in the mid-fourteenth century was not by our standards high, 24 percent on assessed wealth but assessment was at only one-third of real value, and considerable wealth probably escaped assessment. Moreover, the price of bonds in the same period rarely fell below eighty and often rose above ninety, so that the major part of one's contribution could be recovered at will.[434] Although the Monte vecchio revived after the threat caused by the costs of the War of Chioggia, the expenses of the Lombard and Turkish wars of the fifteenth century were too much for it to bear, and by 1474 the bonds paid interest irregularly at 1 percent and had fallen to thirteen. Only as this collapse of the Monte vecchio was occurring did the patrician class consent to direct taxation.[435] It is not difficult to perceive that the system rested on the backs of the middling and the poor.[436] Our concern here, however, is not with the equity of the Venetian system of collecting revenues, but rather with patricians evasion of their responsibilities under that system.

Indirect taxes included those upon wine, various kinds of food, salt, and the like, as well as customs duties upon exports and imports. In 1364 the Great Council objected that many nobles had not bothered to pay the *denarios duodenarum,* which set a bad example for others. They were to pay what they owed within the next eight days. If they did not they might not attend the Great Council or hold any office.[437] The Senate in 1412 decreed that Daniele Loredan, who had been consul in Tana, must pay the *cottimo* upon his own merchandise. He should not have been engaged in commerce at all, but he had done it from the beginning to the end of his office, and he must therefore pay the taxes.[438] The Senate objected in 1419 that governors and officials on the mainland at the end of their terms were bringing home large quantities of wine, which they asked the officials of the wine tax to allow them to take with their baggage directly to their homes. Then the officials could come there later to appraise it, a practice which was open to abuse. The officials were not to allow this, but to appraise the wine at the mooring place where this was customary.[439]

We have notice in 1455 of an unpleasant patrician, Marino Pisani, who was approached by the guards of the *tavola di uscita* while he was returning in his bark from the Flanders galleys. They wanted to examine the bark, obviously suspecting him of evading taxes. He struck them. The Senate voted to convict, but then seems to have been unable to agree upon how many months he should be imprisoned.[440] In 1480 a commander of a ship, Troilo Malipiero, was convicted along with his non-noble patron for using violence against officials who were looking for contraband. The patron and the captain were, in fact, trying to get away with exporting some cloth without paying the tax, and were caught by the employees of the *tavola di uscita*. Malipiero received a sentence of three months in prison and three years' deprivation of captaincies.[441]

The Ten took up in 1484 the problem of nobles and *cittadini* making pleas for immunity from the tax on wine. Provisors had been elected to investigate the poor state of the tax, which was very important, and they found that it was daily less and less enforced. The responsible officials saw no profit in fulfilling their duties and perceived danger to themselves, so they were lax. Henceforth any nobles who were to ask one of these officials to free contraband should be deprived of the Great Council for a year and fined 200 *l. parvorum*.[442] Giovanni Pasqualigo, Francesco Alberti, and Alvise Contarini were convicted by the Ten in 1485 of violating the law of 1484 on the wine tax. They had used insolent and threatening words toward the official, so they suffered an additional fine of 300 *l. parvorum*. This case offers some indication of why officials feared for their lives.[443] In 1500 Geronimo Badoari was found guilty, not only of smuggling wine, but of attacking the officials of the wine tax with a body of armed men. The Ten sentenced him to exile for ten years in Capodistria, with loss of his right hand and an eye if he violated it.[444] One of the many offenses for which Doge Agostino Barbarigo was charged and found guilty was large-scale evasion of indirect taxes.[445]

Evidence on the evasion of forced loans and direct taxes by nobles tends to be late, as already suggested, because the loans were not generally burdensome until the War of Chioggia and because real direct taxes, without claim to repayment, did not exist until the last decades of our period. In 1420 the Senate objected that many citizens, including "many who were powerful and able to lend considerable sums," had failed to turn over to the *savi* responsible for drawing up the assessments of forced loans their estimates of their financial worth. (The *imprestiti* were based on self-assessments.)[446] Again a few weeks later the

Great Council was complaining of those nobles who did not take up the forced loans assigned to them. They should be deprived of the Great Council and all offices.[447]

Another source of revenue was introduced by the Senate in 1434, a tax upon public salaries. The reasoning was that holding public office was a benefit conferred by the state, which, in the state's hour of need, might reasonably be subject to a special tax. As we have seen, the whole system of public employment partook of the nature of a welfare program and many offices were sinecures or near sinecures, so there was a certain logic to this rationale. The initial tax was 10 percent on salaries below four hundred ducats a year and 15 percent on those above four hundred ducats.[448] In November, however, the rates were raised to 30 percent and 40 percent in order to reduce the burden on the loan office.[449]

All this time there had been no general direct tax, although by mid-fifteenth century the value of the bonds was falling seriously. In 1463 Venice finally introduced a *decima* based, not on the self-assessment typical of the forced loans, but upon a relatively sophisticated *catasto* with appraisals made by public officials. There was no expectation that these levies would be repaid.[450] In 1466 the Senate had to take direct action against those who did not pay the tenths. If they did not pay within one week, in addition to monetary penalties, their names were to be read in the Great Council. If they had any office, they were to lose it, and they had to pay the fine, as if they had refused. Until they paid they could not belong to the Great Council or any other council or hold any office.[451] The Senate then recalled that such a penalty was not imposed upon those who owed the tax on public salaries, which was inequitable, since those who had to pay from their own funds were penalized, while those who paid from public funds were not. Much money was owed by the latter group. They were therefore subjected to the same penalties as those who failed to pay the tenths.[452] Sanuto tells us that in 1498 the debt owed by those who had to pay the 30 percent or the 40 percent on public salaries amounted to sixty thousand ducats. The Ten ruled that they should be expelled from office if they did not pay.[453]

In the crisis of 1499, when the Turkish war was at a high pitch, the doge urged everyone to pay the tenths, warning them of the danger of losing the state, of the termination of all those offices and governor-ships which they enjoyed. The government had been able to collect only 64 *l. di grossi* out of 300,000 ducats owed. Obviously, the effort to collect was not doing well.[454] In 1500, debtors on a list of those who had not paid forced loans or taxes were threatened with expulsion.[455] A few days later the Senate actually began to expel senators. Alvise Contarini was expelled, but no one else, because the others either paid or offered acceptable excuses.[456] It is interesting that many somehow found the money when the threat of expulsion became sufficiently real.

Venetian nobles were clearly not anxious to impose taxes upon themselves, coming around very slowly to a direct tax that would bear heavily upon the rich. Not all nobles were rich, of course, but there was a greater proportion of rich nobles than rich commoners, and those who controlled the state were among the wealthy. Nor were nobles eager to pay what had been imposed. There is nothing unique, of course, in dodging taxes. There is ample evidence that rich *cittadini* cheated as much as did the nobles, and poor commoners were no doubt not averse to a bit of smuggling when they had the chance. Florentine businessmen also evaded their taxes, even the *pater patriae* Cosimo de' Medici himself.[457] The rich and powerful elite of Arras cheated fantastically.[458] So do modern Italians, and Americans have also been known to dodge taxes. Venetian patricians were not extraordinarily villainous. The very point of the chapter and the book, indeed, is that the Venetian patriciate was not extraordinary either in its virtues or in its shortcomings.

CONCERNING my earlier, briefer and more limited treatment of refusal and evasion of office,[459] James Bruce Ross wrote: "[H]is emphasis on 'civic irresponsibility' of the patriciate does not seem entirely valid for the early sixteenth century in view of Contarini's persistent efforts after 1515 to secure diplomatic office, not to evade it."[460] Not all nobles, of course, sought to escape their responsibilities. My argument actually was rather carefully qualified:

Enthusiasts for medieval Venetian government have propagated a myth of the patriotic and selfless service of the Venetian nobility, especially as ambassadors. The acts discussed here—as well as an appreciation of human nature as it seems to me—should dispel such fictions. To be sure, when the public stakes are high enough (and sufficiently apparent) Venetian noblemen, and social beings generally, are capable of great self-sacrifice. For the general run of relatively humdrum affairs, however, Venetian noblemen sought desperately to avoid those offices to which a large personal expense was attached, as they sought those (that of the *baiulo* of Constantinople, for example) from which a profit could be made. Even costly offices might be sought, of course, for special motives, as by

wealthy younger men seeking political advancement, or by excep-
tionally public-minded men or for exceptional reasons of state, but
by and large Venetian noblemen went to fantastic lengths to avoid
election to them.[461]

Professor Ross's evaluation of Gasparo Contarini as a worthy gentleman and patriot seems amply justified. He was also a patrician of great
rank, wealth, and ability who might aspire to the highest levels of
public service. He was not unique among the Venetian nobility in his
desire to undertake onerous and expensive offices. But he also was not
typical of the patriciate, who were a much more varied lot than they
have appeared to be.

The thesis presented previously and in this chapter is that *many* nobles
(occasionally the documents say "a majority") *very often* display a remarkable reluctance to accept conscientiously their public responsibilities. Occasionally, like Contarini's friends, they repudiated public service in favor of a religious calling, as Contarini himself, in a sense, was
also eventually to do. More commonly the nobles feared the physical
hazards and hardships of military duty and foreign missions. They also
absented themselves from offices and councils on account of rain or
snow, although it may be deemed doubtful whether Venetian merchants neglected their affairs for similar reasons. By far the most common reason for neglect of civic duties, in fact, was the desire to be
about one's own profitable business, as well as the dread of the very
high out-of-pocket costs of some offices to the individual. Venetian
nobles were not eager to sacrifice their wealth on the altar of St. Mark.
So, in far too many cases, as the documents plainly declare, many
nobles ducked and dodged and squirmed out of their responsibilities in
a manner totally inconsistent with the well-known myth of their singular patriotism.

VI

Corruption

VARIOUS SOURCES, from Boccaccio to the diaries of Malipiero, Priuli, and Sanuto, and not least the legislation and the criminal cases found in the archives, reveal the shady side of Venetian life at all levels.[1] Our concern, however, is not with the 11,654 whores in the city in 1509,[2] the irregular life of the cloistered, or the misdeeds of merchants, but only with those forms of patrician corruption pertaining to civic life. Recent authors have called attention to political corruption among the nobles, although none has approached it as broadly and deeply or within the framework of civic irresponsibility as is attempted here.[3] Even older apologists for the patriciate, like Maranini, saw evidence of evils, but chose to minimize or justify it.[4]

There were, in fact, many and heavy pressures upon the noble office-holder from family, friends, and those with common economic or political interests. Yielding to these pressures was a daily occurrence, and, since so many nobles were involved, it was difficult to crack down on any but the worst offenders. Gaetano Cozzi reminds us of the Venetian maxim, "The wolf does not eat the meat of the wolf."[5]

Of course, the patrician government passed many laws against corruption (so many that they prove that it was a continuing problem), and they did have a fairly sophisticated device for dealing with it in the syndics, who served as a check upon provincial officials. The clamor of the subjects of the newly conquered empire on *terraferma* in 1410 for the appointment of *syndici* like those of the maritime empire suggests that the provincials were already being squeezed by grasping officials, but it also indicates some confidence in the efficacy of the syndics in bringing the culprits to justice.[6] Gasparo Contarini also thought highly of the Venetian practice of condemning a noble who defrauded the Commune to having his offense read annually in the Great Council before his peers.[7]

Unfortunately, much of the evidence of corruption simply does not reveal its nature. A typical charge is brought against a nobleman "formerly *podestà* and captain of Capodistria on account of the things committed by him in the said governorship against the honor of the Signoria." He is convicted, and then the Senate proceeds to vote on his punishment, but nowhere are we told what were his offenses.[8] Another typical document tantalizingly states that a Venetian official "appears to have contravened his commissions *in octo capitulis,*" but does not elucidate.[9] In many other documents, however, we can find enough specific information to enable us to identify the misdeed as embezzlement, bribery, obstruction of justice, or other corrupt practice.

The majority of the offenses were of a financial character. Labalme, following Horatio Brown, believes that signs of corruption began to appear after the aristocracy succeeded in excluding the people from government and restricting the power of the doge, assuring itself of a political monopoly. Since new men no longer rose to the ruling class through wealth and nobles who became poor did not fall from it there arose a wide split within the patriciate itself between the rich and the paupers. The former, not surprisingly, took advantage of their position to enrich themselves further.[10] The latter, equally predictably, welcomed the temptation to escape misery and hunger at the expense of the Republic or the subjects under their jurisdiction.[11] Those of us adhering to a darker view of human nature are more inclined to find corruption a normal state of affairs than to seek its origins; the venality of the Venetian patriciate probably did not begin in 1297–98 (or the early decades of the fourteenth century), although documentation on the subject, as on almost every other, is scarce before the Serrata. It is certainly plausible, however, that the closed character of the nobility and the resulting disparity of wealth within it stimulated political corruption. So, undoubtedly, did the inequalities of remuneration for salaried jobs and the lack of salaries for some positions, plus the fact that the payment of many officials came from the people they administered.[12] Thus, many patrician officials, subject to avarice, plundered the Republic and its subjects.[13]

Once more let it be emphasized that the Venetian patriciate was not unique in its corruption. Lestocquoy recounts the misdeeds of his bourgeois dynasts of Arras, and Gene Brucker reminds us of the corruption of the patrician regime in Florence in the late fourteenth and early fifteenth centuries.[14] Closer to our subject, Cracco tells how the rich and powerful within the Venetian church were accused of stealing from the poor.[15] If the Venetian patriciate was not unique in its corruption, however, it also was not really distinguished for its probity.

EMBEZZLEMENT

The most common form of corruption, at least as reflected in the number of documents dealing with it, was the appropriation of public wealth to private use: a large number of the allegedly self-sacrificing patriciate had their hands badly soiled with ill-gotten public treasure. That is why the noble who nominated a successful candidate was compelled to become his guarantor.[16] Some positions, such as patron of the Arsenal, offered marvelous opportunities for enriching oneself.[17]

As in other chapters, we are not entirely lacking evidence somewhat earlier than the Serrata and the subsequent closing of the patriciate. A law of 1265 on stealing from the Commune remained basic for almost a century, until 1359. Any governor, ambassador, captain, or other official convicted of having stolen or obtained the goods of the Commune contrary to his commission or capitulary, if the amount was above 50 *l.* for those serving abroad or 25 *l.* for those at home, should pay the Republic as much as had been taken and as much more as a fine. Those who wrongfully gave goods of the Commune to others were merely to repay without additional penalty. The penalties seem light, as they should be, to the extent that we are dealing with differences of opinion over expenses. The law also applies, however, to outright stealing of public funds, which would seem to be much more serious.[18] An act of 1273 requires that all officials must report their colleagues if they know them to be receiving, accepting, or giving anything in violation of their capitularies.[19] The Republic took precautions in 1278 against abuses in the mint, providing that when the *massari* turned over silver to the minters, that *massaro* who was entitled to a fifteenth should not weigh the silver, but his colleague should, in the presence of the minter and one or two of the boys. He should also record the weight and cause his scribe to record it, so that there should be no question about it.[20] In 1293 all officials of the mint were prohibited from buying slag left from the process, presumably through fear that they would wrongfully obtain gold or silver belonging to the government.[21]

Baiamonte Tiepolo, ten years before the uprising of 1310 which bears his name, was convicted of misappropriating 2,222 *yperperi* while he was castellan of Modone and Corone. He had felt justified in using the money to maintain an establishment worthy of the grandson of Lorenzo and the son of Giacomo Tiepolo, and his trial may, indeed, have been political in nature. He believed it, at any rate, to have been the work of Doge Pietro Gradenigo. Convictions of his father-in-law, Marco Querini, and his brother-in-law, Pietro Querini, along with his own, lurk in the background of the well-known rebellion.[22] In 1311 we hear of one Giovanni Minio, who, as *vicedomino* of the Fondaco dei Tedeschi had helped himself to 1,140 *l.* of the Commune's money, and who had been sentenced to the customary penalty (2,280 *l.*) under the law of 1265. He was not able to pay, and had therefore been in prison for six months. He was seeking to be released by *grazia,* but was turned down.[23] All officials who drew their incomes from the returns of their offices were forbidden in 1317 to take more than was due them or to borrow anything from those returns for their own use, under penalty of 10 *s.* per *l.*[24] The advocates of the Commune, according to an act of 1325, should prosecute for 12 *d.* per *l.* any official of the city who received or disbursed money without the presence of at least one colleague. The advocates also promised to prosecute for the customary double penalty anyone who disbursed money that he should not.[25] The same penalty should be imposed upon governors who defrauded the Commune or their communities or who alienated public wealth improperly.[26] Provision was made in 1330 for added publicity for the basic act of 1265.[27]

Marco Erizzo was condemned in 1341 to a fine of 1,000 *l.* for the money he had turned to his own use while he was councillor of Crete.[28] Niccoleto Valaresso, who was treasurer of Venice, fell under the penalty for putting his hands into the Commune's money in 1349.[29] In the same year Filippo Venier, formerly *massaro* of the mint, was condemned to 200 *l.* and five years' exclusion from all offices and councils for badly administering the goods of the government and of private persons.[30] In 1354 the Quaranta criminale ordered the advocates of the Commune to arrest and examine Costantino Nani, a money official, and to sequester his goods, because he was accused of receiving public wealth for his own use.[31] Early in the next year three provisors of salt, Pietro Erizzo, Filippo Dandolo, and Giovanni Contarini, were sentenced to deprival for two years of all offices and perpetually of the salt office, as well as to pay two hundred ducats, which they were said to have stolen.[32] The Senate complained in 1355 that the various Venetian officials of Treviso were continually stealing the goods of the Commune. It took measures to see that these officials would be investigated by syndics.[33] Sclavo Bollani, an official of accounts, and his young son, Pietro, were convicted in 1356 for wrongfully receiving the goods of the Commune. The father was sentenced to deprivation of all offices and councils for a year, plus a fine of one hundred ducats, and the son to two months' imprisonment. Sclavo's wife and another son were also charged, but not convicted.[34] In 1358 it was found that some provincial officials were receiving goods of the Republic or of their communities beyond what was allowed by their commissions. This was to be halted under penalty of 300 *l.*[35]

In 1359 the basic act of 1265 and other legislation on the subject were revoked and a new act was passed in the interest of clarifying the subject. Officials, governors, or ambassadors who stole the goods of the Commune were subjected to a graduated scheme of penalties, depending upon the amount involved and whether they confessed or had to be convicted. The penalties ranged from the customary double penalty, plus permanent exclusion from offices and councils and being named before the Great Council as a thief, to payment of the amount stolen, plus a third in addition, and permanent deprivation of office in the place where the offense was committed. Provision was also made for settlement of disputes over what were or were not legitimate expenses. Those who accepted too much money in good faith had only to pay it back.[36] Sclavo Bollani reappears in the record, to his misfortune, as a defendant under the new law. He had stolen 124 ducats belonging to the Commune when he had been official for the wine tax. It is interesting that the Senate declined to convict him under the law that had been passed only two months previously, but after repeated attempts they did convict him on an ad hoc basis. He had to pay the double penalty, but was deprived permanently only of the office of the wine tax and for five years of other offices and councils.[37] I do not think that the Senate in failing to convict under the law of 1359 was concerned about the ex post facto problem, for we have other cases where the Venetians showed no reticence on this score. Perhaps they were hesitant to impose the statutory permanent deprivation of all offices and councils, even upon a noble twice convicted of putting his hand in the public till. Dolfino Dolfin, who had been *vicedomino* of the Fondaco dei Tedeschi, was convicted in 1363 of having failed to keep the money of the Republic in a chest with three keys, instead having misappropriated some 918 *l. ad grossos*. He attempted to cover up through false entries in the books. He had to pay a quarter as penalty and suffer four years' loss of offices and councils. His two colleagues were sentenced to fines of 100 *l.* each for their part in the affair, although they were not accused of receiving money.[38] After ten years, slightly heavier penalties *ad terrorem omnium* were added to the act of 1359. Instead of being read in the Great Council once, the proclamation of theft was to be read annually for five years, and, even if the accused confessed, he was still to be deprived of all offices and councils for five years.[39]

In 1390, after repeated efforts to convict him for taking public money for his own use, Jacopo Trevisan, a loan official, was sentenced to repay the amount plus a half, permanent exclusion from the loan office, and five years' exclusion from all offices and councils. His colleague, Lorenzo Lanzuoli, was sentenced to permanent exclusion from the loan office for failing to report him. For some reason Lanzuoli remained in prison, because nineteen days after his conviction he was moved to a room of the palace on account of sickness, but his sons were made sureties for him.[40] Marco Dandolo, who had been governor of Retimo, was convicted of taking money for himself from a tax on grain. There had also been malfeasance in the building of a villa for himself. He had to restore the money owed to the Republic and pay 200 *l*. in addition, and he was made permanently ineligible for the governorship of Retimo.[41] In 1409 the Senate convicted Giovanni Pasqualigo, formerly a loan official, of misappropriating the funds of his office for his own use, sentencing him to repayment, plus 6 *d*. per *l.,* perpetual exclusion from the loan office, and loss of all offices, but not deprival of the councils, for two years.[42] In the next year it had to cope with a rather large case of embezzlement on the part of Andrea Loredan, who had been *podestà* of Drivasto, where he had stolen over 2,000 *l*. of public money, and had escaped. Like Pasqualigo the year before and many others he was tried in absentia and convicted under the law of 1359.[43]

In 1411 the Senate sought to obviate frauds by requiring all noble officials and judges who were entitled to pay themselves out the incomes of their offices to bring that portion, along with the portions due to subordinate officials, before the treasurers month by month for accounting.[44] The Great Council in 1415 praised the act of 1359 and the raising of penalties in 1369, adding that the officials of old, new, and newest accounts should be responsible for denouncing offenders.[45] In 1416 Antonio da Riva, formerly *massaro* at the gold mint, was convicted of taking a small sum of money for his own use in violation of the act of 1359. He was deprived permanently of all offices of the mint, sentenced to two months in prison, and fined 100 *l*.[46]

In 1416 the penalty for stealing from the Commune was raised again: where under the law of 1369 the convicted embezzler should have his crime declared in the Great Council once a year for five years, henceforth it should be done as long as he lived. The act is most useful to us for its declaration that "many of our nobles have stolen and in an evil way have accepted money belonging to our Commune."[47] Giorgio Bragadin, as official of the salt office, had stolen a large sum of money from the Commune. He had gone to Portogruaro, where he spoke badly and dishonestly of the Republic. A price of 10,000 *l*. was put on his head, he was delivered to Venice, and he was hanged between the two red columns. We have seen case after case of relatively mild punishment for stealing public money, modest fines and exclusion from offices, but the vengeance of Venice for speaking foully of the government was overwhelming.[48]

The Senate noted in 1430 that twenty-five years earlier a certain young noble had misappropriated a large sum of money from the loan office. In the course of the investigation, some errors had been found in the books which would make the state liable to certain claims, but this information was suppressed. Now, some people had gotten wind of the facts and were pressing old claims. The books should not be made public, said the Senate, but kept under lock and key, although anyone who did press his claim should receive justice.[49] In 1431 the Senate complained that in spite of the watchfulness of their ancestors, in recent years many officials had been found with their hands in the public till. This occurred because the books were not sufficiently examined, so the advocates of the Commune had ordered a review of the records for two years. They discovered that the Republic was short four thousand ducats for that period, in spite of the fact that officials of accounts had accepted the books and had written on them that the accounts had been received and were in order. Provision was made, therefore, to investigate the books of the Arsenal, the office of armament, and the *ternaria* (an office over import and export duties), and also the receipts and expenditures of the officials of old, new, and newest accounts since 1415.[50] Andrea Capello, who had been *baiulo* and captain of Negroponte, was charged under thirty-three counts (an unusually large number) in 1433. Among the charges was that he had received eight hundred ducats belonging to the Commune. He was convicted and sentenced to a year in prison, a fine of three hundred ducats, and permanent exclusion from all governorships.[51]

In 1452 we have a rare example of nobles who were not officials engaging in plain robbery, which concerns us only because they tried to rob a public building. Niccolò Erizzo and Giovanni da Mula with a devilish spirit climbed the walls of the vaults of the provisors of the Commune, and with much picking of locks and prying things open they broke in. They were banished for life with provision that if they violated their banishment they should be hanged.[52] A *straordinario*, Francesco Marini, was also convicted in 1455 for taking home money that he was supposed to carry to the treasurers weekly. He had stolen 150 ducats, and, rather surprisingly, he was sentenced only to pay it back with a penalty of a fourth, in spite of the fact that he had also been fiddling with the books.[53] Officials had gotten into the habit of taking for themselves certain new *regaleas,* according to the Senate in 1462.

They had been ordered not to do so, but many had continued the practice, not hiding it but openly recording it in their journals. They were required to restore the value of all taken since the order to desist.[54]

In the late 1470s there was a scandal involving the conversion of the supplies of castellanies to the private use of their commanders. Domenico Vitturi, castellan of Feltre, was guilty of selling the grains and beans turned over to him by his predecessor, of selling wine and other things beyond the circle of his associates, and of absenting himself from the castle without permission of the Council of Ten. He was removed from office and required to replace the foodstuffs.[55] Fantino Coppo, castellan of Peschiera, sold the wheat and disposed of the millet that his predecessor had left him. He also introduced many people into the castle for feasts, and he left the castle by day and opened the bridge by night. He was deprived of his position and other offices and required to replace the grains.[56] Marco Falier, castellan of Padua, converted grain and salt pork to his own profit. Moreover, he used wood, iron, and stone belonging to the government to build a house for himself. He held feasts in the castle, and he too went away from it without permission. He was deprived perpetually of the castellany of Padua, required to pay back his ill-gotten gains, and also to repay the salary given to his son.[57]

In 1497 there was another scandal over provincial governors misappropriating public funds.[58] A former treasurer of Padua, Francesco Cornaro, was convicted in 1499 for having embezzled 4,243 *l.* 10 *s.* He was to repay the capital and as much as penalty, be ineligible for all offices for life, and have his name read as a thief in the Great Council every year.[59] In 1500 the Senate passed an act limiting the expenses of ambassadors, which would not be worthy of notice in the present context except that Priuli complains of the unsupportable expenses, such as four thousand ducats a year by the ambassadors to Rome and Naples, "between expenses and thefts."[60] About the same time Bernardo da Canal, who had been *podestà* and captain of Antivari, and who had stolen money from the Commune and from private citizens, was condemned to a year in prison, repayment plus one hundred ducats, and exclusion from offices and councils for four years. The Senate specified that the money belonging to the Commune should be spent on the fortifications of Antivari, so it appears that his embezzlement probably diverted funds that ought to have been for that purpose.[61] The period from 1486 to 1501 was tainted by the doge's own reputation for corruption. When Agostino Barbarigo died in 1501, the Commune recovered thousands of ducats from the son-in-law who had managed his personal finances.[62]

Bertuccio da Canal embezzled 629 ducats from the Fondaco dei Tedeschi, where he had been an official. In 1502 he was sentenced by the

Quaranta criminale to repay the capital plus one-half, to be denounced in the Great Council annually, and to lose all offices for five years. Not paying, he remained in prison.[63] In 1505 Niccolò Priuli, formerly captain in Famagusta and *luogotenente* in Cyprus, was convicted of taking money from the Commune and from individuals. He was required to pay it back, and was expelled from the Ten and made ineligible for office and for secret councils for two years. He would never be able to hold office in Cyprus again.[64] Antonio da Mezzo, who had been collector for debts owed the Commune, stole a great deal of money, about sixteen hundred ducats, by simply pocketing his collections and making no record. Before he was discovered he skipped town, which was a common and prudent practice. He was offered the option of returning, confessing, and restoring the money, after which he would be banned from public office for life and decried every year as a thief in the Great Council. If he did not, however, he would be banished for life with a heavy price on his head should he ever return to Venetian territory. After the sentence was read in the Great Council, the advocate for the week, Francesco Orio, exhorted the nobles not to misappropriate public money. Priuli also editorializes, commending the government for chastising such persons, and claiming that their ancestors had taken care under severe penalties to see that public officials did not take money home from their offices. The Romans, too, he asserts, had taken severe measures against embezzlement, "because no one ought to take what is not his own."[65]

During our whole period the Venetian Republic struggled against the embezzlement of state funds by noble officials. A basic law on the subject was passed in 1265, and it was replaced by another in 1359. These laws were not unused and forgotten, like so much Venetian legislation, but year after year offenders were convicted under them. They failed to eliminate the vice (as all laws do, of course), or even, it seems, to control it very much, for the offenses recounted here are numerous, even though some of the less interesting have been omitted, and we may assume that many escaped notice. The failure can be attributed in part to the tendency to try offenders on an ad hoc basis, probably for the purpose of imposing a lighter sentence than that provided by law. That very tendency to punish nobles guilty of stealing from the Commune with no greater penalty than exclusion from office for a time and a fine provides a measure of the seriousness with which the offense was taken. To some extent the leniency may have been due to a concern about false prosecutions resulting from political and familial rivalries, for the Venetian nobility is known to have resorted to such weapons in its internecine struggles. Still, even if some convictions resulted from trumped-up charges, it is clear that there was an abundance of very real embezzlement of public wealth.

Chiseling consists of acts near the borderline of corrupt practices, but frequently on the dishonest side of the line. A good example is the venerable practice of cheating on expense accounts, which was not at all unfamiliar to Venetian patricians sent abroad on the business of the Republic. The problem, in fact, was pervasive, and in 1353 the Great Council, complaining of the almost intolerable expense of ambassadors, provisors, and *nuncii,* appointed a commission to investigate the means of controlling "the liberal consciences that they have in expending the wealth of the Commune."[66] This may be somewhat unfair to the patricians, although they clearly exercised much ingenuity in transferring expenses from themselves to the state, for their assignments were often a severe personal or familial financial burden. The probable result of the investigation was the first comprehensive act regulating the expense accounts of ambassadors and officials sent abroad. Despite earlier limited attempts at control, the Senate found no order or method in expense accounts. Some officials, indeed, manifestly a majority, according to the act, ran up enormous expense accounts, chiefly by confounding maintenance expenses, which the ambassador or official was supposed to pay, with expenses of the journey, which could be charged to the Commune. The Senate insisted that expenses should be limited in advance and that careful records of all expenses must be kept by an accompanying notary.[67] Cessi believes, certainly correctly, that the law had its effectiveness limited by the reluctance of the ruling class to see it strictly enforced.[68] It was a common feature of Venetian government to legislate collectively against the evils committed individually by the legislators themselves, then to temper the harshness of the law by lax enforcement. In this manner the patricians achieved some sort of balance between conscience and self-interest.

Public officials entrusted with money belonging to the Commune also sometimes were not prompt to deposit it in the treasury. Three successive *capita* in the thirteenth-century capitulary of the judges of the *avogaria de intus* require officials who receive money for the Republic to turn it in to the treasurers within eight days after the end of every month and the laws provide for the punishment of officials at home and abroad who do not pay what they owe within fifteen days after the ends of their terms.[69] Still, in 1306 the Great Council had to admit: "[O]ur officials who receive money for the Commune do not give it to the treasurers of the Commune as they are held to do." They were again required to turn it in every month under penalty.[70] The *vicedomini* of the sea had acquired the habit by 1307 of lending themselves money out of the pledges that merchants deposited with them for paying their customs taxes. The Great Council prohibited this shady practice or any other means by which the *vicedomini* might put their hands in the money under their care.[71] In 1489 the Senate complained about a certain depraved and pernicious custom according to which many officials who did not turn over the money from their offices at the appropriate time kept it and converted it to their own use.[72] Cessi, in his admirable study of the finances of Venice, has called attention to the squandering of the public treasury systematically brought about by its custodians, in contempt of severe sanctions, at which they brazenly laughed.[73]

A variation upon chiseling by the custodians of the Commune's money was the misuse of materials belonging to the public. Andrea Dandolo, formerly duke of Crete, was sentenced in 1384 by the Senate to pay for the stone and lime that he used for building houses for himself plus 100 *l.* for penalty.[74]

A favorite method of cutting corners was for governors or commanders to fail to provide the required retinue of men and horses. The dignity and even the security of the Republic suffered, but the purse of the individual enjoyed a measure of protection. As early as 1274 the *baiulo* of Acre was warned that if he lacked any of the sergeants he was supposed to have he would receive no money from the Commune as long as they were wanting.[75] In 1361 the Senate noted that some of the patrons of the galleys of Cyprus had not employed the required men. The officials of the Levant, on the day on which the galleys were to sail, should determine by the use of the books and in other ways whether each galley had the requisite number. Any patron who was found undermanned must pay 20 *soldi di grossi* for every missing man.[76] The Great Council objected in 1375 that many governors did not maintain the number of horses and the household that they ought. Since they received the salaries and the perquisites, they must also support the horses, servants, and other burdens.[77] In 1386, the Senate again drew attention to the fact that commanders of galleys were not observing the requirement that their galleys must be fully manned. The captains of the fleets were therefore commanded to make the rounds of their galleys just before their departure, and, if they found men missing, they were to order the commander of the galley to take on additional men at the first place where they could be found. If the galley commander did not obey, the captain himself should enlist and pay the men. Captains were made liable to a fine of five ducats for every missing man. The captain of the Gulf was also authorized to make inspection at his discretion to see that the galleys were properly manned.[78] Donato Giustinian, formerly count of Castello dei Gemelli, was convicted in 1412 for not keeping sufficient troops in the fortress. He had to spend five months in prison, face exclusion from offices abroad for four years, and he should never be eligible to have any fortress *per gratiam*. In addition he was fined 100 *l*.[79] Commanders could also skimp on the required rations for their men, cheating the state and impairing the morale and the effectiveness of the men. In 1423 the Senate made the officials of armaments responsible for punishing patrons of galleys who cheated in this fashion. Both the officials and informers or accusers were to be rewarded for successful prosecutions.[80] Chiseling patrons of galleys learned to leave behind the *balestrieri* qualified at the shooting matches, enrolling in place of them merchants and their servants taking passage on the galleys, so that less than half of the *balestrieri* were real crossbowmen. Such galleys, of course, were not as well prepared for a fight as they should be. The Senate decided in 1440 that one official of armament should accompany as far as Pola each fleet or each galley sailing independently, where he should satisfy himself that the *balestrieri* were bona fide crossbowmen. Any patron caught fudging should pay as a fine the pay of a crossbowmen for the entire voyage and as much more. The officials of armament should also investigate galleys upon their return to see that the *balestrieri* were the same as those originally enrolled.[81] It did not work. At the loss of Negroponte in 1470 the Venetian fleet was handicapped because galley commanders had entered upon the enrollment lists the names of men who never served and because cooks, vintners, and servants were registered as crossbowmen. The Senate was outraged by the corruption, ordered the commanding officer of the fleet, Niccolò da Canal, home for trial, and instructed his successor, Pietro Mocenigo, to stamp it out. Time after time galley commanders had gotten away with such fudging with no ostensible harm. At a crucial moment, however, the deficiencies contributed to one of Venice's most grievous disasters.[82] These forms of defrauding the government by governors and commanders trying to cut their often-oppressive costs are understandable, but they hardly comport with the image of the Venetian patrician willingly sacrificing his family's wealth for the honor of St. Mark.

CONFLICT OF INTERESTS

The Venetian Republic possessed a particularly acute sense of the real and potential conflicts between public and private interests. Alberto Tenenti has recently reminded us in striking terms of the importance in the High Middle Ages of "raison de famille," to which everything else was submitted and by which everything else was inspired. In spite of protestations of love for the *patria,* he sees as profound a gulf between the interests of the *famiglia* of Leon Battista Alberti and of the city-state as between the prince of Machiavelli and the *respublica christiana.*[83] Venice had a plethora of acts attempting to prevent patricians from voting in favor of their relatives.[84] The fear that individual or familial interests would prevail over the public welfare was especially pronounced in the case of ecclesiastical benefices. All who were related to beneficed clergy were known as *papalisti,* and the laws excluding the *papalisti* are famous in the annals of Venetian government.[85] The government made an extremely strenuous attempt to eliminate as many conflicts as possible, but the very mass and confusion of legislation on the subject proves once more that the effort, though impressive, was not successful. Here we shall deal with only a small part of the material on conflicts of interests, that which comes closest to corruption.

Although the acceptance and, indeed, exaction of favors, gifts, and loans by public officials from those subject to their jurisdiction was commonplace in the Middle Ages, the Venetians at an early date recognized that this practice was contrary to the interests of the subjects and the state. The year of an act prohibiting judges from accepting gifts from litigants is not known, for it comes from a capitulary not providing that information, but one would expect it to be very early.[86] The Great Council established in 1256 that the count of Zara could not receive gifts from any Zaran, Slavonian, Dalmation, or anyone else, and within the month were added the *baiuli* and councillors of Acre and Tyre.[87] The rubric of a lost act of 1271 tells us that the *baiulo* of Constantinople could not receive any gift from the emperor after he departed from office nor for a year subsequently.[88] An act of the Great Council in 1273 declared that just as all governors cannot receive any gift during their terms, they cannot do so for six months after they leave office.[89] In 1276 the Great Council commanded that the commissions of all governors contain a clause forbidding them, their unemancipated sons, or business associates from receiving any loans from an inhabitant of their territories or from standing pledge for anyone who would receive such a loan.[90] Mint officials were prohibited from receiving any gift, present, loan, or service.[91] Sometime after 1335 the procurators of San Marco were forbidden to borrow from the estates under their jurisdiction, to have any part in such loans, or to lend to their relatives.[92] The councillors of Crete and their families were prohibited from accepting gifts in 1350.[93] In 1356 the Great Council ruled that no Venetian citizen could receive a loan or a gift from any foreign prince or commune.[94] Apparently this effort was unsuccessful, because the act was essentially repeated in 1375 under threat of perpetual exclusion from all councils (in effect, loss of noble status).[95] An act of 1360 in the capitulary of the officials of accounts prohibited them from receiving gifts or services or permitting them to be received from anyone who had business before such officials.[96] The act of 1273 would seem to have covered the matter, but in 1371 the Senate ordered the prohibition against receiving gifts included in the commissions of all governors.[97] For members of the powerful Ten receiving gifts or provisions was a capital offense.[98]

There were naturally also misgivings about the favors that Venetian officials might bestow, as well as those they might receive. The Great Council held in 1273, for example, that all governors' commissions should state that they might not give, rent, or sell, by *grazia* or otherwise, anything belonging to the Commune to any of their *famiglie* or, indeed, to anyone within their jurisdiction. The same applied to any goods of private persons, living or dead, of which they had the custody.[99] Within six months a special act was passed by the same body commanding that the commission of the *baiulo* of Acre should contain a prohibition against giving anything belonging to the Commune to any business associate or any member of his family. Also, the *baiulo* and his councillors could not initiate a proposal to give anything worth more than ten bezants in value belonging to the Commune to anyone.[100]

One of the most obvious and yet most interesting areas of conflict concerned officials who had business dealings in the field of their jurisdiction. As early as 1248 the Great Council prohibited those who had charge of the taxes on cloth of gold, varicolored silks, or sendal to buy or cause to be bought those cloths or to work them or cause them to be worked. The same applied to those with jurisdiction over those who made fustian or woolen cloth.[101] Ten years later the Great Council declared that officials of the Arsenal should not have any dealings in those things that have to do with the Arsenal, nor should the grain officials deal in grain or the salt officials in salt.[102] Apparently the government was having some difficulty in 1263 over nobles who owned salt in Chioggia being elected as *salinario* there. Before anyone could accept this office he was to swear that he did not own salt.[103] The *vicedomini* of the Fondaco dei Tedeschi, according to an act of 1268, could not buy anything from any merchant coming to the *fondaco*.[104] In 1330 Marino Contarini was convicted for violating it.[105] In 1270 the Great Council legislated that no councillor, head, or member of the Forty should be involved in the sale of salt, wheat or other grain, wood for shipbuilding, or hemp. If he had such interests before he assumed his official post, he should leave the room when these matters came up.[106] The mintmasters of gold had to swear that they would not buy any gold for themselves or for others or take part with any person or commune in money matters.[107] Consuls, *vicedomini,* and other officials who were forbidden to engage in commerce should be fined 10 percent of the value of any merchandise they bought or sold, lose their salaries, and be excluded from all domestic offices for five years if they violated the law. They were not even to approach any broker or foreign merchant about buying or selling.[108] In 1322 the Great Council denied the officials of public loans and their subordinates the right to buy shares in the public debt for resale under penalty of losing their offices.[109] In 1335 the Great Council denied to the grain officials and their sons the right to take part in any voyage chartered by the grain office.[110] The Great Council noted in 1371 that, although the grain officials were prohibited from taking part in any voyage, no penalty had been fixed. They should lose whatever interests they had in such voyages. If they leased ships to the Commune for the transport of grain they should lose whatever they received. They could not engage, of course, in any commerce in grain or flour. Neither could they run a mill.[111] In 1367 the Forty decreed that the officials of butcher shops could not buy meat for anyone or cause it to be given to him.[112] The Senate became considerably exercised in 1427 because some admirals *a parte maris* were involved in commerce pertaining to the Arsenal. Those presently so engaged, the Senate decreed, should have four months to disengage.[113] A senatorial act of 1431 takes us into rather sophisticated affairs. It seems that some members of the Collegio had been buying and selling shares in the public debt, a dubious business, since policies over which the College had influence could add to or detract from the value. The Senate cracked down on them, imposing a fine of one thousand ducats. The chief reason, however, was simply because their buying or selling tipped off foreign observers to Venetian policy.[114] In 1435 the Senate prohibited the consuls and vice-consuls to Damascus and Alexandria and the councillors in those places to buy or sell pepper, spices, or anything else in the lands of the sultan. They should remain above the hurly-burly to oversee the interests of all the Venetian merchants.[115] The Senate decreed in 1449 that officials responsible for selling or renting things belonging to the Commune or the farm of taxes could not themselves have any part in such things. Neither could officials who were responsible for selling or renting things that belonged to private citizens.[116] The Ten objected in 1475 to corruption in the mint in spite of the ineffective laws passed by their ancestors. Things must have been quite bad, because the act speaks of "vice" and of "many enormities committed through desire for money." All officials of the mint were forbidden to engage in any commerce in gold or silver, directly or indirectly, under penalty of loss of all offices for ten years and forfeiture, not only of their profit, but also of the capital.[117] A senatorial decree of 1478 refers to an old act prohibiting patricians from engaging in commerce with princes or other lords, and it extended the act to embrace *condottieri* in Venetian employ. Violators should be ineligible for all offices for five years—ten for those who belonged to the College, held some office, or were members of a secret council. They should also pay two hundred ducats and their contracts with *condottieri* would be unenforceable.[118] The Senate referred in 1495 to a useful series of acts prohibiting nobles from engaging in the salt trade or, in that business, being guarantors, receiving salaries, serving as advocates, procurators, or intercessors, or in any way speaking about it to any governor. The Pregadi decided that similar legislation was needed concerning the stones that were brought to the Lido and the goods that were brought for the Arsenal.[119] Apparently all the earlier prohibitions had not been effective, because Sanuto reports that in 1505 legislation was passed against the grain college and the provisors of grain engaging in the grain trade and also against the officials of the Arsenal being involved in any conflict of interests.[120]

Another reason for conflict was the possession by Venetian nobles of fiefs, gifts, or *grazie* from foreign princes or cities. In 1247 patricians with such holdings worth 100 *s.* or more a year in the march of Treviso, the county of Ferrara, or elsewhere were denied the right to speak for their benefactors or even to accompany them or their envoys before any Venetian council.[121] The ambitious intrigues of Doge Lorenzo Tiepolo caused the Venetians to wish to put some restraints upon his successors, so, after his death in 1275, they added to the ducal *promissione* or coronation oath that neither the doge nor his family might accept fiefs or loans from foreign states. He and his sons were also forbidden to marry foreign wives.[122]

Above all, the Venetian government dreaded entanglement of its nobles with Rome. The papal Curia was the focus of the greatest patronage system of the Middle Ages. Malipiero complained in 1497 that the courier leaving for Rome was more burdened with requests for benefices than the Levantine ships with cargoes.[123] The Venetian government naturally feared that ambassadors to Rome would be concerned with soliciting benefices for themselves, their relatives, or others. Already in 1238 the Great Council legislated against the ambassadors to Rome seeking favors for anyone without the consent of the doge, a majority of his council, and a majority of the Forty.[124] The Great Council realized in 1355 that it was not sound for governors to seek ecclesiastical benefices within their jurisdictions, so they were forbidden to do for themselves or for their sons during their terms of office and for a year afterwards. They also should not have anyone else seek offices for them.[125] The Council of Ten agreed in 1434 that those who would be excluded from the Ten or the Senate for deliberation touching the pope (the *papalisti*) would also be ineligible to be ambassadors to Rome.[126] Late in 1482 the Senate passed an act prohibiting any ambassador from procuring, soliciting, demanding, or accepting any office, dignity, or benefice for himself, a relative, or anyone, except, of course, for those requests committed to him by the Republic. Those who obtained bulls favoring them in such ways should declare them before the Signoria, together with the methods by which they were obtained, and no benefice worth more than one hundred ducats might be kept without the license of the Senate. Eight and a half months later the Great Council approved the measure.[127] In 1487 the Ten decreed that no member of the Pien Collegio, no head of the Ten, or advocate of the Commune could seek or obtain any ecclesiastical benefice for himself or for any relative during his term of office. Neither could he have anyone else seek it for him. Nor could he even receive commendatory letters to that end from the Signoria or the Senate.[128] In 1491 occurred the well-known case of Ermolao Barbaro, noted humanist and one of the preeminent nobles. When the Senate was informed of the death of Cardinal Barbo, Patriarch of Aquileia, it nominated Niccolò Donà, Bishop of Limassol in Cyprus, as his successor. Ermolao Barbaro was sent as ambassador to secure the appointment. Instead, under papal pressure, he accepted it for himself in violation of the laws of Venice and the wishes of the Senate. On 8, 9, and 10 March the Council of Ten with its Zonta met, and Ermolao's father, Zaccaria, was ordered to tell his son to renounce the patriarchate and to come home, but Ermolao would not obey. Reproofs and threats followed. Girolamo Donà, who was a close friend of Barbaro, was sent to persuade him to yield, and, according to Sanuto, on 12 April Ermolao did try to resign the post, but the pope would not allow it. The situation was deadlocked. Ermolao could not resign. Niccolò Donà, of course, could not be promoted. Ermolao could neither return to Venice nor effectively claim his see, which was within the physical control of Venice. He died in Rome in 1493. This is a fascinating case of a very distinguished and admirable noble who defied the laws of the city, not, probably, for gain, but from a mixture of humanistic and religious motives. Virtuous or not, however, he did not place the Republic before all things in accordance with the myth.[129]

If the patriciate could have had its collective will, each patrician would have preserved his uncorrupted purity as much as possible in isolation—one noble from another, judges from litigants, ambassadors from everybody, and all nobles from foreigners. It was not a strange or ignoble aim, but it was an unrealistic one.

GRAFT

Many nobles were guilty of taking graft—and some were even caught. There were opportunities, of course, in various offices, but governorships on *terraferma* were peculiarly subject to this vice. These governors were expected to live in a more ostentatious manner than those *da mare*, but often poor nobles were elected, who went deeply into debt to maintain a state far beyond their means. One means of recovery was to accept or require presents in return for favors.[130]

Of course the Venetian government took precautions against the abuse of their powers by its governors. An act of 1319, for example, provided for the inclusion in the commissions of all governors that they should not compel or cause others to compel fishermen or fishmongers to sell fish to them or to bring their fish to the house of the governor, but should allow them to sell their fish freely in the customary places.[131] Giovanni Querini, an official over gold leaf, was convicted by the Forty in 1353 for accepting gifts in connection with his office and many other wrongful acts. Interestingly, however, he merely lost his office and suffered a fine of 20 *l*.[132] Similarly, Raimondo Dandolo, captain of the tower of San Giuliano, who accepted twelve fish from two fishermen who had been fishing beyond the tower, lost his office in 1359 and had to pay twelve *grossi* for the fish.[133] The principle was affirmed, but the penalty was scarcely harsh. The offense, of course, was not horrendous.

Patrons of galleys had no fear, the Senate declared in 1361, of the various penalties which were intended to deter the carrying of merchandise without the seal showing that export taxes had been paid. Patrons who accepted such merchandise in the future should be subject to a fine of 1,000 *l. parvorum* and permanent exclusion as patrons of the merchant galleys. Subordinate officials who accepted such goods without the knowledge of the patrons should also be punished.[134] Venice continued to have difficulty with evasion of import and export taxes on salt, oil, and other products, due to the collusion of captains, counts, and lesser officials responsible for collecting them. Anyone who would countenance contrabrand in the future because of any gain or benefit given or promised, according to the Senate in 1363, must spend one year in prison and five years in exile for each offense and he should pay to the Commune whatever he had received and as much more out of his own pocket.[135] Marco Morosini was guilty in 1373 of another familiar variety of graft: he was a mint official who bought gold at a low price and sold it to the mint at a high price.[136] Pietro Nani, governor of Canea, had caused or allowed to be built *per grazie* edifices which were harmful and dangerous with regard to the fortifications. Presumably he was paid or otherwise recompensed for the privilege, since he was sentenced to a fine of 600 *l.* and perpetual exclusion from offices in Crete.[137] The Great Council in 1406 called attention to the many frauds committed by customs officials who came to an understanding with merchants. Provisors were made responsible for devising measures to prevent this dishonest practice.[138] Early in 1483 it appears that customs officials were being persuaded to allow some merchants to export goods without paying the customs. New regulations were issued for the purpose of securing the enforcement of the law.[139] In 1497 the Senate found Marino Morosini, who had been treasurer of the Commune, guilty of making deals to his own profit with creditors of the Republic. He was buying loans on the treasury at about 52 percent of the face value, but seeing to it that he then was paid off at full value. He had to pay what he had gained to the Commune, pay an additional fine of one hundred ducats, and was permanently excluded from all positions as treasurer.[140]

Another sort of graft in the fleet was revealed in 1500. Commanders were selling bread, meat, and other items to their men. The poor oarsmen got in debt to the commanders, and the commanders saw themselves paid first out of the money that the government sent for the pay of the oarsmen. This trafficking was also considered degrading to the officers. Any commanders who engaged in it in the future were to lose their positions.[141] One of Doge Agostino Barbarigo's many corrupt practices was to use his authority to compel the treasurers, the salt and grain officials, and the Arsenal to pay in good gold ducats obligations that had been purchased by his relatives and friends for inferior coins.[142]

KICKBACKS

The kickback is a special form of graft by which one party receives back or holds back part of the remuneration of another. Venetian governors and naval commanders, who had been under pressure to lay out large sums of money, were prone to submit to the temptation to recoup out of the salaries of their staffs or crews. Governors would take money from their vicars, judges, and ministers, who in turn, of course, would sell justice or otherwise abuse their offices in order to make up what they had lost.[143] In a similar manner naval commanders sometimes held back from their crews part of the stipend provided by the Republic. Oarsmen were nonetheless willing to enlist, for they were able to turn a profit on the small amount of goods that they were allowed to carry for sale without paying transportation or duties or from the booty they might expect as crews of the war galleys. The kickback to officers of the fleets was not much of a problem, however, before the fifteenth century: in earlier periods the seamen had been conscripted.[144]

In 1401 the Senate passed an act which highlighted kickbacks to governors. Although their commissions established that they should have a certain number of subordinates at fixed salaries, in many cases the governors agreed with these subordinates that they should receive no salaries or expenses. In order to make a living, therefore, the subordinates were reduced to committing illegal and dishonest acts in the performance of their duties. Naturally, the Senate adopted measures to try to end such abuses.[145] A governor named Michele Bon was convicted in 1487 for accepting from his chancellor, as a kickback, twenty "arms" of black velvet worth fifty-four ducats, given to the chancellor by the Council of Ten. Bon was deprived of offices for five years, fined five hundred ducats, and his offense was to be published in the Great Council.[146] Only a few months later he was back before the Ten seeking a pardon. He had suffered great harm to his honor by the publicity in the Great Council, which was not prescribed by the law under which he was convicted. He had loyally served the Republic in other offices. He begged for mercy for himself and his poor and numerous family of ten children. Although he almost had the required two-thirds on the first ballot, he could not muster enough support to prevail.[147]

In an earlier chapter we mentioned the Senate's complaint in 1409 that legislation requiring four noble *balestrieri* on each merchant galley was not being followed. Patrons, who had to stand the costs, had also formed the habit of getting the *balestrieri della popa* to agree that they would not receive payment or that they would return it. The Senate reaffirmed that each merchant galley should enlist four *nobeli di galia,* who should receive the same pay as ordinary *balestrieri,* as well as their food at the captain's table. Patrons of the galleys might not make any agreement with the noble *balestrieri* by which the patrons should receive back all or part of the pay. In fact, the patrons should turn over the money required for the pay of the *balestrieri della popa* to the captain of the fleet, who should pay them.[148] An act of the Senate of 1423 calls to our attention that some of those elected as *balestrieri della popa* were yielding the position to others in exchange for a kickback of part of the pay. This was "against the intention of the Signoria, which in this manner is defrauded." Any noble who did this in the future would be liable for the pay and as much more out-of-pocket. The one elected must go, unless he were ill.[149] There was also a bit of a scandal in 1500 over patrons of galleys paying their oarsmen only 9 *l.* a month, whereas the government allotted 12 *l.* The rowers were anxious for the jobs, and so were willing to accept the subnormal pay. They were to be examined on oath to determine whether there had been cheating, and if there had the patron should be deprived of offices for six years.[150]

BRIBERY

The kickback, of course, is very closely related to simple bribery. The same factors that we have discussed previously, the high cost of living up to the office and the need to recover expenses, as well as sheer greed, disposed patricians to take bribes.[151] Bribery, indeed, was so common throughout the government by the end of the fifteenth century that the Ten did not dare to reveal its secrets, even before the Senate, where it was assumed that there were a number of nobles in the pay of Ludovico il Moro.[152] Ludovico Foscarini wrote in 1453 that, even if other governors were in the habit of accepting gifts, the custom left to him by his father prohibited it.[153]

As early as the ducal *promissione* of Giacomo Tiepolo in 1229, precautions were taken against bribery of the doge. Tiepolo promised that he would accept no presents except strictly limited amounts of food, and not even those from suppliants, but only tokens, such as rose water.[154] In 1260 the Great Council provided that the advocates of the Commune should investigate those who receive money from people having matters before the courts or in the hands of officials, just as they investigate homicides and thefts.[155] The act of 1273 requiring officials to report colleagues who receive or accept anything illegally probably also refers to bribery, as well as embezzlement.[156] The *massari* of the mint and the *vicedomino* of the Fondaco dei Tedeschi took an oath in 1278 that they would not receive any gift at any time in connection with their offices.[157] Roberti's collection of capitularies of the thirteenth century contains so many items of this sort that there is a large entry in the index. They differ somewhat: basically judges, officials, and the like promise that they will not accept gifts from those who have business before them. One capitulary uses the word *pretium,* which can be translated "bribe." Many speak of loans, and some refer to meals and hospitality.[158] The important act of 1359 already discussed with regard to embezzlement probably also covered bribery.[159] One of the four counts against Pietro Giustinian in 1369 was that he had accepted gifts and hospitality.[160] Even more serious, of course, was the corruption of Venetian patricians by foreigners. In 1372 an advocate of the Commune and a member of the Forty were discovered in the pay of Francesco il Vecchio da Carrara.[161]

According to the Senate in 1400 the governors of Treviso and Ceneda were in the habit of selling the captaincies of gates, towers, fortifications, and palaces. It would clearly be better, the act declares, if these posts went to worthy citizens who expose their bodies for the honor of Venice, so an election was established.[162] A series of proceedings extending over a great part of the year 1403 resulted in the conviction of Bertuccio Diedo, vice-captain of the galleys of Romania, and Zanacchio Cornaro of Candia (therefore one of the Venetian nobility of Crete), captain of one of the Cretan galleys. They had accepted money from the Turks for facilitating their passage into Romania. Both were sentenced to heavy fines.[163] One of the best-known bribery trials in Venetian history was that of the great naval hero Carlo Zeno. After the fall of the Carrara it was discovered that Zeno was one of a number of nobles who had received money from Francesco the Younger. His defense was that the money represented the repayment of a small loan made when Carrara was in exile, but the Ten convicted him by a split vote and sentenced the old hero to loss of offices and a year in prison. He served his sentence, which, according to Lane, proves the strength of the Venetian constitution, and at his death a number of years later he received the highest funerary honors. His fundamental loyalty was not really in question: we are very likely dealing with a political prosecution. The Venetian patriciate, however, does not seem to have been particularly conscious of the rule Caesar set for his wife.[164]

There was a big bribery and extortion scandal in Crete in the early 1430s. Three ex-councillors of Crete, Secundo Pesaro, Domenico Bembo, and Lorenzo Avanzago, and two ex-governors of Retimo, Pietro Muazzo and Pietro Dalmario, were convicted. Pesaro's wife was also specifically implicated, though she was not put on trial. A Jew very appropriately named Ottaviano Bonaiuta was found guilty of being a "fixer," who solicited bribes from those with business before the government and tempted the councillors to sell "right and justice, offices and benefices." Among the other charges against the ex-councillors was that in return for money they discounted amounts owed to the treasury and they accepted gifts and hospitality. Each of the guilty except Dalmario was sentenced to pay the amount he had received, plus an equal amount as penalty, to spend two years in prison, and to be permanently ineligible for offices. The sums that each was known to have received were quite large: Pesaro, 796 ducats; Bembo, 800 ducats; Davanzago, 1,500 ducats; Muazzo, 650 ducats. Dalmario was sentenced to spend four months in prison and pay 200 ducats.[165]

In 1437 Pietro Gradenigo was convicted of taking a bribe from Vicenzo Rosso, a scribe at the salt office, or his daughter, to give false testimony against Lucia Avantii. Rosso seems to have been the guardian of Bartolomeo Avantii, who, I think, was the son of Lucia. Gradenigo was exiled for life.[166] Let us pass over the controversial case of the unfortunate Jacopo Foscari, son of Doge Francesco Foscari, who was convicted of taking bribes and of dealing with the Visconti enemy. Very possibly he was guilty, although some authors believe that he was a victim of political hatred against his father.[167] We should bear in mind the possibility that a few of our other examples may be misleading, false actions successfully prosecuted for political or personal reasons, but this is not likely to be true in very many cases. If malicious accusations were the rule, rather than the exception, they would probably not be taken any more seriously than the charges made in modern political campaigns. In 1447 the Ten sentenced Andrea Donà, *cavaliere*, to pay nineteen hundred ducats, to spend a year in prison, and to be ineligible for all offices, because he had accepted nine hundred ducats from Francesco Sforza.[168] In 1448 Benedetto Barbadico was found guilty of accepting a bribe of 500 *l.* to free two thieves when he was *podestà* of Montagnana. He was required to restore the 500 *l.*, which he appeared to have had from the monastery of San Francesco of Montagnana, and to pay 500 *l.* for penalty. He also had to spend a year in prison and was perpetually ineligible to hold any office.[169] One Vincivera Giustinian, who had been vice-councillor of Crete, was convicted in 1456 for having been "corrupted and suborned" by two other nobles, Peraccio Gradenigo and Giovanni Bon.[170]

The Ten discovered evidence in 1471 that Tommaso Zeno was dealing with the cardinal of Santa Maria del Porte in order the sell the secrets of the Venetian councils. Zeno's papers were seized, he was questioned, and he was convicted. He was sentenced to a year in prison and after that five years' exclusion from all secret councils.[171] Then there was an appalling case of bribery of patricians in order to gain the secrets of the Senate for Rome in 1478. The noble Lorenzo Zane, bishop of Brescia, paid Vitale Lando two hundred ducats and gave Lando's son the abbacy of the Umiliati, which was worth seven hundred ducats a year. Giacomo Malipiero also received two hundred ducats. The bishop promised dowries for the daughters of Alvise Loredan and assisted Loredan's brother to benefices worth three hundred to four hundred ducats a year. This was large-scale corruption of the most feared kind.[172]

In 1491 the Ten pursued Andrea Giustinian, count of Lesina, on an accusation that he had been bribed not to proceed against two brothers who were minters and presumably charged with some offense connected with the coinage.[173] A thorough scoundrel was Domenico Bollani, doctor (presumably of laws) and *cavaliere*, formerly advocate of the Commune, who, in that important position, had not only accepted many bribes, but solicited them wholesale through a crowd of "fixers." Bollani was so crooked that he sold justice to both sides in the same case. He was deprived permanently of all offices, exiled for life to Canea, and the advocates were to recover the bribes.[174] Among his accomplices was another nobleman, Pietro Marcello, who also solicited bribes for himself for promoting the client's cause before the advocate.[175] In fact, the names of other associates lead one to suspect that Bollani was heading something like a "franchise operation," for he had agents from Verona, Vicenza, Brescia, Asolo, and elsewhere.[176] In 1495 it was rumored that the duke of Ferrara, who was informed of all the secrets of the Senate, had given an influential senator a pair of capons stuffed with ducats.[177] Only a few years after this Fra Timofeo of Lucca, preaching the Christmas sermon in San Marco, denounced the widespread selling of justice.[178] During this period the doge, Agostino Barbarigo, himself is said to have welcomed bribes.[179] In opposing a continuation of the suspension of government salaries in early 1502, Giovanni Antonio Minio argued that officials deprived of a legitimate income would sell justice and rob the public.[180] As an extreme example, Geronimo Tron was hanged between the two red columns of the ducal palace in 1504. He had been castellan at Lepanto when it was surrendered to the Turks without a fight in 1499, and for that offense he had been exiled to Capodistria. He had broken his exile, a servant had revealed that he had been bribed by the Turks to surrender Lepanto, and under torture he had confessed. He had been receiving an annual payment as the price for his treason.[181]

The evidence proves that many Venetian patricians, from the doge to the poor nobles who took bribes because they had no other means of livelihood, were subject to corruption. No one is claiming, of course, that all patricians took bribes, and it would be rash to assert that a majority were venal, although Ludovico Foscarini's disclaimer, cited above, certainly suggests that large numbers were susceptible. There is no way, of course, in which we can quantify the problem meaningfully, but clearly bribery was widespread.

EXTORTION

In the aftermath of Agnadello, Priuli complained of the officials on *terraferma* who "ate up the poor."[182] This was a long-standing evil, exacerbated by the need of the nobles to recover expenses, and not confined to *terraferma*. For example, the duke of Crete, Fantino Dandolo, complained in 1316 that some of the castellans were unjustly oppressing their poor subjects.[183] Subjects of the governors of Treviso and Ceneda complained bitterly in 1351 and early 1352 about their oppression. The governors had arrogated to themselves many privileges not contained in their commissions. One of the most irksome was that they were impressing transport of wood, grain, hay, and straw, as well as animals, carts, and tools, for their establishments without paying. They were having wood cut that belonged to their subjects. They were accepting things that they needed for a minimum (and presumably coerced) price. They were buying meat, wine, and other necessities without paying the taxes that everyone else had to pay. Subjects had been refused the right to export their wine to Venice and elsewhere. Notaries, under the authority of the governors, charged excessively for their services. The governor of Treviso had contributed to a shortage of grain by not permitting free exchange between areas of surplus and those of need. The Senate elected *savi* to investigate and remedial steps were taken.[184] The investigation that the Senate ordered in 1355 of its officials in Treviso for stealing the goods of the Commune was also directed against dishonest acquisition of the property of the subjects.[185] In 1359 Niccolò Alberti, who had been *podestà* of Pirano, was sentenced to pay a fine and to repay one Stefano 400 *l.* for the cheese which he was missing. We do not know the exact nature of Alberti's offense with regard to the cheese. Very likely he abused his position to take it without payment.[186] Among the ten counts charged against Conte Venier, formerly *podestà* of Isola (d'Istria?), in 1362 was one count of extorting 100 *l.* from Niccoleto Vito and two counts of extorting merchandise from Franceschino Buonsignori for a smaller price than it was worth.[187] In 1367 the Forty took action against Bernardo Duodo, vice-consul at Alexandria. The consul had died, leaving a great quantity of merchandise and money belonging to the accounts of several persons. Duodo had not taken any steps to clear the accounts, and, when the captain of the galleys of Alexandria requested audience with him concerning them, he refused to meet him. The Senate wrote to the duke and councillors of Crete, ordering that if Duodo sent any of the goods or money to Crete they should sequester them, sell the goods, and send the money to Venice.[188]

The Forty in 1370 sentenced Stamato Gradenigo, who had been castellan of Bicorno (Apokoronas), to pay a fine and to pay the six peasants from whom he had exacted services. He also could never again be castellan of Bicorno.[189] Giovanni Diedo, formerly *podestà* of Montona, was sentenced in 1378 for extortion. He was required to restore everything, was deprived of his new office as governor of Pola, and excluded perpetually from the governing of Montona. We do not know the details of the extortions.[190] In 1385 the *giustizieri vecchi* had gotten into the bad habit of adding an extra 4 *d.* onto the accustomed tax of 8 *d.* per load of wood, dividing the supplement among themselves. Similarly they took an illegal addition on the sale of small sticks. The Senate decreed that the extra money should continue to be collected, but should belong to the Commune.[191] In 1392 the Senate convicted Jacopo Suriani, formerly *baiulo* of Cyprus, for taking an illegal cut of the price of sugar bought by Giovanni Michiel from Renaldo Visconti. Suriani was required to pay back what he had accepted and to pay 300 *l. parvorum,* and remained open to further claims.[192] The purpose of all the violence of Niccolò Adoaldo against the men of Isola delle Serafine (*insula Serrphenarum*) in 1393 seems to have been extortion.[193] Pietro Nani, whom we have already mentioned with regard to the probable taking of graft, was also convicted at the same time (1402) of extorting money from the subjects in connection with judgments and in other ways.[194] Andrea Ghisi, who had been *podestà* of Este, was required in 1407 to repay those from whom he had taken wood, as well as those who cut it and those who transported it, and the millers whom he had oppressed, and to pay Berto Masiero for wine. He was sentenced to a year in prison and perpetual exclusion from government positions in the new lands.[195] In 1412 Giovanni Diedo was convicted by the Senate of extorting grain, wine, and other things from the subjects at Motta di Livenza while he was captain of the boats on that river. He received a sentence of a year in prison, a fifty-ducat fine, and exclusion from all offices for five years, and the victims were free to proceed against him.[196] Two months later the Senate sentenced Paolo Morosini to exclusion from offices at Conegliano, a fine of 100 *l.*, and repayment for the enormities and extortion that he committed while governor of that place.[197]

We possess a remarkably detailed indictment, which is a rarity, against Maffeo Capello, governor and *podestà* of Castelbaldo, in 1413. The first two counts were concerned with sixteen *modia* of grain, for which the suppliers had not been paid. He was to pay them, at the price which was customary at the time of delivery, and if any of the grain was found to have been for the public storehouse, then the government would pay for it. Investigation proved that he had received the sixteen *modia,* but had only reported fifteen, so he had to pay 27 *l. parvorum* for the one he had stolen. For twenty-six *staria* of sorghum which he had from Giovanni Marcolino, factor of the sons of Jacopo de Verine, without Marcolino's consent, he was to pay 36 *l.* To complete a payment due to another supplier for two *staria* of sorghum, he had to pay 25 *s. parvorum.* He was also to repay a ducat which he had had by violent means from Pietro de Vataguis. The claims of Martino Dovo di Abbazia for stones and other things supplied to Capello, for which he had not been fully paid, were reserved. One ducat was awarded to Giacomo Becarino, which Capello had received but had not placed in his accounts. Also, 28 *s.* to the same for some plumage. The judgment rendered by Capello against Becarino for 24 *l.* for two guardians of the tower was revoked, and the rights of both parties reserved. Capello had received 71 *l.* 10 *s.* for paying guardians of the tower, as revealed in his records and those of the treasurers of Padua, but he had paid out only 15 *l.* He had to restore the remainder to the guardians, reserving to him any rights he might have against Becarino and others. He owed 84 *l. parvorum* to Deodato the Jew for the remainder of the payment for some linen, which he had to pay, reserving whatever rights he might have against Pietro Polo, to whom he claims to have given part of it. The forced sale of the possessions and meadows of Ambrosino de Marchesini to Lorenzo Crocco was canceled as fraudulent. He was also to pay ser Ambrosino 10 *l. parvorum* for the hay cut from his meadows without permission. He could hold no office until all the above were paid, and he could never serve in Castelbaldo or for two years anywhere else. He also had to pay a fine of 100 *l.*[198]

Just a few days later Niccolò Marcello, *podestà* and captain of Bassano, and Fantino Magno, provisor in the same place, were condemned to pay back all that they had had from the Feltrensi plus one-quarter.[199] In 1415 the Senate recorded that the captaincy of Canea had not been properly filled for twenty years, that of Retimo for three years, and that of Candia since the death of Tommaso Dandolo. In the meantime the rectors had made their sons captains, which was in violation of their commissions and to the great harm of the subjects, who were just fishermen. The so-called captains committed extortionate acts, and the poor subjects had recourse only to the fathers of the wrongdoers. The rectors were warned that they could not make their sons or other members of their families captains, but they must select some other Venetian nobles and pay them the same salaries as their legitimate predecessors.[200] On the same date the Senate reported that castellans of remote fortresses in Crete were heaping fines upon their subjects simply because they were allowed to keep half of what they collected. The oppression was so serious that people were considering leaving their homes to escape. Henceforth castellans who exacted unjust fines should be penalized 500 *l.* to be collected by the advocates, who should have their accustomed portion.[201] In 1416 Paolo Querini, formerly count and captain of Scutari, was condemned for taking a vineyard from Chiurana Fornaria and giving it to Paolo Medono. The vineyard was restored, and Querini was deprived permanently of any offices in Durazzo and Albania and sentenced to six months in prison and a fine of 500 *l.*[202]

In April 1419 we first hear the sad tale of the death of a merchant who had deposited a sum of money and other things with the *baiulo* of Corfu, Niccolò Foscolo. After the merchant's death his sons and his sisters demanded the goods, which, however, the *baiulo* proposed to bring back to Venice at the expiration of his term. The Senate forbade him to do this, but he did it anyway and in October 1420 he was sentenced to restore two hundred ducats to the executors and heirs of the merchant. The remainder owed was to be determined by the advocates of the Commune. Foscolo was also sentenced to a fine of 200 *l.* and perpetual exclusion from office in Corfu.[203] Lorenzo Minio, who was rector and provisor of Bassano and Rovereto, was convicted of extortions in 1421. Minio either had to return to the brothers di Urbano two cuirasses or the equivalent sum of fifty ducats. He also had to pay twenty-eight ducats for some leather work he had from Delaido of Trento. Minio was also sentenced to a 500 *l.* fine and deprival of all offices in perpetuity in Rovereto and the whole Val Lagarina.[204] In 1421 the Senate received reports of "many extortions and violent acts" against its subjects at Brescello. A syndic was assigned to investigate and the process of selection of the rector or castellan was changed.[205] Pietro Diedo, formerly *podestà* and captain of Napoli di Romania, was sentenced in 1422 to be deprived perpetually of governance in that place, to six months in prison, and a fine of 500 *l.*, as well as the restoration to Giovanni Damianto of the dowry of his wife. In motions not adopted there is also mention of profiteering on the sale of raisins—but of this the evidence does not prove that he was convicted.[206]

The *podestà* of Portobuffole, Andrea Cocco, was sentenced in 1424 for seizing wood and sawdust, for cutting wood without permission of the owner of the land, and for taking fodder for his horses without pay. He was required to pay 100 *l.*, never to hold office in Portobuffole, and to make payment for his various extortions.[207] In 1432 the Great Council authorized the Senate to send *sindici* to Bergamo and Brescia to investigate the daily complaints against the Venetian rectors and other officials.[208] Eight months later similar complaints led to authorization of syndics for the entire *terraferma*.[209] We have already considered the bribery scandals in Crete in the early 1430s, in which a Jewish "fixer" had been implicated. As the investigation spread, Venetian provincial officials, especially Pietro Muazzo, who was one of those eventually convicted for taking bribes, took advantage of anti-Semitism to extort money from Jews by such devices as malicious and unfounded proceedings against them.[210] This Muazzo was a thoroughgoing crook and petty tyrant. He also was convicted of charging priests for a license to hear confessions.[211]

The same *podestà* of Montagnana, Benedetto Barbadico, who was convicted of bribery in 1448 was in 1450 charged with extortions and exactions. There is also mention of the improper conviction of a counterfeiter on the basis of a confession gained through the threat of torture without other evidence, but this does not appear in the sentence adopted. He was required to pay 200 *l.* which he had received wrongly and as much for penalty and to complete eighteen months in prison.[212] Likewise Andrea Bragadin had committed a number of offenses against peasants when he had been in the vicariate of the district of Padua, especially against the people of Pernumia. He made them become sureties, he accepted grain, and he bought land and oxen at reduced prices, renting them back to the peasants. He was sentenced in 1457 to spend three months in prison and to pay a fine of 300 *l.*, and measures were taken to undo the harm against the peasants.[213]

A castellan of Brescia, Jacopo Cocco, was found selling bread, wine, cloaks, shoes, and other things to his subordinates in 1473 at inflated prices. The Ten forbade him or his successors to engage in such business under penalty of two hundred ducats and exclusion from all offices for five years. All the subordinates were to receive their pay freely every month. In order that the castellan might live honestly, however, his pay was raised twenty ducats a month.[214] In 1484 Pasquale Querini, *podestà* of Noale, was convicted of extorting and wrongfully accepting money for mortuary payments, things sent to the army, and from bankrupts.[215] At the end of 1499 and the beginning of 1500 Fantino Moro, who had been governor of Arbe, was indicted by two investigating syndics for having robbed the people of the town. Sanuto adds *per esser povero.*[216]

The Quaranta criminale condemned Antonio Moro in 1500 for extortions and thefts committed while in a governorship. He was sentenced to repayment and banishment from office for an unknown number of years.[217] The conviction of Bernardo da Canal in that year was not only for embezzling the money of the Commune, but for his frauds, deception, and cheating against private persons when he was *podestà* and captain of Antivari. The Antivarani complained that he had ruined the land.[218] When Doge Agostino Barbarigo died in 1501 there arose a tide of complaints that the doge, his family, and his servants had demanded gifts from everyone, had extorted money, and had sold justice, so that he had acquired a vast sum of money. He was convicted and penalties were assessed against his estate. It seems reasonably clear that this was not just a political trial, since Sanuto informs us that guilt was proved by the accounts of Barbarigo's son-in-law and accomplice and by many public records, so many that it would have taken three days to read them. There were two hundred witnesses.[219]

Giovanni Antonio Minio's ill-fated argument in the Great Council in 1502 against the suspension of salaries touched upon the temptation for unpaid officials to commit injustices against the people.[220] Things continued to go badly in Antivari. Niccolò Dolfin, who had been one of the syndics who gained the conviction of Bernardo Canal, was sent back to the colony to investigate the complaints against the governor, Giovanni Molin. These complaints from the Antivarani had been backed up by the Venetian castellan, Pietro Bon, but Molin, on the other hand, had lodged complaints against Bon. The syndic was also to visit Alessio and investigate the charges against the Venetian provisor, Antonio Bon, who was accused of having sent a large sum of money home on his own account.[221] In 1505 Niccolò Priuli was convicted of both embezzlement from the government and extorting money from the people when he was captain of Famagusta and lieutenant in Cyprus.[222] At the begining of 1506 Vicenzo Magno was arrested on account of the many complaints from Pago that as the Venetian count he was robbing the poor people there.[223]

From the mid-fourteenth century to the end of our period we find a wide variety of extortionate acts by Venetian officials. The most bizarre is undoubtedly the wickedness of Muazzo, who took bribes, squeezed Jews, and charged priests for the right to hear confessions—behavior which is quite intolerable. In spite of the misdeeds of Venetian governors, those who maintain the myth of Venice often argue that the *popolani* of *terraferma* rallied to St. Mark during the War of the League of Cambrai. Ventura, however, who studied class conflict in the area, retorts that the bitter class enmity between the *popolani* and the *cittadini* simply overwhelmed the common antipathy they felt toward the Venetians as a result of such outrageous behavior.[224]

The punishment for such extortion was not usually very severe. Ineligibility for offices in the place where the offense occurred was common. That corrupt governors remained eligible for other positions, however, shows how strong the patrician right to hold office was. Indeed, without justifying or excusing extortion, there is some basis for understanding why it happened. Consider that quite a few of the documents have to do with the improper acquisition of wood, grain, meat, wine, and other necessities for the governor's household, because, as Sanuto tells us in one case, the governor was poor. Minio was absolutely right, though impolitic, in pointing out the temptations which came to such officials. On the other hand, it appears that in many cases these necessities were not being seized from the rich and influential, although even that is hardly acceptable, but from the poor and the weak.

MISUSE OF JUDICIAL AUTHORITY

Nobles abused the judicial process for corrupt purposes by bringing suits falsely, by obstructing justice, by giving or soliciting false testimony, and by rendering judgments which they knew to be unjust.

A number of cases with which we have already dealt under one rubric or another had as one result the nullifying of some unjust judicial process pursued by extortionate or otherwise crooked magistrates. We can cite a few other examples. In 1390 the judgment against Luca Contarini, former governor of Canea, set aside the sentence that he had improperly and unjustly imposed upon Jacopo Vizzamano.[225] When the *baiulo* and two councillors of Negroponte were convicted in 1394, the Senate decided, among other things, to negate the process brought by the *baiulo*, Gabriele Emo, against Giorgio Maruchai.[226] Judgments of the former governor of Sithia, Ermolao Contarini, against the castellan, Zanacchio Zeno, and his sergeants and against Giorgio di Arbe were also nullified as a consequence of an investigation of Contarini's conduct of office.[227] We have already noticed the infamous Muazzo bringing malicious processes against Jews.[228]

At least as early as the thirteenth century we find a consciousness of the risk that judges would fraudulently obstruct justice.[229] In 1370 we have a case of obstruction by a nonjudicial official. Giovanni Priuli, who was captain of the Gulf, was convicted for refusing to turn over to a lord of the night a certain Lombardino, who was in Priuli's galley in the Canal. Lombardino, who had beaten a whore to death, thus escaped justice, but Priuli was sentenced to a fine of 300 *l. parvorum*.[230] Sometimes, of course, it was a litigant, not a judge or an official, who tried to alter the course of justice, as Zanino Morosini did in 1375 by threatening the judge. He received a three-month term in prison and a 25 *l.* fine.[231]

The thirteenth-century cartularies also reveal an awareness of the risk of perjured testimony. The advocates *del proprio* swore not to make any false instrument or testimony, nor to counsel anyone else to do so. And they promised that if they knew of any such falsehood, they would raise a stir or bring it to the attention of the judge.[232] In 1311 Marino Contarini and Giovanni Arimondo were caught giving false testimony in a case involving a property in the parish of St. John Chrysostom.[233] Several months later Paolo Bembo was convicted of tampering with witnesses before the *corte del proprio*.[234] In a rather tangled case in 1424, Pietro Marcello was charged with inducing Francesco Molin to testify falsely that two other nobles had asked him to witness that Giovanni Marcello, Pietro's son, had told him that Pietro knew of the shipwreck of his ship. Pietro induced Molin to put this in writing according to the wording that Giovanni Marcello read to him. The first attempt in the Senate to convict Pietro Marcello failed, but a second barely passed, reserving to the advocates of the Commune the case against Molin. The only sentence that was accepted, however, was the nullification of Molin's perjured testimony.[235] Andrea Contarini, formerly *podestà* of Padua, was found guilty in 1428 of having given perjured testimony that one Angelino da Allamagna, companion of the abbot of San Niccolò on the Lido, Paolo Trevisan, had confessed to the murder of the abbot's mistress, Madalena.[236] We have already mentioned the bribing of Pietro Gradenigo to give false testimony against Lucia Avantii in a case involving the custody of Bartolomeo Avantii. The Senate authorized his interrogation, with torture if necessary, but he had run away. He was sentenced in absentia to exile for life.[237] Dolfino Dolfin, who had been in the office of the assessors of wine, testified falsely that he had delivered more than 70 *l.* to the treasurers. He was sentenced in 1454 to pay the capital plus fifty ducats.[238]

Like any political society worthy of the name, the Venetian polity sought impartiality in the administration of justice without favoring or doing injustice to anyone, without the magistrates accepting gifts, without procuring improper gains for anyone, as the councillors swore from 1229 on.[239] The oath that "I will neither aid anyone nor injure anyone through fraud" is found throughout the capitularies of various offices in the thirteenth century.[240] No swearing of oaths, of course, is likely to cause magistrates to live up to their duty. Common political or economic interests, the influence of friends, patrons, and clients, and perhaps above all considerations of family solidarity had their weight in the scales of justice.[241] Venetian government, moreover, had a systematic flaw, which encouraged the abuse of legal processes, the *utilitates* or perquisites enjoyed by officials in lieu of a salary or as a supplement, one of which was the right of the magistrate to a portion of the judgment or the fine.[242]

Sometimes, of course, justice miscarried simply because patrician officials were inclined to be lenient toward their fellows.[243] This was probably the case in 1357, when Andrea Paradiso, *podestà* of Farra and Brazza, failed to initiate proceedings against Alvise Michiel, the *podestà* of Lesina, who had killed Marco della Fontana. Paradiso was sentenced to exclusion for life from the government of Farra and Brazza, for five years from all governmental offices, and a fine of 200 *l.*[244] Often justice miscarried through sheer favoritism. One of the offenses for which Cristoforo Marcello, former castellan of Modone and Corone, was sentenced in 1426 was that he had his son Antonio made a canon in the diocese of Modone and then made judgments in favor of that prebend. The father was deprived in perpetuity of the governance of Corone and Modone and the son was expelled from his prebend and required to restore anything he had had from it.[245]

In 1464 the Ten complained of the wrong done by those who besieged judges and officials with their prayers and pleas outside of the court or office, even at their homes. In order that judges and officials could make their decisions sincerely and with uncontaminated minds, the Ten added to the oaths taken by magistrates a penalty for not imposing silence upon such suppliants, negation of any judgment in their favor, deprivation of the Great Council (and all offices) for a year, and a fine of 200 *l.* for the suppliant, if he were a noble.[246] Another means of showing favoritism lay in moving cases up on the calendar, that is, hearing them before others which had been filed earlier. In 1466 the Senate noted that the Quaranta civile, in spite of a law requiring that the cases be heard in order, was yielding through friendship to the pleas of relatives and other nobles for early hearings. The Senate pointed out that "many of the poor, widows, and religious, who cannot take advantage of friendship, are excluded, and their cases never have an end to their very great harm." The old law was reaffirmed and the notary of the Forty was given responsibility for seeing that it was followed. The same rule was also to apply to matters before colleges.[247] Later in the same year the Ten issued a powerful denunciation of rampant favoritism:

> Mandates cannot be made nor penalties imposed too soon in order to put an end to the prayers which certain of our nobles, who presume to be able to do whatever they wish, make daily to prevent officials from doing justice and observing the statutes and ordinances of the Great Council and of their capitularies, which they have sworn to observe. For certain of those nobles assembled together enter the office of the night, or of the heads of the *sestieri,* or of similar offices, whether they impose prison sentences or monetary fines, and they ask, insist, and press vigorously, so that unless provision is made it is not possible for the said officials to exact condemnations or to punish anyone who has any noble favorable to him. And therefore, just as it was provided that they should not make prayers to the Quaranta, as to judges or officials who deal in civil matters, so it is necessary to provide lest they should do it in those offices which judge in criminal matters and exact the penalties and the condemnations of our Signoria.
>
> Let it be enacted that any noble of ours cannot go to the lords of the night, or to the heads of the *sestieri,* or to the five of peace, or to the old justices, or even to the new, and to the officials of the wine tax for pleading for or commending any person having business in any of the aforesaid offices, nor accompanying anyone, nor standing before the said officials on behalf of such persons under penalty of deprivation of the Great Council for a year and of 100 *l.*

Any of the officials who heard such pleas would fall under the same penalty. Nobody appearing before such offices could be accompanied by more than two persons, not counting advocates.[248]

The condemnation of Pasquale Querini in 1484, mentioned earlier, included the revocation of pardons granted by him unjustly and wrongfully to seven homicides condemned by his predecessor.[249] In 1489 Marino Moro, formerly provisor of Veglia, was condemned for rendering unjust judgments on the grounds that the defendants were engaged in illegal assemblies or sects. He, his officials, and the informer had to restore the penalties, and Moro could never be governor in Veglia nor for two years hold office anywhere in Venetian territory.[250] Maranini tells us that at the beginning of the sixteenth century it was common in trials to attempt to influence the poor nobles in favor of the accused.[251]

FALSIFICATION OF DOCUMENTS

Just as by the end of the thirteenth century the advocates *del proprio* swore that they would not bear false witness, they also swore not to make false instruments, to counsel that they be made, or to fail to report any that they discovered.[252] We have a striking case from 1278, when the Great Council convicted Lorenzo Giuliano, who was a salt official in Chioggia. He was guilty of tampering with the books of receipts by erasing entries (scraping the parchment). The sentence was loss of all offices for five years.[253] The advocates of the Commune in 1325 were required to swear, among other things, to be on the watch for any fraud based on false entries in accounts.[254] Dolfino Dolfin, the official of the Fondaco dei Tedeschi whom we discussed in connection with embezzlement of almost 1,000 *l. ad grossos,* tried to conceal his crime by "writing in the books for a long time after his departure some entries (of sums) given to the treasurers without month or day."[255] Chojnacki has drawn from his study of the Raspe the tale of Francesco Contarini, sentenced to a fine of 50 *l.* in 1364 for threatening to put out the eyes of a clerk who refused to alter the transcript of a trial.[256] Stamato Gradenigo, castellan of Bicorno, who was convicted of extortion in 1370, had falsified the records.[257] Nicoleto Cocco, who had been treasurer of Treviso, had falsified the books of the notary and scribe of his office. He was sentenced in 1380 to six months in prison and loss of offices and councils for ten years.[258] Jacopo Grimani was convicted in 1388 of using forged letters, false seals, and false oaths to create documents in his own favor. Naturally all these were nullified, and Grimani was exiled from Crete for life and sentenced to a year in prison.[259] Pietro Dolfin, patron of a ship, and his father, Michele, instigated the scribe of the ship to falsify the ship's books.[260]

We have already mentioned that Francesco Marini, a *straordinario,* was juggling the books in 1455 in order to cover up the fact that he had taken home five thousand ducats that he was supposed to deliver to the treasurers of the Commune, the patrons of the Arsenal, or other officials.[261] A young (twenty-six-year-old) noble named Marco Baffo paid with his life for forging ducal letters in the name of the Ten by virtue of which he had collected five hundred ducats from the governors of Padua, Vicenza, Verona, and Treviso. Like tampering with the coinage, the government took this offense very seriously, and Baffo was sentenced to have "his right hand cut off, so that it would be separated from his arm, and with it hung about his neck, he should be led to the middle of the two columns [the red—or pink—columns of the ducal palace], where he should be hanged by the neck, so that he

should die and his body and soul should be separated." Malipiero specifies also that he was dressed in his patrician robes.[262] In 1489 Niccolò
Bondumier, who was then paymaster for the fleet in Cyprus, was three
hundred ducats short in his accounts. He secured a false document,
which was unknowingly signed by Alvise Pisani of the Pisani bank. It
took over ten years to discover the fraud, but in 1500 he was ordered
from his post in Crete to Venice for trial, and Dolfin notes that he
stood in danger of losing his hand for making the forged document.[263]
In 1504 Benedetto Pesaro, procurator and formerly captain-general of
the sea, was posthumously charged with falsifying his official journals
and books. His scribe was to be examined, if he could be found, for the
books were in his hand. Notice, by the way, that we are here concerned
with a very highly placed noble.[264]

We have some evidence, though not a lot, of Venetian patricians engaged in the crime of counterfeiting or other closely related activities.
In 1353 a young noble named Maffeo Gabrieli was found to have conspired with two subordinates, when he was an official of the assay of
gold, to use in a certain work silver of less fine assay than it was
supposed to be. He was sentenced in absentia, since he was said to be
more afraid of prison than others were of death, and had been abroad
for four years, to loss of offices and councils for six years and a fine of
one hundred ducats.[265] Fantino Morosini and Daniele da Canal, *massari*
at the silver mint, were convicted in 1416 of stamping pieces of silver
that were less good and of less weight than they were supposed to be.
They were sentenced only to permanent exclusion from all offices having to do with gold and silver and to pay a fine of 100 *l.* each.[266]

The cases cited above seem to have been regarded as lightly as the
Venetians regarded many other infractions of law. By the late fifteenth
century, however, we encounter a cluster of counterfeiting cases involving nobles which the government clearly took very seriously. The
series begins in 1473 with Girolamo Querini's buying of counterfeit
money of Ferrara, which he then spent, knowing it to be counterfeit.
He was sentenced to have his right hand cut off and both eyes put out,
and to pay a fine of one thousand ducats.[267] In 1475 Silvestro Contarini
was accused of knowingly spending counterfeit Venetian money. He
failed to appear to defend himself, and he too was sentenced by the Ten
to have his right hand cut off, both eyes put out, and pay a fine of 1,000
ducats.[268] In 1483 the Ten took up the case of Taddeo Gradenigo, who,

when he was castellan of the old castle of Corfu, had been guilty of clipping *troni* and *marcelli* (silver coins named after doges Niccolò Tron and Niccolò Marcello). Gradenigo also prudently declined to appear to defend himself, and he too was sentenced in absentia under the draconian law to loss of his right hand and both eyes, the penalty to be inflicted between the two infamous columns facing the Piazzetta, if he were ever caught.[269] Francesco Bembo was convicted in 1484 of conspiring to make counterfeit coins. He was sentenced to ten years in a prison without a window and, after that, to exile for life in Portogruario.[270] In 1484 Giovanni Geronimo da Riva, who had participated in a counterfeiting scheme with the son and assistant of a mintmaster, had hurried to denounce himself when he sensed that the jig was up. He hoped to get off virtually free of penalty under the law of 1473, but he received a sentence of two years' banishment from Venice and the Veneto.[271] The conviction of Maffeo Soranzo for participation in a conspiracy to produce coins of short weight and inferior alloy in 1490 illustrates the point that not all crimes by nobles, even so sordid a one as counterfeiting, were committed by the destitute. At least we may presume that he was a man of some substance from the fact that his father was both *cavaliere* and procurator of St. Mark.[272]

A few nobles, especially late in the fifteenth century, were thus found tampering with the money. This was a crime that the Republic punished most severely except when there were mitigating circumstances, like the confession of da Riva. It is a crime unlike embezzlement, charges of which could easily arise from an honest (or only slightly dishonest) difference of opinion over what belonged to whom. One does not slide inadvertently into the highly calculated crime of counterfeiting.

VIOLENCE

We are not concerned here with ordinary murders, rapes, thefts, and the like, but with acts of illegal violence which warp the workings of government. Since our rubrics are not mutually exclusive and sometimes not clearly defined, we have already noticed a few such acts, such as the threat to put out a clerk's eye unless he changed the record of a trial. It is worth considering a few more examples of violent civil misbehavior by patricians.

Enrico Ferro, formerly the *podestà* of Rubano, faced charges before the Senate in 1357 for the tortures and other excesses that he had committed against Giacomo di Ceferia, Franceschina, his servant, and Bello da Bologna, his partner. Since he was sentenced to restore some arms to Giacomo, the incident probably had something to do with obtaining them. He was also excluded from all offices and councils for life and fined 100 *l.*[273] The extortions of which Conte Venier was found guilty in 1362 constituted only a few of the charges against him as *podestà* of Isola. He caused injuries to a certain Lucia because she would not let him have his way with her daughter; he imprisoned and fined and struck with his own hands Pencio da Pirano; he caused Giorgio di Guercio of Trieste to be beaten so that he died; he beat a certain mendicant brother with his own hands; he beat Giovanni Scaliono with his own hands. A butcher named Giacomo Groto asked for a license to export animals to Venice, and, because Venier did not wish to give it to him, he imprisoned Groto and then drove him and his animals out of Isola. For this array of violent misdeeds he was banished from Isola, deprived for life of jobs in the provinces, embassies, provisorships, and positions as *sopraconsolo,* also of all offices for two years, and fined 400 *l.*[274] The Senate also found Pietro Giustinian, formerly *baiulo* in Cyprus, guilty in 1369 of striking Maffeo Venier and Pietro Dalpino with a burning, double-branched candlestick, of hitting a physician, Master Alessandro da Pisa, under the loggia of Famagusta, and of giving a blow to a sailor, causing blood to flow. It seems that they were rather lenient in this case, merely fining him 200 *l.*[275] Niccolò Adoaldo was charged in 1393 with excessive iniquities and cruelties against the men of Isola delle Serafine (*insula Serrphenarum*), committing torments and horrible acts against law, justice, and all humanity. He was deprived of all jobs in the provinces for life, denied the right ever to go back to the place, and sentenced to two years in prison.[276] A *collegio* was established in 1402 to look into the misdeeds in office of Eustachio Grioni as *podestà* of Drivasto. He had broken into the house of Giorgio Varsio and raped his wife, Tania, and various other nefarious deeds were charged against him.[277]

Marco Miani, formerly *baiulo* of Corfu, was condemned in 1427 for the damage done to the belts (*suarum centurarum*) of Antonia the baker. Another unadopted punishment would have required him to pay compensation to Maria, a housemaid, for the loss of her finger, but we cannot assume that he was convicted on this count. He was sentenced to perpetual exclusion from the government of Corfu, to pay a fine of 50 *l.,* and to pay twenty-two ducats to Antonia.[278] Miani, however, appears as envoy to the despot of the Morea after about seven months and, after about fourteen months from his sentencing, as *baiulo* of Constantinople, which was a post often considered a great prize.[279] When he had been councillor of Modone, Niccolò Querini had entered into the house of the late chancellor of Modone, Giovanni Cresimbene, and had sex with his daughter, deflowering her. The Senate sentenced him to a year in prison, a fine of 200 *l.*, permanent ineligibility to be rector of Corone or Modone, and to pay 260 ducats into the loan office for an endowment for the dowry of the young women to marry or become a nun.[280] It came to the ears of the Signoria in 1500 that the officers of the fleet were depriving the oarsmen of their fair share of the booty, sometimes injuring and beating them in order to get it. The advocates of the Commune were authorized to hear all the claims of the oarsmen. It was also provided that guilty officers should repay the amount due, plus an additional 25 percent for the advocates. They should also lose their positions and all other offices for five years.[281]

One would not claim that acts of civic violence were commonplace, but nobles in official roles did commit a number of them. The sexual crimes seem especially grievous, although I am not sure that they were considered so.[282]

THE FORMS of corruption practiced by the Venetian patriciate were many and various, covering pretty generally the categories known to us today. If patricians did not take graft on contracts for building bridges, it was because nobles did not build bridges, but they did steal from the Republic as patrons of the Arsenal, they sold military supplies as castellans, and so on, especially after about 1370, when the evidence begins to multiply.

Taking the various sorts of corruption all in all, I do not wish to push too hard the argument that there was anything particularly awful in the corruption of the Venetian patricians, but only that they were subject to the same temptations as other elites and did not resist temptation in any particularly noteworthy manner. To be fair, the evidence presented is a mixture of downright cynical corruption and some cases which represent nothing more sinister than a difference of opinion over legitimate expenses. On the other hand, we should be aware that when we study such a subject as corruption, only a small, though indeterminable, percentage of the cases ever get into the record. Many people get away with corruption, else, we may presume, it would not be done. With regard to corrupt practices involving the acquisition of money, in contrast, for example, to the relatively rare sexual abuses,[283] the Venetian patriciate may have been peculiarly vulnerable, because of the large number of poor men who remained within the patrician elite by right of birth. Unlike most elites, the Venetian patriciate did not adjust itself very readily or very much to changing economic circumstances. The pressure of their poverty tempted—in some cases almost compelled—poor nobles to exploit their offices to eke out a living or to cover the expenses of the office itself. If Venetian nobles were not more wicked than other men, and they probably were not, they were more tempted. The Venetian state was in considerable measure a welfare scheme for the nobility, but because the benefits were often small and usually irregular and unpredictable, many patricians grabbed for themselves what they could when they had the opportunity. The case should not be overstated, but Venetian government probably was more corrupt than the more honest and better administered among modern governments.

VII
Other Uncivil Behavior

Not even the overblown reputation of the Venetian patriciate for wisdom and efficiency in diplomacy can match the strength, I think, of the romantic myth of the noble as the tight-lipped protector of secrets of state. Charles Diehl wondered how secrets could be so well guarded, especially in the relatively large Senate, and he asked whether it was not necessary to find the cause in that firm discipline which from an early hour formed the young Venetian patrician for the service of the Republic and set before him, as the essential rule for his life, absolute devotion to the state.[1] Molmenti exulted that the secrecy of debate in the Senate was never violated.[2] Besta too boasts of Venetian skill in extracting the secrets of others and preserving their own. The ability to dissimulate and to keep silent was greatly prized.[3] The tradition of patrician secretiveness goes back at least as far as the Quattrocento, when Poggio-Bracciolini praised the Venetian government for its investigation of Carmagnola over a period of eight months without any indication that he was under suspicion.[4]

Whatever the virtues of the education of young patricians and the sanction of the myth itself, however, the Venetian system of government presented enormous problems for the preservation of secrets of state: the multiplicity of councils, the size of the Great Council and the Senate, and the rapid rotation of officials.[5] Most violations probably do not stem from such base motives as desire for money or for revenge, although we shall see some examples of perfidy, but from a compulsion to appear important, to set the record straight, to defend the reputation of another or oneself, or simply the inability to lie convincingly. By the end of our period, in any case, everybody knew what was done in the Senate and even the Council of Ten almost immediately.[6] Jacob Burckhardt drew a very different picture than Diehl, Molmenti, and Besta. According to him the Venetian government in the late fifteenth century was so honeycombed with traitors in the pay of pope, prince, or second-rate *condottiere* that the Ten found it prudent to conceal matters of importance from the Senate.[7] The Great Council did not treat much secret business, for, with its two thousand to twenty-five hundred members, it could not be expected to be secure. It was not regarded as a secret council.

The Consiglio dei Pregadi with some three hundred members also was too large to keep secrets, although it did handle a great deal of very sensitive business.[8] The combination of these two factors made the Senate the focus of the Republic's problem concerning violations of secrecy. In 1357 the Senate condemned Angelo Bragadin and Luca Giusti for revealing its secrets, the former to a fine of 100 *l.* and exclusion from all offices and councils for two years and the latter just to the fine of 100 *l.*[9]

The problem does not appear, however, to have become acute until the second half of the Quattrocento. It is not clear why this was so, although the increasing size and importance of the Senate were undoubtedly major factors. From 1449 to 1509 we encounter a rising flood of material on violations of the secrecy of the Senate. In 1449 the Senate lamented the rise of the perilous custom of senators speaking outside the Senate of matters concerning which secrecy had been imposed. Under penalty of 500 *l.* and deprivation of the Senate and ineligibility to be a governor for five years, they were not to speak of these matters, even to members of the Senate or the College.[10] Ten years later the Dieci objected to the "introduction" of the same bad custom, reaffirmed the act of 1449, and increased the fine to 1,000 *l.* The act of 1459 also closed a loophole in the earlier law, since those who left the Senate before secrecy had been imposed had not been covered.[11]

In 1472 the Ten exposed a very high level conspiracy to betray the secrets of the Senate to Rome. It centered upon Elisabetta Zeno, who was the sister of the Barbo Pope Paul II, mother of Cardinal Gianbattista Zeno, and aunt of two cardinals. The lady held a salon attended by important senators and also by two clerks hidden behind a screen. The senators spoke carelessly and the clerks wrote down what they said, in effect reconstituting a record of the proceedings of the Senate. The cardinals were the intermediaries who communicated the secret matter to the Curia. When the Ten discovered the conspiracy, they reinforced themselves with a *zonta* of twenty-five. Elisabetta Zeno was sentenced to exile at Capodistria for life. The cardinals were denied any benefices under the control of the Republic. Pantaleone Barbo received a sentence of a year in prison and exclusion from all offices and councils for ten years. Alvise Barbo was also arrested, but I do not know what became of him. Geronimo Badoari, who was a member of the Ten, was sentenced to six months in prison and permanent exclusion from all offices and councils, in effect deprivation of the rights of nobility. Domenico Zorzi, who was a *savio grande,* and Andrea Trevisan were released. It is likely that they were among the many guests of Elisabetta Zeno seized for questioning who were found not guilty.[12] The incident is instructive in showing the strength and extension of the family and the influence of the pope.

Another rather spectacular case, in 1478, involved three nobles, not members of the Senate, who managed to ascend through the doge's apartments to the roof of the palace, remove some tiles and a skylight, and thus gain access to a place above the ceiling of the Senate chamber, where they could hear the report of Tommaso Malipiero, who had just returned from his embassy to Constantinople. Probably they were seeking information that would give them foreknowledge of events which would affect the economic life of the city. All three, Giovanni Loredan, Jacopo Trevisan, and Daniele Barbaro, were sentenced to six months in prison and deprivation of offices and councils for five years, although we are informed in a later hand that the period of ineligibility was reduced to two years.[13]

The efforts of the government to protect its secrets appear to have been going very badly by this time. Six months later another scandal broke concerning the transmission of state secrets to Rome. Giacomo da Mezzo, Venetian ambassador at the Curia, complained that all the business of the Senate was current at the papal court, and many knew the Senate's action on Roman matters before he did. This really angers an ambassador, because it makes him look like a fool not highly regarded by his government and deprives him of the credibility that he needs for his own gathering of information. Marco Cornaro thereupon felt moved to make a speech in the Senate, not only pleading for senators to keep their mouths shut, but declaring that "when it would be demanded of him, he would reveal what he knew about it." One of the heads of the Ten naturally made such a demand, and Cornaro unfolded enough to set the machinery in motion. A messenger was promptly sent to intercept the courier to Rome at Chioggia or Ravenna. Letters were found that incriminated Alvise and Andrea Zane, brothers of Lorenzo, the bishop of Brescia and titular patriarch of Antioch. They were seized, and so were Giacomo Malipiero, a senator, and Vitale Lando, a ducal councillor and

Malipiero's brother-in-law. The Ten also sent to Brescia to take the bishop, whom the Ten accused of being an assiduous spy and misleader of other nobles for many years. Lorenzo Zane, however, had fled to Mantua. From there he entered Venice secretly and by night, presumably to gather some wealth or settle some affairs, and then he went into hiding. The Ten seized his goods at Brescia, finding among them evidence that the others accused had been sending secret information to the bishop, who relayed it to Rome. Bribery was involved, and on a very large scale. Vitale Lando received two hundred ducats a year and his son received the abbacy of the Umiliati, worth seven hundred ducats a year. That is big money—but then Lando was a member of the Small Council. Giacomo Malipiero received two hundred ducats. Alvise Loredan, who had also become incriminated, obtained a promise from the bishop to dower his daughters. His brother[14] had three hundred to four hundred ducats a year. Although Lando probably received the largest bribe, these are all significant sums. The Ten banished the bishop *in perpetuo* and seized the incomes from his benefices. After the necessary religious expenses were deducted, the remainder went to the Arsenal for the purpose of the Turkish wars. Malipiero, who confessed, was exiled to Arbe for life. Lando was sentenced to exile for ten years in Vicenza and permanent deprivation of all offices and councils. Andrea Zane became ineligible for all offices and councils for two years, but he could never be a member of a secret council as long as his brother Lorenzo lived. Alvise Zane, who knew that the secrets were being revealed and did not report it to the Ten, received the same sentence as his brother Andrea. Alvise Loredan, the brother-in-law of the bishop, who was guilty of sheltering Lorenzo, knowing that he was wanted, was deprived of secret councils for ten years. Francesco Querini also wrote secrets to the bishop and was sentenced to three years' ineligibility for offices and councils and permanent deprivation of secret councils. Domenico Malipiero reports that after the publication of his condemnation Querini died of melancholy. The notary of the ambassador to Rome, a *cittadino,* of course, was also condemned.[15] This case differs a bit from the Zeno case of 1472. Family ties are clear enough, but they are not quite so prominent or widespread as in the case of the Zeno. Neither were so many ecclesiastics of high rank involved. On the other hand, gross bribery is much more prominent in the 1478 case of the bishop of Brescia and the Zane.

In 1482 the heads and inquisitors of the Ten appointed spies to investigate the leaking of secret information to the ambassador of the duke of Ferrara. Dolfino Dolfin and Geronimo Zane were arrested, tortured, and convicted. They were sentenced to exclusion from all secret councils for five years. Nine months later, however, the Ten returned to the case of

Dolfin and exiled him to Friuli for life.[16] The doge complained in 1495 of all the leaks of secret information from the Senate, which then was bruited about the *piazza* and the *campi*.[17] He appears not to have accomplished much by his plea, for in 1496, according to Sanuto, the Senate appointed three investigators to try to put a stop to leaks. They met often, "more to create fear than otherwise," and the diarist adds that there was a reduction in gossip and, in particular, that the members of the Senate were keeping their mouths shut.[18] Dispatches of Duke Ercole's ambassador in the first half of 1497 speak repeatedly of his principal informer, *lo amico*. This chief informer appears to have been corrupted, and, indeed, there was a rumor that the duke had bribed a prominent senator.[19] Another ambassador later in the year also tells of *amici,* some of whom are named, who more or less innocently provide him with information.[20] He tells the duke of secrecy imposed upon the Senate under the most severe penalties ever and then he proceeds to give a full account of the discussion.[21] Malipiero says that secret matters had to be transferred to the Ten, because the duke of Ferrara knew everything that went on in the Senate.[22] Priuli informs us that in 1498 Ludovico Sforza also learned everything that happened in the Senate and was thus able to prepare himself for whatever Venice did. The government could not discover how he was acquiring his knowledge. A secretary named Landi had been caught informing the duke of Milan and had been hanged, but the flow of information continued.[23] In 1499 the Ten objected to the fact that some members of the Senate left the chamber when the door was opened for the entry or exit of the doge or to admit officials who had been summoned or to allow those who had to attend to their offices to go or for other reasons. Those who sneaked out sometimes went about the *piazza* and the *campi* telling about the letters that had been received or even about measures proposed and who spoke pro and con. Very often at the conclusion of the debate the Senate imposed secrecy upon these matters or even exacted an oath, but the wrongdoers had departed and had spread their gossip before this happened. The Ten tried to go to the heart of the matter by prohibiting such departures under penalty of ineligibility for the Senate for a year.[24] The Ten objected in 1505 to the *papalisti,* after their expulsion, sneaking back to a position where they could hear what was said in the chamber. They were to go upstairs to the room called the *cancellaria* and the doors of the upper, middle, and lower stairs should be locked with newly made keys, so that they should not hear anything pertaining to Rome. Any *papalisti* who did not go to the *cancellaria* or who managed to sneak out were to be ineligible for any secret councils or colleges for two years.[25]

Although the Senate does not seem to have had a serious problem of violation of secrecy earlier, it was very acute in the second half of the fifteenth century. It centered upon the papacy and the unreliability of the *papalisti*. It was not excessive precaution to exclude the relatives of clergy from councils, for some did put the interests of their families and the church above that of the state. Other foreign heads of state, such as the duke of Ferrara and the duke of Milan, also gained information from the Senate that should have been kept secret. Finally, we are struck in some of our examples by the complex of relatives, by blood and by marriage, which joined together to sacrifice the security of the state upon the altar of the family's zeal for exalted and remunerative positions in the church.

The Pien Collegio, which served as a probouleutic body for the Senate, was also naturally a sensitive organ of government. As a much smaller group of twenty-six members, however, it could maintain secrecy more readily (and more easily identify leaks) than a body of about three hundred. Nonetheless, it too had security problems from the mid-fifteenth century on.

The act of 1449 already discussed in the preceding section also applied to those of the College "who beyond that College should say to anyone the secret matters treated, read or deliberated in that College." Also subject to penalty, of course, were those who wrote of secret matters to those outside of Venice.[26]

The introduction to a decree of the Ten in 1480 reveals some of the petty problems in maintaining secrecy. It begins by pointing out how important it is to maintain secrecy in the College of the Signoria and the *savi* (the Pien Collegio), since they hear secret letters and they listen to ambassadors. Sometimes, it goes on, they inadvertantly open letters which should be received by the heads of the Ten, and these are read aloud and heard by everybody present. Unfortunately, officials of various sorts are often present, and they hear all this. Afterwards they go to Rialto or elsewhere and tell all that they heard in the Collegio. Henceforth, the decree states, when the College is summoned, the chancellor or a secretary should announce that all who are not members of the Collegio must go out of the room of the two maps or wherever the College is meeting. If officials really do need to appear before the Collegio on matters touching their offices, they should be present only while that business is before the body.[27] But by 1483 the Ten had to return to the problem, reaffirming the act of 1480 but adding that members of the college and any others entitled to be present should keep strict secrecy about all letters and discussions pertaining to the state and all communications from foreign or Venetian ambassadors or envoys. The penalty was to be exclusion from all secret councils and colleges for two years, unless the heads of the Ten should seek a higher penalty.[28] In 1495 Malipiero reported that the duke of Ferrara had enough influence in the Collegio that he knew everything.[29] As it appears, the legislation against nonmembers hearing the secrets of the Pien Collegio was not effective. On 20 November 1499 the Ten was complaining again about the presence of those who did not belong to the Pien Collegio and who revealed its secrets. Once more the Ten took action to exclude everyone except the Signoria and the *savi*.[30] The Ten tried to close the gaps again the following month, asserting that nothing could be worse or more detrimental than the revelation of those things that were done in the Ten and the Pien Collegio. The act employs the familiar argument that when secrecy cannot be trusted the members of those sensitive bodies will be inhibited from giving counsel freely. The revelation of the secrets of the Ten or the College should result in the loss of the offices held and exclusion from all secret councils and colleges for ten years. (Notice that they were still having trouble with officials who were not members of the College.)[31] Already in February 1500 the Ten modified the act of 20 November 1499, having realized that some officials really needed to be present at the meetings of the College. One of the provisors of grain and one of the patrons of the Arsenal were to be allowed to attend, although care should be taken to see that they were present only for the conduct of affairs relevant to their offices, and they should not hear letters, *relazioni,* ambassadors, or consultations not pertinent to them.[32]

The Ten was relatively small—not ten, of course, but seventeen members, usually with a *zonta* for the most serious cases, plus one of the advocates of the Commune, who was not a member but whose presence was required by law. The Ten, moreover, had cultivated and developed a tradition of secrecy renowned in the myth of Venice. Yet even the Ten had difficulty in preserving its secrets in the fifteenth century. In 1440 the Ten convicted five of the six heads of the *sestieri* for revealing what occurred in the Ten. It sentenced them to a month in prison, expulsion from office, and ineligibility for that office for two years.[33] In the case of Niccolò Bernardo in 1441 the Dieci established five years' deprivation of all offices and councils and a month in prison as penalty for anyone who would make public what the members said or how they voted.[34] In 1444 we hear of the Ten imposing secrecy, then discovering at the next meeting that it had been violated. Francesco de Lorenzo, a member of the Ten, was suspected. The process seems to have bogged down over the question of whether the advocates of the Commune, who were to examine witnesses, had the authority to bring a case before the Council of Ten.[35] In spite of its troubles, several days later the Ten turned down a penalty of ten years' deprivation of offices and councils for revealing the particular proceedings, but accepted ten years' exclusion from the Dieci.[36]

In 1445 the Dieci objected that contrary to the law the *papalisti* were not leaving the chamber as soon as matters touching the papacy came up, but were listening to the debate, and leaving only before the voting. Worse, the ambassadors to Rome complained that their mandates were known to the pope before they received them. Although, according to the council, the reputation of Venetian nobles was good, still it would be better if they left the council before these matters were discussed.[37] The act of 1459 on violations of senatorial secrecy also applied to the Council of Ten.[38] On 15 May 1473 Geronimo Molin complained to the Signoria that the recent proceedings over the island of Scarpanto, concerning which the most strict secrecy had been imposed, had been made public outside the council. The Ten sent for Pietro Cornaro, who had told the information to Molin, and it appointed a committee of four to question him.[39]

In spite of the order of the Signoria and the heads of the Council of Ten that nothing should be said outside the Ten concerning Beniamino Judeo and his news of the dealing of the *condottiere* Roberto di San Severino with Lodovico Sforza in 1485, Niccolò Trevisan, a *savio grande* (and therefore a very important politician), had leaked information. The doge and the heads of the Ten were to summon Trevisan and issue a very serious warning that he should say no more under penalty of the indignation of the Council of Ten.[40] In his dispatch of 29 May 1497 the ambassador from Ferrara informed the duke that he had penetrated the secrets of the Ten by means of a relative of *lo amico,* who had entered the council.[41] Late in the same year, the Ten was very upset because someone had not kept information secret according to its command. Secrecy was reimposed under penalty of death and confiscation of property.[42] In 1499 the Ten, as well as the College, was protected in its secret proceedings by a penalty against violators of ten years' exclusion from all secret councils and colleges.[43]

As suggested above, violations of secrecy were not always by any means based on conscious decisions to betray the Republic. Most were probably rooted in carelessness. A provision in an act of the Great Council in 1401 requires that all the documents entrusted to ambassadors must be returned to the government, lest in time they should fall into the hands of those who should not see them.[44] We know that this provision was not always obeyed, for many such documents survive in private archives, some of which can be found in the Museo Correr.[45] In 1437 the Ten prohibited ambassadors, provisors, captains, and others sent abroad on behalf of the Republic from writing to anyone other than the Signoria concerning the business committed to them.[46] Another way in which ambassadors jeopardized secrecy was by bringing flocks of followers to hear them deliver their *relazioni* after the conclusion of their missions. The Ten took action against this custom in 1459.[47] In spite of the act of 1437, the Ten observed in 1464 that ambassadors and provisors continued to write to relatives and friends information concerning their missions that should have remained secret. Once more this was prohibited under threat of action by the Ten.[48] Bad judgment was also shown by orators, according to the Senate in 1468, when they read the letters sent to them by the Signoria to the lords to whom they were accredited. This is not an unthinkable or necessarily treacherous ploy in negotiations. The intention was to convince the other party that the ambassador had already conceded as much as his instructions or his mandates would allow. Sometimes, indeed, an ambassador was provided with several sets of documents, giving him the advantage of what appeared to be a final stand, although he secretly possessed successive fall-back positions. At any rate, Venetian ambassadors were not to show their letters without the express mandate and license of the Senate.[49] A sweeping act of the Senate in 1482 forbade ambassadors to communicate affairs of state to anyone other than those with whom they had to treat and communicate.[50] On 3 March 1497 the doge spoke indignantly in the College against the fact that news from the field was circulating around the city. Letters were sent to the *provveditori* with the army that they must not write news to their relatives or others, according to the act of the Council of Ten, presumably that of 1437. An attempt to agree to a truce had failed, and it would have been better had the abortive effort remained secret.[51]

There does not seem to have been a significant problem with ambassadors or *provveditori* deliberately betraying secrets of state for money or through enmity to the state. These, after all, were men of the establishment, usually wealthy, influential, and politically ambitious men, tied to the interests of the Republic and more disposed than lesser nobles to adhere to the ideal of the Venetian nobleman.[52] They did show irresponsibility, however, in their carelessness concerning secret information, especially in their private correspondence with friends and relatives.

Much of the documentation on violations of secrecy is general in nature, not specifically directed to this or that council, college, or body of officials.

Lords of the *terraferma,* especially Francesco il Vecchio da Carrara, lord of Padua, had their friends, supporters, and paid retainers among the Venetian nobility. In 1372, at the very time when Carrara was attempting to have Venetian patricians who were opposed to him assassinated, other nobles were feeding him secret information. On 26 May Andrea Bassegio informed the Ten that Fra Benedetto of the Order of the Eremitani of San Stefano in Venice was guilty of passing secret information to Moncorso and Bernardo di Lazara, which they in turn delivered to Carrara. Fra Benedetto was taken and he confessed. Four prominent Venetian nobles who had access to secrets of the councils were implicated, tortured, and convicted. Alvise Molin, an *avogadore di Comun,* received a sentence of life imprisonment for being one of Fra Benedetto's informers. His son-in-law, Leonardo Morosini, a member of the Forty, was the other chief informer, and he too was sentenced to prison for life. Fra Benedetto was sentenced to a similar punishment by his prior. Pietro Bernardo, a ducal councillor, and Francesco Barbarigo, a head of the Forty, were convicted of permitting Molin to say things contrary to the honor of the state. They each received a year in prison and permanent deprivation of all secret councils and offices which entailed membership in those councils. From prison the chief informers continued to attempt to correspond with the lord of Padua, with Fra Bonaventura, and with the provincial of the Franciscans via another nobleman, Ramusio Dolfin, who did not deliver the letters, but kept them at home, failing to present them to the Signoria, as he ought to have done. Dolfin, therefore, was also sentenced to two months in prison. Carrara, the beneficiary of the Venetian secrets, wrote that Venice was in worse condition than at the time of the Falier conspiracy.[53] Lazzarini believed that this episode was important in the rise of the influence and power of the Council of Ten, for it acted decisively and effectively to punish a group of highly placed nobles.[54]

In 1384 Carrara was at it again. Pietro Giustinian, advocate of the Commune, was convicted of conveying the secrets of the councils to Padua via one Antonia Marceri of Chioggia. Both were taken and both lost their heads between the two red columns of the ducal palace.[55] Four years later the noble Stefano Manolesso suffered the same fate for sending secrets to Francesco il Vecchio.[56] Once more in 1404 a nobleman, Francesco Muazzo, was convicted of speaking with the lord of Padua without license.[57] We have already mentioned in the preceding chapter the scandal that arose after the fall of the Carrara, when it was discovered that Carlo Zeno and others had received money from the despot of Padua. Although there does not appear to be any suggestion that the hero of the War of Chioggia was selling secrets, the fact does illustrate the Carrara network of influence. Several nobles were convicted, moreover, of revealing secrets.[58]

A proposal defeated in 1425 illustrates the relatively innocent although careless way in which information was spread. There was a bench in the church of San Marco near the font of holy water where nobles were accustomed to sit, and those who were members of the secret councils chatted among themselves, although they could be overheard by others, about the affairs in which the councils were engaged. It was proposed in the Ten that the bench simply be removed—presumably so that the gossiping would at least be dispersed, but the motion did not carry.[59] The Ten complained in 1446 that nothing was discussed concerning others in the councils without immediately being published. Efforts to discover who was leaking secrets had all failed. Now, in some unnamed place where Venice had an ambassador, someone was offering to reveal how the information was getting abroad. The Ten ordered the ambassador to deal circumspectly with the would-be informer, promising that if his information were true he would find the Signoria grateful and generous.[60]

In 1459 the Ten sought to strike against the *papalisti* with a comprehensive act. In spite of the laws requiring their expulsion, the Venetian ambassadors wrote from Rome that the pope knew everything that went on in the councils of Venice, even to the names of those who spoke. Whenever anything touching the pope came before these councils, the chancellor or a notary should admonish the Signoria that the *papalisti* must depart. Nothing should be read until they did. If any ambassador, Venetian or foreign, said anything touching the papacy, the *papalisti* should leave on their own initiative. The colleagues in office of those expelled were to be careful not to say anything in front of them. Notaries who had letters concerning Rome should not read them or show them to *papalisti*. Those of the colleges or councils who spoke to *papalisti* of prohibited matters were to pay a fine of 1,000 *l.* and be deprived of secret councils for a year.[61] We have already referred in Chapter 6 to Tommaso Zeno, who offered to sell state secrets to the cardinal of Santa Maria del Porto.[62] In 1478 the Ten was once more complaining that Venetian secrets were known in Rome. It was rumored that the Venetian ambassador there had some information about it, so the Ten ordered him to write whatever he knew or believed or even suspected concerning whoever was leaking the material, to whom the material was being sent, and by what messengers. Also, of course, he was to give his reasons for his beliefs and suspicions. We would be tempted to believe that this effort led to the exposure of the case of the bishop of Brescia a month and a half later, if we did not know that it was Marco Cornaro's information that broke it open.[63] In 1480 the Ten named a *zonta* of fifteen to consider what to do about the secrets which were known in Rome, Florence, and elsewhere.[64] The act of 12 July

1480 was probably a result of their deliberations. The act complains of the members of the secret councils who discuss affairs of state with ambassadors and other citizens of foreign powers at home, in churches, in the *piazza* and *campi,* and all over town. This should no longer be done, except for the purpose of reporting the discussion to the Signoria or the heads of the Ten. The act provides that anyone who participates in such a discussion and does not report it should pay a fine of one thousand ducats and be exiled from Venice and the Veneto for two years.[65] This is said to have been stringently enforced, at least for a time.[66] It seems that early in January 1485 the Ten came into possession of letters of the bishop of Parenzo in reply to those of Michele Salomon which indicated that the latter was leaking secrets. Salomon was to be seized, examined, and, if necessary, tortured. All his papers were also to be seized and examined.[67]

In May 1486 the Ten broke a rather big case of conveying secret information to Galeotto della Mirandola, a *condottiere* in Venetian employment. Three noblemen and a secretary were involved. The Ten at first could not put hands on the patrician Giovanni da Lezzo, but a few days later he was in custody. On the basis of the testimony of physicians and learned magistrates, the Ten agreed that he was in no condition to be tortured, but they convicted him on the basis of the evidence available. He was exiled for life to Retimo under threat of decapitation if he should ever return. A minority voted in favor of simple capital punishment. A marginal note reports his arrival in Retimo.[68] Giovanni Diedo, another noble, seemed to have been cleared by his denial under torture of correspondence with the *condottiere,* but a few days later he was sentenced to the loss of all councils and offices for three years— which, however, is a lot more lenient than exile for life.[69] Geronimo Leoni, the third nobleman, received the same penalty.[70] The last two were probably guilty of indiscretion or carelessness, but not of treason. A *cittadino,* Francesco da Fin, was chancellor or seneschal to the *condottiere* and the ringleader of the affair. He was sentenced in absentia to perpetual exile, a price was put on his head, and the post that he had from the government (filled through delegates) was taken away.[71] A year later the disgraced secretary put out a feeler to the Ten to the effect that he would turn over information about the leaking of state secrets in return for restoration to favor, and the Ten was quick to follow up the proposal.[72] Five months later, in October 1487, we learn that the Ten had struck a bargain with Francesco da Fin and his brother Giovanni. The latter was to contrive to come secretly to Venice, bringing the documents that Francesco claimed as evidence. If they were useful in uncovering the offenders, Francesco would be absolved in such a way that no one would make a connection between the absolution and the punishment of the wrongdoers. (A rather hard trick to pull off, one would think.) Giovanni would also be restored to favor.[73] Because this material was so touchy, especially with regard to trying to conceal the role of the da Fin in it, the Ten passed a motion that the council members must not speak of it, even to one another, outside the room, or give any indication whatsoever of what was going on.[74] What followed is not known.

In 1489 the Ten convicted the noblewoman Mattea Collalto of having sent a messenger during the recent German war to Count Oderic of Arco, her kinsman, informing him and the captain of Trent of the most secret dealings of the Signoria with the late Roberto of San Severino, which caused the negotiations to abort and resulted in much disorder and peril for the Republic. Although decapitation was proposed, no one voted for it, and she was exiled to Candia for life.[75] Her brother, Count Gianbattista Collalto, who knew what she was doing and did not report it, was exiled permanently to Retimo.[76] Their relative Stefano Celsi, also guilty of failing to report the crime, received a similar sentence to Canea.[77] It is very interesting that all three broke their exile. The two men left their places of exile about a year after arriving there. That their escapes were on the same day strongly suggests that they were planned between them. The lady Mattea, on the other hand, remained in Candia for over seven years before violating her sentence. Count Gianbattista returned to his exile only a few weeks after he left, but he broke it again, taking refuge on the Genoese coast.[78]

The firm patrician discipline which enabled the Republic to guard its secrets so well, according to Diehl's fervid belief, has been shown to have been something less than steadfast, especially after the middle of the fifteenth century. Molmenti's statement that the secrecy of senatorial debate was never violated is pure myth, flatly contradicted by the documents.[79] The problem of keeping state secrets is an extremely difficult one. The Venetians were very conscious of it, but they did not handle it very successfully, a failure of which the government was quite aware and concerning which the documents are quite explicit.

DISOBEDIENCE

Much of the irresponsible behavior previously described, of course, involved disobedience to the laws. In this section, however, we will consider some cases of disobedience which do not involve elections, corruption, and the like.

By 1298 responsibility for enforcing upon officials obedience to their capitularies and commissions had fallen upon the advocates of the Commune.[80] It appears, however, that the advocates were not overly zealous in enforcing obedience upon the ducal councillors. The latter were important political figures, and crossing one of them could have serious political consequences. An act of 1306 provided that if the advocates were notoriously negligent, then the heads of the Forty, or any two of them, should be responsible for admonishing them that they should do their duty, and if within three days they did not, then the heads of the Forty should implead them before the Forty. If found guilty, the advocates should suffer the same penalty as that to which the councillor would have been subject.[81] The advocates were convicted under this act on a close vote in 1349. They had been negligent in enforcing upon the councillors the law that prohibited the latter from hearing ambassadors and other envoys without summoning the heads of the Forty.[82] The advocates, it seems, learned a lesson, but the councillors did not, for shortly afterwards the advocates, as was their duty, initiated a measure to fine each of the councillors for failing to summon the heads of the Forty to hear Raffaino, a papal notary, who had come on behalf of the lord of Padua. One councillor, Paolo Muazzo, did not wish to pay, although he was as guilty as all the others, so his penalty was reaffirmed.[83]

The Senate complained in 1434 that the many regulations concerning the requirement that officials receiving money must bring it weekly to the treasurers, who must expend it only in accordance with the rules, were of no use, since they were circumvented in diverse ways. The Senate repeated the requirements, adding that the officials must settle their accounts monthly. When they did, their books should be signed by the councillor of the month, and after that no treasurer should alter the books.[84] The Senate appears to have been very annoyed in 1444 over the well-known failure of the Venetian government to execute the laws. It observed that the structure of offices was extremely good, and yet daily observation proved that the laws were not carried out. The Senate provided that the College should meet every Thursday, both in the morning and after dinner, to consider the operations of the various offices. Then, on every Friday they must come prepared with written recommendations on the subject.[85] Early in 1445 the Senate called attention to a law of 1429 on the settlement of accounts. The councillor of the month had been required to settle his account on the last day of the month. So had other officials, who were to bring the money they owed to the treasurers on that day. If they did not, the councillor of the month was required to accuse them before the advocates of the Commune. By bad custom, however, the law was not followed. The officials did not settle their accounts or take the money to the treasurers, nor did the councillor of the month accuse them. In fact, everyone did what he pleased, in spite of the laws. The Senate sought to restore the force of the law by a rather sharp increase in the penalties.[86] This was the typical Venetian reaction, which appears ill considered. Raising the cost of disobedience to the law might have a beneficial effect *if* the law had previously been reasonably well enforced but was being disobeyed because the offenders chose to do so at the risk of paying the too-small penalties. (Some people will consistently park illegally, for example, if the fine is too slight.) It would appear to have an effect opposite to that desired, however, if the law is not being enforced regularly because it is felt that the penalties are already too severe (modern laws against the use of marijuana, for example) or where those responsible for enforcement are wary of offending the violators (as in Venice for reasons of *broglio*).

In 1454 the Senate returned to the requirement that officials who received public monies should turn them over to the treasurers every Saturday. This was to prevent thefts and other inconveniences, although stealing by the officials themselves was not what the senators had in mind, at least not primarily. The law was not working satisfactorily, partly because many did not observe it, and partly because many holidays, when thieves might be tempted to get at the public monies, occurred during the week. (There had recently been a break-in of the customs house on such a holiday.) So, the officials were required to carry the money to the treasurers on every Saturday or the eve of any feast under penalty of having to make up any losses out of their own pockets.[87]

A decree of the Ten in 1462 begins by lamenting that some governors do not obey their orders, which, according to the preamble, seem to be worth nothing. This perilous affliction had also infected the judges and officials of Venice, so that it had become necessary "to cut away this disease from our healthy body." Each offending governor, official, or judge, therefore, was subjected to a fine of 200 *l.* or a more severe penalty if the disobedience were extraordinarily serious. If the command could not be carried out, the governor, official, or judge should make his excuses, either by writing or orally, explaining the danger or other legitimate reason.[88]

In 1464 the Ten discovered another dangerous disease to excise. The decree begins by praising obedience to the acts of the councils as the foundation of the state. Nothing, it says, is more perilous and pernicious than that any citizen by his own authority or that of his office or for any reason whatsoever should be permitted to retract, suspend, or impede what has been deliberated and determined by the Great Council, the Senate, the Ten, or the Forty. The advocates of the Commune, who had sworn to uphold the laws, had taken to writing on their own authority to governors telling them to suspend the execution of commands by the councils. In the future this should result in a fine of one hundred ducats. All judges, officials, and governors, moreover, should be informed that they should not heed any such instructions from the advocates, but should instead report the incident to the Signoria and the heads of the Ten.[89]

Once more, in 1469, we discover that officials who received public money were not obeying the old laws requiring them to settle their accounts at the end of every month. The Senate raised the penalty to five hundred ducats.[90] In 1493 Castellano Boldù incurred the wrath of the Ten. He was one of the heads of the Forty, summoned before the doge, who wished something concerning the cardinal of Santa Maria in Portico to be read in the three courts of the Forty. Boldù was directly ordered twice to appear before the doge, but with irreverent words and arguments he dared to set the authority of his office above that of the Signoria, setting a wicked and perilous example. He was deprived of that office in perpetuity.[91]

There was more trouble, it seems, concerning disobedience of governors of the provinces and their subordinates, probably simply because they had to function at a distance from Venice without modern communications, unable to convey their immediate situations and needs to the central government, and compelled to use a certain independence of judgment. This by no means explains all cases of disobedience on the part of governors, but it may account for some of them. For example, in 1330 the Ten took action against Andrea Bragadin, governor of Canea, who had disregarded orders that he should seek out the traitors of Cà Barozzi.[92]

The site of Venice, of course, necessitated the import of grain, and the control of the grain trade was an important function of government. In 1347 Giustiniano Giustinian, *podestà* of Chioggia, was fined 200 *l. di piccoli* for refusing to carry out government grain policy.[93] Governors of the provinces, especially those of the large island of Crete, had been ordered not to impede the shipment of grain to Venice, but rather to assist and favor it. Governors in Crete, however, had refused to give licenses to merchants wishing to ship grain to Venice, even in times of plenty on the island. The Senate ruled in 1349 that governors in Crete must allow Venetians or subjects of Venice to ship grain to Venice as long as the price in Crete was twenty-five hyperpers per *centenaio* or less.[94] The Senate received a complaint in 1363 that the *podestà* of Oderzo had refused a license for sending a quantity of flour from Friuli to Venice. He had been informed that this was against his commission, but, even after receiving a warning, he had not obeyed. The Senate ordered that he should be informed that he would be fined 100 *l.* if he prevented anyone from transporting supplies to Venice.[95] In 1440 the Senate complained bitterly of rectors within the Gulf seizing grain from ships bound for Venice. They had been accustomed to supply their towns with grain from Apulia and other places, but now they had acquired the bad habit of taking it forcefully from ships bearing grain to Venice. The Signoria received many complaints from merchants and Venice itself was short of food. The governors had been warned by the Signoria, but had not heeded. They were not to impede any ships bound with supplies for Venice, and if they did they should suffer a large penalty of one thousand ducats.[96]

The Treaty of Turin, which ended the War of Chioggia, provided that the Venetians should hand over the island of Tenedos to a representative of the Count of Savoy. In pursuance of this agreement the government ordered Zanacchio Muazzo, *baiulo* and captain of Tenedos, to deliver the fortress and the island, which he refused to do, believing that the strategic place, which controlled access to the Dardanelles, would fall into the hands of the Genoese. The government dispatched five galleys under Giovanni Miani and soldiers under Fantino Zorzi and it put a price on Muazzo's head, but he held out for over seven months before yielding the fortress. The government could not get enough votes in the Senate to sentence him, so he went free. Very likely some senators regarded him, as he probably regarded himself, as a Venetian patriot.[97] Not willing to let well enough alone, Muazzo, contrary to the policy of the state, armed a galley to go to Dobruja. He was arrested and sentenced to prison for a year and a fine of 500 *l.*[98] Somewhat less spectacularly, Luca Contarini, rector of Canea, refused to turn over his office to his successor in 1390. The government of Crete had to send a nobleman, Andrea Venier, to make him yield it.[99]

In spite of all the good laws on the subject, the treasurers in the provinces were not making their accounts every month with the *provveditori sopra le camere.* The senators were not at all pleased with the way public money was handled. The treasurers were warned in 1462 that they must balance their accounts monthly and send them to the *provveditori.* If they did not, besides all other penalties they should pay 25 *l.* for each failure.[100] We have mentioned previously the act of the Ten in 1462 imposing a minimum fine of 200 *l.* on officials, judges, or governors who did not obey their orders.[101]

Paolo Querini in 1466 refused to turn over his office as *baiulo* and captain of Durazzo to his successor, as ordered by the Council of Ten. He was sentenced to prison for six months, deprivation of all offices for five years, and permanent exclusion from the government of Durazzo.[102] In 1472 Tommaso Salomon, official of Ternovo, was ordered home to report to prison on account of disobedience to the orders of the Signoria. He was sentenced to three months' confinement.[103] In 1479 a *podestà* named Niccolò Gabrieli failed to obey first the Signoria and then the heads of the Council of Ten, and then he seized the animals of some of the subjects under his jurisdiction. The Ten declared him under the standard penalty of 200 *l.* for disobedience, and said that if he did not pay that and restore everything taken from the subjects plus their expenses within a month, he would be imprisoned until he did.[104] The Ten took umbrage against a former provisor of Veglia, Marino Moro, because he did not take passage immediately from Arbe to present himself for imprisonment in Venice as ordered in 1488. His successor was ordered to take him and send him to Venice, unless he had already departed.[105] Andrea Magno, castellan of Antivari, was disobedient and insolent to his *podestà* and governor in 1494, for which the Ten deprived him of that castellany in perpetuity and of all castellanies for five years.[106] Antonio Baffo and Bernardino Polani, councillors of Retimo, were guilty of refusing to admit into the island Antonio Zancani, then councillor of Crete, who had been assigned to take over the island after the death of the governor. They were sentenced in 1498 to a year in prison and ten years' ineligibility for all offices in Crete.[107] A syndic, Giacomo Barbaro, in 1503 ordered Giovanni Alberto Contarini, *podestà* of Cervia, to report to Venice, because, scorning the syndic, he had used threatening words against a subject. Contarini did return to Venice, but did not report to the prison, as ordered, instead remaining at home.[108]

Although an act of 1268 required that ambassadors at the conclusion of their missions must submit a report in writing, there is no evidence that this was actually done.[109] In 1425 the Senate explicitly stated that while every ambassador naturally made a final report, "of the said *relazioni* nothing is afterward preserved in writing," and therefore, the Senate continued, much useful knowledge was lost. The requirement of written reports was repeated, and it was added that these must be registered, beginning with Paolo Correr's report on Milan, which he must give in writing, in a special volume in the chancery. Interestingly enough, although it would be surprising if some sort of start had not been made on such a register, we have no evidence of its existence, other than the requirement that it had to be done.[110] In fact, we have proof a century later, 1524, that even the requirement of a written report was not being met. Much information was being lost, according to this act, because even those who heard a report could not remember what had been said. Ambassadors must therefore place their *relazioni* in writing *ne le cose substanziali.*[111] It is going beyond our period, but this did not work either—apparently not at all, even for a year or so. The requirement of a written report was read in the Senate in 1533, at which time Marco Foscari, an experienced and distinguished statesman and diplomat, stated that he had been unaware that his missions to Rome in 1526 and Florence in 1528 required written *relazioni*. He made it quite clear that many others were equally unknowing, which is what we ought to expect if a man of Foscari's background was uninformed.[112] I find this a rather remarkable account. No one was committing any awful crimes, of course, but in spite of a history of legislation covering almost two and a half centuries the government simply could not get ambassadors to make reports in writing.

It may be that the most surprising act in the history of Venetian legislation concerning ambassadors is the act of 1478 which indicates that ambassadors acting beyond or contrary to their mandates were not uncommon in Venice. They tried to seem wiser and better, according to the act, than their superiors. Henceforth they were to stay strictly within their orders. The problem, of course, arose largely out of the difficulties of representing the Republic at a distance without adequate communication, although it is undoubtedly true that the ambassadors had become rather careless about adhering to their orders.[113] The law of 1478 was violated within a few months by Francesco Michiel, commissioner in Tuscia, who exceeded the limits of his mandates in his dealings with the *condottiere,* Roberto di San Severino.[114]

The disobedient acts of Venetian ambassadors seem rather mild and generally understandable. Ambassadorships, of course, normally were assigned to important noblemen or those who were destined for prominent roles. The position required men of high prestige and only those of considerable wealth could afford it. These were precisely those patricians of exalted rank who would be most likely, according to Homans's rule, to adhere to the ideals of their society.

A surprising proportion of the problems involving disobedience had to do with captains of fleets, patrons or *sopracomiti* of vessels, or subordinate officers. We have already dealt with some of these under another heading, but there are quite a few examples which did not involve the charge of cowardice in battle.[115]

In 1341 Filippo Contarini, who had substituted for Tommaso Gradenigo as captain of a fleet of three galleys bound for Trebizond, had violated his orders by making for Batum, and doing it twice at that. He was sentenced to a fine of 100 *l. di grossi.* The three ships' commanders, however, were acquitted.[116] Francesco Bon, captain of the Cyprus fleet, was fined 50 *l.* in 1357 for overstaying his term in Cyprus and loading merchandise against his instructions.[117] Marco Duodo, captain of the galleys of Alexandria, was sentenced to a fine of 200 *l.* in 1358 for disembarking from his galley there, badly distributing the shares,[118] and committing other acts contrary to his commission.[119]

We return to the Muazzo case once again, because two *sopracomiti* of galleys were also convicted of disobedience. Enrico Dandolo was sentenced to five years' exile from Crete for giving aid and counsel to Muazzo. Jacopo Vizzamano was deprived perpetually of the command of any armed vessel. He had conspired with Muazzo to land his galley near Tenedos and turn it over to the rebels. The sentences were relaxed as soon as the furor over Tenedos had calmed down. There is some reason to believe, after all, that the participants were regarded as misguided patriots.[120] Paolo Querini and Francesco Bembo were convicted by the Senate in 1386 for leading their galleys in an unauthorized attack on Majorca. Querini, who, it seems, had committed a bit of piracy in addition, received a fine of 300 *l.* and he had to repay all that he had stolen. He could not receive command of a merchant galley for five years and he could never command any vessel headed for Majorca or beyond. Bembo, it appears, had not engaged in any robbery, so he was fined only 100 *l.* in addition to being unable to command a merchant galley for five years or ever to command any vessel to Majorca or beyond.[121]

There must have been a fairly common problem of control of the patrons of the galleys by the captains of the fleets, because in 1392 the Senate referred to the dangers that daily occurred on this account. In order to try to prevent such lack of discipline, the Senate provided that any judgment imposed by a captain upon a disobedient patron could not be ameliorated by *grazia* except with the consent of all six ducal councillors, the three heads of the Forty, thirty-five of the Forty, and three-fourths of the Great Council.[122] In 1431 there occurred the rather bizarre case of Dardo Foscarini, who, against the orders of the government, of the captain of the fleet of Alexandria, and of the patron of the galley, unloaded at Alexandria 255 sacks of soap and three bales of cloth. In the process he attacked the scribe on board, who had tried to stop him. In Venice before their departure he had loaded seven bales of cloth contrary to regulations. The Senate sentenced him to pay 1,500 *l.* and to be ineligible to be a patron of a galley for five years.[123]

An interesting decree of the Senate in 1436 reveals to us that the galleys assigned to go to Tana had not really reached that destination for some years, but under various excuses had gone elsewhere. It was known, moreover, that the patrons of the Tana fleet for the current year had no intention of going there. The Senate did not wish that voyage to be abandoned, so it imposed a fine of five hundred ducats on every patron and captain who did not go to Tana according to their commissions and the terms of the auction.[124]

The Senate protested in 1438 that an old law prohibiting the transport of slaves on armed galleys under penalty of fifty ducats and the loss of the slaves was ignored. This was harmful to the men of the galleys and to the whole city, as was discovered through the recent return of the galleys from Romania. The slaves spread an infection which caused the deaths of many on the galleys and now endangered Venice itself. Henceforth any captain of an armed galley carrying slaves should be fined one hundred ducats per head, the patron of the galley fifty ducats, and the slaves should be confiscated.[125] The Senate was still having difficulty in 1440 with the so-called Tana fleet, which retained a tendency to head for other destinations. It ordered Luca Duodo, the captain of that fleet, to proceed to Tana under penalty of five hundred ducats, to which penalty the two patrons should also be subject.[126] Early in 1498 the Senate had to deal with two cases of insubordination against the captain of the *muda* of Alexandria that had just returned. Sebastiano Contarini, patron of one of the galleys, had used violent and abusive language against the captain, Filippo Tagliapietra, who was merely carrying out his duties. Contarini was sentenced to six months in prison; for ten years he could not be patron, captain, or *sopracomito* of any vessel; for four years he could not hold any office or be in any council; and he had to pay three hundred ducats in fines. The vice-patron of one of the galleys (probably the same one) verbally abused the captain, Tagliapietra, when the latter attempted to board that galley, again in the course of his duties. He received similar punishment, except that he had to spend only three months in prison and to be deprived of offices and councils for one year.[127]

After the Venetians retook Padua in July of 1509 the *provveditore* of the army, Andrea Gritti, accused patricians with the army, especially Sebastiano Bernardo, said by Priuli to be of a "most noble family," and Donato da Lezzo, of plundering houses and even nunneries in violation of orders. Priuli declares them worse than the soldiers, who were at first restrained by fear of hanging but then followed the example of the nobles, whose behavior was worse than that of Turks, Moors, or other infidels. They justified their rapine by claiming that they had been ruined and deprived of a livelihood. They were a disgrace to Venice and to the

nobility, and the public clamored for their deaths. They deserved hanging, according to Priuli, but had no reason to fear it, because they knew
that their status would protect them. Through the machinations of *broglio* Bernardo got off with exclusion from offices and councils for one
year and the payment of claims against him plus 25 percent as penalty.[128]

A few cases of disobedient nobles who were not in offices or commands are worth presenting. The Ten was concerned in 1435 with
many disobedient nobles who stood in the ducal palace one evening and
ignored the doge's command that they should withdraw.[129] In 1473 the
Ten appointed a college to investigate Francesco Minio and others cul-
pable of not obeying, indeed defying, the notaries and officials of the
Ten and of the ducal council representing the majesty of the state.[130] In
1492 a noble named Giovanni Molin was punished by the Council of
Ten for returning to Venice after he had been expelled for pimping. He
must have been part of that large-scale exile of patrician pimps in 1492.
Molin had to spend a year in prison and pay 100 *l. parvorum* to those
who had turned him in.[131] Francesco Contarini and the same Giovanni
Molin who had violated his exile were among a group who had been
convicted in 1500 of "batteries, violences, extortions and other malefac-
tions." They had been sentenced to exile, but Contarini and Molin had
escaped from prison. If they did not turn themselves in within eight
days they would have a price put on their heads, and, if taken alive,
would have their heads cut off between the two red columns.[132] Antonio Grimani, the defeated captain-general, exile, and doge-to-be, broke
his banishment at Cherso and Ossero and went to Rome. The advocates of the Commune introduced in the Great Council a mild measure
to write to Grimani that within a month he must return to his exile, but
twice by a narrow margin the Great Council failed to pass it. This
reflects the sympathy for Grimani that was eventually to lead to his
elevation to the highest office, but it also displays the typical Venetian
lack of respect for orderly legal process.[133]

Venetian patricians, it seems, were not remarkable for their subservi-
ence to the law and to lawful commands. "All do just as they wish,"
according to the Senate.[134] Regular weekly meetings of the Collegio had
to be established to deal with the failure to enforce the laws. One reason
for this was the reluctance of patricians to act against their fellows for
fear of being defeated in their quest for offices by the family and friends
of those prosecuted. It was not only the laws against illegal electioneering that were unenforced, but nobles who owed money to the government were not forced to pay, the misdeeds of governors were over-
looked, and, in general, the domination of political life by *broglio* spread
like a cancer beyond electoral politics to corrupt the entire state.[135]

Another reason why the laws were not obeyed was that the Venetian assemblies legislated too much, so that no one, not even the advocates of the Commune, could keep fully informed on what was legal and what illegal.[136] On various occasions the Great Council admitted such confusion.[137] On one occasion the doge and very many of the Great Council thought they recalled an act, but it could not be found in writing, so the Great Council proceeded to order it set down.[138] So, there was a great deal of honest confusion about the law, but most of the cases cited above reveal intentional disobedience.

VERBAL AND PHYSICAL VIOLENCE

Ruggiero has explained how the Venetian patriciate discerned the dangers of public insults. In an age when outward honor was considered very important—and it is rarely considered insignificant—insulting words could lead to violence, the personal affront spread rapidly to family, followers, and friends, and broad factions would clash in a struggle for power in the halls of government or upon the streets of Venice. This dreaded factionalism would destroy the much-lauded unity of the patriciate, which we have seen to be more fragile than was admitted, and thus endanger its monopoly of political authority. So the state prosecuted and punished, sometimes severely, insulting behavior, but usually only if it was public in nature, and so within our purview, for we are not concerned with noblemen's private misdeeds. Private insults were usually left to be dealt with privately. They, too, might erupt into violence, but it was less likely, because even proud noblemen were usually able to live with an insult that did no harm to their public honor.[139]

It was especially important to preserve the dignity of the government itself against insult. The doge, his councillors, and the Signoria all had their honor protected by the law.[140] The Council of Ten ordered the right hand of Ludovico Contarini cut off in 1464, because he had drawn pictures (presumably caricatures) of Doge Cristoforo Moro and the advocates of the Commune with insulting captions and publicly displayed them.[141] There was no room in Renaissance Venice for the modern political cartoonist. The Ten itself also naturally became the target for insults by individuals and families wounded by its actions.[142]

Examples of patricians verbally abusing lesser officials who were carrying out their duties are understandably common. Haughty nobles took umbrage at being accused, halted, or searched by lesser nobles or commoners. Venetian patricians, like the powerful in other societies, tended to see themselves as above the law, for they were accustomed to making laws, not to being bound by their strictures. In 1349 Maffeo da Mezzo and a commoner friend were halted and searched by a patrol headed by a nobleman named Giovanni Bondumier. The search for concealed arms was quite legal, but da Mezzo took offense, and, when the case was brought before the Forty, he spoke insultingly against Bondumier. Ruggiero sympathetically reconstructs the scene, so that we feel the affront to da Mezzo, who probably supported the laws in general, and even this particular law, but resented being stopped and searched when he knew himself innocent, as, so far as we can tell, he was.[143] The Ten found unbearable the insolence of Michele Morosini in 1477, when he used insulting words against their notary, who addressed him at the order of the heads of the Ten and the advocates of the Commune and in their presence. The Ten sentenced him to six months in prison and another six months' deprivation of all offices and councils.[144] In 1485 the Ten condemned five nobles to fifteen days in prison and the forfeiture of the arms they were bearing on the night on which they used abusive words to the captain of Rialto, who had accosted them in the course of his duty.[145] Three years later the Ten sentenced Dionisio Malipiero to four years' deprivation of offices and councils for defaming the secretaries of the Ten. For once we are informed of the gist, at least, of the offender's words, although this does not appear to be a typical case of name-calling; he had accused the secretaries of revealing the secrets of the Council of Ten.[146] The Ten sentenced Vicenzo Barbaro in 1498 to ten years' exclusion from all offices and councils for insulting a secretary at the office of the Cinque alla pace.[147]

Insults directed against mere citizens or subjects could also result in penalties. Silvestro Trevisan, who had been treasurer of Treviso, and a couple of his friends must have made nuisances and fools of themselves by interrupting the sermon in church in Treviso with insults against the friar and the citizens of the city.[148] In 1488 Filippo Tron, a *savio grande,* one of the weighty men of Venice, was brought before the Ten for his innuendos against the expenditures of Andrea dal Borgo. If he actually had a source of information, he should be compelled to reveal it; if not, he should be admonished that in future he should bring any charges before the heads of the Ten, rather than spreading them around street corners.[149] Sanuto reports a case in 1498 when, at first, Gianpolo Gradenigo, syndic and paymaster at Pisa, was accused before the Ten for his words against Tommaso Zeno, *provveditore* in that place. Upon investigation it proved that Zeno, a choleric gentleman, was the real offender. He abused everybody and threatened to beat a citizen, so he lost his office.[150] The ambassador to Naples complained in 1472 of the actions of Paolo Contarini, an important patrician, son of a procurator of St. Mark, and unfortunately taken for a Venetian ambassador. He insulted the duke of Urbino and the Neapolitan king with rancorous words on behalf of the pope. Venice disowned him to both rulers and promised to punish him.[151]

Insults sometimes escalated into threats and threats into violence. A large majority of the recorded acts of violence and threats by nobles were directed against officials, especially those responsible for the peace of the city and for the customs taxes.[152] When challenged concerning their rowdiness, arms-bearing, or smuggling, nobles were often quick to react with threats and even with drawn daggers or swords. In his study of fourteenth-century violence, Ruggiero discovered that almost 50 percent of the assaults upon communal officials were against police patrollers. Almost 20 percent were committed in the courts, where patrician tempers flashed against unfavorable rulings.[153] A noble, perhaps more than a more modest citizen, might flare up at the attempted enforcement of the law. Sometimes, admittedly, it was a more complex matter than mere umbrage. One of the antecedents of the Querini-Tiepolo conspiracy of 1310 was an incident where Marco Morosini, a lord of the night and a Gradenigo supporter, tried to search Pietro Querini. A shouting match resulted, and Querini even pushed and kicked Morosini around a bit, for which he was duly punished. Very likely the official was using his power to harass a political enemy: Querini reacted like an affronted nobleman.[154] Baseggio Moreto lost a case in 1347 to Catarina, widow of Bartolomeo da Vicenza, but when the communal herald showed up to collect the goods declared confiscated, Moreto met him with a knife and stabbed him. The wound was only superficial, but Moreto fled. He was sentenced in absentia to a minimal fine of 80 *l. di piccoli,* and his wife was ordered to pay it.[155] In 1359 a *custode* for the *signori di notte* stopped and searched a nobleman named Giacomelo Emo, finding him illegally armed with a long sword. As the *custode* took the weapon, Emo snatched it back and seriously wounded the official with it. The Forty fined him 200 *l. di piccoli* for the assault, in addition to the fine, presumably at least 100 *l. di piccoli,* for bearing arms illegally. This was scarcely a heavy penalty for seriously wounding an official.[156] Chojnacki also finds that the patricians of fourteenth-century Venice had little reverence for the law. Twice in the course of a single week in 1361 the Forty had to punish nobles for beating the bailiffs who attempted to serve summonses upon them.[157] In 1363 Vettor Pisani, later the hero of the War of Chioggia, allowed his temper to explode at an affront against his pride. He had been the captain of the *muda* to Tana. One of his galley commanders had been fined for bringing back some dried salt sturgeon in the arms room of the galley, which was against regulations. He appealed to the ducal council, and Pisani was present at the hearing. The ship's scribe claimed that the commander had loaded the sturgeon without the required *bolletta,* the document showing permission to load. Pisani testified that he had issued such a document, and demanded that his word be accepted for it, whereupon Pietro Cornaro, one of the accusing officials and son of Federico Cornaro, by far the richest of all Venetians, sarcastically remarked that the scribe had said otherwise. Later, outside, Pisani stopped Cornaro and threatened him, and that night he waylaid him, dagger in hand. Cornaro fled unharmed, but Pisani was fined two hundred ducats and deprived of an office in Crete to which he had been elected. Clearly it was more serious to attack a son of Federico Cornaro than some commonplace bailiff or patroller. Pisani, however, was promptly elected to another office in Crete.[158] In 1382 Luca Morosini threatened to tear out the eyes of officials who came to collect a fine that he owed. These words of bravado brought him an additional fine of 100 *l. di piccoli.*[159] The *signori di notte* planned to investigate the death of a slave of Francesco and Lorenzo Venier in 1385. The brothers thereupon insulted and threatened Pietro Michiel, one of the *signori.* Michiel, not intimidated, brought the matter before the Forty, who fined each of the offenders 100 *l. di piccoli.* Ruggiero, who has reported the case, speculates how many such threats were both successful and unreported.[160]

Some nobles were exceedingly bad-tempered. The Senate in 1455 sentenced Marino Pisani to two months in prison and a 500 *l.* fine. Pisani had struck the officials who wished to search his bark for contraband; on another occasion he had hit Master Giorgio Onochio in the face in the court of the judges of petitions; and he had also struck in the face Master Boniforte Sartori.[161] Troilo Malipiero, captain of a ship, was convicted in 1480 for attacking with an armed bark officials investigating contrabrand. The Ten sentenced him to three months in prison and three months' ineligibility for being captain of any galley or ship. The patron of his ship was sentenced to four months in prison and two years' banishment from Venice and the Ducato.[162] In 1486 five heads of the *sestieri* and one member of the Criminal Forty serving in place of the sixth were sentenced to deprivation of office and ineligibility for all offices and councils for six months, because they had had bound and lashed a servant of the office of the governors of revenues, who had been sent to them upon the business of that office.[163]

In 1494 the Ten passed a law attempting to protect all officials against intimidation. The preface records the several sorts of unruly behavior against which the act was directed. Many nobles and other citizens, when any magistrate or judge took action against them, apparently threatened such magistrates or judges with failure in the votes of the Great Council or other threats. Other nobles threatened notaries who reminded the Signoria of laws that ran counter to the petitions or desires of those nobles. When scribes of various offices attempted to enforce the rights of the state, many nobles threatened to tear out their eyes or to disfigure them, to deprive them of office or to cause them to fail to be named to other offices. Any noble who in the future threatened any official would be denied offices and councils of the Republic for ten years. If a commoner, he would also be deprived of all offices and benefices for ten years, but in addition he would be banished from San Marco and Rialto for the same period.[164] Pietro, Alvise, and Geronimo Bragadin were sentenced in 1498 under this law for their threatening and injurious words against Niccolò Zorzi, official of new accounts, in his own home.[165] A noble named Geronimo Badoari was found guilty in 1500 of smuggling wine and attacking officials with a body of armed men. He was sentenced to exile at Capodistria for ten years.[166]

It is hardly surprising that on occasion the noble clans attacked rival clans, an outcome against which the Republic constantly strove. The law of 1268 banning the representation of family emblems or coats of arms on the outside of buildings was motivated by a big fight in the Piazza San Marco between the Dandolo and Tiepolo factions.[167] Often, of course, the violence was on an individual level, as when in an inheritance case in 1363 a noble attacked his opponent in the courtroom itself.[168] Ruggiero reports the bizarre case of Antonio Bon in 1371. He tried to intimidate a witness against him, Florentia, wife of Righi ab Aqua. He used both verbal and physical intimidation to try to prevent her from testifying. Florentia, however, was no submissive woman, so she not only persisted in her testimony, but complained to the Cinque alla pace. Bon went to her house, where he beat her again. The charge against him was referred to the Forty, which fined him 50 *l. di piccoli,* a paltry amount, which causes Ruggiero to suppose that many such attempts at intimidation were probably successful.[169]

In 1447 Giovanni Zorzi and others of an armed band freed Alvise Valaresso, who was guilty of homosexual acts with a minor, from the hands of officials.[170] Two nobles of the Contarini and Soranzo families charged with crimes carrying penalties of death or dismemberment, attempted to escape from prison in 1472, killing other prisoners who did not wish to join in the escape.[171] In 1497 Giovanni Raimondo and Tommaso Molin were taken into custody for having snatched a poor smuggler from the hands of officials.[172] This almost surely indicates that they were the principals in the smuggling. The Ten convicted Andrea da Mosto and Alvise Barbadico in 1502 for their attempt to free Alvise's son, Ettore, and others from prison. With the help of an accomplice planted in the new prison, they had the gates unlocked. Da Mosto was exiled to Capodistria for five years and ten additional years of ineligibility for all offices and councils; Alvise Barbadico was sentenced to prison for six months and exclusion from offices and councils for five years.[173]

We would like to know what lay behind the fight at Santa Maria delle Grazie in 1494 when a noble youth, Pietro Muazzo, his younger brother Zaneto, Marimello Spatari, a caulker, and Amadeo, a goldsmith, beat to death a young attendant of the ambassador of the duke of Milan in the presence of the ambassador's wife. Pietro Muazzo was exiled for ten years, and the caulker was sentenced to a year in prison. The other two were released on account of their youth.[174]

On occasion bands of young nobles (let us hope that they were young, and not distinguished elders) simply roamed the streets at night, illegally armed and committing random acts of violence. In 1487 Marco Cornaro *a barba,* Giovanni, Francesco, and Pietro Cornaro, Andrea and Alvise, nephews of the aforesaid Marco, Michele da ca' Greco, and Antonio Abramo were charged before the Ten for an unlawful assembly and nocturnal riot, in that they ran about the city armed with all sorts of weapons committing many crimes and offenses and beatings. Pietro Querini was also inculpated, and was sentenced to six months in prison and three years of banishment. Giovanni Cornaro and Antonio Abramo received the same sentence. Marco and Francesco Cornaro were found innocent. The outcome for the nephews or for Michele is unknown.[175] When the Ten sought to limit the issuance of licenses for bearing arms in 1496, it declared that it was because of daily brawls and homicides.[176]

I think there is little doubt that Ruggiero is correct in asserting that the Venetian nobility did not engage in violence, as a rule, for any reason or policy beyond yeilding to the passion of the moment. They blew up because of some affront, usually from a communal official, or, in the case of random violence, a crowd of presumably young nobles was carried away by irresponsible and destructive high spirits. Ruggiero further points out that most nobles who committed violent acts were merely fined, whereas commoners more often were fined and sent to prison. One can detect a measure of indulgence for these crimes of noble passion, undoubtedly because the judges could identify with the accused. The indulgence and the acts themselves clearly spell irresponsibility on the part of the patriciate.[177]

DISRUPTING THE COUNCILS

The word "decorous" is one of the adjectives that spring to mind in considering the alleged virtues of the Venetian nobility. The *Poema de omni Venetorum excellentia* of Francesco Arrigoni enthuses over the solemnity and majesty when the venerable fathers assemble to conduct affairs of state. No clamor there, no stupid confusion of tongues, no bitter arguments! Everyone takes his seat, and with quiet mind and tranquil spirit they go about their great affairs.[178] Guerdan tells us that "every inconsiderate word was held at Venice for a crime against the State. A speech was never interrupted in the councils—either by an exclamation or by various movements; a speaker never permitted himself an uncivil remark, even an insinuation. . . ."[179] Uncivil behavior in the councils by the patricians, however, was not the rarity that we have been led to believe it was. In the chapters dealing with various kinds of *broglio* we have seen many examples of disorderly conduct: in this section we will not repeat these, of course, but treat only those uncivil acts which have to do with other business of the councils.

As early as 1270 the Great Council legislated against lobbying on the part of councillors, heads of the Forty, and others who carried the voting urns around the councils. They were not to say: "This or that is the better proposal or this or that is the worse," but only "I am going about for such a proposal."[180] The fear of actual violence is shown in an act of the Great Council in 1274 prohibiting anyone from bringing into the Great Council, the Senate, or the Forty any knife more than four fingers long or with a point.[181] The Great Council returned to the subject of prohibited arms in the three councils again during the commotions preceding the uprising in 1310, imposing a fine of 200 *l.* and exclusion from offices and benefices for five years.[182]

The Great Council complained of disturbances in the various councils and colleges in 1441. Whereas the members of the councils and colleges ought to sit and listen to those speaking and to respond only when recognized, the decree stated, the custom had recently arisen that they stood up, wandered about, speaking, thrusting others out of their seats, and generally creating havoc. Telling them that they must sit down and keep quiet did no good. Action had already been taken to punish this sort of misconduct in the new hall of the Great Council, so now the Great Council decreed that if such troublemakers in any councils or colleges did not obey a warning to keep order, they should forthwith be expelled for six months, lose any office by virtue of which they belonged to such council or college, and pay the penalty as if they had refused to serve.[183] The Ten noted in 1451 that heads of the Ten could not impose silence upon someone saying reprehensible things in the Senate or the Great Council, because the heads were scattered about and could not consult together. It provided, therefore, specified places for the heads of the Ten to sit, so that they could help to maintain order and decorum.[184] Cappelletti reports a whole series of acts of the Great Council designed to prevent nobles from interrupting the speeches of others, insulting their colleagues in their speeches, and otherwise disturbing the good order of the councils. He lists acts of 14 August 1490, 5 September 1499, 5 and 20 November 1507, 5 November 1599, 28 June 1604, and 7 June 1715.[185]

The Great Council composed of the whole body of the Venetian patriciate—poor as well as rich, young as well as old, foolish and flighty as well as wise and responsible—was naturally the most turbulent of the Venetian councils. The Great Council legislated in 1251 against those who spoke abusively of others within that body. If the words were displeasing to the doge and a majority of his council, he might order the speaker to sit down and be silent. If the speaker refused, he should be fined 10 s. *grossorum;* a second unheeded warning would raise the fine to 20 s.; a third to 40 s.; a fourth freed the doge and his council to impose any fine wished. This escalation of penalties through a fourth warning by the doge speaks eloquently and negatively of the decorum of the council. If one warning always sufficed, the legislators would have seen no need to take account of a second, a third, and a fourth. In other councils the doge did not have this authority. The same act provided a fine of 100 l., plus the usual prosecution by the venerable lords of the peace, for anyone who left his place, ran about the chamber, and attacked someone.[186] When passions ran high the prohibition was ineffective. In the days before the Tiepolo-Querini conspiracy burst into rebellion in 1310, members of the dissident families, who, of course, belonged to the Great Council, commonly disrupted its proceedings with their angry denunciations of the doge and his policies, so that sometimes the meetings had to be adjourned.[187] Clearly one could argue calmly against the doge, but there was a line beyond which the prudent would not step. In 1362 the Great Council sentenced Niccolò Falier to two years of ineligibility for all offices for his insulting and biting words against the doge.[188]

We wish we knew the scandalous and violent words which Giovanni da Mula and Antonio Contarini used in the Great Council in 1444. They are not reported, but both nobles were deprived of offices for two years and da Mula lost his *regimen,* so we may probably assume that their expression considerably exceeded the limits of decorum.[189] The Ten amended the act on bringing arms to the Great Council in 1455.

Where the law of 1310 spoke of "prohibited" arms, the new one included "every kind of arms."[190] The Ten complained in 1455 of the
"many disorders which were committed by the nobles in the Great
Council." Much legislation had attempted to control such turbulence,
but the officials assigned to control it, the Signoria, the advocates, and
the old and new auditors, sat in the same area and could not see everything, for the hall was wide and the number of nobles great. The Ten
ordered that the new auditors must sit on the side toward San Giorgio.
They must report all violations to the Signoria, the advocates of the
Commune, and the heads of the Ten.[191] A decree of the Ten in 1489
informs us that the retainers of the advocates and the Ten who served as
doorkeepers for the goings and comings of those temporarily excluded
for some reason from the council suffered many insults from expelled
nobles. Upon the mere report of such behavior by the injured retainers
offending nobles should be ejected immediately from the council for six
months.[192]

The Ten reported in 1491 that the laws against bringing arms of any
kind to the Great Council were being contravened, especially, it seems,
with regard to the nominating committees. The Ten assigned one of its
heads and one advocate of the Commune to check the nominating
committees for arms.[193] Bernardino Minotto was perhaps fortunate that
arms were prohibited in the Great Council. He had brought a successful
action against a silver merchant who had sold him fake goods. The
merchant reported his bad luck to his friend Domenico Calbo, a vile-
tempered nobleman, who rushed upon Minotto in the Great Council
before the doors were closed and punched him in the nose, which bled
profusely. When summoned before the Ten Calbo fell to his knees,
confessed his guilt, and begged mercy for himself and his two sons, but
the Ten sent the intolerable fellow into exile on Cyprus for life.[194] In
1502 Giovanni Antonio Minio, when a motion of his was countered by
another motion, made a long and scornful speech full of scandal and
civil discord. The Ten exiled him for life to the island of Arbe, where
he was to report to the governor twice a week.[195]

The Senate had a reputation for the most exalted dignity. Gasparo
Contarini informs us that speeches were made there modestly and with
gravity becoming men of the senatorial order.[196] Francesco Arrigoni,
the fifteenth-century Brescian poet, speaking of the Senate, considered
"the gods to be gathered for arcane matters in such a manner around
the throne of eternal Jove."[197] As we know the classical deities actually
were a rather rowdy lot, and so actually, at least sometimes, were
Venetian senators. Sanuto at various times expresses the exceptional
hold some speaker had upon his audience with the words "no one

spit." Debates, according to Besta, "often degenerated into quarrels and sometimes arrived at deplorable excesses."[198] He was right, of course, although the myth rolls right along regardless of evidence. Let us try once more, however, with additional evidence to dispel it.

The Senate fined Filippo Belegno 100 *l.* in 1336 for his insulting words against the councillors in the presence of the doge and the Senate.[199] In the fifteenth century it was the Ten which tried to enforce discipline in the Senate. In 1438 the Ten protested that recently some nobles used in the Senate words which were quarrelsome, wrongful, and dishonest. If this continued unchecked it would result in great peril and confusion, so the Ten provided for the election of a committee of nobles to investigate the problem.[200] Specifically, charges had been made against some in the grain business who allegedly gave short measures. The Ten passed a comprehensive act, covering not only the Senate but other councils, prohibiting speaking against anyone, or saying anything insulting, or making any improper movement or attack, or moving suddenly from one's place with insulting or threatening words. The penalty was to be 500 *l.* and exclusion from offices and secret councils for a year.[201] According to the Council of Ten in 1441 the Senate was also troubled with untrue statements, and when the heads of the Ten or the inquisitors sought to unravel the matter, senators either lied or refused to say where they obtained their information. Such speakers should be subject to the above penalties unless their statements were true or at least possessed verisimilitude.[202] In 1449 Tommaso Duodo was convicted by the Ten under this act for insulting the doge in the Senate.[203]

There appears to have been a law against disturbances in the Senate passed in 1453, although I have found only a reference to it in a subsequent act of 1477. The latter law by the Ten complained of the uproar and clamor in the Senate, so that those being silent and wishing to hear the speaker could not. The offenders ignored commands that they be silent. One of the heads of the Ten and one advocate of the Commune were to attend every session of the Senate to repress those who walked about and talked or disturbed the speakers while sitting in their places.[204] In 1478 the Ten objected to those nobles who were not members of the Senate, but intruded upon its meetings and mixed among the senators when someone was charged by the advocates, syndics or auditors. It was also directed against those senators who moved from bench to bench forming factions and contradicting the advocates, syndics, or auditors. Some even came before the Signoria with their pleas while it was trying to frame its motions. Defendants were to bring only three companions before the Senate. Anyone who attended illegally or introduced such an intruder would be deprived of all councils for five years and pay a fine of two hundred ducats. So would those members who went about seeking votes against conviction or trying to influence the Signoria.[205]

In 1500 Luca Tron, who had been syndic in the Levant, gave his report in the Senate. He insisted upon insulting the captain, Bernardo Giustinian, and many governors, councillors, and treasurers. He, the syndic, had armed galleys and made necessary provisions, which they had failed to make. On several occasions the heads of the Ten admonished him not to speak badly of persons, but he persevered until one of the heads ordered him to obey, or else.[206] In 1507 two of the *savi grandi,* Leonardo Grimani and Pietro Duodo, spoke against colleagues in the Senate, perhaps against each other. The Ten decreed that henceforth the heads of the Ten should immediately initiate proceedings against such offenders against propriety.[207] An act of the Ten on 5 November 1509 is a bit beyond our usual cutoff point, but it certainly reflects practices that had their origins in the past. It imposed penalties against those who interrupted the speakers in the Senate, who stood on their feet while someone was addressing the house, or who spit. Sanuto greeted the new act with approval, because of the very great confusion and noise among the benches.[208] While the Senate may not have been as rowdy as the Great Council, therefore, it was not always a model of decorum.

There were naturally also disturbances in other councils. Ruggiero reports that Pangrazio Zorzi was fined 100 *l.* in 1358 for getting into a heated argument with the doge in the Forty. The line between vigorous debate and insult, he points out, is a narrow one.[209] The act of 1478 against intrusions by outsiders or disturbances by members of the Senate also applied to the Forty.[210] The Ten complained in 1492 of contentions and disputes in the Quaranta criminale against the presiding councillors and the advocates of the Commune. Such acts were against the decorum and dignity of the council. The members, even if heads or vice-heads of the Quaranta, were not to interrupt or contradict or argue against the councillors or the advocates unless, according to their consciences, they must speak in opposition, and when they should gain recognition and speak from the *arenga.* Violators were to be subject to the penalties under the law of 1478.[211] Francesco Zancani, a head of the Quaranta criminale, acted disrespectfully in 1494 toward Francesco Pasqualigo, doctor and knight and advocate of the Commune, who was speaking in his official capacity from the *arenga* of the council. Zancani was to be reprehended and warned before the doge, the Signoria, and the heads of the Ten that he must not repeat the offense.[212]

In 1465 Niccolò Tron used angry and disrespectful words toward the doge in the College with many people present, both Venetians and foreigners. The Ten considered it a serious enough matter to name a *zonta* of fifteen, but the upshot was that the heads of the Ten were merely to summon Tron and admonish him to go before the doge in the College and beg his pardon.[213] The Senate noted much disorder in the College in 1479 because of a law forbidding the disbursal of funds from the treasury of the Commune (with some specified exceptions) unless authorized by the College. As a result noble creditors daily thronged the Collegio seeking authorization for the payment of what was owed them. They refused to leave until their pleas were granted. The Senate provided that no vote could be taken in the Collegio until all those who were not members and those with conflicts of interests were gone.[214] The Ten in 1498 extended to the Collegio the law of 1438 punishing disgraceful, insulting, and scandalous words spoken against others in the Senate and other councils. Offenders were to be deprived of offices and councils for two years and be fined 1,000 *l. di piccoli*. The mutual insults of three members of the Collegio, one of them a procurator of St. Mark, second in dignity only to the doge, brought on this action.[215]

Even the august and intimate Council of Ten was subject to disruption. Two heads of the Forty, Blasio Venier and Alvise Cornaro, involved in a jurisdictional dispute with the Ten in 1418, angrily interrupted the proceedings of that body and insulted the Ten, the councillors, and the doge. They were merely deprived perpetually of their headships, however.[216]

MISCELLANEOUS UNSEEMLY ACTS

Under this rubric a wide variety of noble behaviors manifesting civic irresponsibility have been grouped. Purely private misdeeds, once again, have been ignored.

In the wake of the treason and execution of Doge Marin Falier, Pietro Badoari, *cavaliere,* who held the important post of duke of Crete, possibly in his cups on the occasion of the feast of St. Lazarus, expressed very strongly his friendship and support for the executed doge. The Ten exiled the indiscreet Badoari from all Venetian territory for life.[217] In 1448 the Ten took up a case concerning letters in the names of many nobles sent to the pope and the cardinals in opposition to the Signoria's nomination for the see of Padua. The Ten imposed severe penalties, five years' deprivation of councils and offices and a five-hundred-ducat fine for nobles writing letters contrary to the recommendations of the government. Investigation proved that these letters were forgeries, not the work of the nobles named.[218] Two nobles were condemned by the Ten in a similar case in 1485. The government had entrusted negotiations for the raising of a papal interdict to the archbishop of Antivari. Ranuzio Cornaro, knowing this to be the case, nonetheless wrote to the bishop of Parenzo, a member of the Curia, and sought to have the matter transferred to the bishop's hands through the influence of the cardinal of San Pietro in Vincoli. Cornaro was deprived perpetually of all councils and offices and exiled to Padua for five years. A senator, Michele Salomon, wrote similar letters, for which he was exiled to Treviso for five years, to be followd by another five years of ineligibility for all offices and councils.[219] The government did not at all like nobles working at cross-purposes in ecclesiastical affairs.

The Senate objected in 1479 that Venetian nobles were in the habit of pleading cases before governors and magistrates in the towns on *terraferma*. Sometimes they adopted an imperious attitude and said things that ought not to have been said. The Senate prohibited such advocacy under penalty of five hundred ducats.[220] On 26 December 1490, the treasurer of Bergamo and others Venetian nobles interfered in the elections in the council of that town. The Ten decreed that only the *podestà,* the captain, and others deputed by the Venetian government should be present in the Bergamese council.[221] In 1501 the Ten wrote to Geronimo Baffo, count of Spalato, that he should cease his misdeeds against the citizens of the city and that he should not take sides among the *polizani*.[222]

Perhaps it is true that the Venetian patriciate was relatively decorous. Certainly they had that reputation before the end of our period. Muir is probably right that the Venetian reputation for political order is reflected in Canon Pietro Casola's comments on the organization, order, and quietness in the Corpus Christi procession in which he participated.[223] Yet, relative to what? Perhaps to other Italians of the Quattrocento. Still, rudeness and insults were commonplace, and proud patricians were all too ready to react with violence or the threat of violence to injuries to their public honor. They especially resented affronts or assumed affronts on the part of officials of lower rank than themselves. It is clear that councils and colleges were often tumultuous, and that on occasions havoc reigned. At any rate, it is not my task to show that Venetian nobles were worse than this or that group, but only that their behavior by no means conformed to the myth.

Conclusion

IT SHOULD now be abundantly clear that far from all Venetian nobles consistently displayed those qualities for which the patriciate has been renowned: dedication, self-sacrifice, bravery, orderliness, gravity, and the rest. Many, no doubt, did exhibit these virtues on critical occasions when extraordinary threats to the Republic called forth the best in men. Some few among those of the highest rank could perhaps boast whole lives nobly dedicated to the service of the state. In general, however, Venetian nobles behaved, in fact, much as ordinary men do. They swiped cheese, smuggled a bit of wine, sneaked from the council chambers, yelled "Gimme!" at voters. They tried to draw more than the one allowable ball from the urn in an effort to get a gold one and they thrust fistfuls of ballots into the receptacles for votes. The very damaging admission is made that unless paid they did not attend to their public duties. A few were real crooks. Most, though, were neither villains nor heroes, but merely part of the everyday, but hardly humdrum, human tragicomedy.

There was a mass of legislation against various patrician failures to live up to the ideal of the myth, and, on the surface, these laws appear admirable. Indeed, their very number does show a persistent collective concern on the nobles' part for the civic virtue which they betrayed by their individual acts. The patricians passed law after law after law. The myth of the patriciate, in fact, not only nourished legislation, but in turn fed upon it. The mythographers have pointed with pride to all these laws as evidence that the Venetian nobles had a profound care for strict morals in politics. In their admiration for Venetian legislation, however, the mythmakers forget the self-mocking maxim: *Una leze veneziana dura una settimana*. This represents a very realistic strain in

Venetian popular wisdom. Unfortunately, such realism is lacking in many intellectuals, medieval and Renaissance as well as modern. The mythographers ought to have observed from the sheer mass and remarkable confusion of the laws that they were simply ineffective. The Venetians clearly legislated much too much. The modern scholar can discover no rational progression from one law to another on the same subject, not primarily because of gaps in the record, although there are some, but because the legislators were unable to keep the legislative record straight. The councils themselves sometimes admitted to confusion concerning the current state of the law. In their muddled and vain attempts to find a way to legislate virtue the lawmakers sometimes turned back to methods that had already been tried and found wanting. They further weakened the structure of law by granting far too many exceptions *per grazie.*[1] Many laws were unenforced almost from the beginning. The legislators piled unenforced penalty upon unenforced penalty without any apparent glimmer of recognition that the laws were not enforced precisely because the penalties already were considered too heavy for the gravity of the offense. Exclusion from office was a common penalty, but, since holding public office meant so much to so many patricians, their fellow nobles, who in the future might need the votes of defendants and their families and friends, were extremely reluctant to deny public office to them completely. A councillor of Modone, for example, who was convicted of raping a virgin, was sentenced to a fine of 200 *l.,* had to pay 260 ducats for the dowry of the victim, and was declared ineligible to be rector at Modone or Corone, but he was left free to be elected to all other offices.[2] This was not exceptional. Time after time the documents drive one to wonder: "What kind of scoundrels were the Venetians willing to accept in public office?"

The cumulative evidence against the myth of the Venetian patriciate is overwhelming. The mass and redundancy of the laws—and the less interesting have been omitted here—striving to restrain nobles' civic misdeeds prove the case. A number of acts, moreover, explicitly declare "many nobles" or even "a majority of our nobles" guilty of this or that. Such statements must have at least a kernal of truth, because the legislators were in a unique position to know the facts and the remarks are anything but self-serving, for they represent the patriciate as a body condemning themselves as individuals. As a body the nobles believed in the ideal of duty owed to the state: individually, when considering their own needs and those of their families, they belied it. Historians of Venice, like most historians of the Age of Nationalism, have stressed too much *raison d'état:* under the influence of the Annalistes and more recently of the anthropologists there is now emerging, even in Venice, a less anachronistic emphasis upon *raison de famille*.[3]

The mythographers, however, will not be denied. Maranini, looking back fondly upon his fifteenth- and sixteenth-century predecessors in the mythmaking tradition, declaims that we should not presume to be able to judge by means of archival documents and critical history better than contemporaries did.[4] To which I reply, "Of course we should!" A sillier statement than Maranini's would be hard to conceive. It calls for the suicide of scholarship. Take Contarini's *De magistratibus,* for example, which is simply one historical document to be evaluated critically, not only as a whole, but bit by bit, to be compared and contrasted with other critically evaluated documents, and then to be employed for whatever purposes it has been found to be useful. Contarini had the advantage of immediacy and intimate knowledge lacking to us, but we have the advantage of perspective and of a critical method unknown to him. Archival documents, moreover, are generally conceded a higher standing for many purposes than narratives, essays, memoirs, and the like, although archival sources, too, of course, must be judged critically. When Contarini tells us that Venetian nobles put aside their private benefit for the sake of the common welfare, it is certainly evidence of something, if only of what Contarini believed or what he wanted his readers to believe (probably the former, since clearly Contarini did not invent the myth). It is not very strong evidence, however, in the face of much archival documentation to the contrary, that the facts were literally and generally as stated by Contarini. If a law declares, on the other hand, that "the majority of our nobles steal from the Commune," especially if it is supported by other documents, then it is highly probable that in fact many nobles (perhaps not literally a majority) were depriving the Commune of money (perhaps not quite literally stealing) that the legislators considered to belong to the public (perhaps there might be a difference of opinion). Even allowing for hyperbole, therefore, the accusation constitutes very strong evidence of widespread patrician civic irresponsibility. This study and its conclusions rest primarily upon archival documents. We must insist that their evidentiary value be respected. Mere assertions of Venetian virtue, unsupported except by tradition and a few exceptional examples, will not do.

We are burdened with the myth of the Venetian patriciate, in part, because sycophantic fifteenth- and sixteenth-century humanists, for whom, in any case, style was more important than truth, sought to win by flattery rewards that they professed could be gained in Venice only by virtue. In part we are encumbered with the bad history of ancient patriots who professedly viewed history as a means for enhancing the importance of their state and society and as a collection of *exempla* for virtuous living. Modern romantics continue the tradition with characteristic gusto. The tendency to fall back upon the traditional view in works of synthesis contributes its share to our problem. The specific critical conclusions of monographs and articles find their way into the common consciousness, even of scholars, only slowly and with difficulty. The inclination to write biographies of precisely those patricians who most conform to the myth, partly because documentation upon them is relatively abundant and partly because of the interests of the biographers, exacerbates our problem. The enduring reputation of the Venetian governing class may also be due in some measure to the extraordinary interest shown over the centuries in the two great city-republics, Florence and Venice, and the consequent tendency to contrast them. The remarkable political failings of the city on the Arno tend to make the government of the city on the lagoons look relatively good.

Patriotic myths, like laws, set forth a desired norm for a society. The myth that functions attracts the behavior of those who accept it toward its norms. The myth of the Venetian patriciate served this purpose with regard to a few among the rich, the well-born, and the powerful, the real elite among the patriciate. A small number of devoted, able, and wealthy nobles carried an enormous burden of political responsibility, so it can be understood if they sometimes refused or evaded offices, although they showed no discernible desire to share their burdens more broadly. Probably most nobles were moved by the myth occasionally. The Venetian ideal as embodied in the myth, however, was so distant from the facts of life for the ordinary run of nobles that they could not, in general, realistically aspire to it, and to that extent it failed to perform its function. An unapproachable goal, in fact, tends to have a negative effect upon behavior. Certainly the incorporation of an unrealistic ideal in laws that are bound to fail creates a mockery of law.

By what right, then, do we judge the Venetian nobility for failing to live up to norms which were for most of them unreasonable and unattainable? We might reply that the patricians lived up neither to their own norms nor to ours, or that since the state was, after all, their possession and increasingly their livelihood, they should have been more willing to sacrifice their individual and familial interests for its sake. A better response, however, is that they should not be condemned too harshly. Venetian patricians were not uniquely irresponsible, although it is likely that their conduct may have been somewhat worse than that of some elites, because of the inflexibility of the patriciate itself, which preserved as nobles large numbers of those who had fallen into poverty and desperation, those for whom the unattainable ideal would tend to work negatively. The decline of commerce in the fifteenth century exacerbated their hardship, and under the pressure of noble poverty in this century we find most of our striking evidence until then of civic irresponsibility. The realization that Venice harbored large numbers of poor nobles is of the utmost importance. The modern scholar simply must keep it in mind that only a very few patricians were among the elite who became doges, ducal councillors, *savi grandi,* and members of the Ten. The evidence is very strong that literally a majority of the patricians were seriously afflicted by poverty. We must have considerable sympathy for their condition and an understanding of the pressures upon them. If we ought to be cautious about judging the nobles, however, it is fair to set the myth alongside their actual behavior, as we have done, and, accepting them for what they were, not much better or worse than the rest of us, judge, not the patricians, but the myth. Possibly this famous myth should even be judged a poor one, because it established an unapproachable norm for all but a few of those whose conduct it was designed to shape. Certainly it must be recognized as myth, and not confused with social and political reality.

The wholesale failure to enforce the norms of civic behavior, expressed not only in the myth, but in the laws, leads us to wonder why Venetian society as a system did not break down. Or was Venice in a state of collapse by the end of the fifteenth century, since the professed norms were not really sanctioned? And, if the Venetian polity had not broken down, why had it not?

Although Venetian society and government were not as unchanging as Contarini would lead us to believe, there is no question that Venice did enjoy a remarkable stability. Lane believes that the closely knit character of the patriciate allowed it to follow a consistent policy century after century.[5] While Chojnacki does not find class solidarity, he does discover an unusual degree of intraclass cooperation and collective political discipline. There was, he believes, a strong commitment to the state, even though it might be sacrificed to or compromised with other commitments, such as that to the lineage.[6] There is much of the myth in these assertions, but there is also some truth—for the myth was never utterly untrue or completely ineffective. Muir finds in the elaborate ceremonial life of Venice a stabilizing factor, and no doubt this is true.[7] Mutual back scratching, in Finlay's eyes, helped to preserve stability,[8] and, of course, it did, although it brought some social evils in its train. Tucci points to the commercial ties among patrician merchants and the feeling of solidarity they gained during years of living abroad.[9] Perhaps the very disparity of the nobility in wealth, social status, and power was an advantage, in a way, because the poor and middling nobles in the Great Council shared some of the concerns, at least, of the non-nobles, who were excluded from political life. Lestocquoy is of the opinion that urban class conflict arose largely from the clash between overbearing entrepreneurs and oppressed industrial workers. Venice, as a commercial rather than an industrial center, was relatively free of such tensions.[10] Some of us believe that the geographical setting and topography of Venice made a significant contribution to stability through protection against foreign assault and discouragement of civil uprising. This is hardly a new or radical suggestion, since in the seventeenth century Giovanni Botero declared that the canals were a major factor in the peaceful condition of Venice, since they prohibited the inhabitants from gathering together without considerable difficulty and delay.[11] Haitsma Mulier has recently revived the argument that Venice's extraordinary geographical situation promotes an untroubled existence.[12] The canals and the lagoons also have a claiming psychological effect which probably has contributed to the tranquility of the city. That peaceful waters had political consequences is perhaps unprovable, but to those who have lived in their presence, at Venice or elsewhere, it will not seem improbable.

The thrust of this book has been both simple and complex. That the myth of the Venetian patriciate does not adequately reflect the character of most actual patricians is a simple, straightforward conclusion, which, it seems to me, is compelled by the evidence. Yet the myth is a historical reality and it had significance. It helped, for one thing, to keep the non-nobles in their decidely subordinate place by persuading them, probably only in part, that they reaped the fruits of good government, while the put-upon patricians spent their labor, their fortunes, and their lives to make this possible. To the extent that the myth was mere propaganda, we must ask ourselves what were the true norms by which most of the patriciate lived. Probably they will be found in the clans or *case,* and not primarily in the state. For at least a small minority, however, the myth was more than just propaganda: to a marked degree it was the guiding star of their lives. We have noted that such men were drawn from the highest rank in the society. It is obvious, however, that we cannot draw a sharp line between the few who were influenced by the myth and the many who were not. The myth was real enough in the minds of most nobles that they voted time after time in the Great Council along with the few to attempt once more to embody it in the law. That their behavior did not conform to it does not prove that it had no influence upon them.

Beyond the attack upon a single myth this study has had a broader aim of insisting that men and societies are more complex than mythographers suppose. This might seen a truism, had not so many scholars, including some of the best, failed to perceive the reality behind the myth. The Venetians had to live with the irreconcilability of the norms established by the myth and the actual civic irresponsibility of many patricians. There was tension between the two, a sort of tension known as well in modern society, and, indeed, as some of us believe, inherent in the human condition. It is the task of any society to struggle with very imperfect success to reconcile private concerns with public order, self-interest with duty, common practice with moral conviction and law. Behind my rather straightforward attack on the myth of the patriciate lies a concern for a more adequate, complex, and indeed ambiguous conception of man and society. Venetian nobles, like the rest of us, were not one-dimensional caricatures of human beings, as the mythographers depict them, but many-sided, complicated, and inconsistent beings caught up in the glory and the tragedy of real life.

Appendix

LAWS AND CONVICTIONS*

	1150-59	1160-69	1170-79	1180-89	1190-99	1200-1209
BROGLIO ONESTO						
Laws						
Convictions						
CORRUPT ELECTIONS						
Laws						
Convictions						
EVASION OF OFFICE						
Laws				I		
Convictions				I		
ABSENTEEISM AND TARDINESS						
Laws						
Convictions						
EVASION OF TAXES AND MILITARY RESPONSIBILITY						
Laws						
Convictions						
CORRUPTION						
Laws						
Convictions						
VIOLATIONS OF SECRECY						
Laws						
Convictions						
DISOBEDIENCE						
Laws						
Convictions						
VERBAL AND PHYSICAL VIOLENCE						
Laws						
Convictions						
DISRUPTING THE COUNCILS						
Laws						
Convictions						

*The laws are relatively complete, the convictions only a sample drawn mostly from the registers of the Great Council, the Senate, and the Ten. Laws and cases not mentioned in the text have been included. The decision whether to count a given bit of evidence as a law or another as a conviction was not always clear-cut. Neither was the placement under one category or another. The numbers, therefore, have no absolute value, but the trends are clear.

	1210–19	1220–29	1230–39	1240–49	1250–59	1260–69
BROGLIO ONESTO						
Laws					3	1
Convictions						
CORRUPT ELECTIONS						
Laws						
Convictions						
EVASION OF OFFICE						
Laws	3	1			8	8
Convictions						
ABSENTEEISM AND TARDINESS						
Laws					2	10
Convictions		1				
EVASION OF TAXES AND MILITARY RESPONSIBILITY						
Laws						
Convictions						
CORRUPTION						
Laws		1	2	3	8	11
Convictions						
VIOLATIONS OF SECRECY						
Laws						
Convictions						
DISOBEDIENCE						
Laws						
Convictions						
VERBAL AND PHYSICAL VIOLENCE						
Laws						1
Convictions						
DISRUPTING THE COUNCILS						
Laws					1	
Convictions						

	1270–79	1280–89	1290–99	1300–1309	1310–19	1320–29
BROGLIO ONESTO						
Laws	5	2	1	2	3	
Convictions						
CORRUPT ELECTIONS						
Laws	1				1	
Convictions						
EVASION OF OFFICE						
Laws	6	12	4	1	4	6
Convictions						
ABSENTEEISM AND TARDINESS						
Laws	9	11	7	12	10	11
Convictions						
EVASION OF TAXES AND MILITARY RESPONSIBILITY						
Laws						
Convictions						
CORRUPTION						
Laws	27	8	9	8	8	11
Convictions	1			4	3	
VIOLATIONS OF SECRECY						
Laws						
Convictions						
DISOBEDIENCE						
Laws	2		2	2		
Convictions						
VERBAL AND PHYSICAL VIOLENCE						
Laws						
Convictions				1		
DISRUPTING THE COUNCILS						
Laws	2				1	
Convictions						

	1330-39	1340-49	1350-59	1360-69	1370-79	1380-89
BROGLIO ONESTO						
Laws		I	2		I	2
Convictions						
CORRUPT ELECTIONS						
Laws				I	3	
Convictions						
EVASION OF OFFICE						
Laws	4	11	4	10	6	6
Convictions						
ABSENTEEISM AND TARDINESS						
Laws	3	7	8	9	8	8
Convictions						
EVASION OF TAXES AND MILITARY RESPONSIBILITY						
Laws			I	I	I	2
Convictions	4		7	4	I	4
CORRUPTION						
Laws	8	4	15	10	20	10
Convictions	I	4	15	4	13	9
VIOLATIONS OF SECRECY						
Laws						
Convictions			2		4	2
DISOBEDIENCE						
Laws		2	I		I	
Convictions	I	11	3	7	4	6
VERBAL AND PHYSICAL VIOLENCE						
Laws						
Convictions		3	I	7	2	3
DISRUPTING THE COUNCILS						
Laws						
Convictions	I		4	I		I

	1390–99	1400–1409	1410–19	1420–29	1430–39	1440–49
BROGLIO ONESTO						
Laws		4	6	11	9	13
Convictions					38	
CORRUPT ELECTIONS						
Laws		2	3		3	5
Convictions		1			40	
EVASION OF OFFICE						
Laws	7	23	15	7	7	15
Convictions						
ABSENTEEISM AND TARDINESS						
Laws	10	11	10	7	6	13
Convictions						
EVASION OF TAXES AND MILITARY RESPONSIBILITY						
Laws	1		1	2	2	
Convictions			2		5	
CORRUPTION						
Laws	5	16	11	10	12	7
Convictions	14	6	19	8	11	7
VIOLATIONS OF SECRECY						
Laws		2	2		4	7
Convictions		3		2		5
DISOBEDIENCE						
Laws	1	1	1	1	7	3
Convictions			1	3	4	3
VERBAL AND PHYSICAL VIOLENCE						
Laws						
Convictions	2	1	2	1	2	
DISRUPTING THE COUNCILS						
Laws					1	5
Convictions			2			3

	1450-59	1460-69	1470-79	1480-89	1490-99	1500-1509
BROGLIO ONESTO						
Laws	8	12	6	24	21	12
Convictions	1		5	3	1	
CORRUPT ELECTIONS						
Laws	11	4	6	7	14	3
Convictions	12	2			7	10
EVASION OF OFFICE						
Laws	11	6	7	14	7	5
Convictions						
ABSENTEEISM AND TARDINESS						
Laws	10	3	8	10	9	8
Convictions			3		2	
EVASION OF TAXES AND MILITARY RESPONSIBILITY						
Laws	2	2	2	3	4	5
Convictions	1			9		8
CORRUPTION						
Laws	5	6	8	10	10	12
Convictions	14	1	13	7	12	15
VIOLATIONS OF SECRECY						
Laws	3	2		5	4	4
Convictions			17	9	1	1
DISOBEDIENCE						
Laws	1	4				
Convictions	1	1	4		8	6
VERBAL AND PHYSICAL VIOLENCE						
Laws	1		1	1	3	
Convictions	3	1	4	19	9	4
DISRUPTING THE COUNCILS						
Laws	4		3	1	6	6
Convictions		2		1	2	2

Notes

PREFACE

1. In another context Peter Laslett has written: "Here again the behaviour or propanganda of an elite is shown to be no reliable indicator of the experience of a whole population, even though they may be related in an interesting way with widely shared aspirations, however unrealistic." "Introduction: The History of the Family," in *Household and Family in Past Time*, ed. Peter Laslett and Richard Walls (Cambridge, 1972), p. 64.

2. Jonathan Swift, *Gulliver's Travels*, ed. Peter Dixon and John Chalker (Baltimore, 1967), pp. 169-70.

3. Girolamo Priuli, *I Diarii*, ed. A. Segre (1494-1500) and Roberto Cessi (1500-1509), in R.I.S.², XXIV, 3 (1912-37), IV, 30-38; Robert Finlay, "The Foundation of the Ghetto: Venice, the Jews, and the War of the League of Cambrai," *Proceedings of the American Philosophical Society*, 126 (1982), 144.

4. The apt words are those of Robert Finlay.

I. THE MYTH OF THE PATRICIATE

1. Donald Weinstein, *Savonarola and Florence* (Princeton, 1970), pp. 35-36 and n. 19. For a brief summary of the reality behind the Florentine myth, see Gene Brucker, *Renaissance Florence* (New York, 1969), pp. 137-38. Alain Dufour, "Le mythe de Genève au temps de Calvin," *Revue suisse d'histoire,* 9 (1959), 489-518, reprinted with revisions in Alain Dufour, *Histoire politique et psychologie historique* (Geneva, 1966), pp. 65-95.

2. On the reasons for its longevity, see Felix Gilbert, "Biondo, Sabellico, and the Beginnings of Venetian Official Historiography," in *Florilegium Historiale: Essays Presented to Wallace K. Ferguson,* ed. J. G. Rowe and W. H. Stockdale (Toronto, 1971), p. 276.

3. Charles J. Rose, "Marc Antonio Venier, Renier Zeno and 'The Myth of Venice,' " *The Historian,* 36 (1974), 480; see also Franco Gaeta, "Alcune considerazioni sul mito di Venezia," *Bibliothèque d'humanisme et Renaissance,* 23 (1961), 60.

4. For a recent survey of the myth, see Edward Muir, *Civic Ritual in Renaissance Venice* (Princeton, 1981), pp. 1-61. Also see Franco Gaeta, "Storiografia, coscienza nazionale e politica culturale nella Venezia del Rinascimento," in *Storia della cultura veneta: dal primo Quattrocento al Concilio di Trento,* ed. Girolamo Arnaldi and Manlio Pastore Stocchi, III, i (Vicenza, 1980-81), pp. 1-91.

5. Gaeta, "Alcune considerazioni sul mito di Venezia," pp. 58-75, esp. p. 60; Gina Fasoli, "Nascita di un mito," in *Studi storici in onore di Gioacchino Volpe* (Florence, 1958), I, 445-79, esp. pp. 451 and 478. In her very erudite survey Fasoli seems to regard every expression of pride or respect for Venice as a manifestation of the myth. See Felix Gilbert, "The Venetian Constitution in Florentine Political Thought," in *Florentine Studies,* ed. Nicolai Rubinstein (London, 1968), p. 466. See also Renzo Pecchioli, "Il 'mito' di Venezia e la crisi fiorentina intorno al 1500," *Studi storici,* 3 (1962), 451-92. Frederic C. Lane points out that at the time of the Falier conspiracy reverence for the aristocratic constitution was not as strong as it would be in the next century. *Venice: A Maritime Republic* (Baltimore, 1973), p. 183.

6. Fasoli, "Nascita di un mito," pp. 448 and 469-70; Giorgio Cracco, *Società e stato nel medioevo veneziano* (Florence, 1967), pp. 270-71, and Cracco, "Il pensiero storico di fronte ai problemi del comune veneziano," in *La storiografia veneziana fino al secolo XVI: Aspetti e problemi,* ed. Agostino Pertusi, (Florence, 1970), pp. 50-52. Both Cracco and Fasoli accuse Martino da Canal of lying. Cracco, "Il pensiero storico e il comune veneziano," p. 52, and Fasoli, "Nascita di un mito," p. 471. Martin da Canal, *Les estoires de Venise: Cronaca veneziana in lingua francese dalle origini al 1275,* ed. Alberto Limentani (Florence, 1972), sec. 1, p. 2, and sec. 2, p. 5. Also in the edition by Filippo-Luigi Polidori, with Italian trans. by Giovanni Galvani, in *Archivio storico italiano,* ser. 1, 8 (1845), 270 and 272.

7. Enrico Besta, "Iacopo Bertaldo e lo splendor Venetorum civitatis consuetudinum," *Nuovo archivio veneto,* 13 (1897), 125.

8. Lane, *Venice,* p. 182; Gaeta, "Storiografia, coscienza nazionale e politica culturale," p. 16.

9. Lorenzo de Monacis, *Chronicon de rebus venetis ab u. c. ad annum MCCCLIV,* ed. by Fl. Cornelius (Venice, 1758), p. 30. Dr. Mark Smith advised me on the translation.

10. Leonardo Giustinian, "Orazione funebre di Giorgio Lauretano," in *Orazioni, elogi, e vite . . . in lode di dogi . . . ,* ed. G. A. Molina, I (Venice, 1795), 12-21.

11. Arnoldo Ferriguto, *Almorò Barbaro, l'alta cultura del settentrione d'Italia nel '400, i "sacri canones" di Roma e le "sanctissime leze" di Venezia* (Venice, 1922) pp. 69-70; Fasoli, "Nascita di un mito," p. 478.

12. Pietro Barozzi, "Orazione in lode di Cristoforo Moro," in *Orazioni, elogi, e vite,* ed. Molina, I, 77-80.

13. William J. Bouwsma, *Venice and the Defense of Republican Liberty* (Berkeley, 1968), pp. 20-21 and 91-92.

14. Bernardo Giustinian, *De origine urbis Venetiarum* (Venice, 1492), 35v and 63v; Patricia H. Labalme, *Bernardo Giustiniani: A Venetian of the Quattrocento* (Rome, 1969), pp. 271-72 and 285-86.

15. Labalme, *Bernardo Giustiniani,* p. 288.

16. Gilbert, "Beginnings of Venetian Official Historiography," pp. 280-81.

17. Gaetano Cozzi, "Cultura politica e religione nella 'pubblica storiografia' veneziana nel '500," *Bollettino dell'Istituto di Storia della Società e dello Stato Veneziano,* 5-6 (1963-64), 221; Gina Fasoli, "La storia di Venezia: Lezioni tenuti nella Facoltà di Magistero di Bologna durante l'anno accademico 1957-58," (Bologna, 1958, Mimeographed), p. 221; Juan Beneyto Perez, *Fortuna de Venecia. Historia di una fama politica* (Madrid, 1947), pp. 43-44; Gaeta, "Storiografia, coscienza nazionale e politica culturale," p. 68.

18. Marcantonio Sabellico, *Rerum Venetarum ab urbe condita libri XXXIII* (Venice, 1718), p. 384. (Henceforth *Decades.*)

19. Marino Sanuto, *Cronachetta,* ed. Rinaldo Fulin (Venice, 1880), pp. 7, 13, 28; id., *De origine, situ et magistratibus urbis venetae ovvero La città di Venetia (1493-1530),* ed. Angela Carraciolo Arico (Milan, 1980), p. 9.

20. Sanuto, *Cronachetta,* p. 16; id., *Città di Venetia,* pp. 13-14.

21. As quoted in Bouwsma, *Venice and the Defense of Republican Liberty,* pp. 63-64, and Giuseppe Maranini, *La costituzione di Venezia dopo la Serrata del Maggior Consiglio* (Rome, 1931), p. 14. (Henceforth *Costituzione di Venezia,* II.)

22. Felix Gilbert, "Venice in the Crisis of the League of Cambrai," in *Renaissance Venice,* ed. John R. Hale (Totowa, N.J., 1973), p. 275.

23. Francesco Arrigoni, *Poema de omni Venetorum excellentia,* B.M., cl. lat. XII, cod. 145 (=4393), 9r, 18r-19r.

24. Ibid., 20r.

25. Francesco Allegri, *La summa gloria di Venetia* (Venice, 1501), n.p. On the superiority of Venice to Rome, see A. Medin, *La storia di Venezia nella poesia* (Milan, 1906), p. 42.

26. Fasoli, "Nascita di un mito," pp. 450-51.

27. Quoted by Fasoli, ibid., pp. 467-68, but attributed incorrectly to Albertus Magnus. David Robey and John E. Law, "The Venetian Myth and the 'De Republica Veneta' of Pier Paolo Vergerio," *Rinascimento,* 15 (1975), 8. The passage quoted by Fasoli is on p. 51. She also has wrongly attributed to Thomas Aquinas a passage that is in the portion of the *De regimine principum* written by Ptolemy of Lucca. "Nascita di un mito," p. 468. In both cases she is following Lorenzo de Monacis. Gilbert, "Venetian Constitution in Florentine Political Thought," pp. 466-67.

28. Rolandinus Patavinus, *Cronica,* ed. Antonio Bonardi, in R.I.S.², VIII, i, 50. Fasoli, "Nascita di un mito," p. 469, also refers to the *Chronicon marchiae Tarvisinae et Lombardiae,* ed. L. A. Botteghi, in R.I.S.², VIII, iii, 3, for another relevant passage and to Antonio Godi, *Cronaca,* ed. Giovanni Soranzo, in R.I.S.², VIII, ii, 3. The latter does not seem to lead to anything relevant. Fasoli

also quotes the passage from Rolandino in her lectures. "Storia di Venezia," p. 25. Stanley Chojnacki has wrongly attributed the quotation to Albertino Mussato. "Crime, Punishment, and the Trecento Venetian State," in *Violence and Civil Disorder in Italian Cities, 1200-1500*, ed. Lauro Martines (Berkeley, 1972), p. 184, n. 7. What he has done is to conflate two notes from Heinrich Kretschmayr, *Geschichte von Venedig*, II (Gotha, 1920), 663, improperly attributing to Mussato (n. 6) the quotation in n. 7.

29. "Lettera pseudo-Dantesca a Guido da Polenta," in *Le opere di Dante,* ed. E. Pistelli (Florence, 1921), pp. 450-51.

30. The Venetians had a certain distaste for windy speeches. Donald E Queller, *The Office of Ambassador in the Middle Ages* (Princeton, 1967), p. 197.

31. Robey and Law, "Venetian Myth and Vergerio," pp. 9 and 56-57. The passage is published here for the first time.

32. Gilbert, "Venetian Constitution in Florentine Political Thought," p. 465. A speech leading to the adoption of the Florentine *catasto* of 1427 referred to Venice as reputedly the best-governed city of all. Quoted in David Herlihy and Christiane Klapisch-Zuber, *Les Toscanes et leurs familles* (Paris, 1978), p. 56, n. 30.

33. Gilbert, "Venetian Constitution in Florentine Political Thought," pp. 466-67; Chojnacki, "Trecento Venetian State," p. 184: D. S. Chambers, *The Imperial Age of Venice, 1380-1580* (London, 1970), pp. 22-23; Pompeo Molmenti, *Venice: Its Individual Growth from the Beginnings to the Fall of the Republic,* trans. H. F. Brown, part I, I (Chicago, 1906), 90-91. I think we may take it that "citizens" here refers to patricians.

34. Pier Paolo Vergerio, *De republica veneta,* in Robey and Law, "Venetian Myth and Vergerio," pp. 36-50, ll. 120-21, 147-51, 143-44, 145-46; Gilbert, "Venetian Constitution in Florentine Political Thought," p. 468. See also Franco Gaeta, "L'idea di Venezia," in *Storia della cultura veneta,* ed. Arnaldi and Stocchi, III, iii, 570-72.

35. Gian Francesco Poggio-Bracciolini, *De nobilitate liber,* in *Opera omnia,* ed. Riccardo Fubini, I (Turin, 1964), 67; Chambers, *Imperial Age of Venice,* p. 25. Lauro Querini responded for the Venetian nobility. Gaeta, "Idea di Venezia," pp. 579-83.

36. Agostino Pertusi, "Gli inizi della storiografia umanistica nel Quattrocento," in *Storiografia veneziana,* ed. Pertusi, pp. 289-90. Pertusi's statement that *In laudem rei publicae Venetorum* was unpublished is incorrect, although it is likely that he had submitted his contribution to this collective volume before the appearance of Fubini's facsimile edition. Gian Francesco Poggio-Bracciolini, *In laudem rei publicae Venetorum,* in *Opera omnia,* II, 917-37.

37. Gilbert, "Venetian Constitution in Florentine Political Thought," pp. 470-71.

38. Poggio-Bracciolini, *In laudem rei publicae Venetorum,* pp. 925-26 and 933.

39. Ibid., pp. 928-29 and 934-35.

40. Ibid., p. 930. He appears to use the word *senatus* for the Great Council.

The doge is elected by the "Senate" (p. 931); there is also a *minor senatus* of 200 members, which is also identified as *rogati* (p. 932).

41. Ibid., p. 931.

42. Quoted (in Italian) in Giovanni Soranzo, "I fattori morali della grandezza e della decadenza di Venezia," *Archivio veneto,* ser. 5, 1 (1927), 284-85; Chambers, *Imperial Age of Venice,* p. 112; Robert Finlay, *Politics in Renaissance Venice,* (New Brunswick, 1980), p. 35. See the negative comment on Venetian oligarchical government. Pius II, *The Commentaries of Pius II,* trans. Florence Alden Gragg with intro. and notes by Leona C. Gabel, Smith College Studies in History, XXII, 1-2; XXV, 1-4; XXX-XXXV; XLIII (Northampton, Mass., 1936-37), p. 241. He also says, however, that the Venetians are a strict people and observe their own laws. Ibid., p. 243.

43. Gilbert, "Venetian Constitution in Florentine Political Thought," pp. 475 and 483; Gilbert, "Florentine Political Assumptions in the Period of Savonarola and Soderini," *Journal of the Warburg and Courtauld Institutes,* 20 (1957), 194-95.

44. Pecchioli, "Mito di Venezia," pp. 469-73; Alberto Tenenti, "Studi di storia veneziana," *Rivista storica italiana,* 74 (1963), 104-5; Tenenti, "La Sérénissime République," in *Venise au temps des galères,* ed. Jacques Goimard (Paris, 1968), p. 165; Gilbert, "Venetian Constitution in Florentine Political Thought," p. 486. Since this deals for the most part, however, with the myth of the constitution, we pass over it briefly.

45. Angelo Baiocchi, "Venezia nella storiografia fiorentina del Cinquecento," *Studi veneziani,* n.s., 3 (1979), 203-81; Fasoli, "Nascita di un mito," pp. 478-79; Gaeta, "Alcune considerazioni sul mito di Venezia," p. 64; Franco Simone, "I contributi della cultura veneta allo sviluppo del Rinascimento francese," in *Rinascimento europeo e Rinascimento veneziano,* ed. Vittore Branca (Florence, 1967), p. 154; Oliver Logan, *Culture and Society in Venice, 1470-1790* (New York, 1972), p. 5; Felix Gilbert, "Venetian Diplomacy before Pavia: From Reality to Myth," in *The Diversity of History: Essays in Honour of Sir Herbert Butterfield,* ed. J. H. Elliott and H. G. Koenigsberger (London, 1970), pp. 115-16; Rudolf von Albertini, *Das florentinische Staatsbewusstsein im Uebergang von der Republik zum Prinzipat* (Bern, 1955), p. 149, n. 3; Federico Chabod, "Venezia nella politica italiana ed europea del Cinquecento," in *La civiltà veneziana del Rinascimento* (Florence, 1958), pp. 49-50. See also on Giannotti, Randolph Starn, *Donato Giannotti and His Epistolae* (Geneva, 1968), pp. 18-22.

46. Albertini, *Florentinische Staatsbewusstsein,* p. 148, n. 2; Gaetano Cozzi, "Domenico Morosini e il 'De bene instituta republica,' " *Studi veneziani,* 12 (1970), 427-28.

47. Machiavelli, *Principe,* quoted in Gaeta, "Idea di Venezia," p. 609. Albertini, *Florentinische Staatsbewusstsein,* p. 148, n. 2.

48. Molmenti, *Venice,* part 1, I, 168; Giuseppe Maranini, *La costituzione di Venezia dalle origini alla Serrata del Maggior Consiglio* (Venice, 1927), p. 168. (Henceforth *Costituzione di Venezia,* I.)

49. Niccolò Macchiavelli, "Lettera a Franc. Vettori," quoted in Giuseppe Toffanin, *Machiavelli e il "Tacitismo,"* 1st ed., 1921; Naples, 1972, p. 20, n. 11. Also in Innocenzo Cervelli, *Machiavelli e la crisi dello stato veneziano* (Naples, 1974), p. 68; Gaeta, "Idea di Venezia," p. 608.

50. Bouwsma, *Venice and the Defense of Republican Liberty,* p. xiii; Gaeta, "Alcune considerazioni sul mito di Venezia," p. 63; Robey and Law, "Venetian Myth and Vergerio," pp. 6-7; Angel A. Castellan, "Venecia como modelo de ordenamiento politico en el pensamiento italiano de los siglos XV y XVI," *Anales de historia antigua y medieval,* 12 (1963-65), 8.

51. Along with the invasions of Italy and the maritime discoveries, this nostalgia of the decadent present for a Golden Age in the past gave rise to the belief that the sixteenth century formed the beginning of the Venetian *decadenza.* Modern scholarship sees Venetian prosperity and vitality continuing through the Cinquecento. Bouwsma, *Venice and the Defense of Republican Liberty,* p. 96.

52. Chambers, *Imperial Age of Venice,* pp. 100-101.

53. Bouwsma, *Venice and the Defense of Republican Liberty,* p. 89. Gilbert settles this issue once and for all, I think. "Beginnings of Venetian Official Historiography."

54. Cozzi, "Pubblica storiografia' veneziana nel '500," pp. 225-27.

55. Lester J. Libby, Jr., "Venetian History and Political Thought after 1509," *Studies in the Renaissance,* 20 (1973), 13.

56. See the bibliographical note in James Bruce Ross, "Gasparo Contarini and His Friends," *Studies in the Renaissance,* 17 (1970), 230, n. 159. Add Myron Gilmore, "Myth and Reality in Venetian Political Theory," in *Renaissance Venice,* ed. Hale, p. 434. Gilmore's essay appeared after Ross surveyed the question.

57. Gasparo Contarini, *De magistratibus et republica Venetorum* (Venice, 1589), 4v-5r; Contarini, *The Commonwealth and Government of Venice,* trans. Lewis Lewkenor (London, 1599; reprint, Amsterdam, 1969), p. 7.

58. Contarini, *De magistratibus,* 4rv (Lewkenor, pp. 5-6); Bruno Dudan, *Il dominio veneziano di Levante* (Bologna, 1938), p. 193. See also Chambers, *Imperial Age of Venice,* pp. 140-42, and Finlay, *Politics in Renaissance Venice,* p. 29.

59. Cozzi, " 'Pubblica storiografia' veneziana nel '500," pp. 234-35.

60. Marco Foscarini, *Della letteratura veneziana ed altri scritti intorno essa,* 2d ed. (Venice, 1854), p. 247, n. 2.

61. Cozzi, " 'Pubblica storiografia' veneziana nel '500," p. 265.

62. Charles J. Rose, "The Evolution of the Image of Venice (1500-1630)" (Ph.D. diss., Columbia University, 1971), pp. 7-8.

63. Brian Pullan, *Rich and Poor in Renaissance Venice* (Cambridge, Mass., 1971), p. 5.

64. Zera S. Fink, *The Classical Republicans: An Essay in the Recovery of a Pattern of Thought in Seventeenth-Century England,* 2d ed. (Evanston, Ill., 1962), pp. 28-51; Fink, "Venice and English Political Thought in the Seventeenth Century," *Modern Philology,* 38 (1940), 155-72; Chabod, "Venezia nella politica italiana ed europea"; William J. Bouwsma, "Venice and the Political Education

of Europe," in *Renaissance Venice,* ed. Hale, pp. 445-66; Eco O. G. Haitsma Mulier, *The Myth of Venice and Dutch Republican Thought in the Seventeenth Century,* trans. Gerard T. Moran (Assen, 1980).

65. Gaeta, "Alcune considerazioni sul mito di Venezia," p. 63; Simone, "I contributi della cultura veneta," pp. 153-54. See Tenenti's criticism of Gaeta in "Studi di storia veneziana," p. 104.

66. Lane, *Venice,* p. 252.

67. Quoted in Molmenti, *Venice,* part 2, I (Chicago, 1907), 15.

68. Benvenuto Cellini, *Autobiography,* trans. with intro. by George Bull (Baltimore, 1969), p. 267.

69. Haitsma Mulier, *Myth of Venice,* p. 42.

70. Ibid., pp. 40-41; Logan, *Culture and Society in Venice,* pp. 6-7; Fink, "Venice and English Political Thought," p. 158.

71. Haitsma Mulier, *Myth of Venice,* p. 44; Logan, *Culture and Society in Venice,* p. 7.

72. Gonzalo Fernandez de Oviedo, *Historia general y natural de las Indias,* ed. Juan Perez de Tudela Bueso (Madrid, 1959), I, lxx, n. 212. I thank Prof. Stelio Cro for the reference.

73. Haitsma Mulier, *Myth of Venice,* p. 57.

74. Ibid., pp. 54-55.

75. Brian Pullan, "Service to the Venetian State: Aspects of Myth and Reality in the Early Seventeenth Century," *Studi secenteschi,* 5 (1964), 98.

76. Muir, *Civic Ritual,* pp. 53 and 55. Brian Pullan, "The Significance of Venice," *Bulletin of the John Rylands Library of the University of Manchester,* 56 (1974), 449-50.

77. *Senatus populusque venetorum,* in imitation of *Senatus populusque romanorum.* Quoted in Bouwsma, "Venice and the Political Education of Europe," p. 456. Chambers calls attention to the device "SPQV" on the opening page (which he has reproduced) of Niccolò da Correggio's *Cephalo e l'Aurora* of 1497. *Imperial Age of Venice,* p. 27 (Illustration 16).

78. Muir, *Civic Ritual,* p. 55. The myth of Venice was also strong in Poland. Ibid., p. 52. It also influenced those who planned the constitutions of Carolina and Pennsylvania. Pullan, *Rich and Poor in Renaissance Venice,* pp. 4-5.

79. "[P]ar les services rendus, par la richesse, par la culture intellectuelle, l'aristocratie vénitienne plus qu'une autre méritait le pouvoir qu'elle ambitionnait. . . ." Charles Diehl, *Une république patricienne: Venise* (Paris, 1915), p. 91.

80. Maranini, *Costituzione di Venezia,* I, 354.

81. Ibid., I, 150, and *Costituzione di Venezia,* II, 137-39; Samuele Romanin, *Storia documentata di Venezia,* 2d ed., III (Venice, 1912), 371; Vincenzo Marchesi, "La Repubblica di Venezia (appunti critici)," *Annali del R. Istituto Tecnico Antonio Zanon in Udine,* 2d ser., 12 (1894), 11.

82. Quoted in Bouwsma, *Venice and the Defense of Republican Liberty,* p. 164.

83. In A. Medin, *La storia di Venezia nella poesia* (Milan, 1906), p. 45; August Buck, "*Laus Venetiae* und Politik im 16. Jahrhundert," *Archiv für Kulturgeschichte,* 57 (1975), 192.

84. Robey and Law, "Venetian Myth and Vergerio," pp. 56-57.

85. Soranzo, "Fattori morali," p. 270; Pompeo Molmenti, *La storia di Venezia nella vita privata*, 6th ed., I (Bergamo, 1922), 66; Rose, "Venice," pp. 7-8.

86. Arrigoni, *Poema*, 9r.

87. Filippo Nani-Mocenigo, "Fonti storiche veneziane," *Ateneo veneto*, 26 (1903), 18.

88. Fasoli, "Storia di Venezia," p. 26.

89. "Care for the people, in peace as well as in war, was characteristic of this government. . . ." Jacob Burckhardt, *The Civilization of the Renaissance in Italy*, trans. S. G. C. Middlemore (New York, 1954), p. 52. See also Romanin, *Storia di Venezia*, III, 371; Vittorio Lazzarini, "Antiche leggi venete intorno ai proprietari nella Terraferma," *Nuovo archivio veneto*, n.s., 38 (1919), 19. It is interesting that the good, bourgeois liberal, Henri Pirenne, waxes just as eloquent over the urban patriciate generally: "It is necessary, in fact, to go back to antiquity to find as much devotion to the public good as that of which they had given proof. *Unus subveniet alteri tamquam fratri suo*—'Let each help the other like a brother'—says a Flemish charter of the twelfth century, and these words were actually a reality. As early as the twelfth century the merchants were expending a good part of their profits for the benefit of their fellow citizens. . . ." *Medieval Cities*, trans. Frank D. Halsey (Princeton, 1972), p. 209.

90. Medin, *Storia di Venezia nella poesia*, pp. 46 and 48.

91. Molmenti, *Venice*, part 2, I, 12; Romanin, *Storia di Venezia*, IV (Venice, 1913), 45-52 and esp. 226-29.

92. Medin, *Storia di Venezia nella poesia*, p. 474; Marchesi, "Repubblica di Venezia," p. 11.

93. Gilbert, "Venetian Constitution in Florentine Political Thought," p. 483.

94. Diehl, *République patricienne*, pp. vii, 118-19, 156, 164-65, and 259-60. Notice the combination of the positive and negative myths.

95. Charles Yriarte, *Vie d'un patricien de Venise* (Paris, 1874), pp. 9, 257, 347-49.

96. Giuseppe Volpi, *La Repubblica di Venezia e i suoi ambasciatori* (Milan, 1928), pp. 45-46; Donald E. Queller, "The Civic Irresponsibility of the Venetian Nobility," in *Economy, Society, and Government in Medieval Italy: Essays in Memory of Robert L. Reynolds*, ed. David Herlihy, Robert S. Lopez, and Vsevelod Slessarev (Kent, Ohio, 1969), p. 223 (=*Explorations in Economic History*, 7 [1969-70]). "Everyone was bound, within the limits of his condition and his ability, to lend service to the state; if anyone refused office to which he had been called, he lost his civil rights." (This was not true.) "Every citizen was inspired by such a lofty sentiment of duty as to feel remorse if he had ever failed to serve his country on every occasion and to the best of his ability." Molmenti, *Venice*, part 1, I, 83. "Venice was an exacting mistress, and all who served her had to abrogate self and devote themselves heart and soul to her service. No individual was of account when weighed in the balance of the state's requirements. . . ." Alathea Wiel, *Venice* (London, 1894), pp. ix-x. "Everyone, noble or plebeian,

lived for VENEZIA, and in return she shed her benefits on everyone." William Roscoe Thayer, *A Short History of Venice* (Boston, 1908), p. x.

97. Pullan, "Service to the Venetian State," p. 127.

98. Enrico Besta, *Il Senato veneziano* (Venice, 1899), p. 22. Active politicians and statesmen are, of course, busy people. When our legislators are in session into the wee hours we regard it as a sign of institutional incompetence, not of civic virtue.

99. G. B. Picotti, "Le lettere di Ludovico Foscarini," *Ateneo veneto,* 32 (1909), 29-31.

100. "[Q]uamprimum provinciam ingressus sum, decrevi Ludovici personam exuere, et publicam induere." Picotti, "Lettere di Ludovico Foscarini," p. 30, n. 2.

101. Gaetano Mosca, *The Ruling Class,* trans. Hannah D. Kuhn, ed. and rev. Arthur Livingston (New York, 1939), p. 62. Rose, "Venier, Zeno and 'the Myth,' " p. 479.

102. Dufour, "Mythe de Genève," pp. 70-71; Gaeta, "Alcune considerazioni sul mito di Venezia," p. 59; F. G. Bailey, "Gifts and Poison," in *Gifts and Poison,* ed. F. G. Bailey (New York, 1971), p. 22.

103. Gaeta, "Alcune considerazioni sul mito di Venezia," p. 59. Dawson and Prewett point to the importance of the ancestors as models of behavior and, therefore, to the stability of social behavior. Richard E. Dawson and Kenneth Prewett, *Political Socialization* (Boston, 1969), p. 8.

104. The Venetian mythologizers have not exactly agreed upon the time of the moral decline, but it ranges from the mid-fifteenth century through the sixteenth. Mid-fifteenth century, Marchesi, "Repubblica di Venezia," p. 51; Cinquecento, Antonio Pilot, "Un capitolo inedito contro il broglio," *Ateneo veneto,* 26 (1903), 544 and 553; Also Romanin, *Storia di Venezia,* VI, (Venice, 1914), 432. Logan points out that these views are not accepted by recent historians. Political decadence is now minimized and economic decline is not seen until the second quarter of the seventeenth century. *Culture and Society in Venice,* p. 24. An idealized foreign society, as in the Florentine use of the Venetian myth, serves much the same purposes. Edward Shils states that "Sometimes these high evaluations of the remote past are more appreciative than actively normative; they serve as standards for the disparagement of the present but not as standards for the guidance of conduct in any specific way." *Tradition* (Chicago, 1981), p. 207. To an extent this is true in Venice, but I would be surprised if it were ever an "either-or" matter.

105. Henry A. Murray has written: "[M]ythic images are the elements, however submerged, by which thought is sustained and propelled, and by means of which ideas—those systems of abstractions, for example, that we call ideologies—activate behavior. . . ." "Introduction to the Issue 'Myth and Mythmaking,' " *Daedalus,* 88 (1959), 212. Vilfredo Pareto expresses this use of myth in the jargon of science. *The Mind and Society: A Treatise on General Sociology,* trans. Andrew Bongiorno and Arthur Livingston (New York, 1963), III-IV, par. 1869, p. 1301.

106. Chambers, *Imperial Age of Venice,* p. 98; Rose, "Venice," p. 479. For another exemplary patrician, Guglielmo Querini, see Giuseppe dalla Santa, "Di un patrizio mercante veneziano del Quattrocento e di Francesco Filelfo suo debitore," *Archivio veneto,* n.s., 11 (1906), 63-90, and esp. 63-64 and 72-74.

107. George C. Homans, *The Human Group* (New York, 1950), p. 126.

108. Ibid., p. 141.

109. Roberto Cessi, *La regolazione delle entrate e delle spese* (Padua, 1925). See Stanley Chojnacki's appreciation of Cessi. "In Search of the Venetian Patriciate: Families and Factions in the Fourteenth Century," in *Renaissance Venice,* ed. Hale, pp. 48-49.

110. Fasoli, "Nascita di un mito"; Gaeta, "Alcune considerazioni sul mito di Venezia"; Pecchioli, " 'Mito' di Venezia."

111. Fasoli, *Storia di Venezia,* pp. 46 and 220-21. On the whole, however, her lectures are in the mythographical tradition. See below, pp. 25-26.

112. Angelo Ventura, *Nobiltà e popolo nella società del '400 e '500* (Bari, 1964), pp. 40-41.

113. Ibid., pp. 39 and 181. He makes an exception of Friuli, where he thinks the Venetian government did act against the oppressive effects of the feudal society.

114. Ibid., pp. 183-84; S. J. Woolf, "Venice and the Terraferma: Problems of the Change from Commercial to Landed Activities," *Bollettino dell'Istituto di Storia della Società e dello Stato Veneziano,* 4 (1962), reprinted in *Crisis and Change in the Venetian Economy in the Sixteenth and Seventeenth Centuries,* ed. Brian Pullan (London, 1968), p. 190.

115. Cracco, *Società e stato;* Chojnacki, "In Search of the Venetian Patriciate," p. 49.

116. Cracco, *Società e stato,* p. 70.

117. Ibid., p. 458.

118. Ibid., pp. 442-43.

119. Donald E. Queller, *Early Venetian Legislation on Ambassadors* (Geneva, 1966); "Newly Discovered Early Venetian Legislation on Ambassadors," ed. Donald E. Queller, in D. E. Queller with Francis R. Swietek, *Two Studies on Venetian Government* (Geneva, 1977), pp. 7-98; Queller, "Civic Irresponsibility."

120. Lane, *Venice,* p. 258.

121. Frederic C. Lane, "Naval Actions and Fleet Organization, 1499-1502," in *Renaissance Venice,* ed. Hale, p. 158.

122. Lane, *Venice,* p. 263.

123. Ibid., p. 174.

124. Ibid., p. 88.

125. Gilbert, "Venetian Diplomacy before Pavia," pp. 101 and 115-16, and nn. 84 and 85.

126. Chojnacki, "In Search of the Venetian Patriciate," p. 48.

127. Chojnacki, "Trecento Venetian State," pp. 186-87.

128. Finlay, *Politics in Renaissance Venice,* esp. pp. 219-22 and 285-88.

129. Guido Ruggiero, *Violence in Early Renaissance Venice* (New Brunswick, 1980), pp. 65-66 and 75.

130. Haitsma Mulier, *Myth of Venice,* p. 4.

131. George O. Sayles, *The King's Parliament of England* (New York, 1974), pp. ix-x.

132. "It is rather amusing, however, how belief in Venetian wisdom and righteousness has continued into the modern treatment of this episode. Heinrich Kretschmayr . . . combines Guicciardini, Sanuto, and Paruta into a mixture that has no relation to fact. But recent Italian historians as well, considerably more steeped in the sources, continue the myth. Roberto Cessi . . . and Cozzi . . . propound the thesis that Venice did not really break the treaty with Charles V because it did not promise assistance to Francis I in the current war. But this thesis is untenable: as the speeches in the Pregadi or, later, Andrea Morosini show, the Venetians themselves did not claim that the treaty with Francis I was compatible with their alliance with Charles V." Gilbert, "Venetian Diplomacy before Pavia," pp. 115-16, n. 84.

133. Molmenti, *Venice,* part 2, I, 11.

134. Ibid., p. 18.

135. Ibid., part 1, I, 177 and 181-82.

136. Ibid., part 2, I, 30.

137. Ibid., pp. 10-11.

138. Ibid., part 2, I, 2 and part 2, II (Chicago, 1907), 229. Some of us, like Shakespeare, may side with York's wife, and not with York. *Richard II,* Act V, sc. 3.

139. Horatio F. Brown, *The Venetian Republic* (London, 1902), p. 138.

140. Ibid., p. 182.

141. Horatio F. Brown, *Studies in the History of Venice* (New York, 1907), I, 84. Yriarte gushed: "La vie de patricien est toute de labeur, . . . son existence intime se disparait dans son existence politique, et on a peine à en retrouver la trace. La famille semble en être absent; on disait que les infirmités humaines elles-mêmes ont été proscrites de par la dure loi qui régit les citoyens nobles." *Patricien de Venise,* p. 257. For a more recent manifestation of this aspect of the myth, see Arthur Livingston: "History shows not a few ruling classes . . . , the Venetian and English aristocracies, for instance, which have been able to lay interests and sentiments aside to a very considerable extent and to govern scientifically and objectively." In Mosca, *Ruling Class,* p. xxii.

142. René Guerdan, *La Sérénissime: Histoire de la République de Venise* (Paris, 1971), p. 148.

143. Ibid., p. 185. Vincent Ilardi, who knows more than anyone about Italian diplomacy in the second half of the Quattrocento, insists that Milan had a much more advanced diplomatic administration.

144. William H. McNeill, *Venice: The Hinge of Europe, 1081-1797* (Chicago, 1974), p. 65.

145. John Julius Norwich, *A History of Venice* (New York, 1982), p. 119.

146. Ibid., p. 155.

147. To the extent that any blame attaches to accepting aspects of the myth, the present author must claim a small share for having accepted the traditional interpretation of the Venetian *relazioni*. Donald E. Queller, *Early Venetian Legislation on Ambassadors* (Geneva, 1966), p. 58; also Queller, *Office of the Ambassador,* p. 142. Detailed scrutiny proved it untrue. Donald E. Queller, "The Development of Ambassadorial Relazioni," in *Renaissance Venice,* ed. Hale, pp. 174-96.

148. Gino Luzzatto, "Les activités économiques du patriciat vénitien (X^e-XIVe siècles)," in *Studi di storia economica veneziana* (Padua, 1954), p. 152. (Reprinted from *Annales d'histoire economique et sociale,* 9 [1937], 25-57.)

149. Ibid., p. 153. Pietro Soranzo was the example of such a noble. Ibid., p. 157.

150. Luzzatto, *Studi di storia economica veneziana,* p. 128.

151. Luzzatto, "Activités économiques," p. 163.

152. "Un inesauribile patrimonio, che perpetua eternamente la memoria di un passato glorioso." He professes not to have any romantic or apologetic intention, however. Roberto Cessi, *Storia della Repubblica di Venezia,* 2d. ed. rev. (Milan, 1968), I, 1.

153. Ibid., I, 183.

154. Ibid., I, 268; Roberto Cessi, *Deliberazioni del Maggior Consiglio di Venezia,* I (Bologna, 1930), xx.

155. Cessi, *Repubblica di Venezia,* I, 268-69.

156. Ibid., I, 270.

157. Ibid., II, 23.

158. Ibid., II, 24-25. The following was written by Luigi Luzzatti, but appears in the preface to Cessi's hardheaded *Regolazione delle entrate e delle spese,* p. x, presumably with the approval of the author: "Nessun falso pudore o peccaminoso sentimentalismo turbavano quelle anime calde d'amor patrio, ma argutamente calcolatrice degli interessi supremi della nazione; avevano anch' esse le loro passioni di parte, sentivano anch' esse gli stimoli degli interessi individuali, ma interessi e passioni, quando era in gioco la fortuna della patria, sapevano espellere con nobile slancio di sacrificio, per rendere la Repubblica più grande, più forte e più rispettata."

159. Yves Renouard, *Les hommes d'affaires italiens du moyen âge,* 1st ed., 1949, revised according to the notes of the author by Bernard Guillemain (Paris, 1968), pp. 82-83.

160. Yves Renouard, "Mercati e mercanti veneziani alla fine del Duecento," in *La civiltà veneziana del secolo di Marco Polo* (Florence, 1955), pp. 98-99.

161. Renouard, *Hommes d'affaires,* p. 293.

162. Ibid., pp. 150-51.

163. Renouard, "Mercati e mercanti veneziani," pp. 99-100. Another learned specialist on urban patriciates, Jean Lestocquoy, wrote: "In Venice the desire for personal gain does not detract from the public utility and each one, while thinking of his personal renown, wishes to increase the glory of the Republic. . . ." *Aux origines de la bourgeoisie: les villes de Flandre et d'Italie sous le gouvernement des patriciens, XIe-XVe siècles* (Paris, 1952), p. 189.

164. Fasoli, *Storia di Venezia,* p. 6.

165. Ibid., p. 35.

166. Ibid., p. 37.

167. Ibid., p. 221. In "Nascita di un mito," p. 450, Fasoli holds that no other modern state has had such an appreciation of the utility of history.

168. Fasoli, *Storia di Venezia,* p. 40.

169. Ibid., p. 54.

170. Ibid., p. 5.

171. This is not intended to point a finger of reproach at Prof. Fasoli or Prof. Cessi, but to suggest a failing common to us all. One good reason for our failure is that a radical revision concerning one aspect of a society usually compels or at least suggests a substantial change in our view of the whole. In the absence of other monographic studies we feel incapable of sweeping changes.

172. Cracco, *Società e stato,* p. 453.

173. Bouwsma, *Venice and the Defense of Republican Liberty,* p. 58.

174. Ibid., pp. 58-59.

175. Ibid., pp. 234-35.

176. Bouwsma, "Venice and the Political Education of Europe," p. 462. See also p. 445.

177. I wish to thank Edward Muir for reading this section in manuscript, especially for his comments on this paragraph.

178. Labalme, *Bernardo Giustiniani,* p. 8.

179. Ibid., p. 244.

180. Ibid., p. 9.

181. Ibid.

182. Ibid., pp. 1-2.

183. Ibid., p. 15.

184. Ibid., p. 231.

II. Welfare Jobs for the Nobles

1. Antonio Stella, "Grazie, pensioni ed elemosine sotto la Repubblica veneta," *Monografie ineditate in onore di Fabio Besta* (Milan, 1912), II, 723; Frederic C. Lane, *Andrea Barbarigo, Merchant of Venice* (Baltimore, 1944), pp. 14-15; Maranini, *Costituzione di Venezia,* I, 330. Even before the so-called Serrata the parishes of S. Martino and S. Antolino in 1285-86 had trouble putting on the feast of the *Marie* "on account of the poverty of the nobles." Cracco, *Società e stato,* p. 316. Cracco has recently indicated the increased demand for public employment during the economic crisis after 1330. Giorgio Cracco, "Patriziato e oligarchia a Venezia nel Tre-Quattrocento," in *Florence and Venice: Comparisons and Relations,* ed. Sergio Bertelli et al. (Florence, 1979), I, 92, n. 34. Jean Georgelin emphatically denies that there was any such thing as a sociologically

distinct group of poor nobles. *Venise au siècle des lumières* (Paris, 1978), pp. 766 and 937, n. 23. He has been severely criticized and, I think, rightly by Piero del Negro, "Il patriziato veneziano al calcolatore: Appunti in margine a Venezia au siècle des lumières di Jean Georgelin," *Rivista storica italiana,* 93 (1981), 838-48.

2. Luzzatto, "Activités économiques," p. 136. Luzzatto says 960, which does not correspond to the above table, where he has obviously shifted two in the lowest category from the non-noble to the noble side. The difference is not significant, at least for our purposes.

3. Ibid., pp. 135-37; Luzzatto, *Storia economica dell'età moderna e contemporea,* I (Padua, 1955), 130. Earlier Luzzatto found these poor nobles "beaucoup plus nombreux qu'on ne pourrait le croire." "Activités économiques," p. 135. Given the nature of the Venetian patriciate, I do not find it at all hard to believe. Lane's description of the distribution of wealth does not quite match Luzzatto's. Frederic C. Lane, "Gino Luzzatto's Contribution to the History of Venice: An Appraisal and a Tribute," *Nuova rivista storica,* 49 (1965), 67. Silvio Borsari mentions that already in the late twelfth and early thirteenth centuries Pietro Ziani helped many poor nobles by providing them money to make profits. "Una famiglia veneziana del medioevo: gli Ziani," *Archivio veneto,* ser. 5, 110 (1978), 44. This sounds generous, and it is, but it should also be understood in the context of a patronage system. On the poverty and dependence upon public offices of the nobles of Dalmatian towns, see Ventura, *Nobiltà e popolo,* pp. 215-26.

4. Luzzatto, *Storia economica dell'età moderna e contemporanea,* I, 83. Priuli, *Diarii,* IV, 297. He later declares that only about one to two hundred *ricchi* pay their taxes, while the rest, *mediocri* and *poveri,* do not. Ibid., IV, 406. I owe both references to Prof. Finlay. See also Ugo Tucci, "Il patrizio veneziano mercante e umanista," in *Venezia centro di mediazione tra Oriente e Occidente (secoli XV-XVI): Aspetti e problemi,* ed. Hans-Georg Beck, Manoussos Manoussacas, and Agostino Pertusi (Florence, 1977), I, 335-36. Jacques Heers gives examples from marginal lands, such as that of the Basques, Poland, the Celtic fringe, and Brittany, where there were numerous poor members of noble clans who appear as peasants, artisans, innkeepers, and the like. *Le clan familial au moyen âge: Etudes sur les structures politiques et sociales des milieux urbains* (Paris, 1974), pp. 28-35. For the Venetians, public employment provided an alternative to working for a living. Sanuto's assertion, if not quite Priuli's, is confirmed by an official act of the Great Council in 1490, which declares that the majority of nobles were dependent upon public office. Maggior Consiglio, Stella, 105(109)v. Although I think the subject of the poor Venetian nobles has not been systematically treated, a general awareness of the problem is hardly new. See Romanin, *Storia di Venezia,* VI, 450.

5. Quoted in Richard Trexler, "Charity and the Defense of Urban Elites in the Italian Communes," in *The Rich, the Well Born, and the Powerful,* ed. Frederic C. Jaher (Urbana, Ill., 1973), p. 73, n. 41. Trexler also points out aid to fallen nobles as examples of saintly charity. Ibid., p. 70. Throughout the article Trexler stresses that poverty was relative to social status.

6. "Per cosa de qualche admiratione, la quale quantucha la mi pare male credibile, tantavolta mi e fermata per persona digna di fede, la quale verisimiliter ne deve havere bona scientia: che per li bandi questi giorni fuoreno dati a ruffiani de questa terra, sono levati de qua sin al presente giorno cento undeci zentilhomeni quali tenevano femine in guadagno et exercivano el ruffianesimo, ultra molti altri quali non erano zentilhomeni, tra quali ce sono trovati molti pretti et fratti. Ben mi e facto sapere che questi ordini et parte sono facte una bona parte per removere zentilhomeni da tale vituperoso et illicito guadagno et offitio." A.S.M. (Milan), P.E., Venezia, cart. 379. Molmenti, *Venice,* part 2, II, 242; Ruggiero Romano, "Des lions affamés," in *Venise au temps des galères,* ed. Goimard, p. 271. I thank Prof. Vincent Ilardi for graciously sending me a photocopy of the dispatch from his vast collection of microfilms. Twelve days before the date of Vimercate's letter the Ten had, indeed, expelled pimps from Venice. Elisabeth Pavan, "Police des moeurs, société et politique a Venise à la fin du moyen âge," *Revue historique,* 264 (1980), 262.

7. Brian Pullan, "Poveri, mendicanti e vagabondi (secoli XIV–XVII)," in *Storia d'Italia. Annali I. Dal feudalesimo al capitalismo* (Turin, 1978), p. 1040.

8. Pietro Barozzi, "Orazione recitata a Papa Paolo II della famiglia veneta Barbo in nome suo e della famiglia in morte de Giovanni suo zio paterno Patriarcha di Venezia," in *Orazioni, elogi, e vite,* ed. Molina, I, 126. See Tucci, "Patrizio veneziano mercante e umanista," pp. 335-36.

9. Gaetano Cozzi, "Authority and Law in Renaissance Venice," in *Renaissance Venice,* ed. Hale, pp. 300-301.

10. See pp. 39-40.

11. Domenico Malipiero, *Annali veneti, 1457-1500,* ed. Tommaso Gar and Agostino Sagredo, in *Archivio storico italiano,* ser. 1, 7 (1843), 691-92; Dieci, Misto, XXV, 141(176)v-142(177)v, 143(178)v-144(179)r, 146(181)v; Pullan, *Rich and Poor in Renaissance Venice,* p. 230; Brian Pullan, "Poverty, Charity and Reason of State: Some Venetian Examples," *Bollettino dell'Istituto di Storia della Società e dello Stato Veneziano,* 2 (1960), 36-37; Philip Longworth, *The Rise and Fall of Venice* (London, 1974), p. 174. Malipiero says that 800 poor nobles might have been drawn to Venice if the measure had passed.

12. Pietro Dolfin, *Annalium Venetorum pars quarta,* fasc. 1, ed. Roberto Cessi and Paolo Sambin (Venice, 1943), p. 252; Malipiero, *Annali veneti,* p. 713; Longworth, *Rise and Fall of Venice,* p. 192; Tucci, "Patrizio veneziano mercante e umanista," p. 336.

13. Dieci, Misto, XIII, 63(93)rv.

14. Ibid., 75(105)r.

15. "[C]um li quali essi nostri nobeli per la mazor parte viveno e sustentano le famiglie loro. . ." Maggior Consiglio, Stella, 105(109)v. Italics in text mine.

16. Dieci, Misto, XXVIII, 136(197)v.

17. Senato, Misti, LVIII, 222(226)v.

18. Pietro Dolfin, *Annalium Venetorum,* pp. 207-8.

19. Marino Sanuto, *I Diarii,* ed. Rinaldo Fulin et al., IV (Venice, 1880), 201-4.

20. Logan, *Culture and Society in Venice*, pp. 26, 273-74; B. Cecchetti, "I nobili e il popolo di Venezia," *Archivio veneto*, 3 (1872), 427-28.

21. Lane, *Venice*, p. 324.

22. Luigi da Porto, *Lettere storiche*, quoted by Rose, "Venice," p. 162, n. 1.

23. Maranini, *Costituzione di Venezia*, II, 8-9; *Costituzione di Venezia*, I, 330. See also F. Marion Crawford, *Venice, the Place and the People: Salve Venetia: Gleanings from Venetian History* (New York, 1909), I, 180. Cecchetti describes the nobles of Crete in the seventeenth century reduced by the cost of the War of Candia to poverty and dependence on officeholding. "I nobili," p. 427.

24. Priuli, *Diarii*, II, 297; IV, 92 and 93.

25. Lane, *Venice*, pp. 226, 323-24; Lane, *Andrea Barbarigo*, p. 12. James Cushman Davis has estimated 800 jobs all together in the Ducato, Terra, and Mar. *The Decline of the Venetian Nobility as a Ruling Class* (Baltimore, 1962), p. 22.

26. Pullan, "Service to the Venetian State," p. 118; Davis, *Decline of the Venetian Nobility*, p. 22; Tenenti, "Sérénissime République," p. 172; Corrado Vivanti, "Pace e libertà in un opera di Domenico Morosini," *Rivista storica italiana*, 84 (1972), 621-22.

27. James Williamson, "Faction and Loyalty in the Venetian State under Doge Foscari" (Paper delivered at the Warwick Symposium, Venice, 29 Nov. 1972). See also, Lane, *Venice*, p. 266.

28. Philip Jones, "Communes and the Despots: The City-State in Late Medieval Italy," *Royal Historical Society. Transactions*, ser. 5, 15 (1965), 84-85.

29. A *grazia* was an act of special legislation granting an office or other privilege or award obviating the normal procedure. Dennis Romano, "*Quod sibi fiat gratia:* Adjustment of Penalties and the Exercise of Influence in Early Renaissance Venice," *Journal of Medieval and Renaissance Studies*, 13 (1983), 252. The same abuse arose in Padua. Ventura, *Nobiltà e popolo*, pp. 87-88.

30. "Cum per nostram dominationem per viam gratie in nostros nobiles multa et multa officia et beneficia diverse conditionis quibus solebant gaudere et vivere populares et alii nostri subditi qui nostro dominio fideliter servierunt dispensata fuerunt contra formam ordinum nostrorum et etiam contra provisiones et concessiones factas subditis terrarum et locorum nostrorum cum magna murmuratione fidelium nostrorum . . . et propter tale inconveniens multi alii nobiles non cessant imo procurant de suprascriptis rebus impetrare. . . ." Dieci, Misto, XV, 39(40)v. Contarini claimed that patrician government maintained harmony among the classes partly by setting aside certain offices for the *popolo*. Muir, *Civic Ritual*, pp. 38-39. This, of course, is what the Ten is trying to do in this act and the following one, but the difficulties are apparent.

31. Dieci, Misto, 40(41)v-41(42)r.

32. Ibid., 45(46)r.

33. "Potestates dicti loci sunt soliti pro maiori parte stare Venetiis et alibi extra regimen suum, quia habent paucum agere, eo quod in littore maiori sunt quinque vel sex familie." Senato, Misti, LV, 65(66)r. After the suppression of the consulates of London, Damascus, and Alexandria after the War of Candia,

the government established the *provveditori al cottimo* of London, Damascus, and Alexandria. They had no duties, but drew thirty silver ducats a month, a sop to the poor nobles. Giuseppe Boerio, *Dizionario del dialetto veneziano,* 2 ed. (1856; reprint, Turin, 1964), p. 204.

34. Senato, Terra, III, 120(122)v.

35. Ibid., 135(137)v.

36. Sanuto, *Cronachetta,* p. 46; id., *Città di Venetia,* pp. 28–29.

37. Contarini, *De magistratibus,* 56rv (Lewkenor, pp. 133–34); Ugo Tucci, "Dans le sillage de Marco Polo," in *Venise au temps del galères,* ed. Goimard, p. 105; Lane, *Andrea Barbarigo,* p. 17. Common sailors had the same right.

38. Lane, *Venice,* pp. 344–45.

39. See p. 37.

40. See pp. 37–38.

41. Lane, *Venice,* p. 344.

42. Maggior Consiglio, Stella, 129(133)r. See also Contarini, *De magistratibus,* 56rv (Lewkenor, pp. 133–34); Priuli, *Diarii,* II, 167–68; Sanuto, *Diarii,* IV, 104; Senato, Mar, XV, 83(94)v–84(95)r; Maggior Consiglio, Stella, 181(185)r; "Traité du gouvernement de la cité et seigneurie de Venise," in P.-M. Perret, *Relations de la France avec Venice* (Paris, 1896), II, 294.

43. "Sit honor et utile terre nostre dare causam nostris nobilibus a quibus ipsam terram gubernari opportet quod inquirant et circhent de mundo, ut possint in agendis communis esse sapienter instructi et probi, ac personas suas exposere in honoribus et laboribus terre quando fuerit necessarium." Maggior Consiglio, Novella, 51(62)v.

44. Lane, *Andrea Barbarigo,* p. 17; Renouard, *Hommes d'affaires,* p. 295.

45. Cozzi, "Authority and Law," p. 297.

46. Lane, *Venice,* p. 345.

47. Sanuto, *Cronachetta,* p. 46; id., *Città di Venetia,* p. 29. He names a salary of sixty ducats. In 1433, on the other hand, the salary was only twenty-five ducats. Senato, Misti, LVIII, 213(217)v. The figure of 100 to 200 ducats can be found in the "Traité du gouvernement de Venise," p. 294, which dates from about the same time as Sanuto. Lane, *Venice,* p. 344, also gives it.

48. Senato, Mar, XV, 83(94)v–84(95)r.

49. *Documents inédits pour servir à l'histoire de la domination vénitienne en Crète,* ed. Hippolyte Noiret (Paris, 1892), p. 86.

50. Lane, *Venice,* pp. 344–45.

51. Senato, Misti, LIII, 102(102)r.

52. Ibid., LVIII, 213(217)v.

53. "Cum multi pauperes juvenes nostri nobiles, sicut omnibus notum esse potest, valde multiplicati sint, propter quod necesse est eis aliqualiter providere. . . ." Ibid., LX, 10(10)v.

54. Dieci, Misto, XV, 41(42)r.

55. Lane, *Venice,* pp. 344–45.

56. Sanuto, *Cronachetta,* pp. 45–46; id., *Città di Venetia,* pp. 28–29.

57. Dieci, Misto, XIII, 87(89)r.

58. Senato, Mar, XV, 83(94)v-84(95)r; Maggior Consiglio, Stella, 181(185)r; Sanuto, *Diarii,* IV, 104; Priuli, *Diarii,* II, 167-68.

59. Contarini, *De magistratibus,* 56v (Lewkenor, p. 134).

60. Noiret, ed., *Documents inédits,* pp. 86-87. I interpret *collegium deputatum* as an ad hoc committee. Lane says "by a committee of the Collegio," which is not at all the same. *Venice,* p. 344. *Collegium* does not always signify the Pien Collegio. The committee appointed by the Ten to investigate criminal charges, for example, is always called a *collegium.*

61. Maggior Consiglio, Stella, 129(133)r. See also Senato, Mar, XV 83(94)v-84(95)r; Maggior Consiglio, Stella, 181(185)r; Sanuto, *Diarii,* IV, 104; Priuli, *Diarii,* II, 167-68. Finlay has misread this passage. *Politics in Renaissance Venice,* p. 242. In addition: Sanuto, *Cronachetta,* pp. 45-46; id., *Città di Venetia,* p. 28; Priuli, *Diarii,* II, 168; "Traité du gouvernement de Venise," p. 294; Finlay, *Politics in Renaissance Venice,* p. 69. We will speak presently of the Quaranta itself as a haven for poor nobles.

62. Senato, Misti, LIII, 165(165)v. "Paucus ordo servatus fuerit, ymo committantur multe inhonestates . . . que volunt quod meliores et sufficientiores balistarii, et magis pauperes accipiantur. Et nota quod ad instantium aliquorum nobilium et aliorum nostrorum semper ibi astantium accipiantur minus sufficientes."

63. "Cum in die palii occurant mille disordines et totidem disobedientie. . . ." Dieci, Misto, XII, 167(168)rv.

64. "[S]icut in similibus casis multis factum est." Senato, Terra, I, 159(160)v.

65. Maggior Consiglio, Stella, 149(153)r, 150(154)v, 151(155)r; Malipiero, *Annali veneti,* p. 645.

66. Sanuto, *Diarii,* I, 906. Actually, one of the grants was to Beneto and Francesco Guoro, sons of the late Pandolfo, jointly. This and many other documents illustrate the importance and the sense of community of the family.

67. Ibid., I, 906.

68. "[E] cosi el thesoro che serve per alimento de poveri Zentilhomeni besognosi, vien despensa a chi non se dovrebbe. . . ." Malipiero, *Annali veneti,* pp. 714-15.

69. Sanuto, *Diarii,* III, 106; Priuli, *Diarii,* I, 267.

70. "[Q]uod communitas eadem semper consuevit remunerire et premiari illos quo personas suas pro statu et honore suo exposuerint." Maggior Consiglio, Novella, 91(102)r. Brian Pullan, "The Occupations and Investments of the Venetian Nobility in the Middle and Late Sixteenth Century," in *Renaissance Venice,* ed. Hale, pp. 395-96. *Balestrierie* were often awarded, but other positions could be used for the same purpose. Priuli, *Diarii,* II, 60, 101; Sanuto, *Diarii,* III, 884, 1406; VI, 107. Of Giovanni Zancani, who was made *provveditore in armata,* Priuli said: "Et tuto fu facto a requisitione di brogij, perche, volendo dir il vero, questo Zantani non valeva un quatrino in armata. . . ." *Diarii,* II, 118. Sanuto says that if he were in the Senate he would not let it pass. *Diarii,* III, 1629.

71. Sanuto, *Diarii*, I, 1003; Malipiero, *Annali veneti*, p. 646.

72. Malipiero, *Annali veneti*, p. 646. Note that the young man was underage.

73. Pietro Dolfin, *Annalium Venetorum*, pp. 219-20; Sanuto, *Diarii*, III, 1241. The sources disagree on the name and the number of positions.

74. Senato, Mar, XV, 83(94)v-84(95)r; Maggior Consiglio, Stella, 181 (185)rv; Sanuto, *Diarii*, IV, 104; Priuli, *Diarii*, II, 168.

75. Contarini, *De magistratibus*, 56rv (Lewkenor, pp. 133-34).

76. Senato, Misti, LIV, 82(83)r. See p. 192.

77. Ibid., LVIII, 132(136)v.

78. Senato, Terra, I, 164(165)v; Maggior Consiglio, Stella, 13(17)v.

79. Maggior Consiglio, Stella, 14(18)v.

80. Ibid., 129(133)r. A few years later fathers could also be substituted. Maggior Consiglio, Stella, 181(185)r; Senato, Mar, XV, 83(94)v-84(95)r.

81. Priuli, *Diarii*, II, 168; Sanuto, *Diarii*, IV, 104; Senato, Mar, XV, 83(94)v-84(95)r; Maggior Consiglio, Stella, 181(185)r. See Lane, *Venice*, p. 345.

82. Sanuto, *Cronachetta*, p. 46; id., *Città di Venetia*, p. 29; Contarini, *De magistratibus*, 56v (Lewkenor, p. 134).

83. "Cum annis preteritis occurerit, et hoc anno (1434) etiam evenit, quod balistarii nobiles electi per collegium non vadunt cum galeis, et illi qui habuerunt plures ballotas sucessive post eos non accipiuntur, et denarii qui ad armamentum pro talium ballistariorum solutione per patrones consignati fuerint postea ab officialibus armamenti restituuntur patronis galearum, que omnia fiunt preter intentionem nostri dominii et preter formam ordinum nostrorum." Senato, Misti, LIX, 68(70)r. Obviously, the *patroni* were inducing those elected not to go. See also the act of 1500: Senato, Mar, XV, 83(94)v-84(95)r; Maggior Consiglio, Stella, 181(185)r.

84. Finlay, *Politics in Renaissance Venice*, p. 69.

85. Senato, Misti, LVIII, 208(212)r.

86. Ibid., LIX, 82(84)v-83(85)r.

87. Senato, Terra, III, 127(129)v. Lane tells us (apparently speaking of the early sixteenth century) that each of the 120 members received more than 100 ducats a year. Lane, *Venice*, p. 324.

88. Priuli, *Diarii*, IV, 93; Finlay, *Politics in Renaissance Venice*, p. 72.

89. Contarini, *De magistratibus*, 41v (Lewkenor, p. 95).

90. Pullan, "Significance of Venice," p. 457.

91. Lewkenor, in Contarini, *Commonwealth of Venice*, p. 164; Pullan, "Occupations and Investments of the Venetian Nobility," pp. 394-95; Lane, *Andrea Barbarigo*, p. 18; Renouard, *Hommes d'affaires*, p. 295.

92. Maggior Consiglio, Presbiter (copia II), 113(151)r and 114(152)r.

93. Ibid., Clericus civicus, 87(135)v.

94. Ibid., 132(180)v.

95. Ibid.

96. Senato, Misti, XLV, 34(34)v.

97. Maggior Consiglio, Ursa, 135(141)r.

98. Senato, Terra II, 154(154)v.

99. Maggior Consiglio, Ursa, 175(181)r.

100. Michiel's daughters were each to receive 1000 ducats for their dowries when they reached ten years of age. Sanuto, *Diarii,* IV, 86; Priuli, *Diarii,* II, 143.

101. Sanuto, *Diarii,* IV, 157; Priuli, *Diarii,* II, 182-83.

102. Maggior Consiglio, Presbiter (copia II), 108(146)rv.

103. Senato, Misti, XXXVII, 92(93)r.

104. This reference is contained in a later act. Ibid., XLII, 148(149)rv.

105. "Cum ducale dominium ex innata sibi clementia consueverit suis civibus nobilibus in eorum necessitatibus benignius suffragari, et specialiter illis qui non suo deffectu ad inopiam devenerunt. Et sicut notum est vir nobilis Raynerus Permarino . . . , qui semper in agendis et servitiis dominii, in quibus fuit fideliter et laudabiliter se gessit, ad debilem conditionem sit deductus propter multam familiam, qua multipliciter est gravatus, cum quatuor creaturas parvulas habeat ad alendum, ex quo pietatis opus sit misericorditer subvenire, quia aliquale onus terre huius est quod nostri nobiles mendicantes in totum deseratur." Maggior Consiglio, Leona, 18(22)v.

106. Ibid., 19(23)r.

107. Ibid., 23(27)r.

108. "Dicta bona et suprascripta provisio non observetur quia capita de XL omni die personis insufficientibus et non bene meritis ponunt partem in consiliis ordinatis de revocando dictam partem et omnes alias stricturas, quia postea petunt gratiam a ducali dominio de dicta pena in qua incurerunt, et sic dicta pars et alie stricture non observantur. . . ." Senato, Misti, XLII, 148(149)rv.

109. Ibid., XLIV, 107(107)r.

110. Ibid., XLV, 44(44)r.

111. Ibid., LIII, 19(19)v.

112. Maggior Consiglio, Regina, 22(28)rv.

113. Maggior Consiglio, Leona, 57(61)v-59(63)v.

114. Maggior Consiglio, Ursa, 136(142)v.

115. Ibid., 151(157)v.

116. Sanuto, *Cronachetta,* p. 215; Davis, *Decline of the Venetian Nobility,* p. 22, n. 16, quoting the *Cronachetta,* p. 178.

117. Senato, Terra, IV, 110(111)v.

118. Dieci, Misto, XVI, 119(156)v.

119. Senato, Misti, XLIII, 31(30)r; Maggior Consiglio, Stella, 105(109)v.

120. Cessi, ed., *Maggior Consiglio,* II (Bologna, 1931), 96. Weakened slightly in 1302. Maggior Consiglio, Magnus, 36(37)v.

121. Maggior Consiglio, Leona, 10(14)r. Notice that we are not here dealing with petty offices for the poor, but with the distribution of honors among the rich.

122. Ibid., Ursa, 90(96)v.

123. Pullan, "Poverty, Charity and Reason of State," pp. 28-30; Brown, *Studies,* I, 312-13.

124. "De hiis beneficiis omnes sentiant et participent de tempore in tempus,

quia quanto brevior erit terminus, quanto plures nobiles in eis beneficiis participabunt." Maggior Consiglio, Ursa, 190(196)v. See also Senato, Terra, VIII, 115(116)r.

125. Maggior Consiglio, Regina, 1(7)v. See also ibid., 31(37)r.

126. "Cum li quali essi nostri nobeli per la mazor part viveno e sustentano le famiglie loro. . ." Maggior Consiglio, Stella, 105(109)v.

127. Cessi, ed., *Maggior Consiglio*, II, 233.

128. Maggior Consiglio, Stella, 16(20)r.

129. Ibid., 53(57)r.

130. Ibid., 129(133)r. The passage "non possi romagnir piui de uno over do al piui" is an example of bad drafting. The limit is either one or two. Such vagueness does not encourage rigorous application of laws.

131. Pullan, *Rich and Poor in Renaissance Venice,* p. 114; Pullan, "Occupations and Investments of the Venetian Nobility," p. 395.

132. Bouwsma finds a dim view of man's capacity for virtue in republicanism. *Venice and the Defense of Republican Liberty,* p. 11.

133. Fink gives a respectable discussion of the more creditable reasons behind *contumacia,* but, following the myth of the magnificent patriciate, never mentions that the nobles were dividing up the spoils. *Classical Republicans,* pp. 31–32. The Venetian patricians were quite honest about what they were doing.

134. Cessi, ed., *Maggior Consiglio,* II, 98.

135. Ibid., II, 42.

136. Ibid., III, 282.

137. *Le deliberazioni del Consiglio dei Rogati (Senato): Serie "Mixtorum,"* I, ed. Roberto Cessi and Paolo Sambin (Venice, 1960), 6.

138. Senato, Misti, XL, 24(27)v.

139. The act (Maggior Consiglio, Leona, 66(70)r) has been published in Giovanni Italo Cassandro, "La Curia di Petizion," *Archivio veneto,* ser. 5, 20 (1937), 171.

140. Maggior Consiglio, Leona, 76(80)v.

141. "Cum antiqui nostri inter alia vigilaverint ad servandum in omnibus equalitatem quantum possent. Et inter alia providerint quod officiales et judices nostri quasi omnes deberent stare extra illa officia et judicatus per unum annum post complementum suorum officiorum et judicatuum, seu per tantum tempus quantum in dictis officiis et judicatibus stetissent, ut quamplures esse possent participarent de honoribus et beneficiis terre." Ibid., 170(175)v.

142. Ibid., Ursa, 22(30)v.

143. Senato, Misti, LIII, 4(4)r. This is an amendment which lacks the cross or the "capta" indicating that it passed.

144. Maggior Consiglio, Ursa, 76(82)v.

145. Ibid., 90(96)v.

146. Ibid., 145(151)v.

147. Ibid., Leona, 193(198)v.

148. Ibid., 194(199)v.

149. Ibid., 195(200)r.

150. Ibid., Ursa, 19(27)v.

151. Ibid., 172(178)r.

152. Priuli, *Diarii*, I, 260.

153. Sanuto, *Diarii*, III, 92.

154. Ibid., III, 808.

155. Senato, Terra, XIII, 151(153)v; Sanuto, *Diarii*, III, 970; Priuli, *Diarii*, II, 66.

156. Cessi, ed., *Maggior Consiglio*, III (Bologna, 1934), 282.

157. Maggior Consiglio, Ursa, 28(36)v.

158. Ibid., Leona, 76(80)v.

159. Ibid., 194(199)v. Also contained in the subsequent amendment. Ibid., 195(200)r.

160. Ibid., Ursa, 145(151)v.

161. Ibid., 172(178)r.

162. Senato, Terra, XV, 114(129)r; Sanuto gives the same act under two dates ten days apart. *Diarii*, VI, 390 and 392.

163. Ibid., IV, 182(183)r.

164. Dieci, Misto, XVI, 80(117)v.

165. Stella, "Grazie, pensioni ed elemosine," p. 723; Cracco, "Patriziato e oligarchia a Venezia," p. 87.

166. Stella, "Grazie, pensioni ed elemosine," pp. 722-23.

167. Vergerio, edited in Robey and Law, "Venetian Myth and Vergerio," p. 46, ll. 228-30.

168. Priuli, *Diarii*, II, 168.

169. Ruggiero Romano, "Lions affamés," p. 284.

170. Cozzi, "Authority and Law," p. 297.

III. Broglio Onesto

1. Ermolao Barbaro, "Orazione funebre di Niccolò Marcello," in *Orazioni, elogi, e vite*, ed. Molina, p. 62.

2. For a typically romantic repetition of the myth, see Fink, *Classical Republicans*, pp. 32-33: "Another notable feature of the Venetian government was that it was in no sense a party system . . . the Venetians had a keen sense of the disasters which factional feuds had brought to other Italian cities and three features of the constitution not only were designed to prevent the rise or existence of political parties, but effectively operated to do so. One of these was the element of lot or chance which was introduced into the election of the Doge. Another was the use of the secret ballot in the form of a box with white and red balls in voting on measures in both the Senate and the Great Council. Under a system in which no one could tell how another had voted, it was impossible to enforce on occasion or assert consistently that party discipline without which political parties do not readily maintain themselves. The third provision was the enactment of the most severe penalties for anything resembling electioneering

or canvassing for votes. Under the Venetian system, a gentleman voted, not as a party member intent on carrying out a political program, but as an individual exercising his own best judgment of the affairs of state."

3. Cessi, ed., *Maggior Consiglio*, II, 87. In paraphrasing this fundamental act, Frederic C. Lane omits *per fraudem*. "The Enlargement of the Great Council of Venice," in *Florilegium Historiale: Essays Presented to Wallace K. Ferguson*, ed. J. G. Rowe and W. H. Stockdale (Toronto, 1971), p. 247. On the act of 1509, Finlay, *Politics in Renaissance Venice*, pp. 205-6.

4. Cozzi, "Domenico Morosini," pp. 421-22; Cozzi, "Authority and Law," pp. 298-99; and Tenenti, "Sérénissime République," p. 172. Sanuto thought the problem had its beginnings in 1448. *Diarii*, XXIV, 657; Finlay, *Politics in Renaissance Venice*, pp. 174-75. Finlay has suggested that the increase in the number of nobles participating in the Great Council was due not only to the financial plight of the patriciate, but also to a marked increase in the number of young patricians, both rich and poor, in the late fifteenth and early sixteenth centuries.

5. As pointed out by Maurice Aymard, "La terre ferme," in *Venise au temps des galères*, ed. Goimard, p. 143.

6. Cozzi, "Authority and Law," pp. 298-300. According to Priuli, importunate nobles were lobbying for office six months before the elections. *Diarii*, IV, 33.

7. Davis, *Decline of the Venetian Nobility*, p. 22; Longworth, *Rise and Fall of Venice*, pp. 192-93; Chambers, *Imperial Age of Venice*, p. 74. On the types of offices involved and the salaries they carried, see Freddy Thiriet, *La Romanie vénitienne au moyen âge: le développement et l'exploitation du domain colonial vénitien (xiie au xv^{e}siècles)* (Paris, 1959), pp. 216 and 194, respectively. Sanuto made up a list of 831 posts elected by the Great Council, 550 within Venice and 281 outside. Finlay, *Politics in Renaissance Venice*, p. 59. He also said that there were about 2420 nobles eligible for office in 1493, rising to 2570 twenty years later. Davis, *Decline of the Venetian Nobility*, p. 55.

8. Malipiero, *Annali veneti*, p. 535. The sale of his house was revoked. Pullan writes of one Francesco di Geronimo Zeno in the later sixteenth century, who had a small income from urban property but who had nothing in the *monte* and nothing in commerce. He had five children and an unmarried sister dependent upon him. He stated that he sought to support himself with public offices, because he certainly could not do without such assistance. "Occupations and Investments of the Venetian Nobility," p. 394.

9. Lane, *Venice*, p. 226.

10. Reinhold C. Mueller, "The Procurators of San Marco in the Thirteenth and Fourteenth Centuries: A Study of the Office as a Financial and Trust Institution," *Studi veneziani*, 13 (1971), 189; Labalme, *Bernardo Giustiniani*, p. 225; Brown, *Venetian Republic*, p. 99.

11. Lane, *Venice*, pp. 262 and 266; Labalme, *Bernardo Giustiniani*, pp. 288-89.

12. Luzzatto, "Activités économiques," pp. 136-37. I think that Chojnacki

puts too generous an interpretation upon his evidence. "In Search of the Venetian Patriciate," p. 69.

13. Lane, *Venice*, p. 264. On the interaction of rich and poor nobles, see Cozzi, "Authority and Law," p. 298. In his *De officio episcopi*, Gasparo Contarini pointed out the special obligation of caring for poor nobles, whose poverty contained a peculiar ignominy. Ross, "Contarini and His Friends," p. 224.

14. Pullan, "Poveri, mendicanti e vagabondi," p. 1040.

15. Robert Finlay, "Venice, the Po Expedition, and the End of the League of Cambrai, 1509-1510," *Studies in Modern European History and Culture*, 2 (1976), 61. This portion of Priuli's *Diarii* has not been published.

16. *Cronaca Bemba*, B.M., cl. ital. VII, cod. 125(=7460), 59r; Romanin, *Storia di Venezia*, II (Venice, 1912), 361-62; Pullan, *Rich and Poor in Renaissance Venice*, pp. 114-15; Pilot, "Capitolo inedito contro il broglio," p. 544; Pompeo Molmenti, "La corruzione dei costumi veneziani nel Rinascimento," *Archivio storico italiano*, ser. 5, 31 (1903), 285. In 1492 the prohibition against *broglio* was extended to ecclesiastical positions. Dieci, Misto, XXV, 129(164)r. The Church of Santa Maria del Broglio was on the site of the present Luna Hotel.

17. Molmenti, *Venice*, II, 235.

18. Finlay, *Politics in Renaissance Venice*, p. 199.

19. Agostino Valiero, "Vita di Bernardo Navagero, P. V. cardinale di Santa Chiesa ed amministrator della chiesa di Verona scritta da Agostino Valiero P. V.," in Molina, ed., *Orazioni, elogi, e vite*, II, 80.

20. *Dominus talis* was all that was allowed. Dieci, Misto, XVI, 142(179)v.

21. Pullan, "Occupations and Investments of the Venetian Nobility," pp. 393-94; Pullan, "The Significance of Venice," pp. 456-57; Cecchetti, "I nobili," 427-28.

22. Priuli, *Diarii*, IV, 200-201.

23. Finlay, *Politics in Renaissance Venice*, p. 197.

24. Ibid., pp. 197-99. The situation in Padua was very similar. Ventura, *Nobiltà e popolo*, pp. 86-87.

25. Lane, *Venice*, p. 262.

26. Boerio, *Dizionario*, p. 791; Romanin, *Storia di Venezia*, II, 361.

27. Rose, "Venice," pp. 483-84.

28. Gilbert, "Venetian Constitution in Florentine Political Thought," p. 476.

29. A convenient listing of the offices to which election was held in the Great Council is provided by Andrea da Mosto, *L'Archivio di Stato di Venezia*, in *Bibliothèque des "Annales Institutorum,"* I (Rome, 1937), 31-33. Brown, *Studies*, I, 313, emphasizes that the tenure of all offices, except the dogeship and the procuratorship of San Marco, was so brief—rarely exceeding a year or sixteen months—that elections in the Great Council must have been virtually incessant.

30. Maggior Consiglio, Fractus, 62(67)v.

31. Cessi, ed., *Maggior Consiglio*, II, 91.

32. Ibid., II, 92.

33. Ibid., II, 97.

34. Cozzi, "Authority and Law," p. 299 and p. 341, n. 25, suggests that the

practice of utilizing four nominating committees rather than two became the norm only toward the close of the fifteenth century. The transition from two to four nominating committees can be seen by comparing the 1493 edition of Sanuto's *Cronachetta* with the revision of 1515. Robert G. Finlay, "The Politics of the Ruling Class in Early Cinquecento Venice" (Ph.D. diss., University of Chicago, 1973), p. 79.

35. It may be read *in toto* in Gasparo Contarini, *De magistratibus* (1589 ed.), pp. 12r-16r (Lewkenor, pp. 23-32). The "Traité du gouvernement de Venise," pp. 259-63, appears to follow Contarini's description with few variations, such as red and green instead of white and green. I believe that this interesting French document could be dated fairly accurately by comparing its provisions to changing Venetian practices.

36. Donato Giannotti, *Della Republica et Magistrati di Venetia,* bound with Gasparo Contarini, *Della Republica et Magistrati di Venetia* (Venice, 1591), p. 156. The process of inscribing the golden balls with a letter code to prevent the presentation of counterfeits is described in some detail by Giannotti, *Libro della Repubblica de'Viniziani,* in *Opere* (Florence, 1850), p. 75. (The occasional use of different editions of a work such as this depending upon availability at Illinois, Princeton, or Venice will be understood by fellow scholars.)

37. See also Giannotti, *Republica di Venetia,* pp. 159-60.

38. It is hardly surprising that, as a result of this procedure, in Venetian parlance the phrase "drawing a golden ball" was proverbially used to indicate any good fortune. Ceccheti, "I nobili," p. 432.

39. Sanuto points out that it was a rare thing for the nominee not to receive the necessary six votes in the nominating committee. *Cronachetta,* pp. 227-29; id., *Città di Venetia,* p. 149. This was, of course, due to the desire of the other members of the nominating committee to have their candidates accepted in turn. Lane, *Venice,* p. 260.

40. The shape of the *bussulus* is described in the "Traité du gouvernement de Venise," pp. 263-64.

41. Some details of the procedure described by Contarini were the result of long-term development. The number of urns and golden balls involved in the first stage (*electio,* or nomination) varied as the number of nominating committees grew from one to two to four. The coded inscription of the golden balls must have begun after the infamous Cicogna conspiracy of 1432 (see pp. 79-80 and 88), which was based on the substitution of such counterfeits. Other such changes in the electoral process will be discussed as we go along. In addition, nominations to many offices were made not only by committees drawn from the Great Council, but also by the Signoria and the Senate. Members of the Signoria simply took turns in choosing nominees, but in 1500 the ducal councillor Antonio Tron persuaded his colleagues in the Signoria to renounce their right to make nominations. The Senate presented nominations by *scrutinio* for a number of important offices. In such cases the four nominees from the committees of the Great Council were joined by a single nomination from the Senate, and the senatorial candidate was usually successful. The Senate never entirely

gave up nomination by *scrutinio,* but toward the close of the fifteenth century introduced attempts to curtail its use. Lane, *Venice,* pp. 259–63.

42. Maggior Consiglio, Leona, 186(191)v.

43. Ibid., 187(192)v.

44. Ibid., Ursa, 53(61)v. The Forty was notorious for its poor nobles engaging in *broglio.*

45. "Et etiam quia pena ipsa in tantum parva est quod multi neque timore ipsius neque respectu honestatis sibi cavent a contrafaciendo dicte parti. . . ." Ibid., 58(66)r. See also ibid., 137(143)v (1442); Dieci, Misto, XVI, 188(225)v (1466). The last act declares: "Multiplicata est presumptio aliquorum nostrorum nobilium et cupiditas regiminum et officiorum nostrorum. . . ."

46. Senato, Misti, LV, 99(100)v.

47. Maggior Consiglio, Ursa, 89(95)v.

48. Dieci, Misto, XII, 162(163)rv.

49. Senato, Terra, II, 132(134)r.

50. Dieci, Misto, XVI, 18(55)v.

51. "Ut electio duci fieret per conscientiam et secundum deum et non per preces." Ibid., XVI, 61(98)v.

52. Ibid., XVI, 117(154)v.

53. Ibid., XVI, 179(216)v. See also ibid., XXXII, 31(81)r (1508).

54. Ibid., XVI, 207(244)r.

55. "Pauci sint qui exacte leges nostras exequantur." Ibid., XX, 9(47)v–10(48)r. The Ten had to return to the same problem in 1497, ibid., XXVII, 130(172)r–131(173)r; Sanuto, *Diarii,* I, 837–38, where it is slightly misdated.

56. "Et multa committuntur ab honestate et modestia aliena. . . ." Maggior Consiglio, Stella, 9(13)v.

57. Dieci, Misto, XXII, 27(63)v.

58. Ibid., XXII, 79(115)r–80(116)r.

59. Ibid., XXIII, 80(110)r.

60. Ibid., XXIV, 62(101)v–63(102)r.

61. Ibid., XXIV, 80(119)v.

62. Maggior Consiglio, Stella, 107(111)v–108(112)r.

63. Dieci, Misto, XXIX, 132(193)r–133(194)r.

64. Maggior Consiglio, Spiritus, 126(127)v.

65. Maggior Consiglio, Novella, 46(57)v and 182(195)v.

66. Senato, Misti, LV, 99(100)v. See above, p. 58.

67. Dieci, Misto, XIX, 61(101)rv; published in Pilot, "Capitolo inedito contro il broglio," pp. 546–47.

68. Dieci, Misto, XXII, 28(64)rv.

69. Ibid., XXIV, 62(101)v–63(102)r. See p. 61.

70. Maggior Consiglio, Presbiter (copia II), 275(314)v.

71. Maggior Consiglio, Leona, 26(30)v; Avogadori di Comun, Capitulare, I 154v.

72. Maggior Consiglio, Leona, 126(130)r; Avogadori di Comun, A, 7(17)r.

73. Maggior Consiglio, Ursa, 44(52)v.

74. See p. 58; Maggior Consiglio, Leona, 187(192)v.
75. Senato, Misti, LV, 98(99)v.
76. Maggior Consiglio, Ursa, 137(143)v.
77. Dieci, Misto, XX, 9(47)v-10(48)v.
78. Ibid., XXII, 88(124)v-89(125)r.
79. Giannotti, *Republica di Venetia,* p. 158.
80. Maggior Consiglio, Leona, 221(226)v; Avogaria di Comun, A, 75.
81. Maggior Consiglio, Ursa, 58(66)r. See p. 58.
82. Ibid., 120(126)r.
83. Dieci, Misto, XXII, 27(63)v. See p. 64.
84. "Novus modus ducendi pueros ad consilium est introductus, ex quo multe incovenientie et multe preces et pratice fiunt. . . ." Maggior Consiglio, Ursa, 120(126)r.
85. "Ab aliquo tempore citra venire ceperit tanta multitudo puerorum nobilium et aliorum, ut fere . . . fit quidam puerilis clamor et strepitus. Preterea quidam ipsorum puerorum audaces loqui ceperunt electoribus. . . ." Ibid., 142(148)v.
86. "Et quoniam dicta pars non habet debitam observantiam s[e] cutum fuerit et sequatur ut in omni maiori consilio multi pueri filii nobilium nostrorum veniant, studiosi introducti ad illud ab parentibus vel aliis suis, qui ultra indecentem strepitum quem in illo faciunt, quidam ipsorum audaces loqui ceperunt electionariis. . . ." Dieci, Misto, XXV, 97(132)v-98(133)r.
87. Maggior Consiglio, Fractus, 71(75)r.
88. Ibid., 73(77)v.
89. Cessi, ed., *Maggior Consiglio,* II, 92.
90. Ibid., II, 96. The Forty, later a much-sought office, was at this time nonsalaried.
91. Dieci, Misto, XX, 32(70)v.
92. Avogadori di Comun, Capitulare, I, 36v-37r. Such protection of an accuser was common.
93. Maggior Consiglio, Novella, 157(168)r.
94. Maggior Consiglio, Ursa, 34(42)r. Since the registered manuscript is partly obliterated, I completed it from the copy in Compilazioni leggi, elezioni, b. 198, no. 161.
95. Dieci, Misto, XVI, 117(154)v.
96. Ibid., XXV, 107(142)rv.
97. Sanuto, *Diarii,* I, 907.
98. See pp. 56-57.
99. Queller, *Early Venetian Legislation,* no. 104, p. 132; Sanuto, *Diarii,* I, 713-14; Finlay, *Politics in Renaissance Venice,* p. 207.
100. Sanuto, *Diarii,* VI, 251 and 254; Finlay, *Politics in Renaissance Venice,* p. 207.
101. Dieci, Misto, XVI, 63(100)v; Guerdan, *Sérénissime,* p. 170; Maranini, *Costituzione di Venezia,* II, 108, refers to a law to this effect in 1365, but his reference is to the Compilazioni leggi, which consists of late copies notoriously

inaccurate on dates and otherwise. He also does not see the real reason behind the legislation.

102. Finlay, *Politics in Renaissance Venice,* p. 207.

103. Maggior Consiglio, Ursa, 16(24)v.

104. "Et multotiens de dictis scruptiniis pro non displicendo dictis taliter querentibus faciunt iuxta eorum rogamina. . . ." Senato, Misti, LV, 99(100)v.

105. Maggior Consiglio, Ursa, 85(91)v; Senato, Misti, LIX, 10(12)r.

106. Maggior Consiglio, Ursa, 100(106)r.

107. Ibid., 137(143)v.

108. Dieci, Misto, XII, 162(163)rv.

109. "[C]hi non priega non pol romagnir. . . ." Ibid., XIII, 131(133)v. The *Summarium legum,* 51v, misdates this act in 1448. *Summarium legum venetarum interius reipublicae regimen spectantium,* B.M., cl. lat. V, cod. 110 (=3035). Other copies: A.S.V., Misc. cod. mss. 146 and 381.

110. Dieci, Misto, XIII, 132(134)v. Strengthened in 1467. Dieci, Miscellanea codici, III, 14r.

111. Dieci, Misto, XIII, 132(134)v.

112. "[I]deo preces ipse quotidie magis solito fiunt sine aliquo respectu ad scalas palatii et alibi in conspectu et oculis omnium." Ibid., XV, 128(129)v-129(130)r. Dieci, Magnus, 86v, misdates the law 19 June, whereas it is clearly 18 June. On signs, see p. 71.

113. Senato, Terra, VI, 69(70)v.

114. Dieci, Misto, XV, 180(181)r. Returned to the problem in 1460. Ibid., XVI, 18(55)b; see p. 59.

115. Ibid., XV, 194(195)r. Dieci, Magnus, 86v, repeats the error mentioned in n. 112.

116. Dieci, Misto, XVI, 63(100)v.

117. Ibid., XVI, 191(228)r.

118. "[M]ulti transeant de bancho ad banchum et illos sequuntur qui ferunt bussulos rogando et promittendo dantibus ballotas suas, et quod longe inhonestius est minantur et iniuriantur qui facere debitum suum et sue satifacere conscientie volunt. . . ." Ibid., XVII, 176(217)v. *Summarium legum,* 51v, misdates this act 7 Sept., rather than 7 Oct.

119. Senato, Terra, VIII, 77(78)v.

120. Dieci, Misto, XX, 9(47)v-10(48)r.

121. Ibid., XX, 187(227)rv. *Summarium legum,* x, gives only the part about the young nobles. More on the young nobles in 1492. Malipiero, *Annali veneti,* p. 689. Again on *broglio* in the Great Council, see Dieci, Misto, XXVII, 133(175)rv (1497).

122. Dieci, Misto, XXI, 155(191)v.

123. The sixteen were the two with the most votes in each of eight committees. Ibid., XXII, 86(122)r.

124. "Vadit pars quod de cetero non detur jusjurandum pro precibus in scrutiniis consilii rogatorum et in scrutiniis maioris consilii nec in collegio

dominii. . . ." Ibid., XXV, 38(73)r. Later legislation suggests that this act was a dead letter.

125. Malipiero, *Annali veneti*, p. 703.

126. Dieci, Misto, XXVII, 130(172)r-131(173)r; Sanuto, *Diarii*, I, 837-38, but there misdated 20 Dec., rather than 19 Dec.

127. Dieci, Misto, XXIX, 37(97)rv.

128. Ibid., XV, 128(129)v-129(130)r. See pp. 68-69.

129. Ibid., XXV, 11(46)v-12(47)r.

130. "Aliquis de ipso maiori consilio presumpserit vel ausus fuerit dare plausum vel se se levare in pedes vel alioquin sedendi facere aliquod soffeo alicuius expresse significationis favoris vel disfavoris. . . ." Ibid., XXV, 70(105)v-71(106)r.

131. Gilbert, "Venice in the Crisis of the League of Cambrai," p. 275.

132. Cessi, ed., *Maggior Consiglio*, II, 86.

133. Maggior Consiglio, Ursa, 85(91)v.

134. Dieci, Misto, XV, 2(3)v.

135. Ibid., XV, 19(20)r.

136. Priuli, *Diarii*, II, 176-77.

137. Dieci, Misto, XXVIII, 191(234)v.

138. Senato, Misti, LV, 98(99)v.

139. Maggior Consiglio, Regina, 106(112)r.

140. Dieci, Misto, XXV, 11(46)v-12(47)r.

141. Ibid., XXVII, 147(189)rv.

142. Maggior Consiglio, Leona, 214(220)r; rather badly abbreviated in Maranini, *Costituzione di Venezia*, II, 117, n. 4; see also Giuseppe Cappelletti, *Relazione storica sulle magistrature venete* (Venice, 1873), pp. 32-33. See for later acts, Dieci, Misto, XIII, 132(134)r, and XV, 66(67)v.

143. Senato, Terra, VI, 69(70)v. Malipiero dates the change in 1467. *Annali veneti*, pp. 655-56. He also records that the task was given to secretaries in 1492. Ibid., p. 689. I am indebted to Robert Finlay for these references. See also, however, the act of 1457 (pp. 98-99), which appears to be inconsistent with those cited here. The government never did settle upon carriers of the *bussuli* in whom it had confidence. At the end of the Republic the job was handled by poor boys chosen at random from orphanages. Guerdan, *Sérénissime*, pp. 169-70.

144. Maranini, *Costituzione di Venezia*, II, 116; Cappelletti, *Relazione storica sulle magistrature venete*, pp. 31-32; *Cronaca Bemba*, 65v-66r.

145. Senato, Misti, LV, 45(46)v.

146. Maggior Consiglio, Ursa, 92(98)v. Repeated in 1442. Ibid, 137(143)v.

147. Dieci, Misto, XIII, 96(98)v.

148. Ibid., XIII, 132(134)r.

149. Ibid., 137(139)v.

150. My research has been predominantly in the archives of the legislating bodies not in those of the judicial bodies. Perhaps a thorough search of judicial records would change this impression, but it is doubtful.

151. Dieci, Misto, XV, 69(70)r.

152. Ibid., XXII, 20(55)v.

153. "Nihil est quod magis cognoscatur pertinere ad justiciam distributivam sanctamque et synceram participationem magistratuum et honorum publicorum per consilia nostra conferendorum secundum bonam rectamque conscientiam ballotantium et pro meritis ballotatorum ad illa, et non per importunitatem, instantiam, gratiam, vel respectum alicuius quam sit ballotatio secreta. . . ." Ibid., XXIII, 161(192)v-162(194)r.

154. Ibid., XXIII, 193(224)r. Additional measures to obtain compliance. Ibid., XXIV, 96(135)v-97(136)r.

155. Since the boys who had been carrying the urns were not big enough to carry the new ones, youths from the chancellery were appointed in their place. Ibid., XXV, 96(131)rv; Sanuto, *Cronachetta,* p. 230; id., *Città di Venetia,* p. 150; "Traité du gouvernement de Venise," pp. 263-64.

156. Dieci, Misto, XXV, 98(133)r. It gives the date of the previous act as 7 June, whereas the act itself says 6 June.

157. Ibid., XXV, 107(142)v. See p. 66.

158. Ibid., XXVIII, 186(229)v. A couple of weeks later a slight change was made in counting. Ibid., 187(230)v.

159. Ibid., XXIX, 132(193)r-133(194)r.

160. Ibid., XXXI, 144(191)v-145(192)v.

161. Cozzi, "Authority and Law," p. 300.

162. It does not completely account, however, for the very widespread tendency of the Venetians and the authorities to ignore the laws.

163. In fact, the clans were so powerful in Genoa that no attempt was made to limit their gatherings. Heers, *Clan familial,* p. 88.

164. Ibid., pp. 88-90 and 242-43.

165. Antonio Pilot, "Ancora del broglio nella Repubblica Veneta," *Ateneo veneto,* 27^2 (1903), 1-2.

166. Avogadori di Comun, Capitulare, I, 19r.

167. Ibid., I, 18v.

168. The "etc." is in the document. On the face of it, this is a badly drafted act. "Three or four" who are not relatives may attend. Participants must leave the Great Council or the Forty, but how is this to be enforced? In fact, a marginal note indicates that the act was not published. Dieci, Misto, XIV, 192(197)v. Still, it is valuable for our purposes.

169. Ibid., XXVI, 129(158)v. The *calze* were founded in the early fifteenth century and continued for about two centuries. Boerio, *Dizionario,* p. 120.

170. Malipiero, *Annali veneti,* p. 704. Finlay translates Malipiero: "He banqueted a hundred or more patricians at a time, for with such guile ambition is exercised, and the guests are more easily bent to his desires and to attend to his requests." *Politics in Renaissance Venice,* p. 204.

171. Dieci, Misto, XXVII, 131(173)r-132(174)r. On the hours during which the *calze* were not permitted to have dinners: "ultra horam vigesimam diei a martio usque ad mensem septembris tempore vere hiemis et septembris usque ad

mensem martii ad horam xxiii diei. . . ." I think this is probably on the basis of the day beginning at 9-10 P.M. in midsummer and 5-6 P.M. in midwinter. Kenneth M. Setton, *The Papacy and the Levant (1204-1571)*, vol. I, *The Thirteenth and Fourteenth Centuries* (Philadelphia, 1976), p. 256, n. 102. Sanuto, *Diarii*, I, 838, refers to this act in a confused way. He also misdates it 23 Dec. instead of 20 Dec.

172. Dieci, Misto, XXXI, 95(142)r. "[N]on debeant in dictis prandiis sociorum intervenire alie mulieres nisi uxores consociorum suorum. . . ." Furthermore, "[V]iri earum mulierum que intervenirent dictis prandiis sociorum non existentes socie eorum incurrant in penas predictas." Bear in mind the exile of a large number of nobles in 1492 for pimping. I think that there was some very nasty business taking place at these dinners of the *calze*. See also Sanuto, *Diarii*, VI, 512-13, and Finlay, *Politics in Renaissance Venice*, p. 204.

173. Maggior Consiglio, Novella, 46(57)v.

174. On *compères* (and *commères*) among the Pyrenean peasants, see Emmanuel Le Roy Ladurie, *Montaillou*, trans. Barbara Bray (London, 1978), pp. 126-28. Prof. Joseph Lynch informs me that according to canon law they were not considered so closely related that they were counted in calculating the prohibited degrees for marriage. On 150 godparents, see Giulio Bistort, *Il magistrato alle pompe nella Repubblica di Venezia* (Venice, 1912), pp. 202-3.

175. Priuli, *Diarii*, II, 385-86; Sanuto, *Diarii*, VI, 215. They do not precisely agree on the date. Also see Finlay, *Politics in Renaissance Venice*, p. 203. Finlay, however, does not appear to see anything in baptisms more dangerous than other sorts of gatherings, whereas the creating of large numbers of *compari* was a very strong means of reinforcing factions.

176. Cessi, ed., *Maggior Consiglio*, II, 212; Heers, *Clan familial*, pp. 110-11.

177. *Consiglio dei Diece, Deliberazioni miste,* ed. Ferruccio Zago, I (Venice, 1962), 7, no. 9; Dieci, Misto, IX, 29(33,35)r and X, 31(35)r.

178. Dieci, Misto, IX, 29(33,35)r and X, 31(35)r.

179. Ibid.

180. Ibid., X, 31(35)r.

181. Ibid., XXIV, 83(122)rv.

182. Ibid., IX, 159(163)r.

183. Ibid., 186(190)v.

184. Ibid., X, 10(14)r.

185. Dieci, Misto, XI, 59(65)r-61(67)rv; 64(70)r.

186. Williamson, "Faction and Loyalty," n.p.; Longworth, *Rise and Fall of Venice,* p. 144.

187. Dieci, Misto, XI, 60(66)r, 61(67)r, and 64(70)r. See n. 188. Zorzi Dolfin, *Chronica,* B.M., cl. ital. VII, cod. 794(=8503), f. 363v.

188. Dieci, Misto, XI, 58(64)r; Zorzi Dolfin, *Chronica,* 363v; Williamson, "Faction and Loyalty," n.p.

189. Dieci, Misto, XI, 58(64)rv.

190. Dieci, Misto, XI, 59(65)r. Romanin is wrong on his sentence. *Storia di Venezia,* IV, 170.

191. Dieci, Misto, XI, 59(65)v, 60(66)r, 60(66)v, and 61(67)r.

192. Ibid., XI, 64(70)r and 65(71)r-66(72)r.

193. Ibid., XI, 63(69)r.

194. Ibid., XI, 147(153)rv; XII, 50(51)r and 65(66)v. In 1434 Barbadeo's request had been refused. Ibid., XI, 85(91)r.

195. Dieci, Misto, XIII, 131(133)r.

196. Ibid., XVIII, 169(225)r-170(226)v and 172(228)r.

197. Ibid., XVIII, 185(241)r.

198. Ibid., XXI, 145(181)r-146(182)v.

199. Ibid., XXI, 147(183)rv.

200. Ibid., XXIII, 144(175)v-145(176)v. Those who were convicted of the lesser offense subsequently had their sentences reduced. Ibid., XXIII, 150(181)r, 151(182)v, and XXIV, 21(60)r.

201. Ibid., XXV, 43(78)v-44(79)r.

202. See p. 105.

203. Maranini, *Costituzione di Venezia,* II, 58, 115-16, 437-38. Lane, however, points out that solicitation of such offices as *sopracomiti, provveditori,* and *capitani* was so repeatedly forbidden that it must have been widely practiced. "Naval Actions and Fleet Organization, 1499-1502," p. 158.

204. Finlay, *Politics in Renaissance Venice,* p. 221. It is taken from the unpublished portion of Priuli, quoted in the original Veneziano by Finlay in his dissertation, "Politics and the Ruling Class," p. 277, n. 1. Another defender was the eighteenth-century Giacinto Tonti, *Trattatello della inosservanza d'un giuramento pubblico e solito praticarsi nel Maggior Consiglio in materia di brogli,* B.M., cl. ital. VII, cod. 1225(=8722), no pagination.

205. "[P]er loqual gran division poria indure in nostro stado e pericolo sel non se oviasse." Dieci, Misto, XIII, 131(133)r: "[Q]uesti brogij et pregierie saranno cauxa de la ruyna veneta che mi meraveglio habia tante durate per queste brogierie et pregierie. . . ." Finlay, "Politics of the Ruling Class," p. 277 (trans. in Finlay, *Politics in Renaissance Venice,* p. 221).

IV. Corrupt Elections

1. Finlay, *Politics in Renaissance Venice.*

2. This chapter is a revised and expanded version of Donald E. Queller and Francis R. Swietek, "The Myth of the Venetian Patriciate: Electoral Corruption in Medieval Venice," in Donald E. Queller with Francis R. Swietek, *Two Studies on Venetian Government* (Geneva, 1977), pp. 99-175.

3. Contarini, *De magistratibus,* 12rv (Lewkenor, p. 24).

4. Ibid., 13r (Lewkenor, pp. 25-26).

5. Ibid., 14v (Lewkenor, p. 29).

6. Ibid., 15v-16r (Lewkenor, p. 31).

7. Dieci, Misto, XXVI, 88(116)r. The same words are repeated in a slightly altered reissue of the statute in 1508: Dieci, Misto, XXXII, 30(80)v.

8. Ibid., XXIV, 173(212)v.

9. Maggior Consiglio, Ursa, 27(35)r.
10. Maggior Consiglio, Regina, 189(197)v-190(198)r, in Queller, *Early Venetian Legislation,* no. 88, pp. 146-47.
11. Dieci, Misto, XVIII, 23(78)v.
12. Maggior Consiglio, Fractus, 28(28)r.
13. Maggior Consiglio, Ursa, 27(35)r. Giannotti points out that officials were appointed to see to it that nobles who failed to draw golden balls returned to the seats they had originally occupied rather than to a different bench from which they would be summoned to the urns a second time and thereby have a second chance to draw a golden ball. *Libro della Repubblica de' Viniziani,* pp. 74-75. On the longitudinal arrangement of the benches at right angles to the front of the dais, see Giannotti, *Republica di Venetia,* pp. 152-53. From the dais attempts to move from bench to bench could be more easily seen than if the benches had been situated in the usual way facing the dais.
14. Maggior Consiglio, Ursa, 82(88)v.
15. See pp. 79-80.
16. Williamson, "Faction and Loyalty," n.p.
17. Dieci, Misto, XI, 59(65)r, 59(65)v-61(67)r, 61(67)v, 63(69)r, 64(70)r, and 65(71)v-66(72)r.
18. One of them, Benedetto Barbadeo, applied for a reduction of his sentence as early as January 1434, but his request was refused: Dieci, Misto, XI, 85(91)r. In September 1436, however, the Ten revoked the sentence of banishment against Barbadeo, Marco Magno, and Zaccaria Contarini, and reduced their originally perpetual exclusion from public office to a period of twelve years from the date of their conviction: ibid., XI, 147(153)rv. At the same time the Ten entertained a plea from Marco Cicogna himself, and decreed that the leader of the conspiracy should be permitted to return to Venice, although he was still to be excluded from all councils and offices for life: ibid., XI, 147(153)v. In January 1440, the sentence against Barbadeo, Magno, and Contarini was further reduced by allowing them to return to the Great Council and to regain eligibility for election to public office at the beginning of 1441: ibid., XII, 50(51)r. The following July, the Ten considered another plea from Cicogna, and decided that he should be allowed to resume his position in the Great Council and to become eligible for election to public office after twelve years had elapsed from the date of his original conviction: ibid., XII, 65(66)v. In each instance the granting of grace required, and won, the consent of the doge, the approval of all six ducal councillors, and the unanimous vote of the Dieci.
19. Senato, Misti, LVIII, 171(175)v.
20. See p. 93.
21. Senato, Misti, LVIII, 188(192)v.
22. Maggior Consiglio, Ursa, 137(143)v.
23. Zorzi Dolfin, *Chronica,* 446r-47r.
24. Dieci, Misto, XV, 128(129)v.
25. Ibid., XV, 130(131)r. Donati's sentence is mentioned only by Zorzi Dolfin, *Chronica,* 447r.

26. See pp. 99-100 and 103.
27. Dieci, Misto, XV, 126(127)r.
28. Ibid., XV, 177(178)v.
29. Ibid., XV, 178(179)r. Within eight months Coppo and Polani were allowed to return *per gratiam* to the Great Council. Ibid., XV, 195(196)r.
30. Ibid., XVII, 52(94)v; misdated 1478 in Compilazioni leggi, elezioni, b 198, 643.
31. Dieci, Misto, XXVIII, 23(78)v. Additional legislation against coming to the urns with benches other than one's own. Ibid., XXI, 49(85)v-50(86)r.
32. Ibid., XXII, 28(66)r.
33. Ibid., XXIV, 51(90)v-52(91)r.
34. Ibid., XXIV, 58(97)v.
35. Ibid., XXIV, 173(212)v.
36. Maggior Consiglio, Stella, 129(133)r.
37. Ibid., 129(133)r.
38. Ibid., 134(138)r.
39. Dieci, Misto, XXVI, 185(214)r.
40. Ibid., XXVII, 102(144)rv.
41. Ibid., XXVIII, 6(49)r.
42. Cessi, ed., *Maggior Consiglio,* II, 88.
43. Ibid., II, 96.
44. Ibid., II, 92.
45. Avogadori di Comun, A, 44(54)r.
46. Senato, Misti, LVIII, 188(192)v.
47. Queller, *Early Venetian Legislation,* no. 60, p. 94. Again on exchanging votes and lots. Maggior Consiglio, Ursa, 183(189)v (1452).
48. Dieci, Misto, XV, 88(89)r.
49. Ibid., XVI, 117(154)v.
50. Queller, *Early Venetian Legislation,* no. 7, p. 61. These positions were often unwanted, and nobles sought to avoid them by alleging irregularities in their elections.
51. Guerdan, *Sérénissime,* p. 169.
52. Sanuto, *Diarii,* XXVIII, 65, 82, 94; Finlay, *Politics in Renaissance Venice,* p. 202.
53. Maggior Consiglio, Spiritus, 137(138)r.
54. A.S.V., Maggior Consiglio, Novella, 147(158)v. The provision that the law be read to the Great Council at regular intervals was a formula employed in numerous statutes, but there is no evidence that it was consistently observed. Given the number of such requirements, this would have consumed a great deal of the council's time.
55. Senato, Misti, XLIII, 156(155)r.
56. Ibid., XLV, 52(52)v.
57. Ibid., XLV, 72(71)r.
58. Maggior Consiglio, Leona, 179(184)v.
59. Maggior Consiglio, Ursa, 92(98)v.

60. Ibid., 140r (146r).
61. Dieci, Misto, XIV, 42(45)rv.
62. Longworth, *Rise and Fall of Venice*, p. 151; See p. 100. It is very difficult to produce evidence of why action was not taken, but a perception that dismemberment was excessive seems to make sense.
63. Dieci, Misto, XV, 116(117)rv. In Queller and Swietek, "The Myth of the Venetian Patriciate," p. 146, the surname "Cornaro" was inadvertently omitted.
64. Dieci, Misto, XV, 116(117)v. It is interesting to note that Giustinian is designated in the act as an inhabitant of the parish of San Barnaba. In later centuries, at any rate, San Barnaba was known as a cheap neighborhood where poor nobles could be found ready to join in conspiracies to rig elections.
65. Ibid., XV, 117(118)r. Zorzi Dolfin, *Chronica,* 444v, reports on Giustinian's sentencing, but gives the date as 7 Jan.
66. Dieci, Misto, XV, 128(129)v.
67. Ibid., XV, 130(131)r. Zorzi Dolfin, *Chronica,* 444v, adds that he was also fined 15,000 *lire,* and again dates the action 7 Jan.
68. Dieci, Misto, XV, 129(130)v.
69. Ibid., XV, 129(130)v. Dolfin does not mention him.
70. Ibid., 130(131)r.
71. Ibid., 117(118)v. See also the act of 1344. See p. 96. The present legislation simply does not square with other acts on the subject of the carriers of the *bussuli.*
72. A full account is given by Zorzi Dolfin, *Chronica,* 446r–47r. Three *capi* are named, Ludovico Lombardo, Francesco Bon, and Lorenzo Baffo, in addition to Pisani. Perhaps Baffo subsequently (*poi*) succeeded Pisani.
73. Dieci, Misto, XV, 124(125)v.
74. Ibid., 126(127)v.
75. Zorzi Dolfin, *Chronica,* 446r–47r.
76. See p. 98.
77. Dieci, Misto, XV, 130(131)rv.
78. See p. 98.
79. Zorzi Dolfin, *Chronica,* 446–47r.
80. Dieci, Misto, XV, 126(127)r. Councillors also were delegated to conduct elections of the *capi* in the Forty.
81. Ibid., XVI, 116(153)v.
82. Ibid., 117(154)v.
83. Maggior Consiglio, Regina, 106(112)v.
84. The best narrative account of the affair is given by Malipiero, *Annali veneti,* pp. 701–2. See also Sanuto, *Diarii,* I, 303, 323–24, and Priuli, *Diarii,* I, 77, n. 1.
85. Dieci, Misto, XVII, 44(63, 85)v.
86. Ibid., XVII, 44(64, 86)r. The Council's provisions to assure Bon's return are also noted by Sanuto, *Diarii,* I, 303.
87. Dieci, Misto, XVII, 47(89)v–48(90)v. These actions were announced in

the Great Council on 18 Sept. Sanuto, *Diarii,* I, 323-24. Priuli, almost certainly incorrectly, has Bon exiled for his insulting speech to the *provveditore* of his fleet. *Diarii,* I, 77. This was itself supposedly a correction of his mistake a few pages earlier. I, 68.

88. Dieci, Misto, XVII, 48(90)v. Frixo's precise ecclesiastical position is unclear. Venetian officials, however, often found a criminal's clerical status an impediment to their execution of penalties. In 1457, for example, the Council of Ten complained that certain persons who had been condemned to exile were having themselves consecrated as clerics in order to return to Venice with impunity. The Dieci decreed that when such exiles were found in Venice, they were subject to a year's imprisonment, followed by return to exile, in spite of their ecclesiastical status. Ibid., XV, 129(130)v.

89. Sanuto, *Diarii,* I, 338.

90. Dieci, Misto, XVII, 80(122)r. Priuli's account is somewhat confused. *Diarii,* I, 77.

91. Dieci, Misto, XXXI, 144(191)v-145(192)r.

92. On *scrutinio,* see Lane, *Venice,* pp. 258 and 260; the description of the process offered by Thiriet, *Romanie vénitienne,* p. 193, n. 2, is not accurate. After 1500 the Senate attempted to curtail nomination by *scrutinio:* see Lane, *Venice,* p. 260.

93. A list of the offices to which the Senate elected is provided by da Mosto, *Archivio di Stato,* I, 37-38. In 1497 the Senate sought to divest itself of the burden of too many elections, decreeing that, with the exception of ambassadors and certain others customarily elected in the Senate, other officials were to be elected in the Great Council: Senato, Terra, XIII, 9(10)v, in Queller, *Early Venetian Legislation,* no. 104, p. 132. The offices listed in this act as remaining under the electoral control of the Senate are far less numerous than those contained in da Mosto's listing.

94. *Deliberations des assemblées vénitiennes concernant la Romanie,* ed. Freddy Thiriet, II (Paris, 1971), 162, no. 1327.

95. Senato, Misti, LX, 240(241)r, in Queller, *Early Venetian Legislation,* no. 54, pp. 89-90.

96. A move to overturn the act of 1442 failed in 1444. Cracco, "Patriziato e oligarchia," p. 86. Besta, *Senato veneziano,* p. 93 and n. 1 and p. 94 and n. 1.

97. Dieci, Misto, XV, 171(172)v.

98. Senato, Terra, VI, 181(181)v.

99. Dieci, Misto, XV, 121(130)v.

100. See p. 99.

101. Zorzi Dolfin, *Chronica,* 446-47r.

102. Dieci, Misto, XXVII, 147(189)rv. These procedures were also to apply to judicial votes taken in the Council of Forty, which were far more common than were elections in that body.

103. Elections to some embassies, for example, were the province of the Signoria, or of the Collegio. In 1495 the Council of Ten complained that the Collegio was violating tradition and law by choosing orators by voice rather

than by ballot or scrutiny. The Ten therefore prohibited the Signoria or Collegio from conducting elections except by scrutiny or ballot: Dieci, Misto, XXVI, 172(201)v-173(202)r, in Queller, *Early Venetian Legislation,* no. 102, p. 130. This action might have been taken because the practice of election by voice could have encouraged corrupt practices by making the electoral process more informal and thereby less subject to effective administrative control.

104. Sanuto, *Diarii,* LIV, 7: "Ma una cosa e di grandissimo momento et non si fa provision, zoe che le balote vien compra per danari. Tutti il sa, et si vade manifesto, che chi non ha la banda di zentilhomeni poveri, ai qual bisogna dar danari avanti tratto et poi la paga poi rimasi, non si pol rimaner in officii da conto. . . ." The translation is from Lane, *Venice,* p. 264.

105. Roland Mousnier, "Le trafic des offices à Venise," *Revue historique de droit francais et étranger,* 30 (1952), 558.

106. Cozzi, "Authority and Law," p. 299 and p. 341, n. 23.

107. Maggior Consiglio, Novella, 92(103)v.

108. Dieci, Misto, XVIII, 76(131)rv. On the provision that the law be read at the Great Council twice a year, see above, n. 54.

109. Ibid., XXI, 62(98)v-63(99)r.

110. Malipiero, *Annali veneti,* pp. 688-89; Finlay, *Politics in Renaissance Venice,* p. 200.

111. Dieci, Misto, XXVI, 88(116)rv. See also, ibid., XXVII, 131(173)r-132(174)r, (1497). The latter is probably the same act to which Sanuto refers under 23 Dec. *Diarii,* I, 838.

112. Pietro Dolfin, *Annalium Venetorum,* pp. 164-65. Both Priuli, *Diarii,* II, 52-53, and Sanuto, *Diarii,* III, 634, 661, and 769-70, deal with the reform at some length, but do not mention bribery. Priuli, in fact, is not certain that it was a good idea. See also Lane, *Venice,* p. 260.

113. Sanuto, *Diarii,* VII, 602-3, 609-11, 616-17.

114. Ibid., VII, 609-11.

115. Ibid., VII, 610.

116. Ibid., VII, 620.

117. Ibid., VII, 603.

118. Dieci, Misto, XXXII, 30(80)v-31(81)r; Sanuto, *Diarii,* VII, 619-20.

119. Finlay, *Politics in Renaissance Venice,* p. 200; Sanuto, *Diarii,* VIII, 387.

120. Sanuto, *Diarii,* XXI, 70. Discussed by Cozzi, "Authority and Law," pp. 312-13.

121. Cozzi, "Authority and Law," p. 313.

122. Gilbert, "Venice in the Crisis of the League of Cambrai," pp. 284-85; Cozzi, "Authority and Law," pp. 332ff.; Lane, *Venice,* pp. 263-64. Finlay believes that the selling of blocs of votes became a serious problem only as a result of the desire for offices arising during the War of the League of Cambrai. *Politics in Renaissance Venice,* p. 200. It is true that the evidence concerning bribery before 1509 displays only a little of the systematic and sophisticated corruption of the *svizzeri.* Lane points out that some attempt was made to curtail the worst abuses of this system—the office of censor, for example, was

instituted in the hope of doing so—after military needs had subsided, but corrupt practices had already reached such epidemic proportions that they could not be successfully combatted. *Venice,* pp. 263-64. On the censors see also Cozzi, "Authority and Law," p. 326.

123. Brown, *Studies,* I, 313.

124. "Et, perdoname li Padri Veneti, quali per cauxa deli brogij stropanno li ochij et non volenno vedere in molte cose. . . ." Priuli, *Diariii,* II, 431. Also, IV, 161. Finlay points out how the influence of *broglio* spread beyond electoral politics, so that officials feared to enforce the laws against patrician debtors to the state, to check the corruption of monasteries inhabited by the members of noble families, or to curb the tyrannies of Venetian governors on the mainland. *Politics in Renaissance Venice,* p. 217.

125. Maggior Consiglio, Spiritus, 137(138)r; Dieci, Misto, XIV, 42(45)rv. These provisions originally applied only to *probe* in the Great Council. They were extended to ballotings and elections in all the councils and colleges of the Republic by the Ten in 1498: ibid., XXVII, 147(189)rv.

126. Dieci, Misto, XV, 88(89)r. This is the act providing for the bottomless *bussulus.*

127. Ibid., XVIII, 52(94)v; XXII, 28(66)r; XXVII, 102(144)rv. The lowering of the sum, especially, may not reflect a conscious decision, but that the earlier act had been forgotten.

128. Ibid., XXVI, 88(116)rv. If the malefactor had already assumed office, the accuser who provided evidence leading to his conviction was also to receive half of any salary and perquisites he would be forced to return to the Commune. Ibid., XXXII, 30(80)v-31(81)r.

129. See, e.g., Maggior Consiglio, Novella, 147(158)v: "Et siquis accusaverit aliquem de contrafacientibus, habeat libras trecentas de bonis illius qui comiserit fallum, si tot reperiuntur. Vel si non reperientur, habeat eas a nostro comuni." This formula is recurrent in the Venetian legislation on electoral corruption.

130. Dieci, Misto, XIV, 42(45)rv. Similar acts: ibid., XXVI, 33(116)rv (bribery); XXVII, 102(144)rv (going to the urns more than once); XXVII, 147(189)rv (casting more than one ballot); XXXII, 30(80)v-31(81)r (bribery).

131. Ibid., XVIII, 23(78)v. Similar provision for drawing more than one ball. Ibid., XXIV, 173(212)v.

132. The sort of *formulae* common in the statutes is that the *pena* stipulated should be "immediata et irremissibili" and that "de quibus quidem penis vel aliqua ipsarum non possit predictis fieri gratis, donum, remissio vel aliqua declaratio." Ibid., XXVI, 185(214)r. These *formulae,* and variants thereof, recur regularly in the legislation against electoral corruption in the Venetian archives.

133. Ibid., XV, 117(118)v.

134. Senato, Terra, VI, 69(70)v.

135. Dieci, Misto, XV, 178(179)r. See also, ibid., XXII, 28(66)r and XXVI, 88(116)rv.

136. Ibid., XXXII, 30(80)v-31(81)r.

137. For example, ibid., XXII, 28(66)r and XXIV, 173(212)v.
138. Ibid., XXVI, 88(116)rv.
139. Ibid., XXVII, 147(189)rv.
140. Ibid., XV, 126(127)r.
141. Maggior Consiglio, Ursa, 27(35)r.
142. Senato, Misti, LVIII, 84(88)v.
143. Dieci, Misto, XXVII, 102(144)rv.
144. Lane, *Venice*, p. 259.
145. Cozzi, "Authority and Law," p. 298.
146. Lane, *Venice*, p. 264. With regard to another subject, prostitution, Pavan writes: "La législation de la commune est, à cet égard, longue et contradictoire, laxiste, puis rigoriste, ponctuées de sanctions jamais ou mal appliquées, de retours en arrière, d'interdits encore renouvelés." "Police de moeurs," p. 247.
147. Probably worse, however, because of the large number of poor nobles, whose poverty did not remove them from the ruling class although they certainly occupied its lowest ranks.

V. EVASION OF PUBLIC RESPONSIBILITIES

1. Peter Riesenberg, "Civism and Roman Law in Fourteenth Century Italian Society," in *Economy, Society and Government in Medieval Italy: Essays in Memory of Robert L. Reynolds,* ed. David Herlihy, Robert S. Lopez, and Vsevelod Slessarev (Kent, Ohio, 1969), p. 250.
2. Ibid., passim, and esp. p. 242.
3. Lane, "Enlargement of the Great Council," p. 250; Lane, *Venice*, p. 109.
4. "[A]l Commun di Venezia per falli di officii o di consei, che io non fosse andato, che fosse tegnudo, lire L." Molmenti, *Storia di Venezia nella vita privata,* I, 65.
5. Pullan, "Service to the Venetian State," p. 117; Lane, *Venice*, p. 109; Davis, *Decline of the Venetian Nobility*, p. 77. At one time lesser governorships on the mainland, as well as those of the maritime empire, were considered not to require the same ostentation and to be profitable. In the fifteenth century, however, the nobles elected to these were maintaining households beyond their means.
6. Bouwsma, *Venice and the Defense of Republican Liberty,* p. 59; Pullan, "Service to the Venetian State," p. 117. See Edward Pessen, "Social Structure and Politics in American History," *American Historical Review,* 87 (1982), 1315.
7. "[S]ed nescio quomodo . . . [*sic*] in omni republica, in quibuscumque magistratibus demandandis, ambitio occupat omnia. Cuius tantum interdum est ardor ut etiam que sine emolumento sunt, ea flagitent homines non idonei, sola cupiditate dignitatis." Domenico Morosini, *De bene instituta republica,* ed. Claudio Finzi (Milan, 1969), p. 88.
8. Lane, *Venice*, p. 259.
9. Norwich, *Venice*, pp. 263-64; Guerdan, *Sérénissime,* pp. 171 and 163-64.

10. Emmanuele A. Cicogna, *Delle inscrizioni veneziane,* VI (Venice, 1853), 93.

11. See pp. 117-18. Davis is not quite correct in saying: "Apparently there was never a problem in finding men who were willing to serve as doges, ducal councillors, members of the Council of Ten, *savi grandi, avogadori del comun,* and in a few other such posts." *Decline of the Venetian Nobility,* p. 92. See also Brian Pullan's review of Davis, *Decline of the Venetian Nobility,* in *Bollettino dell' Istituto di Storia della Società e dello Stato Veneziano,* 5-6 (1963-64), 412-13. Maranini realized that merchants busy making their fortunes would seek to avoid the burdens of the Small Council, although he perversely insists on interpreting the legislation trying to coerce them as evidence of a magnificent system of public law rather than as a series of vain attempts to cope with a messy and nasty reality. *Costituzione di Venezia,* I, 244-45.

12. Steven W. Rowan, "Community Survival: Freiburg im Bresgau from the Black Death to the Reformation" (unpub. ms.), p. 111.

13. Pullan, *Rich and Poor in Renaissance Venice,* pp. 121-23.

14. Refusal and resignation were considered to be the same. We shall treat them as such in this section, although a later section will treat specifically "refusal" after acceptance or during the term of office.

15. Vittorio Lazzarini, "Obbligo di assumere pubblici uffici nelle antiche leggi veneziane," *Archivio veneto,* 19 (1936), 184-98; Maranini, *Costituzione di Venezia,* I, 244-45; Thayer, *Short History of Venice,* p. 225; Soranzo, "Fattori morali," p. 276; Davis, *Decline of the Venetian Nobility,* p. 25.

16. Davis, *Decline of the Venetian Nobility,* pp. 32-33. He continues: "There is very little legislation on the refusals of offices during most of the sixteenth century, and the tone of the preambles to what laws were passed does not suggest that refusals were a serious problem. Furthermore, the diaries of Sanuto and the essays on the constitution by Giannotti and Contarini do not mention any difficulty in finding enough men for offices. Apparently the ruling class was large enough to provide enough men of good calibre for the government." I have examined the registers only for about the first decade of the sixteenth century, but from the twelfth century until that time there is a great deal of legislation on the subject and the preambles display much concern. Sanuto does offer evidence of difficulty in obtaining suitable officials. See *Diarii,* III, 41, 152, 162, 206, 208; IV, 51, 53, 160, 172, for some examples. See also Priuli, *Diarii,* I, 217 and II, 145. Also Malipiero, *Annali veneti,* pp. 305 and 719. Of course, we should not expect to find such material in the mythmakers, Giannotti and Contarini. I do not mean to condemn Giannotti and Contarini for deliberately covering up the difficulties of Venetian government and the irresponsibility of the patriciate, for certainly the Florentine and also the Venetian noble were sincere admirers of the system for which they were propagandists. In addition to having a very pronounced bias in favor of the government, however, they also offer an old-fashioned, "table of organization" view of the constitution without concerning themselves with the question of how it really worked.

17. Cessi, ed., *Maggior Consiglio,* I, 252-53; Lazzarini, "Obbligo di assumere pubblici uffici," pp. 192-93.

18. Cessi, ed., *Maggior Consiglio,* I, 257; Molmenti, *Storia di Venezia nella vita privata,* I, 65.

19. Lazzarini, "Obbligo di assumere pubblici uffici," pp. 193-94.

20. Ibid., p. 195.

21. Cessi, ed., *Maggior Consiglio,* I, 229.

22. Ibid, II, 88.

23. Ibid., II, 89; Lazzarini, "Obbligo di assumere pubblici uffici," pp. 195-96. Cassandro, "Curia di Petizion," 20 (1937), 158-59. The act alludes to the confused state of the legislation. A marginal note in a different hand, not included in the published document, is found in the register, Maggior Consiglio, Fronesis, 111(112). The text refers to a lost act, but the marginal note declares: "Cancelletur pro consilio quod est in Spiritum, 122."

24. Maggior Consiglio, Spiritus, 30(31)r.

25. Ibid., 100(101)r and 116(117)v.

26. Some of the governorships *da mare* did not require great ostentation, so that a governor could get by on his salary and expenses or even make some money.

27. Giovanni Antonio Muazzo, *Historia del governo antico e presente della Republica di Venetia,* B.M., cl. ital. VII, cod. 966(=8406), f. 71; Davis, *Decline of the Venetian Nobility,* pp. 83 and 87. It is not true, however, that the salaries and expenses had been adequate until a relatively late period when they were overwhelmed by the increase of luxury.

28. Cessi, ed., *Maggior Consiglio,* III, 71.

29. Senato, Misti, LIV, 91(92)r. A similar fine for refusing an embassy to Florence. Ibid., LIX, 162(164)r (1436).

30. Queller, *Early Venetian Legislation,* no. 63, p. 96.

31. Ibid., no. 88, pp. 116-17.

32. Sanuto, *Diarii,* IV, 90.

33. "Traité du gouvernement de Venise," p. 289. It is perhaps worth noting that in the Latin Kingdom of Jerusalem in the twelfth century a vassal could have his fief confiscated for refusing to go on an embassy *pro publico bono.* Joshua Prawer, *Crusader Institutions* (Oxford, 1980), pp. 460-61.

34. Cessi, ed., *Maggior Consiglio,* II, 103; Melchiorre Roberti, *Le magistrature giudiziarie veneziane e i loro capitolari fino 1300,* II (Venice, 1909), 184. Fine changed in 1376 to two hundred ducats. Senato, Misti, XXXV, 126(125)v and Maggor Consiglio, Ursa, 123(129)v. Yet Sanuto records a fine of 100 *l. Cronachetta,* p. 98; id., *Città di Venetia,* p. 98.

35. Roberti, *Magistrature giudiziarie,* II, 42-43. The way in which the act of 1263 is described is significant: "[U]num consilium per quod omnes officiales poterant se eicere de officiis pro solidis X grossorum. . . ."

36. Maggior Consiglio, Fractus, 86(90)v.

37. Cessi, ed., *Maggior Consiglio,* III, 173.

38. Maggior Consiglio, Spiritus, 104(105)v.
39. Senato, Misti, XXXIV, 53(53)r.
40. Ibid., XLVII, 108(110)v.
41. Dieci, Misto, IX, 61(65)r.
42. Maggior Consiglio, Ursa, 13(21)r.
43. See pp. 133-36.
44. Maggior Consiglio, Ursa, 70(76)v.
45. Senato, Misti, LX, 227(227)r.
46. Dieci, Misto, XXVII, 132(174)v.
47. Cessi, ed., *Maggior Consiglio,* II, 233; Cassandro, "Curia di Petizion," 19 (1936), 84.
48. Cessi, ed., *Maggior Consiglio,* II, 78.
49. Ibid., III, 173.
50. Roberti, *Magistrature giudiziarie,* III, 187.
51. Ruggiero, *Violence in Early Renaissance Venice,* p. 12. See Dieci, Misto, X, 87(91)r and X, 40(44)v.
52. "Cum iudices proprii habeant parvam penam refutando, scilicet solummodo de soldis decem grossorum:

Vadit pars quod, ut dictum officium non refutetur sic facile, sicut pena erat de soldis X grossorum, sic sit de libris centum pro qualibet iudice proprii qui de cetero eligetur et refutaret. . . ." Maggior Consiglio, Spiritus, 49(51)v.
53. Senato, Misti, XLIX, 70(71)v.
54. Queller, *Early Venetian Legislation,* no. 62, p. 95.
55. Queller, ed., "Newly Discovered Legislation," no. 51, pp. 60-61.
56. Queller, *Early Venetian Legislation,* no. 94, p. 123.
57. Queller, ed., "Newly Discovered Legislation," no. 65, p. 79.
58. This almost certainly means that he would go as an ad hoc ambassador and remain as *baiulo.*
59. Senato, Misti, XXVII, 95(95)r.
60. Ibid., XLI, 54(58)r.
61. Ibid., 56(60)v.
62. Ibid., XLIV, 1(1)rv. The document of 3 June says that seven had refused. Looking at the list, I read six names crossed out, two of those excused for ill health, and two who had accepted.
63. "Cum sicut notum est non sit aliquis qui velit ire ad bailatum Cipri. . . ." Ibid., XLVII, 16(18)r. Ruggero Contarini wrote: "[P]er lo conseio avy day nostri parenti et amixi, refudi. . . ." Giuseppe dalla Santa, "Uomini e fatti dell' ultimo Trecento e del primo Quattrocento. Da lettere a Giovanni Contarini, patrizio venetiano, studente ad Oxford e a Parigi, poi patriarca di Costantinopoli," *Nuovo archivio veneto,* n.s., 32 (1916), 19.
64. "Qua capita sesteriorum per X volunt esse de XXV annis, et hoc tempore non bene reperiuntur dicte etatis qui velint esse. . . ." Dieci, Misto, IX, 19(20)r.
65. *Calendar of State Papers and Manuscripts, Relating to English Affairs, Existing*

in the *Archives and Collections of Venice, and in Other Libraries of Northern Italy*, ed. Rawdon Brown et. al., I (London, 1864), 58.

66. "Cum factis multis electionibus in nostro maiori consilio nullus reperiatur qui velit acceptare potestas Verone. . . ." Senato, Terra, I, 14(15)v.

67. Malipiero, *Annali veneti*, p. 719.

68. Ibid., p. 305.

69. Sanuto, *Diarii*, III, 152, 162, and 208.

70. Ross, "Contarini and His Friends," pp. 200-201.

71. Margaret Leah King, "Caldiera and the Barbaros on Marriage and the Family: Humanistic Reflections of Venetian Realities," *Journal of Medieval and Renaissance Studies*, 6 (1976), 35-43.

72. Riesenberg, "Civism and Roman Law," p. 242.

73. Lane, *Andrea Barbarigo*, p. 19. Recall, however, that his descendants followed a different path.

74. *Cassiere della Bolla Ducale: Grazie—Novus Liber (1299-1305)*, ed. Elena Favaro (Venice, 1962), no. 508, p. 118.

75. Maggior Consiglio, Magnus, 72(73)v.

76. Senato, Misti, XXV, 15(15)r.

77. Ibid., 49(49)r. See Queller, *Early Venetian Legislation*, no. 26, p. 68, for the version passed by the Great Council.

78. Dieci, Misto, V, 8(9)r. Reduced to 30 s. for eight months. Ibid., 12(13)r.

79. Senato, Misti, XXIX, 10(10)r.

80. "Cum officium extimatorum auri sit sine officialibus quia nullus eorum voluit probari isto anno propter modicum salarium istius officii. . . ." Maggior Consiglio, Novella, 85(96)v. For additional examples, see Senato, Misti, XXXI, 1(3)v, 8(10)r; XXXIII, 25(25)r; XXXV, 93(92)r; *Régestes des délibérations du Sénat de Venise concernant la Romanie*, ed. Freddy Thirict, I (Paris, 1958), 105, no. 406 and 122, no. 478.

81. Senato, Misti, XLII, 58(58)r.

82. "Cum multi nostri nobiles refutaverint et continue refutent potestariam Torcelli." Maggior Consiglio, Leona, 65(69)r; "et ad similem conditionem sit potestas Muriani." Ibid. For more examples: ibid., 92(96)r, 98(102)v, 115(119)r, 121(125)v, 131(135)r, and 132(137)v; Senato, Misti, XLIV, 59(59)v.

83. "Quia non invenitur quis velit ire capitaneus armati Padi propter minimam utilitatem." Senato, Misti, XLVII, 24(26)v.

84. "Cum non reperiatur aliquis volens esse judex magni salarii propter minimam utilitatem quam judices habent, nam habere soliti erant ducatos sexaginta in anno pro qualibet, sed propter gueras elapsas detracti fuerunt eis ducati viginti. . . ." Maggior Consiglio, Leona, 168(173)v.

85. "[Q]uamplures ex nostri nobilibus recusant acceptare dictum regimen, quoniam sine gravibus expensis suis in dicto regimine stare non possunt. . . ." Ibid., 172(177)r.

86. "Cum maior pars officiorum et judicatuum Venetiarum propter acceptionem et diminutionem salariorum et utilitatum non ita bene solicitantur nec

administrantur sicut fieri deberet et necesse foret, et ob hoc existentes in judicibus et officiis sunt cohacti pro possendo vivere cum suis familiis attendere etiam ad aliud quam ad officium. Et quia ex hoc sequuntur forte de rebus que cedunt in minus honoris nostri dominii et non modicum dannum introituum nostrorum, ac etiam in tardem expeditionem et gravem expensam specialium personarum. . . ." Avogaria di Comun, Capitolare, I, 171v. For various unwanted positions, see Maggior Consiglio, Ursa, 4(12)v, 12(20)r, 14(22)v; Senato, Misti, LIII, 194(194)r.

87. "Cum multociens facta fuerit electio potestatis et capitanei Casalismaioris, et non inveniatur aliquis qui velit ad dictum regimen ire. . . ." Senato, Misti, LVIII, 13(17)r. See also, ibid., 20(24)r and LIX, 147(149)r.

88. Maggior Consiglio, Ursa, 178(184)r.

89. Senato, Terra, IV, 102(103)r.

90. "Multociens facta fuit electio unius vicedomini Ferrarie loco illius qui ad presens est, qui complevit. Et nemo hucusque acceptavit, solum respectu salarii et limitati, quod ei non sufficit respectu expensarum ei occurentium. . . ." Ibid., 117(118)r.

91. "[P]er la pocha utilita che quelli zudexi hanno, non se trova alcuno che quello officio vogli exercitar. Anci tutti che sono sta electi refudano, perche poco salario e quello che li riman de salario neto. E quello salario che hanno con grandissima difficulta rescuodeno. Le altre sue utilita che hanno sono pochissime a le grande fatiche che lor zudexi hanno per convignir esser presenti a tute stime. . . ." Maggior Consiglio, Regina, 139(145)v.

92. "Electi fuerint ab annis quatuor citra multi nobiles nostri in salinarios nostros Clugie qui continue refutarunt, et hoc ob paucitatem salarii sui. . . ." Maggior Consiglio, Stella, 51(55)rv.

93. Ibid., 54(58)v-55(59)r.

94. "[P]ochi si ritrovano che in quelli officii voglino entrar per la pocha utilita et salario. . . ." Ibid., 55(59)r.

95. "Ad talem conditionem iam reductum est offitium nostrum folee auri ut non reperiatur aliquis qui amplius in illo ingredi velit. Immo, sicut per experientiam videtur, electi ad illud statim renuntiant. Et hoc procedit ob parvitatem salarii. . . ." Ibid., 55(59)v. For another example, see ibid., 71(75)v.

96. Ibid., 81(85)v. Additional examples, ibid., 101(105)v, 102(106)r; Dieci, Misto, XXIV, 159(198)v.

97. "[A] paucis mensibus citra electi fuerunt multi ad castellaniam Montisfalconi, qui omnes refutarunt, nec est aliquis qui ire velit, et hoc propter tenuissimum salarium. . . ." Dieci, Misto, XXIV, 117(121)v.

98. Senato, Terra, XII, 12(12)v.

99. Senato, Misti, XXXVII, 1(1)r-5(5)v; Thiriet, *Romanie vénitienne,* p. 195.

100. Senato, Misti, XLVI, 133(135)r-134(136)r and 150(152)r-154(156)r.

101. Ibid., XLIX, 70(71)r-73(74)v.

102. Thiriet, *Romanie vénitienne,* pp. 195-96. *Camera Inprescriptorum* must be a misreading for *Camera Imprestitorum.*

103. Maggior Consiglio, Stella, 80(84)v.

104. Ibid., 97(101)r.

105. Ibid., 179(183)r; Priuli, *Diarii*, II, 145; Sanuto, *Diarii*, IV, 51 and 53.

106. "[N]on obstante quod in sua esset libertate refutandi supracomitariam lacus sit dispositus alacri et bono animo ire ad serviendum nostro dominio, sed non vellet teneri longo tempore extra, ut possit rebus suis providere. . . ." Senato, Misti, LX 188(188)r.

107. Senato, Terra, IX, 33(33)r.

108. Favaro, ed., *Cassiere della Bolla Ducale*, no. 486, p. 113.

109. Ibid., no. 509, p. 118.

110. Senato, Misti, XLI, 56(60)v and 58(62)r.

111. Ibid., XLIII, 52(51)v; Kenneth M. Setton, "The Catalans and Florentines in Greece, 1380-1462," in *A History of the Crusades*, ed. Kenneth M. Setton, III (Madison, Wis., 1975), pp. 260-61.

112. Senato, Misti, XLIV, 144(144)v and XLV, 1(1)v.

113. Ibid., XLV, 140(139)r.

114. Ibid., XLVI, 3(4)v.

115. Thiriet, ed., *Délibérations des assemblées vénitiennes*, no. 1360, II, 169.

116. Maggior Consiglio, Regina, 104(110)v.

117. Priuli, *Diarii*, I, 217; Sanuto, *Diarii*, III, 41.

118. Sanuto, *Diarii*, IV, 51 and 83; Pietro Dolfin, *Annalium Venetorum*, pp. 282 and 284.

119. Priuli, *Diarii*, II, 145. Pietro Dolfin says the same. *Annalium Venetorum*, p. 282.

120. Sanuto, *Diarii*, IV, 160 and 172.

121. Sanuto also recounts how Alvise Malipiero, elected *provveditore* of the army at Vicenza a couple of weeks after Agnadello, refused, saying, "I'd rather pay money than place my life in danger, seeing that I can't accomplish anything." *Diarii*, VIII, 322. I obtained the reference from Finlay, "Venice and the Po Expedition," p. 41, although he misidentifies the job as *provveditore* at Padua, where, indeed, there was also difficulty in finding a noble willing to go.

122. King, "Caldiera and the Barbaros on Marriage," p. 42.

123. "Cum locus noster Durachii sit male sanus, sicut omnibus clare patet, quia omnes nobiles quos illuc mittimus moriuntur, et a duodus annis citra in dicto regimine quinque nobiles nostri mortui sunt, et ultra mortem dictorum nostrorum nobilium commune nostrum substinet magnam expensam, quia, si obeunt ante complementum unius anni, recipiunt salarium totius anni. Et bonum et pium sit evitare ut dicti nostri nobiles non moriantur. Vadit pars quod decetero non debeant mitti nostri nobiles ad regimen predictum, sed mitti debeant nostri populares. . . ." Senato, Misti, LV, 155(156)v.

124. Davis, *Decline of the Venetian Nobility*, pp. 32-33.

125. Cessi, ed., *Maggior Consiglio*, I, 252-53; Lazzarini, "Obbligo di assumere pubblici uffici," pp. 192-93.

126. Labalme, *Bernardo Giustiniani*, p. 186 and n. 263.

127. Lazzarini, "Obbligo di assumere pubblici uffici," pp. 193-94.

128. Senato, Misti, XLVII, 108(110)v. This was generally considered a desir-

able office for young men, the best initiation to public life. Perhaps they refused because they could not accept without trying to falsify their ages.

129. Maggior Consiglio, Ursa, 13(21)r.

130. Senato, Terra, VI, 38(39)r; Queller, *Early Venetian Legislation,* no. 88, pp. 116–17.

131. Maggior Consiglio, Stella, 54(58)v.

132. Cessi, ed., *Maggior Consiglio,* II, 103; Roberti, *Magistrature giudiziarie,* II, 184.

133. Cessi, ed., *Maggior Consiglio,* II, 89.

134. Ibid., II, 102.

135. Ibid., III, 16. See for an act of 1287, ibid., III, 173.

136. Ibid., III, 142–43; in Queller, *Early Venetian Legislation,* p. 32, n. 107, this is mistakenly recorded as I, 142–43.

137. Maggior Consiglio, Magnus, 71(72)r.

138. Cessi et al., eds. *Consiglio dei Rogati,* I, 250, n. 36.

139. Thiriet, ed., *Délibérations des assemblées vénitiennes,* no. 489, I, 198–99.

140. Cassandro, "Curia di Petizion," 19 (1936), 88.

141. Senato, Misti, XLIV, 1(1)v.

142. Queller, ed., "Newly Discovered Legislation," nò. 28, pp. 34–35.

143. Maggior Consiglio, Leona, 145(150)v. See p. 135.

144. Maggior Consiglio, Stella, 1(5)r.

145. Guerdan, *Sérénissime,* p. 156.

146. Avogadori di Comun, Capitulare, I, 67r. The act does not specify *public* debt, although surely that it is what is intended.

147. Queller, ed., "Newly Discovered Legislation," no. 45, p. 55. Confirmed in 1454. Queller, *Early Venetian Legislation,* no. 63, p. 96.

148. Maggior Consiglio, Novella, 157(168)v.

149. Cessi, ed., *Maggior Consiglio,* I, 103; Roberti, *Magistrature giudiziarie,* II, 184.

150. Queller, *Early Venetian Legislation,* no. 1, p. 59.

151. Actually, the Senate originally excepted only the councillors, procurators, and rectors, and five days later the *Maggior Consiglio* rectified the oversight by adding the others, which, however, were appended in the register of senatorial acts by a sort of footnote. Ibid., no. 26, p. 68.

152. Senato, Misti, XXV, 49(49)r.

153. Maggior Consiglio, Novella, 165(176)v.

154. Maggior Consiglio, Leona, 168(173)v.

155. "[Q]uamplures nostri faciant quotidie se eligi ad castellaniam Durachii causa refutandi sine pena de aliis rebus ad quas sunt electi. . . ." Senato, Misti, LIV, 53(54)r.

156. Queller, ed., "Newly Discovered Legislation," no. 37, pp. 46–47. Also see Maggior Consiglio, Ursa, 114(120)v (1437).

157. Queller, ed., "Newly Discovered Legislation," no. 41, pp. 51–52.

158. Ibid., no. 44, p. 54.

159. Maggior Consiglio, Ursa, 164(170)v.

160. Queller, ed., "Newly Discovered Legislation," no. 63, p. 96.

161. Sanuto, *Diarii*, IV, 90–91, and 99; Finlay, *Politics in Renaissance Venice*, p. 191.

162. Queller, ed., "Newly Discovered Legislation," no. 37, pp. 46–47. See also Maggior Consiglio, Ursa, 114(120)v and 164(170)v.

163. Maggior Consiglio, Stella, 54(58)v.

164. Cessi, ed., *Maggior Consiglio*, II, 50.

165. Ibid., II, 103; Roberti, *Magistrature giudiziarie*, II, 184.

166. Cessi, ed., *Maggior Consiglio*, III, 173.

167. Maggior Consiglio, Spiritus, 38(39)r.

168. Lazzarini, "Obbligo di assumere pubblici uffici," pp. 196–97. See also the act of 1342. Queller, *Early Venetian Legislation*, no. 47, pp. 84–85. I have not been able to find the act itself. I no longer believe that the act of 1342 included a provision that the person must leave within a month after refusing, although the act of 1410 seems to say it. (Ibid., p. 33.) I now believe that this requirement actually comes from the act of 1376. (Ibid., no. 35, p. 76.)

169. The ancient (1269) law: Cessi, ed., *Maggior Consiglio*, II, 234.

170. Queller, ed., "Newly Discovered Legislation," no. 10, pp. 17–18.

171. Cassandro, "Curia di Petizion," 19 (1936), 88; Queller, *Early Venetian Legislation*, no. 35, p. 76 and no. 47, pp. 84–85; Lazzarini, "Obbligo di assumere pubblici uffici," p. 197; Maggior Consiglio, Leona, 5(9)r.

172. "Quia continue eligantur de nostris nobilibus in ambaxatis, provisoriis et aliis officiis et beneficiis communis Venetie, tam intus, quam extra, qui pro maiori parte reffutant pro eundo extra, pro fugiendo penam ordinatam, et vadunt Muranum vel alio, et stant per duos menses solum pro non solvendo penam." Senato, Misti, XL, 146(151)v.

173. Lazzarini, "Obbligo di assumere pubblici uffici," p. 191.

174. Queller, ed., "Newly Discovered Legislation," no. 27, p. 34.

175. Maggior Consiglio, Leona, 143(148)r.

176. Ibid., 145(150)v.

177. Ibid., 170(175)v.

178. Maggior Consiglio, Ursa, 13(21)r.

179. Queller, ed., "Newly Discovered Legislation," no. 37, pp. 46–47. Also see Maggior Consiglio, Ursa, 114(120)v.

180. Ibid., 123(129)v.

181. Ibid., 164(170)v.

182. Queller, *Early Venetian Legislation*, no. 63, p. 96.

183. Senato, Terra, VII, 161(160)r.

184. Queller, *Early Venetian Legislation*, no. 88, pp. 116–17.

185. Cessi, ed., *Maggior Consiglio*, II, 88. Specifically regarding ducal councillors and electors. Ibid., II, 50. Amount changed. Ibid., III, 16.

186. Ibid., II, 233. Reinforced, Queller, *Early Venetian Legislation*, no. 30, pp. 72–73.

187. Cessi, ed., *Maggior Consiglio*, III, 171. Applied to a captain of the galleys. Maggior Consiglio, Spiritus, 30(31)v. Lane points out that many nobles

were reluctant to serve as galley commanders because of the large amount of money they had to spend for outfitting and manning their galleys even before collecting any salary. Others, however, were most eager for the assignment. *Venice,* p. 365. Pietro Soranzo tried to resign his command in 1374, but the Senate ordered him to proceed with his mission under penalty of 1,000 ducats. Senato, Misti, XXXIV, 132(132)v.

188. Queller, ed., "Newly Discovered Legislation," no. 7, pp. 15–16.

189. Maggior Consiglio, Spiritus, 110(111)v.

190. Maggior Consiglio, Novella, 148(159)r.

191. "[P]ostea invento colore recusent prosequi quod promiserant. . . ." Queller, ed., "Newly Discovered Legislation," no. 28, pp. 34–35.

192. Dieci, Misto, XI, 45(51)r.

193. Maggior Consiglio, Ursa, 123(129)v.

194. Dieci, Misto, XV, 52(53)v.

195. In all likelihood "solummodo ad illos qui apud serenissimum dominum ducem et dominos consiliarios ordinarie fecerunt officium" means that they served on the Signoria. Dieci, Misto, XVII, 51(93)r. Within a month the act was modified to except those heads of the civil and criminal branches who served as heads of the courts. Ibid., 53(95)r.

196. Maggior Consiglio, Regina, 107(113)r.

197. Maggior Consiglio, Stella, 80(84)r.

198. Dieci, Misto, XXIV, 154(193)v.

199. E.g., Queller, *Early Venetian Legislation,* no. 94, p. 123.

200. Maggior Consiglio, Capricornus, 18(123)v.

201. Maggior Consiglio, Clericus civicus, 80(128)r.

202. Maggior Consiglio, Leona, 22(26)v.

203. See p. 136.

204. Maggior Consiglio, Spiritus, 157(158)r; summarized in Thiriet, ed., *Délibérations des assemblées vénitiennes,* no. 548, I, 214–15.

205. Maggior Consiglio, Spiritus, 157(158)v. In "Newly Discovered Legislation," p. 22, this is referred to as a lost act, when, in fact, it was only lost in my files.

206. Queller, ed., "Newly Discovered Legislation," no. 15, pp. 22–23.

207. Queller, *Early Venetian Legislation,* no. 48, pp. 85–86.

208. Cessi, ed., *Maggior Consiglio,* III, 307.

209. Compilazioni leggi, elezioni, b. 197, no. 755. I have not found the original.

210. Senato, Misti, XXXIX, 72(76)v; Avogaria di Comun, Capitulare, I, 162v. (I must have missed the original of the latter, which Cassandro cites as Maggior Consiglio, Leona, 86t. It is summarized, but probably dated wrongly, in Maggior Consiglio, Leona, 171(176)r.) Queller, ed., "Newly Discovered Legislation," no. 26, pp. 33–34. There is, however, an error in the last. It should read: "[D]onec solverit in pena libras XXV *pro quolibet vice qua contrafaceret. Et ultra hoc officiales missetarie faciant diligenter cercare si de bonis, tam nobilis,*

quam popularis, poterit aliquid inveniri, et si invenietur, intromittant et faciant quod commune nostrum sit integre satisfatum de eo quod ille solvere debebit. Et ut nemo sub spem ignorantie possit se excusare, teneantur officiales missetarie predicti facere dicti et notificari. . . ." The italicized passage was omitted.

211. Maggior Consiglio, Leona, 171(176)r.

212. Senato, Terra, I, 25(26)r. Repeated in 1444. Ibid., 121(122)r.

213. "[S]int multi nostri nobiles debitores pro refutatione officiorum et aliarum rerum. . . ." Senato, Terra, II, 23(23)v.

214. Sanuto, *Città di Venetia*, p. 215.

215. "Cum officiales, ambaxatores, vel alii Venetiarum quibus imponuntur pene refutandi officia sive ea ad que elliguntur multociens refutent et mittuntur postea camere pro cadutis de pena ut excutiatur. Qui quidem solum scribunt in uno folio quod vadit per cameram. Et in hoc possent multa mala committi, quia quelibet persona posset cancellare quem vellet." Queller, ed., "Newly Discovered Legislation," no. 16, p. 23.

216. Cessi, ed., *Maggior Consiglio*, II, 93-94.

217. "Cum introductum sit per aliquos ex nobilibus nostris quod quando debet eligi aliquis capitaneus, ambassiator, provisor vel tractator pro factis nostris presentis guerre vel aliter, ipsi dicunt aliis nobilibus, non me eleze, vel non me voie. Et non solum ipso hoc dicunt, sed etiam dici faciunt et rogari per illos qui portant bussulos vel per alios, et isto modo habere non possumus de illis nobilibus qui essent accepti terre, et boni et sufficientes pro factis nostris. . . ." Queller, *Early Venetian Legislation*, no. 50, pp. 86-87.

218. Dieci, Misto, XII, 31(32)r.

219. Queller, ed., "Newly Discovered Legislation," no. 42, p. 52.

220. Dieci, Misto, XIII, 132(134)v.

221. Dieci, Misto, XVII, 32(74)v.

222. Queller, *Early Venetian Legislation*, no. 80, p. 109.

223. Dieci, Misto, XXI, 15(51)rv. On the law of 1480, see p. 70.

224. Queller, ed., "Newly Discovered Legislation," no. 62, pp. 74-75. The first reference to the act of 12 Jan. 1483 (1482, Venetian style) dates it correctly, but the second adds ten days and ten years incorrectly.

225. Lazzarini, "Obbligo di assumere pubblici uffici," pp. 193-94.

226. Cessi, ed., *Maggior Consiglio*, II, 90.

227. Ibid.

228. Ibid., III, 207.

229. Ibid., III, 370; Queller, *Early Venetian Legislation*, no. 7, p. 61.

230. Queller, *Early Venetian Legislation*, no. 54, pp. 89-90.

231. Ibid., no. 69, pp. 101-2.

232. Ibid., no. 47, pp. 84-85.

233. "Et multi eliguntur in isto consilio ad diversas res quas refutant pro eundo extra, et tamen non vadunt, quoniam per partem captam in maiori consilio 1410 die ultimo novembris obtinent gratiam prolongationiis termini recedendi. Et denique de gratia in gratiam differendo non recedunt nisi quando

volunt. Ex quo sequitur quod fiunt quodammodo exempti ab exerciis Rei pub-
lice, quia non possunt eligi ad aliquam rem, nec pro sua refutatione penam
patiuntur." Queller, *Early Venetian Legislation,* no. 56, p. 91.

234. Cessi, ed., *Maggior Consiglio,* II, 230.

235. Roberto Cessi, *Problemi monetari veneziani (fino a tutto il sec. XIV)*
(Padua, 1937), no. 25, cap. 77, p. 33. Added to the capitulary of the Council of
Six. Cessi, ed., *Maggior Consiglio,* II, 36. And of the *giudici del proprio.* Roberti,
Magistrature giudiziarie, II, 77.

236. Cessi, ed., *Maggior Consiglio,* III, 173.

237. Ibid., III, 355.

238. Maggior Consiglio, Fronesis, 113(114)r.

239. "Et quia per istud consilium antiquum multi officiales facientes largam
contrafacientiam exeunt de terra et stant per XV dies, et sunt extra officia."
Queller, ed., "Newly Discovered Legislation," no. 10, pp. 17-18.

240. E.g., Senato, Misti, XXIX, 85(81)r; Avogaria di Comun, Capitulare, I,
40v-41r; also, see p. 149.

241. "[M]ulti officiales volentes exire officia et vitare penam refutanti per
indirrectum stant de veniendo ad ea et exeunt sine pena. . . ." Maggior Consiglio, Novella, 89(100)r.

242. Maggior Consiglio, Leona, 5(9)r.

243. Lazzarini, "Obbligo di assumere pubblici uffici," pp. 197-98. This was
passed on the same day that another proposal concerning the use of Murano as a
refuge failed. See pp. 134-35. Extended to *savi del consiglio* and other *savi.*
Senato, Misti, L, 88(88)v. Eight days changed to fifteen in 1458. Queller, *Early
Venetian Legislation,* no. 65, pp. 97-98.

244. Senato, Misti, XLVI, 119(120)v.

245. "Et aliqui, ymo maior pars illorum, qui volunt esse extra quarantiam,
pro non solvendo libras ducentas non veniunt ad consilium et ad campanas
ordinatas tot diebus quod habent puncta XV, et hoc modo sunt extra, et non
solvunt nisi libras centum. . . ." Maggior Consiglio, Leona, 154(159)v.

246. Queller, *Early Venetian Legislation,* no. 55, p. 90.

247. Ibid., no. 61, pp. 94-95.

248. Dieci, Misto, XXIV, 1(41)v.

249. Ibid., XXVI, 25(53)v.

250. Besta, *Senato veneziano,* pp. 85-86.

251. Queller, *Early Venetian Legislation,* no. 10, p. 62.

252. "[Q]uidam nobiles tenentur dare circa libras ii parvorum ab dictum
officium, et non vult solvere, sed vult exire de officio quod eis non multum
placet." Maggior Consiglio, Clericus civicus, 131(180)v.

253. Maggior Consiglio, Fronesis, 11(11)r.

254. Queller, *Early Venetian Legislation,* no. 42, p. 81.

255. Queller, ed., "Newly Discovered Legislation," no. 35, pp. 42-44.

256. "Cum sint capte in preterito diversis temporibus multe partes et ordines
contra debitores nostri communis qui non curant solvere, et vigore ipsarum,
seu aliquarum ex ipsis, nostri nobiles debitores Communis privantur de pos-

sendo elligi ad capitanarias, supracomitarias, provisorias, et ambassiarias, et ad alia offitia et regimina nostra, cum maximo sinistro et incomodo agendorum nostrorum et status nostri dominii, quia ubi intentio terre fuit quod dicti tales debitores privarentur de possendo elligi pro malefaciendos ipsos, ut propterea essent ferventiores ad solvendum debita sua nostro Communi, sequitur totum oppositum, quia sunt multi qui non tantum non curant solvere, sed summo studio querunt esse debitores Communis, ut si eliguntur ad rem aliquam possint sub umbra talis debiti se tueri. . . ." Queller, ed., "Newly Discovered Legislation," no. 36, pp. 44-45. The act sounds curiously as if it were a revocation of the act of 1401, rather than a slightly modified affirmation of it. It seems fairly clear that the Great Council was confused by its own legislation. Since this document was taken from the Compilazioni leggi, the date, at least, could well be inaccurate.

257. Ibid., no. 45, p. 55. Broadened somewhat in 1454 for the needs of the war. Queller, *Early Venetian Legislation,* no. 63, p. 96.

258. "Quia debitores communis non possunt eligi nisi ad Ambaxiarias et provisorias exercitus, evenit sepenumero quod multi de quibus consilia faciunt reputaciones, quando nolunt eligi ad res que sibi non placent, dimittunt se debitores alicuius minimi debiti, et sub isto velamine manent exempti de exertitiis nostri communis." Ibid., no. 65, pp. 97-98.

259. Maggior Consiglio, Regina, 70(76)r.

260. Ibid., 75(81)v-76(82)r.

261. "[P]er fraude se fanno notar debitori de la nostra signoria. . . ." Senato, Terra, VI, 86(87)r.

262. Dieci, Misto, XXVII, 132(174)v.

263. Queller, ed., "Newly Discovered Legislation," no. 69, pp. 85-87.

264. "[M]olti prestantissimi senatori per qualche suo rispetto se mettono debitori per non intrar in collegio in questi importantissimi tempi adesso che le cosse de la signoria nostra grandemente patiscono. . . ." Maggior Consiglio, Deda, 12(27)v.

265. Yriarte, *Patricien de Venise,* p. 257.

266. Cassandro, "Curia di Petizion," 19 (1936), 100. Venice was not unique. Nicolai Rubinstein, "I primi anni del Consiglio Maggiore di Firenze," *Archivio storico italiano,* 112 (1954), 173-74, 181-82, 184-85, and 192-93; Nicolai Rubinstein, "Politics and Constitution in Florence at the End of the Fifteenth Century," in *Italian Renaissance Studies,* ed. E. F. Jacob (London, 1960), pp. 176-78.

267. Cessi, ed., *Maggior Consiglio,* II, 234; III, 390; Roberti, *Magistrature giudiziarie,* II, 106, 167, 243; Cassandro, "Curia di Petizion," 19 (1936), 99 and 20 (1937), 166, no. 36; Maggior Consiglio, Magnus, 10(10)v; Maggior Consiglio, Clericus civicus, 66(114)r; Maggior Consiglio, Novella, 142(253)r; Maggior Consiglio, Leona, 65(69)v; Maggior Consiglio, Deda, 13(28)v; Senato, Misti, LIX, 130(132)v; Senato, Terra, V, 175(175)r; Dieci, Misto, V, 82(83)v; XVIII, 141(196)v; XXX, 172(217)v.

268. Dieci, Misto, VIII, 16(16)v.

269. Ibid., 100(101)r.

270. Maggior Consiglio, Leona, 151(156)v; Cassandro, "Curia di Petizion," 19 (1936), 101.

271. "Cum maior pars officiorum et judicatuum Venetiarum propter acceptionem et diminutionem salariorum et utilitatum non ita bene solicitantur et administrantur sicut deberet fieri. . . ." Maggior Consiglio, Leona, 175(180)v. See also: Senato, Misti, L, 92(92)v–93(93)r; Cassandro, "Curia di Petizion," 19 (1936), 102.

272. "Quoniam sicut per experientiam videtur multi sunt ex officialibus nostris qui stant quinque et sex mensibus in domo nec solidant captas suas, quia super hoc nulla fit conscientia, neque etiam appunctatores de hoc curant, que omnia procedant cum multo interesse et ignominia terre nostre. . . ." Senato, Terra, I, 115(116)v.

273. Dieci, Misto, XII, 167(168)rv. See pp. 36–37.

274. "[M]ulta magna crimina transeunt impunita propter consilium XL criminale, quod non congregatur nisi tribus diebus ebdomade de mane, et tempus non sufficit ad tot agenda, et etiam non congregatur in numero requiritur. Nam XL non habentes salarium aut refutatur consilium aut non veniunt ad consilium." Maggior Consiglio, Ursa, 178(184)r.

275. Priuli, *Diarii*, I, 231.

276. Maggior Consiglio, Presbiter (copia II), 149(187)rv. Cassandro adds to his description of this act: "Accrescendosi le infrazioni, per la facilità con cui si poteva sfuggire all'obbligo, si ripetino le norme, et rafforzono le pene, si creano organi di controlo." "Curia di Petizion," 19 (1936), 99.

277. Maggior Consiglio, Leona, 74(78)v. See also Cassandro, "Curia di Petizion," 19 (1936), 103.

278. Senato, Misti, LIII, 147(147)r, 148(148)v, 149(149)v, 153(153)r. Special provisions were made for some officials, such as the salt officials and those responsible for butcher shops. See also Cassandro, "Curia di Petizion," 19 (1936), 103. A third *appuntatore* was named a month later to share the job at Rialto after Niccolò Barbaro, presumably an elderly noble, resigned because of the difficulty of the stairs there.

279. Senato, Misti, LX, 171(171)v. Prof. Richard Trexler helped me figure out that *hore vintitre* signifies the twenty-third hour beginning at sunset the previous day, or one hour before sunset on the day in question. See also Setton, *Papacy and the Levant*, I, 256, n. 162.

280. Senato, Terra, I, 1(2)v.

281. Ibid., 25(26)v.

282. "Cum ad officia et judicatus nostros non posset peius attendi per officiales nostros, et nobiles et populares, quam fiat, quod procedit quia appunctatores non faciunt debitum suum, imo concordant se cum officialibus nostris et excusant eos in modum quod neque ad exigendum pecunias nostras que ad ministrandum ius attenditur, et omnia in desolationem tendunt. . . ." Ibid., II, 116(116)rv.

283. Senato, Misti, XXIX, 85(81)r. For the evolution, see: Cessi, ed., *Maggior Consiglio*, II, 234 (also published from the *capitolare massarii* by Cessi, *Pro-*

blemi monetari veneziani, no. 25, cap. 77, p. 33); Cessi, ed., *Maggior Consiglio,* III, 88–99 (Cassandro, I believe, has misunderstood this. "Curia di Petizion," 19 (1936), 88); Roberti, *Magistrature giudiziarie,* II, 77 and 288; III, 34; Maggior Consiglio, Fractus, 5(5)v and 73(77)r; Maggior Consiglio, Spiritus, 39(40)v and 82(83)v; Maggior Consiglio, Novella, 62(73)r; Avogaria di Comun, Capitulare, I, 40v-41r.

284. Besta, *Senato veneziano,* p. 85, n. 2. See also, Cessi et al., eds. *Consiglio dei Rogati,* I, 148.

285. Maggior Consiglio, Spiritus, 31(32)v. See also: ibid., 155(156)v; Maggior Consiglio, Novella, 77(88)r; Maggior Consiglio, Leona, 236(241)r.

286. Compilazioni leggi, avogadori, b 66, no number. I could not find the original registered document. These copies are very inaccurate, but the gist of the document must reflect a law, although often misdated.

287. Cessi, ed., *Maggior Consiglio,* II, 104, 231; Dieci, Misto, XIII, 1(2)v.

288. Queller, ed., "Newly Discovered Legislation," no. 65, p. 79.

289. Sanuto, *Diarii,* V, 981. Such tasks were a relatively light burden and not at all unimportant. On diplomatic ceremonial generally, see Queller, *Office of the Ambassador,* pp. 184-208. Pp. 191-94 deal specifically with receptions.

290. Roberti, *Magistrature giudiziarie,* II, 93–94 (*avvocati del proprio*); III, 141 (*giudici del mobile*); III, 154 (*giudici del men*).

291. Robert Finlay, "The Venetian Republic as a Gerontocracy: Age and Politics in the Renaissance," *Journal of Medieval and Renaissance Studies,* 8 (1978), 172.

292. Maggior Consiglio, Leona, 129(133)v.

293. Senato, Misti, LIII, 148(148)v-149(149)v.

294. Gilbert, "Venice in the Crisis of the League of Cambrai," p. 274.

295. Cessi, ed., *Maggior Consiglio,* II, 318.

296. Ibid., II, 357.

297. Ibid., III, 49, 147, 177, 253, and 442; Avogaria di Comun, Magnus, 3(5)r.

298. Maggior Consiglio, Magnus, 67(78)v. Extended to all with appointments abroad. Maggior Consiglio, Capricornus, 35(140)v.

299. Maggior Consiglio, Capricornus, 62(167)r.

300. Thiriet, ed., *Délibérations des assemblées vénitiennes,* no. 420, I, 181. In 1389 *grazie* allowing this were prohibited. Maggior Consiglio, Leona, 29(33)v; Avogaria di Comun, Capitulare, I, 154v. Misdated in the latter. See also Noiret, ed., *Documents inédits,* pp. 307-8 (1425).

301. Maggior Consiglio, Fronesis, 40(40)v. Also in *Summarium legum,* 70v. Quoted in Avogaria di Comun, A, 61(71)r, and Maggior Consiglio, Novella, 162(173)r.

302. "Et contingat multotiens quod in dictis officiis sunt homines vel mercatores vel qui habent sua mercatoria extra et vadunt faciendo facta sua et modicum veniunt ad officium cum magno damno habencium agere ad dicta officia. . . ." Senato, Misti, XXXIII, 90(90)v.

303. Noiret, ed., *Documents inédits,* p. 135; mentioned in Philippe Braunstein

and Robert Delort, *Venise: Portrait historique d'une cité* (Paris, 1971), pp. 98–99. See also Dieci, Misto, XIV, 95(99)v; XV, 45(46)r; and XXIX, 93(154)v.

304. "Quia multum est considerandum et ad providendum quod provisores, capita, capitanei locorum nostrorum, et alii nostri nobiles qui quotidie mittuntur, tam ad exercitum, quam ad alia loca, in presenti guerra, morentur et stent secundem commissiones suas, et quod non recedant de locis et exercitu ubi sunt deputati absque nostro speciali mandato. Nam quotidie contrafit huic nostre intentioni. . . ." Senato, Misti, XLIX, 160(163)v.

305. Senato, Terra, VI, 132(132)v. But see Dieci, Misto, XVIII, 4(59)r, and XIX, 27(67)v-28(68)r, 34(74)v, 50(90)rv, 156(196)v.

306. Queller, *Early Venetian Legislation,* no. 92, p. 122.

307. Priuli, *Diarii,* II, 431.

308. Maggior Consiglio, Spiritus, 144(144)r. Repeated, without recognition of the earlier act. Maggior Consiglio, Novella, 86(97)r. For a similar problem in Padua, see Ventura, *Nobiltà e popolo,* pp. 85-86.

309. Maggior Consiglio, Spiritus, 155(156)v; *Le deliberazioni del Consiglio dei XL della repubblica di Venezia,* ed. Antonino Lombardo, no. 27, II (Venice, 1959), 9. Braudel is therefore incorrect in stating that plague had never emptied the Great Council prior to 1588. Fernand Braudel, *The Mediterranean and the Mediterranean World in the Age of Philip II,* 1st Fr. ed., 1966, trans. Siân Reynolds (New York, 1972), I, 344. See also Maggior Consiglio, Novella, 188(199)r.

310. Maggior Consiglio, Regina, 181(189)v; Andrea Navagero, *Storia della repubblica veneziana,* in R.I.S., 23, col. 1157.

311. "[Q]uando advocator communis de mandato dominii vadit ad faciendum aperiri portam ipsius maioris consilii, emissurus vel sapientes collegii, vel alibi, sicut occurrit, quo tempore fit magnus concursus nobilium nostrorum coram ipsas portas volentium exire. Ex quo sequitur ut aperto hostio fiat tumultuarius impetus et exitus, alienus omnino ab reputatione de maiestate ipsius maioris consilii. . . ." Dieci, Misto, XXI, 9(45)v-10(46)r. See also XXII, 77(113)r.

312. Ibid., XXVI, 67(95)r.

313. Ibid., XXVIII, 40(83)r.

314. Sanuto, *Diarii,* III, 1111.

315. Ibid., III, 1129 and 1401.

316. Priuli, *Diarii,* II, 102. He, himself, was an habitual absentee. See below.

317. Sanuto, *Diarii,* III, 1579.

318. Davis, *Decline of the Venetian Nobility,* p. 23.

319. Sanuto, *Cronachetta,* p. 222; id., *Città di Venetia,* p. 146.

320. Priuli, *Diarii,* IV, 38; Finlay, *Politics in Renaissance Venice,* pp. 21-22.

321. Maranini, *Costituzione di Venezia,* I, 247 and 252; Cessi, ed., *Maggior Consiglio,* II, 36 and III, 282. The Great Council returned again and again to the same issue, as it did in other cases, with previous legislation either unknown or unenforced.

322. Cessi, ed., *Maggior Consiglio,* II, 36.

323. Maggior Consiglio, Presbiter (copia II), 15(53)v-16(54)r.

324. Maggior Consiglio, Spiritus, 142(143)v.

325. Senato, Misti, XXXV, 19(19)v.

326. Dieci, Misto, XXIV, 27(66)r.

327. Ibid., XXV, 40(75)v-42(77)r.

328. "A 10 de Zener, se ha reduto Gran Consegio a numero 1,670; e perche no se ha possu haver altro che 3 Consegieri, e sta licentia." Malipiero, *Annali veneti*, p. 696.

329. "[F]o cativo tempo e non fo se non do consejeri. . . ." Sanuto, *Diarii*, II, 494-95.

330. Ibid., II, 649.

331. "[F]o licentiato il conseio con gran mormoration di tutti, che per consieri eri et ozi non si pol atender a le cosse di la terra. Et il mal era a farli si vechij. . . ." Ibid., III, 87.

332. Ibid., III, 380.

333. "Et cussi fo licentiato con gran mormoration di tutti, che con quel tempo non si dovea sonar gran conseio: e, poi era sonato, li consieri dovea venir." Ibid., III, 1092.

334. Ibid., V, 257 and 401-2.

335. "La matina nevego, et fo solum do consieri. . . ." Ibid., V, 907. Someone has scratched out 27 and written 28 in the margin.

336. Ibid., V, 909.

337. Maggior Consiglio, Capricornus, 57(162)v. A similar act. Maggior Consiglio, Presbiter (copia II), 310(348)rv. Entry into the Great Council after the Serrata was virtually automatic, but it did require approval of twelve of the Forty with at least thirty present.

338. Lombardo, ed., *Consiglio dei XL*, no. 27, II, 9; Maggior Consiglio, Spiritus, 155(156)v, on the following day, but this document says twenty, instead of twenty-five; also see p. 152.

339. Lombardo, ed., *Consiglio dei XL*, no. 223, II, 66-67. Again in 1353. Ibid., no. 112, III, 33.

340. Ruggiero, *Violence in Early Renaissance Venice*, p. 25.

341. Maggior Consiglio, Leona, 18(22)r, 32(36)r and 40(44)r.

342. Ibid., 40(44)v.

343. "[P]ropter quam paucitatem salarij illi de dicto consilio pro maiori parte non curant venire ad campanas. . . ." Ibid., 43(47)v.

344. Ibid., 64(68)v. Refined in 1397 and 1435. Ibid., 85(89)v and Maggior Consiglio, Ursa, 106(112)r.

345. Maggior Consiglio, Leona, 129(133)v.

346. Senato, Misti, LIX, 117(119)v.

347. *Summarium legum*, 114r, citing Maggior Consiglio, Ursa, 178. I have not found the latter.

348. "Verum ipsi XL^{ta} habere debentes de multis pagis non se reducant necque stant ad audiendum cum solita sua attenta audientia, et multi eorum propter hoc aptati recedunt, et solum ad ballotare se reducunt, et non audita causa nec rationibus partium disputantium non fatiunt iuditium, sicut proximis diebus accidit, quod quedam causa cum novem ballotis terminatum fuit cum

maximo damno, periculo, querella, et murmuratione habentium agere coram eis. . . ." Dieci, Misto, XV, 72(73)v.

349. Dieci, Misto, XXV, 40(75)v-42(77)r.

350. Senato, Misti, XL, 41(44)r; XLIII, 72(71)r; XLV, 94(93)r; Senato, Terra, IV, 18(19)v; Zorzi Dolfin, *Chronica,* 445v.

351. "[F]o gran neve, *adeo* non si reduse la mita del collegio. . . ." Sanuto, *Diarii,* II, 479.

352. "Nium se reduse per il tempo cativo. . . ." Ibid., II, 481.

353. Ibid., II, 502-3.

354. Ibid., III, 1165.

355. Ibid., IV, 434.

356. Ibid., V, 336.

357. "[E] questo fo per la gran neve e stranio tempora *etc."* Ibid., V, 840.

358. Zago, ed., *Consiglio dei Dieci,* reg. III, nos. 598-99, p. 198.

359. Dieci, Misto, IX, 95(99)r.

360. Ibid., X, 85(89)r.

361. Ibid., X, 96(100)r.

362. Ibid., X, 98(102)v.

363. Ibid., XI, 90(96)r and 91(97)r.

364. Ibid., XIII, 70(72)v.

365. Ibid., XVI, 18(55)r.

366. Ibid., XVI, 76(113)r. No explanation for what happened to the law of 1447, which was probably neglected and forgotten, like so much Venetian legislation.

367. Ibid., XXII, 169(205)r. Later liberalized. Ibid., XXII, 178(214)r.

368. Ibid., XXIV, 74(113)v-75(114)r. Patricia Labalme concedes that absenteeism was a problem, but believes it was more a matter of overwork than indifference. Her case for overwork, however, is based upon a *capo* of the Ten also assigned to the Committee against Sodomy. "Sodomy and Venetian Justice in the Renaissance," *Tijdschrift voor rechtsgeschiedenis,* 52 (1984), 229-30. The burdens of a *capo* were much greater than those of a mere member. See p. 118. Note, moreover, that some of my documents are directed against members leaving town, presumably on their own affairs.

369. Lane, *Venice,* p. 254. Francis C. Hodgson, *Venice in the Thirteenth and Fourteenth Centuries* (London, 1910), p. 573, asserts that some 140 generally attended. Yriarte finds 178 about average, and he gushes, as usual, over patrician zeal for the public welfare. *Patricien de Venise,* pp. 61-62.

370. Besta, *Senato veneziano,* p. 97, nn. 5 and 6, and p. 99, n. 2.

371. Maggior Consiglio, Capricornus, 49(154)r.

372. Maggior Consiglio, Clericus civicus, 43(91)r; Besta, *Senato veneziano,* p. 99, n. 2, although inaccurate (see Avogaria di Comun, Neptunus, no. 217, 38v and also Maranini, *Costituzione di Venezia,* II, 134); Maggior Consiglio, Fronesis, 145(146)v.

373. Senato, Misti, XIX, 84(84)v. Similar acts, 1351 and 1359; ibid., XXVII, 22(22)r and XXVIII, 102(102)v.

374. Ibid., XXXI, 97(99)v and 103(105)v; XXXII, 50(52)r, 52(54)r, 126 (128)v, and 132(134)r; XXXIII, 15(15)v, 16(16)v, 58(58)v, 68(68)r, 81(81)r, 118(118)r, 121(121)r, 123(123)r, and 124(124)r; XXXIV, 91(91)v, 94(94)v, and 122(122)v; XXXV, 37(37)v and 77(76)r.

375. Besta, *Senato veneziano*, p. 100, n. 2.

376. Maggior Consiglio, Novella, 168(179)v; Besta, *Senato veneziano*, p. 99, n. 3. (The pertinent section is actually on p. 100.)

377. Senato, Misti, XXXVII, 107(107)r; XXXVIII, 48(49)v and 101(102)r; XLI, 52(57)r, 96(99)r, and 96(99)v; XLII, 89(90)r; XLIII, 99(98)r, 132(131)v, and 161(160)v. See also ibid., XLIX, 116(118)r and 190(193)v; L, 135(136)v.

378. Ibid., XLVI, 9(10)r.

379. Maggior Consiglio, Leona, 143(148)v.

380. Senato, Misti, XLVIII, 54(54)r.

381. Ibid., 79(79)v.

382. Avogaria di Comun, Capitulare, I, 176r; Avogaria di Comun, A, 61(71)r.

383. "[P]ropter diversas occupationes terre raro dictum consilium rogatorum congregatur a LXX supra." Senato, Misti, XLIX, 139(141)v and 140(142)rv. (The whole page was recopied.)

384. Maggior Consiglio, Ursa, 8(16)v.

385. Maggior Consiglio, Ursa, 69(75)v.

386. Senato, Misti, LX, 236(236)v. See also, Dieci, Misto, XVIII, 142 (197)rv; "Ex quo lectis litteris, si fores aut remanerent aperte aut aliqua causa de mandato dominii aperiuntur multi discedere conantur."

387. "[C]onsiderato quod numerus nobilium nostrorum . . . et similiter consilii rogatorum est multo maior quam unquam fuerit . . . quod stetur super partibus et ordinibus numeri LXX." Maggior Consiglio, Regina, 179(187)r. On the pestilence and its effects, see Navagero, *Storia veneziana*, col. 1157.

388. Ermolao Barbaro, *Epistolae, orationes et carmina*, ed. Vittore Branca (Florence, 1943), no. XLVI, I, 62; Ferriguto, *Almorò Barbaro*, p. 426, n. 3, and pp. 460–61.

389. Dieci, Misto, XXVIII, 34(77)v. This document is also of great interest regarding the problems the Republic had in preserving secrecy. See p. 216.

390. Senato, Misti, LIV, 128(129)v; Maranini, *Costituzione di Venezia*, I, 290.

391. Sanuto, *Diarii*, XIX, 443; Muir, *Civic Ritual*, pp. 172–73.

392. "[E]t ad presens non sit dictus numerus congregatus, et missum sit pro eis in Rivoalto, quod veniant, et ipsi responderint quod nolunt venire. . . ." Maggior Consiglio, Presbiter (copis II), 26(64)r.

393. Cessi, ed., *Maggior Consiglio*, II, 80–81.

394. Ibid., II, 235–36.

395. Zago, ed., *Consiglio dei Dieci,* reg. III, no. 498, p. 169.

396. Maggior Consiglio, Novella, 142(153)rv.

397. Senato, Misti, XXXV, 142(141)v; Avogaria di Comun, Capitulare, I, 7v–8r.

398. Maggior Consiglio, Novella, 168(179)v; Avogaria di Comun, Capitulare, I, 147v–148r.

399. Maggior Consiglio, Leona, 196(201)v; Avogaria di Comun, A, 54(64)v.

400. Dieci, Misto, XIX, 125(165)v.

401. Senato, Terra, IX, 8(8)r.

402. Ibid., IX, 153(153)v.

403. Cessi, ed., *Maggior Consiglio,* II, 233.

404. "[S]ciunt tenere talos modos et vias quod pro maiori parte nullus vadit ad terminum suum. . . ." Maggior Consiglio, Novella, 139(150)v. Return to the problem in 1408. Senato, Misti, XLVIII, 35(35)v.

405. Senato, Misti, LVI, 120(122)v.

406. "Et etiam sia aproveder sopra quelli che da poi che ihano acceptado istano alcuni uno anno et alcuni do anni che i non vano a isuo Regimenti. . . ." Maggior Consiglio, Regina, 1(7)v; Maggior Consiglio, Stella, 105(109)v, 136(140)v-137(141)r, 157(161)rv; see Queller, *Early Venetian Legislation,* p. 39, n. 143.

407. In a previous section there are a few examples of patricians refusing military service, mostly through fear, especially of the Turks. See pp. 127-29.

408. Molmenti, *Venice,* part 2, II, 43.

409. Donald E. Queller, *The Fourth Crusade* (Philadelphia, 1977), passim. Even if their motives were questioned, their naval skill and valor were not. Donald E. Queller and Irene B. Katele, "Attitudes towards the Venetians in the Fourth Crusade: The Western Sources," *International History Review,* 4 (1982), 1-36.

410. Fasoli, "Storia di Venezia," p. 104.

411. Sanuto, *Diarii,* XXV, 73; Cozzi, "Domenico Morosini," p. 442. Undoubtedly the Venetian was trying to impress the Turk with the invulnerability and wealth of Venice, but there is a sense in which statements taken out of context provide wonderful evidence. With this statement of fact (or, if you wish, near fact) the Venetian has said more than he intended.

412. Priuli, *Diarii,* IV, 44-45; Gilbert, "Venice in the Crisis of the League of Cambrai," p. 275. Elsewhere Priuli calls the Venetian nobles "molto vili d'animo et de choragio et de chore . . . et haranno in simel exercitio et operatione veramente pegio che femine. . . ." Quoted by Cozzi, "Domenico Morosini," p. 441.

413. Niccolò Macchiavelli, *Discorsi,* L. II, c. 10, in *Opere,* ed. Sergio Bertelli, I (Milan, 1968), 255-56; Cozzi, "Domenico Morosini," p. 447.

414. Gian Giacopo Caroldo, *Cronica veneziana,* B.M., cl. ital. VII, cod. 128a (=8639), 248v-249r; Lane, *Venice,* p. 179.

415. Senato, Misti, XXXVI, 81(82)rv; Lane, *Venice,* pp. 192-93.

416. Senato, Misti, XXXVI, 84(85)r.

417. Ibid., 95(96)v.

418. Ibid., 98(99)rv.

419. Ibid, LVII, 183(187)v-184(188)r.

420. Lane, *Andrea Barbarigo,* p. 64.

421. Dieci, Misto, XXI, 139(175)rv.

422. Malapiero, *Annali veneti,* p. 694.

423. Priuli, *Diarii*, I, 182-85, 191-93 and II, 34; Malipiero, *Annali veneti*, pp. 175-79 and 185; Sanuto, *Diarii*, III, 993, 1056, 1106, and 1155; Maggior Consiglio, Stella, 176(180)r; Compilazione leggi, nobili veneti, b 294, nos. 973 and 977; Ester Zille, "Il processo Grimani," *Archivio veneto*, 36-41 (1945-47), 137-94; Finlay, *Politics in Renaissance Venice*, pp. 147-50; Lane, *Venice*, p. 360. Sanuto gives a version of the battle written by Grimani's chaplain for the captain-general's sons. *Diarii*, I, 1230-41.

424. Senato, Terra, XIII, 120(122)rv.

425. Priuli, *Diarii*, II, 109.

426. Lane, *Venice*, p. 414; Jean Claude Hocquet, "Gens de mer à Venise: Diversitè des statuts, conditions de vie et de travail sur les navires," in *Le genti del mare Mediterraneo*, ed. Rosalba Ragosta, I (Naples, 1980), 109-10.

427. Kretschmayr, *Geschichte von Venedig*, II, 120. See Bouwsma, "Venice and the Political Education of Europe," p. 456, on patrician willingness to pay taxes.

428. Sanuto, *Diarii*, VIII, 117; Finlay, *Politics in Renaissance Venice*, p. 33. Finlay's translation. As Alberto Tenenti put it, referring to the Florentine Alberti and the Ragusan Cotrugli: "ils n'excluent pas l'hypothèse d'une concordance entre les intérêts familiaux et les exigences publiques, avec l'éventuelle subordination ou le sacrifice des premiers aux secondes. Mais il s'agit clairement de conjonctures inhabituelles, qui n'appairaissent plus a l'horizon normal et quotidien. En principe, ce type de famille veut compter uniquement sur elle-même, et d'autre part on compte que l'Etat fasse appel à elle le moins possible. Si certaines solidarités sont inéluctables out indispensables il y aura surtout échange de service, mais pratiquement pas communion de valeurs." "Famille bourgeoise et idéologie au bas moyen âge," in *Famille et parenté dans l'occident médiéval*, ed. Georges Duby and Jacques LeGoff (Rome, 1977), pp. 434-35.

429. Priuli, *Diarii*, IV, 77-78.

430. "Traité du gouvernement de Venise," p. 283.

431. "More or less," because the government did have a sinking fund to buy in bonds when the market was low. Lane, *Venice*, p. 184.

432. And then not very enthusiastically. Cracco, *Società e stato*, p. 318.

433. Ibid., pp. 322-23.

434. Lane, *Venice*, pp. 184-85.

435. Ibid., p. 238; Thiriet, *Romanie vénitienne*, p. 219; Brown, *Venetian Republic*, p. 104; Gino Luzzatto, *Il debito pubblico della Repubblica di Venezia* (Milan, 1963), pp. 137-38.

436. Roberto Cessi, *Politica ed economia di Venezia nel Trecento: Saggi* (Rome, 1952), pp. 192-93; Lane, *Venice*, p. 150; Cracco, *Società e stato*, p. 201. Even Maranini perceived where the patricians had placed the tax burden. *Costituzione di Venezia*, I, 272-73. In fairness to the patrician government, poor or middling nobles did not fare better in this respect than commoners. They did have the possibility of government jobs (as, at another level, did the *cittadini*), but, as we shall see (p. 169), when the crisis grew in 1434, these were heavily taxed. For an expression of the belief that the burden ought to be equitable, heavier on those who could afford to pay, lighter on those who could not, see Morosini, *De bene*

instituta republica, p. 201. This progressive notion, however, is followed by an elaboration of the idea (derived from the basic definition of law in the *Corpus juris civilis* taken from Ulpian) that the function of the law is to protect each person's right in what is his own (ibid.) and an explication of the now-familiar "trickle-down" theory of economics (p. 206).

437. Cessi, *Regolazione delle entrate e delle spese,* no. 264, p. 231. I have not succeeded in identifying this levy.

438. Senato, Misti, XLIX, 131(133)v.

439. Ibid., LII, 176(176)v.

440. Senato, Terra, III, 156(158)v.

441. Dieci, Misto, XX, 17(55)r; Malipiero, *Annali veneti,* p. 672. The latter has confused the sentence.

442. Dieci, Misto, XXII, 91(127)rv.

443. Ibid., 149(185)v-150(186)r. Reaffirmation of the law of 1484, ibid., 158(194)rv.

444. Ibid., XXVIII, 86(129)r, 110(153)v, and 111(154)r; Sanuto, *Diarii,* III, 736.

445. Sanuto, *Diarii,* IV, 181-83; Longworth, *Rise and Fall of Venice,* p. 169; Franco Gaeta, "Barbarigo, Agostino," in *Dizionario biografico degli italiani,* VI (Rome, 1964-), 49.

446. Senato, Misti, LIII, 44(44)r. Conviction of Giovanni Zorzi for a false return. Ibid., 44(44)v.

447. Maggior Consiglio, Ursa, 29(37)r.

448. Thiriet, ed., *Régestes des délibérations du Sénat de Venise,* no. 2354, III, 37.

449. Ibid., no. 2370, III, 43.

450. Luzzatto, *Debito pubblico della Repubblica di Venezia,* p. 259.

451. Senato, Terra, V, 151(151)r.

452. Ibid., 157(157)r. Additional problems with nonpayment: ibid., VI, 119(120)rv; 124(124)v; IX, 76(76)rv.

453. Sanuto, *Diarii,* II, 36-37.

454. Ibid., II, 742, 787, 866, and III, 700. "El se attrovano molti zentilho-meni et citadini nostri et altri habitanti in questa cita taxadi anchor fina ne la prima taxa ad restituir, che fina questo zorno non hano pagato soldo alcuno. Ne par se curino pagar non obstante la urgentia et necessita se ha hora del denaro per poter cum el mezo di quelle resister a la rabie de questo imanissimo Turco." Senato, Terra, XIII, 144(146)r. Values of gold and silver coins fluctuated, of course; a half-century earlier the *l. de grossi* had been worth ten ducats. Giovanni di Antonio da Uzzano, *The Practice of Commerce,* trans. in *Medieval Trade in the Mediterranean World,* ed. Robert S. Lopez and Irving W. Raymond (New York, n.d.), p. 148.

455. Sanuto, *Diarii,* III, 763.

456. Ibid., III, 953.

457. Raymond de Roover, *The Rise and Fall of the Medici Bank, 1397-1494* (New York, 1963)., pp. 73-74. The concealing of assets became so widespread that the *catasto* on business investments was abandoned. Ibid., p. 99.

458. Jean Lestocquoy, *Les dynasties bourgeoises d'Arras du XIe au XVe siècle* (Arras, 1945), pp. 51-53 and 63-64. Lestocquoy, however, overrates the sense of financial responsibility of the Venetian patriciate. *Aux origines de la bourgeoisie,* p. 192.

459. Queller, *Early Venetian Legislation,* pp. 30-39.

460. James Bruce Ross, "The Emergence of Gasparo Contarini: A Bibliographical Essay," *Church History,* 41 (1972), p. 37, n. 10.

461. Queller, *Early Venetian Legislation,* p. 31. In the present context it is mildly interesting that one reader paid attention to this passage, which attempts to emphasize the variety and complexity of the patriciate. In a copy from the Princeton University Library some person of questionable ethics, but clear apprehension, has emphasized it with a pencil line down the margin.

VI. CORRUPTION

1. Marchesi, "Repubblica di Venezia," pp. 86-87.

2. Sanuto, *Diarii,* VIII, 414.

3. Longworth, *Rise and Fall of Venice,* p. 151; Cracco, *Società e stato,* p. 377; Chojnacki, "Trecento Venetian State," p. 196, where he points out: "It would be inaccurate to depict noble office holders as generally corrupt. But it is also a misrepresentation to characterize them all as dedicated and selfless public servants. Among Venetian public officials, as among officials of every government, there were those who took advantage of their positions to line their pockets." Basically this is true, although Venetian society, especially from the fifteenth century, tempted its noble officials in special ways.

4. Maranini, *Costituzione di Venezia,* II, 190 and 444-45. This sort of standing of the evidence on its head is typical of the apologists for Venetian government.

5. Cozzi, "Authority and Law," p. 307.

6. Senato, Misti, XLVIII, 154(161,164)v.

7. Contarini, *De magistratibus,* 46v (Lewkenor, pp. 108-9). See also Sanuto, *Cronachetta,* p. 97; id., *Città di Venetia,* and Cozzi, "Authority and Law," p. 322.

8. Senato, Misti, XXIX, 16(16)v.

9. Ibid., 6(6)v.

10. Niccolò Priuli, who had been captain of Famagusta and lieutenant of Cyprus, was charged in 1504 on twenty-seven counts by the syndics. He was an important noble, a member of the Council of Ten. Sanuto, *Diarii,* VI, 113 and 162. Doge Agostino Barbarigo was known for corruption. See p. 201.

11. Labalme, *Bernardo Giustiniani,* p. 226, n. 16. Cracco, *Società e stato,* pp. 381 and 318. On p. 318, n. 5 does not really support the statement in the text, although the statement remains true. Cozzi, "Authority and Law," p. 299, but n. 23 with its five references to Sanuto's *Diarii* also does not support the text, which reads: "According to certain contemporaries, the frequency of cases of

embezzlement in the Venetian administration in this period [the fifteenth century] was due to the fact that many jobs were filled by men forced by their wretchedness to extort profit greater than that offered by the normal salaries." The first three citations refer to corrupt elections, but do not offer any excuses or rationalizations, and offer no specific reference to embezzlement at all. The last two deal with embezzlement, but again offer no excuse or rationalization. They are bare statements of the results of trials. Cozzi's statement is nevertheless true.

12. Thiriet, ed., *Délibérations des assemblées vénitiennes*, no. 692, I, 254-55; Romanin, *Storia di Venezia*, III, 344.

13. Jacopo da Porcia, *De Reipublicae Venetae administratione domi et foris liber* (Treviso, 1492), n.p.

14. Lestocquoy, *Dynasties bourgeoises d'Arras*, pp. 14, 63-64, and 104; Brucker, *Renaissance Florence*, pp. 140-41.

15. Cracco, *Società e stato*, p. 341.

16. Contarini, *De magistratibus*, 14v (Lewkenor, p. 29).

17. Sanuto, *Cronachetta*, p. 121; id., *Città di Venetia*, p. 107.

18. Queller, ed., "Newly Discovered Legislation," pp. 11-13, no. 1; Cessi, ed., *Maggior Consiglio*, II, 28; Roberti, *Magistrature giudiziarie*, II, 43-44. Revisions of the law in 1274, 1280, and 1295. Cessi, ed. *Maggior Consiglio*, II, 235 and 40, III, 385; Roberti, *Magistrature giudiziarie*, III, 164 and 216. The two versions given by Roberti are badly edited: *solvere*, not *salvere; partes* omitted; *habere*, not *habeant*. See also Avogaria di Comun, Capitularie, I, 23v-24r (1301).

19. Cessi, ed., *Maggior Consiglio*, II, 235.

20. Cessi, *Problemi monetari veneziani*, pp. 20-21, no. 25, cap. 22.

21. Roberti, *Magistrature giudiziarie*, III, 46.

22. Brown, *Studies*, I, 69 and n. 2; Cicogna, *Delle inscrizioni veneziane*, III (Venice, 1830), 28-29 and 34; Lane, "Enlargement of the Great Council," p. 240; Hodgson, *Venice in the Thirteenth and Fourteenth Centuries*, p. 214.

23. Maggior Consiglio, Presbiter (copia II), 154(192)r.

24. Avogaria di Comun, Capitularie, I, 69v-70r. At the foot of the page in another hand is a cancellation dated 1405, May 5. Summarized, not quite accurately, in Thiriet, ed., *Délibérations des assemblées vénitiennes*, no. 387, I, 173.

25. Avogaria di Comun, Capitularie, I, 11rv and 15rv.

26. Ibid., I, 14v.

27. Maggior Consiglio, Spiritus, 41(42)v-42(43)r.

28. Thiriet, ed., *Déliberations des assemblées vénitiennes*, no. 482, I, 196.

29. Lombardo, ed., *Consiglio dei XL*, nos. 83-84, II, 25, and no. 134, II, 39-40.

30. Ibid., nos. 242, 248, and 249, II, 72-74.

31. Ibid., no. 185, III, 54.

32. Gian Giacopo Caroldo, *Historia di Venetia*, B.M., cl. ital. VII, cod. 127(=8034), 241r.

33. "[P]er vicarios, judices, socios, notarios et capita baroeriorum potestatum Tarvisii continue committantur multa inhonesta et turpia, tam in accipi-

endo bona specialium personarum, quam in furtando bona Communis quantum possunt. . . ." Senato, Misti, XXVII, 46(46)rv.

34. Dieci, Misto, V, 49(50)v.
35. Senato, Misti, XXVIII, 36(36)r.
36. Cessi, *Regolazione delle entrate e delle spese,* no. 246, pp. 206-9.
37. Senato, Misti, XXIX, 19(19)r.
38. Senato, Misti, XXXI, 44(46)rv. An attempt to convict the notary at the Fondaco failed.
39. Cessi, *Regolazione delle entrate e delle spese,* no. 266, pp. 232-33. Cessi dates the act "1369, die sexto februarii," which would be 6 Feb. 1370 in modern (not Venetian) style. See Maggior Consiglio, Novella, 118(129)v-119(130)r. In a later reference, Maggior Consiglio, Leona, 237(242)v-238(243)r, the first citation is mistakenly to "MCCCLVIII," but subsequently to 1368, which is obviously correct, since it is the act of 1359 which is modified.
40. Senato, Misti, XLI, 101(104)v, 102(105)r, 103(106)r, 103(106)v-104(107)r.
41. Ibid., XLII, 148(149)r.
42. Ibid., XLVIII, 66(66)r.
43. Ibid., 143(148,151)v.
44. Ibid., XLIX, 70(71)v.
45. Maggior Consiglio, Leona, 237(242)v-238(243)r.
46. Senato, Misti, LI, 130(133)v and 132(135)rv.
47. Maggior Consiglio, Ursa, 9(17)v.
48. Dieci, Misto, IX, 162(166)v; Zorzi Dolfin, *Chronica,* 303r.
49. Senato, Misti, LVIII, 7(10)v.
50. "[I]n questi anni mo nuovamente passadi se ha trovado molti officiali aver messo man in le dite pecunie, non habiando teror de dio, ne de la nostra signoria, chomo ancora in le pene in lequal i son cazudi. . . ." Ibid., 88(92)r.
51. Ibid., LIX, 15(17)r.
52. They were driven by a "spirito diabolico." Senato, Terra, III, 56(58)rv. Strictly speaking, of course, this was not embezzlement.
53. Ibid., 188(190)r. See p. 206.
54. Ibid., V, 1(2)r.
55. Dieci, Misto, XIX, 34(74)v.
56. Ibid.
57. Ibid., 50(90)rv.
58. Longworth, *Rise and Fall of Venice,* p. 175.
59. Senato, Terra, XIII, 98(100)rv; Priuli, *Diarii,* I, 225; Sanuto, *Diarii,* II, 940. Sanuto is a little off concerning the penalty.
60. Queller, *Early Venetian Legislation,* pp. 137-39, no. 110. "[C]he non sparagnava chome del suo proprio, et in tal ambasaria di Roma et Napolli spendevanno li oratori ducati 4000 a l'anno, cosa veramente insoportabile, tra spexe et robamenti. . . ." Priuli, *Diarii,* II, 50.
61. Priuli, *Diarii,* I, 217 and II, 56; Sanuto, *Diarii,* III, 39, 813, 835, and 837; Senato, Terra, XIII, 147(149)r-148(150)r.

62. Lane, *Venice*, pp. 268-69.
63. Sanuto, *Diarii*, IV, 249-50. Compilazioni leggi, elezioni, b 197, 150r, dated 4 Dec. 1502, which enacts that noblemen who have been convicted for pocketing public money and defrauding the public cannot, as long as they live, be elected in any office where public funds are managed, is, like so many documents in this collection, misdated. See Maggior Consiglio, Libro d'Oro, XIII, 173rv, dated 31 Aug. 1564.
64. Sanuto, *Diarii*, VI, 162.
65. Priuli, *Diarii*, II, 399 and 401; Sanuto, *Diarii*, VI, 278, 279, 284, and 285, also reports the case.
66. Maggior Consiglio, Novella, 25(36)v.
67. Queller, *Early Venetian Legislation*, no. 27, pp. 69-71. Earlier published by Cessi, *Regolazione delle entrate e delle spese*, no. 236, pp. 191-94.
68. Cessi, *Regolazione delle entrate e delle spese*, p. cxcii.
69. Roberti, *Magistrature giudiziarie*, pp. 144-46; the identical *capita* appear in Avogaria di Comun, Capitolari, I, 11v-12r.
70. Maggior Consiglio, Capricornus, 20(125)r.
71. "Cum ad offitium vicedominorum tabule maris servetur quadam mala consuetudo, videlicet quod in denariis quod vicedomini accipiunt a mercatoribus nomine pignoris pro solvendis suis daciis ponunt manum, et de ipsis denariis accipiunt mutuo, et de ipsis dant et concedant in suis scribanis quamvis bene vendantur. Capta fuit pars quod decetero ipsi vicedomini non possint accipere mutuo vel alio modo possint ponere manum in ipsis denariis datis sibi per pignore. . . ." Ibid., 43(148)r.
72. "Introducta est quadam prava et pernitiosa consuetudo quod multi officiales officiorum huius urbis nostre, tam qui ad presens sunt in officio, quam qui compleverint officia sua, non solidaverant nec solidare curant capsas suas temporibus congruis et debitis iuxta formam legum nostrarum, et pecunias nostras continent penes se illis in eorum usum convertentes. Que res, cum sit pernitiosa et in gravissimum dannum nostri dominii nullo modo tolleranda est." Senato, Terra, X, 146(147)r.
73. Cessi, *Regolazione delle entrate e delle spese*, pp. cclxii-ccxliii.
74. Senato, Misti, XXXVIII, 126(127)v.
75. Cessi, ed., *Maggior Consiglio*, II, 353.
76. Senato, Misti, XXX, 19(19)v.
77. Maggior Consiglio, Novella, 150(161)v.
78. Senato, Misti, XL, 32(35)r.
79. Ibid., XLIX, 105(106)v-106(107)r.
80. Ibid., LIV, 147(148)r; Lane, *Venice*, p. 365.
81. "Cum patroni galearum a mercato non ducant secum ballistarios qui accipiuntur ad barsaleum et dantur sibi per collegium, imo et in Venetiis et quando sunt extra faciunt remanere ballistarios acceptos ad barsaleum et ponunt loco illorum mercatores at famulos mercatorum, ita ut dici potest quod non ducant medietatem ballistrariorum qui sibi dati sunt. . . ." Senato, Misti, LX, 251(252)r.

82. Setton, *Papacy and the Levant,* vol. II, *The Fifteenth Century* (Philadelphia, 1978), p. 303 and n. 117, where the document is printed, at least in part; Marchesi, "Repubblica di Venezia," pp. 51-52; Lane, *Venice,* p. 359.

83. Tenenti, "Famille bourgeoise et idéologie au bas moyen âge," p. 439.

84. Margarete Merores, "Der Grosse Rat von Venedig und die sogennante Serrata von Jahre 1297," *Vierteljahrschrift für Sozial- und Wirtschaftsgeschichte,* 21 (1928), 50. The expelled, or *cacciati,* included in 1260 full brothers, grandsons, nephews, fathers-in-law and sons-in-law, uncles, and any blood relations. Cessi, ed., *Maggior Consiglio,* II, 80. In 1287 a law specified stepfathers for stepsons, grandfathers for grandsons, and vice versa. Ibid., III, 176. For certain cases restricted in 1307 to fathers, sons, and brothers. Senato, Capitolare, 42v.

85. Morosini, *De bene instituta republica,* p. 105; A. Sagredo, "Leggi venete intorno agli ecclesiastici sino al secolo XVIII," *Archivio storico italiano,* ser. 3, 2 (1865), 102; Yriarte, *Patricien de Venise,* p. 61; Besta, *Senato veneziano,* pp. 214-18; Bouwsma, *Venice and the Defense of Republican Liberty,* p. 64; Longworth, *Rise and Fall of Venice,* p. 128.

86. Cassandro, "Curia di petizion," 19 (1936), 94. It was undoubtedly a subsequent act which prohibited judges from receiving gifts from anyone, even from employees of their courts. Ibid.; Roberti, *Magistrature giudiziarie,* p. 243 and n. 3.

87. Cessi, ed., *Maggior Consiglio,* II, 334, 352, and 357.

88. Cessi, ed., *Maggior Consiglio,* II, 401.

89. Ibid., II, 360. Still, in 1281 the Great Council had to decide ad hoc that the *podestà* of Caorle could not accept any of that commune's money. Ibid., II, 321.

90. Ibid., II, 360-361.

91. Cessi, *Problemi monetari veneziani,* no. 37, cap. XVIIII, p. 48.

92. Mueller, "Procurators of San Marco," p. 169.

93. Romanin, *Storia di Venezia,* III, 360.

94. Maggior Consiglio, Novella, 49(60)r.

95. Ibid., 155(166)v-156(167)r; Lazzarini, "Antiche leggi venete," p. 15; Pompeo Molmenti, "Le relazioni tra patrizi veneziani e diplomatici stranieri," in Molmenti, *Curiosità di storia veneziana* (Bologna, 1919), p. 39. Also included in acts of 1380, 1403, and 1406. Compilazioni leggi, nobili veneti, b 294, no. 856; Ferriguto, *Almorò Barbaro,* p. 446, n. 1; Lazzarini, "Antiche leggi venete," no. XVI, pp. 29-30; Molmenti, "Relazioni tra patrizi veneti e diplomatici stranieri," in *Curiosità,* p. 43.

96. Senato, Misti, XXIX, 85(81)r.

97. Ibid., XXXIII, 98(98)r.

98. Romanin, *Storia di Venezia,* III, 53.

99. Cessi, ed., *Maggior Consiglio,* II, 251.

100. Ibid., II, 353.

101. Ibid., II, 306.

102. Ibid., II, 242.

103. Ibid., II, 321. See also ibid., II, 308-9.

104. Cappelletti, *Relazione storica sulle magistrature venete*, p. 106; da Mosto, *Archivio di Stato*, I, 189. Repeated in 1278. Cessi, ed., *Maggior Consiglio*, II, 298.

105. Avogaria di Comun, Raspe, 2495/1, 87rv. I owe this reference to Prof. Guido Ruggiero.

106. Cessi, ed., *Maggior Consiglio*, II, 31.

107. Cessi, *Problemi monetari veneziani*, no. 37, cap. XVIII, p. 48. See also ibid., no. 37, cap. X, p. 46.

108. Roberti, *Magistrature giudiziarie*, II, 147-48.

109. Maggior Consiglio, Fronesis, 100(100)v.

110. Maggior Consiglio, Spiritus, 82(83)v. Also the officials of accounts. Senato, Misti, XXIX, 85(81)r.

111. Maggior Consiglio, Novella, 131(142)v-132(143)r.

112. Lombardo, ed., *Consiglio dei XL,* no. 219, III, 122.

113. Noiret, ed., *Documents inédits*, pp. 317-18.

114. Senato, Misti, LVIII, 31(35)r.

115. Ibid., LIX, 105(107)r.

116. Senato, Terra, II, 112(112)v.

117. Dieci, Misto, XVIII, 100(155)r.

118. Senato, Terra, VIII, 2(2)v.

119. Ibid., XII, 110(110)r. Revoked, as regards hemp and fustian, in 1501. Ibid., XIV, 39(39)v-40(40)r.

120. Sanuto, *Diarii,* VI, 262-63.

121. Maranini, *Costituzione di Venezia*, II, 242. The vital part of the document is printed in Besta, *Senato veneziano*, p. 217.

122. Lazzarini, "Antiche leggi venete," p. 10 and n. 1; Andrea Dandolo, *Chronica per extensum descripta a. 46-128 d. C.,* ed. Ester Pastorello, in R.I.S.², XII, i, 317; Pietro Giustinian, *Venetiarum historia vulgo Pietro Iustiniano Iustiniani filio adiudicata,* ed. Roberto Cessi and Fanny Bennato (Venice, 1964), p. 179; Andrea da Mosto, *I dogi di Venezia nella vita publica e privata* (Milan, 1960), p. 92.

123. Malipiero, *Annali veneti*, p. 494.

124. Cessi, ed., *Maggior Consiglio*, II, 44. Repeated, 1303. Queller, *Early Venetian Legislation*, no. 11, p. 62. Extended to ambassadors to papal legates, 1328. Maggior Consiglio, Clericus civicus, 60(108)r.

125. Maggior Consiglio, Novella, 33(44)v. See also Senato, Misti, XXXIII, 98(98)r.

126. Queller, *Early Venetian Legislation*, no. 52, pp. 88-89. (The word I could not make out is "cognitum.") See also "Traité du gouvernement de Venise," p. 289.

127. Queller, *Early Venetian Legislation*, no. 52, pp. 88-89. Ferriguto, *Almorò Barbaro,* pp. 447-49, has published the version of the Great Council, although he has butchered the text with inappropriate punctuation.

128. Dieci, Misto, XXIII, 118(148)r.

129. Pio Paschini, *Tre illustri prelati del Rinascimento: Ermolao Barbaro, Adriano*

Castellesi, Giovanni Grimani, Lateranum, n.s. 23 (Rome, 1957), pp. 25-28; Ferriguto, *Almorò Barbaro,* pp. 425-26, 429, 436, 445, 455-56, 471.

130. Priuli, *Diarii,* IV, 31-32; Ventura, *Nobiltà e popolo,* pp. 175-76.

131. Maggior Consiglio, Fronesis, 11(11)r; summarized in Thiriet, *Déliberations des assemblèes vénitiennes,* I, 179, no. 410.

132. Lombardo, ed., *Consiglio dei XL,* III, 41, nos. 140-41.

133. Dieci, Misto, V, 78(79)r.

134. Senato, Misti, XXIX, 110(106)v.

135. Ibid., XXX, 147(147)v.

136. Chojnacki, "Trecento Venetian State," p. 196.

137. Noiret, *Documents inédits,* pp. 126-27. Nani was also guilty of extortion.

138. Maggior Consiglio, Leona, 155(159)v.

139. "[O]fficiales doanne non permitterent aliquem extrahere res et mercantias suas nisi in pecuniis numeratis solverint eorum recta et decimas. Et quoniam ipse sanctissime leges et ordines quorumdam malignitate et audatia interrupti sunt et non observantur eque erga omnes." Senato, Terra, VIII, 186(187)r.

140. Ibid., XIII, 19(21)v and 25(27)r.

141. Senato, Mar, XV, 17(28)v-18(29)r. The commanders were also taking the sailors' share of the booty. See p. 210.

142. Priuli, *Diarii,* II, 178.

143. Ibid., IV, 31-32; Ventura, *Nobiltà e popolo,* p. 176.

144. Lane, *Venice,* pp. 160-61 and 365.

145. "[E]t occurat in pluribus quod rectores conveniunt se cum dictis notariis et sociis, et non dant eis aliquod salarium nec expensas prout in commissionibus continetur, et per ipsas conventiones notarii et socii predicti capiunt audatiam et committunt in regiminibus de rebus illicitis et inhonestis. . . ." Senato, Misti, XLV, 120(119)v.

146. Dieci, Misto, XXIII, 131(162)v. A *braccio* was about two feet, although it varied from place to place. Florence Edler, *Glossary of Medieval Terms of Business* (1934; reprint Cambridge, Mass., 1970), p. 52.

147. Dieci, Misto, XXIII, 152(183)r.

148. "Cum antiqui nostri cognoverint esse bonum, ymo necessarium, multis causis et respectibus, et specialiter quod nostri nobiles juvenes facerent se praticos in factis maris, quod quelibet galea a mercato conduceret in numero ballistariorum quatuor pauperes nobiles, et ab aliquo tempore citra non observatur, ymo quod peius est, convenit se cum dictis talibus nobilibus, vz., aut de non dando eis soldum, aut quod teneatur resituere soldum, et etiam alios modos observant qui sunt causa inobservantie dicti ordinis." Ibid., XLVIII, 55(55)r.

149. Ibid., LIV, 82(83)r.

150. Priuli, *Diarii,* I, 325.

151. Gilbert, "Venice in the Crisis of the League of Cambrai," p. 274.

152. Burckhardt, *Civilization of the Renaissance in Italy,* p. 53; Marchesi, "Repubblica di Venezia," p. 87.

153. Picotti, "Lettere di Ludovico Foscarini," p. 30, n. 2.

154. Norwich, *Venice*, p. 175.

155. Maggior Consiglio, Fractus, 85(89)r.

156. Cessi, ed., *Maggior Consiglio*, II, 235.

157. Cessi, *Problemi monetari veneziani*, p. 23, no. 25, cap. 33; Cessi, ed., *Maggior Consiglio*, II, 298.

158. The reference to the index is Roberti, *Magistrature giudiziarie*, III, 262. See especially: II, 74, 95, 211; III, 157, 157-58, 210, 250. Also: II, 108, 109, 148, 158, 206, 289; III, 110(2), 111, 144, 184.

159. See p. 176. Cessi, *Regolazione delle entrate e delle spese*, pp. 206-9, no. 246.

160. Senato, Misti, XXXIII, 18(18)v. See p. 209.

161. See pp. 220-21.

162. Senato, Misti, LXV, 43(43)r.

163. Senato, Misti, XLVI, 68(69)v-69(70)v, 88(89)v, 99(100)v; Thiriet, ed., *Régestes des déliberations du Sénat de Venise*, II, 37, no. 1103-4; II, 42, no. 1127; Noiret, ed., *Documents inédits*, p. 143.

164. Lane, *Venice*, p. 228; Crawford, *Venice*, I, 433. On the general problem of Carrara's friends among the nobility, see Vittorio Lazzarini, "Storie vecchie e nuove intorno a Francesco il Vecchio da Carrara," *Nuovo archivio veneto*, 10 (1895), 325.

165. Senato, Misti, LVIII, 155(159)r, 163(167)v, 164(168)r, 170(174)v, 185 (189)v, 189(193)rv; LIX, 27(29)v; Thiriet, ed., *Régestes des déliberations du Sénat de Venise*, III, 26, no. 2300; 27, nos. 2301 and 2304; 28, nos. 2309-10; 29, nos. 2314 and 2316; 30, no. 2320; 34-35, no. 2338; 44, no. 2376; Noiret, ed., *Documents inédits*, pp. 356-58, 362-63, 369; Thiriet, *Romanie vénitienne*, p. 202; Thiriet, "Le quart et demi di la Romanie," in Goimard, ed., *Venise au temps des galères*, p. 61; Zvi Ankori, "The Living and the Dead: The Story of Hebrew Inscriptions in Crete," *Proceedings of the American Academy for Jewish Research*, 38-39 (1970-71), 82. Both Thiriet and Noiret are sometimes a little inaccurate on details.

166. Senato, Misti, LX, 7(7)v and 21(21)v.

167. Kretschmayr, *Geschichte von Venedig*, III, 363-65; Longworth, *Rise and Fall of Venice*, p. 149.

168. Dieci, Misto, XIII, 71(73)v-72(74)r.

169. Senato, Terra, II, 59(59)r-v.

170. Noiret, ed., *Documents inédits*, p. 452.

171. Dieci, Misto, XVII, 125(167)rv.

172. See pp. 214-15.

173. Dieci, Misto, XXV, 22(57)v.

174. Senato, Terra, XII, 21(21)r-22(22)v.

175. Ibid., 23(23)v.

176. Ibid., 23(23)v-25(25)r.

177. Malipiero, *Annali veneti*, p. 389. I owe the reference to Robert Finlay.

178. Sanuto, *Diarii*, I, 836; Longworth, *Rise and Fall of Venice*, p. 175.

179. Sanuto, *Diarii*, IV, 113; Priuli, *Diarii*, II, 176; Longworth, *Rise and Fall of Venice*, p. 169; Gaeta, "Barbarigo, Agostino," in *Dizionario biografico*, VI, 49.

180. Sanuto, *Diarii*, IV, 203; Finlay, *Politics in Renaissance Venice*, pp. 77-78.

181. Sanuto, *Diarii*, VI, 85-86; Priuli, *Diarii*, II, 359.
182. Priuli, *Diarii*, IV, 31-32; Ventura, *Nobiltà e popolo*, pp. 175-76.
183. Cracco, *Società e stato*, p. 377, n. 1.
184. Senato, Misti, XXVI, 68(68)r-v, 80(80)v, and 81(81)v.
185. Ibid., XXVII, 46(46)rv. See p. 175.
186. Ibid., XXIX, 8(8)r.
187. Ibid., XXX, 118(118)v.
188. Lombardo, ed., *Consiglio dei XL*, nos. 393-94, III, 160-61.
189. Thiriet, ed., *Délibérations des assemblées vénitiennes*, II, 43, no. 813.
190. Senato, Misti, XXXVI, 62(63)v.
191. Ibid., XXXIX, 78(82)r and 124(128)r. The latter is a proceeding against Pietro Morosini.
192. Ibid., XLII, 59(59)v-60(60)r.
193. Ibid., 125(126)v. See p. 209.
194. Ibid., XLIV, 6(7)r; Thiriet, ed., *Régestes des délibérations du Sénat de Venise*, no. 1046, II, 25; Noiret, ed., *Documents inédits*, pp. 126-27.
195. Senato, Misti, XLVII, 138(140)r-v. One of the proposed sentences would have required him to endow dowries for two girls, which suggests that he was accused of deflowering them, but this does not appear in the sentence that was passed.
196. Ibid., XLIX, 103(104)v-104(105)r.
197. Ibid., 122(124)rv.
198. Ibid., L, 16(16)v-17(17)r. The Senate declined to convict Lorenzo Crocco for his part in the quarrel with Ambrosino. Ibid., 17(17)r.
199. Ibid., 18(18)r.
200. Ibid., LI, 57(59)v.
201. Noiret, ed., *Documents inédits*, pp. 238-39. Notice the use of the same pernicious principle by allowing the advocates a share of what they collected.
202. Senato, Misti, LI, 133(136)r.
203. Ibid., LII, 166(166)r and LIII, 84(84)r.
204. Ibid., LIII, 115(115)v-116(116)r.
205. Ibid., 132(132)r.
206. Ibid., LIV, 57(58)v.
207. Ibid., LV, 99(100)v-100(101)r.
208. Maggior Consiglio, Ursa, 90(96)r.
209. Ibid., 92(98)r.
210. Senato Misti, LVIII, 185(189)v; Ankori, "Hebrew Inscriptions in Crete," p. 82.
211. Senato, Misti, LVIII, 185(189)v.
212. Senato, Terra, II, 151(151)v.
213. Ibid., IV, 35(36)v.
214. Dieci, Misto, XVIII, 3(58)v-4(59)r.
215. Senato, Terra, IX, 115(115)r.
216. Sanuto, *Diarii*, III, 74; Priuli, *Diarii*, I, 245-46; Malipiero, *Annali veneti*, p. 720.

217. Priuli, *Diarii*, II, 56. Priuli left the number of years blank, apparently intending to fill it in later.

218. Ibid., I, 217 and II, 56; Sanuto, *Diarii*, III, 39, 813-14, and 835; Senato, Terra, XIII, 147(149)r-148(150)r. See p. 179.

219. Priuli, *Diarii*, II, 176-77; Sanuto, *Diarii*, IV, 181-83.

220. "[C]he ve meteti a pericolo questi che romagnera in officio e rezimento far injustitia, vender la raxon, robar il publico. . . ." Sanuto, *Diarii*, IV, 203. See p. 195.

221. Dieci, Misto, XXIX, 98(159)v-99(160)r.

222. Sanuto, *Diarii*, VI, 162. See p. 180.

223. Ibid., VI, 278; Priuli, *Diarii*, II, 399.

224. Ventura, *Nobiltà e popolo*, p. 179.

225. Senato, Misti, XLI, 111(113)rv.

226. Ibid., XLII, 152(153)r-153(154)v.

227. Ibid., XLIII, 168(167)v.

228. See p. 200. Ankori, "Hebrew Inscriptions in Crete," p. 82.

229. Roberti, *Magistrature giudiziarie*, III, 108.

230. Senato, Misti, XXXIII, 53(53)v.

231. Chojnacki, "Trecento Venetian State," p. 195, n. 24.

232. Roberti, *Magistrature giudiziarie*, II, 95.

233. Maggior Consiglio, Presbiter (copia II), 111(149)rv.

234. Ibid., 117(155)r.

235. Senato, Misti, LV, 13(14)r.

236. Ibid., LVII, 66(68)r.

237. Ibid., LX, 7(7)v and 21(21)v. See p. 194.

238. Senato, Terra, III, 138(140)r.

239. Maranini, *Costituzione di Venezia*, I, 252.

240. Roberti, *Magistrature giudiziarie*, II, 74, 272, 289; III, 30, 110, 157, 184; Avogaria di Comun, Capitulare, I, 8rv.

241. Cozzi, "Authority and Law," p. 307.

242. Thiriet, *Romanie vénitienne*, p. 240. Longworth, *Rise and Fall of Venice*, p. 151.

243. Chambers, *Imperial Age of Venice*, p. 96.

244. Senato, Misti, XXVIII, 11(11)v.

245. Ibid., LVI, 17(19)r; Thiriet, ed., *Régestes des déliberations du Sénat de Venise*, II, 235-36. The son was not bishop of Modone, but a canon.

246. "Quantum nocuerint et noceant justicie tot preces et efficaces pratice que aliquando inhoneste et importune fiunt judicibus et officialibus usque ad eorum domos et alibi extra palatium et extra officia sua omnes intelligunt." Dieci, Misto, XVI, 134(171)r.

247. Senato, Terra, V, 159(159)v.

248. Dieci, Misto, XVI, 207(244)v.

249. Senato, Terra, IX, 115(115)r. See p. 200.

250. Dieci, Misto, XXIV, 99(138)r.

251. Maranini, *Costituzione di Venezia*, II, 124.

252. Roberti, *Magistrature giudiziarie,* II, 195.
253. Cessi, ed., *Maggior Consiglio,* II, 127. The rubric, which says that Giuliano should be *extra Consilium et officia* seems slightly incorrect, since the sentence covers only *officia et regimina.*
254. Avogaria di Comun, Capitulare, I, 14v-15r.
255. "[S]cribendo per multum tempus post suum exitum in quaterno aliquas postas datas camerlengis sine mense vel die." Senato, Misti, XXXI, 44(46)r. See p. 176.
256. Chojnacki, "Trecento Venetian State," p. 195, n. 24.
257. Thiriet, ed., *Déliberations des assemblées vénitiennes,* no. 813, II, 43. See p. 197.
258. Senato, Misti, XXXVI, 94(95)v.
259. Ibid., XL, 106(109)v-107(110)r.
260. Ibid., XLI, 74(77)v-75(78)v.
261. Senato, Terra, III, 188(190)r. See p. 178.
262. Dieci, Misto, XXII, 163(169)v-164(200)r; Malipiero, *Annali veneti,* pp. 675-76. Malipiero is wrong on the amount.
263. Pietro Dolfin, *Annalium Venetorum,* p. 101; Sanuto, *Diarii,* III, 507. Sanuto has him councillor in Canea, Dolfin in Retimo.
264. Senato, Terra, XV, 97(112)v.
265. Lombardo, ed., *Consiglio dei XL,* III, 13-14, nos. 34-36.
266. Senato, Misti, LI, 116(119)v-117(120)r.
267. Dieci, Misto, XVIII, 35(90)v and 37(92)r. This is a rare case where the Venetians showed some consciousness that a defendant should be punished according to the law in effect at the time of his crime, rather than in an ad hoc manner. They were probably no worse in this respect than others; the purpose here, of course, is not to prove the Venetians worse than others, but merely no better.
268. Ibid., 136(191)r. Contarini received the same sentence under the new law as Querini had under the old one.
269. Ibid., XXI, 70(106)r.
270. Ibid., XXII, 7(42)r.
271. Ibid., 60(96)r.
272. Ibid., XXIV, 180(219)v. The assumption, of course, is not absolutely certain.
273. Senato, Misti, XXVIII, 21(21)v.
274. Ibid., XXX, 118(118)v. See pp. 196-97.
275. Ibid., XXXIII, 18(18)v.
276. Ibid., XLII, 125(126)v.
277. Ibid., XLVI, 28(29)r.
278. Ibid., LVI, 66(68)v; summarized in Thiriet, ed., *Régestes des déliberations du Sénat de Venise,* no. 2044, II, 241.
279. Thiriet, ed., *Régestes des déliberations du Sénat de Venise,* no. 2065, II, 244-45; no. 2079, II, 248.
280. Senato, Misti, LX, 24(24)r.

281. "Sono venute ad orechie de la signoria nostra molte exclamation et querelle de molti galioti tornati de armata che tuti le botine et prede che i hano facto i sono sta tolte da li suo capi, i qual non se contentando de la parte a loro spectante hano et tolta quella di galioti contra ogni debito de rason et quod peius est alguni etiam sono ita injuriadi et batudi et tolti per la forza la parte sua. . . ." Senato, Mar, XV, 17(28)v-18(29)r.

282. After reading Ruggiero I am quite certain that my suspicion that sexual crimes were not taken very seriously is correct. *Violence in Early Renaissance Venice*, pp. 156-59 and passim.

283. Chojnacki remarks: "[I]f nobles were not especially inclined toward homicide and theft, they made up for it by their tendencies toward more casual violence and more subtle theft—such as exploiting their official positions." "Trecento Venetian State," p. 199. The registers of the Ten, it is true, are full of sexual (and homosexual) offenses on the part of nobles, as well as commoners, but we are concerned here only with those that involve an abuse of patrician powers.

VII. OTHER UNCIVIL BEHAVIOR

1. Diehl, *République patricienne*, p. 103.
2. Molmenti, *Venice*, part 2, I, 20.
3. Besta, *Senato veneziano*, p. 102.
4. Poggio-Bracciolini, *In laudem rei publicae Venetorum*, p. 934. For other examples of some closely held secrets, see Besta, *Senato veneziano*, pp. 103-4.
5. Fasoli, "Storia di Venezia," p. 48.
6. Gilbert, "Venice in the Crisis of the League of Cambrai," p. 275. Priuli says that the secrets of the Ten and the Senate were known within two days, and he places the blame, for the most part, on aged senators. *Diarii*, IV, 33.
7. Burckhardt, *Civilization of the Renaissance in Italy*, p. 53. I have called attention to the shrewd advice offered to an inexperienced ambassador that he should plant spies on his own government in order to be informed. Donald E. Queller, "How to Succeed as an Ambassador: A Sixteenth Century Venetian Document," *Studia gratiana*, 15 (1972), 662 and 669-70. Burckhardt introduces his paragraph, however, with an example of the unwillingness of young nobles to talk about political matters.
8. Fasoli, "Storia di Venezia," pp. 114-15.
9. Caroldo, *Venetia*, 267v. Giusti is called "Messer Luca Giusti," but Giusti was a *cittadino* name (da Mosto, *Archivio di Stato*, I, 75), not noble (ibid., I, 72), and the fact that he was not deprived of councils suggests that he probably was a *cittadino*. Granted, da Mosto's list of nobles names is imperfect.
10. "Cum introducta sit quedam consuetudo periculosa, videlicet quod res que tractantur et deliberantur in nostro consilio rogatorum de quibus mandatur credentia non tenentur secrete, ymo extra ipsum concilium referuntur et propallantur cum detrimento et onere non mediocri. . . ." Senato, Terra, II, 117(117)r.

11. Dieci, Misto, XV, 192(193)r.

12. Ibid., XVII, 147(188)v and 150(191)rv; Malipiero, *Annali veneti*, p. 661; Sagredo, "Leggi venete intorno agli ecclesiastici," pp. 122-23.

13. Dieci, Misto, XIX, 69(109)v.

14. Malipiero is not absolutely clear. I think he means the bishop's brother, but, if so, which one of them? Probably Andrea, since Alvise was convicted only for failing to report what was going on.

15. Dieci, Misto, XIX, 82(122)v-85(125)v and 90(130)r; Malipiero, *Annali veneti*, pp. 668-70.

16. Dieci, Misto, 104(143)v and 110(149)r-111(150)r; XXI, 11(47)v. There were also proceedings involving a factor of the duke and various members of the household of the duke's ambassador.

17. "El Dose ha parla in Pregadi cerca la secretezza delle cose che se tratta, e s' ha lamenta che le se publica per le piazze; talche e necessario andar purassa volte in Consegio di X, o. ogn' un puo' se lamenta." Malipiero, *Annali veneti*, p. 382.

18. Sanuto, *Diarii*, I, 402; Finlay, *Politics in Renaissance Venice*, p. 218.

19. Archivio di Stato di Modena, Archivio Segreto Estense, Cancelleria Estero: ambasciatori a Venezia, b. 9, c. 13, 32, and 40. I have not seen this collection, but owe the information to the kindness of Robert Finlay.

20. Ibid., b. 10, c. 17, 19, 23, and 31. Malipiero reports that the duke could muster sixty votes in the Senate. *Annali veneti*, p. 530. This reference is also due to Finlay, though I have, of course, seen it.

21. Archivio di Stato di Modena, Archivio Segreto Estense, Cancelleria Estero: ambasciatori a Venezia, b. 10, c. 17.

22. Malipiero, *Annali veneti*, p. 493. The reference is from Finlay.

23. "[O]gni secreto che se trattava nel consiglio di pregadi, de qual importantia se fusse, lo duca de Milano per danari o per altra suo arte lo intendeva. . . ." Priuli, *Diarii*, I, 90.

24. Dieci, Misto, XXVIII, 34(77)v.

25. Compilazioni leggi, leggi, b 236, no. 443. I did not find the full document in the registers of the Ten, but did find a short synopsis at Dieci, Misto, XXX, 118(163)v.

26. Senato, Terra, II, 117(117)r. The act of 1459 doubling the penalty also applied to the College. See p. 213.

27. Dieci, Misto, XX, 20(58)r.

28. Ibid., XXI, 29(65)v.

29. Malipiero, *Annali veneti*, p. 389. Finlay's reference.

30. Dieci, Misto, XXXVIII, 44(87)rv.

31. "Ex quo sequitur hec pessima consequentia ut cives nostri, tam de hoc consilio, quam de collegio, quandoque ex hoc respectu non audeant ita libero ore loqui, dicere et consulere super rebus et materiis que preponuntur, sicut facerent si certo scirent teneri sub illa credentia, que merito debetur huic consilio. . . ." Ibid., XXVIII, 52(95)rv.

32. Ibid., 65(108)v.

33. Ibid., XII, 75(76)v.
34. Ibid., 88(89)v.
35. Ibid., 184(185)v.
36. Ibid., 163(164)v.
37. Ibid., XIII, 10(11)r. Misdated 1440 in Besta, *Senato veneziano*, p. 105.
38. Dieci, Misto, XV, 192(193)r. See p. 213.
39. Ibid., XVIII, 10(65)r.
40. Ibid., XXII, 163(199)r.
41. Archivio di Stato di Modena, Archivio Segrato Estense, Cancelleria Estero: ambasciatori a Venezia, b. 9, c. 32. Information from Prof. Finlay.
42. Dieci, Misto, XXVII, 132(174)v.
43. Ibid., XXVIII, 52(95)rv. See p. 218.
44. Queller, *Early Venetian Legislation*, no. 43, p. 82.
45. Vincent Ilardi, "Fifteenth Century Diplomatic Documents in Western European Archives and Libraries (1450-1494)," *Studies in the Renaissance*, 9 (1962), 78-79.
46. Queller, ed., "Newly Discovered Legislation," no. 40, p. 50.
47. Queller, *Early Venetian Legislation*, no. 66, pp. 98-99.
48. Ibid., no. 72, p. 103.
49. Ibid., no. 76, p. 106; Queller, *Office of the Ambassador*, pp. 121-22 and 125-26. The showing of the first of a series of instructions or mandates, the others of which are concealed (and the second, and so on) is a deceptive device which ought to be discouraged as destructive of the trust necessary for fruitful negotiation.
50. Queller, *Early Venetian Legislation*, no. 91, pp. 120-21.
51. Sanuto, *Diarii*, I, 534.
52. See p. 16.
53. Caroldo, *Venetia*, 350rv; Lazzarini, "Storie intorno a Francesco il Vecchio da Carrara," pp. 325-52; Lazzarini, "Antiche leggi venete," p. 15; Besta, *Senato veneziano*, p. 103; Crawford, *Venice*, I, 426; Dieci, Misto, VI, 103(104)rv.
54. Lazzarini, "Storie intorno a Francesco il Vecchio da Carrara," p. 330. Of course it had already proved its mettle against Doge Falier.
55. Navagero, *Storia veneziana*, col. 1070.
56. Zorzi Dolfin, *Chronica*, 262v.
57. Dieci, Misto, VIII, 97(98)r and 98(99)r.
58. Dieci, Misto, VIII, 124(125)r.
59. "Quia super bancho ubi sedent in ecclesia Sancti Marci nobiles nostri apud pillam ab aqua sancta multociens narrantur de rebus secretis consiliorum nostrorum que audiuntur ab aliis circumstantibus qui non sunt de nostris consiliis cum non parvo periculo agendorum nostrorum. . . ." Ibid., X, 78(82)r.
60. Ibid., XIII, 23(24)r.
61. Ibid., XV, 191(192)v. Besta notes that the Republic never did solve the problem of *papalisti* sending state secrets to Rome in their eagerness to curry favor with the pope. *Senato veneziano*, p. 215.

62. See pp. 194-95. Dieci, Misto, XVIII, 125(167)rv.

63. Dieci, Misto, XIX, 79(119)r. See pp. 214-15.

64. Dieci, Misto, XIX, 184(226)r.

65. Dieci, Misto, XX, 10(48)v. Published in modern Italian in Romanin, *Storia di Venezia,* VI, 116. Also in Molmenti, "Relazioni tra patrizi veneziani e diplomatici stranieri," pp. 38-39. Both incorrectly date it 1481. They have taken the act from the sixteenth-century Capitular delli Inquisitori di Stato, whereas I have used the original register, which leaves no question that 1480 is correct. M. A. R. de Maulde La Clavière is wrong on the amount of the fine. *La diplomatie au temps de Machiavel,* II (Paris, 1892), n. 2.

66. Longworth, *Rise and Fall of Venice,* p. 168.

67. Dieci, Misto, XXII, 99(135)v.

68. Ibid., XXIII, 14(44)v and 18(47)rv.

69. Ibid., XXIII, 17(46)v and 20(49)v.

70. Ibid., 20(49)v.

71. Ibid., 18(47)r.

72. Ibid., 102(132)r.

73. Ibid., 136(167)rv.

74. Ibid., 136(167)v.

75. Ibid., XXIV, 53(92)v.

76. Ibid., 54(93)r.

77. Ibid.

78. See the marginal notes in a later hand in the registers, nn. 70-72 above.

79. See p. 212.

80. Avogaria di Comun, Capitulare, I, 18rv. For earlier legislation, see Roberti, *Magistrature giudiziarie,* II, 159, and Cessi, ed., *Maggior Consiglio,* II, 85.

81. "[A]liquando advocatores communis sunt negligentes in facere observare consiliarios aliquod consilium vel capitulare." Maggior Consiglio, Capricornus, 39(135)rv.

82. Lombardo, ed., *Consiglio dei XL,* no. 125, II, 37. The law was enacted in 1323, but followed a very old custom. Queller, *Early Venetian Legislation,* no. 18, pp. 64-65. Perhaps as a result of this case it was reinforced later in 1349. Ibid., no. 25, pp. 67-68.

83. Lombardo, ed., *Consiglio dei XL,* no. 133, II, 39. Reaffirmation of the law in 1349. Senato, Misti, XXV, 60(60)r.

84. Senato, Misti, LIX, 70(72)rv.

85. "Cum officia huius civitatis nostre optime ordinata sint, sed per ea que quotidie videntur executiones ordinum nostrorum non fiunt in maximum dannum et preiudicium nostri communis." Senato, Terra, I, 113(114)v.

86. "[D]icta optima pars propter malam consuetudinem non observatur, quia neque officiales solidant capsam, neque portant denarios, neque consiliarius mensis accusat, et omnes faciunt sicut volunt, non obstantibus ordinibus et partibus istius consilii. . . ." Senato, Terra, I, 149(150)r.

87. Ibid., III, 124(126)r.

88. "Quamquam sit lex antiqua quod omnes rectores debeant attendere et

observare bona fide et sine fraude omnia que sibi mandantur per dominium, tamen videtur quod disobedientia aliquorum adeo creverit, ut nichil valeant mandata dominii, sed oporteat sibi penam imponi per officium advocatorum communis. Quod quidem apud subditos nostros multum detrahit honori et reputationi dominii nostri, ut plus auctoritatis et potentie habeant libre C et unus advocator communis quam iuramentum et obedientia principis et dominii Venetiarum, cuius honoris omnis rector et officialis et iudex iuravit. . . . Et si huiusmodi periculosus morbus, quis usque ad iudices et officiales Venetiarum pervenit paulatim permittitur crescere, poterit evenire aliquo tempore aliquis casus, qui verteretur in damnum et ruinam nostri status, ad quod primitus obvidandum est quam eveniat et amputare hunc morbum a sano corpore nostro." Dieci, Misto, XVI, 79(116)v.

89. Ibid., 124(161)r.

90. Senato, Terra, VI, 71(72)r.

91. Dieci, Misto, XXVI, 35(63)v.

92. Thiriet, ed., *Délibérations des assemblées vénitiennes*, no. 463, I, 191.

93. Ruggiero, *Violence in Early Renaissance Venice*, p. 128.

94. Senato, Misti, XXIV, 115(115)v.

95. Ibid., XXXI, 33(35)r.

96. Ibid., LX, 209(209)v.

97. Daniele di Chinazzo, *Cronica de la guerra da veniciani a zenovesi*, ed. Vittorio Lazzarini, in *Monumenti storici pubblicati dalla Deputazione di Storia Patria per le Venezie*, n.s., XI (Venice, 1958), 223-28; Navagero, *Storia veneziana*, cols. 1069-70; Raphaynus de Caresinis, *Chronica*, ed. E. Pastorello, in R.I.S.², XII, ii (1922), 58-59 and 61; Setton, *Papacy and the Levant*, I, 323-24; Lane, *Venice*, p. 195; Cicogna, *Inscrizioni veneziane*, VI, 97; Senato, Misti, XXXVIII, 56(57)r and 57(58)v.

98. Senato, Misti, XXXVIII, 146(147)rv.

99. Ibid., XLI, 111(113)rv.

100. Senato, Terra, V, 12(13)v-13(14)r.

101. Dieci, Misto, XVI, 79(116)v. See p. 226.

102. Ibid., 198(235)rv.

103. Ibid., XVII, 174(215)r.

104. Ibid., XIX, 104(144)v.

105. Ibid., XXIV, 5(45)r.

106. Ibid., XXVI, 93(121)v.

107. Ibid., XXVII, 157(199)v.

108. Sanuto, *Diarii*, V, 28.

109. Cessi, ed., *Maggior Consiglio*, II, 102.

110. Queller, *Early Venetian Legislation*, no. 49, p. 86.

111. *Relazioni degli ambasciatori veneti al Senato*, ed. by Arnoldo Segarizzi, I (Bari, 1912), 284.

112. Ibid., III, i, 97-98; *Relazioni degli ambasciatori veneti al Senato*, ed. Eugenio Albèri, ser. 2 (Florence, 1846), III, 137. On this and the note above see Queller, "Development of Ambassadorial Relazioni," p. 187.

113. Queller, *Early Venetian Legislation*, no. 87, p. 116. See my comments on mandates. Ibid., pp. 45-46.

114. Dieci, Misto, XIX, 115(155)v.

115. See pp. 163-66.

116. Bariša Krecić, "Crime and Violence in the Venetian Levant: A Few Fourteenth Century Cases," *Iz Zbornica radova Vizantološkog Instituta,* 16 (1975), 125.

117. Senato, Misti, XXVII, 111(112)v.

118. "[N]on bene fecit ratas. . . ."

119. Senato, Misti, XXVIII, 81(81)v.

120. Ibid., XXXVIII, 47(48)v; Setton, *Papacy and the Levant,* I, 325.

121. Senato, Misti, XL, 34(37)rv.

122. "Cum necessarium sit providere quod patroni galearum a mercato obediant et faciant iuxta mandatum capitaneorum, consideratis periculis et inconvenientiis que possunt occurrere et occurrunt quotidie propter inobedientiam dictorum patronorum." Ibid., XLII, 90(91)r.

123. Ibid., LVIII, 82(86)r.

124. Ibid., LIX, 166(168)v.

125. Ibid., LX, 50(50)v.

126. Ibid., 236(236)r.

127. Senato, Terra, XIII, 29(31)v-30(32)r.

128. Priuli, *Diarii,* IV, 158, 161, 163-64, 232-33; Sanuto, *Diarii,* VIII, 528-29, 534, 550.

129. Dieci, Misto, XI, 115(121)v.

130. Ibid., XVII, 182(223)v.

131. Ibid., XXV, 103(138)v

132. Ibid., XXVIII, 122(165)v-123(166)v.

133. Priuli, *Diarii,* II, 236.

134. See p. 226.

135. Finlay, *Politics in Renaissance Venice*, pp. 217-18; Priuli, *Diarii,* II, 77-78 and IV, 161, 163, 232; Sanuto, *Diarii,* IX, 411 and XXV, 357.

136. Carlo Guido Mor, "Il procedimento per 'gratiam' nel diritto amministrativo veneziano del sec. XIII," in *Cassiere della Bolla Ducale,* ed. Favaro, p. xlvii; Thayer, *Short History of Venice,* p. 221.

137. Maggior Consiglio, Presbiter, (copia II), 23(61)r-24(62)r; Ibid., Fronesis, 79(79)v-80(80)r; ibid., Leona, 220(225)v.

138. Ibid., Clericus civicus, 132(180)r.

139. Ruggiero, *Violence in Early Renaissance Venice*, pp. 129 and 132.

140. Senato, Misti, XXX, 35(35)r and XXXIV, 51(51)r; Cappelletti, *Relazione storica sulle magistrature venete,* pp. 46-47; Dieci, Misto, XXIII, 55(85)v, and 57(87)r; Sanuto, *Diarii,* III, 159.

141. Tenenti, "Sérénissime République," p. 172.

142. Dieci, Misto, IX, 100(104)rv; XV, 42(43)r and 63(64)v; XXVII, 98(140)r, 99(141)r, and 101(143)r; XXII, 104(140)r.

143. Ruggiero, *Violence in Early Renaissance Venice*, p. 134.

144. Dieci, Misto, XIX, 8(48)v-9(49)r.

145. Ibid., XXII, 113(149)v.

146. Ibid., XXIII, 167(199)rv.

147. Priuli, *Diarii*, I, 92. He sued for pardon five years later, but failed to obtain the unanimous support of the Ten. Sanuto, *Diarii*, V, 20.

148. Senato, Misti, LX, 92(92)v-93(93)r.

149. Dieci, Misto, XXIV, 15(55)rv.

150. Sanuto, *Diarii*, I, 1006, 1011, and 1045-46.

151. Dieci, Misto, XVII, 175(216)r. Also see a case against a judge for insulting the Paduan ambassador. Ibid., XXVII, 11(153)r.

152. For examples of violence against officials in connection with smuggling, see p. 168.

153. Ruggiero, *Violence in Early Renaissance Venice*, p. 140.

154. Ibid., pp. 77-78; Longworth, *Rise and Fall of Venice*, p. 90.

155. Ruggiero, *Violence in Early Renaissance Venice*, p. 144. Ruggiero points to a parallel case where a commoner slapped his victim, but received a higher penalty than the noble who stabbed his.

156. Ibid., p. 141.

157. Chojnacki, "Trecento Venetian State," p. 194.

158. Senato, Misti, XXX, 145(145)v; Lane, *Venice*, pp. 190-91.

159. Chojnacki, "Trecento Venetian State," p. 195, n. 24.

160. Ruggiero, *Violence in Early Renaissance Venice*, p. 134-35.

161. Senato, Terra, III, 156(158)v.

162. Dieci, Misto, XX, 17(55)r. There is a +, presumably erroneous, beside a *pars* which did not pass.

163. Ibid., XXIII, 46(76)v-47(77)r; Malipiero, *Annali veneti*, p. 681.

164. Dieci, Misto, XXVI, 62(90)rv.

165. Dieci, Misto, XXVII, 176(218)r; Sanuto, *Diarii*, I, 1015.

166. Dieci, Misto, XXVIII, 110(153)v-111(154)r and Sanuto, *Diarii*, III, 736. See p. 168.

167. Norwich, *Venice*, p. 189.

168. Chojnacki, "Trecento Venetian State," p. 194.

169. Ruggiero, *Violence in Early Renaissance Society*, pp. 146-47.

170. Dieci, Misto, XIX, 8(48)v and 11(51)r-12(52)r.

171. Ibid., XVII, 166(207)v and 174(215)v.

172. Sanuto, *Diarii*, I, 815.

173. Dieci, Misto, XXIX, 95(156)rv.

174. Ibid., XXVI, 84(112)r.

175. Ibid., XXIII, 119(149)v and 128(158)r.

176. Ibid., XXVII, 43(84)v.

177. Ruggiero, *Violence in Early Renaissance Venice*, pp. 142 and 150.

178. "Quenam digna magis visu spectacula queso, / Maiorque maiestas rogo. / Quando cum suscepit venerandos curia patres. / Omnesque suo sedent loco. . . . Non illic clamor: non stulte iurgia lingue: / Non acris altercatio. /

Omnia sedata fiunt, ac mente quieta, / Animoque tranquillo, ut decet." Arrigoni, *Poema*, 9r.

179. Guerdan, *Sérénissime*, p. 172.

180. Cessi, ed., *Maggior Consiglio*, II, 82.

181. Maggior Consiglio, Fractus, 64(69)r.

182. Maggior Consiglio, Presbiter (copia II), 14(15)r. Maranini fails to modernize the date of this act. *Costituzione di Venezia*, II, 104.

183. "Et a poco tempore citra sit introductum quod, tam in consiliis rogatorum et XL^ta, quam collegiis, illi nostri nobiles qui in dictis locis congregati sunt, cum debeant sedere et audire illos qui proponunt, nec respondere nisi ad arrengam, nunc per quandam malam consuetudinem surgunt, et stantes in pedibus vadunt sursum et deorsum, loquendum et exturbando alios sedentes, et aliquando ante dominio veniunt turbati cum modica reverentia, nec valet eis dicere quod sedeant aut taceant." Maggior Consiglio, Ursa, 130(136)v.

184. Dieci, Misto, XIV, 67(71)v.

185. Cappelletti, *Relazione storica sulle magistrature venete*, p. 48.

186. Cessi, ed., *Maggior Consiglio*, II, 20. Maranini dates it 1250. *Costituzione di Venezia*, I, 223. See also pp. 206 and 224.

187. Crawford, *Venice*, I, 229.

188. Caroldo, *Venetia*, 296v; Ruggiero, *Violence in Early Renaissance Venice*, p. 128. The latter took it from the Raspe.

189. Dieci, Misto, XII, 155(156)v-156(157)r.

190. Ibid., XV, 32(33)r. See p. 240.

191. "Cum propter multos disordines qui in nostro maiori consilio per nobiles nostros committebantur, ad quos regulandos diversis temporibus, tam in maiori consilio, quam in isto consilio X et aliis consiliis nostris, multi ordines capti fuerint." Ibid., 64(65)v.

192. Ibid., XXIV, 82(121)v-83(122)r.

193. Ibid., XXV, 12(47)r.

194. Ibid., XXVII, 10(51)v; Malipiero, *Annali veneti*, p. 698. Priuli confused the case with another, but quickly corrected himself. *Diarii*, I, 68 and 77. See also Sanuto, *Diarii*, I, 303 and 323, and Malipiero, *Annali veneti*, II, 701-2. Longworth, *Rise and Fall of Venice*, p. 175.

195. Dieci, Misto, XXIX, 16(76)v.

196. Contarini, *De magistratibus*, 33r (Lewkenor, p. 74); Hodgson, *Venice in the Thirteenth and Fourteenth Centuries*, p. 572.

197. Medin, *Storia di Venezia nella poesia*, p. 44.

198. Besta, *Senato veneziano*, pp. 228-29. The quotation from a humanist of Thessalonica in praise of the Senate, however, is not found in either of the places cited.

199. Senato, Misti, XVII, 60(60)v.

200. Dieci, Misto, XII, 22(23)v.

201. Ibid.

202. Ibid., 90(91)r.

203. Ibid., XIII, 148(150)r.

204. "Nihil est quod magis turbet et noceat rebus status nostri quam strepitus et clamor qui fit in consilio rogatorum cum aliquis est in arenga cum impedimento tacentium et audire volentium et parva obedientia dominii iubentis ut taceatur." Ibid., XIX, 30(70)r.

205. Ibid., 48(88)r.

206. Sanuto, *Diarii*, III, 406.

207. Ibid., VII, 191; Dieci, Misto, XXXI, 172(219)v-173(220)r; Finlay, *Politics in Renaissance Venice*, p. 229.

208. Sanuto, *Diarii*, IX, 292; Finlay, *Politics in Renaissance Venice*, p. 229.

209. Ruggiero, *Violence in Early Renaissance Venice*, p. 128.

210. See pp. 243-44.

211. Dieci, Misto, XXV, 41(76)v.

212. Ibid., XXVI, 79(107)v-80(108)r.

213. Ibid., XVI, 181(218)rv.

214. Senato, Terra, VIII, 65(66)v.

215. Dieci, Misto, XXVII, 192(235)r.

216. Ibid., IX, 172(176)v-173(177)r.

217. Ibid., V, 91(92)v, 107(108)v-108(109)v. This is one of the rare occasions where the offensive words are given.

218. Ibid., XIII, 88(90)4-89(91)r. See a somewhat similar, but perhaps more innocent, case of four councillors who wrote letters in favor of Martin, bishop of Ceneda, to the men of that community and to the *podestà* of Serravalle whereby Perazio Malipiero lost the bishopric. Senato, Misti, XLIII, 169(168)r.

219. Dieci, Misto, XXII, 106(142)rv.

220. Senato, Terra, VIII, 41(42)r.

221. Dieci, Misto, XXIV, 199(238)r.

222. Ibid., XXVIII, 162(205)v-163(206)r.

223. Edward Muir, "Images of Power: Art and Pageantry in Renaissance Venice," *American Historical Review*, 84 (1979), 40 and n. 61.

CONCLUSION

1. Romano believes that *grazie* "allowed the leaders of the regime to make adjustments of the law without undermining the notion that the law was inviolate. . . ." "Grazie in Venice," pp. 266-68. The supposed inviolability of the law is another aspect of the myth of Venice. Venetian laws were quite literally a joke. He is on firmer ground, I think, in arguing that *grazie* (and other forms of patronage) encouraged the patricians to work within the system. Still, few writers display toward Chicago's Daley machine the reverence that so many Venetian historians feel for the Venetian elite, which used very similar methods.

2. In thirteenth-century England the penalty for raping a virgin was blinding and castration. Henry de Bracton, *On the Laws and Customs of England*, trans. with revisions and notes by Samuel E. Thorne, II (Cambridge, Mass.,

1968), 414-15. John Marshall Carter informs me, however, that the English law too was not enforced.

3. John Law has pointed out that historians of Venice have obscured the force of familial interests in opposition to the laws, for they have concentrated upon councils and magistracies or upon the ideas of Venetian and foreign political theorists, and they have been less concerned with the actual behavior of Venetian nobles. John Easton Law, "Age Qualifications and the Venetian Constitution: the Case of the Capello Family," *Papers of the British School at Rome,* 39 (1971), 125. On the general problem of conflicts between the public interest and the family, see Tenenti, "Famille bourgeoise et idéologie au bas moyen âge," esp. pp. 434-35.

4. Maranini, *Costituzione di Venezia,* II, 254, n. 1.

5. Lane, *Venice,* pp. 185-86.

6. Stanley Chojnacki, "Patrician Women in Early Renaissance Venice," *Studies in the Renaissance,* 21 (1974), 200-201.

7. Muir, *Civic Ritual,* e.g., p. 5.

8. Finlay, *Politics in Renaissance Venice,* e.g., p. 286.

9. Tucci, "Patrizio veneziano mercante e umanista," p. 340.

10. Lestocquoy, *Aux origines de la bourgeoisie,* p. 76.

11. Giovanni Botero, *The Reason of State,* trans. by P. J. and D. P. Waley, with an introd. by D. P. Waley (London, 1956), p. 109. Quoted with approval in *Renaissance Venice,* ed. Hale, p. 14.

12. Haitsma Mulier, *Myth of Venice,* pp. 42-43.

Glossary of Venetian Government and Administration

Advocates. *See* avvocati, avogadori, and avogaria.

Appuntatori. Officials assigned to check on whether other officials and judges were present in their offices at the required times and to assign punti to the absent.

Arsenale. The public shipyard.

Auditori nuovi. Three auditors added in 1410 to complement the auditori vecchi by introducing appeals from the newly acquired lands on terraferma in the Quaranta civile nuova.

Auditori vecchi delle sentenze. Three auditors who introduced appeals in civil cases into the Quaranta, later into the Quaranta civile vecchia. Also called avogadori civili.

Avogadori di comun. Board of three magistrates with a wide variety of functions, including those of state's attorneys. Translated here literally as advocates of the Commune.

Avogaria de intus. The avogadori di comun in their capacity of protecting the rights of the Commune against domestic officials.

Avvocato del proprio. Public attorney before the giudici del proprio.

Baiulo. A title for some colonial governors and of the head of the Venetian colony in Constantinople.

Balestrieri della popa. Bowmen of the quarterdeck. Originally young nobles elected to serve on vessels as bowmen in order to gain experience of sailing and trade. They were paid and maintained by the patron and allowed to carry a small amount of goods for trade free of charge.

Camera degl' imprestiti. Officials who administered the public debt.

The information in the glossary is drawn largely from Giulio Rezasco, *Dizionario del linguaggio italiano storico ed ammistrativo* (Bologna, 1881), and da Mosto, *Archivio di Stato*.

Camera dell' armamento. Office responsible for arming and disarming vessels.

Camera imprestitorum. *See* camera degl' imprestiti.

Camerario. Treasurer.

Capi della Quaranta. The Forty, later each of the three Forties, elected three heads. The heads of the Quaranta criminale were members of the Signoria. Where capi della Quaranta is used without qualification, these heads of the Quaranta criminale are meant.

Capi di sestieri. Six, one for each sestiere, to aid the signori di notte.

Captain-general of the sea. *See* capitano generale.

Capitano. (1) Title of the governor of some colonies, possessing civil and criminal, as well as military authority; (2) commander of a fleet.

Capitano generale. The highest naval command.

Castellano. Guardian of a castle and governor of the castellany.

Cattavere. Three officials responsible for watching over the goods of the state. They also had jurisdiction over the Jews.

Cavaliere. An honorific title of great distinction.

Cazude. *See* ufficiali alle cazude.

Chamber of loans. *See* camera degl' imprestiti.

Cinque alla pace. Magistrates with jurisdiction over minor crimes of the popolani.

College. *See* Pien Collegio.

Collegio. *See* Pien Collegio.

Collegio alle biave. Took over the functions of the ufficiali al frumento in 1349. Composed of the councillors, the heads of the Forty, and the ufficiali al frumento.

Consiglio dei Dieci. The Ten. Established in 1310, it consisted of the elected Ten, the doge, and his six councillors, for a total of seventeen. For important cases a zonta was added.

Consiglio dei Pregadi. The Senate. Consisted of sixty elected members, plus a zonta of twenty, forty, and finally sixty, plus the entire Quaranta, plus various officials who sat in the Senate by virtue of their offices.

Consiglio ducale. *See* Minor Consiglio.

Consoli de' mercanti. They examined ships, the prices of ships, their cargoes (so that they would not be overloaded). They were also concerned with the tithe on ships.

Consuls of the merchants. *See* consoli de' mercanti.

Corte del proprio. *See* giudici del proprio.

Corti di palazzo. Collectively, the giudici del proprio, al forestier, di petizion, dell' esaminador, del procurator, and del mobile.

Council of Forty. *See* Quaranta.

Council of Six. *See* Minor Consiglio.

Councillors. Members of the Minor Consiglio.

Doge. The chief of state, elected for life.

Duca di Candia. Governor of Crete.

Ducal Council. *See* Minor Consiglio.

Duke of Crete. *See* Duca di Candia.

Electors of the year. Three electors for naming the members of the Great Council before membership was extended hereditarily to the entire adult male nobility.

Fondaco dei Tedeschi. The building where trade with German merchants was regulated and supervised.

Giudici del procurator. Magistrates with jurisdiction over cases in which the procurators of St. Mark were plaintiffs or defendants on account of their voluntary jurisdiction over wards and wills.

Giudici del proprio. The direct descendant of the old, undifferentiated curia ducis, originally the giudici del proprio had wide jurisdiction, criminal and civil, which was narrowed as other corti del palazzo were established.

Giudici di petizion. They judged questions of debts, of colleganze, and other matters.

Giustizieri vecchi (e nuovi). Magistrates with jurisdiction over guilds (except wool) and weights and measures.

Grain college. *See* collegio alle biave.

Grain office. *See* ufficiali al frumento.

Great Council. *See* Maggior Consiglio.

Heads of the sestieri. *See* capi di sestieri.

Judges of petitions. *See* giudici di petizion.

Judges of the palace. *See* corti di palazzo.

Judges of the procurator. *See* giudici del procurator.

Lieutenant. *See* luogotenente.

Loan official. *See* camera degl' imprestiti.

Lords of the night. *See* signori di notte.

Luogotenente. Governor in Cyprus.

Maggior Consiglio. The sovereign assembly. Although it yielded many of the most important functions to the Senate, it continued to elect to most offices. After the reform of 1297–98 it consisted of all adult male nobles.

Mano. The word has other uses in Venice, but is used here only for a nominating committee.

Massari della zecca. Directors of the Mint. Massari al oro and massari al argento.

Minor Consiglio. The six councillors of the doge. All significant acts, including the opening of correspondence, had to be done by the doge in the presence of at least four councillors. Also called the Ducal Council and the Council of Six. From an early date the three heads of the Forty were joined to the Minor Consiglio and the doge to form the Signoria.

Mintmaster of gold. *See* massari della zecca.

Monte vecchio. *See* camera degl' imprestiti.

New auditors. *See* auditori nuovi.

New justices. *See* giustizieri vecchi (e nuovi).

Nobeli di galia. *See* balestrieri della popa.

Office of armament. *See* pagatori del armamento.

Officials of accounts. *See* ufficiali alle rason vecchie, rason nuove, e rason nuovissime.

Officials of armaments. *See* camera dell' armamento.

Officials of butchershops. *See* ufficiali alle beccherie.

Officials of cloth of gold. *See* ufficiali ai panni d' oro.

Officials of public loans. *See* camera degl' imprestiti.

Officials of the night. *See* signori di notte.

Officials of the salt office. *See* provveditori al sal.

Officials of the wine tax. *See* ufficiali al dazio del vin.

Old justices. *See* giustizieri vecchi (e nuovi).

Pagatori del armamento. Four, later five, officials who attended to the economic administration of warfare.

Patrone of a galley. The merchant who leased a galley at public auction.

Patroni dell' Arsenale. Immediate supervisors of the Arsenale under the general direction of the provveditori.

Pien Collegio. The cabinet or probouleutic body of the Senate, composed of the Signoria and three boards of savi.

Podestà. A title of some provincial governors.

Pregadi. *See* Senato.

Primi. The most important and influential politicians.

Procuratori di San Marco. Eventually nine procurators elected for life, responsible originally for the Basilica, later treasurers of the Republic and custodians of private trusts. After the doge the most respected officials in Venice.

Provisor. See provveditore.

Provveditore. Provincial governor. Often combined with military command. There also were various provveditori in domestic offices.

Provveditori al cottimo. Venetian officials overseeing the accounts of the consuls of Alexandria, Damascus, London, and Constantinople concerning the cottimo, a 2 percent tax on the goods shipped from those places to Venice.

Provveditori al sal. Four provisors with jurisdiction over the production of salt, its acquisition from non–Venetian territories, the fixing of salt prices, and the prevention of contraband salt. The provveditori collected a lot of money, which financed much public building.

Provveditori alle biave. Three provisors, established in 1365, to oversee the accounts of the ufficiali al frumento and to cooperate with the collegio alle biave in supplying the city with grain.

Provveditori del Comune. Superintendents of commerce, navigation, crafts, streets, and the posts.

Provveditori in armata. Civilian officials of fleets, comparable to the provveditori in campo with the armies.

Provveditori sopra le camere. Three officials over the income from terraferma. The office was instituted in 1449.

Quaranta. The Council of Forty, which became the appeals court of Venice. The original council multiplied to three: the Quaranta criminale, the Quaranta civile vecchia (appeals from within Venice), and the Quaranta civile nuova (appeals originating outside Venice). Members served six months each in the Quaranta civile nuova, the Quaranta civile vecchia, and the Quaranta criminale. The Quaranta entered the Senate in 1324. Later only the Quaranta criminale had membership in the Senate. The Quaranta criminale also approved the accession of young nobles to the Great Council.

Rector. *See* rettore.

Rettore. Generic term for a governor of a subject city or territory.

Salinario. *See* provveditori al sal.

Salt officials. *See* provveditori al sal.

Savi. A loose term, which signifies not only members of the three boards of savi but was also used to signify the members of ad hoc commissions.

Savi agli ordini. One of the three boards of savi. Five savi originally responsible for maritime affairs. The office became a training ground in the Pien Collegio for politically promising young patricians.

Savi del consiglio (or del Consiglio dei Pregadi). Another of the three boards of savi. Eventually fixed at six. Alternated in an active role on a weekly basis. The savi del consiglio were the most prestigious and powerful of the three boards of savi, clearly among the primi.

Savi del mar. See savi agli ordini.

Savi di terraferma. Another of the three boards of savi. Five savi, each with a special function.

Savi grandi. See savi del consiglio.

Senato. The chief deliberative assembly, consisting of a basic sixty, a zonta of sixty, the Quaranta (later the Quaranta criminale), and about 140 ex officio members. More properly called the Consiglio dei Pregadi: Senato was a term adopted under the influence of classical humanism.

Signori di notte. Six magistrates basically in charge of enforcing law and order at night, but also receiving jurisdiction over various crimes committed at any time.

Signoria. The probouleutic body of the Maggior Consiglio. It consisted of the doge, the Council of Six, and the three heads of the Quaranta.

Small Council. See Minor Consiglio.

Solutores delle camere nostre de' armamenti. *See* pagatori dell' armamento.

Sopracomito. Commander of a galley.

Sopraconsoli. Three judges over bankruptcies and over the Jewish pawnbrokers.

Straordinario. I believe this refers to the ufficiali all' estraordinario or della tavola da mare, who collected import and export taxes on merchandise carried by sea.

Supraconsuls. See sopraconsoli.

Syndici (or sindici inquisitori). Extraordinary officials who were sent to the provinces to investigate the conduct of the regular officials.

Tavola da mare. See ternaria vecchia e nuova.

Ten. See Consiglio dei Dieci.

Ternaria vecchia e nuova. Officials responsible for import and export duties on oil, timber, and some other items. Ternaria comes from taola (tavola) da mare.

Tractator. One appointed to negotiate on behalf of the Commune.

Ufficiali ai panni d'oro. Officials responsible for seeing that cloth of gold was genuine. They placed a seal on the cloths.

Ufficiali al dazio del vin. Four, later five, officials who collected the tax on wine.

Ufficiali al frumento. Three officials in charge of the camera del frumento. Lost their role after 1349 to the collegio alle biave, of which they were a part.

Ufficiali alle beccherie. Three, after 1363 four, officials charged with the provision of meat, the tax on it, its soundness, and its weight and cost.

Ufficiali alle cazude. Three officials responsible for collecting overdue direct taxes. Established by 1474.

Ufficiali alle rason vecchie, rason nuove, e rason nuovissime. Officials responsible for reviewing the accounts of governors and ambassadors and for debtors of the state. Also, after 1394, for supervising the appuntatori.

Vicedomini. Venetian representatives in various subject cities of terraferma.

Vicedomini al Fontego dei Tedeschi. Venetian magistrates over the Fondaco dei Tedeschi. They lived inside the Fondaco.

Vicedomini alla tavola de' Lombardi. Officials responsible for the taxes from terraferma.

Vicedomini of the Lombards. See vicedomini alla tavola de' Lombardi.

Vicedomini of the sea. See tavola da mare.

Zonta (aggiunta). An addition to any body. The zonta of the Senate became permanent. Ad hoc zonte, on the other hand, were employed for serious cases before the Ten.

Bibliography

Ad D. Ducem Venetorum et Consilium Decem. B.M., cl. ital. VII, cod. 363 (=7386), 72r. Satire on Venetian greed.

Albèri, Eugenio, ed. *Relazioni degli ambasciatori veneti al Senato*. 15 vols. Florence, 1839–63. The great collection of sixteenth-century *relazioni*.

Albertini, Rudolf von. *Das florentinische Staatsbewusstsein im Uebergang von der Republik zum Prinzipat*. Bern, 1955. A fine book, but the author sees the reception of the myth of Venice at Florence only after 1494.

Allegri, Francesco. *La summa gloria di Venetia con la summa de le sue victorie, nobiltà, paesi e dignitè et officii et altre nobilissime illustri cose di sue laude e glorie. . . . Dicta est glorie cronice nove Venetorum*. Venice, 1501. Unadulterated myth.

Anderson, Robert T. *Traditional Europe: A Study in Anthropology and History*. Belmont, Calif., 1971.

Ankori, Zvi. "The Living and the Dead: The Story of Hebrew Inscriptions in Crete." *Proceedings of the American Academy for Jewish Research*, 38-39 (1970–71), 1–100.

Archivi di stato italiani, Gli. Bologna, 1944.

Arnaldi, Girolamo. "Andrea Dandolo doge-chronista." In *La storiografia veneziana*, edited by Agostino Pertusi, pp. 217–68. Florence, 1970.

Arnaldi, Girolamo, and Manlio Pastore Stocchi, eds. *Storia della cultura veneta: dal primo Quattrocento al Concilio di Trento*. III, i–iii. Vicenza, 1980–81.

Arrigoni, Francesco. *Poema de omni Venetorum excellentia*. B.M., cl. lat. XII, cod. 145(=4393). Second half of fifteenth century. Myth.

A.S.M. (Milan). P.E., Venezia, cart. 379.

A.S.V. Avogadori di Comun, Capitulare. The dates are not trustworthy.

———. Compilazioni leggi. Highly inaccurate, especially on dates.

———. Consiglio di Dieci, Magnus (Capitolare del Consiglio dei Deici).

———. Dieci, Misto.

———. Maggior Consiglio.

————. Senato, Mar.

————. Senato, Misti.

————. Senato, Terra.

Aymard, Maurice. "La terre ferme." In *Venise au temps des galères,* edited by Jacques Goimard, pp. 125–49. Paris, 1968.

Bailey, F. G. "Gifts and Poison." In *Gifts and Poison,* edited by F. G. Bailey, pp. 1–25. New York, 1971.

Baiocchi, Angelo. "Venezia nella storiografia fiorentina del Cinquecento." *Studi veneziani,* n.s., 3 (1979), 203–81.

Barbaro, Ermolao. *De coelibatu* and *De officio legati.* Edited by Vittore Branca. Florence, 1969.

————. *Epistolae, orationes et carmina.* Edited by Vittore Branca. 2 vols. Florence, 1943.

————. "Orazione funebre di Niccolò Marcello." In *Orazioni, elogi, e vite,* edited by G. A. Molina, I, 62. Venice, 1795.

Barbaro, Francesco. *Centotrenta lettere inedite di Francesco Barbaro.* Edited by R. Sabbadini. Salerno, 1884.

Barbaro, Marco. *Libro dei matrimoni (Nozze dei nobili).* B.M., cl. ital. VII, cod. 156(=8492).

Baron, Hans. "Cicero and the Roman Civic Spirit." *Bulletin of the John Rylands Library of the University of Manchester,* 22 (1938), 72–97.

————. *The Crisis of the Early Italian Renaissance: Civic Humanism and Republican Liberty in an Age of Classicism and Tyranny.* 1st ed., 1955. Rev. ed., Princeton, 1966.

————. "A Forgotten Chronicle of Early Sixteenth Century Venice." *Essays in History and Literature Presented to Stanley Pargellis,* pp. 19–36. Chicago, 1965.

————. *Humanistic and Political Literature of Florence and Venice at the Beginning of the Quattrocento.* Cambridge, Mass., 1955.

Barozzi, Pietro. "Orazione in lode di Cristoforo Moro." In *Orazioni, elogi, e vite,* edited by G. A. Molina, I, 79–80. Venice, 1795.

————. "Orazione recitata a Papa Paolo II della famiglia veneta Barbo in nome suo e della famiglia in morte di Giovanni suo zio paterno Patriarcha di Venezia." In *Orazioni, elogi, e vite,* edited by G. A. Molina, I, 103-27. Venice, 1795.

————. *Il Vescovo Pietro Barozzi e il trattato "De factionibus extinguendis."* Edited by Franco Gaeta. Venice, 1958. Unoriginal treatise based on Aristotle and Bartolus addressed to Bernardo Bembo, governor of faction-ridden Bergamo.

Bartolomaeus. *Epigramma in laudem Venetiarum.* B.M., cl. lat. XII, cod. 210(=4689), 36r.

Baschet, Armand. *La diplomatie vénitienne: Les princes de l'Europe au XVIe siècle.* Paris, 1862.

Beneyto Perez, Juan. *Fortuna de Venecia: Historia di una fama politica.* Madrid, 1947. Wretched mythography, but Beneyto does offer a lot of information on Spanish views of Venice from the sixteenth to the eighteenth centuries often based on ms. sources in Madrid.

Bertaldo, Jacopo. *Splendor Venetorum civitatis conseutudinum.* Edited by F. Schupfer. Bologna, 1901.

Besta, Enrico. "Iacopo Bertaldo e lo Splendor Venetorum Civitatis Consuetudinum." *Nuovo archivio veneto,* 13 (1897), 109–33.

———. *Il Senato veneziano.* Venice, 1899.

Bilinski, Bronislaw. "Venezia nelle peregrinazioni polacche del Cinquecento e lo Sposalizio del Mare di Giovanni Siemusowski (1505)." In *Italia, Venezia e Polonia tra umanesimo e rinascimento,* edited by Mieczyslaw Brahmer, pp. 233–90. Warsaw, 1967.

Biondo, Flavio. *De origine et gestis Venetorum.* In Graevius, *Thes. Italiae,* V¹, cols. 1–26. Based on extracts on Venice from the *Decades.*

———. *Populi Veneti historiarum liber primus.* In *Scritti inediti e rari di Biondo Flavio,* edited by Bartolomeo Nogara. Rome, 1927. The beginning of his unfinished history of Venice desired by Lorenzo Foscarini and at his instigation ordered by the Senate.

Bistort, Giulio. *Il magistrato alle pompe nella Repubblica di Venezia.* Venice, 1912.

Blockmans, Fr. *Het Gentsche staadspatriciaat tot omstreeks 1302.* Antwerp, 1938.

Boerio, Giuseppe. *Dizionario del dialetto veneziano.* 2d ed., 1856. Reprint, Turin, 1964.

Borsari, Silvio. "Una famiglia veneziana del medioevo: gli Ziani." *Archivio veneto,* ser. 5, 110(1978), 27–72.

Botero, Giovanni. *The Reason of State.* Translated by P. J. and D. P. Waley with an introduction by D. P. Waley. London, 1956.

Botteghi, L.A., ed. *Chronicon Marchiae Tarvisanae et Lombardiae* (Annales S. Justinae). R.I.S.², VIII, iii.

Bouwsma, William J. *Venice and the Defense of Republican Liberty.* Berkeley, 1968.

———. "Venice and the Political Education of Europe." In *Renaissance Venice,* edited by John R. Hale, pp. 445–66. Totowa, N.J., 1973.

Bracton, Henry de. *On the Laws and Customs of England.* Translated with revisions and notes by Samuel E. Thorne. 2 vols. Cambridge, Mass., 1968–.

Brady, Thomas A. *Ruling Class, Regime and Reformation at Strasbourg, 1520–1555.* Leiden, 1978.

Branca, Vittore. "Ermolao Barbaro and Late Quattrocento Venetian Humanism." In *Renaissance Venice,* edited by John R. Hale, pp. 218–43. Totowa, N.J., 1973.

———. "Ermolao Barbaro e l'umanesimo veneziano." In *Umanesimo europeo e umanesimo veneziano,* edited by Vittore Branca, pp. 193–212. Venice, 1963.

———. "Un trattato inedito di Ermolao Barbaro: il *De coelibatu libri.*" *Bibliothèque d'humanisme et de Renaissance,* 14, (1952), 83-98.

———, ed. *Concetto, storia, miti e immagini del Medio Evo.* Florence, 1973.

———, ed. *Rinascimento europeo a Rinascimento veneziano.* Florence, 1967.

Braudel, Fernand. *The Mediterranean and the Mediterranean World in the Age of*

Philip II. 2 vols. !st Fr. ed., 1966. Translated by Siân Reynolds. New York, 1972.

Braunstein, Philippe, and Robert Delort. *Venise: Portrait historique d'une cité.* Paris, 1971.

Brown, Horatio F. "Cromwell and the Venetian Republic." In *Studies in the History of Venice,* edited by Horatio F. Brown, II, 296–321. New York, 1907.

————. "Shakespeare and Venice." In *Studies in the History of Venice,* edited by Horatio F. Brown, II, 159–80. New York, 1907.

————. *Studies in the History of Venice.* 2 vols. New York, 1907.

————. *The Venetian Republic.* London, 1902.

————. *Venice: An Historical Sketch of the Republic.* 2d rev. ed. London, 1895.

Brown, Rawdon, G. Cavendish Bentinck, and Horatio F. Brown, eds. *Calendar of State Papers and Manuscripts, Relating to English Affairs, Existing in the Archives and Collections of Venice, and in Other Libraries of Northern Italy.* 38 vols. to date. London, 1864–1947.

Brucker, Gene. *The Civic World of Early Renaissance Florence.* Princeton, 1977.

————. *Renaissance Florence.* New York, 1969. A good chapter on the Florentine patriciate.

Bruner, Jerome. "Myth and Identity." *Daedalus,* 88 (1959), 349–58.

Brunetti, Mario. "Due dogi sotto inchiesta: Agostino Barbarigo e Leonardo Loredan." *Archivio veneto-tridentino,* 7 (1925), 278–329.

Buck, August. "*Laus Venetiae* und Politik im 16. Jahrhundert." *Archiv für Kulturgeschichte,* 57 (1975), 186–94.

Burckhardt, Jacob. *The Civilization of the Renaissance in Italy.* Translated by S. G. C. Middlemore. New York, 1954.

Burke, Peter. *Venice and Amsterdam: A Study of Seventeenth Century Elites.* London, 1974.

Cairns, Christopher. *Domenico Bollani, Bishop of Brescia: Devotion to Church and State in the Republic of Venice in the Sixteenth Century.* Nieuwkoop, 1976.

Calcagnini, Celio. *Lodi di Venezia* [title by Medin]. In *Componimenti poetici de varii autori in lode di Venezia,* edited by Jacopo Morelli. Venice, 1972.

Cammarosano, Paolo. "Les structures familiales dans les villes d'Italie communales, XIIᵉ-XIVᵉ siècles." In *Famille et parenté,* edited by Georges Duby and Jacques LeGoff, pp. 181–94. Rome, 1977.

Campbell, Joseph. "The Historical Development of Mythology." *Daedalus,* 88 (1959), 232–54.

Canal, Martino da. *Les estoires de Venise: cronaca veneziana in lingua francese dalle origini al 1275.* Edited by Alberto Limentani. Florence, 1972. Also under the title *La cronique des veniciens.* Edited by Filippo-Luigi Polidori, with Italian translation by Giovanni Galvani. *Archivio storico italiano,* ser. 1, 8 (1845), 229–776.

Cappelletti, Giuseppe. *Relazione storica sulle magistrature venete.* Venice, 1873. Static in viewpoint with little sense of development, but there is a long, useful list of offices.

Caresinis, Raphaynus de. *Chronica.* Edited by E. Pastorello. R.I.S.², XII, ii, (1922).

Carile, Antonio. "Aspetti della cronacistica veneziana nei secoli XIII e XIV." In *La storiografia veneziana,* edited by Agostino Pertusi, pp. 75–126. Florence, 1970.

Caroldo, Gian Giacopo. *Cronica veneziana,* B.M., cl. ital. VII, cod. 128a (=8639). The author was secretary of the Ten, and Thiriet rates the chronicle as more valuable than Dandolo or Caresini.

———. *Historia di Venetia.* B.M., cl. ital. VII, cod. 127(=8034).

Carotti, Natale. "Un politico umanista del Quattrocento: Francesco Barbaro." *Rivista storica italiana,* ser. 5, II, ii (1937), 18–37. Based on Barbaro's letters.

Casola, Pietro. *Canon Pietro Casola's Pilgrimage to Jerusalem in the Year 1494.* Translated by M. Margaret Newett. Manchester, 1907.

Cassandro, Giovanni Italo. "Concetto, caratteri e struttura dello stato veneziano." *Rivista di storia del diritto italiano,* 36 (1963), 23–29.

———. "La Curia di Petizion." *Archivio veneto,* ser.5, 19 (1936), 72–144 and (1937), 1–210.

Cassirer, Enst. *The Myth of the State.* 1st ed., 1946. Rpt. Garden City, N.Y., 1955.

Castellan, Angel A. "Venecia como modelo de ordenamiento politico en el pensamiento italiano de los siglos XV y XVI." *Anales de historia antigua y medieval,* 12 (1963–65), 7–42. The myth in its rankest form. Venice equated with Sparta.

Cecchetti, B. "I nobili e il popolo di Venezia." *Archivio veneto,* 3 (1872), 421–48. Slightly documented and a quaint conclusion.

———. "La vita dei Veneziani fino al secolo XIII." *Archivio veneto,* 2 (1871), 63ff.

Cellini, Benvenuto. *Autobiography.* Translated and with introduction by George Bull. 1st ed., 1956. Rpt. Baltimore, 1969.

Cervelli, Innocenzo. *Machiavelli e la crisi dello stato veneziano.* Naples, 1974.

Cessi, Roberto. "La finanza veneziana al tempo di la guerra di Chioggia." In *Politica ed economia di Venezia nel Trecento: Saggi,* edited by Roberto Cessi, pp. 179–248. Rome, 1952.

———. " 'L'officium de navigantibus' e i sistemi della politica commerciale veneziana nel sec. XIV." In *Politica ed economia di Venezia nel Trecento: Saggi,* edited by Roberto Cessi, pp. 23–61. Rome, 1952.

———. *Politica ed economia di Venezia nel Trecento: Saggi.* Rome, 1952.

———. "Politica ed economia veneziana del Trecento." In *Politica ed economia di Venezia nel Trecento: Saggi,* edited by Roberto Cessi, pp. 7–22. Rome, 1952.

———. "Prestiti pubblici e imposta diretta nell'antica Repubblica Veneta." In *Politica ed economia di Venezia nel Trecento: Saggi,* edited by Roberto Cessi, pp. 123–78. Rome, 1952.

———. *Problemi monetari veneziani (fino a tutto il sec. XIV).* Padua, 1937.

———. *La regolazione delle entrate e delle spese.* Padua, 1925. A strong rejection of class solidarity and civic loyalty.

————. "Le relazioni commerciali tra Venezia e le Fiandre nel sec. XIV." In *Politica ed economia di Venezia nel Trecento: Saggi,* edited by Roberto Cessi, pp. 71–172. Rome, 1952.

————. *Storia della Repubblica di Venezia.* 2 vols. 1st ed., 1944–46. 2d ed. rev., Milan, 1968.

————. ed. *Deliberazioni del Maggior Consiglio di Venezia.* 3 vols. Bologna, 1930–34.

Cessi, Roberto, Paolo Sambin, and M. Brunetti, eds. *Le deliberazioni del Consiglio dei Rogati (Senato): Serie "Mixtorum."* 2 vols. Venice, 1960–61.

Chabod, Federico. "Venezia nella politica italiana ed europea del Cinquecento." In *La civiltà veneziana del Rinascimento,* pp.27–55. Florence, 1958. Rise of the myth of the constitution in the sixteenth century, when Venice became the defender of "liberty."

Chambers, D. S. *The Imperial Age of Venice, 1380–1580.* London, 1970. Excellent survey by no means traditional in its view of the patriciate.

Chinazzo, Daniele di. *Cronica de la guerra da veniciani a zenovesi.* Edited by Vittorio Lazzarini. In *Monumenti storici pubblicati dalla Deputazione di Storia Patria per le Venezie,* n.s., XI. Venice, 1958.

Chojnacki, Stanley. "Crime, Punishment, and the Trecento Venetian State." In *Violence and Civil Disorder in Italian Cities, 1200–1500,* edited by Lauro Martines, pp. 184–228. Berkeley, 1972. He regards patrician misdeeds as more exceptional than I do, because he has used judicial records, whereas I have used primarily the more generalized legislation.

————. "In Search of the Venetian Patriciate: Families and Factions in the Fourteenth Century." In *Renaissance Venice,* edited by John R. Hale, pp. 47–90. Totowa, N.J., 1973. Argues that the Great Council was not really "closed" until 1381.

————. "Patrician Women in Early Renaissance Venice." *Studies in the Renaissance,* 21 (1974), 176–203.

Cicogna, Emmanuele A. *Delle inscrizioni veneziane.* 6 vols. Venice, 1824–53.

Clarke, Maude V. *The Medieval City-State.* London, 1926.

Clough, Cecil H. Review of *Nobiltà e popolo,* by Angelo Ventura. *Studi Veneziani,* 8 (1966), 526–44. Quite critical.

Commynes, Philippe de. *Memoires.* Edited by J. Calmette and G. Durville. 3 vols. Paris, 1924–25. More recently edited by Samuel Kinser and translated by Isabelle Cazeaux. 2 vols. Columbia, S.C., 1973. Praise for Venice, even for its reverence toward God.

Contarini, Gasparo. *De magistratibus et republica Venetorum.* Venice, 1589. Translated as *The Commonwealth and Government of Venice* by Lewis Lewkenor. London, 1599; reprint, 1969. See ch. I, "The Developed Myth: Venice."

————. *Opera.* Paris, 1571; reprint, 1968.

Corso [?], Bernadino. *Ad dominium Venetorum.* B.M., cl. ital. IX, cod. 363 (=7386), 123v.

Cozzi, Gaetano. "Authority and Law in Renaissance Venice." In *Renaissance Venice,* edited by John R. Hale, pp. 293–345. Totowa, N.J., 1973.

————. "Cultura politica e religione nella 'pubblica storiografia' veneziana nel '500." *Bollettino dell' Istituto di Storia della Società e dello Stato Veneziano,* 5–6 (1963–64), 215–94. Excellent long article on public historians from Sabellico through the sixteenth century with frequent comments on other historians, such as Sanuto.

————. *Il Doge Nicolò Contarini: Ricerche sul patriziato veneziano agli inizi del Seicento.* Venice, 1958.

————. "Domenico Morosini e il 'De bene instituta republica.' " *Studi veneziani,* 12 (1970), 405–58. An extraordinarily useful article.

————. "Marin Sanudo il Giovane: dalla cronaca alla storia." In *La storiografia veneziana,* edited by Agostino Pertusi, pp. 333–58. Florence, 1970.

Cracco, Giorgio. "Mercanti in crisi: Realtà economiche e riflessi emotivi nella Venezia del tardo Duecento." In *Studi sul medioevo veneto,* edited by Giorgio Cracco, pp. 1–24. Turin, 1981.

————. "Patriziato e oligarchia a Venezia nel Tre-Quattrocento." In *Florence and Venice: Comparisons and Relations,* edited by Sergio Bertelli, Nicolai Rubinstein, and Craig Hugh Smyth. Vol. I, *Quattrocento.* Florence, 1979.

————. "Il pensiero storico di fronte ai problemi del comune veneziano." In *La storiografia veneziana,* edited by Agostino Pertusi, pp. 45–74. Florence, 1970.

————. *Società e stato nel medioevo veneziano.* Florence, 1967. Accepts the myth of selfless service, but recognizes and strongly disapproves the oppression of all but the *potenti.*

Crawford, F. Marion. *Venice, the Place and the People: Salve Venetia: Gleanings from Venetian History.* 2 vols. New York, 1909.

Cronaca Bemba. B.M., cl. ital. VII, cod. 125(=7460). One of the more useful chronicles, since it contains some information on domestic politics and the constitution.

Cronaca di Venezia in terza rima. B.M., cl. ital. VII, cod. 728(=8070).

Da Canal, Martin. *Les estoires de Venise: Cronaca veneziana in lingua francese dalle origini al 1275.* Edited by Alberto Limentani. Florence, 1972. Also an older edition by Filippo-Luigi Polidori, with Italian trans. by Giovanni Galvani, in *Archivio storico italiano,* ser. 1, 8 (1845), 229–776.

Dalla Santa, Giuseppe. "Commerci, vita privata e notizie politiche dei giorni della lega di Cambrai (da lettere del mercante veneziano Martino Merlini)." *Atti del Reale Istituto Veneto di Scienze, Lettere ed Arti,* 75 (1917), 1547–1605.

————. "Di un patrizio mercante veneziano del Quattrocento e di Francesco Filelfo suo debitore." *Nuovo archivio veneto,* n.s., 11 (1906), 63–90.

————. "Uomini e fatti dell' ultimo Trecento e del primo Quattrocento. Da lettere a Giovanni Contarini, patrizio venetiano, studente ad Oxford e a Parigi, poi patriarca di Constantinopoli." *Nuovo archivio veneto,* n.s., 32 (1916), 5–105.

Da Mosto, Andrea. *L'Archivio di Stato di Venezia: Indice generale, storico, descrittivo ed analitico.* In *Bibliothèque des "Annales Institutorum."* 2 vols. Rome, 1937.

————. *I dogi di Venezia nella vita pubblica e privata*. Milan, 1960.

Dandolo, Andrea. *Chronica brevis*. Edited by Ester Pastorello. R.I.S.², XII, i, 329–73.

————. *Chronica per extensum descripta a. 46–1280 d.C*. Edited by Ester Pastorello. R.I.S.², XII, i, 1–327.

Davis, James Cushman. *The Decline of the Venetian Nobility as a Ruling Class*. Baltimore, 1962. From the sixteenth century to the fall of the Republic.

————. *A Venetian Family and Its Fortune, 1500–1900: The Donà and the Conservation of their Wealth*. Philadelphia, 1975.

————, ed. *Pursuit of Power: Venetian Ambassadors' Reports on Spain, Turkey, and France in the Age of Philip II, 1560–1600*. New York, 1970.

Dawson, Richard E., and Kenneth Prewett. *Political Socialization*. Boston, 1969.

Dazzi, Manlio. "Leonardo Giustinian." In *Umanesimo europeo e umanesimo veneziano*, edited by Vittore Branca, pp. 173–92. Venice, 1963.

Del Negro, Piero. "Il patriziato veneziano al calcolatore: Appunti in margine a 'Venise au siècle des lumières' di Jean Georgelin." *Rivista storica italiana*, 93 (1981), 838–48.

De Roover, Raymond. *The Rise and Decline of the Medici Bank, 1397–1494*. New York, 1963.

Derville, Alain. "Pots-de-vin, cadeaux, racket, patronage: Essai sur le mécanisme de decision dans l'Etat bourgignon." *Revue du Nord*, 56 (1974), 341–64.

De Valous, Guy. *Le patriciat lyonnais aux xiiiᵉ et xivᵉ siècles*. Paris, 1973.

Diehl, Charles. *Une république patricienne: Venise*. Paris, 1915. Declares that he will not write on the "romantic Venise" of Byron et al., and proceeds to do just that. A terrible book by a distinguished historian.

Dizionario biografico degli italiani. Rome, 1960–.

Dolfin, Pietro. *Annalium Venetorum pars quarta*. Fasc. 1. Edited by Roberto Cessi and Paolo Sambin. Venice, 1943. Fourth and last part, 1500–1501, of Dolfin's chronicle.

Dolfin, Zorzi. *Chronica*. B.M., cl. ital. VII, cod. 794(=8503).

Dollinger, Philippe. "Le patriciat des villes du Rhin supérieur et ses dissensions internes dans le première moitié du XIVᵉ siècle." *Schweizerische Zeitschrift für Geschichte*, 3 (1953), 248–58.

Dorson, Richard N. "Theories of Myth and the Folklorist." *Daedulus*, 88 (1959), 280–90.

Duby, Georges, and Jacques LeGoff, eds. *Famille et parenté dans l'occident médiéval*. Rome, 1977.

Dudan, Bruno. *Il dominio veneziano di Levante*. Bologna, 1938. An apologist for Venetian imperialism. Not very well done.

————. "Il 'Liber secretorum fidelium crucis super terrae sanctae recuperatione et conservatione' ed alcuni aspetti del pensiero politico veneziano nel secolo XIV." *Atti del Reale Instituto Veneto di Scienze, Lettere ed Arti*, 95 (1935–36), 665–70.

Dufour, Alain. "Le mythe de Genève au temps de Calvin." *Revue suisse d'histoire*, 9 (1959), 489–518. Reprinted with revisions in Alain Dufour, *Histoire politique et psychologie historique*, pp. 65–95. Geneva, 1966. Sophisticated treatment of historical mythology.

Edler, Florence. *Glossary of Medieval Terms of Business*. 1st ed., 1934. Reprint, Cambridge, Mass., 1970.

Eliade, Mircea. *Myth and Reality*. Translated from French by William R. Trask. New York, 1963.

———. "The Yearning for Paradise in Primitive Tradition." *Daedalus*, 88 (1959), 255–67. Not specifically useful to me, but very interesting.

Fasoli, Gina. "Nascita di un mito." In *Studi storici in onore di Gioacchino Volpe*, I, 445–79. Florence, 1958. A fundamental article on the development of the myth from its beginnings to about 1500. Very learned.

———. "*La storia di Venezia: Lezioni tenuti nella Facoltà di Magistero di Bologna durante l'anno accademico, 1957–58.*" Bologna, 1958. Mimeo.

Favaro, Elena, ed. *Cassiere della Bolla Ducale: Grazie—Novus Liber (1299–1305)*, Venice, 1962.

Fernandez de Oviedo, Gonzalo. *Historia general y natural de las Indias*. Edited by Juan Perez de Tudela Bueso. 4 vols. In Biblioteca de autores españoles, cvii-cxx. Madrid, 1959.

Ferriguto, Arnoldo. *Almorò Barbaro, l'alta cultura del settentrione d'Italia nel '400, i "sacri canones" di Roma e le "sanctissime leze" di Venezia*. Venice, 1922.

Fink, Zera S. *The Classical Republicans: An Essay in the Recovery of a Pattern of Thought in Seventeenth-Century England*. 1st ed. 1945. 2d ed., Evanston, Ill., 1962.

———. "Venice and English Political Thought in the Seventeenth Century." *Modern Philology*, 38 (1940), 155–72.

Finlay, Robert. "The Foundation of the Ghetto: Venice, the Jews, and the War of the League of Cambrai." *Proceedings of the American Philosophical Society*, 126 (1982), 140–54.

———. "Politics and History in the Diary of Marino Sanuto." *Renaissance Quarterly*, 33 (1980), 585–98.

———. "Politics and the Family in Renaissance Venice: The Election of Doge Andrea Gritti." *Studi veneziani*, n.s., 2 (1978), 97–117.

———. *Politics in Renaissance Venice*. New Brunswick, 1980. A fine book.

———. "The Politics of the Ruling Class in Early Cinquecento Venice." Ph.D. diss., University of Chicago, 1973. The dissertation which after much revision became *Politics in Renaissance Venice*.

———. "The Venetian Republic as a Gerontocracy: Age and Politics in the Renaissance." *Journal of Medieval and Renaissance Studies*, 8 (1978), 157–78.

———. "Venice, the Po Expedition, and the End of the League of Cambrai, 1509–1510." *Studies in Modern European History and Culture*, 2 (1976), 37–72.

Fortes, Meyer. "The Structure of Unilineal Descent Groups." *American Anthropologist*, 55 (1953), 17–41.

Foscarini, Marco. *Della letteratura veneziana ed altri scritti intorno essa*. 2d ed. Venice, 1854.

Gaeta, Franco. "Alcune considerazioni sul mito di Venezia." *Bibliothèque d'humanisme et Renaissance,* 23 (1961), 58–75. Development of the constitutional myth in political tracts of the fifteenth to the eighteenth centuries.

———. "Barbarigo, Agostino." In *Dizionario biografico degli italiani.* Rome, 1960–.

———. "L'idea di Venezia." In *Storia della cultura veneta,* edited by Girolamo Arnaldi and Manlio Pastore Stocchi, III, iii, 565–641. Vicenza, 1980–81.

———. Review of "Il 'mito' di Venezia e la crisi fiorentina intorno al 1500," by Renzo Pecchioli. *Bollettino dell'Istituto di Storia della Società e dello Stato Veneziano,* 4 (1962), 387–93.

———, ed. *Relations des ambassadeurs vénitiens.* Translated by Jean Chuzeville. Paris, 1970.

———. "Storiografia, coscienza nazionale e politica culturale nella Venezia del Rinascimento." In *Storia della cultura veneta,* edited by Girolamo Arnaldi and Manlio Pastore Stocchi, III, i, 1–91. Vicenza, 1980–81.

Gallo, Rodolfo. "Una famiglia patrizia: i Pisani ed i Palazzi di Santo Stefano e di Stra." *Archivio veneto,* ser. 5, 34–35 (1944), 65–228.

Garin, Eugenio. *L'umanesimo italiano.* Paris, 1952.

Georgelin, Jean. *Venise au siècle des lumières.* Paris, 1978.

Giannotti, Donato. *Della Republica et Magistrati di Venetia.* Bound with Gasparo Contarini, *Della Republica et Magistrati di Venetia,* pp. 108–229. Venice, 1591. Also under the title *Libro della Repubblica de'Viniziani.* In *Opere.* Florence, 1850. Notes where no edition is specified refer to the edition of 1591.

Gianturco, Elio. "Bodin's Conception of the Venetian Constitution and His Critical Rift with Fabio Albergati," *Revue de littérature comparée,* 18 (1938), 684–95. Bodin's opposition to the myth of the mixed constitution.

Gilbert, Felix. "Biondo, Sabellico, and the Beginnings of Venetian Official Historiography." In *Florilegium Historiale: Essays Presented to Wallace K. Ferguson,* edited by J. G. Rowe and W. H. Stockdale, pp. 275–93. Toronto, 1971. Biondo and Sabellico were not official historians but lecturers at the school of San Marco. Navagero was the first official historian.

———. "The Date of the Composition of Contarini's and Giannotti's Books on Venice." *Studies in the Renaissance,* 14 (1967), 172–84.

———. "Florentine Political Assumptions in the Period of Savonarola and Soderini." *Journal of the Warburg and Courtauld Institutes,* 20 (1957), 187–214.

———. *History: Choice and Commitment.* Cambridge, Mass., 1977.

———. *Machiavelli and Guicciardini: Politics and History in Sixteenth Century Florence.* Princeton, 1965. Good material on Florentine imitation of Venice.

———. "Machiavelli e Venezia." *Lettere italiane,* 21 (1969), 389–98. Machiavelli opposed the myth of Venice as in conflict with his Florentine patriotism.

———. "Religion and Politics in the Thought of Gasparo Contarini." In *Action and Conviction in Early Modern Europe: Essays in Memory of E. A. H. Harbison,* edited by Theodore K. Rabb and Jerrold E. Seigel, pp. 90–116. Princeton, 1969. Also in Felix Gilbert, *History*, pp. 247–67. Cambridge, Mass., 1977.

———. "The Venetian Constitution in Florentine Political Thought." In *Florentine Studies*, edited by Nicolai Rubenstein, pp. 463–500. London, 1968. Also in Felix Gilbert, *History*, pp. 179–214. Cambridge, Mass., 1977. Admiration of the Florentines, especially the aristocrats, for the Venetian constitution, or, until Giannotti, for their misunderstanding of it. There are extensive quotations from the sources in the notes.

———. "Venetian Diplomacy before Pavia: From Reality to Myth." In *The Diversity of History: Essays in Honour of Sir Herbert Butterfield*, edited by J. H. Elliott and H. G. Koenigsberger, pp. 79–116. London, 1970. Also in Felix Gilbert, *History*, pp. 295–321. Cambridge, Mass. 1977.

———. "Venice in the Crisis of the League of Cambrai." In *Renaissance Venice*, edited by John R. Hale, pp. 274–92. Totowa, N.J., 1973. Also in Felix Gilbert, *History: Choice and Commitment*, pp. 269–91. Cambridge, Mass., 1977.

Gilmore, Myron. "Myth and Reality in Venetian Politican Theory." In *Renaissance History*, edited by John R. Hale, pp. 431–44. Totowa, N.J., 1973. On the constitutional myth.

Giustinian, Bernardo. *De origine urbis Venetiarum*. Venice [1492]. Also in Graevius, *Thes. Italiae*, V, i, cols. 1–172. Labalme calls it the first well-ordered history of Venice. It ends, however, with the victory over Pepin.

Giustinian, Leonardo. "Orazione funebre di Giorgio Lauretano." In *Orazioni, elogi e vite*, edited by G. A. Molina, I, 12–21. Venice, 1964.

Giustinian, Pietro [?]. *Venetiarum historia vulgo Pietro Iustiniano Iustiniani filio adiudicata*. Edited by Roberto Cessi and Fanny Bennato. In *Mon. Dep. veneta*, n.s., XVIII.

Godi, Antonio. *Cronaca*. Edited by Giovanni Soranzo. R.I.S.², VIII, ii, 1–51.

Goimard, Jacques, ed. *Venise au temps des galères*. Paris, 1968.

Grendler, Paul F. "Francesco Sansovino and Italian Popular History, 1560–1600." *Studies in the Renaissance*, 16 (1969), 139–80.

Guerdan, René. *La Sérénissime: Histoire de la République de Venise*. Paris, 1971.

Guicciardini, Francesco. *Dialogo e discorsi del reggimento di Firenze*. Edited by Roberto Palmarocchi. Bari, 1932.

———. *History of Italy*. Translated by Cecil Grayson with *History of Florence*. New York, 1964.

Haitsma Mulier, Eco O. G. *The Myth of Venice and Dutch Republican Thought in the Seventeenth Century*. Translated by Gerard T. Moran. Assen, 1980.

Hale, John R. *England and the Italian Renaissance*. London, 1963.

———, ed. *Renaissance Venice*. Totowa, N.J., 1973.

Hazlitt, W. C. *The History of the Origin and Rise of the Venetian Republic*. 1st ed., 1858. 4th ed., 1915. Reprint, New York, 1966.

Heers, Jacques. *Le clan familial au moyen âge: Etudes sur les structures politiques et sociales des milieux urbains*. Paris, 1974.

———. *Parties and Political Life in the Medieval West*. Translated by David Nicholas. New York, 1977.

Herlihy, David. "Family Solidarity in Medieval Italian History." In *Economy, Society and Government in Medieval Italy: Essays in Memory of Robert L. Reynolds*, edited by David Herlihy, Robert S. Lopez, and Vsevelod Slessarev. Kent, Ohio, 1969. (Also in *Explorations in Economic History*, 7 [1969–70], 173–84.)

Herlihy, David, and Christiane Klapisch-Zuber. *Les Toscanes et leurs familles.* Paris, 1978.

Hieronimus Atestinus. In *Cronica della antiqua citta de Ateste*, edited by F. Franceschetti. Este, 1899. Volume includes two poems in praise of Venice and the Venetian Senate.

Hocquet, Jean Claude. "Capitalisme marchand et classe marchande à Venise au temps de la Renaissance." *Annales: Economie, sociétés, civilisations*, 34 (1979), 279–304.

———. "Gens de mer à Venise: Diversité des statuts, conditions de vie et de travail sur les navires." In *Le genti del mare Mediterraneo*, edited by Rosalba Ragosta, I, 103–68. Naples, 1980.

Hodgson, Francis C. *Venice in the Thirteenth and Fourteenth Centuries.* London, 1910.

Homans, George C. *The Human Group.* New York, 1950.

Hyde, John K. *Society and Politics in Medieval Italy: The Evolution of the Civil Life, 1000–1350.* New York, 1973.

Ilardi, Vincent. "Fifteenth Century Diplomatic Documents in Western European Archives and Libraries (1450–1494)." *Studies in the Renaissance*, 9 (1962), 64–112.

Jaher, Frederic C., ed. *The Rich, the Well Born, and the Powerful.* Urbana, Ill., 1973.

Jones, Philip. "Communes and Despots: The City-State in Late Medieval Italy." *Royal Historical Society. Transactions.* ser. 5, 15 (1965), 71–96.

Kedar, Benjamin Z. *Merchants in Crisis: Genoese and Venetian Men of Affairs and the Fourteenth Century Depression.* New Haven, 1976. Failure of confidence and enterprise.

King, Margaret Leah. "Caldiera and the Barbaros on Marriage and the Family: Humanistic Reflections of Venetian Realities." *Journal of Medieval and Renaissance Studies*, 6 (1976), 19–50.

———. "The Patriciate and the Intellectuals: Power and Ideas in Quattrocento Venice." *Societas*, 5 (1975), 295–312.

———. "Personal, Domestic and Republican Values in the Moral Philosophy of Giovanni Caldiera." *Renaissance Quarterly*, 28 (1975), 535–74.

Kluckhohn, Clyde. "Recurrent Themes in Myth and Mythmaking." *Daedalus*, 88 (1959), 268–79.

Koranyi, Karol. "La costituzione di Venezia nel pensiero politico della Polonia." In *Italia, Venezia, e Polonia tra umanesimo e Rinascimento*, edited by Mieczyslaw Brahmer, pp. 206–14. Warsaw, 1967. Admiration for the Venetian constitution in sixteenth- and early seventeenth-century Poland.

Krekić, Bariša. "Crime and Violence in the Venetian Levant: A Few Fourteenth

Century Cases." *Iz Zbornika radova Viznatološkog Instituta*, 16 (1975), 123–29.

Kretschmayr, Heinrich. *Geschichte von Venedig.* 3 vols. I–II, Gotha, 1905–20. III, Stuttgart, 1934.

Labalme, Patricia H. *Bernardo Giustiniani: A Venetian of the Quattrocento.* Rome, 1969. Follows the myth, but contains lots of useful material.

———. "Sodomy and Venetian Justice in the Renaissance." *Tijdschrift voor rechtsgeschiedenis*, 52 (1984), 217–54.

Lamansky, Vladimir. *Secrets d'état de Venise.* St. Petersburg, 1884.

Lane, Frederic C. *Andrea Barbarigo, Merchant of Venice.* Baltimore, 1944.

———. "At the Roots of Republicanism." In Lane, *Venice and History*, pp. 520–39. Baltimore, 1966.

———. "The Enlargement of the Great Council of Venice." In *Florilegium Historiale: Essays Presented to Wallace K. Ferguson*, edited by J. G. Rowe and W. H. Stockdale, pp. 236–74. Toronto, 1971. The so-called Serrata was originally an enlargement, not a closing.

———. "The Funded Debt of the Venetian Republic, 1262–1482." In Lane, *Venice and History*, pp. 87–98. Baltimore, 1966.

———. "Gino Luzzato's Contribution to the History of Venice: An Appraisal and Tribute." *Nuova rivista storica*, 49 (1965), 49–80.

———. "Investment and Usury in Medieval Venice." In Lane, *Venice and History*, pp. 56–68. Baltimore, 1966.

———. "Medieval Political Ideas and the Venetian Constitution." In Lane, *Venice and History*, pp. 205–308. Baltimore, 1966.

———. "Naval Actions and Fleet Organization, 1499–1502." In *Renaissance Venice*, edited by John R. Hale, pp. 146–73. Totowa, N.J., 1973.

———. "Recent Studies on the Economic History of Venice." *Journal of Economic History*, 23 (1963), 312–34.

———. "Venetian Bankers, 1496–1533." In Lane, *Venice and History*, pp. 69–86. Baltimore, 1966.

———. *Venice: A Maritime Republic.* Baltimore, 1973.

———. *Venice and History: Collected Papers of F. C. Lane.* Baltimore, 1966.

Laslett, Peter. "Introduction: The History of the Family." In *Household and Family in Past Time*, edited by Peter Laslett and Richard Walls, pp. 1–89. Cambridge, 1972.

Law, John Easton. "Age Qualifications and the Venetian Constitution: The Case of the Capello Family." *Papers of the British School at Rome*, 39 (1971), 125–37.

———. "Verona and the Venetian State in the Fifteenth Century." *Bulletin of the Institute of Historical Research*, 52 (1979), 9–22.

Lazaroni, Pietro. *De clarissimis magistratibus venetis.* B.M., cl. lat. X, cod. 240(=3370), 40(24)r–48(32)r. First half of the fifteenth century. Addressed to the doge, the Signoria, and the Senate.

Lazzarini, Vittorio. "Antiche leggi venete intorno ai proprietari nella Terraferma." *Nuovo archivio veneto*, n.s., 38 (1919), 6–31. Reprinted in Lazzarini,

Proprietà e feudi, offizi, garzoni, carcerati in antiche leggi veneziane, pp. 9–41. Rome, 1960.

––––––. "Beni carraresi e proprietari veneziani." In *Studi in onore di Gino Luzzatto,* I, 274–88. Milan, 1950.

––––––. *Marin Faliero.* Florence, 1963. A major work.

––––––. "Obbligo di assumere pubblici uffici nelle antiche leggi veneziane." *Archivio veneto,* 19 (1936), 184–98.

––––––. "Le offerte per la guerra di Chioggia e un falsario del Quattrocento." *Nuovo archivio veneto,* n.s., 4 (1902), 202–13.

––––––. "Possessi e feudi veneziani nel Ferrarese." In Lazzarini, *Proprietà e feudi, offizi, garzoni, carcerati in antiche leggi veneziane,* pp. 31–48. Rome, 1960. Also in *Miscellanea di studi storici in onore di Roberto Cessi.*

––––––. *Proprietà e feudi, offizi, garzoni, carcerati in antiche leggi veneziane.* Rome, 1960.

––––––. "Storie vecchie e nuove intorno a Francesco il Vecchio da Carrara." *Nuovo archivo veneto,* 10 (1895), 325–63.

Le Roy Ladurie, Emmanuel. *Montaillou.* 1st Fr. ed., 1975. Translated by Barbara Bray. London, 1978.

Lestocquoy, Jean. *Aux origines de la bourgeoisie: les villes de Flandre et d'Italie sous le gouvernement des patriciens, XIᵉ-XVᵉ siècles.* Paris, 1952.

––––––. *Les dynasties bourgeoises d'Arras du XIᵉ au XVᵉ siècle.* Arras, 1945. Good material on the civic responsibility of the patriciate of Arras, although the author tries not to overstress it.

"Lettera pseudo-Dantesca a Guido da Polenta." In *Le opere di Dante,* edited by E. Pistelli, pp. 450–51. Florence, 1921. Anti-Venetian.

Levin, Harry. *The Myth of the Golden Age in the Renaissance.* Bloomington, Ind., 1969.

––––––. "Some Meanings of Myth." *Daedalus,* 88 (1959), 223–31.

Lévi-Strauss, Claude. *The Elementary Structures of Kinship.* 1st Fr. ed., 1949. Translated from the revised French text of 1967 by James Harle Bell, John Richard von Sturmer, and Rodney Needham. Boston, 1969.

Libby, Lester J., Jr. "The Reconquest of Padua in 1509 according to the Diary of Girolamo Priuli." *Renaissance Quarterly,* 28 (1975), 323–31. Uses the unpublished portion of Priuli's *Diarii* to show the factionalism of the Venetian nobility after Agnadello.

––––––. "Venetian History and Political Thought after 1509." *Studies in the Renaissance,* 20 (1973), 7–45.

Lodi di Venezia [title by Medin]. B.M., cl. ital. IX, cod. 363(=7386), 44v–45r.

Logan, Oliver. *Culture and Society in Venice, 1470–1790: The Renaissance and Its Heritage,* New York, 1972. Slightly documented, but judicious.

––––––. "The Ideal of the Bishop and the Venetian Patriciate, c. 1430–c. 1630." *Journal of Ecclesiastical History,* 29 (1978), 415–50.

Lombardo, Antonino, ed. *Le deliberazioni del Consiglio dei XL della Repubblica di Venezia.* In Mon. Dep. veneta, n.s., 3 vols. to date, 9, 12, and 20. Venice, 1957–.

Longworth, Philip. *The Rise and Fall of Venice*. London, 1974.

Lopez, Robert S., and Irving W. Raymond, eds. *Medieval Trade in the Mediterranean World*. New York, n.d.

Lorenzo de Monacis. *Chronicon de rebus venetis ab u. c. ad annum MCCCLIV*. Edited by Fl. Cornelius. Venice, 1758.

Luttrell, Anthony. "Venezia e il principato di Acaia: secolo XIV." *Studi veneziani*, 10 (1968), 407–14.

Luzzatto, Gino. "Les activités économiques du patriciat vénitien (X^e-XIVe siècles)." In Luzzatto, *Studi di storia economica veneziana*, pp. 125–65. Reprinted from *Annales d'histoire économique et sociale*, 9 (1937), 25–57.

———. "L'attività commerciale di un patrizio veneziano del Quattrocento." In Luzzatto, *Studi di storia economica veneziana*, pp. 167–93. Padua, 1954. Reprinted from *Rivista di storia economica*, 8 (1943), 1–22 (under pseudonym of G. Padovan).

———. "Il costo della vita a Venezia nel Trecento." In Luzzatto, *Studi di storia economica veneziana*, pp. 285–97. Padua, 1954. Reprinted from *Ateneo veneto*, 125 (1934), 213–24.

———. *Il debito pubblico della Repubblica di Venezia*. Milan, 1963.

———. "Il debito pubblico nel sistema finanziario veneziano." In Luzzatto, *Studi di storia economica veneziana*, pp. 211–24. Padua, 1954. Reprinted from *Nuova rivista storica*, 13 (1929).

———. "La decadenza di Venezia dopo le scoperte geografiche nella tradizione e nella realtà." *Archivio veneto*, ser. 5., 84 (1955), 162–81.

———. "L'economia," In *La civiltà veneziana del Trecento*, edited by José Ortega y Gasset et al., pp. 85–109. Florence, 1968.

———. "L'oro e l'argento nella politica monetaria veneziana dei secoli XIII e XIV." In Luzzatto, *Studi di storia economica veneziana*. Padua, 1954. Reprinted from *Rivista storica italiana*, ser. 5, 2 (1937), 17–29.

———. *I prestiti della Repubblica di Venezia (sec. XIII-XV)*. Padua, 1929.

———. *Storia economica dell'età moderna e contemporanea*. 2 vols. Padua, 1955–60.

———. *Storia economica di Venezia dall'XI al XVI secolo*. Venice, 1961.

———. *Studi di storia economica veneziana*. Padua, 1954.

———. "Tasse d'interesse e usuria a Venezia nei secoli XIII-XV." In *Miscellanea in onore di Roberto Cessi*, I, 191–202. Rome, 1958.

Machiavelli, Niccolò. *The Discourses*. Translated by Leslie J. Walker. 2 vols. New Haven, 1950.

———. *Opere*. Edited by Sergio Bertelli. 10 vols. Milan, 1968–79.

Malipiero, Domenico. *Annali veneti, 1457–1500*. Edited by Tommaso Gar and Agostino Sagredo. *Archivio storico italiano*, ser. 1, (1843), 1–720.

Maranini, Giuseppe. *La costituzione di Venezia dalle origini alla Serrata del Maggior Consiglio*. Venice, 1927.

———. *La costituzione di Venezia dopo la Serrata del Maggior Consiglio*. Rome, 1931. Tiresome glorification of Venetian government. Subject needs redoing.

Marchesi, Vincenzo. "La Repubblica di Venezia (appunti critici)." *Annali del R.*

Istituto Tecnico Antonio Zanon in Udine, ser. 2, 12 (1894), 5–100. Views the patriciate before the mid-fifteenth century in traditional terms.

Maulde La Clavière, M. A. R. de. *La diplomatie au temps de Machiavel.* 3 vols. Paris, 1892–93. A wonderful old book.

Mauss, Marcel. *The Gift: Forms and Functions of Exchange in Archaic Societies.* 1st Fr. ed., 1925. Translated by Ian Cunningham. New York, 1967.

McNeill, William H. *Venice: The Hinge of Europe, 1081–1797.* Chicago, 1974. Generally repeats the old mythological view of the patriciate. Even a brilliant and suggestive mind like McNeill's is no substitute for reading the sources.

Medin, A. *La storia di Venezia nella poesia.* Milan, 1906.

Merlini, Martino. *La Liga di Cambrai e gli avvenimenti dell'anno 1509.* Edited by Giuseppe dalla Santa. Venice, 1903. Letters of a prosperous, non-noble merchant to his brother in Beirut.

Merores, Margarete. "Der Grosse Rat von Venedig und die sogenannte Serrata von Jahre 1297." *Vierteljahrschrift für Sozial- und Wirtschaftsgeschichte,* 21 (1928), 33–113.

———. "Der venezianische Adel." *Vierteljahrschrift für Sozial- und Wirtschaftsgeschichte,* 19 (1926), 193–237.

Michele, Agostino. "Letter to Francesco Barbaro." *Epistolae, carmina et orationes variorum auctorum.* B.M., cl. lat. XIV, cod. 221(=4623), 3v–4v. Congratulating Barbaro on his embassy to Rome.

Molina, G. A., ed. *Orazioni, elogi, e vite . . . in lode di dogi.* I, Venice, 1795.

Molmenti, Pompeo. "La corruzione dei costumi veneziani nel Rinascimento." *Archivio storico italiano,* ser. 5, 31(1903), 281–307.

———. "Le relazioni tra patrizi veneziani e diplomatici stranieri." *Nuova Antologia,* 272 (1917), 3–17. Also in *Curiosità di storia veneziana,* pp. 25–63. Bologna, 1919.

———. *La storia di Venezia nella vita privata.* 3 vols. 1st ed., 1880. Vol. I, 6th ed., Bergamo, 1922; vols. II and III, 7th ed., Bergamo, 1928–29. Outstanding example of traditional view.

———. *Venice: Its Individual Growth from the Beginning to the Fall of the Republic.* 1st Ital. ed., 1880. Translated by Horatio F. Brown. Part 1, 2 vols.; part 2, 3 vols. Chicago, 1906–8.

Mor, Carlo Guido. "Il procedimento per 'gratiam' nel diritto amministrativo veneziano del sec. XIII." In *Cassiere della Bolla Ducale,* edited by Elena Favoro, pp. v–xlviii. Venice, 1962.

Morosini, Domenico. *De bene instituta republica.* Edited by Claudio Finzi. Milan, 1969. Began it in 1497 and worked on it until his death in 1509.

Mosca, Gaetano. *The Ruling Class.* Translated by Hannah D. Kuhn, edited and revised by Arthur Livingston. New York, 1939.

Mousnier, Roland. "Le trafic des offices à Venise." *Revue historique de droit français et étranger,* 30 (1952), 552–65.

Muazzo, Giovanni Antonio. *Historia del governo antico e presente della Republica di Venetia.* B.M., cl. ital. VII, cod. 966(=8406). Seventeenth-century treatise.

————. *Raccolta di parti ed ordini in materia della nobiltà veneziana.* B.M., cl. ital. VII, cod. 196(=8578).

Mueller, Reinhold C. "The Procurators of San Marco in the Thirteenth and Fourteenth Centuries: A Study of the Office as a Financial and Trust Institution." *Studi veneziani,* 13 (1971), 105–220.

Muir, Edward. *Civic Ritual in Renaissance Venice.* Princeton, 1981.

————. "Images of Power: Art and Pageantry in Renaissance Venice." *American Historical Review,* 84 (1979), 16–52.

Murray, Henry A. "Introduction to the Issue 'Myth and Mythmaking.' " *Daedalus,* 88 (1959), 211–22.

"Myth and Mythmaking." Special issue of *Daedalus,* 88 (1959), 211–30. The introduction seems to promise an examination of ethical or even political myths, which the authors do not fulfill.

Nani-Mocenigo, Filippo. "Fonti storiche veneziane." *Ateneo veneto,* 26 (1903), 7–24.

Navagero, Andrea. *Storia della repubblica veneziana.* R.I.S., XXIII, cols. 923–1216.

Newett, M. Margaret. "The Sumptuary Laws of Venice in the Fourteenth and Fifteenth Centuries." In *Historical Essays by Members of the Owens College, Manchester,* edited by T. F. Tout and James Tait, pp. 245–78. London, 1902.

Noiret, Hippolyte, ed. *Documents inédits pour servir à l'histoire de la domination vénitienne en Crète.* Paris, 1892. Not entirely reliable in detail.

Norwich, John Julius. *A History of Venice.* New York, 1982.

Olivieri, Achille. Review of *Renaissance Venice,* edited by John R. Hale. *Studi veneziani,* 16 (1974), 574–82.

Ourliac, Paul. Review of *Le patriciat lyonnais aux XIIIe et XIVe siècles,* by Guy de Valous. *Journal des savants,* 1973, 228–32.

Pagello, Bartolomeo. *De laudibus urbis Venetiarum.* Edited by F. Zordan. Vicenza, 1856. From Vicenza, late fifteenth or early sixteenth century.

Pansolli, L. *La gerarchia delle fonti di diritto nella legislazione medievale veneziana.* Milan, 1970.

Paolino Minorita, Fra. *Trattato de regimine rectoris.* Edited by Adolfo Mussafia. Vienna-Florence, 1868. Early fourteenth-century scholastic treatise on governance of oneself, the family, and the state. Based upon Colonna's *De regimine principum.*

Pareto, Vilfredo. *The Mind and Society: A Treatise on General Sociology.* Translated by Andrew Bongiorno and Arthur Livingston. 4 vols. 1st ed., 1935. New York, 1963.

————. *The Rise and Fall of the Elites.* Translated from *Un applicazione di teorie sociologiche* (1902). Totowa, N.J., 1963.

Paschini, Pio. *Tre illustri prelati del Rinascimento: Ermolao Barbaro, Adriano Castellesi, Giovanni Grimani.* Lateranum, n.s. 23 (Rome, 1957).

Pavan, Elisabeth. "Police des moeurs, société et politique à Venise à la fin du moyen âge." *Revue historique,* 264 (1980), 241–88.

Pecchioli, Renzo. "Il 'mito' di Venezia e la crisi fiorentina intorno al 1500." *Studi storici,* 3 (1962), 451–92.

Perkinson, Richard H. " 'Volpone' and the Reputation of Venetian Justice." *Modern Language Review,* 35 (1940), 11–18.

Perret, P. M. *Histoire des relations de la France avec Venise.* 2 vols. Paris, 1896.

Pertusi, Agostino. "Gli inizi della storiografia umanistica nel Quattrocento." In *La storiografia veneziana,* edited by Pertusi, pp. 269–332. Florence, 1970.

―――, ed. *La storiografia veneziana fino al secolo XVI: Aspetti e problemi.* Florence, 1970.

Pessen, Edward. "Social Structure and Politics in American History." *American Historical Review,* 87 (1982), 1291–325.

Picotti, G. B. "Le lettere di Ludovico Foscarini." *Ateneo veneto,* 32 (1909), 3–31.

Pignatti, Terisio. *Venice,* Translated from Italian by Judith Landry. New York, 1971.

Pillinini, Giovanni. "Marino Falier e la crisi economica e politica del '300 a Venezia." *Archivio veneto,* ser. 5, 84 (1968), 45–71. The "Falier conspiracy" was actually a conflict between two factions of rich nobles with the victors pulling over the struggle a mask of conspiracy to overthrow the patrician republic.

Pilot, Antonio. "Ancora del broglio nella Repubblica Veneta." *Ateneo veneto,* 27^2 (1904), 1–22.

―――. "Ancora notizie di versi e di prose sul broglio nella Republica Veneta." *Ateneo veneto,* 31 (1908), 259.

―――. "Un capitolo inedito contro il broglio." *Ateneo veneto,* 26 (1903), 544–55.

―――. " 'Disordini e sconcerti' del broglio nella Republica Veneta." *Ateneo veneto,* 27 (1904), 295–301.

―――. "La teoria del broglio nella Repubblica Veneta." *Ateneo veneto,* 27 (1904), 176–89.

Piovane, Guido. "Anacronismo della Venezia quattrocentesca." In *La civiltà veneziana del Quattrocento,* pp. 1–21. Florence, 1957.

Pirenne, Henri. *Early Democracies in the Low Countries.* Translated by J. V. Saunders. New York, 1963.

―――. *Medieval Cities.* Translated by Frank D. Haley. 1st ed., 1925. Princeton, 1972.

Pius II, Pope. *The Commentaries of Pius II.* Translated by Florence Alden Gragg with introduction and notes by Leona C. Gabel. Smith College Studies in History, XXII, 1–2; XXV, 1–4; XXX-XXXV; XLIII. Northampton, Mass., 1936–57.

―――. *Memoirs of a Renaissance Pope: The Commentaries of Pius II.* An abridgement, translated by Florence Alden Gragg, edited with introduction by Leona C. Gabel. 1st ed., 1959. Reprint, New York, 1962.

Pocock, J. G. A. *The Machiavellian Moment: Florentine Political Thought and the Atlantic Republican Tradition.* Princeton, 1975.

Poggio, Francesco. *Momenti di storia veneziana: la riforma del 1297.* Alessandria,

1960. A few undocumented pages setting forth the modern version in outline of the reform of 1297.

Poggio-Bracciolini, Gian Francesco. *In laudem rei publicae Venetorum*. In *Opera omnia*, facs. of 1538 ed., edited by Riccardo Fubini, II, 917–37. Turin, 1964–69. Praise of Venice in contrast to villainous Florence.

———. *De nobilitate liber*. In *Opera omnia*, facs. of 1538, ed. edited by Riccardo Fubini, I, 64–83. 4 vols. Turin, 1964–69. Negative opinion of Venice here.

Porcia, Jacopo da. *De Reipublicae Venetae administratione domi et foris liber*. Treviso, 1492.

Prawer, Joshua. *Crusader Institutions*. Oxford, 1980.

Priuli, Girolamo. *I Diarii*. Edited by A. Segre and Roberto Cessi. R.I.S.², XXIV, 3 (1912–37). Very critical of Venetian nobility. The last part of the *Diarii* remains unedited.

Pullan, Brian. "The Occupations and Investments of the Venetian Nobility in the Middle and Late Sixteenth Century." In *Renaissance Venice*, edited by John R. Hale, pp. 379–408. Totowa, N.J., 1973.

———. "Poveri, mendicanti e vagabondi (secoli XIV-XVII)." In *Storia d'Italia. Annali I. Dal feudalesimo al capitalismo*, edited by Ruggiero Romano, pp. 981–1047. Turin, 1978.

———. "Poverty, Charity and the Reason of State: Some Venetian Examples." *Bollettino dell'Istituto di Storia della Società e dello Stato Veneziano*, 2 (1960), 17–60.

———. *Rich and Poor in Renaissance Venice*. Cambridge, Mass., 1971.

———. "Service to the Venetian State: Aspects of Myth and Reality in the Early Seventeenth Century." *Studi secenteschi*, 5 (1964), 95–147. Emphasizes the different opportunities for rich and poor nobles to serve the state and thus to rise to the highest offices.

———. "The Significance of Venice." *Bulletin of the John Rylands Library of the University of Manchester*, 56 (1974), 443–62.

———. Review of *Decline of the Venetian Nobility*, by James Cushman Davis. *Bollettino dell'Istituto di Storia della Società e dello Stato Veneziano*, 5–6 (1963–64), 406–25.

———, ed. *Crisis and Change in the Venetian Economy in the Sixteenth and Seventeenth Centuries*. London, 1968.

Queller, Donald E., "The Civic Irresponsibility of the Venetian Nobility." In *Economy, Society, and Government in Medieval Italy: Essays in Memory of Robert L. Reynolds*, edited by David Herlihy, Robert S. Lopez, and Vsevelod Slessarev. Kent, Ohio, 1969. (Also in *Explorations in Economic History*, 7 [1969–70], 223–35.)

———. "The Development of Ambassadorial Relazioni." In *Renaissance Venice*, edited by John R. Hale, pp. 174–96. Totowa, N.J., 1973.

———. *Early Venetian Legislation on Ambassadors*. Geneva, 1966.

———. *The Fourth Crusade*. Philadelphia, 1977.

———. "How to Succeed as an Ambassador: A Sixteenth Century Venetian Document." *Studia gratiana*, 15 (1972), 653–71.

————. *The Office of the Ambassador in the Middle Ages.* Princeton, 1967.

————, and Irene B. Katale. "Attitudes towards the Venetians in the Fourth Crusade: The Western Sources." *International History Review,* 4 (1982), 1–36.

————, and Francis R. Swietek. "The Myth of the Venetian Patriciate: Electoral Corruption in Medieval Venice." In Queller with Swietek, *Two Studies on Venetian Government,* pp. 95–175. Geneva, 1977.

————, with Francis R. Swietek. *Two Studies on Venetian Government.* Geneva, 1977.

————, ed. "Newly Discovered Early Venetian Legislation on Ambassadors." In Queller with Swietek, *Two Studies on Venetian Government,* pp. 7–98. Geneva, 1977.

Renouard, Yves. *Les hommes d'affaires italiens du moyen âge.* 1st ed., 1949. Revised according to notes of the author by Bernard Guillemain. Paris, 1968. A fine book, but it does adopt the romantic view of the patriciate.

————. "Mercati e mercanti veneziani alla fine del Duecento." In *La civiltà veneziana del secolo di Marco Polo,* pp. 83–108. Florence, 1955. Romantic and unoriginal. Renouard felt himself a foreign representative honoring Venice at a session sponsored by the Cini Foundation.

Reumont, Alfred von. *Della diplomazia italiana da secolo XIII al XIV.* Revised ed. of *Dei diplomati italiani e delle relazioni diplomatiche italiane dal 1260 al 1550* of 1850. Florence, 1857.

Rezasco, Giulio. *Dizionario del linguaggio italiano storico ed amministrativo.* Bologna, 1881.

Riesenberg, Peter. "Civism and Roman Law in Fourteenth Century Italian Society." In *Economy, Society and Government in Medieval Italy: Essays in Memory of Robert L. Reynolds,* edited by David Herlihy, Robert S. Lopez, and Vsevelod Slessarev. Kent, Ohio, 1969. (Also in *Explorations in Economic History,* 7 [1969–70], 237–54.)

Roberti, Melchiorre. *Le magistrature giudiziarie veneziane e i loro capitolari fino 1300.* In Mon. Dep. veneta, 2d ser. I. Padua, 1907. II and III. Venice, 1909–11.

Robey, David, and John E. Law. "The Venetian Myth and the 'De Republica Veneta' of Pier Paolo Vergerio." *Rinascimento,* 15 (1975), 3–59. Excellent article on the myth of Venice before the League of Cambrai. Includes a critical edition of Vergerio's treatise.

Rodenwaldt, Ernst. "Untersuchungen über die Biologie des venezianischen Adels." *Homo: Zeitschrift für die vergleichende Forschung Menschen,* 7 (1957), 1–26.

Rolandinus, Patavinus. *Cronica.* Edited by Antonio Bonardi. RIS², VIII, i, 1–174.

Romanin, Samuele. *Storia documentata di Venezia.* 1st ed., 1853–61. 2d ed., 10 vols., Venice, 1912–25.

Romano, Dennis. "Charity and Community in Early Renaissance Venice." *Journal of Urban History,* 2 (1984), 63–82.

―――. "*Quod sibi fiat gratia:* Adjustment of Penalties and the Exercise of Influence in Early Renaissance Venice." *Journal of Medieval and Renaissance Studies,* 13 (1983), 251–68.

Romano, Ruggiero. "Des lions affamés." In *Venise au temps des galères,* edited by Jacques Goimard, pp. 205–85. Paris, 1968.

Rosand, Ellen. "Music and Myth of Venice." *Renaissance Quarterly,* 30 (1977), 511–37.

Rose, Charles J. "The Evolution of the Image of Venice (1500–1630)." Ph.D. diss., Columbia University, 1971.

―――. "Marc Antonio Venier, Renier Zeno and 'the Myth of Venice.'" *The Historian,* 36 (1974), 479–97.

Ross, James Bruce. "The Emergence of Gasparo Contarini: A Bibliographical Essay." *Church History,* 41 (1972), 22–45.

―――. "Gasparo Contarini and His Friends." *Studies in the Renaissance,* 17 (1970), 192–232. A solid study which provides some basis for an attack upon the myth.

Rowan, Steven W. "Community Survival: Freiburg im Bresgau from the Black Death to the Reformation." Unpub. MS.

Rubinstein, Nicolai. "Italian Reactions to Terraferma Expansion in the Fifteenth Century." In *Renaissance Venice,* edited by John R. Hale, pp. 197–217. Totowa, N.J., 1973.

―――. "Marsilius of Padua and Italian Political Thought of His Time." In *Europe in the Late Middle Ages,* edited by John R. Hale, pp. 44–75. London, 1965.

―――. "Politics and Constitution in Florence at the End of the Fifteenth Century." In *Italian Renaissance Studies,* edited by E. F. Jacob, pp. 148–83. London, 1960. The author argues convincingly that the Florentine *ottimati* for their own political ends persuaded Savonarola to push the Venetian model of government.

―――. "I primi anni del Consiglio Maggiore di Firenze." *Archivio storico italiano,* 112 (1954), 151–94. Interesting for me for the problem of absenteeism in Florence.

Ruggiero, Guido. "Modernization and the Mythic State in Early Renaissance Venice: The Serrata Revisited." *Viator,* 10 (1979), 245–56.

―――. "Sexual Criminality in Early Renaissance Venice, 1338–58." *Journal of Social History,* 8 (1975), 18–37. Sexual crimes, except sodomy, were considered relatively minor, especially the rape of lower-class women by nobles.

―――. *Violence in Early Renaissance Venice.* New Brunswick, 1980. Much interesting material for my subject—and Ruggiero has investigated, for the most part, different collections of documents than I have.

Ruskin, John. *The Stones of Venice.* 1st ed., 1851. 2 vols. New York, 1884.

Sabellico, Marcantonio. *De Venetis Magistratibus.* Venice, 1488. A listing with a few words on the responsibilities of each office. Criticized by Giannotti.

―――. *Rerum Venetarum ab urbe condita libri XXXIII.* Venice, 1718. Not much touching the myth.

Sagredo, A. "Leggi venete intorno agli ecclesiastici sino al secolo XVIII." *Archivio storico italiano*, ser. 3, 2 (1865).

Sansovino, Francesco. *Venetia città nobilissima et singolare*. Venice, 1581.

Sanuto, Marino. *Cronachetta*. Edited by Rinaldo Fulin. Venice, 1880. Dedicated in 1493, when Sanuto was twenty-eight.

————. *I Diarii*. Edited by Rinaldo Fulin, Federico Stefani, Nicolò Barozzi, Guglielmo Berchet, and Marco Allegri. 58 vols. Venice, 1879–1903. Uniquely rich in material.

————. *Libro dei magistrati*. B.M., cl. ital. VII, cod. 761(=7959). Ca. 1515. Similar to the *Cronachetta*, but the information is sometimes inconsistent in the two. Making use of these two and a third version, Angela Carraciolo Arico has recently published a critical edition, *De origini, situ et magistratibus urbis venetae ovvero la città de Venetia (1493–1530)*. Milan, 1980.

————. *La spedizione di Carlo VIII in Italia*. Edited by Rinaldo Fulin. *Archivio veneto*, suppl., 1873.

Sanuto, Marino (Torsello). *Liber secretorum fidelium crucis super Terrae Sanctae recuperatione et conservatione*. Hanover ed. of 1611. Toronto, 1972.

Sapori, Armando. *The Italian Merchant in the Middle Ages*. 1st French ed., 1952. Translated by Patricia Ann Kennan. New York, 1970.

Savonarola, Girolamo. *Trattato circa il reggimento e governo della città di Firenze*. 6th ed., 1847. Reprint, Turin, 1963. Translated by Renée Watkins in *Humanism and Liberty: Writings on Freedom from Fifteenth Century Florence*. Columbia, S.C., 1978.

Sayles, George O. *The King's Parliament of England*. New York, 1974.

Sayous, André. "Aristocratie et noblesse à Gênes." *Annales d'histoire economiques et sociales*, 9 (1937), 366–81.

Schumpeter, Joseph A. *Imperialism and Social Classes*. Translated by Henry Norden, edited by P. M. Sweezy. New York, 1951.

Segarizzi, Arnoldo, ed. *Relazioni degli ambasciatori veneti al Senato*. 3 vols. Bari, 1912–16.

Sestan, Ernesto. "La politica veneziana nel Duecento." *Archivio storico italiano*, 135 (1977), 295–331.

Setton, Kenneth M. "The Catalans and Florentines in Greece, 1380–1462." In *A History of the Crusades*, edited by Kenneth M. Setton, III, 225–77. Madison, Wis., 1975.

————. *The Papacy and the Levant (1204–1571)*. Vol. I, *The Thirteenth and Fourteenth Centuries*. Philadelphia, 1976. Vol. II, *The Fifteenth Century*. Philadelphia, 1978. Third vol. not yet published.

Shils, Edward. *Tradition*. Chicago, 1981.

Simmel, Georg. *Conflict*, translated by Kurt H. Wolf, and *The Web of Group-Affiliations*, translated by Reinhard Bendix. 1st ed., 1955. New York, 1966.

Simone, Franco. "I contributi della cultura veneta allo sviluppo del Rinascimento francese." In *Rinascimento europeo e Rinascimento veneziano*, edited by Vittore Branca, pp. 137–58. Florence, 1967.

Skinner, Quentin. *The Foundations of Modern Political Thought*. 2 vols. Cambridge, 1978.

Bibliography

Soranzo, Giovanni. "I fattori morali della grandezza e della decadenza di Venezia." *Archivio veneto*, ser. 5, I (1927), 266–93. Not very good.

Starn, Randolph. *Donato Giannotti and His Epistolae*, Geneva, 1968.

Stella, Antonio. "Grazie, pensioni ed elemosine sotto la Repubblica veneta." *Monografie ineditate in onore di Fabio Besta*, II, 715–85. Milan, 1912.

Summarium legum venetarum interius reipublicae regimen spectantium. B.M., cl. lat V, cod. 110(=3035). Also A.S.V., Miscellanea codici mss. 146 and 381.

Swift, Jonathan. *Gulliver's Travels*. Edited by Peter Dixon and John Chalker. Baltimore, 1967.

Tamassia, Nino. *La famiglia italiana nei secoli decimoquinto e decimosesto*. 1st ed., 1911. Reprint, Rome, 1971.

Tenenti, Alberto. "Famille bourgeoise et idéologie au bas moyen âge." In *Famille et parenté*, edited by Georges Duby and Jacques LeGoff, pp. 431–40. Rome, 1977.

———. "The Sense of Space and Time in the Venetian World of the Fifteenth and Sixteenth Centuries." In *Renaissance Venice*, edited by John R. Hale, pp. 17–46. Totowa, N.J., 1973.

———. "La Sérénissime République." In *Venise au temps des galères*, edited by Jacques Goimard, pp. 161–83. Paris, 1968.

———. "Studi di storia veneziana." *Rivisti storica italiana*, 75 (1963), 97–111. Bibliographical article.

———. Review of *Nobiltà e popolo*, by Angelo Ventura. *Studi storici*, 7 (1966), 401–8.

———. Review of *Società e stato*, by Giorgio Cracco. *Studi veneziani*, 11 (1969), 665–74.

Thayer, William Roscoe. *A Short History of Venice*. Boston, 1908. A popularizer with a romantic admiration for the Venetian oligarchy.

Thiriet, Freddy. "Les chroniques de la Marcienne et leur importance pour l'histoire de la Romanie gréco-vénitienne." *Mélanges d'archéologie et d'histoire de l'Ecole Française de Rome*, 66 (1954), 241–92.

———. *Histoire de Venise*. 1st ed., 1952. 4th ed., Paris, 1969. Thoroughly traditional, not only on the patriciate, but on the Serrata, the role of the Senate, *relazioni* and *dispacci*, etc.

———. "Le quart et demi de la Romanie." In *Venise au temps des galères*, edited by Jacques Goimard. pp. 57–79. Paris, 1968.

———. *La Romanie vénitienne au moyen âge: le développement et l'exploitation du domain colonial venetien (xiie au xve siècles)*. Paris, 1959.

———. ed. *Délibérations des assemblées vénitiennes concernant la Romanie*. 2 vols. Paris, 1966–71.

———, ed. *Régestes des délibérations du Sénat de Venise concernant la Romanie*. 3 vols. Paris, 1958–61. Good introduction and useful appendices.

Thrupp, Sylvia L. *The Merchant Class of Medieval London (1300–1500)*. Chicago, 1948.

Toffanin, Giuseppe. *Machiavelli e il "Tacitismo."* 1st ed., 1921. Naples, 1972.

Tonti, Giacinto. *Trattatello della inosservanza d'un giuramento pubblico e solito praticarsi nel Maggior Consiglio in materia di brogli*. B.M., cl. ital. VII, cod.

1225(=8722). An eighteenth-century priest, basically against the oath and in favor of *broglio*. Arguments based on theological analogies.

"Traité du gouvernement de la cité et seigneurie de Venise." In P.-M. Perret, *Relations de la France avec Venise*, II, 239–304. 2 vols. Paris, 1896. Excerpts from a much larger work. Perret dates it before 1485. Excellent.

Trexler, Richard. "Charity and the Defense of Urban Elites in the Italian Communes." In *The Rich, the Well Born, and the Powerful*, edited by Frederic C. Jaher, pp. 64–109. Urbana, Ill., 1973.

Tucci, Ugo. "Dans le sillage de Marco Polo." In *Venise au temps des galères*, edited by Jacques Goimard, pp. 89–110. Paris, 1968.

———. "Il patrizio veneziano mercante e umanista." In *Venezia centro di mediazione tra Oriente e Occidente (secoli XV-XVI): Aspetti e problemi*, edited by H. G. Beck, M. Manoussacas, and A. Pertusi, I, 355–57. 2 vols. Florence, 1977.

Valeri, Nino. "Venezia nella crisi italiana del Rinascimento." In *La civiltà veneziana del Quattrocento*, edited by Guido Piovane, pp. 23–48. Florence, 1957.

Valiero, Agostino. "Vita di Bernardo Navagero, P.V. cardinale di Santa Chiesa ed amministrator della chiesa di Verona scritta da Agostino Valiero P.V." In *Orazioni, elogi e vite*, edited by G. A. Molina, II, 74–110. Venice, 1795.

Valsecchi, Antonio. "Bibliografia analitica della legislazione della Repubblica di Venezia." *Archivio veneto*, 2 (1871), 50–62; III (1872), 16–37; IV (1872), 258–88. There is more, but the University of Illinois Library lacks the following volumes, and I did not find it especially valuable.

Ventura, Angelo. *Nobiltà e popolo nella società veneta del '400 e '500*. Bari, 1964. Fine book on Venetian government of the Terraferma.

———. "Scrittori politici e scritture di governo." In *Storia della cultura veneta*, edited by Girolamo Arnaldi and Manlio Pastore Stocchi, III, iii, 513–63. Vicenza, 1980–81.

Vergerio, Pier Paolo. *De republica veneta*. In Robey and Law, "Venetian Myth and Vergerio." *Rinascimento*, 15 (1975), 36–50.

Vivanti, Corrado. "Pace e libertà in un opera di Domenico Morosini." *Rivista storica italiana*, 84 (1972), 617–24.

Volpe, Gioacchino. "L'Italia e Venezia." In *La civiltà veneziana del Trecento*, edited by José Ortega y Gasset et al., pp. 23–83. Florence, 1968.

Volpi, Giuseppe. *La Repubblica di Venezia e i suoi ambasciatori*. Milan, 1928.

Walser, Ernst. *Poggius Fiorentinus: Leben und Werke*. Berlin, 1914.

Weinstein, Donald. "The Myth of Florence." In *Florentine Studies*, edited by Nicolai Rubinstein, pp. 15–44. London, 1968.

———. *Savonarola and Florence*. Princeton, 1970.

Wiel, Alathea. *Venice*. London, 1894.

Williams, Raymond. *Keywords: A Vocabulary of Culture and Society*. New York, 1976. See "myth," pp. 176–78.

Williamson, James. "Faction and Loyalty in the Venetian State under Doge Foscari." Paper delivered at the Warwick Symposium, Venice, 29 Nov. 1972.

Woolf, S. J. "Venice and the Terraferma: Problems of the Change from Commercial to Landed Activities." *Bollettino dell'Istituto di Storia della Società e dello Stato Veneziano,* 4 (1962). Reprint in *Crisis and Change,* edited by Brian Pullan, pp. 175–203. London, 1968.

Yriarte, Charles. *Vie d'un patricien de Venise.* Paris, 1874. Full of patriotic fervor and dotted with small errors.

Zago, Ferrucio, ed. *Consiglio dei Dieci, Deliberazioni Miste.* 2 vols. Venice, 1962–68.

Zannoni, Maria. "Giorgio Dolfin, cronista del sec. XV." *Memorie della R. Accademia di Scienze, Lettere e Arti in Padova,* n.s., 58 (sc. mor.) (1941–42), 5–23.

Ziliolo, Andrea. *Delle guerri dei suoi tempi.* B.M., cl. ital. VII, cold. 328(=8513).

Zille, Ester. "Il processo Grimani." *Archivio veneto,* 36–41 (1945–47), 137–94.

Index

I have treated homonyms as referring to a single person only when there is good reason to believe that it was so. Occasionally this is based only upon proximity of dates and compatibility of behaviors, but usually upon more solid evidence. Otherwise, I list them separately with the dates of the documents in parentheses.

A Note on the Author

DONALD E. QUELLER is professor of history at the University of Illinois at Urbana-Champaign. He is the author of many books and scholarly articles on the office of the ambassador, Venice, and the Fourth Crusade.